"I'm In The Army Now"

World War I Veterans
of
Transylvania County, NC

Compiled and Published by Jan C. Plemmons

Unknown Transylvania World War I Soldiers

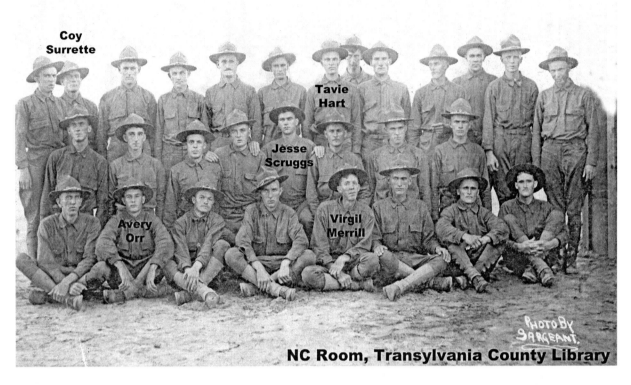

Coy Surrette

Tavie Hart

Jesse Scruggs

Avery Orr

Virgil Merrill

NC Room, Transylvania County Library

Allen McCall Files

Gillespie Files
Vicky Trent Photo

Allen McCall files

Cover Photo: Sylvester Winchester and George W. Reese. Courtesy of Frances Reese.

"I'm In The Army Now"
World War I Veterans
of Transylvania County, NC

Compiled and Published by: Jan C. Plemmons

in association with WorldComm, ISBN 978-1-56664-290-3

For information contact:
Jan C. Plemmons

Summer Address:
897 North East Shore Drive
Lake Toxaway, NC 28747
or
Winter Address:
4996 1st Coast Highway
Fernandina Beach, FL 32034

Acknowledgments

Research Assistants: Norma Surrette and Helen Ingle

Typing Assistant and Proof Reader: Jo Anne "Jan" Warren

Cover Design: Yvonne Dickson

To all the families that so graciously shared their family photos, World War I artifacts and family stories with me. The photos in the book will identify both the veteran and family member that shared the photo for the book.

To the *Transylvania Times* and all previous owners of the newspaper for the excellent coverage of our citizens and events through all the many years.

Knitting for the Red Cross

Introduction

2 Apr 1920   Brevard News

SOUVENIR OF THE GREAT WAR

"All the soldiers and sailors who volunteered or were drafted into the U.S. Army or Navy, whether they actually took part in the conflict or not, are asked to see Mr. Ralph Fisher, Mr. Verne Clement or Mr. Louis Loftis about having their record inserted in the beautiful Souvenir of the Great War: which is to be gotten out for our Transylvania Heroes.

"Each man will be asked to contribute a cut made from his photograph to be put in the book, together with an account of his life and war record. Those who make "the supreme sacrifice" will be given the place of honor in the front pages.

"The souvenir will have a map of Transylvania County showing the homes of our boys, a map of the battlefields in France and Belgium; pictures of airplanes, tanks and men in battle; a short history of the Great War and poems about it. The book will be edited by E.H. Norwood, assisted by Messrs. Fisher, Clement and Loftis and will be gotten up in handsome style so as to make a suitable souvenir to hand down to your children's children.

"In order to make the publication of this book possible each soldier and sailor must do his part. The cuts of the photographs of each man will be furnished at cost, be paid for by himself and remain his property after the book is published. If there are any of the men too poor to pay for their pictures the cost of it will be divided up among the rest."

Special Note: To date no record can be found that this souvenir book was printed. If anyone has any knowledge of this booklet or of any work that was done on it would you PLEASE contact Jan Plemmons (janplemmons@yahoo.com) or the librarian at the NC Room at the Transylvania County Public Library.

Ninety-three years later a book honoring World War I soldiers of Transylvania County, NC is available. Jan Plemmons, compiler, has taken a slightly different format than the proposed 1920 book. There will be no "bloody war battles " presented, only information of the soldiers and "interesting" facts of the United States' participation in the war.

The very first challenge for this publication was to identify the subjects who were in the military between April 6, 1917 and November 11, 1918. There is no source for ONE COMPLETE list. The list of 470 individual soldiers was compiled from many sources.

The primary source of the soldiers' records came from the World War I Service Record Cards (SRC). Congress ordered the Adjutant General of the United States to provide each state with a statement of service from the War Department for each individual who served in the U.S. Army during the war. Cards for individuals serving in the Navy, Coast Guard and Marines were also created. In 1924 these records were sent to North Carolina and in 1960 the cards were transferred to the State Department of Archives and History. The cards can be viewed at the Archives or from 50 rolls of microfilm that can be purchased from the Archives. The cards for the entire state of North Carolina are filed in alphabetical order by last name, not by county. To find the Transylvania men, every roll of film had to be viewed.

Unfortunately, there is not a Service Record Card for each soldier. With the assistance of two outstanding researchers, Norma Surrette and Helen Ingle, we realized we must find additional sources to identify World War I soldiers. A list was created from the 1930 Census that collected military service data. Once again, many errors were made because often the man thought if he did not serve overseas he should say NO.

Another list was compiled using Frankie Monteith's Transylvania County North Carolina Cemetery Survey, published in 1985. We elected to include ALL veterans who served in World War I and are buried with a military marker in Transylvania County, as well as those who enlisted in Transylvania County.

World War I files in the NC Room, Transylvania County Library were researched and a third list was compiled from names that were found on loose papers in the files. Very poor quality microfilm of the

Introduction

Brevard News (present **Transylvania Times**) was read and all legible articles for WW I were saved, creating a fourth list.

The four lists were combined into one and everyone who was on the original SRC list was scratched from the newly created #2 list. The remaining men were thoroughly researched using the birth records, death certificates, marriage records, census records, discharge papers, obituaries, heritage books, the Internet and personal accounts of people who knew them.

Ancestry.com and FamilySearch.org provided draft registrations, applications for military headstones and findagrave.com helped locate burial places. These sources verified many men on the lists. The death certificates indicated place of death, specifically naming veterans hospitals; many had a block to indicate military service and some stated specifically that they served in WW I.

Once the military service was documented the name was added to the original Service Record Card list. A biographical summary was written for each individual to include birth and death information, spouse(s), parents and a brief summary of the Draft Registration Card. The Draft Registration Card is NOT a record of service; it is a record of compliance with the law requiring every young man between the ages of 21 and 31 to register. Each biographical summary indicates the sources used to obtain the data.

The Service Record Card is printed just as it appears from the microfilm with SRC Notes to explain abbreviations used on the card. Obituaries have been edited to the basic facts. The obituary source will be the **Transylvania Times** unless otherwise stated. If a photo of the individual was obtained it is included stating the name of the donor.

News items and letters to the **Brevard News** were extracted and are reprinted on the appropriate soldier's page. Interesting facts of World War I and old photographs were added to complete the page.

Disclaimer: We found in our research conflicting birth and death dates on documents for some individuals. The obituaries often named spouse(s) we were unable to confirm. We did not try to resolve these issues, but instead printed conflicting dates/names so that each reader can pursue further research if desired.

After eight months of intense research this book was created from the names of soldiers that were found. If an individual served in World War I but enlisted in another county or state and is buried in a Transylvania County Cemetery without a military marker he will not be recognized in this book. I extend my sincere apologies to any family that has a World War I veteran of Transylvania County who does not appear in this volume.

I have thoroughly enjoyed getting to know the 470 veterans as I did the biographical research. There are 468 men and two women: Corrine Anderson and Tessie Prue Crowder Wiley. I have had the pleasure of meeting many of the families as I searched for photographs. The greatest treat for me was hearing the wonderful family stories and seeing the artifacts that are now family treasures.

The World War I veterans certainly earned a place in history and I hope this volume will serve as a reminder to all of us of the sacrifices they made for the United States of America and for the freedom we enjoy today.

Jan C. Plemmons

Andy ADAMS

Born:	14 May 1893, Jackson County, NC
Died:	25 Apr 1967, Oteen VA Hospital, Buncombe County; age 73
Buried:	Pisgah Gardens Cemetery
Occupation:	Carpenter
Spouse:	**Pearl OWEN**
Father:	**Allen ADAMS**
Mother:	**Nancy HASKINS**
Draft Registration:	Jackson County, 21, single, farmer

[Documentation: Buncombe County DC, Transylvania County Cemetery Survey, Ancestry.com]

```
                                                                        1
      Adams,         Andy       3,278,153    • White • Colored.
    (Surname)     (Christian name)  (Army serial number)
Residence: _____ East Laport   Jackson  NORTH CAROLINA
        (Street and house number)  (Town or city)  (County)      (State)
                            Sylva N C June 25/18
• Enlisted • R. A. • N. G. • E. R. C. • Inducted at _____ on _____, 19__
Place of birth: East Laport N C _____ Age or date of birth: May 14/1893
Organizations served in, with dates of assignments and transfers: _____
      45 Co 12 Bn 156 Dep Brig to July 21/18; Hs School FA Repl
      Draft Camp Jackson S C to Aug 7/18; Btry 7 Arty Repl(Over)

Remarks (continued): _____
_____
_____
      Draft to Jan 22/19; Co B 324 Inf to May 8/19; 81 Div Hq
      Tr Rear Echelon to disch.
_____
Wounds or other injuries received in action: None.
Served overseas from †Aug 22/18 to †June 20/19, from †_____ to †_____
Honorably discharged on demobilization __June 28/19__, 19____
In view of occupation he was, on date of discharge, reported ____0____ per cent disabled.
Remarks: _____

Form No. 724-1, A. G. O.   • Strike out words not applicable.   † Dates of departure from and arrival in the U. S.
Nov. 22, 1919.                                                    3—7342
```

SRC Note: HS School (Horseshoer School) FA (Field Artillery) Tr Rear (Troop Rear)

Spring 1918   Brevard News

Ernest Lafayette AIKEN

Born:	16 Mar 1888, Transylvania County, NC
Died:	8 Jan 1946, Transylvania County, NC; age 57
Buried:	Carr's Hill Baptist Church Cemetery
Father:	**Randell Theodore AIKEN**
Mother:	**Susan Virginia WILSON**
Draft Registration:	29, single, barber and farming with his father, R. T. Aiken

[Documentation: obituary; Transylvania County DC; Transylvania County Cemetery Survey, Discharge]

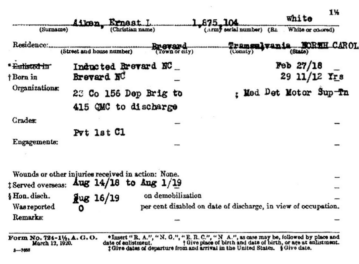

1/10/1946
ERNEST L. AIKEN

Funeral services for Ernest Aiken, 57, who died in the Brevard hospital, were held at Carr's Hill Baptist Church, Wed. afternoon. Burial was in the church cemetery. He had been ill for some time.

Mr. Aiken, a native of Brevard had always lived here. He was a veteran of World War I and members of the American Legion served as pallbearers and were in charge of the gravesite.

Surviving are two brothers: Randall and Ruel Aiken; and one sister Mrs. Selina Grant. He was the son of Mr. and Mrs. Theodore Aiken.

SRC Note: Med Det Motor Sup TN (Medical Detachment Motor Supply Train)

31 Mar 1919   Brevard News
Mrs. R.T. Aiken has had a recent letter from her son, Ernest Aiken, who is on the Rhine in Germany in which he states that he is in excellent health and enjoying life.

NEWS ON THE STREET

23 Apr 1917   Brevard News

EVIDENCE OF PATRIOTISM IS SEEN IN BREVARD

Brevard has not held any public patriotic demonstrations but flags can be seen waving in the breezes in various parts of town, from residences, places of business and autos. Lapels and hatbands bear small flags.

People are talking war on every side and reading the newspapers with interest. A few citizens have offered their services to the county and to various authorities, in the event of need, among them being Joseph S. Silversteen, T.H. Shipman, Ora L. Jones, W.E. Breese and Thomas Teague.

George Harry Lake AIKEN

Born:	3 Apr 1895, Transylvania County, NC
Died:	unknown
Race:	Colored
Father:	**James P. AIKEN**
Mother:	**Mary AIKEN**
Draft Registration:	22, single, mechanic for A.H. King Co.
Enlistment Notes:	A note in the WW I file, signed by J.I. Watson, Chief Clerk of the local Draft board stated, "George was to be entrained for Camp Dix, Wrightstown, NJ on 18 Jul 1918." It stated he was living in Washington, DC at that time. 1930 Census has him in Bay County, FL and no further records found.

[Documentation: Ancestry.com, 1910, 1930 censuses, WWI files in NC Room Transylvania County Library]

Dr. Julius Luther AIKEN

Born:	16 Sep 1897, Transylvania County, NC
Died:	11 Dec 1979, Pickens County, SC; age 82
Buried:	Hillcrest Memorial Park, Pickens, SC
Occupation:	Dentist
Spouse:	**Beatrice PEIRANO**
Father:	**William Luther AIKEN**
Mother:	**Mary Jane LANKFORD**
Draft Registration:	Julius was a dental student at that time.

[Documentation: findagrave.com; SSDI]

Aiken, Julius L(uther)			5,582,000	white [1/2]
(Surname)	(Christian name)		(Army serial number)	(Race: White or colored)

Residence:		Brevard · · · · · · · NORTH CAROLINA
	(Street and house number) (Town or city)	(County) (State)
* Enlisted in	Inducted Atlanta Ga Oct 15/18	—
† Born in	Brevard NC Sept 16 1897	—
Organizations:	SATC Atlanta Southern Dental College to discharge	—
Grades:	Pvt —	—
Engagements:	—	—

Wounds or other injuries received in action: None. —
‡ Served overseas: none — —
§ Hon. disch. Dec 8/18 on demobilization —

SRC Note: SATC (Student Army Training Corps)

12/13/1979
JULIUS AIKEN

Dr. Julius Luther Aiken, 83, retired dentist of Pickens, SC died Tuesday. He was a native of Transylvania County, the son of the late William Luther and Mary Jane Lankford Aiken.

Dr. Aiken attended Brevard Institute, Berea College and was a graduate of Atlanta Southern Dental College. He was a World War I veteran and a member of Grace United Methodist Church in Pickens.

Dr. Aiken was a charter member of Pickens Rotary Club, a life member of Keowee Lodge #78 A.F.M., a past commander of American Legion Post #11, past president of the Piedmont Dental Society, and a member of the South Carolina Dental Association.

Surviving is a daughter, Mary Aiken; two sisters: Miss Hattie Aiken and Mrs. Arabella Houston; and a half brother, W.L. Aiken.

Funeral services will be held Friday in the Grace United Methodist Church with entombment in Hillcrest Memorial Park Mausoleum at Pickens.

When the United States entered into World War I the Army Medical Department consisted of less than 1,000 personnel but it numbered over 350,000 when peace returned in November 1918. By the end of World War I the U.S. Army had enlisted a total of 4,620 dentists, 21,480 nurses and 2,234 veterinarians.

Dr. Julian L. Aiken became one of the 4,620 dentists but he was in the Army less than two months and was stationed at the Southern Dental College in Atlanta.

Richmond Pierce AIKEN

Born:	26 Jan 1894, Transylvania County, NC
Died:	8 Dec 1965, Transylvania County, NC; age 71
Spouse:	**Rozella MEECE**, m. 31 Mar 1921, Transylvania County, NC
Father:	**William Calhoun AIKEN**
Mother:	**Hester Delia Ann POWELL**
Buried:	Old Toxaway Baptist Church Cemetery
Draft Registration:	Single, employed as a laborer for R.M. Powell of Rosman; mother was a dependent

[Documentation: Transylvania County DC, Discharge; Transylvania County Cemetery Survey, Cowart's Index to Marriages]

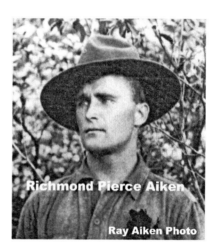

Aiken, Richmond P   1,876,460   white   1½

(Surname)   (Christian name)   (Army serial number)   (Race: White or colored)

Residence: Rosman   NORTH CAROLINA

(Street and house number)   (Town or city)   (County)   (State)

Enlisted in / Inducted Brevard NC Sept 18/17

†Born in Rosman NC 22 9/12 yrs

Organizations: FH 324 306 Sn Tn to discharge

Grades: Cook July 2/18

Engagements: —

Wounds or other injuries received in action: None.

‡Served overseas: Aug 8/18 to June 20/19

§Hon. disch. June 29/19 on demobilization

Was reported   per cent disabled on date of discharge, in view of occupation.

Remarks: 0%

Form No. 724-1½, A. G. O.
March 12, 1920.
3—1988

Richmond Pierce Aiken

Ray Aiken Photo

SRC Notes: Sn Tn (Sanitation Train)

21 Sep 1917   Brevard News
THIRTY-ONE MEN TO CAMP JACKSON

Forty percent of the certified draft, making 31 men, was ordered to report on Tuesday at 5 P.M. at the office of the local enlistment board and to leave for Camp Jackson, S.C. Wednesday morning. . . . Richmond Pierson Aiken . . .

Tuesday night at the Aethelwold Mrs. J. S. Silversteen, Chairman of the National League of Woman's Service, presented the men with comfort kits prepared by the women of the league.

On Wednesday morning 31 men formed a line at the rooms of the War Department and marched to the depot. There was no roll of drums nor blare of horns but it was, nevertheless, an impressive spectacle. A large crowd was on hand for the good-byes and the young men were cheerful.

7 Dec 1917   Brevard News
COUNTY CITIZEN VISITS CAMP BOYS

R.M. Powell of Rosman was here last week in his return from Columbia, SC, where he had been to visit some of the Transylvania boys at Camp Jackson. The boys to whom he made a special visit were his son R.C. Powell, Pierce Aiken, Wiley Owen, Walter Whitmire and Bill Bowman. Mr. Powell spent three days in camp and was much pleased with what he saw, especially with the good treatment the boys were receiving from Uncle Sam.

Ruel Elkins AIKEN

Born:	30 Jun 1894, Transylvania County, NC
Died:	4 Feb 1958, Oteen VA Hospital, Buncombe County; age 63
Buried:	Carr's Hill Baptist Church Cemetery
Spouse:	**Ada ALLISON**, m. 6 May 1920, Transylvania County, NC
Father:	**Randell Theodore AIKEN**
Mother:	**Susan Virginia WILSON**
Draft Registration:	Otsego, NY, 22, single, employed by Charles Coe and the town of Exeter, NY

[Documentation: Buncombe County DC, Transylvania County Cemetery Survey, US Headstone Application, Cowart's Index to Marriages, Ancestry.com, Discharge, TT obituary]

2/13/1958
RUEL E. AIKEN

Funeral services for Ruel E. Aiken, 63, were held at the Carr's Hill Baptist Church on February 6. Burial was in the church cemetery. Mr. Aiken was a carpenter by trade and he died at a veterans' hospital following a long illness.

He is survived by his widow, Mrs. Ada Allison Aiken; two daughters: Hattie Sue and Mrs. Clifton Ashe; a son, Edgar; one brother, Randal and one sister, Mrs. Salina Grant.

1 Aug 1918   Brevard News

Mr. and Mrs. Theo. Aiken has received word that their son, Ruel, has arrived safely overseas.

News on the Street

15 Sep 1918   Brevard News

INFORMATION TO MERCHANTS, HOUSEWIVES

Until further notice the Food Administration allows the merchants to sell to any housewife a fifteen-day's supply of sugar, based on two pounds per month for each member of the family.

Each housewife is allowed to buy not more than sixty-day's supply of flour. If buying flour that does not contain the 20 percent substitutes our Government asks that every hotel, boarding house and individual mix with wheat flour not less than 20 percent of corn meal or some other substitute, as all of the allied nations have agreed to make their bread on this basis, so that you will be eating the same kind of bread in your home that our soldier boys are eating in the trenches.

Any further information that any citizen or merchant wishes I will be glad to furnish it.

Thomas H. Shipman
Food Administration
Transylvania County

James Cecil AKERS

Born:	20 Jun 1895, Pennsylvania
Died:	25 May 1970, Transylvania County, NC; age 74
Buried:	Pisgah Gardens Cemetery
Occupation:	Painting contractor
Spouse:	**Helen Gertrude MEACHAM**
Father:	**Ellis AKERS**
Mother:	**Edith Nancy JACKSON**
Draft Registration:	Crystal Springs, PA, 21, single, painter for B.S.Jackson in Everett, PA
Military Marker:	PVT US Army WW I

[Documentation: FamilySearch.com, Ancestry.com, 1900-1940 censuses, Transylvania County Cemetery Survey, tombstone data, findagrave.com (mother), TT obituary, wife's NC DC]

4/6/1970
JAMES C. AKERS

James C. Akers, age 74 of Rosman died suddenly at his home on May 25. Mr. Akers, a native of Pennsylvania, had resided in the Rosman area part time for the past 10 years. He was a retired painting contractor, a veteran of World War I and a member of the American Legion, Elks, VFW and the Forty and Eight Club.

His wife, Mrs. Helen M. Akers and one brother, Merle Akers survive him.

Funeral services were held in the chapel of the Frank Moody Funeral Home, followed by burial in Pisgah Gardens.

---

20 Apr 1917   **Brevard News**
STATE NOW READY TO RAISE HER SHARE
GUARDS ON SPECIAL DUTY

Raleigh---With Camp Glenn, Morehead definitely designated by the War Department as the point of mobilization for troops in this state and practically all of the North Carolina Guard units now in service assigned to special guard duties at various points in the state to protect properties that might be molested by agents and sympathizers of the Germans, the National Guard authorities now have their definite lines to which to work in getting out this state's quota of whatever troops the Federal Government will raise in prosecuting the war.

It is not likely that Camp Glenn will be called into service until there comes from Washington the call for the raising of the 500,000 men to augment the regular army and the National Guard forces, and this is not expected to come until summer, possibly June or July. The task pressing upon the Guard authorities now is the enlistment of recruits to get the units of the Guard up to even the peace strength of 56 men each, to say nothing of the full war strength, which is 150 men. Numbers of the officers are free to say that they do not believe the enlistments can be completed through the ordinary volunteer channels and they believe there will have to be a call from the Governor and something in the way of a conscription by lot before the work will be completed.

The trouble seems to be that there is a general holding back to join entirely new units that it has been expected would be called for. Men in all parts of the state are ready to join new organizations, but they seem to be balking at the idea of all entering as "green privates" in old organizations with so many trained men in line ahead of them. The Guard authorities are much encouraged over the outlook, however, and there are daily indications of increased response to the call to arms through regular channels.

John Estes AKINS/AIKENS

Born: 2 Oct 1890, Jackson County, NC
Died: 16 Jul 1972, Pickens, SC; age 81
Burial: Hillcrest Memorial Park, Pickens, SC
Spouse: **Nancy Etta STEWART**
Father: **A.J. (Jack) AKINS/AIKENS**
Mother: **Callie Modena COGDILL**
Draft Registration: Self-employed farmer, married with no children.

[Documentation: Ancestry.com; SSDI Jackson County Birth Index]

Akins,	John Estis	1,316,125	White 1½
(Surname)	(Christian name)	(Army serial number)	(Race: White or colored)

NORTH CAROLINA

Residence: Lake Laxaway, Transylvania Co.
  (Street and house number) (Town or city) (County) (State)

Enlisted in: Inducted Brevard, N.C.   Oct 4/17 —
Born in: Jackson Co, NC   26 yrs —
Organizations: Hq Co 316 FA to Discharge —

Grades: — —

Pvt

Engagements: — —

Wounds or other injuries received in action: None. —
Served overseas: none —
Hon. disch. Mch 29/19   on demobilization —
Was reported 0   per cent disabled on date of discharge, in view of occupation.
Remarks: — —

Form No. 724-1½, A. G. O.
March 12, 1920.
3—7685

*Insert "R. A.," "N. G.," "E. R. C.," "N. A.," as case may be, followed by place and date of enlistment. †Give place of birth and date of birth, or age at enlistment.
‡Give dates of departure from and arrival in the United States. §Give date.

SRC Note: FA (Field Artillery)

Greenville News (SC)
7/20/1972
JOHN E. AIKEN

John Esley Aiken, 82, Easley, died Wednesday. Born in Transylvania County, NC, son of Jackie Aiken, he was an employee of Arial Mill and a taxi driver.

Surviving are a daughter, two brothers, Marshall and Walter Aiken; and two sisters, Stella Wimpy and Becky Queen.

Services were held on Friday at Elljean Baptist Church and burial in the Hillcrest Memorial Park.

Members of 119th Infantry at Woodpile

Haywood County Digital Collection

Julian Leftwich ALBERT

Born:	4 Jul 1899, Interior, VA
Died:	3 Feb 1968, Los Angeles, CA; age 68
Buried:	Williamette National Cemetery, Portland, OR
Father:	**Sidney ALBERT**
Mother:	**Martha LEFTWICH**
Draft Registration:	**No**
Military Marker:	PFC US Army World War I

[Documentation: Ancestry.com: findagrave.com, Discharge, US Veterans Gravesites]

Albert, Julian L   1,305,668   White
(Surname)   (Christian name)   (Army serial number) (Race: White or colored)

Residence:_____Pisgah Forest,_____NORTH CAROLINA
              (Street and house number)   (Town or city)   (County)   (State)

* Enlisted in NG   Asheville, N C   —   July 24/17 —
† Born in   Interior, Va   —   18 yrs   —
Organizations:
    Co F 1 Inf NC NG to Sept 12/17; 14 Co 4 Bn 155 Dep Brig to
    Oct 24/17; Co C 113 M.G. Bn to Mch 1/18; Co D 115 MG Bn to
                                                   Discharge —

Grades: Pvt 1 cl Sept 28/17; Pvt Oct 26/ 17

Engagements: —   —

Wounds or other injuries received in action: None.   —
‡ Served overseas: May 11/18 to Mch 22/19   —
§ Hon. disch.   Apr 2/19   on demobilization   —
Was reported   0   per cent disabled on date of discharge, in view of occupation.
Remarks: —   —

Form No. 724-1½, A. G. O.   *Insert "R. A.", "N. G.", "E. R. C.", "N A.", as case may be, followed by place and
    March 12, 1920.   date of enlistment.   † Give place of birth and date of birth, or age at enlistment.
    3—7668   ‡ Give dates of departure from and arrival in the United States. § Give date.

SRC Note: NC NG (North Carolina National Guard) MG (Machine Gun)

TRAFFIC POLICE Camp Hancock Augusta, Ga.

1919 Post Card

Sidney M. ALBERT

Born:	Dec 1898, Roanoke, VA
Died:	28 May 1945, Manila, Philippines; age 47
Buried:	Ft. William McKinley Cemetery, Manila
Occupation:	Career military, cook and baker for the unit
Notes:	Divorced; ex-wife and children in Buncombe County
Draft Registration:	No

[Document sources: web page hhtp;://www.mm.org/duffyamerlead.html; ancestry.com, Discharge from WW I, Census records]

Albert, Sidney M.   717,517   White
  (Surname)   (Christian name)   (...my serial number) (Race: White or colored)

Residence: Pisgah Forest   NORTH CAROLINA
  (Street and house number)   (Town or city)   (County)   (State)

*Enlisted in   N G   Hendersonville N C   Aug 21/17
†Born in   Roanoke Va   19 8/12 years
Organizations:

6 Co CAC FT Caswell N C to Sept 9/18; Unit L Sept Aut Repl
Draft CA Ft Caswell No Oct 16/18; Heavy Arty Tng Bn
Grades: APO 733 To Nov 25/18; Btry C Tractor Arty Repl Bg 1 –
Army to dec 17/18; 54 Arty CAC to disch

Engagements: (Over)

Wounds or other injuries received in action: None.
‡Served overseas: Sept 25/18 Moh 7/19
§Hon. disch. Moh 18/19   on demobilization
Was reported   0   per cent disabled on date of discharge, in view of occupation.
Remarks:

Remarks (continued):

Pvt lcl Feb 1/18; Corp Feb 9/18; Sgt July 27/18;
Pvt Nov 25/18

SRC Note: CAC (Coast Artillery Corps) Tng (training) Arty (artillery)

Kitchen Police 105th Engineer Train Company E

Haywood County Digital Collection

Bowen ALEXANDER

Born:	23 Nov 1892, Oconee, SC
Died:	23 Oct 1918 at military camp; age 25
Buried:	Hamburg Cemetery, Jackson County, NC
Father:	**William P. ALEXANDER**
Mother:	**Susan Belle CABE**
Registration Card:	26, single, employed by W.P. Alexander, gave Glenville, Jackson County, NC, place of residence

[Documentation: Ancestry.com]

8

Alexander, Bowen   4,159,758   *White *Colored*
(Surname)   (Christian name)   (Army serial number)

Residence: _____ Saphire Transylvania NORTH CAROLINA
(Street and house number) (Town or city) (County)   (State)

*Enlisted *R. A. *N. G. *E. R. C. *Inducted at Sylva, N C   on July 24 19 18
Place of birth: Oconee Co., S C   Age or date of birth: Nov 23, 1891
Organizations served in, with dates of assignments and transfers:
        20 Co Rct Receiving Dep Camp Hancock, Ga to Aug 28/18;
        72 Co 6 Grade M Trk Det to death
Grades, with date of appointment:
        Pvt

Engagements:

Wounds or other injuries received in action: *None.
Served overseas from †   to †   , from †   to †
Died of _____ Influenza - lobar pneumonia _____ Oct 23 , 19 18
(Cause and date of death)
Person notified of death: _____ Perry Alexander _____ Father
(Name)   (Degree of relationship) N . C.
_____ Saphire _____
(No. and street or rural route)   (City, town, or post office)   (State or country)
Remarks :
Form No. 724-S, A. G. O.   *Strike out words not applicable.   † Dates of departure from and arrival in the U. S.
Nov. 22, 1919.   3—7359

<u>23 Nov 1917</u>   <u>Brevard News</u>

OUR OWN BOYS MUST HAVE CAMP COMFORTS
National League For Women's Service Makes The Appeal To People Of County To Contribute Produce–Every Boy And Enlisted Should Have Sweaters And Kits

The National League of Women's Service of Transylvania County has been working along all patriotic lines for the past seven months and recently made and equipped 82 comfort kits, to give to each one of the last drafted boys.

The league now has the names and addresses of the boys who enlisted from this county and are working to make each one of them a comfort kit. The boys come from all parts of the county and we need funds to carry on the work. We asked that the farmers help us by donating corn, potatoes, butter, pumpkins or canned fruit. The league will find a sale for these things and will use the money in this way to equip the balance of the comfort kits. We will also buy yarn to be made into sweaters for the Transylvania boys and donations of money, no matter how small, will be gratefully accepted.

Any who want to make their boys happier and more comfortable may send donations to the president Mrs. Joseph S. Silversteen or the store of C.M. Doyle, Brevard.

Elizabeth M. Silversteen, Pres. National League for Women's service of Transylvania County

Bowen Alexander died at Camp Hancock, GA of influenza and lobar pneumonia 23 Oct 1918.

James William ALLENDER

Born:	25 May 1896, Spring City, TN
Died:	15 Sep 1978, Buncombe County, NC; age 82
Buried:	Pisgah Gardens
Occupation:	Retired papermaker
Spouse:	**Annie Glendola MATTHEWS**
Father:	**Myron Eugene ALLENDER**
Mother:	**Mary Kate DOTSON**
Draft Registration:	21, Single, working for Wolf River P&F Company, Shawano, WI

[Documentation: Roster of WWI Veterans from American Legion 50th Anniversary celebration; NC Death Collection; Son Ronnie's obit; BIRLS Death File; Transylvania County Cemetery Survey; 1900-1920 Censuses and 1940 Census; Marriage records of parents; obit]

9/21/1978
ALLENDER, JAMES W.

James William Allender, age 82, of Pisgah Forest, died Friday evening in Memorial Mission Hospital in Asheville after a period of declining health. He was a native of Spring City, Tenn. and had lived in Transylvania County for some 20 years. He was a son of the late Eugene and Mary Kate Dotson Allender. He was a retired papermaker and a veteran of World War I.

Surviving are the widow, Glendora Matthews Allender; two sons, Ronald and Danny Allender; a brother, Robert Allender; and three sisters: Sally Westpall, Lois Raasch, and Hazel Montour.

Services were held Sunday at the Brevard Wesleyan Church and the burial was in Pisgah Gardens.

Eugene ALLISON

Born:	Sep 1892, Brevard, NC
Died:	2 Jun1939, Nantahala, Swain County, NC; age 46
Buried:	Rutherford County Memorial Cemetery
Spouse:	**Byrd LAMBE**
Father:	**William Hix ALLISON**
Mother:	**Mattie YONGUE**
Draft Registration:	Single, 24 years of age, attorney and manager of a 300 acre farm
Note:	Eugene served in both WWI and WWII.

[Document sources: Swain County DC, Dunn's Rock Masonic Lodge Archives]

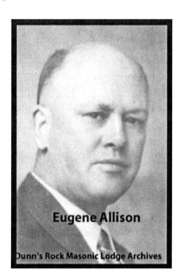

Eugene Allison

Dunn's Rock Masonic Lodge Archives

		OFFICER—NG
Allison	Eugene	White
(Surname)	(Christian name)	
Residence	Buvard	NORTH CAROLINA
(Street and house number)	(Town or city) (County)	(State)

• Born in **Buvard N C** **Sept 12/92**

† Drafted into Federal service Aug. 5, 1917, as **2 Lt F A; N G**

Promotions: **1Lt Dec 25/17**

Organizations and staff assignments: **113 F A to disch**

Principal stations: **Mooresville N C, Camp Sevier S C; AEF**

Engagements:

Wounds received in action: None.

‡ Served overseas **May 27/18 to Mch 19/19**

Hon. disch. (date) **Mch 28/19** for convenience of the Government, services no longer required.

Was reported **0** per cent disabled on date of discharge, in view of occupation.

SRC Note: FA (field artillery) AEF (American Expeditionary Forces)

3 Aug 1917   Brevard News
EUGENE ALLISON RECEIVED LIEUTENANTS COMMISSION
    The News inadvertently overlooked the name of Eugene Allison in the list of volunteers last week. Mr. Allison rendered valuable aid in recruiting a machine-gun company and was promised a lieutenants commission if he would enlist 20 men for a field artillery company. He raised more than the required number and has received his commission as 2nd Lieut. He is stationed for training for about 2 weeks at Mooresville.
    Lieut. Allison writes his people that he has scored the highest points in physical examination of any man in the battery of 119 men and that every one of the 25 boys who went with him from Transylvania passed the examination successfully and that he had been commended for the fine type of boys he enlisted from this county. He reported that they were all getting along fine.

24 Aug 1917   Brevard News
Lieut. Eugene Allison, who has been stationed at Mooresville, for a few weeks, requested a change of address to Camp Sevier, Greenville South Carolina. The other boys from Brevard who were with Lieut. Allison are also at Greenville.

14 Sep 1917   Brevard News
A.H. Allison and Ralph Fisher motored on Saturday to Greenville and Camp Sevier near that city. They returned the same day, accompanied by Lieut. Eugene Allison, who stayed over Sunday, to visit here.

19 Oct 1917   Brevard News

Lieut. Eugene Allison, Ralph Duckworth, Horace Davis, Carl and George Fortune and Dahl Swangim of Camp Sevier, Greenville, spent Saturday night and Sunday in Brevard, returning Sunday night.

28 Dec 1917   Brevard News

Eugene Allison who was commissioned last summer as second lieutenant, has received, it is reported, the commission of first lieutenant in the field artillery.

3 Mar 1918   Brevard News

A private letter from Lieut. Eugene Allison, from which we take the liberty to comment upon, says: "you have no idea the pleasure I derive from the paper. It brings more news than can be written in a letter." He says the boys are doing fine work. Scarcely any sickness at all since the warm weather has set in.

He says it helps all the boys to have their friends from home visit them. It makes them think that the home people are behind them in the movement to further the cause of democracy.

21 Jun 1918   Brevard News

Lieut. Eugene Allison has arrived safely in France.

14 Nov 1918   Brevard News

Mrs. W.H. Allison has had recent letters from her sons Eugene and Haskell. Both are well and enjoying France.

Eugene Allison
Source: Catherine Merrill Watkins scrapbook at Transylvania County Library

Large Throng Attends Eugene Allison Rites

Funeral services for Eugene Allison, 45, deputy United States Marshal of Asheville, were held at Brevard Methodist Church Sunday afternoon at 2 o'clock. Mr. Allison died suddenly of a heart attack on Thursday night while on duty investigating a robbery in Swain County.

Interment was in Oak Grove Cemetery, North Brevard with Masonic rites. (Later moved to Rutherford County Memorial Cemetery)

Attesting to the high esteem in which Mr. Allison was held was the fact that it was one of the largest funerals said to have been held at the local church. A large number of those in attendance included his numerous friends from various sections of Western North Carolina, particularly those from Forest City, Rutherfordton and Alexander, where he taught school for a number of years and his business associates from Asheville. The many handsome floral pieces were also a tribute of loving friendship.

High tribute was paid Mr. Allison at the funeral service. The following statement from U.S. Marshal Charles R. Price of the western district of the Department of Justice of N.C. (with which Mr. Allison was connected) has since been made: "I had known Mr. Allison for about ten years and held him in the highest esteem. His amiable disposition endeared him to all who knew him. He made friends easily and held them. Mr. Allison joined my force a little more than a year ago and proved a capable and efficient officer. I feel that his death, tragic as it was, came as he would have desired - while on the job".

Surviving are the widow; one son, Eugene, Jr., two daughters: Mary Lambe and Hix; his mother, Mrs. W.H. Allison of Brevard; a brother, Major Haskell Allison; two sisters: Mrs. T.A. Dekle and Mrs. Earl Boyd.

Mr. Allison was a native of Brevard and lived here at the home of his mother, Deer Park Home, until moving to Forest City about 15 years ago. He served overseas in the World War and was married soon after his return home after the signing of the Armistice. He practiced law in Brevard for a number of years and later was principal of the Davidson River School for several years. He was a former member of the Brevard Methodist Church and was at all times active and deeply interested in church and civic affairs. He was a Mason.

Haskell ALLISON

Born:	26 Dec 1895, Transylvania County, NC
Died:	23 Jun 1973, Lake County, FL; age 77
Buried:	Raleigh National Cemetery, Raleigh, NC
Spouse:	**Rose Alberta LAUTERWASSER**
Father:	**William Hix ALLISON**
Mother:	**Mattie YONGUE**
Draft Registration:	Single, a student at a government training camp, Ft. Oglethorpe, GA.

[Documentation; Ancestry.com, Findagrave.com]

18 May 1917   Brevard News
Haskell Allison left on Saturday for Ft. Oglethorpe, GA to take training preparatory for making a commissioned officer.

17 Aug 1917   Brevard News
Haskell Allison, who left Clemson College in the spring with other seniors to enter the training camp at Fort Oglethorpe, has received a second lieutenant's commission in the United States regular army. He is expected home on a visit this week.

14 Nov 1918   Brevard News
Mrs. W.H. Allison has had recent letters from her sons, Eugene and Haskell. Both are well and enjoying France.

---

8 Jun 1917   Brevard News
TOTAL WAR REGISTRATION FOR COUNTY WAS 850.

15 Jun 1917   Brevard News
MORE THAN 200,000 WERE ENROLLED IN NORTH CAROLINA

James Stanley ALLISON

Born:	1 Jan 1893, Transylvania County, NC
Died:	28 Nov 1961, Oteen VA Hospital, Buncombe County; age 68
Buried:	Evergreen-Gillespie Cemetery
Occupation:	Farmer
Spouse:	**Kitty Elizabeth HIGGINS**, m. 1 Nov 1919, Transylvania County, NC
Father:	**William S. ALLISON**
Mother:	**Flora TOWNSEND**
Draft Registration:	Henderson County, 24, single, farmer

[Documentation: Buncombe DC, Discharge, findagrave.com, Ancestry.com, Cowart's Index to Marriages, TT obituary]

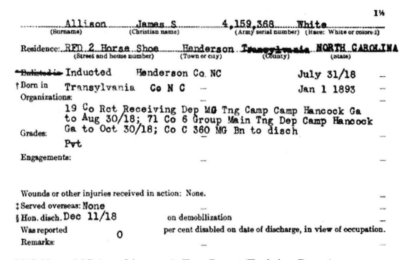

SRC Note: MG (machine gun) Tng Depot (Training Depot)

11/28/1968
JAMES S. ALLISON

Funeral services for James Stanley Allison, age 68, will be held Thursday afternoon at Forge Valley Baptist Church with burial following in the Gillespie Evergreen Cemetery.

Mr. Allison died Tuesday in the Oteen Veterans Hospital. For a number of years he had made his home with a son William in Mountain Home. Mr. Allison was a native of Transylvania County and also a member of the Pisgah Forest Baptist Church. His wife, Kitty Higgins Allison, predeceased him.

Survivors include three daughters: Mrs. Elizabeth Morgan, Mrs. Ruby Little and Mrs. Mary Sue Dalton; three sons: James S, Jr., Harold and William Allison; two brothers: Arthur and Turner; three sisters: Mrs. Emmett Reece, Mrs. Joe McCrary and Mrs. Fred Manley.

<u>5 Sep 1918</u>   **Brevard News**
RED CROSS SENDS SOCKS TO SOLDIERS

The Transylvania Red Cross last week sent 130 pairs of hand-knit woolen socks to Atlanta to be sent to France for American soldiers. This box of socks is the twenty-ninth Red Cross box sent from the local chapter to Atlanta since the first of January.

Julian Thomas ALLISON

Born:	3 Mar 1888, Transylvania County, NC
Died:	10 Jan 1963, Henderson County, NC; age 74
Buried:	Boylston Baptist Church Cemetery, Henderson County, NC
Occupation:	Retired state employee
Spouse:	**Zora Jane LEDBETTER**
Father:	**Benjamin Franklin ALLISON**
Mother:	**Martha ALLISON**
Draft Registration:	30, single, farming
Discharge:	Enlisted Nov. 5, 1917 in Brevard. Private Quartermaster Corps, National Army. Discharged Dec. 20, 1917 due to health problems.

[Documentation: Henderson County DC, Discharge paper, Henderson County, North Carolina Cemeteries, Ancestry.com, Discharge, Henderson T-N obituary]

2 Nov 1917   **Brevard News**
LOCAL BOARD ORDERS THIRTEEN MORE MEN
All men whose names appear here are ordered to report to the Local Board at 5 P.M. on Monday, November 5, 1917 for transportation for Camp Jackson. They will leave for Camp November 6 at 8 A.M. . . . J.T. Allison . . .

10/12/1963
JULIAN ALLISON

Julian Thomas Allison, 75, a resident of Mountain Home and a retired state employee, died at his home Tuesday after a period of declining health.

Funeral services will be held Wednesday at 3 p.m. in the Boylston Baptist Church in Pisgah Forest. Burial will be in the church cemetery.

Surviving Mr. Allison are the wife, the former Zora Ledbetter; two daughters: Mrs. C.V. Nicholson and Mrs. J.H. Huggins Jr.; and a son, R.M. Allison.

A member of Boylston Baptist Church, Mr. Allison was employed as a bridge construction worker by the state before he retired.

---

24 Oct 1918   **Brevard News**

THE LOCAL EXEMPTION BOARD

Since the United States entered into this struggle for democracy the News has given considerable space to patriotic causes and has also given some space to patriotic citizens who have neglected their businesses to take up patriotic work. Yet there are some for whose work we have errored and fallen short in showing the proper appreciation, and the News feels it should take this written method of expressing its appreciation for the work done by the Local Exemption board.

These gentlemen Dr. J. W. Wallis, Messrs. J. I. Watson, T. S. Wood and F. E. Shuford have not only neglected their businesses, but they have neglected their homes and loved ones for this work and have spent many nights until one, two and three o'clock laboring over the questionnaires, etc., and the compensation they will realize for their service is nothing to compare with the sacrifices they have made. They have proven their worth and have shown their patriotism by their untiring efforts as our local exemption board and we feel we speak the sentiments of the whole community in this little tribute to them.

Richard Edgar ALLISON

Born: 3 Aug 1890, Transylvania County, NC
Died: 11 Jun 1950, Oteen Veteran's Hospital, Buncombe County; age 59
Buried: Boylston Baptist Church Cemetery, Henderson County, NC
Occupation: Carpenter
Spouse: **Sarah Ellen ALLISON**
Father: **Richard I. ALLISON**
Mother: **Sarah Rebecca BANNING**
Draft Registration: Single, carpenter for the Transylvania Tanning Co. of Brevard

[Documentation: Buncombe County DC; TT obituary, Cowart's Index to Marriages, Discharge]

Allison, Richard E.   4,159,449   White   1¼
(Surname)   (Christian name)   (Army serial number)   (Race: White or colored)
Residence: Route 1   Etowah   Transylvania   NORTH CAROLINA
(Street and house number)   (Town or city)   (County)   (State)
Enlisted in   Inducted at Brevard Transylvania Co N C   July 24/18
Born in   Blantyre N C   Aug 3, 1890
Organizations: School Co 1 MG Tng C to Nov 16/18; Co M Group 2 Main Tng;
Dep MG Tng C to Dec 24/18; C o C Provisional Group 2
Main Tng Dep to Feb 6/19; Co A Provisional Group 2
Camp Hancock Ga to disch
Grades: Pvt

Engagements: —

Wounds or other injuries received in action: None.
Served overseas: None
Hon. disch. Feb 12/19   on demobilization
Was reported 0   per cent disabled on date of discharge, in view of occupation.
Remarks:

Form No. 724-1¼, A. G. O.
March 12, 1920.

SRC Notes: MG Tng (Machine Gun Training)

6/22/1950
RICHARD EDGAR ALLISON
Last rites for Richard Edgar Allison, age 60, a veteran of World War I, were held at Boylston Baptist Church with burial in the Boylston church cemetery. Mr. Allison died at Oteen Veterans Hospital following a lengthy illness. He was a carpenter and had made his home near Etowah.

He is survived by seven daughters: Mrs. Virginia Garren, Mrs. Margaret Rollins, Mrs. Lucille Watkins, Esther, Beulah, Lois and Nancy Allison; six sons: Richard, James, Robert, Ralph, Charles and David; one sister, Mrs. Sophia Griffin; and a brother, Walter Allison.

18 Jul 1918 Brevard News
23 MORE MEN TO LEAVE JULY 24, 1918
Following is a list of white registrants for induction on July 24th, 1918 for Camp Hancock, Ga., who will leave on the 3:13 train:
. . . Richard Edgar Allison, Etowah R.F.D. . . .

TRANSPORTATION CORPS

The French railroad had dangerously deteriorated during the war and it was necessary for the United States to provide both personnel and supplies to bring the system up to a high state of efficiency.

It was early decided, as expedient for our purposes, to use American rolling stock on the French railroads, and approximately 20,000 cars and 1,500 standard gauge locomotives were brought from the United States and assembled by our railroad troops. We assisted the French by repairing with our own personnel 57,385 French cars and 1,947 French locomotives. The lack of rolling stock for allied use was at all times a serious handicap, so that the number of cars and locomotives built and repaired by us was no small part of our contribution to the allied cause.

Orcutt, Louis E., **The Great War Supplement**, published 1920, p. 278.

Robert Thomas ALLISON

Born:	14 Oct 1890, Henderson County, NC
Died:	14 Jan 1969 in Oteen VA Hospital, Buncombe County; age 78
Buried:	Pisgah Gardens Cemetery
Occupation:	Retired carpenter
Spouse:	**Jettie FAHNESTOCK**
Father:	**Samuel Franklin ALLISON**
Mother:	**Evelyn ANDERS**
Draft Registration:	Single, self-employed farmer, claimed sister and children as dependents

[Documentation: Buncombe County DC; Transylvania County, DC]

Allison, Robert Thomas   1,865,835   White   1¼
(Surname)   (Christian name)   (Army serial number)   (Race: White or colored)

Residence: RFD 1   Etowah   Henderson   NORTH CAROLINA
(Street and house number)   (Town or city)   (County)   (State)

Enlisted in   Inducted at Brevard NC   Apr 1/18
Born in   Blantyre NC   28 7/12 yrs
Organizations: 29 Co 8 Tng Bn 156 Dep Brig to Apr 22/18; Sn Squad
1 81 Div Camp Sevier SC to June 13/18; 322 Amb Co 306
Sn Tn to July 18/18; 1 Development Bn Camp Sevier SC to
Aug 6/18; 4 Bn US Guards New Orleans La to Sept 1/18; #
Grades: Sgt Oct 21/18

Engagements:
Remarks (continued):
Co A 35 Bn US Guards Camp Beauregard La to disch

Served overseas: None
Hon. disch.   Jan 6/19   on demobilization
Was reported   0   per cent disabled on date of discharge, in view of occupation.
Remarks:

SRC Note: SN Squad (Sanitation Squad) Sn Tn (Sanitation Train)

2/15/1969
ROBERT ALLISON

Robert T. Allison, 78, died January 14th in an Asheville hospital after a long illness. Mr. Allison was a World War I veteran and a member of the American Legion. He belonged to the Glady Branch Baptist Church in Brevard.

Survivors include the wife, Jettie F. Allison; two daughters: Mrs. Rowe Cantrell and Mrs. Reynolds Bush; one son, Thomas E. Allison; and one sister, Mrs. Henrietta Dalton.

Funeral services were conducted January 17th in the Glady Branch Baptist Church and burial followed in the Pisgah Gardens Cemetery.

---

31 Jan 1919   Brevard News

The Red Cross will sell at AUCTION ON Monday, FEB 2ND at 12:30 noon, one Registered Shorthorn Cow and one four month old Calf. This cow is known as Lorora Banff. She is four years old, was bred in Wisconsin and bought by Mr. R.W. Everett at a sale in Asheville. She brought at that sale $250. She will weigh about 1400 pounds, is fine type of beef stock. All the money goes to the RED CROSS. Mr. Everett gave her to the RED CROSS.

Thos. H. Shipman, C.E. Orr and C.M. Doyle: Committee

Samuel Benjamin ALLISON

Born:	25 Mar 1899, Transylvania County, NC
Died:	7 Oct 1962, Corvallis, OR; age 63
Buried:	Oaklawn, Corvallis, OR
Occupation:	Retired State Highway Dept. employee
Spouse:	**Sallie ZACHARY**
Father:	**Benjamin L. ALLISON**
Mother:	**Sallie LITTEN**
Draft Registration:	No

[Documentation: obituary; application for headstone; Ancestry.com, Discharge]

Name ALLISON- SAMUEL BENJIMAN   Service Number   100-57-23
Enlisted
Enro XXX'   RECRUITING STATION RALEIGH NC   Date   5-10-17
Age at Entrance   24 YRS 1 MO   Rate   U.S.N.
Home Address   **   APPRENTICE SEAMAN   XXX N. R. F
A.   Served at TRANSYLVANIA   State BREVARD
                                    From   To   Served as   NC   No. Days

TRAINING STATION NORFOLK	5-10-17	6-6-17	APPRENTICE SEAMAN	27
RECEIVING SHIP NORFOLK	6-6-17	6-6-17	FIREMAN 3 CLASS	25
U S S NEW YORK	6-6-17	6-15-17	FIREMAN 2 CLASS	498
U S S WISCONSIN	6-15-17	7-7-17		
RECEIVING SHIP NEW ORLEANS LA	7-7-17	8-25-17		
U S S BRIDGEPORT	8-25-17	11-11-18		

Remarks:

Date   Discharge   11-13-19   FIREMAN 1 CLASS
Place   Inactive D XXX   U S S BRIDGEPORT AT NEW YORK N Y Rate at Discharge

Oct. 12, 1962
SAMUEL ALLISON
Funeral services for Samuel B. Allison, age 73, of Corvallis, Oregon were held Tuesday afternoon in the McHenry Chapel in Corvallis. Burial was in the Oaklawn Cemetery.

Mr. Allison died Sunday in the Good Samaritan Hospital following a lingering illness.

A retired employee of the State Highway department, he had been a resident of Transylvania County until moving to Oregon a few years ago.

Surviving are the widow, Mrs. Sally Zachary Allison; one daughter, Mrs. Betsy Beddingfield; two sons: Hugh and Sgt.. Robert L. Allison of the US Army; and one brother: James L. Allison.

18 May 1917   Brevard News
BREVARD YOUNG MEN ANSWER WAR'S CALL
   The call to arms continues to meet with response of one kind or another in Brevard. Since the last issue of the News several applications for a chance to serve the country have been made
. . . . Sam D. Allison . . . passed examinations for Naval service successfully.

18 May 1917   Brevard News
The news is informed by the Navy recruiting station at Raleigh that Samuel B. Allison enlisted on the 10th from this county.

2 Nov 1917   Brevard News
 Sam Allison was here recently on leave. He is now a fireman on the U.S. ship, USS Bridgeport, the converted German vessel, *Breslau*, and is stationed at Boston, Mass.

> Upon the entrance of the United States into World War I, customs officials seized *Breslau*, but not before her German crew had done considerable damage to her machinery. She was assigned Identification Number (Id. No.) 3009, renamed *Bridgeport* on 9 June 1917, and commissioned into service on 25 August 1917.

Walter Dakota ALLISON

Born:	22 Jun 1897, Transylvania County, NC
Died:	9 Nov 1980, Hendersonville, NC, age 83
Buried:	Boylston Baptist Church Cemetery, Henderson County, NC
Father:	**Richard I. ALLISON**
Mother:	**Sarah Rebecca BANNING**
Draft Registration:	No

[Documentation sources: Henderson County DC, Henderson T-N obituary]

```
                                                          5¾
--------------Allison,    Walter          _____White_____
      (Surname)     (Christian name)      (Army serial number)  (Race: White or colored)

Residence:_____Penrose_____NORTH CAROLINA
      (Street and house number)    (Town or city)    (County)      (State)

*Enlisted in     NG at Goldsboro, N.C.         June 21/17       —
†Born in         Penrose, N.C.      —          19 10/12 yrs     —
 Organizations:
                 Co F 2nd InfN.C.N.G.to Aug 31/17; Co F 119 Inf   —
                 to desertion

Grades:
                 Pvt 1st cl Oct 18/17      —

Engagements:                       —                            —


Wounds or other injuries received in action: None.
‡Served overseas: None           —                             —
§Deserted        Dec 17/17 at Camp Sevier, S.C.                —
 Remarks:

Form No. 724-5½, A. G. O.    *Insert "R. A.", "N. G.", "E. R. C.", "N A.", as case may be, followed by place and
  March 12, 1920.             date of enlistment.    †Give place of birth and date of birth, or age at enlistment.
  1—7882                      ‡Give dates of departure from and arrival in the United States.  §Give date and place.
```

Hendersonville Times-News
11/10 /1980
WALTER D. ALLISON

Walter D. Allison, 83, of Dillard Avenue, Hendersonville, died Sunday at his residence following a long illness. He was a native of Transylvania County and was the son of the late Richard and Sarah Banning Allison. Surviving are several nieces and nephews.

Services will be held at 2 pm Tuesday in the Antioch Baptist Church, of which he was a member. Burial will be in Boyleston Baptist Church Cemetery.

---

11 Aug 1918   Brevard News
WAR WORK IN WASHINGTON

If you are not called upon to fight for your country, you may earn good money in transportation work, which is equally essential to victory. Our war for liberty and democracy is administered from the United States government and the Nation's capital, and countless workers have been brought into Washington for this purpose. These workers, as well as the normal population of the city, must be carried daily to and from their offices by the street railways, many of whose employees have been drafted.

It is vital that the transportation system on the capital should be kept in a state of maximum efficiency and that the place of employees who are offering their lives for our country should be filled without delay.

The Washington Railway Electric Company now offers excellent positions as conductors and motorman to men between the ages of 17 and 50. The work is considered essential by the Government authorities. It is pleasant, helpful, and permanent, and gives ambitious men the opportunity to learn the street railway business.

The rate of pay, after instruction for a period equal to 60 hours, is $.32 an hour to start. Men may then earn from $80-$100 monthly. Wages are paid daily.

If you want to engage in pleasant and healthful work in the most beautiful city in the United States, apply in person or by letter to the Chief Instructor, Washington Railway and Electric Company, 14th and E. Capitol St., Washington DC.

Wave Jefferson ALLISON

Born:	21 May 1889, Transylvania County, NC
Died:	26 Feb 1963, NC Cancer Institute, Robeson County; age 73
Buried:	Piney Grove Cemetery, Talley Rd., Penrose, NC
Spouse:	**Maggie BRADLEY**, m. 19 Dec 1909, Transylvania County
Father:	**William Marion ALLISON**
Mother:	**Sallie PARKER**
Draft Registration:	Married, fireman for Southern RR Co, asked for exemption because of his wife and child
Note:	His death certificate has the name ROBERT QUEEN and not Wave Jefferson ALLISON.

[Documentation: Robeson County DC, Cowart's Index to Marriage, Ancestry.com]

```
                                                             J½
        Allison,  Wave J.                      White
       (Surname)    (Christian name)   (Army serial number) (Race: White or colored)

Residence: R-1      Penrose           Transylvania NORTH CAROLINA
          (Street and house number)  (Town or city)  (County)     (State)

Enlisted in  Inducted at Brevard N C.              Oct 4/17        -
†Born in     Penrose N C            -              28 4/12 yrs     -
Organizations: Hq Co 316 FA to Oct 16/17;Co D 119 Inf to desertion -

Grades:     Pvt                     -                              -

Engagements:                        -                             -


Wounds or other injuries received in action: None.               -
‡Served overseas:  None             -                             -
§Deserted    Dec 7/17 at Camp Sevier S C                          -
Remarks:                            -                             -
```

SRC Notes: FA (Field Artillery)

2/26/1963
ROBERT E. QUEEN
AKA: WAVE JEFFERSON ALLISON

Last rites for Robert Ernest Queen, age 73, of Route 1, Pisgah Forest, will be held Thursday morning at Turkey Creek Baptist Church. Burial will be in Piney Grove Cemetery. Mr. Queen died early Tuesday morning in a Lumberton hospital following a long illness

A lifelong resident of Transylvania County, he was a retired carpenter and a member of Turkey Creek Baptist Church.

Survivors include one son, Layton Allison and one brother, Dewey Allison.

---

12 Apr 1918   **Brevard News**
REWARD OFFERED FOR TRANSYLVANIA DESERTER

The following man from Transylvania County has deserted from Camp Sevier, South Carolina:
Allison, Wave J., Company D, 119th Infantry, deserted Dec. 7, 1917. Age 28, height 5 ft. 7 ½ in., brown hair, brown eyes, weight 140 lbs.: home address Penrose, R.F.D. 2.

A reward of $50.00 will be paid to any person for the delivery of the above deserter to the nearest army post or camp.
William G. Green   Capt. 119th Infantry

Bud (Justin) ANDERS

Born:	28 Aug 1892, Transylvania County, NC
Died:	25 May 1958, Richmond County, GA; age 65
Burial:	Macedonia Church Cemetery
Spouse:	**Norma OWEN**, m. 16, Jan 1926, Transylvania County
Father:	**Phillip M. ANDERS**
Mother:	**Mary Jane HEAD**
Draft Registration:	Single, farming, and claimed his mother as a dependent
NOTE:	Three members of this family were killed when their auto crashed into a freight train near Augusta, GA, 25 May 1958.
Military Marker:	N.C. PVT 3CO 1 Development BN WW I

[Documentation: application for headstone, Ancestry.com, Cowart's Index to Marriages, Discharge, Hendersonville, T-N obituary]

Justin "Bud" Anders

Gertrude Morgan Photo

Anders, Bud   4,773,497   White
  (Surname)   (Christian name)   (Army serial number)   (Race: White or colored)

Residence: Lake Toxoway Transylvania NORTH CAROLINA
               (Street and house number)   (Town or city)   (County)   (state)

Inducted
~~Enlisted in~~   Brevard ,Transylvania Co., N.C.   Aug 30/18
Born in   Lake Toxoway N C   26 yrs
Organizations: 3 Co 1 Development Bn Camp Greene N C to disch

Grades: Pvt

Engagements:

Wounds or other injuries received in action: None.
Served overseas: None
Hon. disch.   Feb 7/19   on demobilization
Was reported 20   per cent disabled on date of discharge, in view of occupation.

Hendersonville Times News
5/27/1958
ANDERS' TRIPLE FUNERAL

Triple funeral services for three members of a Pisgah Forest family who were killed in a train-auto collision near Augusta GA on Sunday will be held Wednesday at 2 p.m. in Macedonia Baptist Church in Transylvania County. Interment will follow in the church cemetery.

The three victims are Mr. and Mrs. Bud Anders and their son, Coy. Two other members of the family remain in critical condition in an Augusta hospital, where they underwent brain surgery following the accident. They are Lois, 13, and Harold, 11. Another son, Alvoid, 23, the driver of the Anders car at the time of the accident, was not seriously injured. Two older children, Gertrude Morgan and Vernon Anders also survive.

The family had been employed on a gladiolus farm at Cocoa FL during the winter and was returning to their Pisgah Forest home because Alvoid was to be inducted into the armed forces on Tueday.

---

23 Jan 1918   Brevard News
SOLDIERS ADVISED TO INSURE LIVES
Dr. Hunt Advises All Soldiers To Get Government Insurance At Once.

Charlie ANDERS

Born:	24 Apr 1896, Henderson County, NC
Died:	13 Mar 1974, Polk County; age 77
Buried:	Evergreen Memorial Gardens, Landrum, SC
Spouse:	**Lillie Mae FORRESTER**
Father:	**O. Frank ANDERS**
Mother:	**Mary Elizabeth HENRY**
Draft Registration:	21, single, listed mother as a dependent
Discharge:	Enlisted Oct 4, 1917 at Brevard, assigned as Private, Battery "C", 316th Field Artillery, National Army. He was discharged Oct. 10, 1917 as being physically unfit for military service.

[Documentation: Polk County DC, Discharge, Ancestry.com, findagrave.com, TT obituary]

3/13/1974
CHARLIE C. ANDERS

Charlie C. Anders, age 77, of Landrum, S.C. died Wednesday at St. Luke's Hospital, Landrum, S.C. He was the son of the late Frank and Elizabeth Henry Anders of Etowah, a retired textile worker and a World War I veteran. His wife was the late Lillie Mae Forrester Andrews.

He is survived by six daughters: Mrs. Lydia Brian, Mrs. Thelma Abernathy, Mrs. Evelyn Wilson, Mrs. Margie Pittman, Mrs. Louise Howard and Mrs. Mary Barton; and one sister, Mrs. Leona Harvey.

Services were held at Petty Funeral Home and burial was in Evergreen Memorial Gardens, Landrum, S.C.

---

15 Aug 1918 Brevard News
SOLDIER'S POLE TAX
Brevard, North Carolina, August 14, 1918
Hon. J.H. Pickleshimer, Chairman
Transylvania County Republican Executive Committee
Brevard North Carolina
Dear Sir:

In behalf of the Transylvania boys who are now serving their country in the Army and Navy, I desire to submit the following proposition to you as chairman of the Republican executive committee of Transylvania County.

It is not right, patriotic or in keeping with the duty we owe our country at the present time that any truly technical objection be raised to prevent our soldiers and sailors from voting if they so desire.

Representing the Democratic executive committee of Transylvania County and the Democratic nominee I therefore propose that neither political party nor its representatives challenge any soldiers or sailors vote at the coming election in the fall for the reason that said soldier or sailor has failed to pay his poll tax as required by law.

Please write me at your earliest convenience as to whether your party will agree to this proposition are not.

Respectfully,
W.E. Breese
Chairman of the Democratic Executive Committee
Transylvania County

Loonie Monroe ANDERS

Born	16 Mar 1897, Transylvania County, NC
Died	May 1956, undetermined; age 58
Buried	Rehoboth Baptist Church Cemetery, Greenville County SC
Spouse(s):	**Birdell PATTERSON**, m. 17 Oct 1920, Transylvania County
	H. Elizabeth TINSLEY
Father:	**Wash ANDERS**
Mother:	**Sarah SMITH**
Draft Registration:	21, single, employed by Brevard Land and Timber Co.

[Documentation: Ancestry.com; findagrave.com, Discharge, <u>Cowart's Index to Marriages</u>]

Name ANDERS- LOONIE MONROE		Service Number 100-21-05	
Enrolled At RECRUITING STATION RALEIGH NC	Date 7-3-18	XXXX	
Age at Entrance 21 YRS 3MO Rate SEAMAN 2 CLASS	Town LAKE TOXAWAY State N C	U.S.N.R.F.	
Home Address A Served at TRANSYLVANIA From To	Served as	No. Days	

	From	To	Served as	No. Days
NAVAL TRAINING STATION HAMPTON ROADS VA	8-8-18	11-1-18		
U S S MICHIGAN	11-1-18	11-11-18	SEAMAN 2 CLASS	131

Remarks:

HAMPTON ROADS VA SEAMAN 2 CLASS

Date Discha XXX 2-27-19
Place Inactive Duty HEADQUARTERS 5 NAVAL DISTRICT- Rating at Discharge

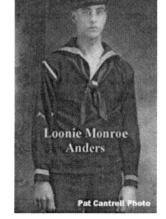

Loonie Monroe Anders

Pat Cantrell Photo

Greenville News (SC)
5/3/1956
L.M. ANDERS

Loonie M. Anders, 59, died at a Greenville hospital Wednesday following six months of illness. Mr. Anders, a native of Transylvania County, NC, had lived in Piedmont for the past 27 years. He was a veteran of World War I and the son of the late Washington A. Anders and Mrs. Sarah E. Anders.

Surviving are his wife, Hattie Anders; three daughters: Pauline Miller, Hazel Hill and Dellie Mae Morton; three sons: William L., Franklin D. and Robert H. Anders; two sisters, Elsie White and Nancy Monroe; and one brother, Luther F. Anders.

Photo # NH 75529 USS Michigan March 1920

Naval History Archives

The USS Michigan was commissioned 4 January 1910. She was the first battleship in the world to be commissioned with superfire type turrets.

In late December 1918 the battleship was assigned to the Cruiser and Transport Force. She made two voyages to Europe transporting 1,052 troops to the United States.

Merida Linsey ANDERS

Born:	23 Mar 1889, Henderson County, NC
Died:	16 Nov 1963, Transylvania County, NC; age 74
Buried:	Blue Ridge Baptist Church Cemetery
Spouse:	**Ada ROBINSON**
Father:	**William ANDERS**
Mother:	**Ann UNDERWOOD**
Draft Registration:	27, single and farming
Service Record Card:	No
Note:	Gravestone gives NO military information.
Discharge:	Enlisted July 6, 1918, Brevard; saw no battles and was discharged April 19, 1919. PVT in Medical Department

[Documentation: Transylvania County DC, Transylvania County Cemetery Survey, Ancestry.com, Familysearch.com, TT obituary, Discharge]

11 Jul 1918   **Brevard News**

Twelve Transylvania boys left on last Saturday for Fort Oglethorpe, Ga., to begin their careers as defenders of democracy. The boys left on the afternoon train . . .
. . . Merida Anders, Cedar Mountain . .

11/23/1963
ANDERS FUNERAL

Services for M.L. Anders, 74, of Brevard, were held Monday in the Blue Ridge Baptist Church and the burial followed in the church cemetery. Members of the Brevard American Legion Post were pallbearers. He was a veteran of World War I. Mr. Anders died unexpectedly at his home Saturday afternoon.

Surviving are six daughters: Mrs. Ralph Green, Mrs. Lewis Roberts, Mrs. Richard Sexton, Mrs. J.C. Robertson, Mrs. Pearline S. . . and Mrs. Melvin Galloway; two sons: Perry and Charles; three brothers: Bunyan, Carlos, and John; and one sister, Mrs. Marjorie Bishop.

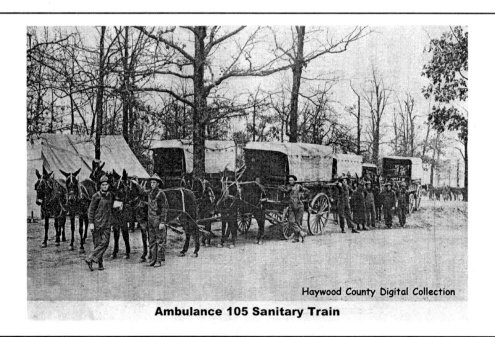

Haywood County Digital Collection

Ambulance 105 Sanitary Train

Corrine W. ANDERSON

Born:	19 March 1873
Died:	29 Apr 1928, undetermined location: age 55
Buried:	Arlington National Cemetery, Arlington, VA
Occupation:	Navy nurse
Father:	**James Blair ANDERSON**
Mother:	**Henrietta Porcher HERIOT**
Draft Registration:	No
Notes:	Birth year was determined to be between 1873 and 1875 according to Census Records and 19 March 1873 from the Cannon Family Tree

[Documentation: application for military headstone, Ancestry.com, 1880-1020 Censuses, Cannon Family Tree (ancestry.com)]

Name ANDERSON-	CORINNE W.			Service Number	415-02-60		
APPOINTED at	HANMELS - LONG ISLAND NY		Date	11-15-12			
Age at Entrance 45 YRS.	Rate NURSE					U.S.N.	
Home Address XX A	County TRANSYLVANIA		Town State	BREVARD N.C.			
Served at	From	To		Served as			No. Days
NAVAL HOSPITAL- NEW YORK N.Y.	4-6-17	12-10-17					
NAVAL HOSPITAL-	12-10-17	11-18-18	NURSE				585

Date Discharge 12-31-19
Place Inact NAVAL HOSPITAL- HAMPTON ROADS VA Rating at Discharge NURSE

22 Aug 1918   Brevard News

Recent arrivals at the Hunt Cottage are Judge A.D. Sayne, Montgomery, Ala. and Mrs. Hunt's sister, Miss Corinne Anderson, U.S. Hospital, Hampton Roads, VA.

Miss Corinne Anderson was one of the two ladies from Transylvania County that volunteered for military service for World War I. Miss Anderson was the sister-in-law to Dr. Charles Hunt, a very prominent doctor in Transylvania County at that time. She gave Brevard, NC as her home address at the time of her appointment at Long Island, NY. but there is some question to her being a native of Transylvania County.

In 1899 the United States acquired Tutuila and several smaller islands in the South Seas. The same year we built a new Naval Station Tutuila. The Navy felt compelled to improve living standards for the Polynesians and health care was a major concern. In 1906 the navy authorized funds for a permanent dispensary and medical supplies. Vaccination against smallpox was mandatory and sewerage and water treatment were high priorities.

In 1911 the Samoans financed and built a new hospital. In 1913 Nurse Mary H. Humphreys and Nurse Corinne W. Anderson sailed from San Francisco to establish a school to train young women in nursing. The all male medical staff put many obstacles in the way of the nurses but on February 23, 1914 four students began a two-year course in nursing. The two nurses had to work an eight-hour shift as nurses and teaching was after the nursing shift. Nurse Humphrey appealed to the Secretary of the Navy for an additional nurse. In August of 1914 he was so moved by their work that he sent two additional nurses to assist Humphreys and Anderson.

Corinne Anderson remained in Samoa until November 1915 and returned to the States.

Serving Proudly A History of Women in the US Navy, Godson, Susan, pub. 2001, p. 52.

Furman ANDERSON

Born:	27 Feb 1896, Pickens, SC
Died:	Mar 1966, Philadelphia, PA
Race:	Colored
Spouse:	**Bessie COOK**
Father:	**Robert ANDERSON**
Mother:	**Easter UNKNOWN**
Draft Registration:	21, single, Ethiopian, day laborer for the Transylvania Tanning Co., dependent mother

[Documentation: Ancestry.com, 1910-1940 Censuses, Draft Registration, SSDI]

Anderson, Furman   3,098,631   Colored
(Surname)   (Christian name)   (Army serial number)   (Race: White or colored)

Residence: _____ Brevard _____ NORTH CAROLINA
(Street and house number)   (Town or city)   (County)   (State)

* Enlisted in   Inducted at Transylvania Co N.C. on June 21/18
† Born in   Pickens S.C. 22 6/12 yrs
Organizations: 72 Co 18 Tng Bn 159 Dep Brig to June 29/18; 4 Co Devel-
opment Bn 1 Camp Z Taylor Ky to Aug 27/18; 7 Co Develop-
ment Bn 2 Camp Z Taylor Ky to Dec 23/18; Co C 442 Re- *
Grades: Pvt   —   —

Engagements: —   —

Wounds or other injuries received in action: None.   —
‡ Served overseas: None   —   —
§ Hon. disch.   May 5/19   on demobilization   —
Was reported   0   per cent disabled on date of discharge, in view of occupation.

21 Jun 1918   Brevard News
COLORED REGISTRANTS TO LEAVE FOR CAMP TAYLOR, KY
ON FRIDAY, JUNE 21, 1918.
. . . Furman Anderson, Brevard . . .

NEW OPPORTUNITIES FOR BLACK AMERICANS

At the beginning of World War I most blacks lived in the rural South. They were held to jobs considered disagreeable to whites and their wages were extremely low. There were better paying jobs in the North but those jobs were usually filled by immigrants from European countries.

When the war broke out the immigrants stopped coming to the United States. Now the jobs were open to blacks. From 1918 to 1920 more than 350,000 blacks went north. They went to railroad and industrial centers for the sole purpose of obtaining a job with a good wage.

They did obtain jobs but they found that life in the North was not a great deal different than the South with the prejudice factor. In neighborhoods blacks seldom found acceptance. Blacks and whites fought each other and full-scale riots between black and white gangs often resulted in hundreds of people being injured or killed.

Even with the disappointments and hardships black people faced in the war years most did not return to the South after the war was over. Life in the North still provided more opportunities and access to political power than the South had traditionally offered.

Ligon Briggs ARD

Born:	3 Mar 1890, Dale, Alabama
Died:	4 Feb 1988, Transylvania County, NC; age 97
Buried:	Pisgah Gardens Cemetery
Spouse:	**Helen LITSPEICH**, m. 25 Oct 1947, Dale, Alabama
Father:	**Eratus Byron ARD**
Mother:	**Zenada Belle BYRD**

[Documentation: Ancestry.com, TT obituary]

2/6/1988
Ligon B. Ard

Ligon B. Ard, 97, died Thursday. A native of Ozark, Ala., he was a retired Rear Admiral in the U.S.N.R. and a graduate of the U.S. Naval Academy. He was an executive officer in World War I and a member of the Naval Reserve. He was former district manager of Chase Brass & Cooper Co. and commander of several naval bases. He was the recipient of the Mexican Service Medal, Bronze Star and Croix de Guerre. He was a member of American Legion, VFW and North Carolina Literary and Historical Association. He was past president of Western North Carolina Historical Association, Blue Ridge chapter of SAR and Asheville chapter of Naval League of U.S. He was a former board chairman of Transylvania County Library and a former board member of Transylvania County American Red Cross. He was a former member of Local Humane Society and a senior member of Brevard Kiwanis Club.

Surviving are his wife, Helen Letspeich Ard; a daughter, Nancy Gray; and a sister, Eva Mae Kelly. Services will be Sunday in St. Phillip's Episcopal Church. Burial will be in Pisgah Gardens with military rites by the American Legion.

Ligon Ard

TT Photo

THEY DIED FOR YOU

What Are You Going To Do About It?

JUNE 23rd TO 28th
North Carolina War-Savings Week

North Carolina's quota in War-Savings Stamps is forty eight million dollars. This must be raised during the period, June 2 rd to 28th, by pledge and purchase.

6/27/1918 Brevard News

Wade Cameron ARMFIELD

Born:	9 Dec 1898, Waxhaw, NC
Died:	6 Dec 1974, Transylvania County, NC; age 75
Buried:	Gillespie-Evergreen Cemetery
Occupation:	Linotype machinist
Spouse:	**Mary Osborne WILKINS**
Father:	**William J. ARMFIELD**
Mother:	**Mollie SNIPES**
Draft Registration:	No
Military Marker:	PFC US Army

[Documentation: Transylvania DC, Transylvania County Cemetery Survey, US Veterans BIRLS, Ancestry.com]

U.S. Department of Veteran Affairs BIRLS Death File about Wade Armfield

Name:	Wade Armfield
Birth Date:	9 Dec 1898
Death Date	6 Dec 1974
SSN:	41900793
Enlistment Date 1:	20 Apr 1917
Release Date 1:	18 July 1919

---

25 May 1917   **Brevard News**
REGISTRARS FOR ARMY DRAFT ARE NAMED
Sheriff, Clerk of Court and Health Officer name registrars who register all males for Army draft between 21 and 31 on June 5, 1917.

Pres. Wilson's proclamation for a selective draft registration of eligibles for military service has become a state and local matter by Governor Beckett's appointing a registration board in each county. The board consists of the Sheriff, clerk of court and the County physician, and is proposed to appoint precinct registrars whose duty it will be to register eligibles for service in the Army–that is, who had passed their 21st have not yet reached their 31st birthday.

In adhering to the proclamation the Sheriff, the clerk of the court and the County physician organized and made appointments of the registrars on Tuesday. The registrars according to the precincts are as follows:

Brevard – F.F. Shuford, T.H. Hampton, and Bill Jones
Boyd – L.F. Lyday
Cathy's Creek – L.W. Brooks, J.L. Waldrop
Cedar Mountain - Ralph L. Lee
Dunn's Rock – William Maxwell
Eastatoe - Jordon Whitmire
East Fork – Charlie Gravely
Gloucester – J.H. House
Hogback – W.H. Nicholson
Rosman – J.M. Zachary
Little River – H.P. Nicholson

Isaac ARROWOOD

Born:	2 Feb 1898, Cocke County, TN
Died:	21 Apr 1966; undetermined, age 68
Buried:	Cross Plains Baptist Church Cemetery, Greenville County, SC
Spouse:	**Hester BISHOP**
Father:	**C.H. ARROWOOD**
Mother:	**Eliza Abigail RAINES**
Draft Registration:	No
Military Marker:	SC Pvt. Btry. B 113 Fld. Arty. WW I

[Documentation: Ancestry.com, findagrave.com]

Arowood, Isaac A	1,324,473	white[1½]
(Surname) (Christian name)	(Army serial number)	(Race: White or colored)

Residence: Brevard   NORTH CAROLINA
(Street and house number)   (Town or city)   (County)   (State)

* Enlisted in   NG at Brevard NC   July 24/17.
† Born in   Cocke Co Tenn   19 2/3 yrs
Organizations: Btry F 1st Regt FA NC NG (Btry F 113 FA) to disch.

Grades: Pvt

Engagements:

Wounds or other injuries received in action: None.
‡ Served overseas: July 16/18 - Apr 27/19
§ Hon. disch.   May 8/19   on demobilization
Was reported   0   per cent disabled on date of discharge, in view of occupation.
Remarks:

SRC NOTES: NG (National Guard) FA (Field Artillery)

Greenville News (SC)
4/22/1966
I.A. ARROWOOD

Isaac Anderson Arrowood, 68, retired farmer of the Cross Plains Community, Travelers Rest, died at a local hospital yesterday after four days of serious illness and eight months of declining health.

Born Feb. 21, 1898 in Del Rio, Tenn., he was a son of the late James Chrisley and Abbey Gill Arrowood. Most of his life was spent in Greenville County and he had lived in the Cross Plains Community 31 years. During World War I he served with the Army.

Surviving are his wife, Hester Bishop Arrowood; three daughters: Alberta Seay, Susie Pittman and Edna Wright; five sons: William H., John Robert, Woodrow, Benjamin A. and Gene A. Arrowood; and one sister, Cassie A. Orr.

Under the direction of Secretary of the Navy Josephus Daniels, the Navy's active fleet grew between 1916 and 1919 from 331 to 752 vessels. The largest increases occurred with destroyers whose numbers swelled from 63 to 161 and submarines, which rose from 38 to 91. The number of battleships remained at 36. The fastest growing segment of navel power was the Flying Corps., which expanded from 54 planes to 2,107 aircraft, including planes, blimps and balloons. Manning the vastly expanded fleet demanded a huge increase in personnel, and from the declaration of war on April 6, 1917 until Armistice on November 11, 1918, the Navy grew from 5,243 to 32,483 regular and reserve officers, and from 65,789 to 469, 965 enlisted personnel.

Serving Proudly, Godson, Susan, pub. 2001, p. 59.

Clyde ASHWORTH

Born:	2 Nov 1889, Transylvania County
Died:	30 Dec 1941, Transylvania County; age 52
Buried:	Gillespie-Evergreen Cemetery
Father:	**William S. ASHWORTH**
Mother:	**Celia ORR**
Draft Registration:	27, single, merchant in Brevard, NC

[Documentation: Transylvania County Cemetery Survey; Transylvania County DC, Discharge]

Ashworth, Clyue   1.860.453   White   1½
_____
    (Surname)   (Christian name)   (Army serial number) (Race: White or colored)

Residence: PO Box 423   Brevard   NORTH CAROLINA
    (Street and house number)   (Town or city)   (County)   (State)

~~Enlisted by~~ Inducted NC   Brevard NC   Oct 4/17 —
Born in   Brevard NC   —   27 11/12 yrs
Organizations:
                Hq Co 316 FA to discharge

Grades: Corp Feb 21/18; Sgt Apr 1/18; RegtlSgt Maj Oct 1/18 —

Engagements: —   —

Wounds or other injuries received in action: None.
Served overseas: Aug 5/18 to Mch 6/19   —
Hon. disch.   Mch 24/19   on demobilization   —
Was reported   0   per cent disabled on date of discharge, in view of occupation.

SRC NOTES: FA (Field Artillery)

15 Feb 1918
Brevard News
Clyde Ashworth is spending sometime with his parents and friends. He makes a fine looking soldier.

11 Apr 1919
Brevard News
Clyde Ashworth has returned from overseas to his home here.

Haywood County Digital Collection

Camp Scene Company E, 120th Infantry

Winston ASHWORTH

Born:	15 Jun 1897, Transylvania County, NC
Died:	28 Mar 1949, Oak Ridge, Tennessee; age 51
Buried:	Gillespie-Evergreen Cemetery
Occupation:	plumber and steam fitter
Spouse:	**Mae DUNCAN** m. 5/12/1930
Father:	**Perry Jackson ASHWORTH**
Mother:	**Lula BRACKEN**
Draft Registration:	22, single, worked in Azalea, NC
Note:	Grave marker gives NO military information
Discharge Notes:	Winston registered for the draft 24 Aug 1918. He was inducted in the Army 10 Nov 1918. The Armistice was 11 Nov 1918 and the draft officially ended and Winston was discharge 14 Nov 1918. Technically he was in the Army for 5 days

[Documentation: Ancestry.com, TT obituary]

3/31/1949
WINSTON ASHWORTH

Funeral services for Winston Ashworth, 51, a native of Brevard, who died of a heart attack Monday night in a hospital at Oak Ridge, TN, were held Wednesday in the First Baptist Church here. Burial followed in the Gillespie Cemetery.

Ashworth was a plumber and pipe fitter. He left Brevard in 1943 for Knoxville, TN, moving later to Oak Ridge. He was a member of Highland View Baptist Church.

Surviving are the widow; on son, Charles Winston Ashworth; the parents, Mr. and Mrs. P.J. Ashworth and five brothers and four sisters.

Late 1917

This pen sketch was printed in the **Brevard News** inthe fall of 1917 with the following caption:

AFTER FIVE MONTHS

The two pictures are of the same young man. The first was taken on the day he enlisted and the second after he had five months' military training. His home is in North Carolina.

William Charles AUSTIN

Born:	7 Nov 1884, New York
Died:	10 Sep 1954, Fort Wayne, Indiana; age 69
Buried:	Gillespie-Evergreen Cemetery
Spouse:	**Mildred GALBRAITH**
Father:	**David Orville AUSTIN**
Mother:	**Nettie BUELL**
Draft Registration:	No
Note:	Grave stone gives NO military information

[Documentation: Ancestry.com, Transylvania County Cemetery Survey, TT obituary]

9/16/1954
AUSTINS FATALLY INJURED IN WRECK
Impressive Rites Held Tuesday Morning
Well Known in Business Circles

Final rites for Mr. and Mrs. W. C. Austin, who were killed last Friday night in an automobile accident at Fort Wayne, Indiana, were held Tuesday morning at the Gillespie cemetery.

The firing squad of the Monroe Wilson post of the American Legion, of which Mr. Austin was a member, gave a three-gun salute, followed by taps by the bugler to close the service.

When the Austins were killed in the head-on collision near Fort Wayne, Mr. Austin was en route to a reunion of his overseas army unit. Mr. Austin was 69, while Mrs. Austin was 65.

Mr. Austin served with the Sixth Engineers with the Third Division in France and Germany. He was wounded and received the Purple Heart. He was in seven different campaigns.

Mr. and Mrs. Austin were professional photographers and had operated the Austin Art Shop here for more than 23 years. They were both natives of the state of New York.

Survivors include one son, William St. Clair Austin, three daughters, Jeanette Austin, Patricia Austin, and Jean Austin. Mr. Austin is also survived by one brother and Mrs. Austin by two brothers.

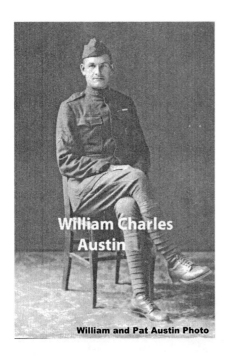

William Charles Austin

William and Pat Austin Photo

13 Mar 1919   Brevard News

THE HOME PORTRAITURE—THE KODAK WAY

Pictures taken in the home atmosphere and home surroundings have a quality and charm of their own. The Kodak enables you to take just such pictures of your family and friends, indoors or out.

Kodaks and Kodak Supplies of all kinds—the Kodak name is a guarantee of quality—that's why we sell the genuine Eastman goods.

FRANK D. CLEMENT
Buy in Brevard   **The Jeweler**

Augustus Littleton BAGWELL

Born:	30 Nov 1894, Transylvania County
Died:	1 Jan 1978; Transylvania County, age 83
Buried:	Gillespie-Evergreen Cemetery
Spouse:	**Beulah Irene REID**, m. 22 Feb 1936, Transylvania County, NC
Father:	**Marcus BAGWELL**
Mother:	**Emma CONLEY**
Draft Registration:	22, single, self-employed farmer in the Cathy's Creek Township

Documentation: Transylvania County DC, Transylvania County Cemetery Survey, Discharge]

Augustus Bagwell

Ann Stamey & Judy Bagwell

SRC Note: HqCo (Headquarters Company) FA (Field Artillery)

Asheville Citizen Times
1/2/1978
AUGUSTUS L. BAGWELL

Augustus "Gus" Littleton Bagwell, 83, died in Asheville VA Hospital after an extended illness. He was a lifelong resident of Transylvania County, the son of the late Marcus and Emmily Connolly Bagwell. He was a veteran of World War I, a member of the V.F.W. and the American Legion. He was a retired employee of Olin Corporation and was a member of Carson's Creek Baptist Church.

He s survived by his wife, Beulah Reid Bagwell; a son, Lane Bagwell; a daughter, Mrs. Ann B. Stamey; a brother, Wade; and a sister, Mrs. Carrie Powell.

Services were held in the chapel of Moody-Connolly Funeral Home. Burial was in Gillespie-Evergreen Cemetery with full military rites.

---

30 Aug 1918
Brevard News

Word has been received that Augustus L. Bagwell has landed safely in France.

---

8 Aug 1918   **Brevard News**
FOLLOW-UP THE SOLDIERS

The Y.M.C.A. workers in France are not making special efforts to dodge bullets or the fearful gas, but follow the soldiers into the trenches and upon the field of battle. These noble workers are receiving high commendations from the French authorities. They are not quitters and they refuse to be relieved, saying where the troops go the Y.M.C. A will stick.

Lambert Ellim (Ellison) BAGWELL, Sr.

Born:	7 Aug 1892, Transylvania County, NC
Died:	20 Apr 1953, Transylvania County, NC; age 60
Buried:	Gillespie-Evergreen Cemetery
Occupation:	Contractor and lumberman
Spouse:	**Mayo Helen BATSON**, m. 10 Aug 1919, Transylvania County, NC
Father:	**John BAGWELL**
Mother:	**Mary Adlyn CISOM**
Draft Registration:	21, single and farming
Discharge:	Inducted 6 Jul 1918: Discharged from the draft due to hyperthyroidism.

[Documentation: Ancestry.com, Transylvania County DC, Transylvania County Cemetery Survey, Cowart's Index to Marriages, 1930 Census indicates military service in WW I, Discharge]

11 Jul 1918   Brevard News

Twelve Transylvania boys left on last Saturday for Fort Oglethorpe, Ga., to begin their careers as defenders of democracy. The boys left on the afternoon train . . .

. . . Lambert Elam Bagwell, Brevard . . .

Hendersonville Times-News
4/20/1953
LAMBERT BAGWELL

Brevard, April 21 (Special) Lambert E. Bagwell, 60, died at his home here Monday after a long illness.

A gravesite service was held this afternoon in Green Acres Cemetery. Mr. Bagwell was engaged in the lumber business in this county for many years.

Surviving are the widow; two sons: L.E., Jr. and Harrell; and a daughter, Mrs. Jene Nicbergall.

25 Apr 1919   Brevard News
PICTURE SHOWS MEN IN ACTION

Here are some of the thrills and "punches" that the spectator will find in "The Price Of Peace," the new film history of the great war just issued by the Treasury Department in connection with the Victory Loan campaign. The picture will be shown all over the United States.

Embarkation of thousands upon thousands of the 2 million soldiers sent to France, including the first pictures ever released showing the great "Leviathan," formerly the "Vaterland," sailing from the port of Hoboken for Brest, in all her war camouflage.

Thrilling scenes of how the Marines fought at Balleau Wood, with machine guns in action, close up, just like a box seat in the war.

The "Lost Battalion" on the scene of the famous stand against the Germans, Major Whittlesey, his men and the graves of their comrades. A battle in the air and the falling of an enemy plane-an American air squadron in action, photographed from a plane.

Captured German balloons used for front observation in the American sector and a tremendous artillery barrage put up to protect the big gun bags from an attack by enemy planes.

How an American battery went into action on one of the war's very last mornings-pouring mustard gas shells into the enemy at the rate of eight a minute per gun.

American Army of Occupation marching across the Rhine into Germany-a wonderful parade financed on Liberty Bonds.

Thomas BAGWELL

Born:	13 Feb 1900, Transylvania County, NC
Died:	4 Jan 1955, Transylvania County, NC; age 54
Buried:	Gillespie-Evergreen Cemetery
Occupation:	Military and plasterer
Father:	**Marcus BAGWELL**
Mother:	**Emily CONLEY**
Draft Registration:	No
Military Marker:	NC CO 1 Discharge Camp WW I

[Documentation: Transylvania County DC, 1910 census, Application for Military Headstone, Ancestry.com,
Transylvania County Cemetery Survey, TT obituary]

```
                                                                                        1
_____ Bagwell, Thomas _____ 717,536 _____ * White * Colored.
            (Surname)         (Christian name)      (Army serial number)
Residence: _____ Brevard _____ NORTH CAROLINA _____
                      (Street and house number)  (Town or city)   (County)      (State)
* Enlisted *R. A.* N. G. *E. R. C. *Inducted at __Hendersonville N C __ on Aug 15, 1917
Place of birth: __Brevard N C _____ Age or date of birth: _18 6/12 yrs_____
Organizations served in, with dates of assignments and transfers: _6 Co C A C N C N G to
_____May 11/18; 11 AA Btry C A C to discharge_____

Grades, with date of appointment: ___Pvt_____

_____

Engagements: _____

Wounds or other injuries received in action: None.
Served overseas from † July 14/18 † Dec 22/18 from †_____ to †_____
Honorably discharged on demobilization __Jan 7/19·_____, 19_____
In view of occupation he was, on date of discharge, reported _____0_____ per cent disabled.
Remarks: _____
```

SRC Note: CAC NC NG (Coast Auxiliary Corps North Carolina National Guard)

1/6/1955
THOMAS BAGWELL

Thomas Bagwell and Fred Whitmire perished in a fire that completely destroyed the home of Mr. Whitmire in the Cherryfield section of the county. The bodies of the men were burned beyond recognition but the men were seen together late in the afternoon prior to the fire.

Mr. Bagwell was a veteran of World War I and World War II. He was a retired plasterer and was about 55 years old.

Survivors include two brothers: Gus and Wade Bagwell; and two sisters: Mrs. Albert Fortune and Mrs. Fields Powell. Burial was in the Gillespie-Evergreen cemetery.

<u>7 May 1918</u>   <u>Brevard News</u>

TRANSYLVANIA PREPARING TO RAISE HER SHARE OF WAR FUND

Committees Have Been Appointed To Canvas County And Raise Apportioned
$2,000 "Over the Top" War Fund

Arthur Harlow BANTHER

Born:	19 Oct 1895, Transylvania County
Died:	16 Apr 1963, Transylvania County, age 67
Buried:	Little River Baptist Church Cemetery
Spouse:	**Essie SCOTT**, m. 26 May 1918, Transylvania County, NC
Father:	**Christopher Columbus BANTHER**
Mother:	**Delia Ann GRANT**
Draft Registration:	"Otter" Harlow, 23, single, section laborer for Southern Railway Co., Transylvania Division, Brevard

[Documentation: Transylvania County DC; <u>Transylvania County</u> <u>Cemetery Survey;</u> Discharge, TT obituary]

Robert L. Banther Photo

Arthur Banther

Banther, Arter H		1,315,304	White	
(Surname)	(Christian name)	(Army serial number)	(Race: White or colored)	
Residence: Quebec	Quebec		NORTH CAROLINA	
(Street and house number)	(Town or city)	(County)	(State)	
†Born in	Inducted at Brevard NC Oct 4/17			
Organizations:	Lake Toxaway NC 23 11/12 yrs			
	Btry D 316 FA to Oct 16/17; Co D 119 Inf to Disch			
Grade:	Pvt			
Engagements:				

Wounds or other injuries received in action: None.

‡ Served overseas: None

§ Hon. disch. Mch 1/19 on demobilization

Was reported 0 per cent disabled on date of discharge, in view of occupation.

4/16/1963
ARTHUR H. BANTHER

Funeral services for A.H. Banther, a resident of Transylvania County, who died Tuesday, will be held Friday afternoon at the Little River Baptist Church and interment will be in the church cemetery. He was a veteran of World War I and the Brevard American Legion post will conduct military graveside services.

Surviving are the wife, Mrs. Essie Banther; two sons: Robert and William; four daughters: Martha Hoxit, Loraine Fisher, Geneva Stepp and Julia Gray; a sister, Prudence Early; and two brothers: Pierson and Taylor Banther.

<u>14 Nov 1918</u>   **Brevard News**
VICTORY GIRLS

When a girl enrolls in the Victory Girls she pledges herself to work and give a stated sum for war work. She should make good her pledge out of money earned, paying in full or in three installments at the time when subscriptions to the men's and women's campaign are payable.

She will receive a Victory Girl's button; also a banner to hang in the window of her home saying a girl there is enlisted for victory. On full payment she will receive a receipt certificate.

Each girl in Transylvania County will be one of an army of "Girls Pulling for Victory" and whether that pull registers five dollars or fifty, if it represents your highest power of sacrifice, you will have achieved good in earning as well as in giving.

The United War Work committee has appointed Mary Jane King as Director of Victory Girls in Transylvania.

Dock BANTHER

Born:	11 Jan 1895, Transylvania County, NC
Died:	29 May 1946, Transylvania County, NC; age 51
Buried:	Macedonia Church Cemetery
Occupation:	Farmer
Spouse:	**Bertha PATTERSON,** m. 13 Jan 1918, Transylvania County, NC
Father:	**Christopher Columbus BANTHER**
Mother:	**Delia Ann GRANT**
Draft Registration:	No
Note:	Grave marker has NO military information
Discharge:	Discharged May 22, 1919 at Fort D.A. Russell, Cheyenne, Wyoming. He was a Private and enlisted June 23, 1918. He participated in active battles Sept. 26 and 27, 1918 in the Argonne offensive.

[Documentation: Transylvania DC, <u>Transylvania County Cemetery Survey</u>, Familysearch.com, ancestry.com, TT photo, Discharge, TT obituary]

This is to Certify, that *Dock Barnes*

Private Quartermaster Corps

National Army

as a TESTIMONIAL OF HONEST AND FAITHFUL SERVICE, is hereby HONORABLY

DISCHARGED from the military service of the UNITED STATES by reason of *S.C.D. Brown*

Said *Dock Barnes* was born

in *Andrews*, in the State of *Georgia*

When enlisted he was *23 3/12* years of age and by occupation a *Farmer*

He had *Blue* eyes, *Dk. Brown* hair, *Fair* complexion, and

was *Five* feet *Ten* inches in height.

Given under my hand at *Camp McClellan, Alabama* this

Ninth day of *April*, one thousand nine hundred and *Eighteen*.

Oscar Bell

Captain 2 M. N.A.

Commanding

ENLISTMENT RECORD

Name: *Dock Barnes*   Grade:

Enlisted *Dec 11th 1917* at *Fort Oglethorpe Georgia*

Serving in *First*   enlistment period at date of discharge.

Prior Service:* *None*

Noncommissioned officer: *Never*

Marksmanship, gunner qualification or rating:† *Not taken*

Horsemanship: *Not Mounted*

Battles, engagements, skirmishes, expeditions: *None*

Knowledge of any vocation: *None*

Wounds received in service: *None*

Physical condition when discharged: *Poor*

Typhoid prophylaxis completed: *Not taken*

Paratyphoid prophylaxis completed: *Not taken*

Married or single: *Single*

CHARACTER: *Excellent*

Remarks: *Disability incurred in line of duty. Soldier entitled to travel allowance from Anniston, Alabama to Fort Oglethorpe, Georgia. No R.M.O.L.*

Signature of Soldier: *Dock Barnes*

Augustus F. Gerken

Captain Infantry, N.C.

Commanding *Q.M. Dept.*

*Give company and regiment or corps or department, with inclusive dates of service in each enlistment.
†Give date of qualification or rating and number, date, and source of order announcing same.

Filed *Dec 29th 1934 4:00 P.M.* Recorded *Jan 3rd 1935*

Camp McClellan Ala. Apr. 9 1918

Paid in full $17.95

R.G. Winman

Jess C. Galloway Clerk.

Ellis Freeman BARTON

Born:	2 Nov 1890, Transylvania County, NC
Died:	27 Jun 1921, Transylvania County, NC; age 30
Buried:	Cathey's Creek Baptist Church Cemetery
Occupation:	Lumberman
Father:	**George T. BARTON**
Mother:	**Elizabeth McCALL**
Draft Registration:	25, single, worker at Carr Lumber Company
Note:	Ellis spent some months in a Veteran's hospital in TN with a respiratory problem.

[Documentation: Transylvania County DC, <u>Transylvania County Cemetery Survey</u>, Ancestry.com, FamilySearch.org, Brevard News obituary]

<u>21 Jun 1918</u>   <u>Brevard News</u>
WHITE REGISTRANTS WHO ARE TO LEAVE FOR CAMP JACKSON, S.C.
TUESDAY, JUNE 25th, 1918 AT 3:13 P.M.
. . . Ellis Freeman Barton, Selica . . .

7/1/1921
SELICA SOLDIER LAID TO REST

Ellis F. Barton died Sunday night at Selica at the home of his uncle Henry Barton. He was twenty-nine years of age. Funeral services were held Monday afternoon at Cathey's Creek Church and the interment took place at the church cemetery.

Ellis Barton was the son of G.T. Barton, who now lives on the Clough place. Beside this parent, his mother having preceded him to the grave, he is survived by five brothers and two sisters who are: Julius, Rufus, H.W., Seldon and Lewis Barton, Mrs. Fannie Stepp and Miss Pauline Barton.

Ellis was one of those young Transylvanians who answered their country's call for fit men to defend world democracy against the atrocity of the Germans. He had training at Camp Wadsworth and then was sent overseas with his division. While fighting on the fields of Flanders late in the fall of 1918, he was gassed and taken to a hospital. This was only a few days before the armistice, so that he was among the last of the American boys to be numbered among the casualties of the Great War.

After being brought back to this country he was placed in one government hospital after another, the last being the Old Soldiers' Home of Johnson City, Tenn. Finally he was brought back to his old home at Selica where he lay for months before the end came.

While dying more than two years after the close of the conflict young Barton was truly one of the Transylvania boys who made the supreme sacrifice to make the world safe for democracy.

Seldon Monroe BARTON

Born: 6 Aug 1893, Transylvania County
Died: 7 Jan 1936, Transylvania County, age 42
Buried: Cathey's Creek Baptist Church Cemetery
Father: **George T. BARTON**
Mother: **Elizabeth McCALL**
Draft Registration: 23, single, timber man for Carr Lumber Co

[Documentation: Transylvania County DC; <u>Transylvania County Cemetery Survey</u>; Discharge, TT obituary]

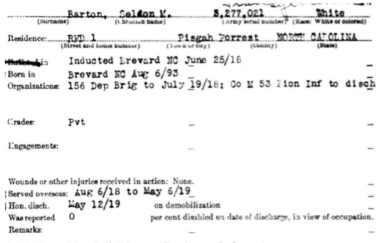

SRC Note: Pion Inf (Pioneer Regiment Infantry)

<u>21 Jun 1918</u>   **<u>Brevard News</u>**
WHITE REGISTRANTS WHO ARE TO LEAVE FOR CAMP JACKSON, S.C.
TUESDAY, JUNE 25th, 1918 AT 3:13 P.M.
. . . Seldon Monroe Barton, Selica . . .

1/9/1936
SELDON BARTON

Seldon Barton, 42, died Tuesday morning at his home at Davidson River following several months of ill health. Funeral services were held Wednesday afternoon at the Cathey's Creek Baptist Church and burial was in the church cemetery.

Mr. Barton was the son of the late Mr. and Mrs. Timothy Barton of Davidson River. He is survived by several brothers and sisters. The Masons had charge of the services.

Charlie Cleveland BATSON

Born:	13 Nov 1892, Transylvania County
Died:	22 Aug 1955, Moore General Hospital, Buncombe County; age 58
Buried:	Old Toxaway Baptist Church Cemetery
Spouse:	**Agnes CHAPPELL**
Father:	**Barney C. BATSON**
Mother:	**Rachel ORR**
Draft Registration:	24, birth year military records 1893, single, self-employed farmer
Note:	Buncombe County DC gives 1894 as birth year.

[Documentation: ***Transylvania County Cemetery Survey;*** *TT obituary, Discharge, Buncombe County DC]*

Batson, Charlie C   2,587,019   white
(Surname)   (Christian name)   (Army serial number)   (Race: White or colored)

Residence: Cherryfield Transylvania NORTH CAROLINA
(Street and house number)   (Town or city)   (County)   (State)

Inducted
*Enlisted in   July 6/18 Transylvania Co Brevard N C   —
†Born in   Brevard N C 25 8/12 yrs
Organizations: Instruction Co 2 Med Dept Camp Greenleaf Ga to July 25,
18; Med Dept Office of Surgeon Ft Monroe Va to Sept 8/
18; 302 Water Tank Tn Med Dept to disch   —
Grades:
Pvt 1 cl Apr 16/19   —
Engagements: —   —

Wounds or other injuries received in action: None.   —
‡Served overseas: Sept 28/18 to Sept 19/19   —
§Hon. disch.   Sept 29/19   on demobilization
Was reported   0   per cent disabled on date of discharge, in view of occupation.   —
Remarks:

8/30/1951
CHARLIE BATSON

Funeral services for Charlie C. Batson, 58, who did last Wednesday night at Moore General hospital, were held Saturday afternoon at the Old Toxaway Baptist Church. The American Legion conducted graveside rites. Mr. Batson, a farmer, had been a patient at Moore General for the past eight months.

Survivors include the widow; two sons: Charlie C., Jr., and Bill; three sisters: Mrs. Clara Nelson, Mrs. Allen Sisk and Mrs. Elam Galloway; and one brother, Nathan Batson.

11 Jul 1918   Brevard News

Twelve Transylvania boys left on last Saturday for Fort Oglethorpe, Ga., to begin their careers as defenders of democracy. The boys left on the afternoon train . . .
. . . Charlie C. Batson, Cherryfield . . .

Standard FORD ambulance with storm curtains   *Army Archives*

The Ambulance Corp graduated from horse drawn to motorized vehicles. Ford, Fiat, Peugeot and General Motors Company ambulances were all used in Europe during World War I. The Ford was used extensively because it sat high and could get through flooded roads not accessible by lower vehicles. French soldiers accused the Americans of painting water marks on their vehicles and depth gauges and some calls for evacuation would request the ambulance "boats." If the roads were blocked, the "T" could go cross-country. It was light enough that three or four soldiers could pick it up and move it if it were stuck in a ditch or shell hole.

Fred Blythe BAUER

Born:	27 Dec 1896, North Carolina
Died:	30 May 1971, Transylvania County, NC; age 74
Buried:	Pisgah Gardens Cemetery
Spouse:	**Catherine DOTTERWEICH**
Father:	**Adolphus Gustavus BAUER**
Mother:	**Rachel BLYTHE**
Draft Registration:	No
Military Marker:	NC CPL Inf WWI

Documentation: Transylvania County DC, Transylvania County Cemetery Survey, Veteran Affairs BIRLS Death File, Ancestry.com]

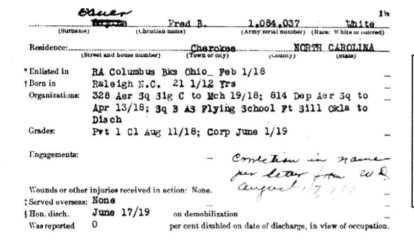

The U.S. Army Insignia
For the Aviation Section of the
Signal Corps.

6/3/1971
FRED BAUER

Fred Blythe Bauer, 74, died in a local hospital Sunday afternoon after an extended illness. He was a native of Raleigh and had lived in Cherokee and Fontana before coming to Brevard in 1953.

He was Assistant Chief of the Cherokee from 1935 to 1939, a member of the Monroe Wilson Post #88, Charter member of the Steve Youngdeer Post of Cherokee, life member of the Mt. Pleasant, Michigan Masonic Lodge. He authored the book **Land of the North Carolina Cherokees**, published in 1970. He was a veteran of World War I Air Force.

He is survived by the wife, Catherine A. Bauer; one son, Frederick William Bauer; one daughter, Mrs. Wade Mitchem, Jr.; one sister, Mrs. Roy Frye and one brother, Chief Jarrett Blythe.

Graveside services were conducted Tuesday at Pisgah Gardens.

Docsouth.unc.edu/   THE DIGITAL BLUE RIDGE PARKWAY

A very interesting article titled "Parkway Development and the Eastern Band of Cherokees" tells the story of Fred and Catherine Bauer and their opposition to the American Indian Federation (AIF), formed in 1934, and the Government's proposed **Indian New Deal**.

It was through their tireless efforts that the Blue Ridge Parkway was rerouted from the heavily Indian populated Soco Valley and did not disrupt the Indian way of life in the valley. They argument was it would split the Reservation and the Indians would loose prime property and tourist attractions.

GEORGE BELL   Aka Thomas George Fleetwood BELL

Born: 11 Nov 1894, Transylvania County
Died: 15 Sep 1975, Transylvania County; age 80
Buried: Enon Baptist Church Cemetery
Spouse: **Cannie HOLDEN**
Father: **William T. BELL**
Mother: **Rachel BANKS**
Draft Registration: 23, single, laborer for Southern Railroad Co.   Listed a six year old brother as a
                       dependent and requested to be exempt from the draft.
Military Marker: CPL US Army WW I

[Documentation: Discharge, Transylvania County DC; Transylvania County Cemetery Survey]

Bell, George	1,853,507		White
(Surname)	(Christian name)	(Army serial number)	(Race: White or colored)
Residence:	Penrose		NORTH CAROLINA
	(Street and house number)	(Town or city) (County)	(State)

Inducted at Brevard N C Oct 3/17
† Born in   Penrose N C 23 11/12 yrs
Organization: M D F Hosp 323 to disch

Grade: Corp Feb 13/19

Engagements:

Wounds or other injuries received in action: None.
† Served overseas: No
† Hon. disch.   Apr 3/19   on demobilization
Was reported   0   per cent disabled on date of discharge, in view of occupation.

26 Sep 1918   Brevard News
   Private Bell of Camp Jackson was in on furlough visiting his father and mother and returned Tuesday.

9/18/1975
GEORGE BELL

George Bell, 80, died Monday evening in Transylvania Community Hospital after a short illness. Mr. Bell was a life long resident of Transylvania County. He was a veteran of World War One.

Surviving are one daughter, Mrs. Leota C. Soles; a son, Thomas E. Bell; and a brother, Grady Bell.

Funeral services were held Wednesday in the chapel of Moody Funeral Home and burial followed in the Enon Church Cemetery.

At the beginning of the war hospital construction was considered a very high priority. The goal was that in no case should the Army lack facilities to the care of its sick and wounded.

On December 1, 1918, there were available in Army hospitals 399,510 beds, or 1 bed for every 9 men in the Army. Of these, 287,290 were overseas and 112,220 were in the United States. The hospital capacity only exceeded that capacity in this country during the influenza epidemic when it became necessary to take over barracks for hospital purposes. Except during two weeks in October 1918, at the height of the attack on the Hindenburg Line, the hospitals overseas never reached capacity. At the fullest time there remained 60,000 unused emergency beds.

Orcutt, Louis E., **GREAT WAR HISTORY**, 1920, p. 130.

Gream Hasker BENJAMIN

Born:	25 Oct 1894, Transylvania County, NC
Died:	27 Sep 1943, Los Angeles, California; age 48
Buried:	Los Angeles National Cemetery
Race:	Colored
Father:	**BENJAMIN**
Mother:	**RICHARDSON**
Draft Registration:	22, single, working as a chauffer and mechanic for A.H. King

[Documentation: Ancestry.com, Application for Headstone, findagrave.com, California Death Index]

Notes from Headstone Application: Hasker served with the Medical Department in the Animal Debarkation Depot in Charleston, SC. He apparently died in a Soldier's Home in Los Angeles, California and the headstone was requested by the administrator of the facility.

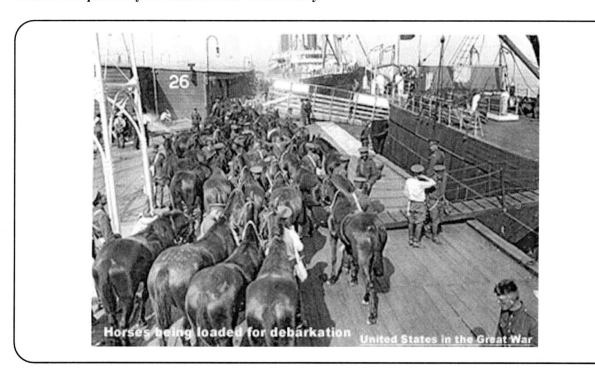

Samuel BENJAMIN

Born:	25 Nov 1895
Died:	14 Feb 1957, Veteran's Hospital, Buncombe County; age 61
Buried:	Cooper Cemetery
Race:	Colored
Occupation:	Mechanic
Spouse:	**Belle MOONEY**, 8 Oct 1919, Transylvania County
Father:	**Alfred BENJAMIN**
Mother:	**Matilda JOHNSON**
Draft Registration:	22, single, Brevard, a mechanic employed by King Motor Co.

[Documentation: Transylvania County Cemetery Survey, Ancestry.com-VA headstone application, Buncombe County DC, Cowart's Index to Marriages, TT obituary]

Benjamin Sam   3,098,632   colored   1½
(surname)   (christian name)   (army serial number)   (Race: White or colored)

Residence: Brevard   Transylvania NORTH CAROLINA
(Street and house number)   (Town or city)   (County)   (State)

• Enlisted in   Inducted at Transylvania CoℓC   June 21/18
† Born in   Brevard NC   22 7/12 yr
Organizations: 159 Dep Brig to July 13/18; Co C 801 Pion Inf to disch

Grades: Corp Aug 24/18; Sgt Oct 8/18

Engagements:

Wounds or other injuries received in action: None.
‡ Served overseas: Sept 8/18 to June 5/19
§ Hon. disch.   June 13/19   on demobilization
Was reported   0   per cent disabled on date of discharge, in view of occupation.

SRC Notes: Dep Brig (Depot Brigade)   Pion Inf (Pioneer Regiment Infantry)

2/21/1957
SAMUEL BENJAMIN

Samuel Benjamin, 61, well known colored resident of Brevard, died Thursday afternoon in a veterans' hospital. He had suffered from a lingering illness.

The deceased was a mechanic by trade. He was a veteran of World War I.

Funeral services were conducted Sunday afternoon at the Bethel "A" Baptist church and burial was in the Cooper cemetery.

Survivors include his wife, Belle Mooney Benjamin; and one daughter, Mrs. Anne Branham.

21 Jun 1918   Brevard News
COLORED REGISTRANTS TO LEAVE FOR CAMP TAYLOR, KY
ON FRIDAY, JUNE 21, 1918.
. . . Sam Benjamin, Brevard . . .

46

Walter L. BENJAMIN

Born:	3 Aug 1885, Transylvania County
Died:	3 Jan 1932, Transylvania County, age 46
Buried:	Cooper Cemetery
Race:	Colored
Occupation:	Employed by the town of Brevard
Spouse:	**Dikie HUTCHISON**, 21 Nov 1925, Transylvania County
Father:	**Alfred BENJAMIN**
Mother:	**Matilda JOHNSON**

Draft Registration: No

[Documentation: Transylvania County DC; TT obituary, <u>Cowart's Index to Marriages</u>]

	Benjamin, Walter L.	3,674,395	Colored
(Surname)	(Christian name)	(Army serial number)	(Race: White or colored)

Residence: Brevard   Transylvania   NORTH CAROLINA
      (Street and house number)   (Town or city)   (County)   (state)

* Enlisted in   NA at Brevard NC   July 19/18
† Born in   Brevard NC   25 11/12 yrs
Organizations: 153 Dep Brig to disch.

Grades: Pvt

Engagements:

Wounds or other injuries received in action: None.
‡ Served overseas: No
§ Hon. disch.   Nov 26/18   on demobilization
Was reported   0   per cent disabled on date of discharge, in view of occupation.
Remarks:

1/7/1932
WALTER BENJAMIN

The death of Walter Benjamin on Sunday night at 8 o'clock caused quite a stir among our colored people. Funeral services were held Tuesday. He was 47 years of age and for some time had been an employee of the town of Brevard.

21 Jun 1918   **Brevard News**
COLORED REGISTRANTS TO LEAVE FOR CAMP TAYLOR, KY ON FRIDAY, JUNE 21, 1918.
. . . Walter Lewis Benjamin, Brevard

Calisthenics Camp Zachary Taylor, Louisville, Ky.   **1918 Postal Card**

Dr. Charles Crawford BENNETT

Born:	16 Mar 1891, Ola, NC
Died:	31 Mar 1962, Buncombe County; age 71
Buried:	Green Hills Cemetery, Asheville, NC
Spouse:	**Lillian WEST**
Father:	**Andrew Carson BENNETT**
Mother:	**Jane Elizabeth RUSSELL**
Draft Registration:	26, single, occupation listed as a senior dental student

[Documentation: Buncombe County DC, Ancestry.com]

```
                                                                    1½
  Bennett,  Charles C              2,576,490            White
     (Surname)          (Christian name)    (Army serial number)  (Race: White or colored)

Residence:_____Brevard_____NORTH CAROLINA
               (Street and house number)      (Town or city)      (County)        (state)

* Enlisted in    ERC at Camp Jackson NC Octb26/17               —
† Born in        Ola NC 26 7/12 yrs
  Organizations: Med Sec ERC Charleston SC to Sept 2/17; Student Army
                 Tng C Agricultural Mechanical College Orangeburg SC
                 to Nov 19/18; 42 Co US Gds to Disch

  Grades:        Pvt

  Engagements:

  Wounds or other injuries received in action: None.
‡ Served overseas:  No                                          —
§ Hon. disch.       Dec 31/18      on demobilization             —
  Was reported      0              per cent disabled on date of discharge, in view of occupation.
```

SRC Note: ERC (Enlisted Reserve Corps)

2 Nov 1917   Brevard News

Charles Bennett, who went with the last call to Camp Jackson was given a discharge to finish his dental studies and be ready for a commission in the medical reserve corps. After a visit home, he left Thursday to re-enter the Atlanta Dental College

19 Sep 1918   Brevard News

One of our efficient dentist, Dr. Chas. E. Bennett, has been called to the colors and is stationed at Orangeburg, SC.

Asheville Citizen-Times
April 1, 1962
Dr. C.C. BENNETT

Services for Dr. C.C. Bennett, 71, Asheville dentist for 45 years, will be held Monday in the First Presbyterian Church. Dr. Bennett died in an Asheville hospital after an illness of several weeks.

A native of Haywood County, he was a graduate of Emory University's School of Dentistry, where he was valedictorian of his class. He had attended Mars Hill College, Old Weaverville College and Western Carolina University.

Surviving are the widow, Lillian Bennett; three sons: Rev. Harold, Richard and Ralph Bennett; three stepsons: Walter N., Joseph C., and Frank W. Bennett; two sisters, Lela Clark and June Parks; and two brothers, J.W. and G.R. Bennett.

Gola Robert BENNETT

Born:	5 Dec 1896, Haywood County
Died:	11 Jan 1974, Buncombe County, NC; age 77
Buried:	Green Hills Cemetery, Asheville, NC
Occupation:	Grocery store business
Spouse:	**Mary F. GARDNER**
Father:	**Andrew Carson BENNETT**
Mother:	**Jane Elizabeth RUSSELL**
Draft Registration:	21, employed by Asheville Power and Light Co.

[Documentation: Buncombe DC, Ancestry.com; findagrave.com]

Name	BENNETT- GOLA ROBERT		Service Number	111-44-92	
XXXX Enrolled	at RECRUITING STATION RALEIGH N.C.		Date 7-20-18		
Age at Entrance 21 YRS 7 MO.	Rate APPRENTICE SEAMAN			XXXX U.S.N.R.F.	
Home Address XXX		Town BREVARD			
8	County TRANSYLVANIA	State N.C.			

Served at	From	To	Served as	No. Days
5TH NAVAL DISTRICT NORFOLK VA.	7-20-18	11-11-18	APPRENTICE SEAMAN	114

Remarks:

SEAMAN 2 CLASS

Date Dis XXXX 12-9-18
Place Inactive Duty 5TH NAVAL DISTRICT NORFOLK VA.   Rating at Discharge

Asheville Citizen-Times
1/12/1974
GOLA R. BENNETT

Services for Gola R. Bennett, 77, who died Friday will be held Monday at St. Joan of Arc Catholic Church, of which he was a member. Burial will be in Green Hills Cemetery.

A native of Haywood County, he had lived in Buncombe County for 55 years. He was a Navy veteran of World War I, a retired grocery man and restaurant operator. His wife, Marcelle Grimes Bennett, died in July 1970.

Surviving are a daughter, Rita Durner; a son, Jack Bennett; and two sisters: Lela Clark and June Parks.

---

22 Aug 1918   **Brevard News**
CONSERVATION OF PAPER

The United States Government has issued orders to all newspapers that the consumption of news print paper must be reduced at least 15 percent in order to prevent a paper famine.

A number of the weekly papers of the state have reduced their size to just half the regular size. We do not intend to cut ours down to one half the regular size, but it is necessary for us to reduce it in order to save our share of the paper. We are going to cut down to six pages for the duration of the war, or until the paper supply is replenished.

We expect to give our readers about the same amount of home news, however, and how that the will appreciate our position.

Dr. John Glenn BENNETT

Born:	26 Feb 1893, Haywood County, NC
Died:	31 Mar 1961, Henderson County, NC; he was 68
Buried:	Oakdale Cemetery, Henderson County, NC
Occupation:	Dentist
Spouse:	**Edna Mae RICE**
Father:	**Andrew Carson BENNETT**
Mother:	**Jane Elizabeth RUSSELL**
Draft Registration:	24, single, working as a motor man for Asheville Power and Light Co.
Note:	Death Certificate states served in WW I

[Documentation: 1900-1940 Census, Ancestry.com

Hendersonville Times News
4/1/1961
Dr. J.G. BENNETT

Dr. John Glenn Bennett, 68, died unexpectedly last night at his home. He had been in declining health and had limited his practice for several years. He was in his office yesterday.

He had been a resident here 37 years. He was a native of Haywood County, the son of A.C. and Jane Russell Bennett. He graduated from Western Carolina University in 1915 and taught school a year in Haywood County before entering the Atlanta Dental College and graduating in 1919. He began his practice in Franklin, moved to Asheville and practiced two years before coming to Hendersonville in 1922.

Dr. Bennett was active in the First Baptist Church and many civic affairs. He was an ardent golfer and outdoorsman and a former city golf champion.

Surviving are the wife, Edna Rice Bennett; a daughter, Mrs. E.W. Wilder; a son, Ed Bennett; three brothers: Dr. C.C., J.W. and G.R. Bennett; two sisters, Mrs. J.L. Parks and Mrs. Leila Clark.

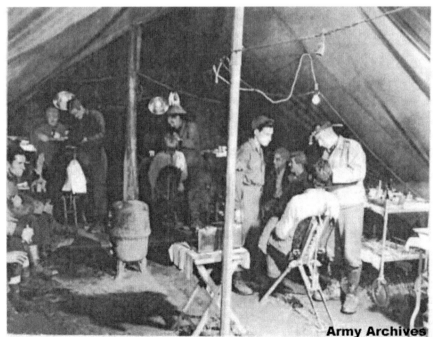

Dental Clinic 9th Evacuation Hospital France 1944

Raymond Franklin BENNETT

Born:	9 May 1896, Clayton County, Ohio
Died:	2 Jan 1980, Transylvania County; age 83
Buried:	Pisgah Gardens Cemetery
Spouse:	**Jessie Elizabeth SYMONS**
Father:	**Charles Victor BENNETT**
Mother:	**Bera Viola MITCHELL**
Draft Registration:	Fayette, Ohio, 21, single
Military Marker:	US Navy WW I

[Documentation: Transylvania County DC, <u>Transylvania County Cemetery Survey</u>, Ohio Soldiers in WW I, Ancestry.com]

BENNETT, RAYMOND FRANKLIN, 111-46-38, White, Columbus Ave., Washington C. H., O. USN Rctg Sta Cincinnati, O. Dec 14/17. Br Clinton Co, O. May 9/96. Receiving Ship Norfolk Va to Feb 15/18; USS Kearsarge to Mch 3/18; USS Solace to Mch 4/18; Naval Hosp Norfolk Va to Mch 12/18; USS Kearsarge to Apr 19/18; Receiving Ship Boston Mass to Apr 30/18; USS Shawmut to Nov 11/18. F 2c 108 days; F 1c 224 days. Ordinary disch Apr 30/19. Demob. USS Shawmut North River NY. Eng 2c.

Asheville Citizen Times
1/4/1980
RAYMOND F. BENNETT

Raymond Franklin Bennett, 83, former mayor of Brevard, died mid-week at Transylvania Community Hospital. Bennett was mayor of Brevard from 1965 to 1971. During his terms of office the new Brevard city hall was built and the Brevard ABC board was established. Olin Corporation, formerly Ecusta Paper Corporation, employed him where he served as plant manager, general and manufacturing superintendent.

A native of Clayton County, Ohio, he had been a resident of Brevard since 1939.

He was elected national president of the Paper Management Association in 1947 and was a past president and director of Brevard Chamber of Commerce. A trustee for Transylvania County Community Hospital, he had served as a director for First Union National Bank in Brevard.

A veteran of World War I, he was a post commander of the Brevard American Legion, of which he was a life member and trustee. He was co-founder of Transylvania County Shriner's Club and was a life member of Dunn's Rock Masonic Temple. He was also a member of Brevard's Veterans of Foreign Wars.

Surviving is a daughter, Mrs. Carl Avra.

Memorial services were held at Brevard-Davidson River Presbyterian Church with burial in Pisgah Gardens. The Brevard American Legion conducted graveside services.

Raymond F. Bennett
The Echo Anniversary Edition 1949

Of the 42 American divisions which reached France 36 were organized in the summer and early autumn of 1917. The other 6 were organized as divisions by January, 1918, but had been in training as separate units month before that time.

The average division had been organized eight months before sailing for France.

Orcutt, Louis, **The Great War History**, pub. 1920, p. 70

John Norris BERKSHIRE, Sr.

Born:	29 Jan 1900, Petersburg, KY
Died:	11 Nov 1965, Buncombe County, NC; age 65
Buried:	Pisgah Gardens Cemetery
Occupation:	Self-employed home builder
Spouse:	**Julia PARKER**
Father:	**Benjamin H. BERKSHIRE**
Mother:	**Ethel Gay NORRIS**
Draft Registration:	Boone, KY, 18, farmer
Military Stone:	Kentucky PVT US Marine Corps WW I

[Documentation: Buncombe County DC, Transylvania County Cemetery Survey, Ancestry.com, TT obituary]

11/18/1965
JOHN N. BERKSHIRE

Funeral services for John Norris Berkshire, 63, of Rosman were held Sunday at Moore Funeral home. Burial was in Pisgah Garden. Military rites were conducted at the grave. Mr. Berkshire died November 11th in an Asheville hospital after a brief illness.

A native of Petersburg, KY, Mr. Berkshire lived in Rosman for the past 19 years.

Survivors include the widow, Julia Parker Berkshire; two sons: Charles and John, Jr.; and two sisters: Mrs. Mellicent Palmer and Mrs. Cordelia Woodruff.

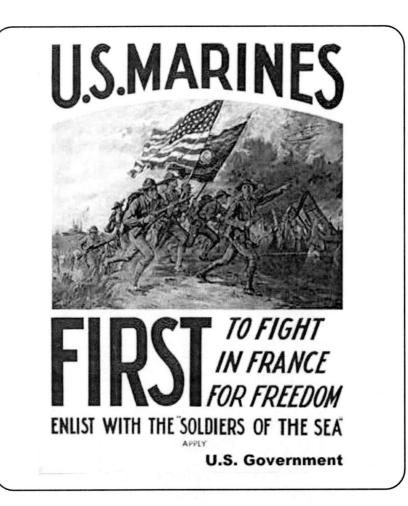

Walton BERKSHIRE

Born:	19 Jul 1892, Indiana
Died:	21 Feb 1985, Henderson County, NC; age 92
Buried:	PIsgah Gardens Cemetery
Spouse:	**Hazel SNIPES**
Father:	**William Terrell BERKSHIRE**
Mother:	**Rosella STEWART**
Draft Registration:	Boone, KY, 24, single, farming

[Documentation: Hendersonville T-N Obituary, Henderson County DC, Ancestry.com]

Hendersonville Times News
February 21, 1985
WALTON BERKSHIRE

Brevard: Walton "Pat" Berkshire, 90, died Thursday 21 Feb. 1985 in Pardee Hospital, Hendersonville, NC after a period of declining health

He was a native of Rising Sun, Ind. and the son of the late William Terrell & Rosella Stewart Berkshire.

Survivors include his wife, Hazel Snipes Berkshire; his daughter, Beulah Wynn; his brother, Stuart Berkshire; and a half sister Frances Kiem.

Funeral services will be held at p.m. Sunday at Moody-Connolly Funeral Home Chapel. Burial will be held in Pisgah Gardens with full military rites conducted by the American Legion Post 88.

George Hamlin BISHOP

Born:	31 Jul 1896, Transylvania County
Died:	7 Sep 1921, Transylvania County, NC; age 25
Buried:	Rocky Hill Cemetery
Occupation:	Deputy Sheriff of Transylvania County
Father:	**George BISHOP**
Mother:	**Alice HAMLIN**
Draft Registration:	No

[Documentation: Transylvania DC; Transylvania County Cemetery Survey; TT obituary]

George Hamlin Bishop

Mary A. Bishop Photo

Name BISHOP- GEORGE HAMLIN			Service Number	111-52-64		
NAVY RECRUITING STATION COLUMBIA S.C. Date 5-30-18					U.S.N. U.S.N.R.F.	
Age at Entrance 21 YES 10 MO. Rate SEAMAN 2 CLASS				Town CEDAR MOUNTAIN		
Home Address XXX County TRANSYLVANIA			State N. C.			
8 Served at	From	To	Served as			No. Days
NAVAL TRAINING CAMP CHARLESTON S.C.	5-30-18	11-11-18	SEAMAN 2 CLASS			165

Remarks:

CARPENTERS MATE 3 CLASS

Date X 2-8-19
Place Inactive Duty NAVAL TRAINING CAMP AT CHARLESTON S.C. Rating at Discharge

SRCNote: Carpenters Mate on reverse side

9/23/1921
HAMLIN BISHOP

On 17 Aug 1921, death claimed Hamlin Bishop, oldest son of Mr. and Mrs. George W. Bishop of Cedar Mountain NC. He was in the mountain sanitarium for 14 days where everything that could be done by human power for his relief was adopted; but disease had too strong a grippe and at 6:30 pm he passed to that great beyond. Hamlin was born on 31 Jul 1896 was a faithful member of Rocky Hill Church.

When the world war broke out and our country called for volunteers, Hamlin was among the first to enlist in the Navy. At the time of his death, he was a member of the Naval Reserve. In 1920, he served as a deputy sheriff.

He is survived by his parents; two brothers: Wilkie and Boyce; three sisters: Idell, Eldean and Laura Jane; and two half sisters: Mrs. M.R. Osborne and Mrs. W.W. Byars, Hamlin also leaves a heart-broken girl, Miss Corrie Smith of Toccoa, GA who will also mourn his death.

The remains were carried to the Rocky Hill Cemetery on Friday at 11 a.m.

---

18 Jun 1917   **Brevard News**
HOW SHALL WE PAY FOR THE WAR?
A Constructive Criticism on the House Revenue Bill
LOANS BETTER THAN TAXES

Jerry Hobert BISHOP

Born:	28 Jul 1895, Transylvania County
Died:	17 Aug 1988, Charleston, SC, age 93
Buried:	Woodlawn Memorial Park, Greenville County, SC
Spouse:	**Susie HUFFMAN**
Father:	**Jeremiah BISHOP**
Mother:	**Nancy BURNS**
Draft Registration:	21 (birth year 1896), single, a carpenter for E.A. Heath at Caesar's Head, SC

[Documentation: SSDI; Ancestry.com; findagrave.com]

```
............        Bishop    Jerry H.          1,876,280        White
             (Surname)     (Christian name)    (Army serial number)  (Race, White or colored)

Residence.....  R F D #1 ......Pisgah Forest  Transylvania  NORTH CAROLINA
             (Street and house number)    (Town or city)    (County)    (State)

Enlisted in    Inducted Brevard N.C. Sept 18/17
Born in        Little River N.C. 22 2/12 Yrs
Organizations: MD F Hosp Camp Jackson S.C. to Nov 11/17; Amb Co 324
               306 Sn Tn to May 3/18; Bkry Co 329 to May 7/18; Bkry
               Co 380 to Mch 25/19; School for Bkrs & Cks QMC**
Grades:        Pvt 1 Cl July 22/18; Corp Oct 12/18; Sgt Feb 26/19

Engagements:

Wounds or other injuries received in action: None.
Served overseas: None
Hon. disch.    July 25/19      on demobilization
Was reported   0               per cent disabled on date of discharge, in view of occupation.
Remarks:
```

SRC Note: MD F (Medical Department Field)   Bkrs (Bakery Company)

21 Sep 1917   Brevard News
THIRTY-ONE MEN TO CAMP JACKSON
    Forty percent of the certified draft, making 31 men, was ordered to report on Tuesday at 5 P.M. at the office of the local enlistment board and to leave for Camp Jackson, S.C. Wednesday morning.
. . . Jerry Hobert Bishop . . .

Greenville News (SC)
8/20/1988
JERRY H. BISHOP, SR.

    Charleston--Jerry Hobart Bishop, Sr., 93, formerly of Greenville, died August 17, 1988 at his home after a period of declining health. He was a retired construction employee, a US Army veteran of World War I and a member of Rocky Mountain Baptist Church in Cedar Mountain, NC.

    Surviving are his wife, Susie Huffman Bishop; and a son, Jerry H. Bishop, Jr.

    Services were Saturday at Thomas McAfee Funeral Home Chapel with burial in Woodlawn Memorial Park.

    On 21 March 1917, Loretta Perfectus Walsh, a civilian clerk, became the first chief yeoman (F) in the Naval Reserves. When the United States declared war on 6 April 1917, there were 201 women in the Naval Reserve. By Armistice Day, their numbers had reached 8,997; three weeks later, 11,275. Altogether 11,880 women served in the Navy.
    Serving Proudly, Godson, Susan H., p. 60

Perry Raymond BISHOP

Born:	26 Jun 1897, Transylvania County, NC
Died:	21 Nov 1965, Greenville, SC; age 68
Buried:	Rocky Hill Cemetery
Spouse:	**Sarah WARREN**, 8 Aug 1918, Transylvania County
Father:	**Jeremiah BISHOP**
Mother:	**Nancy Anna BURNS**
Draft Registration:	21, self employed
Note:	Grave marker gives NO military information
Draft Registration:	No
Service Record Card:	No

[Documentation: NC Birth Index, Transylvania County Cemetery Survey, Ancestry.com, Discharge, Cowart's Index to Marriages, TT obituary]

14 Nov 1918   Brevard News
   On Monday morning a crowd of relatives, friends and well-wishers were at the depot to bid God Speed to the following young men who were leaving for Camp Green, Charlotte: . . . Raymond Bishop . . .
   Mrs. Silversteen, on behalf of the National League for Woman's Service, presented them with comfort kits. Mr. R.H. Zachary furnished matches, tobacco, cigarettes, chewing gum, etc to cheer them on their way. Miss Annie T. Colcock sent socks.

11/25/1965
BISHOP RITES
   Last rites for Raymond P. Bishop of Cedar Mountain were held Tuesday afternoon at the Rocky Hill Baptist Church. Burial followed in the church cemetery.
   Mr. Bishop died Sunday morning in a Greenville Hospital after a lengthy illness. He was in the lumber business prior to his retirement.

   After reviewing Perry Raymond Bishop's discharge certificate that is on file at the Transylvania County Register of Deeds Office, we find he was exempted from military service May 18, 1917 but was recalled by the Local Draft board and was inducted at Brevard November 10, 1918. He went to Camp Green, Charlotte. NC where he received the discharge November 14, 1918 but was still subject to the Exemption Board of Transylvania County.

> Even if the United States had had the manpower for war, its soldiers would most likely have marched off empty-handed. In the whole U.S. Army, there were fewer than fifteen hundred machine guns and five hundred light field guns. The United States did not possess a single flamethrower and had no tanks.
> Stewart, Gail B., **World War I,** Lucent Books, Inc. 1991

John BLYTHE

Born: Abt 1892 in Transylvania County, NC
Death: Undetermined
Race: Colored
Draft Registration: No
Note: Unable to find much information about John. His military
                 record states he enlisted in the regular Army in Columbus, Ohio at
                 the age of 21 years and 10 months. He was honorably discharged and may have
                 re-enlisted. The 1900 Federal Census of Pumpkintown, Pickens County, SC, re-
                 cords John as a stepson (last name Tomson) in the household of William and
                 Mary Blythe with siblings, Sally and Hosea Tomson. The 1910 Federal Census,
                 Transylvania County, NC, had a John Blythe living in the Boyd Township with
                 his stepfather William Blythe and Mary (siblings Sally, Hosea and Mamie Bly-
                 the). South Carolina is recorded as his state of birth on this census.

[Documentation: Ancestry.com]

Blythe,	John	335,811	Colored
(Surname)	(Christian name)	(Army serial number)	(Race: White or colored)

Residence: _____ Brevard _____ NORTH CAROLINA
                (Street and house number)   (Town or city)   (County)   (State)

Enlisted in   RA Columbus Bks Ohio_Dec 10/13
Born in   Brevard N C 21 10/12_yrs
Organizations: Co E 25 Inf to disch_

Grades: Pvt 1cl Mch 20/19 _

Engagements: _

Wounds or other injuries received in action: None.
Served overseas: None
Hon. disch.   Mch 31/19 for Immediate Re-enlistment
Was reported   0   per cent disabled on date of discharge, in view of occupation
Remarks: _

---

7 Dec 1917   **Brevard News**
                        WE ARE AT WAR

And the United States Government has efficiently
recognized the American Red Cross as part of
America's Inner Line of Defense.

Transylvania boys at the front will offer their lives
to help keep the Outer Lines Safe.

All who stay within Transylvania's unmenaced borders can help make the Inner Line a strong support to
the Outer Line by giving 10 minutes or several weeks
work, 10 cents or several hundred dollars to the
Transylvania Chapter America Red Cross

William Hershel BLYTHE

Born:	28 Dec 1895, Henderson County, NC
Died:	10 Mar 1932, Oteen VA Hospital, Buncombe County; age 36
Buried:	Davidson River Cemetery
Occupation:	Steam Shovel Operator
Spouse(s):	**Gladys BLEVINS**
Father:	**J.V. BLYTHE**
Mother:	**Martha HOOD**
Draft Registration:	Henderson County, 22, single farmer
Military Marker:	NC PVT 359 M.G. BN 95 Div

[Documentation: Buncombe County DC, Transylvania County Cemetery Survey, Ancestry.com, Brevard News obituary]

Brevard News
3/17/1932
HERSHELL BLYTHE

Funeral services for Hershell Blythe, 38 years old, of Etowah, were held at the Davidson River Presbyterian Church Friday afternoon at 1:30 o'clock, and surrounded by friends and relatives the body was laid to rest in the Davidson River Cemetery.

Tealer BOSTICK

Born:	11 Nov 1890, Transylvania County, NC
Died:	21 Dec 1952, Oteen VA Hospital, Buncombe County; age 62
Buried:	Davidson River Cemetery
Race:	Colored
Occupation:	Tailor
Spouse:	**Isabella**
Father:	**James BOSTICK**
Mother:	**Sallie SMITH**
Draft Registration:	Buncombe County, 27, married, waiter at Battery Park Hotel

[Documentation: Buncombe County DC, 1900-1940 Censuses, Ancestry.com]

Bostick, Tealer   2,430,116   Colored
(surname)   (Christian name)   (Army serial number) (Race: White or colored)

Residence: 118 Church St   Asheville   NORTH CAROLINA
(Street and house number)   (Town or city)   (County)   (State)

Enlisted in   Inducted LB#2 Ashland N C Apr 20/18
Born in   Revard N C 28 7/12 yrs
Organizations: 158 Dep Brig to July 17/18; Co H 802 Pion Inf to disch

Grades: Corp Nov 27/18

Engagements:

Wounds or other injuries received in action: None.
Served overseas Sept 1/18 to June 28/19
Hon. disch. July 13/19   on demobilization
Was reported 0   per cent disabled on date of discharge, in view of occupation.
Remarks:

William McKinley BOWMAN

Born:	7 Apr 1895, Hickory, NC
Died:	Undetermined
Buried:	Undetermined
Occupation:	Working at lumber company at time of enlistment in Army
Father:	**Robert BOWMAN**
Mother:	**Mary FOX**
Draft Registration:	22, single, teamster for H. Cook Lumber Co. of Rosman
Note:	Names of parents were obtained from a Bowman Family Tree, Ancestry.com

[Documentation: Ancestry.com]

Bowman   William M   1,876,301   White
(surname)   (Christian name)   (Army serial number) (Race: White or colored)

Residence:_____Breward_____Transylvania____NORTH CAROLINA
         (Street and house number)   (Town or city)   (County)   (State)

*Enlisted in   Inducted Breward N C Oct 3/17   —
†Born in   Hickory N C 22 7/12 yrs   —
Organizations: Med Dept Field Hosp Camp Jackson S C to Nov 11/17;
                 Amb Co 324 - 326 Sn Tn to disch

Grades: Wag Sept 25/18   —   —

Engagements: —   —

Wounds or other injuries received in action: None.
†Served overseas: Aug 7/18 to June 16/19   —
§Hon. disch.   June 24/19   on demobilization   —
Was reported   0   per cent disabled on date of discharge, in view of occupation.

SRC Note: Sn Tn (Sanitary Train)

7 Dec 1917   Brevard News
COUNTY CITIZEN VISITS CAMP BOYS
R.M. Powell of Rosman was here last week in his return from Columbia, SC, where he had been to visit some of the Transylvania boys at Camp Jackson. The boys to whom he made a special visit were his son R.C. Powell, Pierce Aiken, Wiley Owen, Walter Whitmire and Bill Bowman. Mr. Powell spent three days in camp and was much pleased with what he saw, especially with the good treatment the boys were receiving from Uncle Sam.

---

2 May 1919   Brevard News

HORSES FOR SALE
Beginning Monday, May 5th, 1919

R.R. Deaver returned yesterday from Camp Wadsworth, where he purchased a carload of very fine horses, which he will offer for sale to the farmers of our county, beginning Monday, May 5th. The horses were shown on Main Street after they were unloaded and seemed to be a very fine selection of animals.

Robert F. BOYD

Born:	8 Dec 1895, Buncombe County, NC
Died:	Mar 1947
Buried:	Undetermined
Father:	**Berry Marcus BOYD**
Mother:	**Amanda DUCKETT**
Draft Registration:	21, farmer, single
Service Record Card:	No
Note:	Last known location of Robert was 1930 census in Huntington, NY

[Documentation: Ancestry.com, 1930 Census, Discharge, SSDI]

Boyd   Robert F.   4,159,457   White
(Surname)   (Christian name)   (Army serial number)   (Race: White or colored)

Residence: R F D #1   Etowah   Transylvania   NORTH CAROLINA
               (Street and house number)   (Town or city)   (County)   (State)

* Enlisted in   Inducted Brevard N.C. July 24/18
† Born in   Sandy Mush N.C. Dec 8/1895
Organizations: 71 Co 6 Gp Main Tng Dep Camp Hancock Ga to Oct 30/18;
                  Co B 358 MG Bn to Dec 13/18; Hq Tr 95 Div to Disch

Grades: Pvt

Engagements:

Wounds or other injuries received in action: None.
‡ Served overseas: None
§ Hon. disch.   Jan 4/19   on demobilization
Was reported   0   per cent disabled on date of discharge, in view of occupation.

18 Jul 1918   Brevard News
23 MORE MEN TO LEAVE JULY 24, 1918 for induction on July 24th, 1918 for Camp Hancock, Ga., . . . Robert Frank Boyd, Etowah . . .

Haywood County Digital Collection

Boys of the 120th Infantry Buying Stamps and Stationary from Y.M.C.A.

James Orlando BRACKEN

Born:	30 Nov 1893
Died:	20 Oct 1965, Kingston, NY; age 71
Buried:	Cathey's Creek Baptist Church age Cemetery
Occupation:	Carpenter
Spouse:	**Ellen J. McCARTHY**
Father:	**John Dillard BRACKEN**
Mother:	**Florida BROWN**
Draft Registration:	No
Military Marker:	NC CCM US Navy WW I

[Documentation: Transylvania County Cemetery Survey; TT obituary, Ancestry.com]

Name	BRACKEN- JAMES ORLANDO		Service Number	112-85-66	
Enlisted XXXXX at	USS BARNEY AT WASHINGTON D.C.		Date	8-2-15	
Age at Entrance	25 YRS 9 MO.	Rate SEAMAN			U.S.N. XXXKKJ
Home Address	XX		Town	BREVARD	
B	County	XX	State	N.C.	
	Served at	From	To	Served as	No. Days

USS VESTAL	4-6-17	11-11-18	CARPENTERS MATE 2 CLASS	131
			CARPENTERS MATE 1 CLASS	427
			CHIEF CARPENTERS MATE	26

Remarks:

Date Discharge 6-25-19
Place XXXXXX ty   USS VESTAL AT NEW YORK N.Y

CHIEF CARPENTERS MATE
Rating at Discharge

15 Mar 1918   Brevard News
J.O. Bracken, of the U.S. Navy, spent a few days with his mother and sister and other relatives during the past week. The Navy seems to agree with him.

11 Apr 1919   Brevard News
J.O. Bracken of the U.S.S. Vestal is at home on a furlough of thirty days. He was called home on account of the illness of his mother.

10/28/1965
James Bracken

Funeral services for James O. Bracken, age 71, of Kingston, New York, were held last Sunday in the Frank Moody Funeral Home Chapel. Burial was in Cathey's Creek Cemetery. Mr. Bracken died October 20th, after a lingering illness.

Survivors include one sister, Mrs. G.W. Trent; and three daughters: Helen, Margaret and Florence, all of Boston, Mass.

He was a carpenter and a veteran of World War I and a member of the Thomasville Orphanage Baptist Church.

> The USS Vestal was a repair ship in service with the US Navy from 1913 to 1946. She was damaged during the Japanese attack on Pearl Harbor and was decommissioned 14 August 1946.

William C. BRACKEN

Born:	17 Sep 1896, Transylvania County, NC
Died:	20 Jun 1958, Alameda, CA; age 61
Buried:	Golden Gate National Cemetery, San Bruno, CA
Occupation:	Switchman for the Union Pacific RR
Spouse:	**Ruth GARDNER**
Father:	**William O. BRACKEN**
Mother:	**Carrie Lee BURRELL**
Draft Registration:	No

[Documentation: CA Death Index, US National Cemetery Interment Control Form, Ancestry.com, 1910- 1940 Censuses, Parent's NC Death Certificates, Discharge, TT obituary]

6/26/1958
W.C. BRACKEN

Last rites for William Clarence Bracken, 62, native of Brevard, were held Monday at the Golden Gate National Cemetery, San Bruno, Calif.

A semi-retired implement salesman and former railroad man, Mr. Bracken died last Friday in the Oakland, California Veteran's hospital. Mr. Bracken's mother and other survivors live in Brevard.

Bracken moved to the San Jose, Calif., area a year ago from Oregon where he was employed by International Harvester Co. Previously he worked for the Union Pacific Railroad in Wyoming.

SRC Note: CAC (Coast Artillery Corps)

Gaither Henry BRANCH

Born:	20 Sep 1899, Caldwell County, NC
Died:	12 May 1966, Burke County, NC; age 66
Buried:	Pisgah Gardens Cemetery
Occupation:	Retired farmer and barber
Spouse:	**Priscilla Dean WARREN**, Feb. 3, 1926 in Buncombe County
Father:	**James Wesley BRANCH**
Mother:	**Mary Loucinda CLONTZ**
Draft Registration:	No
Military Marker:	N.C. PFC L Co 120 Inf 30 Div WW I PH

[Documentation: Burke County DC, <u>Transylvania County Cemetery Survey</u>, Ancestry.com]

Wash Day Camp Hancock, Augusta, GA.

Carl Cleveland BREEDLOVE

Born:	26 Sep 1894, Transylvania County, NC
Died:	10 Dec 1972, Transylvania County, NC; age 78
Buried:	Lakeside Cemetery
Spouse:	**Annie Virginia OWEN**, m. 30 Jan 1916, Transylvania County, NC
Father:	**James Arthur BREEDLOVE**
Mother:	**Ruanna WHITMIRE**
Draft Registration:	22, married, farmer
Military Marker:	SC PVT US Army WW I

[Documentation: Transylvania DC, Upper Transylvania County, NC Remembered, Ancestry.com, TT obituary, Discharge]

21 Sep 1917   Brevard News
THIRTY-ONE MEN TO CAMP JACKSON
Forty percent of the certified draft, making 31 men, was ordered to report on Tuesday at 5 P.M. at the office of the local enlistment board and to leave for Camp Jackson, S.C. Wednesday morning.
. . .Carl Cleveland Breedlove . . .

12/14/1972
CARL C. BREEDLOVE

Carl Cleveland Breedlove, 78, of Lake Toxaway, died Sunday evening at Transylvania Community Hospital after a short illness. He was caretaker of the Nunnley Estate and was a life-long resident of Transylvania County. He was a veteran of World War I and a deacon of Lake Toxaway Baptist Church.

He is survived by his widow, Mrs. Annie Owen Breedlove; two sons: James R. and Jesse M Breedlove; one daughter, Mrs. Leo Powell; and one sister, Mrs. Annie Galloway.

Funeral services were held Tuesday in the Lake Toxaway Baptist Church with burial in the church cemetery.

James Breedlove home

Fred Breedlove

Edna Owen Breedlove

Jesse Franklin Breedlove

James Breedlove

Carl Breedlove

Susan Breedlove Photo

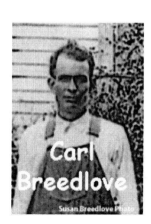

Carl Breedlove

Susan Breedlove Photo

Charles Fredrick BREEDLOVE

Born:	27 Oct 1896 in Transylvania County, NC
Died:	5 Nov 1966, Transylvania County, NC; age 70
Buried:	Lakeside Cemetery
Occupation:	Stonemason
Spouse:	**Nancy THOMAS**, m. 4 Jul 1922, Transylvania County, NC
Father:	**James Arthur BREEDLOVE**
Mother:	**Ruanna WHITMIRE**
Draft Registration:	No

[Documentation: Transylvania County DC; <u>Upper Transylvania County, NC Remembered</u>, TT obituary, Discharge]

Charles F. Breedlove

Susan Breedlove Photo

Name BREEDLOVE - CHARLES FREDRICK   Service Number 113-07-84

Enlisted XXXXX at RECRUITING STATION RALEIGH N.C.   Date 11-9-17   U.S.N. XXXX

Age at Entrance 21 YRS   Rate APPRENTICE SEAMAN

Home Address XX   County TRANSYLVANIA   Town LAKE TOXAWAY   State N.C.

B Served at	From	To	Served as	No. Days
RECEIVING SHIP AT NORFOLK VA.	11-9-17	12-23-17	APPRENTICE SEAMAN	84
NAVAL TRAINING STATION NORFOLK VA.	12-23-17	2-4-18	SEAMAN 2 CLASS	181
NAVAL HOSPITAL AT HAMPTON ROADS VA.	2-4-18	2-18-18	SEAMAN	102
NAVAL TRAINING STATION NORFOLK VA.	2-18-18	3-1-18		
USS MAINE	3-1-18	11-11-18		

Remarks:

Date Discharge 7-5-19 NAVY RECRUITING STATION
Place XXXXXy   ATLANTA GA.   Rating at Discharge SEAMAN

31 Oct 31 1918   Brevard News
Fred Breedlove, who is in the U.S. Navy, writes his parents Mr. and Mrs. James A. Breedlove, the he is well and enjoying life.

5 Apr 1919   Brevard News
Fred Breedlove is home for a few days. He has served 18 months in the Navy on the U.S.S. Maine.

11/6/1966
CHARLES F. BREEDLOVE

Charles Fredrick Breedlove, age 70 died at his home Saturday afternoon at Lake Toxaway after a short illness. He was a lifelong resident of Transylvania County, a veteran of World War I and a stonemason by trade.

Surviving are two daughters: Mrs. Julia Fisher and Mrs. Cecil Fisher; two sons: Ben and Frank; three brothers: Carl, Jess and Ward; and one sister, Mrs. Ira Galloway.

Funeral services were conducted at the Lake Toxaway Baptist Church and burial was in the church cemetery.

> The USS Maine was taken out of service in 1909 but brought back into service in 1911 and stayed on the East Coast. During WW I she was used to train engineers, armed guard crews and midshipmen. She was decommissioned at Philadelphia Navy Yard January 23, 1922 and sold for scrap.

William Edmond BREESE

Born:	1 Jul 1900, Transylvania County, NC
Died:	28 Sep 1958, Miami, Florida; age 58
Buried:	Evergreen Cemetery, Jacksonville, FL
Spouse:	**Elizabeth BROOME**
Father:	**William E. BREESE, Sr.**
Mother:	**Rebekah WOODBRIDGE**
Draft Registration:	18, Citadel student, employed at S.W.C. Camp Plattsburg Bliss, NY

[Documentation: Florida Death Index, Parent's NC Death Certificates, 1900 census, Ancestry.com, Findagrave.com]

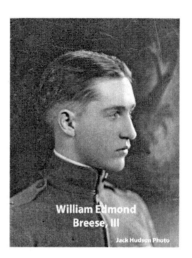

William Edmond Breese, III
Jack Hudson Photo

Breese   William (Edmond)   White
(Surname)   (Christian name)

Brevard   NORTH CAROLINA

Residence..
(Street and house number)   (Town or city)   (County)   (State)

Born in Brevard NC July 1/1900
Appointed 2d Lt Inf Sept 16/18 fr CL   Plattsburg Bks N Training Cam

Promotions :

Organizations and staff assignments : SATC University of Maine to disch

Principal stations : Orono Me.

Engagements :

Wounds received in action : None.

Served overseas No

Hon. disch. (date) Dec 16/18   for convenience of the Government, services no longer requir

Was reported O   per cent disabled on date of discharge, in view of occupation.

27 Apr 1917   Brevard News

Last week the News published the names of those who, to its knowledge, had offered their services to the government in various branches.....W.E. Breese. "Mr. Breese was outstanding in the performance of important assignments in the United States and abroad," wrote his former State Dept. Chief, Howard Flynn, under whom Breese served in the picture division OWI, overseas   He interrupted his college work to serve for a time during 1918 as a second lieutenant of infantry.

October 2, 1958
DICK BREESE, 58,
Prominent Newspaperman Was A Native Of Brevard. Career Noted

Edmond (Dick) Breese, 58, news editor of Pan American World Airways public relations department and a veteran well-known Southern newsman, died early Monday after a courageous two-year fight against cancer at Miami, Florida.

His news career had spanned the work from the banks of the Mississippi to Belgrade, Yugoslavia. He was born here in Brevard.

During his 15-year association with the Memphis Commercial Appeal, from 1929 to 1944, Mr. Breese rose from reporter to city editor and news editor of that influential mid-south daily.

He left the staff of the Tennessee Daily during World War II to join the Office of War Infor-

mation, handling assignments in Washington and Rome, Italy. From Rome, Breese went to Belgrade, serving there during 1946 as director of the United States Information Service and press attaché for the U.S. Embassy in Belgrade.

In the war-torn Yugoslav capital, Breese, with a staff of 20, handled news releases, pictures, features, recordings and documentary movies, photo exhibits and displays – a complete information program spotlighting the American way of life to a country struggling in the throes of reconstruction.

"Mr. Breese was outstanding in the performance of important assignments in the United States and abroad," wrote his former State Dept. Chief, Howard Flynn, under whom Breese served in the picture division OWI, overseas branch.

Returning to this country, Mr. Breese joined PAA's Latin American division public relations department in April 1947. He served as news editor since 1955.

Combining an incisive wit - that even his fatal malady could not dim – with scholarly background. Breese was born here on July 1, 1900. He attended schools in Brevard, the Citadel military college in South Carolina, and the University of North Carolina. He was the son of the late Edmond W. and Rebekah W. Breese of Brevard.

He interrupted his college work to serve for a time during 1918 as a second lieutenant of infantry in the U.S. Army.

For a time he engaged in farming with his father in Brevard before becoming, as he put it, "fed up with farming" and deciding to enter the newspaper profession.

Breese, who lived at 615 Gondoliere, Coral Gables, was married in January 1932, to Elizabeth Broome, of Jacksonville. They have a son William E. Breese, 22, and a daughter Sarah Elizabeth, 19.

Other survivors include a brother Lt. Col. E.W. Breese, and a sister Mrs. Martha Fraser.

Services were held in St. Stephens Episcopal Church, Coconut Grove and the burial was in the Evergreen Cemetery, Jacksonville, Florida.

---

14 Nov 1917   **Brevard News**

OUR HOME DEFENDERS ANSWER THE SUMMONS
Local Company Of Home Guards Organized Last Week
J. W. Burnett Elected Lieutenant
25 Men Selected From National Council Of Defense

A branch of the 38th division of Home Guards was organized at the rooms of the Brevard Club last Friday night by the enrollment of 25 representative men from this community as member of the body and by the election of J. W. Burnett as the 1st Lieut.

The men who were selected by the Council for National defense as follows: J. W. Burnett, J. E. Waters, W. E. Breese, Robert Orr, Fred Johnson, P. H. Galloway, M. M. Chapman, J. S. Silversteen, W. W. Croushorn, E. F. Wellman, T. E. Patton, Junior, John O. Cantrell, B. J. Sitton, C. C. Yongue, J.A. Miller, Jr., J.M. Allison, E.F. Moffett, C.E. Orr, C.B. Deaver, R.L.Gash, C.M. Doyle and F.E. Slatton.

The members of the guard, as now constituted, are above the national draft age--their ages ranging from 34 to 45 years. They will be included in the Hendersonville Company and subject to call from the captain of the company; but locally they will constitute an independent company, commanded by Mr. Burnett.

Mr. Burnett, who will also appoint others, has appointed one other local officer. This officer is J. A. Miller, Jr., 1st Sgt.

J. S. Silversteen has offered the upper floor of the tannery as a meeting and drilling place for the company, and there the men will assemble every Thursday night for military drill. This place has approximately an acre of floor space.

Mr. Burnett elected 1st Lieut. and local commanding officer has had the advantage of military training, which was taken in his college course.

The question of uniform in the men is one of great importance. Gov. Bickett has given assurance that he will endeavor to have an appropriation made by the Legislature for this purpose. In the meantime it has been decided to apply to the city and county officials for the funds needed on the condition that if the legislature makes the appropriation, the city and county will be reimbursed. A committee was appointed to make this application. The committee consists of J.S. Silversteen, J.A. Miller, Jr., C.B. Deaver, J.M. Allison and C.M. Doyle.

James Allen BREWER

Born:	21 Jun 1890, Manning, South Carolina
Died:	7 Aug 1969, Transylvania County, NC; age 79
Buried:	Montvale Cemetery, Whitewater, NC
Occupation:	Farmer
Spouse:	**Pearl Ella Mae KINSEY, m.** 21 Mar 1925, Transylvania County
Father:	**Thomas Franklin BREWER**
Mother:	**Maggie TENNANT**
Draft Registration:	No
Note:	Grave marker gives NO military information
Discharge:	Enlisted July 14, 1917 in Manning, SC. He was on American Expeditionary

Forces from July 17, 1918 until June 1, 1919. Discharged Aug 29, 1919 at Ft.
McPherson, Ga., PVT Co K 52nd Inf AEF U.S. Army

*[Documentation: Transylvania County DC, Upper Transylvania County, NC Remembered, Discharge,
Ancestry.com, TT obituary]*

8/14/1969
JAMES A. BREWER

James Allen Brewer, age 80, of Sapphire Whitewater Community died early last Thursday morning following a lingering illness.

He had resided in Transylvania County for a number of years. He was World War I veteran, was active in the Sapphire-Whitewater Community activities and was a retired farmer.

Survivors include three daughters: Mrs. A.V. Yancey, Mrs. Doyle Rice and Mrs. Ford Rice; and eight sons: Gordon, Edwin, Eugene, Don, Ronald, Gary, Wallace and Harry Brewer.

The funeral was conducted at the Whitewater Baptist Church with burial following in he Whitewater Church Cemetery.

Camp Scene

Julius Leander BRITTAIN

Born:	11 Sep 1896, Horse Shoe, NC
Died:	5 Nov 1965, Henderson County, NC; age 69
Buried:	Mills River Pres. Church Cemetery, Henderson County, NC
Spouse:	**Ella GILLESPIE**
Father:	**George BRITTAIN**
Mother:	**Rose Ann CORPENING**
Draft Registration:	21, single and self employed

[Documentation: Henderson County Delayed Birth Index, Henderson County DC, <u>Henderson County NC Cemeteries</u>, Hendersonville T-N obituary, Ancestry.com]

```
                                                                    1½
        Brittain    Julius Lee           4,070,829  White
         (Surname)     (Christian name)      (Army serial number) (Race: White or colored)

Residence:                   Brevard    Transylvania Co  NORTH CAROLINA
                       (Street and house number)  (Town or city)    (County)        (State)

Enlisted:           Inducted  Aug 5/18  Transylvania Co NC
Born in             Hendersonville  N C   Sept 11/1896
Organizations:      Co M 5 Pion Inf to Aug 29/18; Co F 56 Pion to Disch


Grades:             Pvt

Engagements:

Wounds or other injuries received in action: None.
Served overseas:    Sept 4/18 to June 9/19
Hon. disch.         June 16/19 on demobilization
Was reported        0           per cent disabled on date of discharge, in view of occupation.
Remarks:
```

SRC Note: Pion Inf (Pioneer Regiment Infantry)

Hendersonville Times-News
11/6/1965
J.P. BRITTAIN KILLED IN FARM ACCIDENT

A 69-year-old Horse Shoe farmer was killed Friday afternoon in a tractor accident at the home of his son in Horse Shoe. J. Neal Grissom, acting county coroner, said that Julius Lee Brittain, Sr., died due to massive internal injuries. In attempting to set up a portable feed mill, Mr. Brittain was wedged against the side of a farm building as his son, J.L. Brittain Jr., was backing the tractor into position to make the attachment.

A resident of Route 1, Horse Shoe, Mr. Brittain was a Henderson County native and son of the late George and Rosa Corpening Brittain. He was a member of the Mills River Presbyterian Church where he had served as an elder for the past 25 years.

Funeral services will be held at 2 p.m. Sunday in the Mills River Presbyterian Church Burial will take place in the church cemetery.

<u>14 Nov 1918</u>   **Brevard News**
DOYLE WANTS SOLDIERS PICTURES

C.M. Doyle is urging everyone who has a picture of his Transylvania Soldier Boy to bring it in to the Brevard Hardware Company. Mr. Doyle has quite a few pictures already in his large show window but wants to turn the whole window over to this purpose.

It is believed that there are at least three hundred pictures of our Transylvania Soldier boys and as everyone would like to see and know "our heroes" it is hoped that the relatives and friends will bring these pictures in at once.

Paul BROOKS

Born: 30 Dec 1896, Transylvania County, NC
Died: 27 Mar 1992, Greenville, South Carolina; age 95
Buried: Graceland West Cemetery, Greenville County, SC
Spouse: **Callie Mae SMITH**, 7 Sept 1929, Greenville, SC
Father: **Whitfield BROOKS**
Mother: **Susan Ella WERTZ**
Draft Registration: 21, employed at Gloucester Lumber Company
Military Marker: PVT US ARMY World WAR I

[Documentation: Transylvania County Birth Index, SC Findagrave.com, 1900 census, Greenville, SC Marriage Records, Ancestry.com]

Brooks, Paul 4,480,508 White

Residence: Rosmar Transylvania NORTH CAROLINA
Enlisted R.A. N.G. E.R.C. Inducted at Brevard NC on Aug 26/19 18
Place of birth: Davidson River NC Age or date of birth: Dec 31/1896
Organizations served in, with dates of assignments and transfers:
156 Dep Brig to disch
Grades, with date of appointment: Pvt
Engagements:
Wounds or other injuries received in action: None.
Served overseas from † No to † , from † to †
Honorably discharged on demobilization Dec 19/ , 19 18
In view of occupation he was, on date of discharge, reported 0 per cent disabled.
Remarks:

SRC NOTES: Dep Brig (Depot Brigade)

7 Mar 1919   Brevard News
SERIOUS ACCIDENT

An almost fatal accident occurred near the Gloucester Lumber Company's Camp last Friday morning when Paul Brooks was caught beneath a falling tree. The victim suffered a skull fracture and numerous other serious injuries. Dr. English reached the scene of the accident within a short time and immediately left with the injured man for Asheville where he was taken to the Mission Hospital. Mr. Brooks had been in training at Camp Sevier for several months and had received honorable discharge from the Army but a few weeks ago. Latest advices from Asheville are to the effect that hope is now entertained for his recovery.

Greenville New (SC)
3/29/1992
PAUL BROOKS

Paul Brooks, 95, of 101 Bud Street, Union Bleachery, died March 27, 1992 at his home. He was a retired employee of Cone Mill, a member of Paris View Baptist Church and served with US forces during World War I.

Surviving are his wife, Callie Mary Smith Brooks; and two daughters, Mary Louella Gibson and Paula Patricia Brooks.

Services were Monday at Parris View Baptist Church with burial in Graceland West Cemetery.

James Luther BROWN

Born:	1 Jul 1902, Henderson County, NC
Died:	3 Oct 1978, Henderson County, NC; age 76
Buried:	Little River Baptist Church Cemetery
Spouse:	**Willie Mae PRIDMORE**
Father:	**John Luther BROWN**
Mother:	**Addie DRAKE**
Draft Registration:	No
Service Record Card:	No
Military Marker:	CSM US Navy WW I & II

[Documentation: Henderson County Delayed BC, findagrave.com, NC Death Collection, Transylvania County Cemetery Survey, Hendersonville T-N, Ancestry.com]

Hendersonville Times-News
10/3/1978
JAMES L. BROWN

James Luther Brown, 75, of Route 3, a retired farmer, died Tuesday evening in the veteran's hospital, Asheville, following a long illness.

Mr. Brown was a lifelong resident of Henderson County, a son of the late John and Addie Drake Brown. He was a veteran of World Wars I and II and was a member of Pleasant Hill Baptist Church. He was a member of Hedrick-Rhodes Post 5206, Veterans of Foreign Wars and Hubert M. Smith Post 77, American Legion.

He is survived by four sisters: Rosa Schwarz, Lois Mullis, Nettie Ward and Gertrude Fleming.

Graveside services will be held at 4 p.m. Thursday at Little River Baptist Church Cemetery.

3/1/1918

W.S.S.
WAR SAVINGS STAMPS
ISSUED BY THE
UNITED STATES
GOVERNMENT

It Is Your Duty

*To Know about War Savings Stamps
The Thrift Stams cost 25 cents each and pave the way to systematic saving. The War Stamps are $4.12 each, bear interest at 4 per cent and will be exchanged for sixteen Thrift Stamps plus $2. in cash. They are for sale at the Post Office and Banks and all stores will soon have them.*

Get The Saving Habit

Buy a THRIFT STAMP every day, help yourself and help your government win the war. Remember that if every person in the United States bought a 25 cent Thrift Stamp it would mean $25,000,000 for our country.

*WAR SAVINGS COMMITTEE
Transylvania County*

John Heyward BROWN, Sr.

Born:	22 Sep 1890, Transylvania County, NC
Died:	20 Nov 1976, Buncombe County, NC; age 86
Buried:	Gillespie-Evergreen Cemetery
Spouse:	**Callie GALLOWAY**, m. 14 Feb 1922, Transylvania County, NC
Father:	**William Alexander BROWN**
Mother:	**Drucilla Caroline MEECE**
Draft Registration:	27, single, painter for Gillespie & Harris in Brevard
Note:	1930 Census say NO to military service

[Documentation: 1900-1940 Censuses, Ancestry.com]

11/23/1976
JOHN BROWN

Services for John Heyward Brown, Sr., 86, who died Saturday were held Monday at Glady Branch Baptist Church. Burial was in the Gillespie-Evergreen Cemetery.

A lifelong resident of Transylvania County, he was a retired painter and paperhanger. He was a veteran of World War I.

Surviving are a daughter, Elizabeth Sellers; three sons: John H, Jr., Heyward S. and Lawrence E. Brown; a sister, Iantha Scruggs; and two brothers, Herman H. and Austin A. Brown.

John H. Brown
Elizabeth Sellers Photo

---

17 May 1918 Brevard News
NURSES PRETTY
Red Cross Hospital Uniform Most Becoming in History of World

In a recent newsletter from the front the war correspondent of the Philadelphia North American helps to explain the song, "I'm in Love With a Beautiful Nurse."

"There are 62 Red Cross nurses at this place," says the dispatch. "They are cheerful, obedient, brave and competent. And those who weren't pretty to begin with became so the moment they donned the uniform that is the most becoming in all the history of costumes devised for the mystification and beguiling of men.

"In the officers' ward was a colonel with bronchitis. 'I've seen them in the Philippines, and I've seen them in China,' he told me. 'I suppose I've seen about all the existing types, but I never yet saw one that wasn't pretty inside of 24 hours.'

"He reminded me of an Irish Tommy, who, so his major told me, woke up in a hospital in 1916 and, seeing the nurses in the ward, exclaimed, 'May the holy Virgin bless us, but the angels have come down to the Service!'"

Hundreds of Red Cross nurses however, are doing work abroad in which their looks are less eagerly considered. Finding and caring for war orphaned babies, fighting tuberculosis, reestablishing homes in shell wrecked villages; these are some of the big tasks of mercy which, thanks to American contributions the Red Cross sets for its nurses.

John Robert BROWN

Born:	1 Feb 1893, undetermined
Died:	27 Oct 1976, Buncombe County, NC; age 83
Buried:	Shoal Creek Baptist Church Cemetery
Spouse:	**Clercie Ellen ASHE**
Father:	**Manley A. BROWN**
Mother:	**Sophia SHELTON**
Draft Registration:	No
Service Record Card:	No
Military Marker:	PVT U.S. Army WW I

[Documentation: Buncombe County DC, Transylvania County Out County DC, Transylvania County Cemetery Survey, Ancestry.com, findagrave.com]

10/29/1976
JOHN ROBERT BROWN

John Robert Brown, 83, died Wednesday in a Brevard hospital after an extended illness. A native of Jackson County, and a Transylvania County resident for many years, he was a retired lumberman and a World War I veteran.

Surviving are the widow, Clercie Ashe Brown; two sons: Chester and Wendell Brown; seven daughters: Nora Hall, Irma McCall, Edith Chapman, Katie Perkins and Sue Bishop, Etta Owen and Mary Ellen Hartmann; seven brothers: Tinsley, Fonnie, Clarence, Clyde, Floyd and Griffin; two sisters: Mrs. Royal Lowe and Mrs. Ralph Broom.

Services will be held at 2 p.m. Friday at Shoal Creek Baptist Church, where he had been a deacon for 60 years. Burial will be in the church cemetery.

---

5 Aug 1918   **Brevard News**

RED CROSS TO FILL VACANT PLACE

The Home Service section of the Transylvania Chapter of the American Red Cross wishes to again call the attention of all soldiers' families to the effort that this committee is eager to help all soldiers' families in any way possible to them. Anyone wishing information and advice, or in need of help because of conditions existing in their home since their husband or son has been called to "the Colors," may come to the U.D.C. Meeting Room on any Tuesday morning from 10:30 to 12:30 or Friday afternoon from 4 to 6 o'clock.

Letters will be written, information given and help extended to any soldier's family in need. The Home Service Committee will be glad to receive information regarding soldiers families from any reliable person, as it is a duty not only of the members of this committee but of every citizen and this County, to help inspire confidence in the hearts and minds of our soldiers and their dear ones, confidence in the fact that the Red Cross will stand ready at all times to help at home as well as at the front.

The committee simply asks that all who can will please come to us or send some trustworthy person. If unable to do this, the committee will send a representative to them if notified.

Most sincerely,
Mrs. J. Silversteen

Homer Jerome BRYAN

Born:	16 May 1895, Madison County
Died:	28 Mar 1977, Transylvania County; age 81
Buried:	Pisgah Gardens Cemetery
Spouse:	**Lonnie WEST**
Father:	**Levi Jackson BRYAN**
Mother:	**Maria Eliza RECTOR**
Draft Registration:	Madison County, 22, single, farmer
Military Marker:	PVT US Army WW I

[Documentation: North Carolina Birth Index, Transylvania County DC, <u>Transylvania County Cemetery Survey</u>, Ancestry.com, findagrave.com]

Bryan, Homer Jerome	5,349,120	• White ☒Colored
(Surname) (Christian name)	(Army serial number)	

Residence: _____Route 2_____ _____Marshall_____ _____ __NORTH CAROLINA__
(Street and house number)   (Town or city)   (County)   (State)

*Enlisted *R. A. *N. G. *E. R. C. *Inducted at __Madison Co NC__ on __Aug 5__, 19__18__

Place of birth: __Marshall NC__   Age or date of birth: __May 16/1895__

Organizations served in, with dates of assignments and transfers:
__Co H 5th Pion Inf to Aug 25/18; Co M 4th Pion Inf to__
__Aug 30/18; Co C 331st Inf to disch.__

Grades, with date of appointment: _____

Engagements: _____

Wounds or other injuries received in action: None.

Served overseas from †Sept 23/18† Jan 26/19 from †_____ to †_____

Honorably discharged on demobilization __Feb 8__, 19 19

In view of occupation he was, on date of discharge, reported __10__ per cent disabled.

Remarks: _____

SRC Note: Pion Inf (Pioneer Infantry)

3/31/1977
HOMER BRYAN

Homer Jerome Bryan, 81, died Monday in a Brevard hospital after a period of declining health. A native of Madison County and a resident of Brevard for the past 30 years, he was a veteran of World War I. He was a member of Legion Post 88 of Brevard.

Surviving are the widow, Lonnie West Bryan; a daughter, Frances Costes; a son, Troy J. Bryan; and a sister, Sally Sprinkle.

Memorial services were held Wednesday at Brevard First Baptist Church and burial followed in the Pisgah Garden Cemetery

---

ARMISTICE

Within a few days of the fighting at Argonne, the German government asked the Allied commanders for a cease-fire. Terms for the settlement of the war needed to be worked out and it was decided by the two sides that the war would end. On the eleventh of November 1918 at exactly 11:AM the guns were to be silent.

When 11:AM came it was all over. Both the Germans and Allies emerged from the trenches and met as if they were best friends ever. They exchanged souvenirs and celebrated together. The war had at last ended but the important work of determining what the war had decided was far from being settled.

Harry Lambert BRYSON

Born:	20 Sep 1900, Jackson County, NC
Died:	22 Jan 1989, Transylvania County, NC; age 88
Buried:	Cremation
Occupation:	Retired logger
Spouse(s):	**Roxie E. GALLOWAY**, m. 9 Jul 1922, Transylvania County
	Leota Alice REID
Father:	**Robert Lee BRYSON**
Mother:	**Alice NICHOLSON**
Draft Registration:	No

[Documentation: Roster of WWI Veterans from American Legion 50ᵗʰ Anniversary celebration; NC Birth Index; NC Death Collection; 1910, 1930 and 1940 Censuses; TT obit]

1/26/1989
HARRY L. BRYSON

Harry Lambert Bryson, 88, of Sapphire died Monday. A native of Jackson County, he had lived most of his life in Transylvania County. He was a logger and a veteran of World War I, U.S. Navy.

Surviving are his wife, Leota Reid Bryson; one daughter, Anita Louise Bryson; two sons, Harold and Ernest Bryson; one brother, Lloyd Bryson; and one sister, Mildred Winthrop.

Memorial services will be held at 3 p.m. Sunday in Lake Toxaway Baptist Church.

<u>**9 May 1919**</u>   <u>**Brevard News**</u>

EVERY SOLDIER WILL RECEIVE VICTORY METAL

In compliance with an order recently issued by the War Department every Transylvania boy who served the colors during the recent conflict with Germany will be given a Victory Metal. These metals are to be awarded to every soldier of the Allied governments. After prolonged conferences with representatives of all the countries recently fighting against the Huns, General March, who helped the Americans to victory, has announced the design for the Victory Medal has been approved for issuance to every soldier in commendation of his service to the cause. The design is to be similar for all countries but may differ in detail for the various armies.

The obverse side of the metal will bear a winged victory and on the reverse will be, in the language of the country by which it was issued, the words: "The Great War Of Civilization," and the arms on the Allies. A campaign ribbon also has been adopted to consist of a "double rainbow" series of colors. This ribbon will be similar for all armies and is to be issued in the United States very soon. To indicate participation in the more important engagements, extra clasps will be attached to the ribbons. For the Americans these clasps will bear the names of the battles selected by General Pershing as the most important engagements of the War. Special clasps will indicate the place of service, as in France, Italy, England or Siberia. Citations for individual soldiers will be shown by attaching a small silver star for each citation. These ribbons and medals are to be awarded to all officers, enlisted man, and Army nurses who served on active duty for at least 15 days in the Army of the United States with an honorable record. Is it will take some time to make the metals the ribbons will be awarded first.

James McKinley BURGESS

Born:	24 Feb 1897, Polk County
Died:	8 Sep 1942, Johnson City, Tennessee; age 45
Buried:	Carr's Hill Baptist Church Cemetery
Spouse:	**Lola HOGSED**, m. 12 Feb 1927 Transylvania County
Father:	**Nathan Columbus BURGESS**
Mother:	**Elsie Ann SALMON**
Draft Registration:	No
Service Record Card:	No
Note:	Grave marker has NO military information and there is an application for a military headstone.

[Documentation: Discharge, Application for Military Headstone, TT obituary, Ancestry.com]

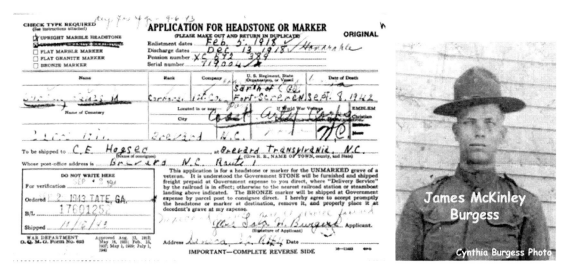

James McKinley Burgess

Cynthia Burgess Photo

9/16/1942
JAMES McKINLEY BURGESS

James Burgess, 45, died at the Veterans' Hospital in Johnson City, Tenn., on Tuesday following a lingering illness. Funeral services were held Thursday afternoon at Carr's Hill Baptist Church with interment in the church cemetery. The American Legion was in charge of the cemetery service.

Mr. Burgess had been an invalid the past two years or more, following injuries suffered to his back in a fall at the Ecusta plant. He was a veteran of World War I and had been in a number of government hospitals in recent months for treatment. He was a native of Polk County but had made Brevard his home for some time.

Survivors are his widow, Lola Hogsed Burgess: four children Newland, Sadie, Anthony and Charles Burgess; two brothers and two sisters also survive: Walter and John Burgess, Mrs. J.E. Martin and Mrs. W.J. Ridings.

In 1917 at the Declaration of War the United States Army had a force of only 80,000 while our total population was over 70 million people. These troops were all volunteer and were scattered around the world, doing routine tasks in China, Mexico and the Canal Zone in Panama. They had not been called upon to perform any real combat duty, so their experience was very limited. The officers had not been responsible for more than a few thousand soldiers where their counterparts in Europe were commanding units of one million or more soldiers.

Clingman Starnes CAMP

Born:	3 May 1894 in Buncombe County, NC
Died:	31 May 1956, Henderson County, NC; age 62
Buried:	Dana Methodist Church Cemetery, Henderson County, NC
Father:	**George W CAMP**
Mother:	**Mary HAMMETT**
Draft Registration:	23, single, a laborer at the Carr Lumber Company. Card states his birth date is MARCH 5, not May as DC states.
Note:	DC stated he shot himself in the neck, severed the artery and jugular vein.

[Documentation: Henderson County DC; Ancestry.com, military headstone]

SRC Notes: MD (Medical Department) Med Det (Medical Depot)

June, 1956
C.S .CAMP

The body of Clingman S. Camp, 61, of North Blue Ridge community was found yesterday at 5 p.m. on the bed at his home, according to Chief Deputy Sheriff Selden Clark of the Henderson County Sheriff's Department. Death resulted from a shotgun wound in the throat, according to Clark, called to the scene by Lee McAbee, a tenant in the Camp home, who found the body.

He was a World War I veteran and a bachelor and lived alone. Surviving are two half-brothers: John and Joe Camp; and a brother-in-law, John Turner.

Funeral services will be held Sunday afternoon at Refuge Baptist Church and burial will follow in the Blue House Cemetery.

Josephus Floyd CARMICHAEL

Born:	20 Apr 1896
Died:	3 May 1947, Alameda, CA; age 51
Buried:	Golden Gate National Cemetery, CA
Spouse:	**Elsie L. KAY**, m. 1917, Pasquotank County, NC
Father:	**Willis L. CARMICHAEL**
Mother:	**Mary M. CLAYTON**
Draft Registration:	No
Note:	The application for his headstone indicated he re-enlisted in Portsmouth, VA in the Navy for WW II.

[Documentation: Ancestry.com-military headstone, NC Marriage Collection, U.S. Veterans Gravesites]

United States Naval definitions:
   Landsman – preliminary rank for new recruits
   Yeoman – performs secretarial and clerical duties
The great majority of Yeoman during World War I were assigned duties at Naval Installations in the Continental United States.

Frank Brown CARR

Born:	13 Jul 1890 in Maraus, Italy
Died:	16 Aug 1965, Burke County, NC; age 75
Buried:	Gillespie-Evergreen Cemetery
Spouse:	**Elizabeth Mae McLEAN**, m. 15 Oct 1919, Transylvania County, NC
Father:	**Mike CARR**
Mother:	**Caroline**
Draft Registration:	26, single, chief clerk and director of Carr Lumber Co. He asked for an exemption from the draft because he was in charge of supplying poles to Southern Bell.

[Documentation: Burke County DC; Ancestry.com; <u>Transylvania County Cemetery</u> <u>Survey</u>; TT obituary, Discharge]

Carr, Frank B.	867,966	White	
(surname)	(Christian name)	(Army serial number)	(Race: White or colored)

Residence: Pisgah Forest   NORTH CAROLINA
(street and house number)   (Town or city)   (County)   (State)

* Enlisted in   RA at Ft Thomas Ky Dec 13/17

† Born in   Cosinza Italy 27_5/12 yrs

Organizations: 602 Sup Sq Sig v to Mch 24/18; 11 Provisional Aer Cons Regt (76 Spruce Sc) to Sept 20/18; 146 Spruce Sq to disch

Grades: Sgt Apr 1/18; Sgt 1 cl Sept 10/18

Engagements: —

Wounds or other injuries received in action: None.

‡ Served overseas: No

§ Hon. disch.   June 3/19   on demobilization

Was reported   0   per cent disabled on date of discharge, in view of occupation.

Remarks: —

SRC Notes: Sup Sq (Supply Squadron) Sig (Signal Corps) Aer Cons Regt (Aero Construction Regiment)

<u>21 Feb 1919</u>   <u>Brevard News</u>

Sgt. F.D. Carr, who volunteered from Transylvania County the fall of 1917, was honorably discharged January 3rd, 1919 at Vancouver Barracks, Washington, where he served for over a year in the aviation section Spruce Production Division, U.S. Army and is now back with the Carr Lumber Company.

8/19/1965
F. BROWN CARR

Funeral services for Frank Brown Carr, age 75, were held Tuesday afternoon in the First Baptist Church of Brevard. Burial was in the Gillespie-Evergreen Cemetery.

Mr. Carr died Monday morning in a Western North Carolina hospital after a lingering illness.

Mr. Carr was associated with the Carr Lumber Company of Pisgah Forest for several years. He was a nephew of Louie Carr. He was a member of the Brevard Kiwanis Club and the Dunn's Rock Masonic Lodge.

Surviving are the widow Mrs. Betty McLean Carr and three brothers and sisters

The Spruce Production Division was a unit of the US Army established in 1917 to supply the Army with high quality spruce needed for the production of aircraft for the United States war efforts in World War I. The headquarters were in Portland. Oregon and its main operations center was at Vancouver Barracks in Vancouver, Washington.

Carl Hamilton CASE

Born:	4 Oct 1887 in Transylvania County, NC
Died:	26 Aug 1978, Douglas, GA, age 90
Buried:	Valleytown Cemetery, Andrews, NC
Spouse:	**Cullie FRANKS**
Father:	**Caldwell C. CASE**
Mother:	**Emily M. HAMILTON**
Draft Registration:	29, single, time keeper for Carr Lumber Company

[Documentation: Ancestry.com; findagrave.com, Discharge]

8/27/1978
CARL H. CASE

Carl H. Case, 91, of Weston, GA, formerly of Andrews, died at his home after a long illness. A native of Cherokee County he was a retired lumber merchant and restaurant owner. He was a member of Douglasville, GA. Baptist Church.

The wife, Cullie Franks Case and two daughters, Mrs. Glen Gunter and Nell McLeroy, survive him.

Services were held in the chapel of J. Cowan Whitley Funeral Home in Douglasville. Burial was in Valleytown Cemetery.

SCR Notes: MG (Machine Gun) Tng (Training Company)

18 Jul 1918   Brevard News
23 MORE MEN TO LEAVE JULY 24, 1918
Following is a list of white registrants for induction on July 24th, 1918 for Camp Hancock, Ga., who will leave on the 3:13 train:
. . . Carl Hamilton Case, Brevard . . .

---

15 Aug 1918   Brevard News

HOSPITAL GARMENT ROOMS CLOSED

The Transylvania Red Cross has received instructions from headquarters that work in the hospital garment department is to be discontinued until further corrections are received from the government in regard to what the Red Cross will be expected to furnish the Army and Navy during the period beginning November 1. The Red Cross has filled all orders made by the government to that date.

While the local Red Cross workers are asked to stop sewing for short time, they are asked to continue the making of sweaters and socks with all speed possible.

Wool for these garments may be obtained in the Transylvania Red Cross headquarters on Tuesday and Saturday mornings from 10 to 12 and on Monday, Wednesday and Friday afternoons from 3:30 to 5:30. Miss Delia Gash, chairman of the Wool Garment Committee, will be at the Red Cross to give

Clyde CASE

Born	16 Nov 1891, Transylvania County, NC
Died:	5 Jan 1977, Buncombe County, NC, age 85
Buried:	Oakdale Cemetery, Henderson County, NC
Occupation:	U.S. Game Warden
Spouse:	**Annie LESLIE** m. 13 May 1919, Henderson County, NC
Father:	**Caldwell C CASE**
Mother:	**Emily M. HAMILTON**
Draft registration:	25, single, a clerk in the store of W.S. Ashworth in Pisgah Forest

[Documentation: Buncombe County DC; Henderson County OCDC; Ancestry.com, Hendersonville T-N obituary]

Clyde Case

Ruth Gray Photo

Case, Clyde 1,865,838 1
(Surname) (Christian name) (Army serial number) • White • Colored.
Residence: Pisgah Forest NORTH CAROLINA
(Street and house number) (Town or city) (County) (State)
Brevard N C
•Inducted at on Apr 1 19 18
Place of birth: Brevard N C Age or date of birth: 26 5/12 yrs
Organizations served in, with dates of assignments and transfers:
156 Dep Brig to Apr 17/18; Co C 318 F Sig Bn to
Mch 23/19; 153 Dep Brig to Disch
Grades, with date of appointment: Pvt

Engagements:

Wounds or other injuries received in action: None.
Served overseas from † July 14/18 to † Mch 22/19, from † to †
Honorably discharged on demobilization Apr 3/19, 19
In view of occupation he was, on date of discharge, reported 0 per cent disabled.

SRC Notes: Dep Brig (Depot Brigade) Sig Bn (Signal Battalion)

<u>**14 Feb 1919   Brevard News**</u>
NEWS FROM OVER THERE
Bonnetable, France
Jan 11, 1919
Editor Brevard News

I am by no means a writer, but a few words might be of interest to the people back home, even if I do make mistakes. During my time of nearly six months over here I have experienced lots of things I never did before. Some of which are to be well remembered. But I have had more pleasure and fewer hardships than many of the boys.

I sailed from New York on the English ship, Khyber, carrying a little over two thousand men. There were fourteen ships in the convoy when we started, but for some reason one turned back the second day out. Of the thirteen that continued the trip, there were over twenty six thousand yanks and about five hundred Red Cross ladies. All reached this side safely, except for one man. We all had to wear our life preservers all the time, in case of danger by meeting with the enemy, but they were not needed. The ninth day, a convoy of submarines were located ahead of us by another ship and reported back but this only caused us to go a little distance out of our way. The next day we were joined by a number of submarine chasers that guarded us into Liverpool.

We got a hearty welcome while we were in England but only got to spend three days there. I got to see some of the country while we were crossing it, while I like France, it is very different to the States.

At South Hampton we took a boat across the channel to Le Havre, France. There is where I heard my first "Jerry" airplane. He came out the second night we were there but the only damage done was by the civilians in town, a little way from camp. I was in four different places in France during the time I was in training before going to visit the Huns. Most of the time being in small towns where there were only a few soldiers. When our battalion went to the front, it was to join the Second Army Corps directing the twenty-seventh and thirtieth divisions that were working with the English. At that time they had just crossed the Hindenburg Line. At Belecourt, about five miles back of where we were stationed, is where they lost so heavily because the Germans were in an underground tunnel and coming out behind them.

They had only been there a few days when they were relieved and sent back to rest. While they were making their way past us they didn't look like they were going to a picnic. They were making their way along steadily in a continuous rainfall. There was nothing to keep one's face from showing the tired worn out feeling from the long hike with a pack on their back and after being in the trenches. Sometimes it was almost impossible to have meals just at the desired time. I was never any closer to the front lines than Corps Headquarters and while our officers were doing everything possible to avoid this we were not surprised if we had a breadless meal. But we can all feel proud now that the war is over and hope that no one will ever have to face another one like it.

Thanking you for the pleasure I have gotten out of your paper that has been sent to me regularly and for allowing me the space for this letter.

Clyde Case.

Hendersonville Times-News
1/5/1977
CLYDE CASE

Clyde Case, 85, of 2521 Haywood Road, died Wednesday morning in Asheville VA Hospital. He was a native of Brevard, a son of the late C.C. and Emily Hamilton Case. Mr. Case retired from Tennessee Valley Authority in Morristown, TN, in 1954. Prior to his employment with the TVA, he was with the U.S. Forest Service stationed at the Pink Beds in Pisgah National Forest. He was an Army veteran of World War I and a member of the American Legion and Disabled American Veterans in Morristown. He was a member of Valley Hill Baptist Church and was active in the extension programs of the church.

Surviving are the widow, Ann Leslie Case; a daughter, Mrs. Doyal Gray; a sister, Mrs. Lessie Guffee and a brother, Carrol H. Case.

Funeral services will be conducted Thursday in Shepherd's Church Street Chapel. Burial will be in Oakdale Cemetery.

Haywood County Library Digital Collection

105th Field Signal Battalion Post Exchange

Floyd CASSADA

Born:	16 Feb 1892, Madison County, NC
Died:	3 Apr 1975, Henderson County; age 83
Buried:	Pisgah Gardens Cemetery
Spouse:	**Lillian Inez ROBESON**
Father:	**Abe CASSADA**
Mother:	**Henrietta ROBERTS**
Draft Registration:	No
Military Marker:	SGT U.S. Army WW I

[Documentation: Henderson County DC, Transylvania County Cemetery Survey, Ancestry.com, Henderson T-N obituary]

Cassada, Floyd   655,016   white   2½

(Surname)	(Christian name)	(Army serial number)	(Race: White or colored)

Residence: _____ Marshall Madison   NORTH CAROLINA

(Street and house number)   (Town or city)   (County)   (State)

* Enlisted in N C olumbus Bks Ohio   —   Dec 31/15
† Born in   Marshall N Car   —   2d 10/12 Yrs
Organizations   4 4 Engrs Ponton Tn to —   ; Co 2 6 Engrs To
                May 17/17; Co 2 6 Engrs To disch

Grades: Pvt 1cl Feb 20/17; Sgt My 13/17; Stable Sgt May 31/ 7; Sgt
Engagements: V 5/17; Sgt 1cl Mch 2/13

Wounds or other injuries received in action: None.
‡ Served overseas: July 14/18 to Apr 27/19   —
§ Hon. disch. June 4/20 abolishment of BAR   —
Was reported _____ per cent disabled on date of discharge, in view of occupation.
Remarks: 0   —

Hendersonville Times-News
4/5/1975
FLOYD CASSADA

Floyd Cassada, 83, of Etowah, died Thursday in a Hendersonville hospital after a brief illness. A native of Madison County, he had lived in Henderson County for 16 years. He was a son of the late Abe and Henrietta Roberts Cassada and was a supervisor of the Malaria Control US Government for 24 years before retiring in 1958. He was a veteran of World War I.

Mr. Cassada is survived by his widow, Inez Roberson Cassada.

Funeral services will be held at 2 p.m. Saturday at Shepherd's Church Street Chapel. Burial will be in Pisgah Gardens.

---

17 Aug 1917   **Brevard News**

RED CROSS BOOSTED BY 816 ARTICLES

Mrs. J.S. Silversteen, chairman of the National League of Woman's Service, recently shipped to the Red Cross supply depot at New York a box of articles prepared by the women of the league.

The box contained 816 articles for the use of at Army hospitals and was valued at $70. The list included arm slings, fracture pillows, head, abdominal and T Bandages, and many plain bandages—nearly enough to supply one Army hospital for a week

Carl CHAPMAN

Born:	29 Apr 1889, Quebec, NC
Died:	24 Jun 1927, Oteen VA Hospital, Buncombe County; age 38
Buried:	Oak Grove Baptist Church Cemetery Quebec, NC
Occupation:	Railroad worker
Father:	**James Haygood CHAPMAN**
Mother:	**Martha GALLOWAY**
Draft Registration:	23, single, worked for Southern Railroad
Note:	Grave marker gives NO military information

[Documentation: Buncombe County DC, Upper Transylvania County, NC History, Discharge, draft registration, Ancestry.com]

19 Sep 1918   Brevard News
News has been received recently that Carl Chapman, son of Mr. and Mrs. James Chapman of Quebec has arrived safely overseas.

28 Feb 1919   Brevard News
Carl Chapman, who is now with the Army of Occupation in Germany, writes that he is enjoying the best of health.

Brevard News
7/7/1927
CARL CHAPMAN

Carl Chapman, son of Mr. and Mrs. James Chapman of Quebec, died Friday afternoon, June 24, 1927. The funeral services were conducted from Oak Grove Baptist Church Sunday, the 26th.

When this country entered the World War, Carl enlisted for service, taking his training at Camp Jackson. He sailed for France in the late summer of 1918, arriving on the 4th of September, where he took additional training. As his assigned Division was to move to the front the Armistice was signed. After the Armistice was signed, Carl was with the 50th Division of the Army of Occupation in Germany for some time before sailing for America. He reached home June 22, 1918 after an absence of thirteen months.

During the seven years from 1919 to 1926 Carl remained with his parents. In October 1926 he became ill, his affliction lingering for eight months. During the last days of his illness he was taken to Oteen Veterans Hospital where he received the best of medical attention.

Jesse Cannon CHAPMAN

Born:	28 Jan 1894, Transylvania County, NC
Died:	31 Oct 1966, Transylvania County, NC; age 72
Buried:	Galloway Cemetery in Middlefork
Spouse:	**Bertha GALLOWAY**, m. 31 Jul 1921, Transylvania County, NC
Father:	**Maxwell CHAPMAN**
Mother:	**Nancy S MOORE**
Draft Registration:	21, single, farmer with his dad, claimed exemption due to broken breastbone
Military Marker:	NC PVT 319 Field Artillery WW I

[Documentation: Ancestry.com; Transylvania County DC; Transylvania County Cemetery Survey; TT obituary, Discharge]

11/3/1966
JESSIE CHAPMAN

Jessie C. Chapman died at his home in Rosman early Monday morning, October 31st, after a brief illness. He was a native of Transylvania County and a veteran of World War I.

Surviving are two brothers: Lon and W.M. Chapman.

Funeral services were conducted at Middle Fork Baptist Church Wednesday afternoon, November 2nd. Burial was at Galloway Memorial Cemetery.

SRC Notes: FA (Field Artillery) Btry (Battery)

21 Jun 1918   **Brevard News**
WHITE REGISTRANTS WHO ARE TO LEAVE FOR CAMP JACKSON, S.C.
TUESDAY, JUNE 25th, 1918 AT 3:13 P.M.
. . . Jesse Chapman, Calvert . . .

---

5 Sep 1918   Brevard News

HOME GUARD 8   PISGAH CAMP 2

Labor Day was celebrated by the Brevard people with a ball game between the Brevard Home Guards and the officers of Pisgah Forest Camp. The game was played on the diamond of the camp and was a very interesting and fast game, considering that the home team had had no practice. But, in spite of this fact, they held their opponents down to "0" until the 8th inning when they made two runs. The score at the end of the 9th inning stood 8 to 2 in favor of the home guards.

The battery for the home guards: Grady Kilpatrick and Harry Patton. For the soldiers: we did not learn.

Ralph Herman CLEMENT

Born: 23 Aug 1895, Vermont
Died: 28 Dec 1940, San Diego, CA; age 45
Buried: Ft. Rosencrans National Cemetery, CA
Spouse: **Eleanor**
Father: **Frank CLEMENT**
Mother: **Blanche DODGE**
Draft Registration: No
Note: Frank retired from the US Navy Dec. 1, 1939 as a Chief Electrician's Mate.

[Documentation: Ancestry.com; findagrave.com, California Death Index]

Name CLEMENT RALPH HERMAN			Service Number 121-64-75	

Enlisted at RECRUITING STATION RALEIGH N.C.   Date 5-31-17   U.S.N.
Age at Entrance 21 YRS 9 MOS.   Rate APPRENTICE SEAMAN   R.F.
Home Address --- Town BREBARD -
County TRANSYLVANIA   State N.C.

Served at	From	To	Served as	No. Days
HOME AWAITING ORDERS	5-31-17	7-19-17	APPRENTICE SEAMAN	215
TRAINING STATION NEWPORT R.I.	7-19-17	8-23-17	ELECTRICIAN 3 CLASS	151
U S S NEBRASKA	8-23-17	11-11-18	ELECTRICIAN 2 CLASS	163

18 May 1917   Brevard News
BREVARD YOUNG MEN ANSWER WAR'S CALL
    The call to arms continues to meet with response of one kind or another in Brevard. Since the last issue of the News several applications for a chance to serve the country have been made. Clarence Duckworth, Ralph Clement, Sam D. Allison and Carl Fortune passed examinations for Naval service successfully, and the last two left Monday for Asheville for the expressed purpose of entering the service.

24 Aug 1917   Brevard News
Ralph Clement, who enlisted in the Navy has notified his father, Frank D. Clement, that he has been transferred to the battleship Nebraska.

Photo #NH 101205 USS Nebraska in camouflage paint WW I

Verne Pearson CLEMENT

Born:	4 Nov 1898, Orleans, Vermont
Died:	7 Jul 1953, Transylvania County, NC; he was 54
Buried:	Gillespie-Evergreen Cemetery
Spouse:	**Elizabeth Love HAMILTON**
Father:	**Frank CLEMENT**
Mother:	**Blanche DODGE**
Draft Registration:	No
Note:	Draft registration card for WWII. He lived in Brevard and operated Clemson/Co-ed Theatre.
Military marker:	NC CPL 10 Co 155 Depot Brig WW I

[Documentation: Ancestry.com; Transylvania County DC; <u>Transylvania County</u> <u>Cemetery Survey,</u> Discharge]

Transylvania Times June 29, 1939
VERNE P. CLEMENT

	Clement, Verne P	2,295,786	White	
(Surname)	(Christian name)	(Army serial number)	(Race: White or colored)	
Residence:	Brevard	Tvansylvania	NORTH CAROLINA	
(Street and house number)	(Town or city)	(County)	(State)	

* Enlisted in RA at Ft Screven Ga Feb 1/18 —
† Born in Orleans Vt 19 2/12 yrs —
Organizations: Co H Sig C Ft Wood N Y to Apr 1/18; 22 Serv Co Sig C to Feb 1/19; QMC Det #15 Jersey City N J to disch

Grades: Pvt 1 Cl Apr 15/18; Corp Dec 16/18 —

Engagements: — —

Wounds or other injuries received in action: None. —
‡ Served overseas: No — —
§ Hon. disch. Mch 14/19 on demobilization —
Was reported 0 per cent disabled on date of discharge, in view of occupation. —
Remarks: ... —

SRC Notes: Sig C (Signal Corps)   Serv Co (Service Company)   QMC (Quartermaster Corps)

7/8/1953
VERNE P. CLEMENT

First Methodist Church this morning was the scene of funeral rites for Verne P. Clement, 54, Brevard businessman who died suddenly at his home on Tuesday. A former mayor of this city, Mr. Clement played a vigorous role in political and civic affairs here and represented this district as senator for one term in the N.C. General Assembly. Clement was formerly active in the Kiwanis Club, the Brevard Chamber of Commerce and the Brevard Federal Savings and Loan Association and other organizations.

Prior to his retirement he and his father owned and operated the theaters here. A native of Orleans, Vt., he came to Western North Carolina about 40 years ago.

Surviving are the widow Mrs. Love Clement; the father, Frank D. Clement; and one brother, Ted Clement.

---

22 Aug 1918   **Brevard News**
ENTERTAIN SOLDIERS
The Pisgah Forest branch of the Red Cross will entertain the soldiers stationed at that place with a watermelon feast and corn roast Saturday evening at the Davidson River School house.

Walter Meynardie CLOUD

Born:	29 Jul 1898, McLeod, FL
Died:	28 Nov 1957, Transylvania County, NC; age 59
Buried:	Arlington National Cemetery, Arlington, VA
Spouse(s):	**Ethel Louise POPE**
	Ruth NELSON
Father:	**Walter CLOUD**
Mother:	**Allie Belle McNEIL**
Draft Registration:	No

Documentation: Transylvania County DC; Ancestry.com, Interment record, Discharge]

Name CLOUD WALTER MEYNARDIE JR.   Service Number 121-73-41
Enlisted at RECRUITING STATION RALEIGH N.C.
Enlisted XXX   Date 4-16-17
Age at Entrance 18 YRS 8 MOS.   Rate LANDSMAN ELECTRICIAN GENERAL   U.S.N. U.XXXXF.
Home Address ---   Town BREVARD
D   County ---   State N.C.

Served at	From	To	Served as	No. Days
RECEIVING SHIP AT NEW YORK	4-16-17	3-9-18	LANDSMAN ELECTRICIAN	
U S S CANONICUS	3-9-18	10-22-18	GENERAL	219
NAVY BASE HOSPITAL NO 2.	10-22-18	11-11-18	ELECTRICIAN 3 CLASS GENERAL	255

Remarks:

Date Discharge 8-4-19
Place InacXXXXX U S S CANONICUS   Rating at Discharge ELECTRICIAN 2 CLASS GENERAL.

27 Apr 1917 Brevard News
MORE TRANSYLVANIANS READY FOR WAR

   Last week the News published the names of those who, to its knowledge, had offered their services to the government in various branches.

   M. Walter Cloud enlisted in the Navy at Brooklyn, NY.

19 Apr 1918 Brevard News
ON HIS WAY TO WAR ZONE

W. M. Cloud, Jr., who enlisted in the Navy a year ago, is now an electrician on a mine-layer, now on its way to the war zone. Mr. Cloud was the first to enlist from Transylvania County.

Photo # NH 106362 USS Canonicus 10 July 1919

Naval History Archives

Allison CLOUGH

Born:	21 Jan 1893, Union City, Erie, PA
Died:	20 June 1947, New York; age 54
Buried:	Maple Grove Cemetery, Carroll, NY
Spouse(s):	**Ellen Rice SMATHERS**, m. 5 Sept 1913
	Minnie DUFF
Father:	**Levi S. CLOUGH**
Mother:	**Dora M DAVIS**
Draft Registration:	24, married with one child, working in Pisgah Forest in the lumber industry

*[Documentation: Ancestry.com, 1920 & 1940 Census, rootsweb. <u>History of NC</u>, Vol. 4,
ancestry.com/cemetery/mapleg]*

Clough Allison C		White	
(Surname)	(Christian name)		
Residence	Brevard	NORTH CAROLINA	
(Street and house number)	(Town or city)	(County)	(State)

* Born in   Union City Pa   Jan 21/93   —

† Appointed   2 Lt   Engrs   Aug–5/18 NA   ‡ Training Camp.

Promotions: 1 Lt   May 6/19   —   ....

Organizations and staff assignments: 20 Engrs to disch—   —

Principal stations: AE.   —   —

Engagements: —   —

Wounds received in action: None.

‖ Served overseas   Feb 1/18 to June 26/19   —

Hon. disch. (date)   July 16/19   for convenience of the Government, services no longer required.

Was reported   0   per cent disabled on date of discharge, in view of occupation.

Remarks: Enl Serv   —   ....

SRC Notes: Engrs (Engineers)

11/21/1918 Brevard News

PEACE

Has been declared, but

THE WAR IS NOT OVER YET

There will be war in merchandising for some time to come. Prices will no doubt go higher and higher.

We have a splendid line of Groceries that we can sell you at very reasonable prices. We also carry all kinds of Country Produce.

OUR FRESH AND CURED MEATS CAN'T BE BEAT—AND WE SELL FOR LESS.

F. P. SLEDGE

Robertson B. COLE

Born:	3 Mar 1901, Elizabethton, Tennessee
Died:	10 Feb 1961, Ferguson, Missouri; age 59
Buried:	Jefferson Barracks National Cemetery, St. Louis, MO
Occupation:	Switchman for railroad
Spouse:	**Zella**
Father:	**Robert COLE**
Draft Registration:	No

[Documentation: MO Death Certificate, 1920 Census, U.S. National Cemetery Interment Form]

Cole Robertson B 1,324,496 White
(Surname) (Christian name) (Army serial number) (Race: White or colored)

Residence: Rosman NORTH CAROLINA
(Street and house number) (Town or city) (County) (State)

Enlisted in NG Rosman NC July 18/17
Born in Colesville Tenn 18 4/12 yrs
Organization: Btry F 1 FA NC NG (Btry F 113 FA) to disch

Grade: Pvt

Engagements:

Wounds or other injuries received in action: None.
Served overseas: May 26/18 to Mon 19/19
Hon. disch. Moh 28/18 on demobilization
Was reported 0 per cent disabled on date of discharge, in view of occupation.
Remarks:

SRC Notes: NG (National Guard) FA (Field Artillery) Btry (Battery)

COLE, Robertson B. PFC R-1324496 JEFFERSON BARRACKS

DATES OF SERVICE
ENLISTMENT SEPARATION ☐ RETIRED
5 Jan 1920 4 Jan 1923 ☐ DIED ON AD

SERVICE DATA (Company, Regiment, Division, or other organization and basic arm of service):
4 CO COAST DEFENSES OF MANILA & SUBIC BAYS COAST ARTY CORPS

☑ WW I ☐ WW II ☐ KOREA ☐ OTHER (Specify)
STATE MISSOURI
EMBLEM (Check one) ☐ HEBREW ☐ OTHER (Specify) ☑ CHRISTIAN ☐ NONE

DATE OF BIRTH DATE OF DEATH DATE OF INTERMENT
Mar 3 1901 Feb 10 1961 Feb 14 1961

GRAVE LOCATION
Section D GRAVE NO 1115 DEPTH OF GRAVE 5'
CASKET IN ☐ BOX ☑ VAULT ☐ NONE

NAME AND ADDRESS OF NEXT OF KIN OR MARKER ORDERED
Mrs. Zella Cole (Wife)
829 Carson Road
Ferguson 35, Missouri

REMARKS (Authority for interment, disinterment)
AUTH:TWX-GSA MPRC ARMY BR STL
Dated 13 Feb 1961
Grave 1114 Reserved for Wife

HEADSTONE OR MARKER ORDERED
Pfc Co F ww I
COLUMBUS MARBLE WORKS
COLUMBUS, MISSISSIPPI

SHIPPING POINT FOR HEADSTONE (Nearest freight station)
Missouri Pacific R.R.
Jefferson Barracks, Mo. A-3453052
MAR 3 - 1961

PLACE OF DEATH
829 Carson Road, Ferguson 35, Missouri
RELIGIOUS DENOMINATION OF DECEDENT
Baptist

NAME OF FUNERAL DIRECTOR
White-Mullen
NAME OF CHAPLAIN OFFICIATING AT BURIAL SERVICE
Rev. F. Denton

TYPED NAME OF SUPERINTENDENT
Martin T. Corley
SIGNATURE OF SUPERINTENDENT
Martin T. Corley

---

8 Mar 1918   Brevard News

AMERICAN RED CROSS TO
ENROLL 24,000,000 SCHOOL
CHILDREN IN JUNIOR AUXILIARIES

Luther F. COOPER

Born:	4 Mar 1893, Brevard, NC
Died:	20 Nov 1962, Oteen VA Hospital, Buncombe County; age 69
Buried:	Gillespie-Evergreen Cemetery
Spouse:	**Eunice DUCKWORTH**
Foster Father:	**T.W. WHITMIRE**
Foster Mother:	**Mattie COOPER**
Note:	Obituary states he was the foster son of Mr. and Mrs. T. W. Whitmire
Draft Registration:	Buncombe County, 24, single, mechanic for Whitmire Motors in Brevard
Service Record Card:	No
Military Marker:	NC PVT CO F 3 Engr. TNG REGT WW I

[Documentation: Buncombe County DC, Transylvania County Cemetery Survey, US Headstone Application, Ancestry.com]

Luther Cooper

Tom Cooper Photo

11/29/1962
LUTHER F. COOPER

Funeral services for Luther Franklin Cooper, 69, of Brevard were held Friday morning at the Brevard Methodist Church. Burial followed in the Gillespie-Evergreen Cemetery. He died at a veterans' hospital following a long illness.

Mr. Cooper was a veteran of World War I and was the foster son of the late T.W. and Mattie Cooper Whitmire. For many years he was the head mechanic for the Transylvania Tanning Company.

Survivors include his widow, Mrs. Eunice Duckworth Cooper; one daughter, Mrs. Betty Taylor; and two sons, Thomas and Joe Cooper.

---

3 Oct 1918   Brevard News
GIVE THE BOYS SOMETHING TO READ

Mr. Hay of the Army Y.M.C.A. serving in Pisgah Forest is anxious to secure at once an abundance of reading matter for the men. The regular Y.M.C.A. supply of reading material has not begun to come in yet and the men must have something to read. Any readers of the News who have recent magazines and periodicals or old magazines with lots of pictures can serve Uncle Sam and the soldiers by turning such over at once to Mr. J.F. Henry on Probart Ave. Brevard or Mrs. T.E. Patton, Pisgah Forest.

Joseph Elias CORBETT

Born:	15 May 1891, Charleston, SC
Died:	22 Mar 1962, Buncombe County, NC; age 70
Buried:	Oak Grove Cemetery, Brevard
Occupation:	Employed at Olin Mathieson Chemical Corp.
Spouse:	**Julia Anna JOHNSON**, m. 19 Dec 1923, Transylvania County, NC
Father:	**James CORBETT**
Mother:	**Minnie BRYANT**
Draft Registration:	No
Service Record Card:	No
Military Marker:	Pvt. Co. C1 PROV DEV REG

[Documentation: Buncombe County DC, South Carolina Delayed Births, Application for Veteran Headstone, Transylvania County Cemetery Survey, Ancestry.com, TT obituary, Discharge]

3/29/1962
JOE CORBETT

Funeral services for Joseph Corbett, 70, were held Saturday afternoon at the Oak Grove Methodist Church. Mr. Corbett died early Thursday morning in an Asheville hospital from injuries received when a car struck him near his home November 8th. He has been hospitalized since the accident.

He is survived by one son, Joseph Corbett, Jr.; one daughter, Mrs. Bernice Taylor; one step daughter, Mrs. Anna Belle Allison; two stepsons: Ernest and Charles Allison; and one sister, Mrs. O.R. Blackwell.

Mr. Corbett was a veteran of World War I and a retired employee of Olin Mathieson Chemical Corporation. He was a native of South Carolina and a member of the Oak Grove Methodist Church.

---

26 Sep 1918   Brevard News

TO HELP MAKE WAR MASKS

The Food Administration is calling on Transylvania people to save all fruit pits from peaches, prunes, etc. an acid is extracted from these that is used in making gas masks. Receptacles for these seed will be placed in convenient places.

Ralph Clingman CORDELL

Born:	10 Apr 1889, Buncombe County
Died:	16 Oct 1961, Oteen VA Hospital, Buncombe County; age 72
Buried:	Cathey's Creek Baptist Church Cemetery
Spouse:	**Aileen WILSON**, m. 13 Dec 1924, Transylvania County, NC
Father:	**John Asbury CORDELL**
Mother:	**Alice Melissa GRAGG**
Draft Registration:	Buncombe County, 21, single, farmer
Service Record Card:	No
Note:	Grave stone gives NO military information. Death Certificate states he was in WW I.

[Documentation: Buncombe County DC, <u>Transylvania County Cemetery Survey</u>, TT obituary, Ancestry.com]

10/20/1960
RALPH CORDELL

Funeral services for Ralph C. Cordell, 71, of Route 2, Brevard, were held Tuesday afternoon at the Cathey's Creek Baptist Church and burial was in the church cemetery. Mr. Cordell died Sunday morning in the Veterans Hospital at Oteen. A native of Buncombe County he was a veteran of World War I. He was a farmer and a member of the Berar Baptist Church in Asheville.

Survivors include the widow, Mrs. Aileen Wilson Cordell; one daughter, Mrs. Thelma Kinsey; two sisters: Mrs. Frank Porter and Mrs. H.C. Creasman; and four brothers, J.H, Lester, Harold and L.H Cordell.

Ralph C. Cordell

Cora Reess Photo

9/5/1918   Brevard News

Pictures from home give cheer to the boys at the front, or to the boys waiting in camp. There are likely to be some tedious homesick days and a little cheer-up in the way of photographs of the home-folks and the home doing will do them a lot of good.

And some day when you want to give something a little more substantial send along a Kodak and ask your Soldier Boy to send pictures to you.

Brownie Cameras $2.00 to $12.00; Kodaks $7.50 and up.

FRANK D. CLEMENT
The Jeweler

Buy in Brevard

Benjamin Franklin COX

Born:	18 Oct 1895, Henderson County, NC
Died:	6 Oct 1947, Augusta, GA; age 51
Buried:	Enon Baptist Church Cemetery
Occupation:	Telegraph operator
Spouse:	**Sula HAMET**, m. 14 Feb 1925, Transylvania County
Father:	**Marshall E. COX**
Mother:	**Martha DALTON**
Draft Registration:	No
Service Record Card:	No
Military Marker:	NC CPL 105 Field SIG BN 30 Div WW I

[Documentation: US Headstone Application, Georgia Death Index, Ancestry.com, Discharge, 1900-1930 Censuses, Cowart's Index of Marriages, TT obituary]

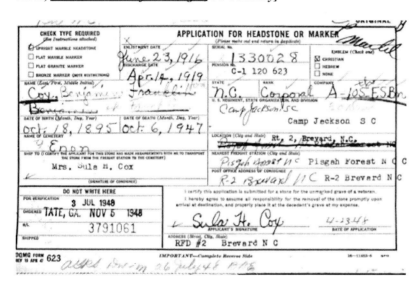

Benjamin F. Cox
Lucille C. Cooper Photo

10/16/1947
BENJAMIN F. COX

Funeral services were held last Wednesday afternoon for Benjamin Frank Cox, 51, Henderson County native, who died in a Veteran's hospital in Augusta, Ga., on Monday following an extended illness. The service was conducted at Enon Baptist Church and burial followed in the churchyard cemetery with The American Legion chapter in charge.

Mr. Cox, who was a veteran of World War I, had been a patient at the veterans' hospital for eight years. Prior to his illness he was a telegraph operator serving in Buncombe, Henderson and Transylvania counties.

He is survived by his widow, Mrs. Sula Hamet Cox; two daughters: Lucille and Claudia Cox: two sons: Frazier and Eddie Cox; three sisters: Mrs. Lillie Banning, Mrs. Ada Parvis and Mrs. Gertrude Dowling; and three brothers: James M., Thomas and George Cox.

NATIONAL ARMY CANTONMENT (CAMP)

Camp Devens   Location: Ayers, Mass   Organization: 76th Division
Troops from Maine, New Hampshire, Vermont, Massachusetts, Rhode Island and Connecticut

---

Roy Edward CRARY

Born:	27 Sep 1897, Transylvania County, NC
Died:	26 Feb 1976, Colonial Beach, VA; age 78
Buried:	Ft. Lincoln Cemetery, Brentwood, MD
Spouse:	**Sarah FULLBRIGHT**
Father:	**Truman Bishop CRARY**
Mother:	**Edna Callie JONES**
Draft Registration:	No
Service Record Card:	No

[Documentation: NC Birth Index, SSDI, Veteran's BIRLS Death file, Ancestry.com]

U.S., Department of Veterans Affairs BIRLS Death File, 1850-2010 about Roy Crary

Name:	Roy Crary
Gender:	Male
Birth Date:	27 Sep 1897
Death Date:	26 Feb 1976
SSN:	579011685
Branch 1:	ARMY
Enlistment Date 1:	17 Oct 1917
Release Date 1:	14 Mar 1919

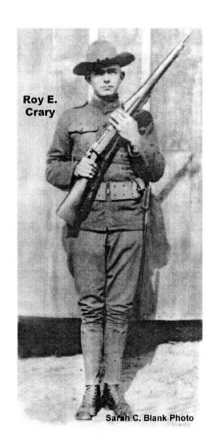

Roy E. Crary

Sarah C. Blank Photo

James Allen CRISP

Born:	30 Apr 1892, Newberry, SC
Died:	11 Oct 1987, Buncombe County, NC ; age 95
Buried:	Green Hill Cemetery, Waynesville NC
Occupation:	Retired from Ecusta Paper Corp.
Spouse:	**Nellie BURGIN**
Father:	**John Hedley CRISP**
Mother:	**Constance B. WILLIAMS**
Draft Registration:	25, single, letter carrier, Tift County, GA

[Documentation: Roster of WWI Veterans from American Legion 50th Anniversary celebration; SC Delayed Births; NC Death Collection; U.S. National Homes for Disabled Volunteer Soldiers; 1900, 1910, 1930 and 1940 Censuses; obit]

10/15/1987
JAMES A. CRISP

James Allen Crisp, Sr. 95, of Brevard died Sunday in an Asheville hospital. A native of Newberry County, S.C., he had lived in Transylvania County since 1937. He retired from Ecusta Paper Corp. and attended the University of Georgia. He served as service officer for the American Legion and was a member and deacon of Brevard First Baptist Church. He was a veteran of World War I and the husband of Nellie Burgin Crisp who died in 1986.

Surviving are a son, Rev. James A Crisp Jr.; and two brothers, John Kibler Crisp and Pinckney F. Crisp.

Services were held Wednesday in the chapel of Garrett Funeral Home in Waynesville. Burial was in Green Hill Cemetery.

French Military Aeroplane.

WW I Postal Card

Sherman CRITE

Born:	5 Jun 1896, Langland, GA
Died:	12 Sep 1959, Oteen VA Hospital, Buncombe County; age 63.
Buried:	Cooper Cemetery
Race:	Colored
Spouse:	**Mary WINN**, m. 6 Feb 1932, Transylvania County, NC
Father:	**Sherman CRITE**
Mother:	**Patience WRIGHT**
Draft Registration:	Lincoln, GA, 21
Service Record Card:	No

[Documentation: Buncombe County DC, Application for Military Headstone, Ancestry.com, Discharge]

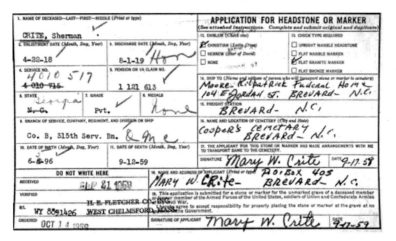

A little recreation for soldiers of the 23rd Engineers Regiment

1919 Postal Card

Henry W. CROW

Born:	11 Dec 1890, Oconee, SC
Died:	1 Jul 1935, Oteen VA Hospital, Buncombe County; age 44
Buried:	Whitmire Cemetery, Eastatoe
Father:	**Will CROW**
Mother:	**Emily LUSK**
Draft Registration:	27, married, sawmilling
Notes:	DC stated he was divorced at time of his death
Military Notes:	Pvt, Camp Prov. Guard Co., Camp Sevier, SC

Documentation: Buncombe County DC, findagrave.com, Ancestry.com, Transylvania County Cemetery Survey, TT obit]

7/11/1935
HENRY CROW

Funeral services for Henry Crow, 44-year-old, World War veteran who died at Oteen on Monday night of last week were held at Zion Baptist Church.

One brother, Loran Crow of Rosman, a sister and two brothers at Salem, SC survive. He was unmarried.

Remount Station Hospital

Robert Loran CROW

Born:	3 Jul 1893, Salem, SC
Died:	27 Apr 1947, Transylvania County, NC; age 54
Buried:	Mt. Moriah Baptist Church Cemetery
Spouse:	**Beulah POWELL**
Father:	**Will CROW**
Mother:	**Emily LUSK**
Draft Registration:	Salem, SC, 23, single and working as a sawmiller
Military Marker:	US ARMY World War I

[Documentation: Transylvania County DC, <u>Transylvania County Cemetery Survey</u>, Discharge, Ancestry.com]

5/1/1947
R.L. CROWE

Robert Loran Crowe, 53, died at his home near Rosman Sunday morning following a cerebral hemorrhage. He was a native of Salem, S.C., son of the late Mr. and Mrs. William Crowe. He was a World War I veteran, a member of Middle Fork Baptist Church, a member of W.O.W. and an employee of Toxaway Tanning Company.

He is survived by the wife Beulah Powell Crowe and five children: Shirley Ann, Lin, Lynell, Elmo and Howard Crowe; one sister, Bessie Spearman and one brother, Jim Crowe.

Funeral services were held Monday afternoon and the burial followed in the Whitmire Cemetery.

1/25/1919 Brevard News
The Lee Kiddies Coming to Town.

AUDITORIUM
SATURDAY, JANUARY 25th.

William Fox presents the "Lee Kiddies" in

"DOING THEIR BIT"

In the war just closing most of us bought a bond. The greater part of us bought some Thrift Stamps. All the ladies knitted a sweater. Probably 99 per cent. did "their bit". These two children, strangers in a strange land, did more.

Come and see how these children turned a slacker into a real man and how Jane captures the real spies.

Matinee 3:30 - - Night 7:30
Admission 5 cents

SAVE YOUR NICKELS AND BUY THRIFT STAMPS.
Uncle Sam Still Needs Them.

Joe CURTO

Born:	25 Nov 1895, Patalia Ploposto, Italy
Died:	7 Dec 1962, Oteen VA Hospital, Buncombe County; age 67
Buried:	Pisgah Gardens Cemetery
Occupation:	Farmer
Spouse:	**Leila SEXTON**
Father:	**Vess CURTO**
Mother:	**Carmen**
Draft Registration;	21, single; lumber laborer for Carr Lumber Company, Pisgah Forest, NC. Born in Italy, came to this country at age 16
Note:	Gravestone gives NO military information
Discharge:	Enlisted 26 Feb 1918 Brevard; Pvt, Arty, Btry "A" Arty CAC, United States Army; discharged 15 March 1919 Camp Jackson, SC

[Documentation: Ancestry.com, Buncombe County DC, <u>Transylvania County Cemetery Survey</u>, Discharge, TT obituary]

12/12/1962
JOE CURTO

Funeral services for Joe Curto, 67, were held Sunday afternoon at the Brevard Wesleyan Methodist Church. A military burial was conducted at Pisgah Garden Cemetery. Mr. Curto was a veteran of World War I.

He died in an Asheville hospital early last Friday morning after a lengthy illness. He was born in Pola Castra, Italy and came to the United State some 51 years ago, and has resided in Transylvania since coming to America.

He is survived by the widow, Mrs. Lelia Sexton Curto; two sons: Joseph Edward and Henry Franklin; six daughters: Mrs. Coy K. Brown, Mrs. George D. McCall, Mrs. Roy Haskett, Jr., Mrs. Gene Lovell, Miss Josephine Curto and Miss Martha Ann Curto.

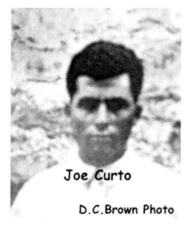

Joe Curto

D.C. Brown Photo

Who were the HUNS?

The Huns were a tribe of people who lived in what is now Germany in A.D. 400. They were known for their cruel and ruthless tactics in war. The committee responsible for raising money to support the war, the CPI (Committee on Public Information) tried to paint all Germans as HUNS but there is no evidence that German soldiers were any crueler than the French, British or American soldiers.

This was a scare tactic to urge the American public to WANT to support the war efforts by purchasing Liberty Bonds.

Lemuel Loyd DANIELS

Born:	7 Aug 1896, Dobbins, Grant County, West Virginia
Died:	20 Nov 1973, Oteen VA Hospital, Buncombe County; age 77
Buried:	Pisgah Gardens Cemetery
Spouse:	**Olivia MORRIS**
Father:	**William Benjamin DANIELS**
Mother:	**Margaret MONTONY**
Draft Registration:	W.VA, 21, working in coal mine
Military Marker:	West VA S2 US Navy WW I
Note:	Enlisted in US Navy at Elkins WVA in June 1918; discharged 3 Sep 1919; served aboard the USS Mount Vernon.

[Documentation: Buncombe County DC, <u>Transylvania County Cemetery Survey</u>, Discharge, Mary Galyon, Ancestry.com]

Hendersonville Times News
Nov 21, 1973
LEMUEL L. DANIELS

Lemuel Lloyd Daniels, 77 of Rt. 1, Pisgah Forest, died Tuesday in an Asheville hospital after a long illness. He was a member of Turkey Creek Baptist Church and a retired employee of Olin Mathieson Corp.

He is survived by his wife, Mrs. Olivia Daniels; four daughters: Carolyn Owen, Mary Ann Galyon, Thelma Siniard and Helen Peeler; one brother, William Daniels; and three sisters: Mrs. Roy E. Miller, Mrs. Ralph Lyday and Mrs. James Fleet.

Graveside services were conducted Tuesday at Turkey Creek Baptist Church Cemetery.

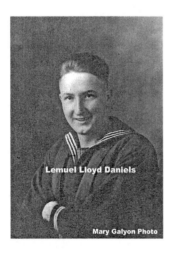

Lemuel Lloyd Daniels

Mary Galyon Photo

USS Mount Vernon   Naval History Archives

On the morning of 5 Sep 1918 *USS Mount Vernon* was hit by a single torpedo fired from a German U-82 boat. The USS Winslow, Conner, Nicholson and Wainwright responded immediately and started dropped depth charges. The U boat escaped but was not allowed to surface and fire additional shots at the *USS Mount Vernon.*

The *USS Mount Vernon* was able to steam back to Brest, France with the loss of 36 out of 1,450 persons aboard. Thirteen others were wounded. The ship suffered considerable damage but was repaired but did not returned to battle.
Wikipedia

Dalphin Alston DAVIS

Born: 6 Sep 1890, Virginia
Died: 30 May 1978, last residence Baltimore, MD, age 87
Buried: Undetermined location
Spouse: **Virginia GIBBS**
Father: **William Henry DAVIS**
Mother: **Harriett FEASTER**
Draft Registration Card: Gloucester County, NJ; 26, single, roofing superintendent
                                for a Philadelphia, PA company; listed sister as a dependent.

[Documentation: Charlotte County VA Birth Index, SSDI, SAR Membership Application, 1900-1940 Censuses, Ancestry.com]

```
(Surname)  Davis      Dalphin Alston        (Christian name)   white

Residence _____ Pisgah Forest  NORTH CAROLINA
          (Street and house number)   (Town or city)   (County)      (State)

* Born in          Charlotta Va Sept 6/90
† Called into active service as   2 Lt AS May 31/18 ERC          ‡ Training Camp.
Promotions :

Organizations and        271 Aero Sq to disch
staff assignments :

Principal
stations :         Ellington Fld Tex; Aberdeen Proving Ground Md

Engagements :

Wounds received in action : None.
§ Served overseas    no
‖ Hon. disch.      Jan 10/19    for convenience of the Government, services no longer required.
Was reported      0     per cent disabled on date of discharge, in view of occupation.
Remarks :         Enl Serv Over

* Enlisted in      RA at Columbus Bks on July 31/17  Ohio
† Born in          Charlotte Court, House Va  26 10/12 yrs.
Organizations:     38 Aero Sqd to disch.

Grades:            Pvt

Engagements:       none.

Wounds or other injuries received in action: None.
‡ Served overseas:  none.
§ Hon. disch.      May 30/18 to accept commission.
Was reported      0         per cent disabled on date of discharge, in view of occupation.
Remarks:          For commissioned service see card previously sent
```

17 Aug 1917   **Brevard News**

Alston Davis, son of Rev. W.H. Davis of Pisgah Forest, is reported to have joined an aviation corps and is now in San Antonio, Texas.

18 Jul 1918   **Brevard News**

Lieut. Alston Davis was the guest last week of his parents, Rev. and Mrs. W.H. Davis at Pisgah Forest. Lieut. Davis was en route from Ellington Field, Texas, where he received his commission in the aviation corps, to Aberdeen, MD., where the largest aviation school in the country is located, as well as the largest aerial supply base in the United States. Here Lieut. Davis will serve as inspector of Lewis Machine guns, airplanes, motors, bombs, etc.

Horace Augustus DAVIS

Born:	15 Jul 1894, Greenville, South Carolina
Died:	2 Jan 1942, Charleston, SC; age 47
Buried:	West View Cemetery, Pickens County, SC
Spouse:	**Emmie SMITH**
Father:	**James W. DAVIS**
Mother:	**Nancy Jane HARRISON**
Draft Registration Card;	22, single, worked as a printer for the **Brevard News**

[Documentation: South Carolina Death Index, US Headstone Application, findagrave.com, 1910-1930 Censuses]

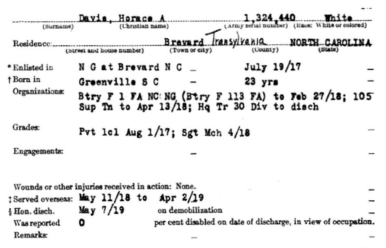

SRC Notes: Btry (Battery) FA CN NG (Field Artillery North Carolina National Guard) Sup Tn (Supply Train) Hq Tn (Headquarters Train)

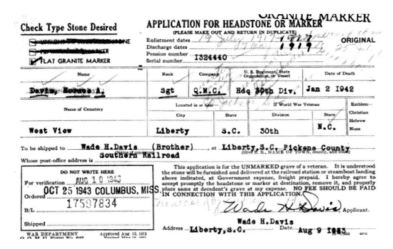

12 Oct 1917   Brevard News
A party of boys from Camp Sevier, Greenville, came home for a short visit Saturday, returning Sunday afternoon. There were Horace Davis, . . . The boys seemed to be in good spirits and enjoying camp life.

16 Nov. 1917   Brevard News
Horace Davis, Ralph Duckworth, Perineau Lankford and Mack Sitton came from Camp Sevier for a visit home at the week-end

Theodore Nelson DAVIS

Born:	18 Feb 1883, Swain County
Died:	23 Jul 1972, Oteen VA Hospital, Buncombe County; age 89
Buried:	Oak Grove Cemetery Brevard
Spouse(s):	**Roxanna TEAGUE**
	Marie KILPATRICK
Father;	**John E DAVIS**
Mother:	**Fannie WALLS**
Draft Registration:	Swain County, 30, single; civil engineer for the Appalachian Railway Company of Cherokee, NC
Note:	1940 Census: living in Brevard, NC with his second wife
Military Marker:	PVT U.S. Army WW I

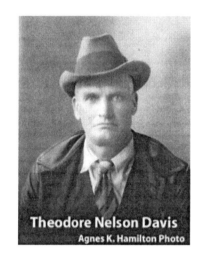

Davis, Theodore   4070952   • White • ~~Colored.~~
  (Surname)   (Christian name)   (Army serial number)

Residence: _____ .Pisga Forrest, _____ NORTH CAROLINA
           (Street and house number) (Town or city)   (County)   (State)

~~• Enlisted • R. A. • N. G.~~ • E. R. C. •Inducted at Transylvania Co NC on Aug 5, 1918

Place of birth: _____ Buncoumbe Co NC _____ Ag~~e or date of birth~~ 4 Yrs

Organizations served in, with dates of assignments and transfers:
    Co M 5 Pion Inf to Aug 25/18; Co K 4 Pion Inf
    to Sept 1/18; Sup Co 55 Pion Inf to Disch.

Grades, with date of appointment: _____
    Pvt

Engagements: _____
    xx

Wounds or other injuries received in action: None.
Served overseas from † Sept 15/18, June 18/19 from † _____ to † _____
Honorably discharged: July 3, 19 19 _____ ETS
          (Date)
In view of occupation he was, on date of discharge, reported _____ (Cause) _____ per cent disabled.

Theodore Nelson Davis
Agnes K. Hamilton Photo

SRC Notes: Pion Inf (Pioneer Infantry)

18 Jul 1918   **Brevard News**
23 MORE MEN TO LEAVE JULY 24, 1918
Following is a list of white registrants for induction on July 24th, 1918 for Camp Hancock, Ga., who will leave on the 3:13 train:
. . . Theodore Davis, Azalea . . .

7/27/1972
T.N. Davis

Theodore N. Davis, 89, died Sunday afternoon in Oteen Hospital after a long illness. He was a native of Swain County and had resided n Transylvania for a number of years. He was a veteran of World War I, having served with the U.S. Army. Before his retirement several years ago, he was a civil engineer.

Surviving are the wife, Marie Kilpatrick Davis; one son, James E; one daughter, Mrs. Anna Hamilton; one brother, C.A. Davis; and one sister, Miss Addie Davis.

Graveside services were conducted Wednesday in Oak Grove Cemetery of Brevard.

NATIONAL ARMY CANTONMENT (CAMP)
Camp Upton   Location: Yaphank, Long Island, NY   Organization: 77th Division
Troops from Metropolitan portions of New York

Wiley DEVORE

Born:	7 Jul 1891, Transylvania County, NC
Died:	21 Dec 1979, Oteen VA Hospital, Buncombe County; age 88
Buried:	Macedonia Baptist Church Cemetery
Spouse:	**Emma WOODRING**, m. 11 May 1918, Transylvania County, NC
Father:	**John DEVORE**
Mother:	**Margaret Louise SMITH**
Draft Registration:	24, single; self-employed farmer in the Gloucester, NC community; lists his brother as a dependent
Note:	Gravestone gives NO military information

[Documentation: Discharge, Buncombe County DC, Transylvania County Cemetery Survey, Discharge, Ancestry.com]

Devore, Wiley   3,277,075   * White * Colored.
(Surname)   (Christian name)   (Army serial number)

Residence: RFD 1   Lake Toxway   NORTH CAROLINA
(Street and house number)   (Town or city)   (County)   (State)

* Enlisted ~~R. A. at~~ *Inducted at Brevard N C   on June 25 19 18

Place of birth: Lake Toxway NC   Age or date of birth: July 7/1893

Organizations served in, with dates of assignments and transfers:
156 Dep Brig to Oct 22/18; Camp Humphreys Va Co 1
Oct Aut Repl Draft Engrs to Nov 25/18; Co D 5 Engrs

Grades, with date of appointment: Tng Regt to Disbh

Pvt

Engagements:

Wounds or other injuries received in action: None.
Served overseas from †NO to †   , from †   to †
Honorably discharged on demobilization   Dec 27 19 18
In view of occupation he was, on date of discharge, reported   0   per cent disabled.

Wiley DeVore

James DeVore Photo

SRC Notes: Pion Inf (Pioneer Regiment Infantry)

21 Jun 1918   Brevard News
WHITE REGISTRANTS WHO ARE TO LEAVE FOR CAMP JACKSON, S.C.
TUESDAY, JUNE 25th, 1918 AT 3:13 P.M.
. . . Wiley Devore, Lake Toxaway . . .

31 Jan 1919   Brevard News
We are glad to have Wiley Devoe with us again after a few months in the service of his country, although he did not get to go to France.

Asheville Citizen Times
2/23/1979
WILEY DEVORE

Wiley Devore, 88, died in Asheville VA Medical Center after an extended illness. A native of Transylvania County, he was a son of the late John and Louise Smith Devore. He was a retired farmer.

Surviving are three sons: Wiley, Jr., Carlee, and John Edward Devore; four daughters: Ethel Anders, Effie Hogsed, Eunice Anders and Aileen Cane.

Services were held in Macedonia Baptist church, of which he was a member. Burial was in the church cemetery.

Thomas Lawrence DILLARD

Born:	24 Aug 1895, Cashiers, NC
Died:	31 Jan 1998, Anderson, SC, age 102
Buried:	Hillcrest Memorial Park, Pickens, SC
Spouse:	**Annie WILLIMON**
Father:	**William L. DILLARD**
Mother:	**Bertha HOOPER**
Draft Registration:	21, single, logger in Pisgah Forest

[Documentation: WW I Service Record Card; Ancestry.com, findagrave.com, SSDI]

Name DILLARD - TOM LAWRENCE   Service Number 31-27-79
Enlisted at NAVY RECRUITING STATION COLUMBIA S.C.   Date 11-26-17
XXXled
Age at Entrance 22 YRS. 3 MOS.   Rate HOSPITAL APPRENTICE 2ND.CLASS   U.S.N. UXXXX.
Home Address ___   ___   Town PISGAH FOREST
E   County   State N.C.

Served at	From	To	Served as	No. Days
NAVAL TRAINING STATION NEWPORT R.I.	11-26-17	8-26-18	HOSPITAL APPRENTICE 2ND.CLASS	248
NAVAL HOSPITAL PARIS ISLAND S.C.	8-26-18	11-11-18	HOSPITAL APPRENTICE 1ST CLASS	97
			PHARMACIST MATE 3RD.CLASS	5

Remarks:

Date Discharge 8-25-19 USS TROY AY HOBOKEN N.J.   PHARMACIST MATE
Place XXXXXXXX   Rating at Discharge 3RD.CLASS

Greenville News (SC)
2/2/1998
THOMAS L. DILLARD

Thomas L. Dillard, 102, formerly of Six Mile, died Saturday at Richard M. Campbell Veterans Nursing Home in Anderson. He was retired from the Six Mile Post Office and a member of Six Mile Baptist Church where he was a former deacon. He was a member of Six Mile Masonic Lodge for 79 years, a former mayor of Six Mile and a former member of the Pickens County School Board. He was a US veteran of World War I and a former partner of Roper-Dillard, Inc.

Surviving are three sisters: Mildred Sanders, Lillian Liddane and Lucille Crespin.

Services will be Tuesday at Dillard Memorial Funeral Home and burial in Hillcrest Memorial Park.

The steamship *Minnesota*, a passenger-cargo ship, was built in 1904 at New London, Connecticut, for the Great Northern Steamship Company. In November 1915 she broke down and was towed to San Francisco for repairs for the year of 1916 she sat awaiting legal action against her owner. The Atlantic Transport Company purchased the *Minnesota* in January 1917 and began her first trans-Atlantic passage in late March 1917.

In early 1919 *Minnesota* was chartered by the Navy, renamed *USS Troy*, she was placed in commission in late February. After conversion to a troop transport she made three passages from France to the US, bringing home more that 14,000 veterans of World War I. *USS Troy* was decommissioned in mid September 1919, returned to her owners and again became *S.S. Minnesota*.

James Perry DODGIN

Born:	4 Aug 1896, Transylvania County, NC
Died:	6 Mar 1924, Transylvania County, NC; age 27
Buried:	Oak Grove Baptist Church Cemetery, Quebec, NC
Occupation:	Farmer
Spouse:	**Arlissa MILLER**, m. 14 Jul 1917, Transylvania County, NC
Father:	**Richard DODGIN**
Mother:	**Jane FISHER**
Note:	Grave marker gives NO military information. There is record of a military marker ordered by his wife in 1947.
Discharge:	Enlisted 23 June 1916 at High Point, NC and was discharged 13 Oct 1917. Technically he was in the Army at the beginning of World War I. He did see action in the Mexican Border activities prior to US declaring war. PVT 20th Co 5th Training BATT 55th Depot BRIG

[Documentation: Discharge, Transylvania County DC, Upper Transylvania County, NC Remembered, Ancestory.com]

James Perry Dodgin

Margaret C. Dills Photo

---

27 Jun 1918   **Brevard News**

NATIONAL LEAGUE W. S. MEETING

An important business meeting of the National League of Women's Service of Transylvania County was held on Thursday afternoon, June 20, at the home of the chairman Mrs. J. S. Silverstein. Various committees were appointed to carry on the general work taken up by the League, and a motion passed to hold meetings on the 4th Thursday of each month at the home of the chairman. All members of the League are requested to attend these meetings, as they will, at such times, take up the business side of the work. All persons interested in making comfort kits for our boys and in Food Conservation will be most welcome.

Elizabeth M Silverstein, Chairman

Clarence Edward DUCKWORTH

Born:	3 Aug 1897, Transylvania County, NC
Died:	17 Sep 1976, Buncombe County, NC; age 79
Buried:	Beaverdam Community Cemetery, Canton
Spouse:	**Mabel WILLIAMS**
Father:	**William H. DUCKWORTH**
Mother:	**Roxie PICKELSIMER**
Draft Registration:	21, single and farming with his dad
Military Proof:	Only record found is that Clarence was inducted 24 Aug 1918.

[Documentation: Ancestry.com, 1900-1940 Censuses]

9/2//1976
CLARENCE DUCKWORTH

Clarence E. Duckworth, 79, died Friday in an Asheville hospital after an illness of two weeks. Born in Brevard and a Haywood County resident for 43 years, he was a self employed carpenter and painter and a member of Canton First Baptist Church. He was a son of the late William and Roxie Pickelsimer Duckworth.

Surviving are the widow, Mabel Williams Duckworth; a daughter, Mrs. Bruce L. Corzine; two sons; Jack and Neil Duckworth; and three brothers: Walter, Frank and Robert Duckworth.

Services were held Sunday in the Wells Funeral Home Chapel and burial followed in the Beaverdam United Methodist Church Cemetery.

Clarence Duckworth
V. Frank Duckworth Photo

Ralph Jennings DUCKWORTH

Born:	26 Jun 1899, Transylvania County, NC
Died:	12 Sep 1970, Buncombe County, NC; age 71
Buried:	Gillespie-Evergreen Cemetery
Occupation:	Banker
Spouse:	**Kathleen VAUGHAN**
Father:	**William H. DUCKWORTH**
Mother:	**Roxie PICKELSIMER**
Draft Registration:	No
Military marker:	NC PVT 113 FLD ARTY WW I

[Documentation: Buncombe County DC, Discharge, <u>Transylvania County Cemetery Survey</u>, Ancestry.com]

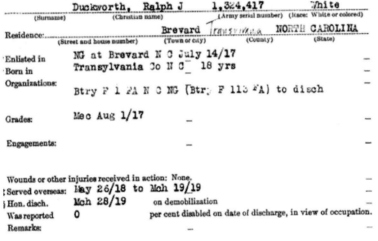

Ralph Duckworth

V. Frank Duckworth Photo

SRC Notes: FA NC NG (Field Artillery North Carolina National Guard)

21 Jun 1918   <u>Brevard News</u>
Ralph Duckworth has landed safely over seas according to a message received here Saturday.

7 Mar 1919   <u>Brevard News</u>
Ralph Duckworth, who has been in France for several months, writes that he expects to return to the US about the middle of March.

16 May 1919   <u>Brevard News</u>
Ralph Duckworth are home after several months service with the colors. Ralph was a member of the 113th Field Artillery, which was on the front the day the armistice began.

9/17/1970
RALPH J. DUCKWORTH

Ralph Jennings Duckworth, Sr., 71, retired banker, died last Saturday night in an Asheville hospital after a long illness. Mr. Duckworth, a native of Transylvania County, was a banker for 34 years in Brevard. He retired as Vice-president of the Brevard office of the First Union National Bank.

Surviving are his widow, Kathleen Vaughan Duckworth; a son, Ralph, Jr.; a sister, Helen

Russel; and four brothers: Clarence, Frank, Walter and Robert Duckworth.

A veteran of World War I, he was a member of the Monroe Wilson Post. He was also a member of the Brevard Elks Lodge and served three terms as a Brevard alderman.

Services were held Monday in the First Baptist Church of Brevard and the burial was in the Gillespie-Evergreen Cemetery.

William Walter DUCKWORTH

Born:	24 Jul 1895, Transylvania County, NC
Died:	28 Dec 1979, Oteen VA Hospital, Buncombe County; age 84
Buried:	Gillespie-Evergreen Cemetery
Spouse:	**Jean HARRIS**, m. 8 Oct 1924, Transylvania County, NC
Father:	**William H. DUCKWORTH**
Mother:	**Roxie PICKELSIMER**
Draft Registration;	21, single, worked as a clerk in the Duckworth Drug Store, Brevard, NC
Military Marker:	US Marine Corps WW I

[Documentation: Buncombe County DC, <u>Transylvania County Cemetery Survey</u>, Discharge, <u>Cowart's Index to Marriages</u>, Ancestry.com]

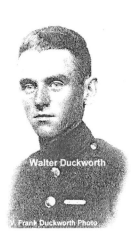

DUCKWORTH   William Walter LCR   White
(Surname.)   (Christian name.)   (Army serial number.)
Residence: _____ Brevard _____ N.C.
              (Street and house number.) (Town or city.)   (County.)   (State.)
Enlisted } in the United States Marine Corps at Asheville, N.C. on 2-8-18.
                                     (Place of application.)   (Date of oath.)
Place of birth: Brevard, N.C.   Date of birth: 7-24-1895.
Organizations served in, with dates of assignments and transfers: Paris Island, S.C.:
USS Pennsylvania 4-20-18: New York 1-28-19:

Grades, with date of appointment: _____
Pvt 1st Cl 10-1-18

Engagements: _____

Wounds or other injuries received in action: _____
Served overseas from _____ to _____
Exit from service: To inactive status 4-19-19: RD #21
Remarks: _____

Walter Duckworth

V. Frank Duckworth Photo

16 May 1919   Brevard News

Ralph and Walter Duckworth are home after several months service with the colors. Walter was in the Naval Corps and Ralph was a member of the 113th Field Artillery, which was on the front the day the armistice began.

12/31/1979
WALTER DUCKWORTH, Sr.

William Walter Duckworth, Sr., 84, died last Friday in the Asheville VA Medical Center. A lifelong resident of Transylvania County, he was the son of William Henry and Roxie Pickleseimer Duckworth and the husband of the late Jean Harris Duckworth. He was owner and operator of Duckworth Motor Company in Brevard for 30 years and was a World War I veteran. He was a former alderman of Brevard and a member of the American Legion Post of Brevard.

He was a member of Dunn's Rock masonic Lodge and also a Shriner. He was a member of the Brevard Elks Lodge and a member of Brevard First Baptist Church.

Surviving are a daughter, Ann Runyan; a son William Walter Duckworth, Jr.; two brothers Frank and Robert Duckworth.

Graveside services were held Sunday in Gillespie-Evergreen Cemetery.

USS Pennsylvania was launched 16 March 1915 and commissioned 12 June 1916. She ran on fuel oil, not coal and served as an escort ship for the President of the United States during the war.

Nathan P. DWORETZKY

Born:	4 Jan 1895, New York
Died:	30 Sep 1976, New York; age 81
Buried:	Undetermined
Spouse:	**Felice AUSLANDER**
Father:	**Morris DWORETZKY**
Mother:	**Theresa SILVERSTEEN**
Draft Registration:	22 years, single, worked as a tanner of leather & assistant general manager for Toxaway Tanning Company, Rosman, NC.
Draft Registration:	WW II: 47, lived in New York City and worked for Toxaway Tanning Company with a business address in New York City.
Note:	He was a nephew of Joseph Silversteen

[Documentation: Ancestry.com, BIRLS Death File, 1900-1940 Censuses]

SRC Notes: Ord Dep (Ordnance Depot)

19 Oct. 1917   **Brevard News**
N.P. DWORETZKY ENLISTS IN ORDNANCE SERVICE

Nathan P. Dworetzky, who has been for the last few years assistant to J.S. Silversteen in the tanning business, recently offered his services to the country, passed the examination at Greensboro, and was given the position of sergeant in the ordnance department of the Army.

Mr. Dworetzky will report for duty at Camp Lee, Virginia on October 22. From information he received from headquarters, he expects an early call to active service. His duties will be connected with the handling and supplying of ammunition and will be charged with much responsibility.

19 Sep. 1918   **Brevard News**
Word has been received that Nathan Dworetzky has arrived safely overseas.

NATIONAL ARMY CANTONMENT (CAMP)

Camp Lee   Location: Petersburg, Va.   Organization: 80th Division
Troops from New Jersey, Virginia, Maryland, Delaware and the District of Columbia

John Young ELLER

Born:	21 Dec 1896, New York
Died:	3 Apr 1976, Transylvania County, NC; age 79
Buried:	Gillespie-Evergreen Cemetery
Occupation:	Federal Game Warden for the US Forestry Service
Spouse:	**Eileen CRISPIN**
Parents:	**John J. ELLER**
Military Marker:	CPL US Army WW I

[Documentation: Transylvania County DC, 1940 Census, Ancestry.com, <u>Transylvania County Cemetery Survey</u>]

Eller, John Y 4,236,529 • White • Colored
(Surname) (Christian name) (Army serial number)

Residence: RFD #3 Greensboro Guilford NORTH CAROLINA
(Street and house number) (Town or city) (County) (State)

██████████. •Inducted a Guilford Co NC on Aug 5, 19 18

Place of birth: Liberty NJ   Age or date of birth: Dec 21/1896
Organizations served in, with dates of assignments and transfers: Co B 57 Pion Inf to Aug
28/18; 55 Pion Inf to ----; 331 Inf to Nov 27/18; 57 Gd
Co Army Serv C to Disch.

Grades, with date of appointment:
Corp Oct 17/18.

Engagements:

Wounds or other injuries received in action: None.
Served overseas from † Sept 15/18 † July 11/19 from † _____ to †_____
Honorably discharged on demobilization July 21/19 , 19____
In view of occupation he was, on date of discharge, reported 0 per cent disabled.
Remarks:

SRC Notes: Pion Inf (Pioneer Regiment Infantry)

4/5/1976
JOHN ELLER

John Young Eller died Saturday at his home after a period of declining health. Born in New York and a Transylvania County resident for 41 years, he was an Army veteran of World War I and a retired employee of the U.S. Forestry Service with 31 years of service.

Surviving is the widow, Eileen Crispin Eller. Graveside services were held Monday in the Gillespie-Evergreen Cemetery.

In 1918 the U.S. Army Service of Supply instituted a salvaging unit near the French city of Tours that employed hundreds of French women and a number of idle "Sammies" in order to eradicate Army waste. It was there that the millions of discarded uniform elements were re-fashioned into other useful items.

The need for a hospital slipper became an issue and they "invented" a hospital slipper with a sole made from a torn and discarded campaign hat and old canvas leggins. It was such a good slipper, and easy to make that St. Pierre-des-Corps soon reached quantity production of it.

Stars and Stripes, 1918

Dr. Ernest Lafayette ENGLISH

Born:	29 Jun 1886, Madison County, NC
Died:	11 Jan 1934, Buncombe County, NC; age 47
Buried:	English Cemetery, Madison County, NC
Occupation:	Physician
Spouse:	**Inez GLAZENER**, m. 3 Apr 1920, Transylvania County
Father:	**William M. ENGLISH**
Mother:	**Julia HOLCOMBE**
Draft Registration;	30, single, living in Rosman, NC

[Documentation: Buncombe County DC, <u>Cowart's Index to Marriages</u>, Ancestry.com, Asheville Citizens obituary, TT obituary]

English, Ernest L   4,159,453   • White • Colored.
    (Surname)   (Christian name)   (Army serial number)

Residence: _____ Rosman Transylvania NORTH CAROLINA
            (Street and house number)   (Town or city)   (County)   (State)

████████████ •Inducted at Brevard NC _____ on July 24 18

Place of birth: Faust NC _____ Age or date of birth: June 29/86

Organizations served in, with dates of assignments and transfers: _____
    Main Tng Dep MC Tng Center Camp Hancock Ga to Aug 29/18
    MD Camp Greenleaf Ga to Sept 27/18; Motor Co 14   over

Grades, with date of appointment: _____
    Pvt

Remarks (continued): _____
    Sec E Camp Greenleaf Ga to Oct 24/18; Motor Co 16
    Sec B Camp Greenleaf to Nov 12/18; Gen Hosp 14
    to Nov 24/18; Base Hosp 158 to disch

Wounds or other injuries received in action: None.
Served overseas from †_NONE____ to †_____, from †_____ to †_____
Honorably discharged on demobilization _____Dec 13/18_____, 19____
In view of occupation he was, on date of discharge, reported __0_____ per cent disabled.

18 Jul 1918   Brevard News
23 MORE MEN TO LEAVE JULY 24, 1918

Following is a list of white registrants for induction on July 24th, 1918 for Camp Hancock, Ga., who will leave on the 3:13 train:

. . . Ernest Lafayette English, Rosman . . .

11 Jan 1934
Asheville Citizens
DR. ERNEST L. ENGLISH

Rites for Dr. Ernest L. English, 47, retired physician, who died yesterday morning at his home, 147 Clinton Street, West Asheville, were set for 2 PM this afternoon at the home of his mother, Mrs. W.M. English at Faust, Madison County.

Surviving Dr. English are his mother, Mrs. W.M. English, a son Ernest B.; a brother, E.B. English and four sisters: Mrs. J.E. Sams (missing the ending)

25 Jan 1934
Brevard News

. . Dr. English was a former resident of this county, and his wife was a Transylvania County girl, Miss Inez Glazener, eldest daughter of R.F.

Glazener of Rosman. For several years Dr. English was a physician in Rosman.
(missing the ending)

Harvey Eugene ENGLISH

Born:	20 Jun 1984, Transylvania County, NC
Died:	14 Dec 1989, Henderson County, NC; age 95
Buried:	Boylston Baptist Church Cemetery
Spouse:	**Cora MAXWELL**
Father:	**Daniel ENGLISH**
Mother:	**Alice Eleanor CAGLE**
Draft Registration:	22, single, teamster for Charlie Hollingsworth at Pisgah Forest, NC

[Documentation: Roster of WWI Veterans from American Legion 50th Anniversary celebration; NC Birth Index; NC Death Collection; 1910-1940 Censuses; obit]

Hendersonville Times News
12/15/ 1989
HARVEY E. ENGLISH

Harvey E. English, 95, died Thursday, Dec. 14, 1989, at Pardee hospital after a sudden illness. He was a native of Transylvania County and a son of the late Weldon and Alice Cagle English. He was the husband of Cora Maxwell English who died in 1987. He was a retired carpenter and a member of Boylston Baptist Church where he served as a deacon and Sunday school teacher. He was an Army veteran of WWI.

Survivors include a son, Roger English; two brothers: Tom and Lester; and two sisters: Louise Wilkie and Rachel English.

A funeral service will be held at 4 pm Saturday at Boylston Baptist Church. Burial will follow in the church cemetery.

115

Paul Wallace ENGLISH

Born:	4 Nov 1897, Transylvania County, NC
Died:	10 Feb 1978, Magnolia, Arkansas; age 80
Buried:	Shepherd's Memorial Park, Henderson County
Spouse:	**Mary Isabelle JACKSON**, m. 15 Nov 1922, Spartanburg, SC
Father:	**Preston Brooks ENGLISH**
Mother:	**Julia SHEPHERD**
Draft Registration:	No
Military Marker:	US Army WW I

[Documentation: NC Birth Index, NC Death Collection, findagrave.com, 1900-1940 Censuses, Ancestry.com, FamilySearch.org]

---

18 Nov 1917   **Brevard News**
APPEAL TO WOMEN OF TRANSYLVANIA
Wool Sweaters Badly Needed By Men In Camp
TransylvaniaWomen Should Knit Sweaters And Socks For Transylvania Boys
Wool Offered At Reduced Prices

Sisters of Transylvania, how many of you are knitting for the boys in camp? More than 100 young men have gone from our County into the Army, and there ought to be more than 100 sweaters and mufflers, more than 100 pairs of knit woolen socks ready right now to send them.

Perhaps you have sent your boy a sweater. Perhaps you are knitting one now for the Red Cross. Perhaps you are intended to knit but you haven't got started yet. Just remember one thing, we haven't any time to lose! Winter has come; the boys in the camps need all the warm things we can send. The Red Cross is doing its best, but perhaps they haven't gotten around to your boy yet. Are you going to sit and hold your hands and just let him shiver? Don't you think it is up to you to send him his 1st sweater from home? We, Transylvanian women, whether we belong to the Red Cross or not, ought to be able to make 100 sweaters for our boys before Christmas. We can send them sweaters to keep them warm until they get ready to go across the ocean. That may be sooner than any of us believe. Once they are on the other side, the Red Cross will have to supply them with new sweaters and socks.

Perhaps you are willing enough to knit, but can't get any wool. That's the problem we have all been worrying over. But there's a way to settle it if we all work together and do our best. Let us call ourselves the "Get Together Family of Transylvania County" and invite every woman to help.

There are several ways of getting wool yarn--we can buy it or have it given to us. We ought to get together and buy a lot of it at the wholesale price because even so it cost about $1.50 to make a sweater and $.85 to make a pair of socks. Some of us have already ordered a lot of wool yarn and Mrs. H.A. Plummer and O.L. Erwin have kindly offered to get us some more at the lowest possible price. If you're going to buy any, let us know and we will order it for you. We will send you the directions with the yarn and you can make some of the sleeveless sweaters that are easy to make if you know how to knit.

How many of you can knit socks? Get busy. Your boy's feet will be much warmer in the home knit socks than in the ones the government buys from a factory.

Come, now, let the "Get Together Family" begin to work. Buy enough for two sweaters if you can afford to and give half to your neighbor. If you have no boy in the war - then knit a sweater or pair socks for a friend. Whether you live in Brevard, Rosman, Pisgah Forest or Toxaway, get together and get busy.

Mrs. Fitch Taylor   Mrs. O.L. Erwin   Miss Annie Colcock

Herbert Carlyle ENLOE

Born:	13 Nov 1892, Swain County, NC
Died:	1 Oct 1975, Buncombe County, NC; age 82
Buried:	Pisgah Gardens
Occupation:	Retired farmer
Spouse:	**Annie COCHRAN,** 31 May 1920, Johnson City, TN
Father:	**Aesop William ENLOE**
Mother:	**Clarinda Margaret CONNOR**
Draft Registration:	24, agriculture student, working for father in Judson, NC

[Documentation: Roster of WWI Veterans from American Legion 50th Anniversary celebration; NC Death Cer-tificate Transylvania County Cemetery Survey; 1900-1940 Censuses; obit]

10/2/1975
H.C. ENLOE

Herbert Carlyle Enloe, 82, died Wednesday in an Asheville hospital after a long illness. Mr. Enloe was a native of Swain County, retired farmer and a veteran of World War I.

Surviving are four daughters: Mrs. Harold R. Hogsed, Mrs. William A. Surrett and Mrs. Parks Hunter; and four sons, Carl A., Roland H., Robert Doyle and Judson H. Enloe Funeral services will be held Saturday at 2 p.m. in the First United Methodist Church of which he was a member. Burial will follow in Pisgah Gardens Cemetery.

Herbert C. Enloe

Roland Enloe Photo

Charles ERWIN

Born:	27 Aug 1894, Transylvania County, NC
Died:	6 Dec 1966, Transylvania County, NC; age 72
Buried:	Cooper Cemetery
Occupation:	Worked at Transylvania Tanning Company, Brevard, NC
Race:	Colored
Spouse:	**Delsey CUNNINGHAM**, m. 25 Jun 1922, Transylvania County
Father:	**William ERWIN**
Mother:	**Harriett SLOAN**
Draft Registration:	22, single, lived in Brevard
Note: Military:	NC PVT CO G 369 Inf WW **I**

[Documentation: Transylvania County DC, Cowart's Index to Marriages, Transylvania County Cemetery Survey, Ancestry.com, TT obituary]

12/15/1956
CHARLES ERWIN

Charles C. Erwin, 72, died unexpectedly Tuesday in the home of his sister, Mary E. Smith. Mr. Erwin was a native of Brevard, a son of the late William and Harriett Sloan Erwin. He was a World War I veteran, having served with Company G of the 369th Infantry.

Surviving is addition to the sister, are the widow, Delsey Erwin; a brother, Howard; and a stepson, Charles Erwin.

Services were held Sunday at Bethel Baptist Church and the burial followed in the Cooper Cemetery.

1919
369th Arriving Home

21 Jun 1918   Brevard News
COLORED REGISTRANTS TO LEAVE FOR CAMP TAYLOR, KY ON FRIDAY, JUNE 21, 1918.
. . . Charles Erwin, Brevard . . .

The 369th Infantry is known for being the first African-American regiment to serve with the American Expeditionary Force during World War I. The regiment was nicknamed the **Harlem Hellfighters** and the **Black Rattlers**

118

Overton Lewis ERWIN

Born:	29 Jan 1896, Transylvania County
Died:	8 Aug 1930, Oteen VA Hospital, Buncombe County; age 34
Buried:	Davidson River Cemetery
Occupation:	Worked as a clerk for his father, O.L. Erwin
Father:	**Overton L. ERWIN, Sr.**
Mother:	**Verona PATTON**
Draft Registration:	21, single
Military Marker:	NC SGT ANTIACFT BTRY CAC WW I

[Documentation: Discharge, Buncombe DC, Application for Veteran's Headstone, <u>Transylvania County Cemetery Survey</u>, Ancestry.com]

Erwin	Overton L	756,981	White
(Surname)	(Christian name)	(Army serial number)	(Race: White or colored)

Residence: **Brevard** Transylvania **NORTH CAROLINA**
(Street and house number) (Town or city) (County) (State)

Enlisted in **NG Hendersonville N C** June 14/17
Born in **Calvert N C** 21 5/12 yrs
Organizations: **6 Co CAC NC NG (6 Co Cape Fear) to Jan 8/18; 2 Co. ROTC Ft Oglethorpe Ga to Apr 18/18; 6 Co C Def Ft Caswell NC to May 11/18; 13 A A Btry CAC to disch**
Grades: **Pvt 1cl Aug 6/17; Corp Oct 6/17; Sgt Oct 21/18**

Engagements:

Wounds or other injuries received in action: None.
Served overseas **July 14/18 to Dec 21/18**
Hon. disch. **Jan 7/19** on demobilization
Was reported **0** per cent disabled on date of discharge, in view of occupation.
Remarks:

SRC Notes: CAC NC NG (Coast Artillery Corps North Carolina National Guard)

3 May 1918   Brevard News
Overton Erwin of Fort Caswell is at home on a few days furlough.

24 Jan 1919   Brevard News
Sgt. Overton Erwin has arrived from France after receiving an honorable discharge from the National Army. His many friends here are particularly proud of his record that was officially stated 100 percent perfect.

8/13/1930
OVERTON LEWIS ERWIN, Jr.

Overton Lewis Erwin, Jr., 34, died suddenly last Friday morning at Oteen Veterans Hospital. While he had not been well for the past several years, there was no thought of the seriousness of his illness. His parents had spent the day before with him at Oteen and his death the following morning was shocking to the family and to Transylvania county friends and business associates.

He volunteered his services to the United States government in the early days of America's entrance into the World War, being placed later with the anti-aircraft division. He was a Mason, a member of the American Legion, a young businessman, and a friend to many. He operated a Standard Oil service station on East Main Street.

Funeral services were held at the historic Davidson River Presbyterian church. It was estimated that more than fifteen hundred people gathered into and about the church, only a few hundred were able to enter the church during services. Burial followed in the Davidson River cemetery.

Surviving are the parents, Mr. and Mrs. O.L. Erwin, three sisters, Miss Katherine Erwin, Mrs. A.K. Lewis and Mrs. L.E. Lewis.

Mitchel Monroe EUBANKS

Born:	6 Aug 1893, Transylvania County, NC
Died:	4 Jan 1962, Transylvania County, NC; age 68
Buried:	Dunn's Creek Baptist Church Cemetery
Occupation:	Worked as a farmer for his father
Spouse:	**Eva RAINES**, 31 May 1919, Transylvania County
Father:	**Elijah EUBANKS**
Mother:	**Delia RAXTER**
Draft Registration:	24, single, lived and worked in Selica, NC

[Documentation: Transylvania County DC, <u>Cowart's Index to Marriages</u>, <u>Transylvania County Cemetery Survey</u>, Ancestry.com, Discharge, TT obituary]

SRC Notes: Tng Dep MG (Training Depot National Guard)

18 Jul 1918   **Brevard News**
23 MORE MEN TO LEAVE JULY 24, 1918
Following is a list of white registrants for induction on July 24th, 1918 for Camp Hancock, Ga., who will leave on the 3:13 train:
. . . M. Monroe Eubanks, Selica . . .

17 Jan 1919   Brevard News
Chester Fenwicke, Elzie Mull and Monroe Eubanks have returned home from the training camps. Their many friends are glad to see them home again.

1/11/1962
MONROE EUBANKS

Last rites for Monroe M. Eubanks, 68, were held Friday at the Dunn's Creek Baptist Church and the burial followed in the church cemetery. A native Transylvanian, Mr. Eubanks died Thursday at the home of Mrs. Effie Eubanks, a sister-in-law. He had been in ill health for several years. Mr. Eubanks was a farmer.

Survivors include the widow; three brothers: Jimmie, McKinley and Robert.

William McKinley EUBANKS

Born:	6 Jun 1897, Transylvania County, NC
Died:	15 Nov 1967, Buncombe County, NC; age 70
Buried:	Glazener Cemetery
Spouse(s):	**Bessie GLAZENER**
	Mattie Alma LONDON
Father:	**Elijah EUBANKS**
Mother:	**Delia RAXTER**
Draft Registration:	No
Discharge:	William was inducted 10 Nov 1918, the Armistice was signed 11 Nov 1918; discharged 14 Nov 1918 as the draft had been cancelled.

[Documentation: Buncombe DC, Findagrave.com, Ancestry.com, Discharge, Brevard News]

14 Nov 1918   **Brevard News**

On Monday morning a crowd of relatives, friends and well-wishers were at the depot to bid God speed to the following young men wh owere leaving for Camp Green, Charlotte:
. . . William McKinley Eubank . . .

11/23/1967
WILLIAM EUBANKS

William McKinley Eubanks, 70, died last Wednesday in an Asheville hospital following a long illness. He was a native of Transylvania County and a retired farmer.

Survivors include his wife Mattie Alma London Eubanks; two daughters, Katie Sue Toole and Martha Van Horn; six sons: Alton, Doyle, Lewis, Weldon, Daniel and Russell Eubanks; and two brothers, Jimmy and Robert Eubanks.

Funeral services were conducted on Friday in the Cherryfield Baptist Church and burial was in the Glazener Cemetery.

Angelo FALCO

Born:	17 Oct 1892, Italy
Died:	27 Nov 1974, Transylvania County, NC; age 82
Buried:	Pisgah Gardens Cemetery
Occupation:	Maintenance at Naval Base in Oregon
Spouse:	**Bessie FRADY**
Father:	**Joseph FALCO**
Mother:	**Marie PERIA**
Draft Registration:	Orena, Nev., 26, single, worked for railroad
Military Marker:	PVT US Army

[Documentation: Transylvania County DC, <u>Transylvania County Cemetery Survey</u>, Ancestry.com]

---

30 May 1919 Brevard News

TRY TO BE PATIENT

Do not get mad and criticize the Government because a relative or a friend may have failed to secure his discharge from the Army. This is a tremendous enterprise which the United States has been engaged the past two years and the people ought to stop long enough to consider the utter unpreparedness of the country for the struggle it faced when Congress sustained the call to arms. It takes time to muster out millions of men in the regular way and the military authorities are doubtless, making the best of an unusual situation. Bear in mind, too, that the government is experiencing great difficulty in getting men capable of relieving trained men at the various hospitals. Many of the hospitals are full of wounded soldiers from the battlefields of France, numbers of who are bedridden and helpless and the best attention possible is due them. Take comfort from the good that your son, or your relative, has escaped injury and will be restored to you in due course. You will receive him with open arms when he does come home.

If you have contracted the habit of vilifying the Government upon one pretext or another it might not be amiss to remember than no feat of construction has ever approached that of the United States involved in the completion of sixteen cantonments for the National Army in ninety days at the beginning of hostilities in which this country participated. The completion of this program, together with the building of sixteen tent cities for the National Guard, involved the erection and equipment of thirty-two cities capable of accommodating 40,000 persons each. Every one of these had to be provided with requisite water, lights, sewerage, hospital and heating utilities, and the preparation of military features, such as parade grounds and gun ranges.

The War Department points with pride to the contrast between the creature comforts enjoyed by the American soldier of 1917 and those afforded the men of the (18)sixties. Substantial barracks, heated by steam or stoves, took the place of tents; chemically pure water replaced that secured from the casual spring or stream; scientific laundries cared for the National Army recruit's clothing and field bakeries gave him the modern successor to the ashy hoecake. It is figured that the lumber alone used in the construction of the cantonments was equivalent to a boardwalk twelve inches wide and one inch thick, "to the moon and half way back."

The cantonments occupied 167,741 acres of land, which cost an average of $3.93 per acre, while the entire expenditures represented only seventy percent of the total cost for the building of the Panama Canal which required ten years for completion. The war-building program also included the construction of great storehouses, factories for various purposes, docks, magazines, railroads, aviation fields, proving grounds, arm posts, embarkation facilities and hospitals. Five hundred and thirty-five operations in 442 localities were in progress simultaneously, touched every state except one and called for the expenditure of a billion dollars a month during the latter part of the year 1918.

Let us not become impatient because some of our boys have not been given their freedom. "There's a reason."

Le Moyne Angus FARRIOR

Born:	18 Feb 1897, Dardanelle, Arkansas
Died:	14 Sep 1953, Jefferson, KY; age 56
Buried:	Davidson River Cemetery
Spouse:	**Geneva NEILL**
Father:	**Edwin Walton FARRIOR**
Mother:	**Estella BROWN**
Draft Registration:	Hardaville, Arkansas 21, single
Military Marker:	NC S2 USNRF WW I

[Documentation: Kentucky Death Record, Application for Veteran Headstone, <u>Transylvania County Cemetery Survey</u>, Ancestry.com, <u>Heritage of Transylvania County</u>, Vol. 1]

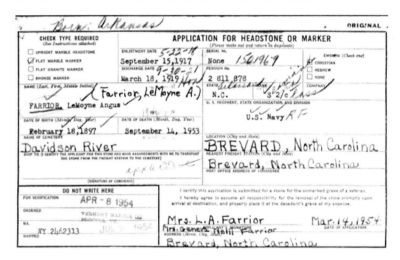

9/17/1953
LE MOYNE A. FARRIOR

LeMoyne Angus Farrior died Monday in a veterans' hospital in Louisville, Ky., where he had been undergoing treatment for two weeks following surgery. Funeral services were held at the First Baptist Church in Brevard with burial in the Davidson River Cemetery.

He is survived by his widow, Geneva Neill Farrier; two sisters: Mrs. Jan Classing and Miss Bonnie Lee Farrior; and two brothers: J. H. Farrior and K. W. Farrior.

Chester Collingwood FENWICKE

Born:	15 Aug 1897, Transylvania County, NC
Died:	24 Dec 1979, Transylvania County, NC; age 82
Buried:	Gillespie-Evergreen Cemetery
Spouse(s):	**E. Vernoie ASHWORTH**, m. 11 Jun 1922, Transylvania County, NC
	Beatrice GALLOWAY, m. 11 Jan 1947, Transylvania County, NC
Father:	**Henry FENWICKE**
Mother:	**Emma Jane TINSLEY**
Draft Registration:	21, single

[Documentation: Transylvania County DC, NC Birth Index, Transylvania County Cemetery Survey, Cowart's Index to Marriages, Ancestry.com]

Chester Fenwicke

Marie Cison Photo

10 Oct 1918   Brevard News
Mr. Chester Fenwick left for Camp Sevier Tuesday. We all certainly do miss him .

17 Jan 1919   Brevard News
Chester Fenwicke, Elzie Mull and Monroe Eubanks have returned home from the training camps. Their many friends are glad to see them home again.

Asheville Citizen Times
12/25/1979
C.C. FENWICKE

Chester Colingwood Fenwicke, 82, of Carolina Trailer Court died Monday in the Brevard hospital. He was a native of Transylvania County and the son of the late Harry C. and Emma Tinsley Fenwicke. He was a veteran of the U.S. Army and was a retired mechanic. Services were at Morningside Baptist Church with burial in Gillespie Evergreen cemetery.

Survivors are his wife, Beatrice Bruner Fenwicke; two sons: Jack S. and Richard H. Fenwicke; a daughter, Mrs. J. E. Driscole; a stepson, Charles W. Galloway; and a brother, Frank Fenwicke.

Mr. Fenwicke was preceded in death by his sister, Ada Fenwicke Barton.

Christopher McDaniel FISHER

Born: 25 May 1895, Transylvania County, NC
Died: 2 Dec 1958, Richmond, VA; age 63
Buried: Toxaway Lakeside Cemetery
Occupation: Timber cutter for J. McCall of Gloucester, NC
Spouse: **Clara MILLER**
Father: **Simpson M. FISHER**
Mother: **Mary Etta LEE**
Draft Registration: 22, single, lived at Lake Toxaway, NC

[Documentation: TT obituary, Upper Transylvania County, NC Remembered, Ancestry.com, discharge]

Fisher Christopher McD 2,994,475 *White *Colored

Residence: Balsam Grove (Town or city) NORTH CAROLINA (State)

*Inducted at Brevard NC on May 24/18

Place of birth: Lake Toxaway NC Age or date of birth: 23 Yrs

Organizations served in, with dates of assignments and transfers: 156 Dep Brig to disch

Grades, with date of appointment: Pvt

Engagements:

Wounds or other injuries received in action: None.
Served overseas from † none to †, from † to †
Honorably discharged on demobilization Dec 30/18, 19
In view of occupation he was, on date of discharge, reported 0 per cent disabled.

APPLICATION FOR HEADSTONE OR MARKER

1. NAME OF DECEASED: Fisher, Christopher M.
2. ENLISTMENT DATE: 5-24-1918
3. DISCHARGE DATE: 11-15-1918
4. SERVICE NO.: 2994475
5. PENSION OR VA CLAIM NO.: C-1455527
6. STATE: N. C.
7. GRADE: Pvt.
8. MEDALS: None
9. BRANCH OF SERVICE, COMPANY, REGIMENT, AND DIVISION OR SHIP: Army 3 rd. Co. 8 th. Div.
10. DATE OF BIRTH: 5-25-1895
11. DATE OF DEATH: 12-2-1958

12. EMBLEM: CHRISTIAN (Latin Cross)
13. CHECK TYPE REQUIRED: FLAT MARBLE MARKER

14. SHIP TO: Mr. M. O. McCall Jr. Lake Toxaway N. C.
15. FREIGHT STATION: Rosman, N. C.
16. NAME AND LOCATION OF CEMETERY: Lake Side Cem. Lake Toxaway, N. C.

SIGNATURE: M.O. McCall Jr. DATE 12-4-1958

DO NOT WRITE HERE
RECEIVED: DEC 9 1958
VERIFIED: JAN 1959
WY-7934226
MOUNTAIN MARBLE CORP. RUTLAND, VT.
SIGNATURE OF APPLICANT: M.O. McCall Jr. 12-4-1958

12/11/1958
CRIS M. FISHER

Funeral services for Cris M. Fisher, 63, of Lake Toxaway, were held last Friday afternoon at the Lakeside Baptist Church at Lake Toxaway and burial was in the Lakeside Cemetery. Mr. Fisher died last Tuesday afternoon at the Veterans Hospital at Richmond, Virginia.

Survivors include the widow; four daughters: Mrs. Clara Bell Alexander, Mrs. Bonnie F. Hampton, Mrs. Belva McCall and Mrs. Bobbie Nell Holden; two sons: Vaughn and Donald; and one sister and five brothers.

Mr. Fisher was a farmer and he was a member of the Lakeside Baptist Church.

Cyrus Watha FISHER

Born:	15 Jan 1893, Transylvania County, NC
Died:	6 Jul 1972, Buncombe, NC; age 79
Buried:	Quebec Oak Grove Cemetery
Occupation:	Common laborer for B. P. Thomas at Quebec, NC
Spouse:	**Fannie E. POWELL**, M 29 Aug 1920, Transylvania
Father:	**John Barry FISHER**
Mother:	**Nancy Ann CHAPMAN**
Draft Registration:	24, single; lived and worked in Quebec, NC

[Documentation: Transylvania County DC, Discharge, Upper Transylvania County, NC Remembered, Cowart's Index to Marriages, Ancestry.com]

Fisher	Cyrus W	106,792	White
(Surname)	(Christian name)	(Army serial number)	(Race: White or colored)

Residence: _____ Quebec Transylva_ NORTH CAROLINA
(Street and house number) (Town or city) (County) (State)

Enlisted in   RA   Ft Thomas Ky   June 16/17
Born in   Transylvania Co NC _   24 5/12 yrs _
Organizations:

Co K 4 Inf to Oct 2/17; Co A 4 MG Bn to disch

Grades:

Pvt 1cl Sept 1/17; Sag May 6/18; Corp July 10/18;
Engagements: Sgt Sept 1/18;

Wounds or other injuries received in action: None.
Served overseas: Dec 24/17 to Aug 4/19
Hon. disch.   Aug 14/19   on demobilization
Was reported   0   per cent disabled on date of discharge, in view of occupation.
Remarks:

7/16/1972
CYRUS W. FISHER

Cyrus Watha Fisher, 79, Lake Toxaway, died last Thursday evening in a VA Hospital after a long illness. Mr. Fisher was a veteran of World War I.

Surviving are the following: one daughter, Mrs. Veardrey Hoxit; one half brother, Austin Waldrop; and one half sister, Mrs. Ruth Lowe.

Funeral services were held Saturday in the Oak Grove Baptist Church at Quebec. Burial followed in the church cemetery.

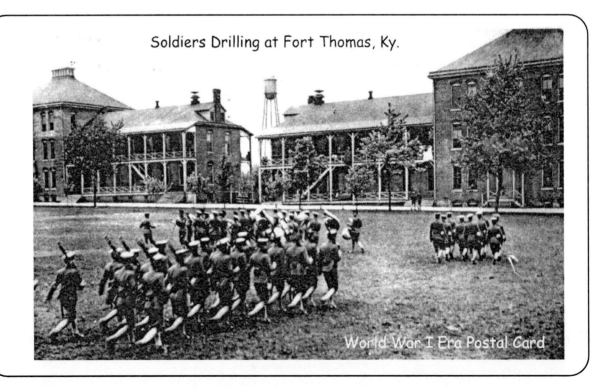

Soldiers Drilling at Fort Thomas, Ky.

World War I Era Postal Card

Earley Dillie FISHER

Born:	7 May 1897, Transylvania County, NC
Died:	20 Jan 1967, Buncombe County, NC; age 69
Buried:	Quebec Oak Grove Cemetery
Spouse:	**Callie THOMAS**, m. 16 Mar 1917, Transylvania County
Father:	**John Barry FISHER**
Mother:	**Nancy Ann CHAPMAN**
Draft Registration:	No

[Documentation: Upper Transylvania County, NC Remembered, Buncombe DC, Cowart's Index to Marriages Discharge, Ancestry.com]

Fisher	Early D		White
(Surname)	(Christian name)	(Army serial number)	(Race: White or colored)

Residence: Quebec Transylvania NORTH CAROLINA
(Street and house number) (Town or city) (County) (State)

* Enlisted in   RA   Ft Thomas Ky   June 16/17
† Born in   Quebec NC   20 1/12 yrs
Organizations:
                 Co K 4 Inf to disch

Grades:
                 Pvt
Engagements:

Wounds or other injuries received in action: None.
‡ Served overseas: None
§ Hon. disch.   Sept 14/17 on S C D
Was reported   75   per cent disabled on date of discharge, in view of occupation.
Remarks:

1/27/1967
E.D. FISHER

Earley Dilly Fisher, 71, of Lake Toxaway, died last Friday in a Buncombe County hospital following a long illness. Mr. Fisher was a retied North Carolina State Prison guard, a World War I veteran, and a member of the Oak Grove Baptist Church.

Surviving are the widow, Mrs. Callie Thomas Fisher; three sons: John, M.C. and Perry; three daughters: Mrs. Dorene Chapman, Mrs. Beatrice Mason and Mrs. Martha Netherton; a half-brother, Auston Waldrop; two sisters: Mrs. Ida Lee Phillips and Mrs. Ruth Lowe.

Note: Earley was inducted at Fort Thomas, Ky June 16, 1917 and was awarded an Honor Discharge September 14, 1917 on S C D. "Surgeon's Certificate of Disability."

FORT THOMAS, KENTUCKY   1919 Postal Card

John Thomas FISHER

Born:	9 May 1894, Transylvania County, NC
Died:	11 Feb 1964, St. Petersburg, FL; age 69
Buried:	Royal Palm Cemetery, St. Petersburg, FL
Spouse:	**Sybil SHAY**
Father:	**William Clark FISHER**
Mother:	**Rhoda WALKER**
Draft Registration:	No

[Documentation: Transylvania County Birth Index, Florida Death Index, TT obituary, Evening Independent, St. Petersburg, FL obituary, Ancestry.com]

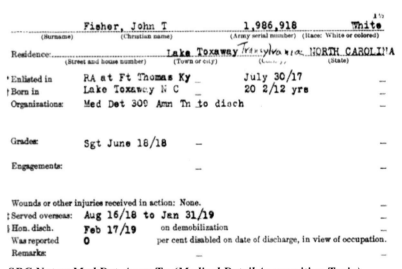

John Fisher

Tony Fisher Photo

SRC Notes: Med Det Amm Tn (Medical Detail Ammunition Train)

16 Nov 1917   Brevard News
John T. Fisher of the United States regular Army, recently stationed at Camp Taylor, KY., is in this county visiting his mother, Mrs. J.B. Neal, of Lake Toxaway and his brother, Ralph R. Fisher of Brevard.

7 Dec 1917   Brevard News
John Fisher who has been visiting his mother, Mrs. J.B. Neal of Lake Toxaway, has left this week for Camp Taylor, KY.

10 Oct 1918   Brevard News
Mrs. J.B. Neal of Lake Toxaway has received word that her son Sgt. John T. Fisher has arrived safely overseas.

14 Mar 1919   Brevard News
John Fisher has returned to his home at Lake Toxaway from France.

18 Apr 1919   Brevard News
John Fisher who has been home for a few weeks with friends after a few months service in France left Thursday for Nashville, Tenn.

Evening Independent, St. Petersburg, FL
2/11/1964
EX-MAGISTRATE JOHN FISHER DIES

Former St. Petersburg magistrate John Thomas Fisher, 67, died today at his residence. He was a cattle rancher and had been active in the real estate business.

Judge Fisher had been ill for more than a month. He was taken to Bay Pines Veterans Hospital early in January suffering from a heart attack and pneumonia. He returned home last week.

He served as Justice of the Peace in Dist. I from 1936 to 1948. During that time the district embraced a considerable Northside area. Boundary lines were shifted as population increased.

Well-known for his handling of juvenile cases before the Pinellas Juvenile Court was instituted, he prided himself on handling cases "with horse sense."

He retired in 1953 but continued to manage his property and cattle interest.

Judge Fisher was born in Lake Toxaway, NC, May 9, 1897, the son of Dr. William C. and Rhoda Fisher. He came to Pinellas County in 1924. He went to the Mexican border in 1916 as First Sergeant with a North Carolina National Guard Infantry Company. In World War I he served 14 months in France with the 77th Field Artillery Headquarters Battalion. He was discharged with the rank of Sergeant Major.

He was a Mason, Elk and a member of the American Legion, VFW, DAV, 40 and 8, Exchange Club and Lakewood Country Club.

Survivors include his wife Sybil Shay Fisher; two daughters: Mrs. Robert Atwood and Mrs. H.R. Anderson; and a sister, Mrs. Spencer Welborn.

Perry Hillie FISHER

Born:	25 Dec 1895, Transylvania County, NC
Died:	13 Dec 1966, Oteen VA Hospital, Buncombe County; age 70
Buried:	Quebec Oak Grove Cemetery
Occupation:	Farmer
Spouse:	**Marie THOMAS**
Father:	**John Barry FISHER**
Mother:	**Nancy Ann CHAPMAN**
Draft Registration:	No

[Documentation: <u>Upper Transylvania County, NC Remembered</u>, Buncombe County DC, Ancestry.com, Discharge]

<table>
<tr><td colspan="2">Fisher Perry H</td><td>106,920</td><td>White</td></tr>
<tr><td>(Surname)</td><td>(Christian name)</td><td>(Army serial number)</td><td>(Race: White or colored)</td></tr>
<tr><td>Residence:</td><td>Quebec</td><td>Transylvania</td><td>NORTH CAROLINA</td></tr>
<tr><td></td><td>(Street and house number)</td><td>(Town or city)   (County)</td><td>(State)</td></tr>
<tr><td>Enlisted in</td><td>R / Ft Thomas Ky</td><td>-</td><td>June 16/17</td></tr>
<tr><td>Born in</td><td>Transylvania N C</td><td>-</td><td>21 5/12 yrs</td></tr>
<tr><td>Organizations:</td><td colspan="3">Co K 4 Inf to Oct 2/17; Co A 4 M G Bn to disch</td></tr>
<tr><td>Grades:</td><td colspan="3">Pvt 1cl Sept 1/17; Wag May 6/18; Corp June 11/18; Sgt Sept 1/18</td></tr>
<tr><td>Engagements:</td><td colspan="3">-</td></tr>
</table>

Wounds or other injuries received in action: None.
Served overseas: Dec 24/17 to Apr 27/19
Hon. disch. May 27/19   on S C D
Was reported 16 2/3 per cent disabled on date of discharge, in view of occupation.
Remarks: *Awarded Croix-de-Guerre /ar 9/19*

Note: Perry was inducted into the Army 16 Jun 1917 at Ft. Thomas, Ky. The record states he served overseas from 24 Dec 1917 until 27 Apr 1919. He received an Honorable Discharge 27 May 1919 with the phrase: S C D "Surgeon's Certificate of Disability". He was rated as being 16 2/3 percent disable on his Discharge.

Most notable Perry Fisher was awarded the **Croix de Guerre** metal, a French military decoration. The French **Croix de Guerre** was instituted on 8 April 1915 by the French Government to recognize acts

of bravery in the face of the enemy specifically mentioned in dispatches.

It was awarded to soldiers, sailors and airmen of all ranks, and of any Allied Army, with various types of **Croix de Guerre** available: the bronze, was awarded by the Army; the silver was awarded by a division; the silver-gilt was awarded by a corps; the silver star was awarded by a division and a bronze star was awarded by a regiment. The metal was attached to decorative ribbon pin. The reverse was dated with one of four dates: "1914-1915', '1914-1916', '1914-1917' or '1914-1918'.

Fisher Brothers from Upper Transylvania County

  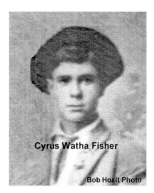

Very early photos of the three Fisher brothers

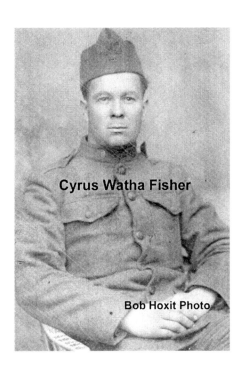 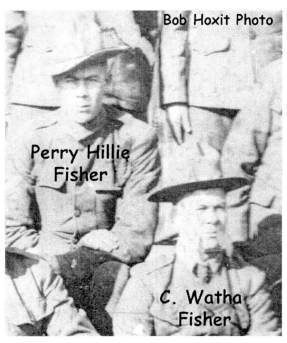

The three Fisher brothers enlisted in the Army at Fort Thomas, Kentucky 16 June 1917. Early Dillie, the youngest brother was 20 1/2 years of age at the time of his enrollment. His Service Record indicates he was discharged 14 September 1917 with a 75% disability.

Both Watha and Hillie remained in the military until 1919 and both men served overseas for almost two years. They served in the same company and remained together throughout the war. Both men received outstanding decorations for their gallant service for the United States Army and Perry received a medal from the French government for his acts of bravery.

Bob Hoxit, grandson of Watha, shared a photograph of the 4th Infantry that is approximately four feet long and one foot tall. The picture above that includes Perry and Watha together was scanned from this large photograph. He shared his grandfather's military Bible that has an engraved metal front cover. He also has his grandfather's metal doughboy helmet.

Ralph Rudolph FISHER

Born:	3 Feb 1892, Greenville, South Carolina
Died:	17 Sep 1955, Transylvania County, NC; age 63
Buried:	Gillespie-Evergreen Cemetery
Occupation:	Attorney in practice for himself in Brevard, NC
Spouse:	**Thelma RICHARDSON**
Father:	**William Clark FISHER**
Mother:	**Rhoda WALKER**
Draft Registration;	25, single
Military Marker:	NC PFC 19 Co 20 ENG WW I

[Documentation: Transylvania County DC, <u>Transylvania County Cemetery Survey</u>, TT Obituary, Discharge, Ancestry.com]

Fisher Ralph R   289,690   White
(Surname)   (Christian name)   (Army serial number)   (Race: White or colored)

Residence: Brevard Transylvania NORTH CAROLINA
(Street and house number)   (Town or city)   (County)   (State)

*Enlisted in   N A Ft Thomas Ky-   Dec 13/17
†Born in   Greenville Co S C   25 10/12 yrs

Organizations: Co A 20 Engrs to June /18; 19 Co 20 Engrs to disch

Grades: Pvt 1cl Sept 22/18

Engagements:

Wounds or other injuries received in action: None.
‡Served overseas: Feb 17/18 to May 29/19
§Hon. disch.   June 21/19   on demobilization
Was reported 0   per cent disabled on date of discharge, in view of occupation.
Remarks:

Form No. 724-1½, A. G. O.   *Insert "R. A.," "N. G.," "R. C.," "N. A.," as case may be, followed by place and
March 12, 1920.   date of enlistment.   †Give place of birth and date of birth, or age at enlistment.
5—7288   ‡Give dates of departure from and arrival in the United States.   §Give date.

Ralph R. Fisher

Tony Fisher PHoto

11 Dec 1917   Brevard News
Ralph R. Fisher left Tuesday for Fort Thomas, KY., to enlist in the 20th Forestry regiment of the regular Army. Mr. Fisher's training as woodsman and lumberman before studying law led him to choose this branch of the service.

28 Dec 1917   Brevard News
INTERESTING LETTER FROM RALPH R. FISHER   "Just allow an echo from a boy from Western North Carolina to blow in on a breeze and please receipt the same by mailing a card or writing a letter to the address given below. Now please don't fail to write to me if you know me; if you don't know me, write anyway 'cause I am in the Army now." 13th Co., 1st Platoon, 313 Squad. Ft. Thomas, KY

18 Jan 1918   Brevard News
Word has just reached us that Ralph R. Fisher, who is stationed at Fort Thomas, KY is seriously ill with pneumonia. Hope this report is not true.

1 Feb 1918   Brevard News
Ralph R. Fisher, who was reported to be dangerously ill a few weeks ago at Fort Thomas, KY has returned to Brevard Wednesday afternoon much improved, in fact he is able to be out.

8 Feb 1918   Brevard News
Ralph R. Fisher wrote a letter of a patriotic character to the News from the aviation camp in Kentucky, about the first of January, and has since that time received letters innumerable congratulatory of his character. This not only shows the patriotism of our people all over the country, but it shows that the Brevard News is an excellent advertising medium. On account of illness, Mr. Fisher is now at home for recuperations.

15 Feb 1918   Brevard News
Ralph Fisher left on Thursday for Fort Thomas, KY., after spending a short furlough with relatives here.

22 Feb 1918   Brevard News
Ralph R. Fisher has been transferred from Fort Thomas, KY., to New York. His address now is Private Ralph R. Fisher, Co A, 7Bn, 20 Eng. Via New York, A.E.F.

9/22/1955
HUGH CROWD ATTENDS FUNERAL SERVICES FOR RALPH R. FISHER

Final rites for Ralph R. Fisher, 63, prominent Brevard attorney, politician and civic leader, were held Sunday afternoon, with several thousand persons paying last respects.

Services were held at 4 PM in the First Baptist Church, with graveside rites being conducted at the Gillespie Cemetery by local, district and state legionnaires. State legion commander, Paul Robertson, Chapel Hill, presided over the graveside rites.

Mr. Fisher died late Saturday afternoon at his home following a serious illness of several months. Mr. Fisher resigned as a member of the House of Representatives April 16 because of ill health. He underwent several operations and had been in critical condition for some time prior to his death.

Although a native of Greenville, SC, he had resided in Brevard since childhood. He was the son of Dr. W.C. and Rhoda Emma Walker Fisher. He attended Columbus Institute 1903-1904, Furman Fitting School 1909-1910, Mars Hill College 1910-1914 and Wake Forest College 1917.

Haywood County Digital Collection

Truck Company No 2 105 Ammunition Train

Streeter Gerald FISHER

Born: 14 Feb 1895, Transylvania County, NC
Died: 23 Jan 1953, Transylvania County, NC; age 57
Buried: Gillespie-Evergreen
Spouse: **Dovie Jane GARREN**
Father: **John FISHER**
Mother: **Mamie TURNER**
Draft Registration: No
Military Headstone: NC PFC CO H 21 Inf Reg WW I

[Documentation: Transylvania County DC, Transylvania County Cemetery Survey, Application for Military Headstone, Ancestry.com]

Fisher	Streeter	2,366,870	White
(Surname)	(Christian name)	(Army serial number)	(Race: White or colored)

Residence: RFD 1 Box 54 Etawah *Henderson* NORTH CAROLINA
(Street and house number) (Town or city) (County) (State)

Enlisted in   RA Columbus Bks Ohio   Aug 26/14
Born in   Transylvania Co N-C   19 6/12 yrs

Organizations:

Grades: Co E 13 Inf to Oct 18/18; Provost Guard Co Camp
               Fremont Calif to Mch 25/19; Co E 21 Inf to disch
               Pvt 1 cl Jan 7/18

Engagements:

Wounds or other injuries received in action: None.
Served overseas: No
Hon. disch.   Oct 20/19 for reenlistment
Was reported   0   per cent disabled on date of discharge, in view of occupation.

1/28/1954
STREETER FISHER

Funeral services for Streeter Gerald Fisher, 58, well known paperhanger and painter of Brevard, will be held Thursday afternoon, January 18, at the First Baptist Church of which he was a member. Burial will be in Evergreen Cemetery.

Mr. Fisher, a native Transylvanian, died suddenly at his home Saturday afternoon. A veteran of World War I, he was active in legion affairs and a popular member of Monroe Wilson Post No. 88.

Survivors include the widow, Mrs. Dovie Garren Fisher; three daughters: Mrs. Louis Kilpatrick, Mrs. Richard Bollinger and Mrs. James Bowen.

1918   BREVARD NEWS
ANNOUNCEMENT

The recent War Tax on Theatres and Moving Pictures necessitates an increase in the price of admission. The law requires that all children not in arms as well as adults shall pay the tax. The greater part of exhibitors have advanced their 10 cents admission to 15 cents and are keeping the 5 cents admission the same.

Whether we can give you a high class feature at 15 cents remains to be seen, but we shall endeavor to do it. The admission for a time will be adults 15 cents. Children not in arms and under 12 years of age 5 cents.

Brevard Amusement Co.
F.D. Clement, Manager

Warren Isiah FISHER

Born:	4 Jun 1895, Transylvania County, NC
Died:	20 Feb 1974, Transylvania County, NC; age 78
Buried:	Toxaway Lakeside Cemetery
Occupation:	Farmer at Lake Toxaway, NC
Spouse:	**Edith MONTEITH**
Father:	**Isiah FISHER**
Mother:	**Caroline LEE**
Draft Registration;	22, single
Military Marker:	NC PVT US Army WW I

[Documentation: Transylvania County DC, Upper Transylvania County, NC Remembered, Ancestry.com]

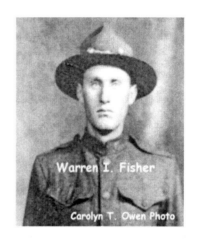

Fisher, Warren I   1,986,995   White
(Surname)   (Christian name)   (Army serial number)   (Race: White or colored)

Residence: _____ **Lake Toxaway** _____ **NORTH CAROLINA**
(Street and house number)   (Town or city)   (County)   (State)

* Enlisted in   RA at Ft Thomas Ky   July 30/17
† Born in   Lake Toxaway N C   22 1/12 yrs
Organizations: M D to disch

Grades: Pvt

Engagements:

Wounds or other injuries received in action: None.
‡ Served overseas: Sept 16/18 to June 6/19
§ Hon. disch.   June 21/19   on demobilization
Was reported   0   per cent disabled on date of discharge, in view of occupation.
Remarks:

SRC Notes: M D (Medical Department)

2/20/1974
Hendersonville Times News
WARREN I. FISHER

Warren I. Fisher, 78, of Lake Toxaway, died Wednesday in a Brevard hospital after a long illness. A lifelong resident of Transylvania County, he was a retired farmer and an Army veteran of World War I.

Mr. Fisher is survived by his wife, Edith Monteith Fisher; four daughters: Mrs. Ford Owen, Mrs. Allen Bryson, Mrs. Robert Pruitt and Mrs. Wolfe Rogers; four sons: Howard Ray Fisher, Ben Fisher, Warren E. Fisher and James Joseph Fisher; one sister, Beulah McNeely.

Funeral services will be at 2 p.m. Friday at Lake Toxaway Baptist Church, of which he was a member. Burial will be in Toxaway Lakeside Cemetery. Grandsons will be pallbearers.

Fort Thomas is a city in Campbell County, Kentucky, located only four miles south of Cincinnati, Ohio. The military facility of Fort Thomas was constructed on the southern bank of the Ohio River in 1890 with the first unit assigned there being the 6th Infantry. The 6th Infantry gained its' fame from the Spanish-American War. They joined Col. Teddy Roosevelt and his "Rough Riders" at Santiago, Cuba and brought an end to that war. On December 10, 1898 a peace treaty was signed ending the war and Spain gave up Cuba, Guam, Puerto Rico and the Philippines, which became U.S. Possessions

The Spanish-American War in 1898 between Spain and the United States lasted only ten weeks. Only 385 soldiers died from actual combat but thousands died from diseases, such as yellow fever, dysentery and other causes.

Carl Lavender FORTUNE

Born:	26 Jul 1899, Transylvania County, NC
Died:	13 Jun 1927, Ocala, FL; age 27
Buried:	Oak Grove Cemetery-Brevard
Father:	**Sidney FORTUNE**
Mother:	**Elizabeth WILSON**
Note:	Grave marker has NO military information
Draft Registration:	No

[Documentation: <u>Transylvania County Cemetery Survey</u>, 1900-1920 Census, Brevard News obituary, Ancestry.com]

Fortune   Carl L   1,324,478   White
(Surname)   (Christian name)   (Army serial number)   (Race: White or colored)

Residence: Brevard   Transylvania   NORTH CAROLINA
(Street and house number)   (Town or city)   (County)   (State)

Enlisted in   NG Brevard NC   July 18/17:

Born in   Brevard NC   18 1/12 yrs

Organizations: Btry F 1 FA NC NG (Btry F 113 FA) to disch

Grades: Pvt

Engagements:

Wounds or other injuries received in action: None.
Served overseas: May 26/18 to Mch 19/19
Hon. disch. Mch 28/19   on demobilization
Was reported 0   per cent disabled on date of discharge, in view of occupation.
Remarks:

SRC Notes: FA NC NG (Field Artillery North Carolina National Guard)

6/23/1927
CARL FORTUNE

Funeral services for Carl Fortune, 28, who was killed instantly at Ocala, Fla. on Monday of last week while doing electrical work, were held Saturday at Oak Grove Methodist Church, Brevard. Burial followed in the Oak Grove Cemetery. Following the news of the death his brother, Albert left for Ocala to accompany the body back to Brevard.

Surviving are the parents, Mr. and Mrs. S.L. Fortune and five brothers and five sisters: William, Claude, Albert, Mitchell, George, Mrs. Felix Norton, Mrs. J.N. Siniard, Mrs. Hale Siniard, Mrs. Zeb Kilpatrick and Mrs. Andy Erwin.

18 May 1917   Brevard News
BREVARD YOUNG MEN ANSWER WAR'S CALL
The call to arms continues to meet with response of one kind or another in Brevard. Since the last issue of the News several applications for a chance to serve the country have been made. Clarence Duckworth, Ralph Clement, Sam D. Allison and Carl Fortune passed examinations for Naval service successfully, and the last two left Monday for Asheville for the expressed purpose of entering the service.

28 Sep 1917   Brevard News
Claude, George and Carl Fortune, all in the field artillery stationed at Camp Sevier, Greenville, SC, came home last week to visit their mother, Mrs. S.E. Fortune, who at that time was critically ill. Her condition has since improved considerably and the three young men have returned to camp.

19 Oct 1917   Brevard News
Lieut. Eugene Allison, Ralph Duckworth, Horace Davis, Carl and George Fortune and Dahl Swangim of Camp Sevier, Greenville, spent Saturday night and Sunday in Brevard, returning Sunday night.

27 Jun 1918   Brevard News
Mrs. Sydney Fortune has received cards from her three sons of their safe arrival in France.

Claude Erwin FORTUNE

Born:	17 Feb 1885, Transylvania County, NC
Died:	30 Jul 1961, Transylvania County, NC; age 76
Buried:	Oak Grove Cemetery-Brevard
Occupation:	Lumberman
Father:	**Sidney FORTUNE**
Mother:	**Elizabeth WILSON**
Draft Registration:	29, single, sawmill work
Military Marker:	PVT BTRY F113 Field Arty WW I

[Documentation: Transylvania County DC, Transylvania County Cemetery Survey, Discharge, Application for Veteran Headstone, Ancestry.com, TT obituary]

Fortune	Claude E	1,324,494	White	
(Surname)	(Christian name)	(Army serial number)	(Race: White or colored)	

Residence: _____ Brevard Transylvania NORTH CAROLINA
(Street and house number) (Town or city) (County) (State)

* Enlisted in   NG Brevard, NC   _   July 19/17   _
† Born in   Brevard, NC   _   29 7/12 yrs   _
Organizations: Btry F 1 FA NC NG (Btry F 113 FA) to disch   _

Grade: Pvt   _   _

Engagements: _   _

Wounds or other injuries received in action: None.   _
‡ Served overseas: May 26/18 to Mch 19/19   _
§ Hon. disch. Mch 28/19   on demobilization   _

28 Sep 1917   Brevard News
Claude, George and Carl Fortune, all in the field artillery stationed at Camp Sevier, Greenville, SC, came home last week to visit their mother, Mrs. S.E. Fortune, who at that time was critically ill. Her condition has since improved considerably and the three young men have returned to camp.

27 Jun 1918   Brevard News
Mrs. Sydney Fortune has received cards from her three sons of their safe arrival in France.

8/5/1961
CLAUDE E. FORTUNE

Funeral services for Claude Erwin Fortune, 76, Brevard, were held Tuesday in the Oak Grove Methodist Church. Burial was in the church cemetery.

Mr. Fortune died Sunday afternoon in the Transylvania Community Hospital following a lengthy illness. He was a lumberman, a World War I veteran and a member of the American Legion.

Survivors include two sisters; Mrs. J.M. Siniard and Mrs. Zeb Kilpatrick; and three brothers: M.W., Albert and Bill Fortune.

NATIONAL ARMY CANTONMENT (CAMP)

Camp Dix   Location: Wrightstown, NJ   Organization: 78th Division
Troops from Remainder of New York and Northern Pennsylvania

George FORTUNE

Born:	18 Aug 1889, Transylvania County, NC
Died:	4 Aug 1939, Transylvania County, NC; age 49
Buried:	Oak Grove Cemetery Brevard
Occupation:	Worked at the cotton mill
Spouse:	**Lura HUGGIN**
Father:	**Sidney FORTUNE**
Mother:	**Elizabeth WILSON**
Draft Registration:	28, single, worked at a sawmill

[Documentation: Transylvania County DC, <u>Transylvania County Cemetery Survey</u>, Application for Veteran Headstone, discharge, TT obituary, Ancestry.com]

```
                                                                    1½
       Fortune      George W         1324500      white
         (Surname)      (Christian name)      (Army serial number)  (Race: White or colored)

Residence:_____ Brevard_____  NORTH CAROLINA
                (Street and home number)    (Town or city)    (County)       (State)

*Enlisted in   NG Camp Sevier S C  _                    Aug 28/17  _
†Born in       Brevard N C         _                    28 yrs     _
Organization:  Btry F 113th F A  to_discharge                      _


Grade:     Pvt             _                                       _

Engagements:  Toul Defensive St Mihiel Offensive; Meuse-Argonne    _
              Offensive; Troyon Defensive; Offensive of the Woevre

Wounds or other injuries received in action: None.
Served overseas: May 26/18 to Mar 19/19                            _
Hon. disch.    Mar 28/19      on demobilization                    _
Was reported   - -           per cent disabled on date of discharge, in view of occupation.
Remarks:                    _
```

SRC Note: FA (Field Artillery)

28 Sep 1917   Brevard News
Claude, George and Carl Fortune, all in the field artillery stationed at Camp Sevier, Greenville, SC, came home last week to visit their mother, Mrs. S.E. Fortune, who at that time was critically ill. Her condition has since improved considerably and the three young men have returned to camp.

27 Jun 1918   Brevard News
Mrs. Sydney Fortune has received cards from her three sons of their safe arrival in France.

8/10/1939
GEORGE FORTUNE

George Fortune, 50 died at his home Friday night, following an illness of several weeks, during which time he had been a patient at Oteen. Funeral services were held Sunday from Oak Grove Methodist Church and interment was made in the cemetery nearby.

Mr. Fortune was a son of the late Sidney E. Fortune and as a young man he volunteered for service in the World War, along with three of his brothers. He was a member of the 113th Field Artillery, 30th division and saw active service in France until the conflict ended.

Surviving are five sisters: Mrs. J.N. Siniard, Mrs. Hale Siniard, Mrs. Felix Norton, Mrs. Zeb Kilpatrick and Mrs. A.J. Erwin; and four brothers: William, Mitchell, Albert and Claude.

William C. FORTUNE

Born:	14 Jan 1885, Transylvania County, NC
Died:	15 Sep 1966, Oteen VA Hospital, Buncombe County; age 81
Buried:	Oak Grove Cemetery-Brevard
Occupation:	Retired lineman
Spouse(s):	**Ida MURPHY**, m. 16 Jun 1902, McDowell County, NC
	Sarah Jane DAVEY
Father:	**Sidney FORTUNE**
Mother:	**Elizabeth WILSON**
Military Marker:	CPL Co F 17 ENG WW I

[Documentation: Buncombe County DC, McDowell County Marriage Collection, Transylvania County Cemetery Survey, Discharge, TT obituary, Ancestry.com]

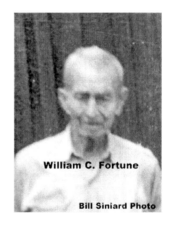

William C. Fortune

Bill Siniard Photo

Fortune	William B	168,722	white
(Surname)	(Christian name)	(Army serial number)	(Race: White or colored)

Residence: Brevard Transylvania NORTH CAROLINA
(Street and house number) (Town or city) (County) (State)

' Enlisted in   NA Knoxville Tenn   July 6/17
† Born in   Brevard NC   31 6/12 yrs
Organizations: Co F 17 Engrs to disch

Grades: Pvt 1/cl Oct 14/17; Corp Apr 15/18

Engagements:

Wounds or other injuries received in action: None.
‡ Served overseas: July 28/17 to Mch 25/19
‡ Hon. disch.   Apr 11/19   on demobilization
Was reported   0   per cent disabled on date of discharge, in view of occupation.

SRC Note: Engrs (Engineers)

19 Oct 1918   Brevard News
C.M. Siniard has heard for a second time from his son Robert in France. The letter said that he was running an engine and that Will Fortune was with the electric line workers.

28 Dec 1918   Brevard News
Robert G. Siniard and Will C. Fortune write letter from "somewhere in France".

   "We have been here at this place for some time, and things are pretty good for us. We are rather busy all the time and therefore, one does not have time to think of the few things that are not as one would like. We have had but little cold weather here and plenty of rain. If you can give us any information as to what regiment the boys who have left there belong to we would appreciate it very much. We would then have a chance to be on the lookout for them.. We would be glad to see the boys should they come our way. We will close wishing you all a Merry Christmas."

9/22/1966
WILLIAM FORTUNE

   Funeral services for William C. Fortune, 81, Brevard, were held last Friday in the Oak Grove Church, North Brevard and burial followed in the church cemetery. Mr. Fortune died last Thursday in a veteran's hospital at Oteen after a lingering illness. He was a lifelong resident of Transylvania County and a retired watchman for the town of Brevard. He was also a veteran of World War I. Survivors include a brother, Albert and a sister, Mrs. J.N. Siniard.

Ernest P. FOWLER

Born:	13 Jun 1886, Transylvania County, NC
Died:	29 Oct 1926, Augusta, GA; age 40
Buried:	West View Cemetery, Augusta, GA
Spouse:	**Maggie Ada WILSON**, m. 27 Aug 1911, Transylvania County, NC
Father:	**David FOWLER**
Mother:	**Myra GALLOWAY**
Draft Registration:	30, married, lived in Cedar Mountain and worked for Gloucester Lumber Co.
Note:	Georgia Death Index gives death date 26 Oct 1926

[Documentation: Georgia Death Index, findagrave.com, 1900 & 1920 Censuses, Discharge, Ancestry.com, Cowart's Index to Marriages]

Fowler Ernest P   1,865,837   • White • Colored.
(Surname)   (Christian name)   (Army serial number)

Residence: _____ Brevard   Transylvia   NORTH CAROLINA
(Street and house number)   (Town or city)   (County)   (State)

• ▓▓▓▓▓▓▓▓ •Inducted at Brevard N C __ on Apr 1, 19 18
Place of birth: Cedar Mountain N C   Age or date of birth: 31 9/12 yrs
Organizations served in, with dates of assignments and transfers: 156 Dep Brig to May
25/18; Btry F 317 F A to July 19/18; 156 Dep Brig to
Sept. 17/18; Hq Co 11 Regt F A Repl Depot to disch
Grades, with date of appointment: Pvt

Engagements: _____

Wounds or other injuries received in action: None.
Served overseas from tNo ____ to † _____, from † _____ to † _____.
Honorably discharged on demobilization Dec 8/18 ____, 19 ____.
In view of occupation he was, on date of discharge, reported 0 ____ per cent disabled.
Remarks: _____

SRC Notes: FA (Field Artillery) Dep Brig (Depot Brigade) Repl Depot (Replacement Brigade)

Haywood County Library Digital Collection

105th Ammunition Train at one of the Y.M.C.A.Buildings

Oliver FOWLER

Born:	17 Jan 1891, Transylvania County, NC
Died:	11 Dec 1971, South Carolina; age 80
Buried:	Highlands Baptist Church Cemetery, Greenville County, SC
Spouse:	**Viola BULLOCK**, m. 24 Dec 1925, Greenville County, SC
Father:	**Mont FOWLER**
Mother:	**Naomi BRYSON**
Draft Registration:	26, single, cutting chestnut wood for Al Bryson
Military Marker:	NC PVT US Army WW I

[Documentation: 1900-1930 Censuses, findagrave.com, SSDI, Ancestry.com, greenvillecounty.org]

Fowler,	Oliver		1,324,507	White	I
(Surname)	(Christian name)		(Army serial number)	(Race: White or colored)	

Residence:	Main St	Brevard	Transylvania	NORTH CAROLINA
	(Street and house number)	(Town or city)	(County)	(State)
Enlisted in	NC Camp Sevier SC			Sept 11/17
Born in	Brevard NC			26 9/12 yrs
Organizations:				
	Btry F 1 FA NC NG (Btry F 113 FA) to disch			
Grades:				
	Pvt			
Engagements:				

Wounds or other injuries received in action: None.

Served overseas: May 26/18 to Mch 19/19

Hon. disch. Mch 26/19 on demobilization

Was reported 0 per cent disabled on date of discharge, in view of occupation.

Remarks:

SRC Notes: FA NC NG (Field Artillery North Carolina National Guard)

12 Oct 1917   **Brevard News**
A party of boys from Camp Sevier, Greenville, came home fro a short visit Saturday, returning Sunday afternoon. There were ....Oliver Fowler, ...The boys seemed to be in good spirits and enjoying camp life.

Greenville News (SC)
12/9/1971
OLIVER FOWLER

Oliver Fowler, 81, formerly of Greenville, died Wednesday in Easley. Born in Transylvania County, NC, son of the late P. Mont and Naomi Bryson Fowler, he was a retired textile operator and a veteran of World War I

Surviving are a daughter, Mrs. Bradbury Webber; and three brothers: William, John and Baxter Fowler.

Burial was in Highlands Baptist Church Cemetery, Greenville County, SC.

On the outbreak of World War I there were on hand nearly 600,000 Springfield rifles, model #1903. This number was sufficient for the initial equipment of an army of 1,000,000 men. What no one foresaw was that we should be called upon to equip an army of nearly 4,000,000 men in addition to furnishing rifles for the use of the Navy.

Orcutt, Louis E., **The Great War Supplement**, published 1920, p. 83.

Robert John FRANKS

Born:	5 Dec 1894, Georgia
Died:	22 May 1983, Buncombe County, NC; age 88
Buried:	Whitewater Baptist Church Cemetery
Spouse:	**Georgia Ann UNDERWOOD**
Father:	**James B. FRANKS**
Mother:	**Rebecca PLOTT**
Draft Registration:	22, single, farmer in Union County, GA

[Documentation: Roster of WWI Veterans from American Legion 50th Anniversary celebration; NC Death Collection; obit; 1930 Census; Transylvania County Cemetery Survey]

5/26/1983
R. J. FRANKS

Robert John Franks, 88, died Sunday in the Asheville VA Medical Center after a period of declining health. Franks, a native of Georgia, had resided in Transylvania County for the past 40 years. He was a veteran of World War I.

Surviving are five sons: George, Edgar, Earl, John Jr. and Clarence Franks; two daughters, Jessie Beddingfield and Lucille Powell; and a sister, Iva Underwood.

Services were held Tuesday in Whitewater Baptist Church, of which he was a member. Burial was in the church cemetery.

Robert J. Franks
Jessie Beddingfield Photo

Robert T. FRAZIER, Jr.

Born: 7 Oct 1889, Washington, DC
Died: 22 Sep 1970, Transylvania County, NC; age 80
Buried: St. Paul-in-the-Valley
Occupation: Manufacturing Executive
Spouse: **Ethel THOMPSON**
Father: **Robert T. FRAZIER, Sr.**
Mother: **Corinne REID**
Draft Registration: Training at Ft. Oglethorpe, GA; Dependent wife and child
Military marker: District of Columbia Capt. US Army Res WW I

[Documentation: Transylvania County DC, <u>Transylvania County Cemetery Survey</u>, Ancestry.com]

9/24/1970
R.T. FRAZIER

Robert Thomas Frazier, 80, died unexpectedly Tuesday, September 22nd. He was a native of Washington, DC and had made his home in Transylvania County since his retirement. He was a retired manufacturing executive and a veteran of World War I.

He is survived by his wife Ethel Thompson Frazier; four daughters: Katherine Wilson, Ethel Cornwell, Corinne Kilgore and Harriet Patterson; and one sister, Ida Russell.

Graveside services will be conducted at St. Paul's Cemetery September 25th.

Fort Oglethorpe was an Army post established in 1902 and opened in 1904. It served as a cavalry post for the 6th Cavalry. Fort Oglethorpe housed approximately 4,000 enemy military personnel as prisoners of war and civilian detainees during World War I. The military prisoners included the German sailors while the civilian internees included businessmen and individuals charged with a variety of offenses under the Espionage Act of 1917.

The war camp was surrounded by two barbed-wire fences, about ten feet tall and had tripod watch towers outside the fencing. Each tower was equipped with a searchlight, telephone and a machine gun. The camp was divided into two parts. Camp A, the "millionaire's camp," housed the wealthy prisoners in private rooms who paid for their own food and also retained cooks and servants recruited from the stewards and sailors of the German maritime fleet. Camp B consisted of some thirty barracks that house the majority of the 4,000 prisoners.

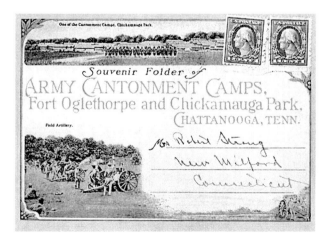

Bert Harold FREEMAN

Born: 13 Jul 1896, Pickens, SC
Died: 15 Oct 1965, Transylvania County, NC; age 69
Buried: Woodlawn Memorial Park, Greenville, SC
Occupation: Police work
Spouse: **Melonee LOOPER**
Father: **William T. FREEMAN**
Mother: **Hattie ADDINGTON**
Draft Registration: No

[Documentation Roster of WWI Veterans from American Legion 50th Anniversary celebration, NC Death Certificate; 1900-1940 Censuses; obit]

10/21/1965
BERT H. FREEMAN

Last rites for Bert Harold Freeman were held last Saturday afternoon at First Baptist Church. He was a native of Pickens County, SC and had lived in Brevard since 1926. He was in law enforcement in South Carolina before coming to Brevard. He served as Chief of Police, Transylvania County Sheriff (1943 to 1954) and District Superintendent with NC State Prison Department. He served as mayor of Brevard from 1957 to 1961 and was a veteran of World War I.

Burial was in Woodlawn Cemetery, Greenville SC and military graveside rites were con-

ducted by legionnaires of the Monroe Wilson post of the American Legion.

Mr. Freeman died last Friday at his home on West French Broad Street unexpectedly, after an apparent heart attack. Surviving are the widow, Mrs. Melonee Looper Freeman; a daughter, Mrs. Juanita Freeman Cox; four sisters: Eula McJunkin, Iola, Sallie Looper and Mrs. Willie Bloodworth; and two brothers, Oscar and Waco Freeman

Bert Freeman
Transylvania Sheriff's Archives

In August 1917 the first 200 men called for the draft under went a physical examination in Brevard to determine their physical fitness to serve as soldiers. The physical exams were administered by local physicians but adhered to the standards mandated by the United States Military.

No record has been located to indicate that the physical examinations ever took place locally after the initial draft call. From that date the men were officially inducted into the Army and rode the train to the assigned military base where they underwent their first official physical examination.

The Service Record Cards and Discharge Records indicate in some cases, that some individuals were found physically unfit for military service and discharged with as few as five days military duty.

Because these individuals had been officially sworn into the military service they automatically became eligible for all military benefits granted to soldiers that served in the military. This included medical benefits, pension benefits and a military headstone.

John Mannon GAINES

Born:	11 May 1898, Arkansas
Died:	19 Aug 1973, Transylvania County, NC; age 75
Buried:	Pisgah Gardens Cemetery
Occupation:	Branch Manager for Duke Power
Spouse:	**Kathleen BELCHER**
Father:	**John S. GAINES**
Mother:	**Florence COOK**
Draft Registration:	No
Service Record Card:	No
Military Marker:	Arkansas CPL US Army WW I

[Documentation: Military Marker, Transylvania County DC, Transylvania County Cemetery Survey, 1900-1940 Censuses, Greenville County SC Marriage Records, WW 2 Draft Card, TT obituary]

8/23/1973
JOHN MANNON GAINES

Graveside rites for John Mannon "Jim" Gaines, 73, were held Tuesday afternoon in Pisgah Gardens. Mr. Gaines was a prominent executive with Duke Power Company, serving as manager of the Brevard branch for most of the 35 years that he was with Duke. Before joining Duke Power Company he was with Westinghouse Electric and Manufacturing and Florida Power Company.

Mr. Gaines was a native of Texarkana, Arkansas and a graduate of the Institute of Technology.

He was a veteran of World War I, serving overseas and participated in five major engagements. He was a member of the First United Methodist Church of Brevard and served two terms as President of the Brevard Chamber of Commerce.

Mr. Gaines is survived by his wife, Kathleen Belcher Gaines; by three daughters: Mrs. Robert L. Honeycutt, Mrs. J. R. Mitchell and Mrs. Elon Abernathy; and one sister, Mrs. Russell Reeves.

food
1 - buy it with thought
2 - cook it with care
3 - use less wheat & meat
4 - buy local foods
5 - serve just enough
6 - use what is left

don't waste it

U.S Government
Food Administration

145

Arthur Carson GALLOWAY

Born:	14 Jun 1893, Transylvania County, NC
Died:	17 Apr 1969, Johnson City, Tennessee; age 75
Buried:	Mountain Home National Cemetery, Johnson City, TN
Spouse:	**Hattie**
Father:	**James M. GALLOWAY**
Mother:	**Martha Jane AIKEN**
Draft Registration:	No
Note:	Death Certificate stated he was divorced at time of death

[Documentation: US Veterans Gravesites.com, 1900 & 1920 Censuses, SSDI, Ancestry.com]

Galloway, Arthur C. 56,655 *White *Colored
(Surname) (Christian name) (Army serial number)

Residence: Rosman NORTH CAROLINA
(Street and house number) (Town or city) (County) (State)

*Enlisted *R. A. *N. G. *E. R. C. *Inducted at Ft. Thomas Ky on Mch 30 19 17
Place of birth: Transylvania Co N C Age or date of birth: 23 9/12 years
Organizations served in, with dates of assignment and transfers:
Co A 28 Inf to July 12/19; Co K 62 Inf to Furlough
to Reserve
Grades, with date of appointment:
Pvt, Pvt 1cl

Engagements:

Wounded in action (degree and date) slightly July 18 July 19 19 18
Served overseas from †June 14/17 to †Apr. 19/19, from † to †
*Honorably discharged Furloughed to Reserve Mch 31/2019
In view of occupation he was, on date of discharge, reported 0 per cent disabled.
Remarks:

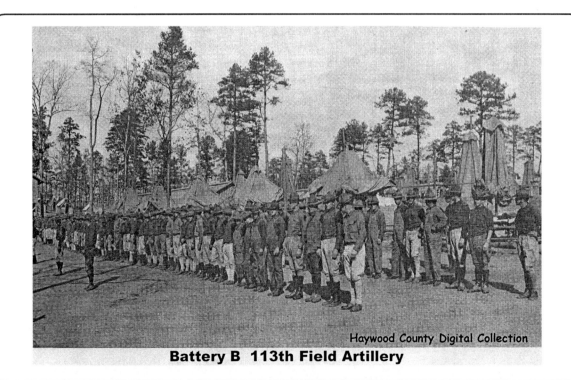

Haywood County Digital Collection

Battery B 113th Field Artillery

Carl Fred GALLOWAY

Born:	3 Feb 1893, Transylvania County, NC
Died:	4 Oct 1962, Transylvania County, NC; age 69
Buried:	Galloway Cemetery in East Fork
Occupation:	Carpenter
Spouse(s):	**Etta McCALL**, m. 17 Sep 1911, Transylvania County, NC
	Ola WHITMIRE
Father:	**James GALLOWAY**
Mother:	**Sarah AIKEN**
Draft Registration:	24, married with 1 child, farming
Note:	Grave marker has NO military information
Discharge:	Inducted 3 July 1918 at Brevard. Served in 27th Co., 7th BN 30 July 1918 through 12 July 1919

[Documentation: Transylvania County DC, <u>Cowart's Index to Marriages</u>, Discharge, 1930 Census, Ancestry.com, <u>Transylvania County Cemetery Survey</u>]

Galloway Carl		2,758,454	• White • Colored	1
(Surname)	(Christian name)	(Army serial number)		

Residence: _____ **Selica Transylvania NORTH CAROLINA**
 (Street and house number)   (Town or city)   (County)   (State)

_____ *Inducted at **Brevard N C** on **July 30, 18**

Place of birth: **Brevard N C** Age or date of birth: **Feb 8/91**

Organizations served in, with dates of assignments and transfers: **341 G & F Co to disch**

Grades, with date of appointment: **Prt 1cl Nov 19/18**

Engagements: _____

Wounds or other injuries received in action: None.
Served overseas from † **No** to † _____ from † _____ to † _____
Honorably discharged on demobilization **July 12/19** , 19___
In view of occupation he was, on date of discharge, reported **0** per cent disabled.
Remarks: _____

SCR Notes: G&F (Guard and Fire Company)

10/11/1962
CARL GALLOWAY

Last rites for Carl F. Galloway, 69, of Brevard were held Saturday afternoon at the King Street Baptist Church. Burial was in Galloway Memorial Park. Mr. Galloway died Thursday at his home.

A carpenter by trade, he was a life long resident of Brevard and was a member of the Zion Baptist Church of Rosman.

Survivors include the widow, Mrs. Ola Whitmire Galloway; six daughters: Mrs. Alma Bruner, Mrs. Effie Fisher, Mrs. Essie Whitmire, Mrs. Estell Brotherton, Mrs. Gertrude McCall and Mrs. Frankie McElrath; three sons: Freeman, Clifton and Garfield; three brothers: Jesse A., Grady and Welch Galloway

---

NATIONAL ARMY CANTONMENT (CAMP)

Fort Meade Location: Annapolis Junction, Md. Organization: 79th Division
Troops from Southern Pennsylvania

Charles Zackary GALLOWAY

Born:	18 Dec 1888, Transylvania County, NC
Died:	14 Jul 1942, Richland County, SC; age 53
Buried:	Graceland Cemetery, Greenville County, SC
Spouse:	**Rose TENCH**
Father:	**Marcus GALLOWAY**
Mother:	**Nancy McCALL**
Draft Registration:	No

[Documentation: South Carolina Death Record, 1900 & 1910 Censuses, US Headstone Application, Findagrave.com, Ancestry.com]

Galloway Charles		1,896,514	white	2 1/
(Surname)	(Christian name)	(Army serial number)	(Race: White or colored)	

Residence: _____ Quebec *Transylvania* NORTH CAROLINA
(Street and house number) (Town or city) (County) (State)

Enlisted in RA Charlotte N C___ Nov 29/12 —
Born in Quebec N C — 23 11/12 yrs
Organizations: Hq Tr 11 Cav to Aug 12/17; Tr A 11 Cav to Sept 8/17; Co C 320 MG Bn to disch

Grades: Corp Oct 7/17; Stable Sgt Oct 15/17; Sgt July 6/18 Stable Sgt July 19/18;

Engagements: — —

Wounds or other injuries received in action: None. —
Served overseas: Apr 25/18 to May 6/19 —
Hon. disch. Nov 28/19 ETS —
Was reported 0 per cent disabled on date of discharge, in view of occupation.
Remarks: — —

SRC Notes: HQ Tr (Headquarters Troop) CAV (Cavalry) MG (Machine Gun)

Greenville News (SC)
7/15/1942
CHARLES Z. GALLOWAY

Charles Zackary Galloway passed way yesterday in Richland County, SC after a short illness. He was born in Transylvania County, NC December 18, 1888, a son of the late Marcus and Elizabeth McCall Galloway. He had lived in Greenville a number of years and was connected with the Hupmobile agency as a mechanic. During the First World War he saw service and spent 18 months overseas.

Mr. Galloway is survived by his wife, Rose Tench Galloway; four children: John, Bruce, Betty Joe and Bessie Lou Galloway; one brother Chester A. Galloway; and two sisters, Flora McCall and Bessie Meece.

---

22 Aug 1918   Brevard News

U.D.C. ENTERTAINS MEN FROM CAMP

On Saturday evening the Transylvania Chapter United Daughters of the Confederacy entertained at the library in honor of the non-commissioned offers stationed at Pisgah Forest.

The building was decorated throughout with clematis, goldenrod and other wild flowers. There with the numerous softly colored lights, made a pleasing setting for the scene. Numbers of guest filled the building and grounds. Over two hundred people were present during the evening.

Miss Annie Jean Gash, president of U.D.C., presided as hostess for the occasion. She was assisted by Miss Martha Boswell, Miss, Kathleen Erwin and a number of other young ladies of the town.

Frank Curva GALLOWAY

Born:	1 May 1898, Transylvania County, NC
Died:	30 Nov 1934, Greenville, South Carolina; age 36
Buried:	Springwood Cemetery, Greenville County, SC
Married:	**Ina WELLS**
Father:	**James GALLOWAY**
Mother:	**Sarah AIKEN**
Draft Registration:	No

Documentation: South Carolina Death Record, findagrave.com, US Headstone Application, Ancestry.com]

Galloway, Frank C	1,322,749	White	
(Surname) (Christian name)	(Army serial number)	(Race: White or colored)	

Residence:	Rosman		NORTH CAROLINA
(Street and house number)	(Town or city)	(County)	(State)

* Enlisted in   **NG Rosman NC**   —   July 10/17   —
† Born in   **Transylvania Co NC**   19 2/12 yrs   —
Organizations: **Co 6 NC Cav (Co A 115 MG Bn to Disch)**   —

Grades: **Pvt**   —   —

Engagements: **xx**   —   —

Wounds or other injuries received in action: None.   —
‡ Served overseas: **May 11/18 to Apr 18/19**   —
§ Hon. disch.   **Apr 24/19**   on demobilization   —
Was reported   **0**   per cent disabled on date of discharge, in view of occupation.
Remarks: —

SRC Notes: NC CAV (North Carolina Cavalry) MG Bn (Machine Gun Battalion)

Greenville News (SC)
12/1/1934
FRANK C. GALLOWAY

Funeral services for Frank Curva Galloway will be held today at the Trinity Lutheran Church and the interment will be made in Springwood Cemetery. The Veterans of Foreign Wars and local Legionnaires will form the honorary escort.

The death of Mr. Galloway occurred early Friday morning at a local hospital. He had only been ill for the past three weeks. Mr. Galloway was a native of Rosman, NC, and had been in Greenville since 1919. He was a World War I veteran, having served with the Thirtieth Division, with thirteen months service overseas. Since he had been in Greenville he had engaged I the dental mechanic business.

Mrs. Ina Wells Galloway, his wife, survives him, with one son, Frank Curva Galloway, Jr. He is also survived by his mother, Mrs. James Galloway and five brothers: Grady, Welch, Carl J.C. and Jesse.

NATIONAL ARMY CANTONMENT (CAMP)

Camp Gordon   Location: Atlanta, Ga   Organization: 82nd Division
Troops from Georgia and Alabama

James Erwin GALLOWAY

Born:	9 Nov 1892, Transylvania County, NC
Died:	29 Aug 1978, Transylvania County, NC; age 85
Buried:	Gillespie-Evergreen Cemetery
Spouse:	**Annie SMITH**
Father:	**Early GALLOWAY**
Mother:	**Mary Jane SIZEMORE**
Draft Registration:	24, single, carpenter for Toxaway Tanning Company
Military marker:	PVT US Army WW I

[Documentation: Transylvania County DC, Transylvania County Cemetery Survey, Cowart's Index of Marriages, Discharge, Ancestry.com]

Galloway, J(ames)Erwin 3,034,121 • White • Colored:
(Surname) (Christian name) (Army serial number)

Residence: Brevard Transylvania NORTH CAROLINA
(Street and house number) (Town or city) (County) (State)

*Inducted at Brevard N C on July 15, 19 18

Place of birth: Brevard N C Age or date of birth: Nov 9/1892

Organizations served in, with dates of assignments and transfers:
CAC Unasgd to Sept 20/18; ' Co CAC Charleston S C
to Sept 25/18; Btry A 26 Arty CAC to Sept 27/18;

Grades, with date of appointment:
Pvt

Remarks (continued):

Btry C 6th Trench M Bn to disch

Wounds or other injuries received in action: None.
Served overseas from †Nov 2/18 to †Jan 8/19, from †_____ to †_____
Honorably discharged on demobilization Jan 19/19, 19____
In view of occupation he was, on date of discharge, reported 0 per cent disabled.
Remarks:

SRC Notes: CAC (Coast Artillery Corps)

Sandra L. Reid Photo

21 Jun 1918   Brevard News
WHITE REGISTRANTS WHO ARE TO LEAVE FOR CAMP JACKSON, S.C.
TUESDAY, JUNE 25th, 1918 AT 3:13 P.M.
. . . James Erwin Galloway, Brevard . . .

Asheville Citizen Times
8/30/1978
JAMES ERWIN GALLOWAY

James Erwin Galloway, 85 died Tuesday at his home in Brevard. A lifelong resident of Transylvania County, he was a son of the late Pick and Janie Sizemore Galloway. He was associated with Colwell and Galloway Construction Company. An Army veteran of World War I, Galloway was a member of the American Legion Post and VFW Post of Brevard.

He was a member of Glady Branch Baptist Church and Woodmen of the World Balsam Camp. Graveside services were held at Gillespie-Evergreen Cemetery. The Rev. Tommy Owen and members of the American Legion and VFW posts of Brevard officiated.

Surviving are his wife, Annie Smith Galloway; two daughters, Mrs. Albert Williams and Mrs. Robert Eason; two sons, James P. and Bud Galloway; two sisters, Emma Rheinhart and Mrs. Tom McKinney and two brothers, Ralph Galloway and Troy Galloway.

Jesse Monroe GALLOWAY

Born:	18 May 1895, Transylvania County, NC
Died:	5 Sep 1968, Transylvania County, NC; age 73
Buried:	Oak Grove Cemetery, Brevard
Spouse:	**Josie PRESSLEY**, m. 13 Dec 1919, Transylvania County
Father:	**Tom GALLOWAY**
Mother:	**Ella BARTON**
Draft Registration:	22, single employed by E.L. Gaston
Grave marker:	PVT US Army WW I

[Documentation: Transylvania County DC, Transylvania County Cemetery Survey, Cowart's Index to Marriages, Ancestry.com, TT obituary]

```
                                                                          1
       Galloway        Jesse M        2,587,021   • White • Colored.
        (Surname)         (Christian name)   (Army serial number)
Residence: _____ Selica _____ NORTH CAROLINA
               (Street and house number)   (Town or city)   (County)   (State)
ENLISTED N.G.- R.C. *Inducted at Transylvania NC      on July 6  19 18
Place of birth: Transylvania NC        Age or date of birth: 23 yrs
Organizations served in, with dates of assignments and transfers: Med Dept Cp Greenleaf
     Chicamaugo Pk 7/25/18; Ft Monroe Va 12/16/18; New Cumberland
     Pa to Disch
Grades, with date of appointment: Pvt.
_____
_____
Engagements: XX
_____
_____
Wounds or other injuries received in action: None.
Served overseas from †____None____ to †_____, from †_____ to †_____
Honorably discharged on demobilization   Jan 24            , 19 19
In view of occupation he was, on date of discharge, reported _____0_____ per cent disabled.
Remarks: _____
```

SRC Notes: FA (Field Artillery)

11 Jul 1918   Brevard News

Twelve Transylvania boys left on last Saturday for Fort Oglethorpe, Ga., to begin their careers as defenders of democracy. The boys left on the afternoon train . . .
. . . Jess M. Galloway, Selica . . .

2 Feb 1919   Brevard News

Pvt. Jesse Galloway returned home Sunday noon from Fort Oglethorpe where he has been stationed in camp for several months.

9/16/1968
JESS M. GALLOWAY

Jess M. Galloway, 73, died in the Transylvania Community Hospital last Thursday after a lengthy illness. Mr. Galloway was a native of Transylvania County and a retired employee of the Moland-Drysdale Corporation of Etowah.

Survivors include his widow, Mrs. Josie Galloway; one daughter, Elsie O'Shields and one son, Roy Galloway; two brothers, Frank and Wayman Galloway; and one sister, Mrs. Nancy White.

Funeral services were conducted last Saturday in the Temple Baptist Church. Burial was in the Oak Grove Cemetery.

Lee Grady GALLOWAY

Born:	15 Nov 1889, Transylvania County, NC
Died:	21 Feb 1963, Johnson City, Tennessee; age 73
Buried:	Mountain Home National Cemetery, Johnson City, TN
Father:	**James GALLOWAY**
Mother:	**Sarah AIKEN**
Draft Registration:	27, single, worked at Rosman Tanning Extract Co.

[Documentation: Transylvania County Birth Index, Transylvania County DC, Application for Veteran Headstone, Veterans Gravesite, 1900-1940 Censuses, TT obituary, Ancestry.com]

The Purple Heart is a United States Military decoration awarded in the name of the President to those who have been wounded or killed while serving on or after April 5, 1917. Lee Galloway was severely wounded 15 Sept 1918 while serving overseas.

2/28/1963

Grady Galloway

Last rites for Lee Grady Galloway, a native of Transylvania County, were held Monday at the Veterans Cemetery at Mountain Home, Tennessee. Mr. Galloway died last Thursday in the Government hospital at Mountain Home after a lengthy illness.

He is survived by two brothers, A.N. and Welch Galloway.

He was a veteran of World War I and he was awarded the Purple Heart during the first conflict. Several years ago he was employed at the Rosman Tanning and Extract Plant at Rosman.

Sylvester Merrimon GALLOWAY

Born:	16 Aug 1896, Transylvania County, NC
Died:	17 Jul 1962, Oteen VA Hospital, Buncombe County; age 65
Buried:	Galloway Cemetery in East Fork
Spouse:	**Mamie HENSLEY**, m. 4 Jun 1918, Transylvania County
Father:	**Thomas GALLOWAY**
Mother:	**Selena Jane WHITMIRE**
Draft Registration:	21, married and worked at Gloucester Lumber Company
Note:	Death Certificate stated he was divorced

[Documentation: Buncombe County DC, Transylvania County Cemetery Survey, Cowart's Index of Marriages, Discharge, Ancestry.com]

Galloway, Sylvester M. 4,480,509 • White • Colored

Residence: P O Box 108 Rosman Transylvania NORTH CAROLINA
(Street and house number) (Town or city) (County) (State)

*Inducted at Brevard N C on Aug 28, 19 18

Place of birth: Rosman N C Age or date of birth: Aug 16/1896

Organizations served in, with dates of assignments and transfers:
Btry C 1st Regt F A Repl Regt to Nov 6/18, 4 Btry
Camp Jackson S C Nov Repl Draft to Nov 23/18,

Grades, with date of appointment:
Pvt

Remarks (continued):

Btry C 1st Regt F A Repl Depot to disch

Wounds or other injuries received in action: None.
Served overseas from † No to †_____, from †_____ to †_____
Honorably discharged on demobilization Dec 14/18, 19_____
In view of occupation he was, on date of discharge, reported 0 per cent disabled.
Remarks:

SRC Notes: FA (Field Artillery)

26 Aug 1918   Brevard News
TWELVE MORE MEN LEFT MONDAY for Camp Jackson
. . . Sylvester M. Galloway, Brevard . . .

Y.M.C,A. Amusement Tent

Thomas Coleman GALLOWAY

Born:	12 Aug 1889, Jackson County, NC
Died:	23 Sep 1958, Transylvania County, NC; age 69
Buried:	Gillespie-Evergreen Cemetery
Spouse;	**Stella YOUNG**
Father:	**James A. GALLOWAY**
Mother:	**Martha BROWN**
Draft Registration:	29, single, attorney

[Documentation: Transylvania County DC, Transylvania County Cemetery Survey, 1900-1940 Censuses, Discharge, Ancestry.com, TT obituary]

Galloway, Thomas C. 4,774,766 • White • Colored.
(Surname) (Christian name) (Army serial number)

Residence: Whitmore St Brevard Transylvania NORTH CAROLINA
(Street and house number) (Town or city) (County) (State)

C. *Inducted at Transylvania Co N C on Sept 7, 1918
Place of birth: Jackson Co N C Age or date of birth: Aug 12/1889

Organizations served in, with dates of assignments and transfers:
Rct Camp #4 Ca p Greene N C to disch

Grades, with date of appointment:
Pvt

Engagements:

Wounds or other injuries received in action: None.
Served overseas from † NO to † , from † to †
Honorably discharged on demobilization Dec 13/18 , 19
In view of occupation he was, on date of discharge, reported O per cent disabled.
Remarks:

T. Coleman Galloway
Transylvania Times Photo

SRC Notes: Rct Camp (Recruit Camp)   *T.C. Galloway was Postmaster in Brevard from 1933-1955*

14 Nov. 1918   Brevard News

T. Coleman Galloway, who is stationed with the local exemption board at High Point, has been at home on a few days leave. He is happy to be home, and his friends are happy to greet him.

9/25/1958
T.C. GALLOWAY

Last rites for T. Coleman Galloway, 71, former postmaster and well-known Brevard attorney and political figure, will be held Thursday morning at the First Baptist Church. Burial will follow in the Gillespie-Evergreen Cemetery. He was a member of the First Baptist Church and was also a veteran of World War I.

Mr. Galloway died Tuesday afternoon at his home here, following an illness, which had kept him confined for the past two months. Mr. Galloway served as postmaster of Brevard from July 1, 1933 to January 1, 1956. Prior to that time he was engaged in the general practice of

law from 1916 until 1933, and following his retirement from the post office, he again opened his law office.

Survivors include the widow, Stella Young Galloway; two daughters, Mrs. Spencer Macfie and Mrs. Herbert Allen; and one son Thomas Y. Galloway.

A native of Jackson County, he came to Transylvania in his early teens, and he was educated in the public schools here and at Brevard Institute. In 1916 he received his law degree from Wake Forest College.

Frank Mitchell GARREN

Born:	22 Mar 1893, Transylvania County, NC
Died:	21 Jul 1952, Transylvania County, NC; age 59
Buried:	Gillespie-Evergreen Cemetery
Spouse(s):	**Altha Jean HOLDEN, Myrtle BROWN**
Father:	**Robert A. GARREN**
Mother:	**Amy GARREN**
Draft Registration:	24, single, sawmilling for W.M. Sitton
Military Marker:	NC Cook 113 Field ARTY 30 Div WW I

[Documentation: Transylvania County DC, <u>Transylvania County Cemetery Survey</u>, Application for Veteran Headstone, Discharge, 1910-1940 Censuses, Ancestry.com, TT obituary]

```
                Garren, Frank M           1,324,442          White        1ℎ
        (Surname)      (Christian name)       (Army serial number) (Race: White or colored)

Residence:_____ Brevard  Transylvania   NORTH CAROLIN
        (Street and house number)      (Town or city)     (County)       (State)

Enlisted in   NG Brevard NC        _       July 7/17;           _
Born in       Brevard NC           _       24 4/12 yrs.         _
Organizations: Btry F 1 FA NC NG (Btry F 113 FA) to disch.      _

Grades:       Pvt 1cl Oct 1/17; Ck Dec 16/18;

Engagements:               _                        _

Wounds or other injuries received in action: None.
Served overseas: May 26/18 t-Mch 19/19              _
Hon. disch.   Mch 28/19       on demobilization     _
Was reported  0       per cent disabled on date of discharge, in view of occupation.
Remarks:                   _                        _
```

SRC Notes: FA NC NG (Field Artillery North Carolina National Guard)

4 Apr 1919   Brevard News
Frank Garren and Elmer Gillespie have received honorable discharges from the Army and are at home here. They served in France as members of the famous 30th Division.

18 Apr 1919   Brevard News
Frank Garren, who has just returned from overseas, visited his sister, Mrs. H. Garren, last week.

7/24/1952
FRANK GARREN

Funeral services for Frank Garren, 59, who died at his home Monday morning after a heart attack, were held Wednesday morning at the home on Country Club Road. Burial followed in the Gillespie Cemetery. He was a veteran of World War I.

For several years Mr. Garren drove a taxi in Brevard and he was also engaged in the floor sanding business for some time.

Survivors include the wife; two sons, Frank and Wayne; two daughters, Mrs. Mike Colvin and Sandra; one brother, Tom; two sisters, Mrs. H. Garren and Mrs. T.W. Tinsley; six stepchildren: Paul Meece, Mrs. Carl Magolia, Charles Lee Meece, Billy Meece, Mary Meece and David Meece.

Henry Edgar GARREN, Sr.

Born:	5 Aug 1892, Transylvania County, NC
Died:	7 Oct 1968, Transylvania County, NC; age 76
Buried:	Gillespie-Evergreen Cemetery
Spouse:	**Eva E. GALLOWAY**, m. 15 Aug 1917, Transylvania County, NC
Father:	**John GARREN**
Mother:	**Nancy WILSON**
Draft Registration:	23, single, driver and mechanic for Brevard Transfer Co.

[Documentation: Transylvania County DC, <u>Transylvania County Cemetery Survey</u>, Discharge, Ancestry.com, TT obituary]

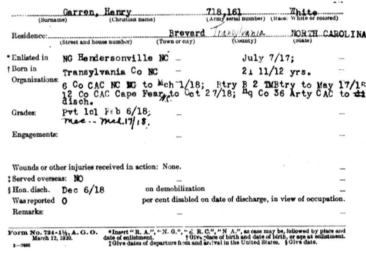

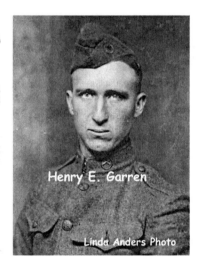

Henry E. Garren

Linda Anders Photo

SRC Notes: TM Btry (Trench Mortar Battery)

26 Apr 1918   Brevard News

Henry Garren, one of our boys from Fort Caswell, was in Brevard on a furlough for several days recently.

10/10/1968

HENRY E. GARREN, SR.

Henry Edgar Garren, Sr. 76, of Jordon Road, died at his home early Monday after a short illness. He was a life-long resident of Transylvania County and before retirement was connected with the Silversteen Industries and Carr Lumber Company. He was a veteran of World War I and served with the 9th Company, Headquarters Artillery.

Surviving are the following: one daughter, Eva Elizabeth Garren; five sons: Henry E., Jr., John R., Carl E., Marc, and Craig; and one sister, Mrs. Ida Tinsley.

Funeral services were held Wednesday at the First Baptist Church and burial followed in Gillespie-Evergreen Cemetery.

Fort Caswell was located on Oak Island, Brunswick County, NC. The fort was closed after the Civil War but in 1896 it was rebuilt and became one of the most important military posts on the East Coast. The fort was used as an Army Training camp during the World War I. After the War, Fort Caswell was abandoned. World War II brought the Fort back on line as an Army base and submarine lookout. In 1946, the federal government designated Fort Caswell as war surplus and it was assigned for disposal. In 1949 the Baptist State Convention purchased the property for $86,000.

James William GARREN

Born:	4 Mar 1896, Transylvania County, NC
Died:	31 Mar 1958, Greensburg, Kansas; age 62
Buried:	Cathey's Creek Baptist Church Cemetery
Spouse(s):	**Annie COPE**, m. 14 Feb 1920, Transylvania County, NC
	Elizabeth WARREN, m. 6 May 1934, Transylvania County, NC
Father:	**Thomas Leander GARREN**
Mother:	**Sarah WILSON**
Draft Registration:	21, single, farming for J.M. Bryson
Military Marker:	NC PVT TRENCH MORTAR BN WW I

[Documentation: Transylvania County Birth Index, Cowart's Index to Marriages, Transylvania County Cemetery Survey, Discharge, Ancestry.com, TT obituary]

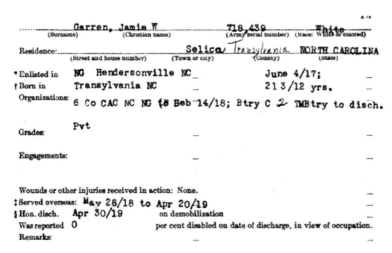

<u>9 May 1919</u>   **Brevard News**

Cpt. James Garren has arrived at home from overseas. We all are glad to see him back once more in the good old U.S.A

4/10/1958
James Garren

Funeral services for James W. Garren, 62, were conducted Friday afternoon, April 4th at the Cathey's Creek Baptist Church. Burial followed in the church cemetery.

A native of Transylvania County, Mr. Garren died suddenly on March 31st at his home near Greensburg, Kansas.

He was a member of the Cathey's Creek Church and also the American Legion.

Surviving are the widow, Mrs. Nella Garren; a son, Frank; a daughter, Mrs. Lucille Jones; the father, Tom Garren; three brothers: Robert, Luther and Walter; two sisters, Mrs. Clate Osteen and Mrs. Willine Pegues.

James was in the TMB (Trench Mortar Battalion). A mortar is a short, stumpy tube designed to fire a projectile at a steep angle so that it falls straight down on its target. One advantage of the mortar was that it could be fired from the safety of the trench, avoiding exposure of the soldiers to the enemy. And, with a lot of good luck, the mortar bomb would fall almost straight down and land in the enemy trench. They were undeniably effective in terms of trench warfare.

Thomas S. GASH

Born:	10 Feb 1894, Transylvania County, NC
Died:	15 May 1931, Transylvania County, NC; age 37
Buried:	Undetermined
Occupation:	Laborer at the foundry
Race:	Colored
Spouse:	**Ossie MOONEY**
Father:	**Millard F. GASH**
Mother:	**Harriett HEMPHILL**
Draft	Registration: No
Note:	Thomas' parents are buried at the New French Broad Cemetery

[Documentation: Transylvania County DC, Ancestry.com]

Gash, Thomas S. 3,545,090 *White *Colored.
(Surname) (Christian name) (Army serial number)

Residence: _____ Pisgah Forest _____ NORTH CAROLINA
(Street and house number) (Town or city) (County) (State)

* ▓▓▓▓▓▓▓ *Inducted at #20 Philadelphia Pa on Aug 15, 1918
Place of birth: _____ Pisgah Forest NC _____ Age or date of birth: _ Jan 24/94 _
Organizations served in, with dates of assignments and transfers: _____
_____ Co M 813 Pion Inf to July 15/19; Co D 323 Service Bn _____
_____ QMC to disch _____
Grades, with date of appointment: _____

Engagements: _____

Wounds or other injuries received in action: None.
Served overseas from Sept 15/18 to July 13/19, from † _____ to † _____
Honorably discharged on demobilization _____ July 21/19 _____, 19 _____
In view of occupation he was, on date of discharge, reported _____ 0 _____ per cent disabled.

SCR Notes: Pion Inf (Pioneer Infantry)

158

Albert GASTON

Born:	25 Mar 1887, Transylvania County, NC
Died:	July 1965, Virginia; age 77
Buried:	Undetermined
Race:	Colored
Spouse(s):	**Adell POWELL**, m. 7 Aug 1912, Transylvania County, NC
	Effie DARITY, m. 7 May 1921, Transylvania County, NC
Father:	**Alex GASTON**
Mother:	**Mary GASTON**
Draft Registration:	30, married, farming for J.K. Barclay

[Documentation: FamilySearch.org, Cowart's Index to Marriages, National Homes for Disabled Volunteer Soldiers, Ancestry.com]

Gaston   Albert   3,098,534   * ~~White~~ * Colored.
(Surname)   (Christian name)   (Army serial number)

Residence: _____ Brevard Transylvania NORTH CAROLINA
(Street and house number)   (Town or city)   (County)   (State)

_____ *Inducted at Transylvania Co. NC on June 21 19 18

Place of birth: ____ Brevard NC ____ Age or date of birth: ____ 31 4/12 yrs.

Organizations served in, with dates of assignments and transfers: Co D 801 Pion Inf to disch

Grades, with date of appointment: Pvt 1cl Nov 6/18

Engagements: _____

Wounds or other injuries received in action: None.
Served overseas from † Sept 8/18 † June 5/19, from † _____ to † _____
Honorably discharged on demobilization _____ June 13, 1919
In view of occupation he was, on date of discharge, reported ____ 0 ____ per cent disabled.
Remarks: _____

---

21 Jun 1918   Brevard News
**COLORED REGISTRANTS TO LEAVE FOR CAMP TAYLOR, KY
ON FRIDAY, JUNE 21, 1918.**
. . . Albert Gaston, Brevard . . .

Albert Gaston /.   (Colored)   0.00   37-2?   Va 3394

MILITARY HISTORY

Time and Place of Each Enlistment	Rank	Company and Regiment	Time and Place of Discharge	Cause of Discharge	Disabilities when Admitted to the Home
June 21, 1918 Brevard, NC	Pvt 1cl	801st Pioneer Infty	June 13, 1919 Camp Lee Va.	Demobilized	Arthritis mod. severe Rt ankle. Traumatic, claims injury to ankle in France, observation for tertiary syphilis

DOMESTIC HISTORY

Where Born	Age	Height	Complexion	Color of Eyes	Color of Hair	Read and Write	Religion	Occupation	Residence Subsequent to Discharge	Married or Single	Name and Address of Nearest Relative
Brevard. NC	47		Colored	Brown	Black	yes	Prot.		Brevard. NC	married	Effie Gaston (wife) Brevard. NC

HOME HISTORY

Rate of Pension	Date of Admission Re-Admission and Transfer	Conditions of Re-Admission	Date of Discharge and Transfer	Cause of Discharge	Date of Death	Cause of Death
	Adm. Va Home Va Aug 30. 1933.					

Page from Ledger of

National Homes for Disabled
Volunteer Soldiers 1866-1938

Hampton, Virginia

Claud Elmer GILLESPIE

Born:	17 Sep 1895, Transylvania County, NC
Died:	16 Jul 1951, VA Hospital, Buncombe County; age 55
Buried:	East Fork Methodist Cemetery
Occupation:	Salesman
Spouse(s):	**Victoria GILLESPIE**, m. 26 May 1919, Transylvania County, NC
	Norma E. BRITTAIN
Father:	**Joseph GILLESPIE**
Mother:	**Margaret CRANSHAW**
Draft Registration:	21, single
Military Marker:	NC PFC 113 Field Arty 30 Div WW I

[Documentation: Buncombe County DC, Transylvania County Cemetery Survey, Cowart's Index to Marriages, Application for Veteran Headstone, Discharge, Ancestry.com, TT obituary]

Claude Elmer Gillespie
Victoria Trent Photo

Gillespie	Claud	E	1,324,443	White
(Surname)	(Christian name)	(Army serial number)	(Race: White or colored)	

Residence: Brevard *Transylvania* NORTH CAROLINA
(Street and house number) (Town or city) (County) (State)

Enlisted in N G Brevard N C July 7/17

Born in Transylvania Co N C 21 10/12yrs

Organization: Btry F 1 F A N C N G (Btry F 113 F A) to disch

Grades: Pvt 1/cl Oct 1/17 Pvt May 10/18

Engagements: --

Wounds or other injuries received in action: None.

Served overseas: May 26/18 to Mch 19/19

Hon. disch. Mch 28/19 on demobilization

Was reported 0 per cent disabled on date of discharge, in view of occupation.

Remarks:

SRC Notes: FA NC NG (Field Artillery North Carolina National Guard)

---

21 Mar 1919   **Brevard News**

J.A. Gillespie has gone to Columbia, SC to visit his son, Elmer who is expected to arrive from France about the 17th of this month.

4 Apr 1919   **Brevard News**

Frank Garren and Elmer Gillespie have received honorable discharges from the Army and are at home here. They served in France as members of the famous 30th Division.

2/19/1951
CLAUDE E. GILLESPIE

A military funeral was held for Claude Elmer Gillespie, 54, at the Rosman Methodist Church on Wednesday afternoon. Burial followed in the East Fork Cemetery. Mr. Gillespie died Monday at Moore General Hospital where he was taken on Sunday following a stroke. He had been failing in health for several years.

Mr. Gillespie was a native of Transylvania County. He had been a farmer and clothing salesman during his lifetime. He was a veteran of World War I and served overseas.

Survivors include his widow; ten children: John, Joseph, Mrs. Paul McCarthy, Mrs. Lloyd Trent, Mrs. Ransler King; by a former marriage C.E., Alvin, Mildred, Zandra and Edith; and two brothers, Leon and Ernest Gillespie.

Branch Loranzo GLAZENER

Born:	23 Jun 1895, Transylvania County
Died:	2 Mar 1918, somewhere in France, age 22
Buried:	Glazener Cemetery
Father:	**Benjamin GLAZENER**
Mother:	**Martha E. KUYKENDALL**
Draft Registration:	21, single, worked at Gloucester Lumber Co.

[Documentation: Transylvania County Cemetery Survey, Application for Veteran Headstone, Ancestry.com, Soldiers of the Great War Vol 2, NC, page 404]

Glazener, Branch L.   294,780   • White ~~Colored~~.
(Surname)   (Christian name)   (Army serial number)

NORTH CAROLINA

Residence: _____ Brevard   Transylvania   CAROLINA
          (Street and house number)   (Town or city)   (County)   (State)

~~Enlisted in N. C. E. R. C.~~ Inducted at Brevard N C   on Nov 5, 1917

Place of birth: Transylvania Co. N C.   Age or date of birth: 22 1/3 Yrs

Organizations served in, with dates of assignments and transfers: Co E 324 Inf Nov 5/17
to Feb 5/18; Co E 8 Bn 20 Engrs to Mch 24/18.

Grades, with date of appointment: _____
          Pvt

Engagements: _____

Wounds or other injuries received in action: * None.

Served overseas from † Feb 26/18 to † Mch 24/18 from † _____ to † _____

Died of _____ pneumonia _____ March 24, 1918
          (Cause of death)   (date of death)

Person notified of death: Benjamin Glazener   Father
          (Name)   (Degree of relationship)

          Brevard   N.C.
(No. and street or rural route)   (City, town, or post office)   (State or country)

Remarks: _____

2 Nov 1917   Brevard News
LOCAL BOARD ORDERS THIRTEEN MORE MEN
   All men whose names appear here are ordered to report to the Local Board at 5 P.M. on Monday, November 5, 1917 for transportation for Camp Jackson. They will leave for Camp November 6 at 8 A.M.
. . . Branch L. Glazener . . .

5 Apr 1918   Brevard News
DIED IN FRANCE
Brance Lorenzo Glazener, son of B.J.Glazener, Brevard, NC died somewhere in France March 2nd of pneumonia.

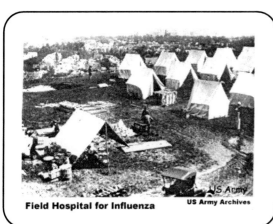

Field Hospital for Influenza   **US Army Archives**

   The flu epidemic broke out in the summer of 1918 and unexpectedly disappeared in 1919. It claimed up to 70 million lives in the world
   Measles and influenza were the most significant diseases for the Army in World War I due to the pneumonia that usually followed.
   The flu epidemic of 1917-18 killed over 24,500 soldiers.

Julian Austin GLAZENER

Born:	11 Mar 1894, Transylvania County, NC
Died:	18 May 1986, Raleigh, NC; age 92
Buried:	Mountlawn Memorial Park, Raleigh, NC
Spouse:	**Margaret STRAYHORN**, m. 12 Jun 1920
Father:	**Edward GLAZENER**
Mother:	**Florence JUSTUS**
Draft Registration:	23, single, a student
Discharge:	Enlisted, 12 Sept 1917 at Raleigh, NC for four years. Total Naval Service 1 1/2 years; Discharged from U.S. Naval Hospital, Norfolk, Va. April 9, 1919.

[Documentation: Discharge, North Carolina Death Collection, Mother's name from father's DC, wife's name from son's DC, Ancestry.com, Heritage Of Transylvania County, NC, Vol.2:154:42]

13 Dec. 1918   **Brevard News**

Pvt. Julian Glazener, who is connected with the Hospital Corps A.E.F. Somewhere in France, has notified his relatives that he will return at an early date.

2 May 1919   **Brevard News**

Julian Glazener is expected home next week from Virginia, where he is in the Naval hospital.

May 22, 1986
JULIAN A. GLAZENER

Julian Austin Glazener, 92, Raleigh, a native of Brevard died Monday in a Raleigh hospital. He was the son of Edward and Florence Thomas Glazener of the Cherryfield community. He was a veteran of World War I, a Mason and a 1922 graduate of North Carolina State University.

He taught vocational agriculture in Ellerbe High School and at Brevard High School before becoming County Agent for Transylvania County. He went to Raleigh in the mid-50's as a community development specialist with the Extension Service where he worked until he retired.

Mr. Glazener is survived by his wife, Margaret; three sons: Bruce, Dr. Edward and Dr. Fred Glazener.

The funeral service was held at the Forest Hills Baptist Church and burial followed in Montlawn Memorial Park in Raleigh.

Julian A. Glazener

10 Oct 1918   **Brevard News**

AMERICAN SOLDIERS ANXIOUS FOR BOOKS
American Library Association Providing Reading Matter
Boys On The Battle Front

The American Library Association which has shouldered the responsibility of collecting books magazines and newspapers by the millions in every city and town throughout the country is distributing this vast quantity of reading matter to the men in France through the Y.M.C.A., the Red Cross, the Knights of Columbus and the Salvation Army

Robert Lewis GOODSON

Born:	19 Nov 1894, Haywood County, NC
Died:	17 Jul 1970, Transylvania County, NC; age 75
Buried:	Crab Creek Baptist Church Cemetery, Henderson County
Occupation:	Lumberman
Spouse:	**Ella RAINES**, m. 10 Apr 1917, Transylvania County, NC
Father:	**James GOODSON**
Mother:	**Martha MILLER**
Draft Registration:	No

[Documentation: Transylvania County DC, <u>Henderson County Cemeteries</u>, <u>Cowart's Index to Marriages</u>, Discharge]

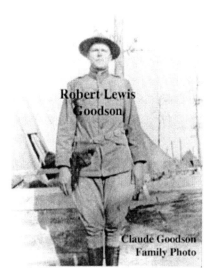

Goodson, Bob		1,324,511		White
(Surname)	(Christian name)	(Army serial number)		(Race: White or colored)

Residence: _____ Brevard   NORTH CAROLINA
(Street and house number) (Town or city) (County) (State)

Enlisted in   NC Brevard N C July 18/17

Born in   Buncombe N C   22 Yrs.

Organizations: Btry F 1 FA N C NG (Btry F 113 FA) to disch

Grades: Pvt

Engagements:

Wounds or other injuries received in action: None.
Served overseas: May 26/18 to Mch 19/19
Hon. disch.   Mch 28/19   on demobilization
Was reported   per cent disabled on date of discharge, in view of occupation.
Remarks: 0

Robert Lewis Goodson

Claude Goodson
Family Photo

7/30/1970
ROBERT L. GOODSON

Robert Lewis Goodson died unexpectedly at his home Friday. He was a native of Haywood County and had resided in Transylvania County for a number of years. He was a veteran of World War I and retired lumberman.

Survivors include one daughter, Mrs. Mary Edwards; four sons: Lewis, Floyd, Claude and Clarence; and one brother, Jake Goodson.

Graveside services were conducted Sunday afternoon at Crab Creek Cemetery.

---

6 Apr 1917   **Brevard News**

PRESIDENT WILSON ASKS FOR WAR

Congress convened in extra session Monday and was urged by President Wilson to declare war on Germany. Congress is debating the matter and will most likely declare a state of war while big warlike preparations are being made.

Champ Clark was elected Speaker of the House.

Charles Bryan GRAVELY

Born:	10 Jul 1896, Transylvania County, NC.
Died:	15 Oct 1980, Cleveland County, NC; age 84
Buried:	Hillcrest Memorial Gardens, Spartanburg, SC
Spouse:	**Callie**
Father	**Joseph B. GRAVELY**
Mother:	**Delia Ann SCRUGGS**
Draft Registration:	No

[Documentation: NC Death Collection, findagrave.com, Ancestry.com]

Charles Bryan Gravely

Fran Johnson Photo

Gravley, Charles B.	1,324,512	White	A 78
(Surname) (Christian name)	(Army serial number)	(Race: White or colored)	

Residence: _____ Brevard *Transylvania* NORTH CAROLINA
(Street and house number)   (Town or city)   (County)   (State)

Enlisted in   NG Brevard NC   —   July 18/17   —
Born in   Transylvania Co NC   —   21 yrs   —
Organizations: Btry F 1st FA NC NG (Btry F 113 FA to disch   —

Crades: Pvt   —   —

Engagements: —   —

Wounds or other injuries received in action: None.   —
Served overseas: May 26/18 to Mch 19/19   —
Hon. disch.   Mch 28/19   on demobilization   —
Was reported   0   per cent disabled on date of discharge, in view of occupation.   —
Remarks: —   —

SCR Notes: FA NC NG (Field Artillery North Carolina National Guard

12 Oct 1917   Brevard News
A party of boys from Camp Sevier, Greenville, came home for a short visit Saturday, returning Sunday afternoon. There were … Bryan Gravely …. The boys seemed to be in good spirits and enjoying camp life.

5 Apr 1918   Brevard News
Bryan Gravley, who is in the training camp at Greenville, spent a day or two at home the past week.

14 Jun 1918   Brevard News
Bryan Gravley, of Brevard, along with a host of other boys, is either in France or on his way there.

Greenville News (SC)
10/16/1980
BRYAN GRAVELY

Bryan Gravely, 84, Greer, husband of Callie Center Gravely, died Wednesday. Born in Brevard, NC, he was a veteran of World War I. He was retired from the plaster business.

Surviving also are stepsons, Ivan and J.D. Neely; and two sisters, Gertrude Garland and Ethel Morgan. Burial was in the Hillcrest Memorial Gardens, Spartanburg County, SC.

James Harrison GRAVELY

Born:	26 May 1891, Transylvania County, NC
Died:	29 May 1942, Transylvania County, NC; age 51
Buried:	Dunn's Rock-Connestee Cemetery
Spouse:	**Eloree PERRY**
Father:	**John H GRAVELY, Sr.**
Mother:	**Syda Belle CRENSHAW**
Draft Registration:	No

[Documentation: Transylvania County DC, Transylvania County Cemetery Survey, Application for Veteran Headstone, Ancestry.com, Heritage to Transylvania County Vol. 2:254:718]

Gravely, James H. • White • Colored

(Surname) (Christian name) (Army serial number)

Residence: Brevard Transylvania NORTH CAROLINA
(Street and house number) (Town or city) (County) (State)

•Inducted at Brevard N C on Oct 3, 19 17

Place of birth: Brevard N C Age or date of birth: 26 6/12 yrs

Organizations served in, with dates of assignments and transfers: MD to disch

Grades, with date of appointment: Pvt

Engagements:

Wounds or other injuries received in action: None.
Served overseas from † None to †____, from †____ to †____
Honorably discharged: Feb 16, 19 18 on SCD
(Date) (Cause)
In view of occupation he was, on date of discharge, reported ____ per cent disabled.
Remarks:

21 Sep 1917   Brevard News
THIRTY-ONE MEN TO CAMP JACKSON
   Forty percent of the certified draft, making 31 men, was ordered to report on Tuesday at 5 P.M. at the office of the local enlistment board and to leave for Camp Jackson, S.C. Wednesday morning.
. . James Harrison Gravely . .

> James Gravely's entire military time was with the Medical Department in the United States Army. He spent no time overseas and he was discharged with a Surgeon's Certificate of Disability.
>
>   Hospitalization represented one of the largest and most difficult of the medical problems in the American Expeditionary Forces. There was always a surplus of several thousand beds as the result of great effort and planning to make the utmost of the resources available.
>   Evacuation of the sick and wounded was another difficult problem, especially during the battle periods. The total number of men evacuated was 214,467, of whom 11,281 were sent in hospital trains to base ports. The number of sick and wounded sent to the United States up to November 11, 1918 was 14,000. Since the Armistice 103,028 patients have been sent to the United States.
>   The Army and Medical Department was fortunate in obtaining the leading physicians, surgeons and specialists in all branches of medicine and the Army Nurse Corps shared the challenge and duties of caring for the soldiers.
>   Orcutt, Louis E., **The Great War Supplement**, published 1920, p. 2

John Lemuel GRAVELY

Born: 25 Oct 1894, Transylvania County, NC
Died: 24 Jul 1948, Memphis, Tennessee; age 53
Buried: Glazener Cemetery
Occupation: Brick mason
Spouse: **Mary CLARK**, m. 19 Apr 1919, Transylvania County, NC
Father: **Joseph B. GRAVELY**
Mother: **Delia Ann SCRUGGS**
Draft Registration: No

[Documentation: Tennessee Death Records, Application for Veteran Headstone, <u>Cowart's Index to Marriages,</u> <u>Transylvania County Cemetery Surveys</u>, Ancestry.com]

John Lemuel Gravely

Delia A. G. Byrd Photo

The form reads:

Gravley John L   1,338,698   White *~~Colored~~.   1
(Surname)   (Christian name)   (Army serial number)

Residence: __xx__ Brevard *Transylvania* NORTH CAROLINA
(Street and house number)   (Town or city)   (County)   (State)

†Enlisted‡ R A * N G * E R C *Inducted at Brevard N C on Feb 27 19 18
Place of birth: __Transylvania Pa__   Age or date of birth: __23 4/12 yrs__

Organizations served in, with dates of assignments and transfers:
8 Const Bricklaying Co to disch

Grades, with date of appointment:
Pvt

Engagements: __xx__

Wounds or other injuries received in action: None.
Served overseas from †~~June 30/18~~₀ †Dec 11/18, from † _____ to † _____
Honorably discharged on demobilization __Dec 23__, 19__18__
In view of occupation he was, on date of discharge, reported _____0_____ per cent disabled.
Remarks: _____

22 Feb. 1918   <u>Brevard News</u>
John Gravely left Brevard Monday evening for Greenville where he will become one of the boys in Uncle Sam's service.

July 26, 1948
JOHN L. GRAVELY

John L. Gravely, 53, died in Kennedy's Veteran Hospital in Memphis, Tenn., last Saturday and funeral services were held at Glady Branch Baptist Church Wednesday and interment followed in Glazener Cemetery. The American legion Post was in charge of the graveside rites.

A native of Transylvania, the deceased was a rock mason in this county for many years. He was a veteran of World War I.

He is survived by his widow, Mary Gravely; three sons: Jack, Joe and Mack Gravely; and four daughters: Lucille Peavy, Louise Jones, Alta May and Delia Ann Gravely. Surviving brothers and sisters are Bryan, Joe and Dewey Gravely, Ethel Morgan and Gertrude Carland.

NATIONAL ARMY CANTONMENT (CAMP)

Camp Doniphan Location: Fort Sill, Oklahoma   Organization: 35th (old 14th) Division
Troops from Missouri and Kansas

Perry Fields GRAVELY

Born:	24 Jun 1893, Pickens County, SC
Died:	14 Sep 1972, Oteen VA Hospital, Buncombe County; age 79
Buried:	Galloway Cemetery in East Fork
Spouse(s):	**Emma CANTRELL, Ella SMITH, Charlotte AIKEN**
Father:	**Richard GRAVELEY**
Mother:	**Elizabeth GILSTRAP**
Draft Registration:	Pickens, SC, 23 single, farming
Service Record Card:	No
Military Marker:	SC PVT CO H 118 Inf WW I

[Documentation: Buncombe County DC, Discharge, TT obituary, Ancestry.com]

9/21/1972
PERRY F. GRAVELY

Perry Fields Gravely, 79, Rosman, died last Thursday evening in the Oteen VA Hospital. Mr. Gravely was a native of Pickens, S.C., but had resided in Transylvania County for the past 43 years. He was a veteran of World War I, serving in Europe with the 30th Division, a member of the Monroe Wilson American Legion and a member of the Old Toxaway Baptist Church.

Surviving are the widow, Mrs. Charlotte Aiken Gravely; three daughters: Mrs. Gladys Moss, Mrs. Dallas Powell and Mrs. Bessie Lee Anders; three sisters: Mrs. Nora Reeves, Mrs. Virgie Hooper and Mrs. Beulah McJunkin; and two brothers: Ed and Benson Gravely.

Funeral services were held Saturday in the Middlefork Baptist Church and burial followed in the Galloway Memorial Park.

Perry Fields Gravely

Joyce Suddeth Photo

Andy F. GREEN

Born:	29 Dec 1892, Otto, NC
Died:	26 Mar 1971, Rabun County, GA; age 78
Buried:	Flats of Middle Creek Missionary Baptist Church Cemetery
	Macon County, NC
Married:	**Harriett BROWN**
Father:	**Judson GREEN**
Mother:	**Ruth E. WATKINS**
Draft Registration:	24, single, railroading for Gloucester Lumber Co.

[Documentation: North Carolina Death Record, findagrave.com, Ancestry.com]

Green   Andy F   1,872,943   * White * Colored.
(Surname)   (Christian name)   (Army serial number)

Residence: _____ Balsam Grove _____ NORTH CAROLINA
              (Street and house number)   (Town or city)   (County)   (State)

████████████████████ C. *Inducted at Brevard, NC _____ on Apr 26, 1918
Place of birth: Otto, NC _____ Age or date of birth: ____ 24 4/12 yrs

Organizations served in, with dates of assignments and transfers: _____
_____ MD to disch _____

Grades, with date of appointment: _____
_____ Pvt _____

Engagements: _____

Wounds or other injuries received in action: None.
Served overseas from Aug 23/18 to Aug 3/19, from † _____ to † _____
Honorably discharged on demobilization Aug 11/19 _____, 19_____
In view of occupation he was, on date of discharge, reported __0__ per cent disabled.
Remarks: _____

German Cannon

Robert Merrill Collection

Walter GRIFFIN

Born:	13 Mar 1892, Atlanta, GA
Died:	30 Jan 1956, Oteen VA Hospital, Buncombe County; age 65
Buried:	Cooper Cemetery
Race:	Colored
Married:	**Ella**
Father:	**Billy GRIFFIN**
Draft Registration:	No
Service Record Card:	No
Military Marker:	NC PVT SUP. Co. 810 Pioneer Inf. WW I

[Documentation: Buncombe County DC, Application for Veteran Headstone, 1930 Census,

Supply Train Company No. 4 Repair Department

Oliver Gaston GROGAN

Born: 13 May 1894, Transylvania County, NC
Died: 30 Dec 1970, Haywood County, NC; age 76
Buried: Oak Grove Cemetery, Brevard
Occupation: Retired textile worker
Spouse: **Bessie SENTELLE**, m. 20 Apr 1918, Transylvania County, NC
Father: **Thomas GROGAN**
Mother: **Susan AIKEN**
Draft Registration: 23, single, firing a sawmill for O.V. Summey
Military Marker: NC PVT 18 CO 156 Depot Brig WW I

[Documentation: Haywood County DC, <u>Transylvania County Cemetery Survey</u>, <u>Cowart's Index to Marriages</u>, Ancestry.com]

Grogan, Oliver G   1,891,607   * White *Colored
(Surname)   (Christian name)   (Army serial number)

Residence: Brevard   Transylvania   NORTH CAROLINA
(Street and house number)   (Town or city)   (County)   (State)

▬▬▬▬. *Inducted at Salica NC   on May 24, 19 18

Place of birth: Salica NC   Age or date of birth: 24 yrs

Organizations served in, with dates of assignments and transfers: _____
_____156 Dep Brig to disch _____

Grades, with date of appointment: _____
_____Pvt _____

Engagements: _____

Wounds or other injuries received in action: None.
Served overseas from †_None____ to †_____, from †_____ to †_____
Honorably discharged on demobilization _____Dec 7, 19 18
In view of occupation he was, on date of discharge, reported _____0_____ per cent disabled.
Remarks: _____

Form No. 724-1, A. G. O.   *Strike out words not applicable.   †Dates of departure from and arrival in the U.S.
Nov. 22, 1919.

SRC Notes: Dep Brig (Depot Brigade)

1/7/1971
OLIVER GROGAN

Oliver Gaston Grogan, 76, died last Wednesday evening in a Haywood County rest home following a long illness. Mr. Grogan was a retired textile worker and a veteran of World War One.

Survivors include two sons: George and Jim Grogan; one daughter, Jessie Miller; four brothers: T., Fred, Bunt and Brance Grogan; three sisters: Dicie Waters, Sallie Owens, and Etta Shelton.

Funeral services were held January 2nd in the Chapel of Frank Moody Funeral home and burial followed in the Oak Grove Cemetery.

NATIONAL ARMY CANTONMENT (CAMP)

Camp Hancock   Location: Augusta, Ga.   Organization: 28th (old 7th) Division
Troops from Pennsylvania

Walter Perry GROGAN

Born:	1 Sep 1895, Transylvania County, NC
Died:	12 May 1934, Seminole County, FL; age 38
Buried:	Evergreen Cemetery, Seminole County, FL
Spouse:	**Mamie**
Father:	**William H. GROGAN**
Mother:	**Ann Hassie KING**
Draft Registration:	Wildwood, FL, 21, single, working in orange groves

[Documentation: Florida Death Collection, findagrave.com, Census Records, Ancestry.com]

Grogan   Walter Parry   3,871,759   * White * Colored
(Surname)   (Christian name)   (Army serial number)

Residence: _____ Brevard _____ NORTH CAROLINA
(Street and house number)   (Town or city)   (County)   (State)

Enlisted R. A. National. *Inducted a Bushnell Fla _____ on July 15 18

Place of birth: Brevard N C _____ Age or date of birth: Sept. 1, 1895

Organizations served in, with dates of assignments and transfers: 4 Provisional Bn Engrs
Ft Benj Harrison Ind to Oct 31/18; Co C 87 Engrs to
disch

Grades, with date of appointment: _____
Pvt

Engagements: _____

Wounds or other injuries received in action: None.

Served overseas from † None ____ to † ____, from † ____ to † ____

Honorably discharged on demobilization ____ Dec 6/18 ____, 19__

In view of occupation he was, on date of discharge, reported ____ O ____ per cent disabled.

Remarks: _____

1920 Postal Card

COMPANY STREET, FT. BENJAMIN HARRISON, INDIANA

171

Clarence F. HALL

Born:	20 May 1897, Transylvania County, NC
Died:	11 Sep 1979, Umatilla, Oregon; age 82
Buried:	Olney Cemetery, Umatilla County, Oregon
Spouse:	**Norah ENGLISH** m. 18 Jul 1920, Transylvania County, NC
Father:	**George W. HALL**
Mother:	**Eva Ann BAYNARD**
Draft Registration:	No
Note:	Grave marker gives NO military information
Discharge:	Enlisted 1 June 1918 Columbus, Ohio; Pvt. in Battery "E" 53rd Artillery; discharged Camp Eustis, Va 14 April 1919

[Documentation: Discharge, <u>Cowart's Index to Marriages</u>, Oregon Death Index, findagrave.com, FamilySearch.com, Ancestry.com, Rowan County NC BC]

9/20/1979
CLARENCE HALL

Clarence F. Hall of Pendleton, Oregon, died September 13, 1979. Funeral Services were held in Pendleton, Oregon. He had lived in Brevard most of his life. Survivors include the widow Nora English Hall; two sons, Gene and Luther Hall; three sisters; Mrs. Yancy McCrary, Mrs. Mirtie Roberson and Maggie Storm; and a brother, Harbin Hall.

Edmond D. HALLENBERG

Born:	June 1896, Louisville, KY
Died:	8 May 1958, Dallas County, TX; age 62
Buried:	Undetermined
Spouse:	**Lillian**
Father:	**Henry HALLENBERG**
Mother:	**Anna**
Note:	His family was in the tanning business in Louisville, KY and one can suspect he was in Transylvania County representing his family business.

[Documentation: 1900 and 1930 Census, Ancestry.com. Texas Death Index]

Hallenberg, Edmond D.   160,328   ..hite   1¼
(Surname)   (Christian name)   (Army serial number)   (Race: White or colored)

Residence:_____ Pisgah Forest Transylvania   NORTH CAROLINA.
(Street and house number)   (Town or city)   (County)   (State)

Enlisted in Ft Thomas Ky Aug 5/17   —
Born in Louisville Ky 21 1/12-yrs   —
Organizations: Co A 10 Engrs to Oct 22/17; Co C 10 Engrs to Nov 29/18;
Hq Det 20 Engrs to Dec 31/18; Base Hos 208 to disch

Grade:
..ag Apr 1/18   —   —

Engagements: —   —

Wounds or other injuries received in action: None.   —
Served overseas: Sept 6/17; Feb 22/19   —
Hon. disch. Mch 26/19   on demobilization   —
Was reported 0   per cent disabled on date of discharge, in view of occupation.
Remarks: —   —

27 Apr 1917   Brevard News
MORE TRANSYLVANIANS READY FOR WAR
Last week the News published the names of those who, to its knowledge, had offered their services to the government in various branches.
..Elda Hallenburg. ….

The Wristwatch Comes of Age

Before World War I most men preferred to use the pocket watches on chains, attached to a vest or overall bibs as a means of telling time. The chains and pocket watch was not acceptable with military uniforms, therefore the wristwatch was the alternative. The wristwatch was redesigned during the war to make it more masculine and practical for the American soldier.

Prior to World War I, a man who wore a wristwatch was ridiculed as being feminine and unmanly. One magazine wrote that wristwatches were worn only by women or "by boys who had their handkerchief tucked up their sleeves."

Once our American soldiers started wearing the wristwatch they became very popular with the men and women in the United States. Young boys were especially fond of the wristwatches, believing that it made them look older and more sophisticated.

Clyde HAMILTON

Born:	9 Aug 1895, Henderson County, NC
Died:	27 Jan 1983, Transylvania County, NC; age 87
Buried:	Little River Baptist Church Cemetery
Spouse:	**Hyburnia SHIPMAN**, m. 4 Jul 1938, Transylvania County, NC
Father:	**Manson HAMILTON**
Mother:	**Mary PATTERSON**
Draft Registration:	21, single, farmer
Military Marker:	PFC US Army WW I

[Documentation: North Carolina Death Index, Cowart's Index to Marriages, 1900-1940 Censuses, Transylvania County Cemetery Survey, Ancestry.com, Hendersonville T-N obit]

Clyde Hamilton

Lois H. Hannah Photo

Hendersonville Times-News
1/28/1983
CLYDE HAMILTON

Brevard - Clyde Hamilton, 87, of 58 East Main Street, died Thursday at his home after a period of declining health. A native of Transylvania County, he was a son of the late Manson and Mary Patterson Hamilton. He was a veteran of World War I and a member of Little Cove Baptist Church.

Surviving are his wife, Hyburnia Shipman Hamilton; three daughters: Lois Hannah, Anna Setzer and Mary Ella Sweat; a son, Otis Hamilton; and three sisters: Hester Hart, Gladys Whitlock and Lora Patterson.

Services will be held at 2 p.m. Saturday in Little River Baptist Church. Burial will be in the church cemetery. Memorials may be made to Little Cove Baptist Church or to a favorite charity.

---

30 Nov 1917   Brevard News

GIVE PRODUCE OR MONEY
TO MAKE BOYS COMFORTABLE

The sale of produce, collected by the National League of Women's Service, began Wednesday at the Brevard Hardware Company store. The women's committee of the League urges all citizens to contribute produce or money so that the boys in camp are supplied with sweaters and comfort kits.

William Neal HAMILTON

Born:	13 Mar 1892, Transylvania County, NC
Died:	21 Nov 1978, Buncombe County, NC
Buried:	Crab Creek Baptist Church Cemetery, Henderson County NC
Occupation:	Farmer
Spouse:	**Loveda McCRARY,** m. 18 Dec 1917, Hendersonville, NC
Father:	**Manson HAMILTON**
Mother:	**Mary PATTERSON**
Draft Registration:	25, single, no dependents, employed at Little River
Military Service:	Served his entire military time at Camp Croft, Spartanburg, SC with the duties of guarding the conscientious objectors.

[Documentation: Hendersonville Times-News obit; Henderson County NC Heritage, Vol. 2:235:155]

Hendersonville Times News
11/21 1978
W. NEAL HAMILTON

After a long illness, Neal W. Hamilton, 86, died Monday in Asheville VA Medical Center. For many years he was disabled after suffering two serious falls resulting in a broken back and broken left arm. Mr. Hamilton was a native of Transylvania County, a son of the late Manson and Mary Patterson Hamilton, the grandson of Voltaire Condorsed Volney and Elizabeth Evans Hamilton and the great-grandson of Robert and Ann Orr Hamilton.

He was an Army veteran of World War I and a retired farmer. He finished public school at Little River, then Fruitland Institute in Henderson County. He attended Little River Baptist Church. He was an active member of the choir and Sunday school class. For many years he sang in quartets. He loved reading, writing, and music. He played several instruments including the organ, piano, guitar, and mandolin. His great joy in his last years was to play piano and sing with his granddaughters, Marsha and Suzanne Rhodes.

Surviving are his widow, Love McCrary Hamilton; two daughters: Juanita Webster and Mary Lou Rhodes; a son, Coman Hamilton; a brother, Clyde Hamilton; and three sisters: Hester Hart, Gladys Whitlock and Lora Patterson

Services will be held Wednesday in Shepherd's Church Street Chapel. Burial will be in Crab Creek Baptist Church Cemetery.

William Neal Hamilton

Mary Lou Rhodes Photo

World War I Conscientious Objectors

"As a Mennonite, much of my research has been done at Mennonite archives and historical libraries. The archives I work in at the Swarthmore College Peace Collection also influenced it.

"An unofficial source states that 3,989 men declared themselves to be conscientious objectors when they reached the camps: of these, 1,300 chose noncombatant service; 1,200 were given farm furloughs; 99 went to Europe to do reconstruction work for the American Friends Service Committee (AFSC); 450 were court-martialed and sent to prison; and 940 remained in camps until the Armistice was signed."

Anne Yoder, compiler   **www.swarthmore.edu**

Charles Amos HAMRICK

Born:	17 Feb 1892, Ellenboro, NC
Died:	13 Dec 1962, Rutherford County, NC; age 70
Buried:	Rutherford County Memorial Cemetery
Occupation:	Barber
Spouse:	**Ella SMART**
Father:	**Preston HAMRICK**
Mother:	**Margaret DEDMOND**
Draft Registration:	25, single, barber in Brevard

[Documentation: Rutherford County DC, Application for Veteran Headstone, Ancestry.com]

```
                                                                    1
          Hamrick,        Charles {.   1,875,231        * White * Colored.
          (Surname)       (Christian name)  (Army serial number)
Residence: _____ Brevard Transylvania NORTH CAROLINA
          (Street and house number)  (Town or city)   (County)      (State)
    * ▮▮▮▮▮▮▮▮▮▮▮▮▮*Inducted at  Brevard, N. C.     on Sept 7, 19.17
Place of birth: Ellenboro, N. C.    Age or date of birth: 28  7/12 yrs.
Organizations served in, with dates of assignments and transfers: MD Fld Hosp Camp
          Jackson SC to Nov 11/17., Amb Co. 324 306 Sn Tn to
          disch.
Grades, with date of appointment: Pvt 1 cl Dec 1/17.

Engagements: _____

Wounds or other injuries received in action: None.
Served overseas from † Aug 8/18. to † June 20/19 from †_____ to †_____
Honorably discharged on demobilization  June 29/19  19_____
In view of occupation he was, on date of discharge, reported _____ per cent disabled.
```

SRC Notes: Amb Co (Ambulance Company)

14 Sep 1917   Brevard News
THE GOING OF SOLDIERS

John Hyder, Ernest Miller, Harold Hardin and Charles Hamrick, the first of the regular draft to be called to the colors left Saturday morning for Camp Jackson, Columbia, S.C.

When the nine o'clock train rolled in the station, a crowd of relatives and friends of the departing boys thronged the platform, each one striving to get a parting handshake.

17 Dec 1917   Brevard News
Charles Hamrick is at his home in Forest City for a short furlough.

Army Auto Ambulance in Action

Charles A. HANNAH

Born:	26 Jan 1885, Daretown, NJ
Died:	11 Jul 1968, Lakeland, Florida; age 83
Buried:	Lakeland Memorial Gardens, Lakeland, FL
Spouse:	**Margaret AGNER**
Father:	**Charles HANNAH**
Mother:	**Mary**
Draft Registration:	No

[Documentation: Ancestry.com, NJ US Army Register of Enlistments]

Hannah, Charles A.   White
(Surname)   (Christian name)   (Army serial number)   (Race: White or colored)

Residence: Rosman,   NORTH CAROLINA.
     (Street and house number)   (Town or city)   (County)   (State)

Enlisted in   R.A. at Columbus Bks-O. Jan 22/16

Born in   Salem N.J. Age 30 11/12 yrs

Organizations: Co G, 313 Inf to disch

Grades: Sgt

Engagements: xx

Wounds or other injuries received in action: None.

Served overseas: none

Dishon. disch.   May 13, 1921 G.C.M.O. #500

Remarks: xx

NOTE: Charles Hannah received a Dishonorable Discharge by GCMO (General Court Martial Order)

177

Edward R. HARBISON

Born:	3 Jan 1893, Burke County, NC
Died:	3 Sep 1959, Burke County, NC; age 66
Buried:	Harbison Family Cemetery, Burke County, NC
Race:	Colored
Father:	**Molton HARBISON**
Mother:	**Margaret Louise REID**
Draft Registration:	23, single, working for Carr Lumber Co.
Military Marker:	PFC US Army WW I

[Documentation: NC Birth Index, NCfindagrave.com, Application for Veterans Headstone, 1910-1940 censuses, Ancestry.com]

SANITARY CORPS

War Department General Orders No. 80 dated 30 June 1917, created an important precursor of the Medical Service Corps. The newly created organization was called the Sanitary Corps, "for want of a better name," and it enrolled newly commissioned officers with special training in sanitation engineering, in bacteriology, or other related sciences to sanitation and preventative medicine. The officer force was set at a maximum of 1 per 1000 total Army active duty strength, and the grades were initially capped at Major. The order also provided for a support team of 3,905 enlisted personnel in grades from private to hospital sergeant.

The Sanitary Corps began with nine officers on active duty and one year later there were 1,345 officers. It reached its peak strength in November 1918 with 2,919 officers.

Ginn, Richard V.N., **The History of the U.S. Army Medical Service Corps,** Office of the Surgeon General and Center of Military History United States Army, Washington, D.C., 1997

Dr. Carl HARDIN

Born:	26 Dec 1896, Transylvania County, NC
Died:	4 Feb 1962, Oteen VA Hospital, Buncombe County; age 65
Buried:	Gillespie-Evergreen Cemetery
Occupation:	Dentist
Spouse:	**Mae HARRIS**
Father:	**A.L. HARDIN**
Mother:	**Bertha McGAHA**
Draft Registration:	21, single, barber in Brevard
Military marker:	NC PFC BTRY B 2 TM BN CAC WW I

[Documentation: Buncombe County DC, Transylvania County Birth Index, Transylvania County Cemetery Survey, Discharge, Ancestry.com]

Hardin, Carl   718,165   white
(Surname)   (Christian name)   (Army serial number)   (Race: White or colored)

Residence: Brevard Transylvania NORTH CAROLINA
(Street and house number)   (Town or city)   (County)   (State)

* Enlisted in   NG Hendersonville NC   June 14/17
† Born in   Cedar Mountain NC _   21 6/12 yrs
Organizations: 6 Co CA NC NG (6 Co CAC) Feb 14/18; Btry B 2 TM Bn to disch

Grades: Pvt 1st Cl Feb 1/18; Pvt Dec 18/18;   —

Engagements: —   —

Wounds or other injuries received in action: None.   —
‡ Served overseas: May 29/18 to Apr 20/19;   —
§ Hon. disch.   May 7/19   on demobilization   —
Was reported   0   per cent disabled on date of discharge, in view of occupation.
Remarks: —   —

2/8/1962
DR. CARL HARDIN

Funeral services for Dr. Carl Hardin, 65, a former mayor of Brevard, were held Tuesday afternoon at the First Baptist Church of which he was a member. Burial followed in the Gillespie-Evergreen Cemetery.

Dr. Hardin died early Sunday morning in the Veterans hospital at Oteen, following a lengthy illness. Dr. Hardin was a native of Transylvania County and was educated in the local schools and at Brevard Institute. He received his degree in dentistry at the Atlanta Dental College, Atlanta, Ga.

He first practiced here and for one year, 1938, in Canton. From that time until 1956, when he retired he had dental offices here in Brevard.

Dr. Hardin was a veteran of World War I, and since his discharge, he had been active in veterans' affairs. Because of his record of service to the Monroe Wilson Post No. 88, Dr. Hardin was given a life membership in the American legion. He was also a member of the Lewis Earl Jackson Post of Veterans of Foreign Wars.

He is survived by the widow, Mae Harris Hardin, a native of Georgia; one son, Stanford; two daughters, Jean Dixon and Mrs. Robert May: and two brothers, Harold and Dr. Hubert C. Hardin.

For years he had collected antiques and relics of pioneer days in American history, and his huge collection included everything from household items to farm equipment, guns, etc.

Harold HARDIN

Born:	7 Feb 1894, Transylvania County, NC
Died:	30 Oct 1977, Cabarrus County, NC; age 83
Buried:	Undetermined
Spouse:	**Dolly FOLKES**
Father:	**A.L. HARDIN**
Mother:	**Bertha McGAHA**
Draft Registration:	23, single, carpenter for T.B. Summey, Jr.

[Documentation: Transylvania County Birth Index, 1900-1940 Censuses, TT obituary, Ancestry.com]

Hardin, Harold 1,876,246 • White • ~~Colored~~.
(Surname) (Christian name) (Army serial number)

Residence: Brevard Transylvania NORTH CAROLINA
(Street and house number) (Town or city) (County) (State)

• ▮▮▮▮▮ *Inducted at Brevard NC on Sept 7 19 17
Place of birth: C. Adar Mountain NC Age or date of birth: 23 7/12 yrs
Organizations served in, with dates of assignments and transfers: Amb Co 324 306 Sn Tn to Disch

Grades, with date of appointment: Pvt 1cl Feb 12/18

Engagements:

Wounds or other injuries received in action: None.
Served overseas from † Aug 8/18 to † June 20/19 rom † _____ to † _____
Honorably discharged on demobilization June 29 19 19
In view of occupation he was, on date of discharge, reported 0 per cent disabled.
Remarks:

Form No. 724-1, A. G. O. *Strike out words not applicable. †Dates of departure from and arrival in the U.S.
Nov. 22, 1919.

SRC Notes: Amb Co (Ambulance Company) Sn Tn (Sanitary Train)

14 Sep 1917   Brevard News
THE GOING OF SOLDIERS FOUR

John Hyder, Ernest Miller, Harold Hardin and Charles Hamrick, the first of the regular draft to be called to the colors left Saturday morning for Camp Jackson, Columbia, S.C.

12 Dec 1917   Brevard News

Harold Hardin who had a few days leave of absence from Camp Jackson, Columbia, SC, visited his parents Mr. and Mrs. A.L. Hardin and left again for camp on Christmas Day.

10/30/1977
HAROLD HARDIN

Word has been received here of the death of Harold Hardin, 83 of Concord, a summer resident of Hendersonville, Sunday night in a Concord hospital after a brief illness.

Mr. Hardin was a native of Transylvania County and had spent his summers in Hendersonville for the past five years, where he was active in the Shuffle Club. He was owner and operator of a dry cleaning business in Concord.

Surviving are the widow, Mrs. Dolly Folkes Hardin; two nieces and a nephew, Stan Hardin.

Services will be held Tuesday in Trinity Reformed Church at Concord.

Ernest B HARKINS

Born:	1900, Transylvania County, NC
Died:	Undetermined
Buried:	Undetermined
Spouse:	**Dueretta PEGUMP, m.** 19 Oct 1923, Billings, Montana
Father:	**William HARKINS**
Mother:	**Martha ASHWORTH**
Note:	Census records show Ernest traveled around and was in Michigan in 1940. Can find no further information.

[Documentation: FamilySearch.org, Ancestry.com]

Harkins, Ernest B   2,337,957   White

(Surname)   (Christian name)   (Army serial number)   (Race: White or colored)

Residence: Brevard Transylvania   NORTH CAROLINA

(Street and house number)   (Town or city)   (County)   (State)

Enlisted in   RA Ft Screven Ga Feb 5/18

Born in   Brevard NC 18 yrs

Organizations: Co A 4 Inf to disch

Grades: Pvt

Engagements:

Wounds or other injuries received in action: None.
Served overseas: Apr 6/18 to July 25/18
Hon. disch. Dec 31/18   on demobilization
Was reported 10%   per cent disabled on date of discharge, in view of occupation.
Remarks: Indefinite furlough from Oct 26, 19...

Transylvania County Library NC Room- Family Files – Ernest B. Ashworth/Harkins
August 29, 1918

Mr. J.C. Logan, Director Civilian Relief
Southern Division
Healy Building
Atlanta, Ga.
Dear Sir:

When Mr. Fulton visited Brevard, he told us to take up all cases to be investigated through your office, and I will act accordingly.

I wish to have the allotment of Ernest B. Harkins hurried, if possible, as he has been in the service since Feb. 5, 1918, and his mother has not received the money he allotted to her from his pay.

This man entered the service under the name of Ernest B. Ashworth and was first in the Recruit Company #1 at Ft. Scevens, Ga., and then he was sent to Newport News, Va. From there to France. He is now in this country in the Walter Reed American Hospital at Washington, D.C. When he first signed himself Ernest B. Harkins I do not know, nor under which name he asked for the allotment to be made to his mother, who is Martha Ashworth.

She came to us with his letters in which he stated he had made an allotment to her from his pay of $15.00 per month, but she has never received any of this money. I will write to the boy and ask for his allotment number, as his mother cannot write. I will also learn, if possible, under which name he signed the allotment papers, hoping that in the meantime you can start the Bureau of War Risk and Insurance working on this case so that Martha Ashworth, mother of Ernest B. Harkins may soon be receiving the allotment made her by her son.

Sincerely yours,
Chairman Civilian Relief Committee
Elizabeth M. Silversteen

Response from Boyce Edens to Mrs. Silversteen's letter on behalf of Martha Ashworth

Civilian Relief – Brevard, N.C.
Re: Ernest B. Harkins or Ashworth
Sept. 7, 1918
Mrs. J.S. Silversteen
Civilian Relief Committee]
American Red Cross
Brevard, N.C.
Dear. Mrs. Silversteen:

　We have your letter of August 29th concerning the non-receipt of allotment and allowance by the mother of the above named soldier.

　If you cannot learn his full military designation from the mother, I refer you to paragraph 16, Supplement 32 to ARC 207, Handbook of Information, wherein explicit directions are given for obtaining this information. After you have found out the full name under which he enlisted and the full military designation, please fill out carefully a form 296, following closely the instructions on the back thereof. Send this to us and we will make inquiry concerning the allotment through the proper channels.

Very truly yours,
Boyce M. Edens
Assistant to Director,
Civilian Relief

Richard Edward HARRISON

Born:	8 Mar 1898, Mississippi
Died:	14 Dec 1935, Spartanburg, SC; age 37
Buried:	Oak Grove Baptist Church Cemetery, Quebec, NC
Spouse:	**Louise MILLER**
Father:	**James T. HARRISON**
Mother:	**Fannie MOORE**
Draft Registration:	Lowndes, MS, 20, single, just discharged from Army

[Documentation: South Carolina DC, Application for Veteran's Headstone, FamilySearch.org, Ancestry.com]

12/19/1935
RICHARD E. HARRISON

Richard E. Harrison, 37, teacher in Polk County and former resident of Transylvania, was killed Saturday night near Campobello, SC, when the car he was driving, collided with a truck driven by G.C. Small on the Spartanburg-Asheville Highway. Facts established at the coroner's inquest held Sunday were to the effect that the driver of the truck was blameless and he was released.

Mr. Harrison was survived by his widow, Mrs. Louise Miller Harrison of this county, and a small son Richard Harrison, Jr.; two brothers, J.T. Harrison, postmaster of Sapphire and Eugene Harrison; and one sister Fannie Baker.

Mr. Harrison saw service in World War I, having been a first class petty officer in the Coast Guard.

Funeral services were held Wednesday at Oak Grove Baptist Church, Quebec, with interment in the cemetery nearby.

May 1917	**Brevard News**

WILSON ISSUES BIG ARMY DRAFT PROCLAMATION
President Designates June 5, 1917 as Registration Day
HEAVY PENALITIES FOR FAILURE TO ENROLL
All Males Between 21 and 30, Inclusive are Liable
Absentee Registration May Be Done By Mail
Federal and State Officials to Appoint Registrars

Tavie Harold HART

Born:	26 Oct 1895, Transylvania County, NC
Died:	29 Apr 1968, Transylvania County, NC; age 72
Buried:	Orr Cemetery
Occupation:	Farmer
Spouse:	**Hester HAMILTON**, m. 20 Apr 1924, Transylvania County, NC
Father:	**Ladson Mills HART**
Mother:	**Flora LINDSEY**
Draft Registration:	21, single, farmer

[Documentation: Transylvania County DC, Transylvania County Cemetery Survey, Cowart's Index to Marriages, Discharge, FamilySearch.org, Ancestry.com]

Tavie Harold Hart

Walt Hart Photo

```
                                                                        1
      Hart      Tavie H.          1,876,329  * White * Colored.
        (Surname)   (Christian name)    (Army serial number)
                              Pisgah  Randolph   NORTH CAROLINA
Residence: _____
              (Street and house number)   (Town or city)   (County)   (State)
      ▆▆▆▆▆▆▆.  *Inducted at  Brevard N.C.        on Sept 18 1917
Place of birth: Pisgah N.C.        Age or date of birth: 21 10/12 Yrs
Organizations served in, with dates of assignments and transfers: MD Field Hosp 321
        386 Sn Tn to Disch

Grades, with date of appointment:       Cfr Mch 24/18



Engagements: _____


Wounds or other injuries received in action: None.
Served overseas from Aug 8/18 to June 20/19, from †_____ to †_____
Honorably discharged on demobilization       June 29, 19 19
In view of occupation he was, on date of discharge, reported __0__ per cent disabled.
Remarks: _____
```

SRC Notes: Sn Tn (Sanitation Train)

21 Sep 1917   Brevard News
THIRTY-ONE MEN TO CAMP JACKSON
. . .Tavie Harold Hart . . .

March 2, 1968
TAVIE H. HART

Tavie Harold Hart, 72, of Little River community died at his home Monday after an extended illness. He was a lifelong resident of Transylvania County, a retired farmer and a veteran of World War I. A memorial service was conducted Wednesday at Little River Baptist Church.

He is survived by his wife, Hester Hamilton; one daughter, Flora Marie Hart: three sisters: Inez Hart, Rowena Summey and Polly Jerome; and one brother, Walter F. Hart.

"**Garbage is Valuable, Don't Waste It.** Explosives, fertilizers, soaps--vital war necessities are being made from kitchen refuse. Clean garbage is also excellent food for hogs. Keep it free from broken crockery-glass-tin cans-sweepings and other household rubbish. Use every ounce of food fat for human consumption, then make the garbage pail do its part."
United States Food Administration Poster

Miles Early HEAD

Born:	13 May 1894, Transylvania County, NC
Died:	25 Nov 1958, Oteen VA Hospital, Buncombe County; age 64
Buried:	Gillespie-Evergreen Cemetery
Occupation:	Barber
Spouse:	**Carletta BRYSON**
Father:	**William HEAD**
Mother:	**Margaret BARNES**
Draft Registration:	23, single, farming in the Sapphire area

[Documentation: Buncombe County, DC, <u>Transylvania County Cemetery Survey</u>, Application for Veteran Headstone, Ancestry.com]

Carol Nesby Photo

11/27/1958
M.E. HEAD

Last rites for Miles Early Head, 64, well known Brevard barber, were held last Friday morning here at the First Baptist Church. Officials of the Monroe Wilson Post of the American Legion conducted graveside rites at the Gillespie-Evergreen Cemetery.

Mr. Head died late Tuesday in the Veterans Hospital at Swannanoa, after a brief illness.

A native of Transylvania, Mr. Head was a former commander of the local post. He was a veteran of World War I and served in Europe.

Survivors include the widow, Mrs. Carletta Bryson Head; two daughters, Mrs. Orville McKelvin and Mrs. Marcus Brown; two sons, Robert and Roy; and one brother W.B. Head.

---

21 May 1918 Brevard News
U.S. ENGINEERS NEED MEN

The 28th Reg. U.S. Engineers at Woodbridge, Va., needs 375 recruits to fill out the Regiment. No man under the present draft can enlist: only men from 18 to 21 or 31 to 45. Good chance for promotion and grand chance to see service as miners, as this is a mining regiment. There is an excellent opportunity for married men. The Government will help you take care of your family. So be patriotic, enlist now and fight for your country.

For further information see a recruiting officer or write Capt. Monteith, E.R.C., Woodbridge, Va., 28th Reg. C.S. Engineers.

Samuel Otis HEAD

Born:	30 Nov 1888, Buncombe County, NC
Died:	15 Jan 1943, Augusta, GA; age 54
Buried:	Undetermined
Father:	**Milllard Filmore HEAD**
Mother:	**Mary Jane RAY**
Draft Registration:	28, single, log scaler for Gloucester Lumber Co.
Special Note:	Samuel was a patient at a Veterans Hospital in Augusta, Georgia according to 1940 census

[Documentation: Ancestry.com, Georgia Deaths, 1900-1940 censuses]

STATE OF NORTH CAROLINA, COUNTY OF TRANSYLVANIA TEACHERS, 1918-1919.

SCHOOLS:

TURKEY CREEK—Miss Mary Belle Orr, Prin., No. 2, Brevard.

BLANTYRE—Miss Clell Watson, Prin., Miss Lillie Picklesimer, Blantyre.

PENROSE HIGH SCHOOL—Miss Parham, Prin., Mrs. Harley Lyday, Mrs. Maggie Wilson, No. 2, Brevard.

BOILSTON—Miss Cnnie Glazener, Prin., Horse Shoe.

BREVARD HGH SCHOOL—Miss Cora L. Tyner, Prin., Miss Myrtle Rhodes, Miss Elizabeth Morton, Miss Janie F. Moseley, Miss Louise Townsend, and Miss Carrie Hornaday, all of Brevard.

DAVIDSON RIVER—Mr. J. W. Bennett, Prin., Miss Emma Bell, Miss Julia Deaver, and Miss Maxine Reece, all of Pisgah Forest.

ENGLISH CHP.—Miss Etta McCall, Prin., No. 2, Brevard.

PINK BEDS—Miss Ruth Brooks, Prin., Pisgah Forest.

ASHWORTH CAMP—Mr. W. L Carmichael, Prin., Pisgah Forest

HEDDEN CAMP—Miss Ollie Owen, Prin., Pisgah Forest.

SELICA—Mr. A. J. Hamilton, Prin., Miss Mary Orr, Miss Mattie Pearle Lyday, all of Selica.

CALVERT—Miss Maude Allison, Prin., Mrs. A. P. Bell, all of Calvert.

ROSMAN HIGH SCHOOL—Miss Clarice Guthrie, Prin., Miss Sallie Merrill, Miss Bella Gillespie, Miss Beulah Whitmire, Miss Bessie Poole, all of Rosman.

ROUND TOP—Mr. F. L. Wilson, Prin., Miss Mae Quiett, Brevard, No. 1.

ISLAND FORD—Miss Dora Reece, Prin., No. 1, Brevard.

DUNNS CREEK—Miss Ella Hollingsworth, Prin., Pisgah Forest.

CARSON CREEK—Miss Mary Lilly Barringer, No. 1, Brevard.

EAST FORK—Miss Georgie Burrell, Prin., No. 1, Brevard.

OAK FOREST—Miss Lucile Wilson, Prin., No. 1, Brevard.

OLD TOXAWAY—Miss Roxie Reece, Prin., Miss Marie Thomas, both Rosman.

PLEASANT HILL—Miss Dovie Garren, Prin., Rosman.

ROBINSON SCHOOL—Miss Grace Gillespie, Prin., Balsam Grove.

PINE GROVE—Miss Fannie Beggs, Prin., Lake Toxaway.

SHOAL CREEK—Miss Janie Gillespie, Prin., Balsam Grove.

OWENS SCHOOL—Mr. H. P. Nicholson, Prin., Lake Toxaway.

QUEBEC—Mr. W. C. Reid, Prin., Miss Norma Chapman, Miss Victoria Gillespie, all of Quebec.

OAKLAND—Miss Sue Heath, Prin., Namur, N. C.

MONTVALE—Miss Alta Younger, Prin., Namur, N. C.

LAKE TOXAWAY—Mr. D. H. Picklesimer, Prin., Miss Rosa Hamilton, Lake Toxaway.

UNION SCHOOL—Miss Stella Reid, Prin., Sapphire.

CEDAR MOUNTAIN—Miss Texie Briggs, Prin., Cedar Mountain.

LAUREL CREEK—Miss Emma Brown, Prin., Pisgah Forest.

LITTLE RIVER—Miss Hattie Henson, Prin., Miss Greta Picklesimer, both of Etowah.

MINE MT.—Miss Geneva Wilson, Prin., Cedar Mountain.

STOVEN CAMP—Miss Mildred Bryant, Prin., Balsam Grove.

GLADE CREEK—(Col.) Miss Jessie B. Saville, Prin., Miss Viola Saville, both Davidson River.

BREVARD SCHOOL—(Col.) Principal G. W. Thompson, Assistants Mrs. J. H. Johnstone, and Miss Preston Mills, all of Brevard.

The above list of teachers in my opinion are much above the average County teachers.

Most Cordially and Sincerely Yours,

A. F. MITCHELL, County Sup't Pub. Inst. Trans. Cty.

William Burley HEAD

Born:	25 May 1897, Transylvania County, NC
Died:	21 Mar 1978, Transylvania County, NC; age 80
Buried:	Pisgah Gardens Cemetery
Spouse:	**Minnie GILLESPIE**, m. 17 Aug 1924, Transylvania County, NC
Father:	**William HEAD**
Mother:	**Margaret BARNES**
Draft Registration:	21, single, working for Vernon Neill

[Documentation: Transylvania County DC, <u>Transylvania County Cemetery Survey</u>, <u>Cowart's Index to Marriages</u>, Discharge, Ancestry.com]

SRC Notes: Pion Inf (Pioneer Infantry)

3/27/1978
WILLIAM B. HEAD

William Burley Head, 80, died last Tuesday in the Transylvania Community Hospital after a long illness. He was a native and lifelong resident of Transylvania County and a son of the late William and Margaret Barnes Head. He was a veteran of World War I and a member of East Fork Baptist Church.

Surviving are two grandchildren. Full military graveside services were held Thursday at Pisgah Gardens.

A morale booster for the men of the Eighty-first Division at Camp Jackson, SC came about when the men began referring to themselves as "wildcats". The name sounded mean and tough, and it made the soldiers feel a little braver.

One of the men in the division fashioned a piece of fabric into the shape of a wildcat ready to pounce and he sewed it on the sleeve of his uniform. It became popular and other men of the Division wanted patches for their uniforms also. Eventually other divisions came up with names and symbols for their men and the soldier patch came into permanent being.

William Harvey HEAD

Born:	22 May 1891, Pickens County, SC
Died:	15 Dec 1931, Pickens County, SC; age 40
Buried:	Bethel Church Cemetery, Pickens, SC
Spouse:	**Myrtle PORTER**
Father:	**John Washington HEAD**
Mother:	**Malinda ELLENBURG**
Draft Registration:	26, married, working at Rosman Tanning Extract Company

[Documentation: South Carolina Death, Application for Veteran Headstone, findagrave.com, Ancestry.com

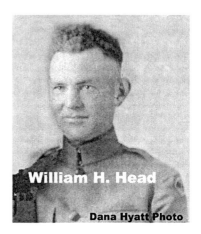

William H. Head
Dana Hyatt Photo

Head	William H	1,324,446	White
(Surname)	(Christian name)	(Army serial number)	(Race: White or colored)

Residence: Rosman Transylvania NORTH CAROLINA
(Street and house number) (Town or city) (County) (State)

Enlisted in NG Brevard, N.C. July 18/17
Born in Pickens, Co, S.C. — 26 2/12 yrs

Organizations: Btry F 1st Regt N.C. FA (Btry F 113 FA) to disch

Grades: Pvt 1/cl Oct 1/17; Pvt July 25/18

Engagements: —

Wounds or other injuries received in action: None. —
Served overseas: May 26/18 to Mch 19/19 —
Hon. disch. Mch 26/19 on demobilization —
Was reported 0 per cent disabled on date of discharge, in view of occupation.
Remarks: —

SRC Note FA (Field Artillery)

WILLIAM H. HEAD

William Head, 40, died at his home near Crete, Pickens County, December 15, 1931, after a two-week illness. Funeral services were held the following day from Bethel Church.

Mr. Head leaves to mourn his passing his wife, who before marriage was Miss Myrtle Porter, and five children: Harold, Jack, Marilyn, Billy and Helen; his aged father and mother and six brothers and sisters: J. Wesley, R.T. Head; Mrs. W.B. Cantrell, Mrs. A.A. Ellenberg, Mrs. Mary Mosley and L.P. Head.

Mr. Head was a World War veteran and served with the 30th Division overseas.

At Drill with Wooden Guns

Joseph McKinley HEATH

Born:	11 Aug 1896, Greenville County, SC
Died:	5 Jun 1983, Transylvania County, NC; age 86
Buried:	Little River Baptist Church Cemetery
Spouse:	**Bessie LEE**, m. 2 Oct 1931, Transylvania County, NC
Father:	**Charles M. HEATH**
Mother:	**Mary E. McCRARY**
Draft Registration:	21, single, self-employed
Military Marker:	PVT US Army WW I

[Documentation: North Carolina Death Index, Discharge, <u>Transylvania County</u> <u>Cemetery Survey</u>, Ancestry.com, TT obituary]

```
                                                                              1
       Heath, Joseph Mc          4,480,510
                                                           * White  *Colored
        (Surname)      (Christian name)    (Army serial number)
                    Route #1    Etowah  Henderson   NORTH CAROLINA
Residence: _____
            (Street and house number)  (Town or city)  (County)        (State)
                            *Inducted at  Brevard  NC          on Aug 28, 19  18
Place of birth: ___Greenville,  N C____  Age or date of birth: __Aug 11/96___
Organizations served in, with dates of assignments and transfers: _____
       FA Repl Dep Camp Jackson SC to disch

Grades, with date of appointment: _____
_____Pvt_____

Engagements: _____

Wounds or other injuries received in action: None.
Served overseas from  None       to †_____ from †_____ to †_____
Honorably discharged on demobilization   Dec 11/18       , 19____
In view of occupation he was, on date of discharge, reported __0_____ per cent disabled.
Remarks: _____
```

SRC Notes: FA Repl Dep (Field Artillery Replacement Depot)

26 Aug 1918   Brevard News
TWELVE MORE MEN LEFT MONDAY
The following men were entrained for Camp Jackson Monday afternoon:
. . . Joseph M. Heath, Etowah R.F.D. . . .

6/3/1963
JOSEPH M. HEATH

Joseph McKinley Heath, 86, of Hart Road, died Sunday in a Brevard hospital. The son of the late Charles and Mary McCrary Heath, he was a Greenville, SC native and had lived in Transylvania County most of his life. He was a retired farmer, well driller and World War I Army veteran.

Surviving are his wife, Bessie Lee Heath; four sons: Bobby, Wayne, Billy Joe and Randy; three daughters: Betty Whitmire, Jene Crossley and Ann Gosnell; and a sister, Sue H. Shipman.

Graveside services will be held at 3 p.m. Tuesday in Little River Cemetery.

NATIONAL ARMY CANTONMENT (CAMP)
Camp Taylor   Location: Louisville, Ky.   Organization: 84th Division
Troops from Indiana and Kentucky

Leonard Bert HEATH

Born:	20 Sep 1893, Transylvania County
Died:	16 Nov 1951, Transylvania County, NC; age 58
Buried:	Dunn's Creek Baptist Church Cemetery
Occupation:	Farmer
Father:	**Americus HEATH**
Mother:	**Athalinda McCALL**
Draft Registration:	25, single, farming with his father
Military marker:	NC Cook 306 SN TRAIN 81 DIV WW I

[Documentation: Transylvania County DC, <u>Transylvania County Cemetery Survey</u>, 1900-1940 Censuses, Application for Veteran's Headstone, Ancestry.com]

Leonard B. Heath
Eileen Summey Photo

SRC Notes: Amb Co (Ambulance Company) SnTn (Sanitation Train) Ck (Cook)

21 Sep1917   Brevard News
THIRTY-ONE MEN TO CAMP JACKSON
    . . . Leonard Bert Heath . . .

19 Apr 1918   Brevard News
Leonard Heath from Camp Jackson, Columbia, SC is at home on a five-day's furlough visiting his parents.

11/22/1951
L.B. HEATH

Leonard B. Heath, 58, well-known farmer of Transylvania and a veteran of World War I was buried Sunday afternoon at the Dunn's Creek Baptist Church. Members of the Monroe Wilson Post of the American Legion held graveside rites for Mr. Heath.

Mr. Heath was found dead last Friday afternoon in a cornfield about two miles out on the Greenville highway by a sister-in-law, Mrs. Charles Heath. Acting coroner, E. McGaha, who investigated, contributed death to natural causes.

Mr. Heath is survived by his mother, Mrs. Renda Heath; three brothers: Charles, Elzie and William; and one sister.

Azalea Hospital was opened at Asheville August 1918 for tubercular soldiers and sailors.

Newton Lee HEATH

Born:	4 Jun 1896, Transylvania County, NC
Died:	7 Jul 1954, Transylvania County, NC; age 58
Buried:	Carr's Hill Baptist Church Cemetery
Spouse:	**Nora CISON**
Father:	**Monroe HEATH**
Mother:	**Rachel ALLISON**
Draft Registration:	21, single, farming for Wm. P. Allison

[Documentation: Transylvania County DC, Transylvania County Cemetery Survey, FamilySearch.org, Ancestry.com, Discharge]

Newton L. Heath

Marjorie W. Masters Photo

Heath, Newton L   1,863,404   *White *~~Colored~~
(Surname)   (Christian name)   (Army serial number)

Residence: Brevard *Transylvania*   NORTH CAROLINA
(Street and house number)   (Town or city)   (County)   (State)

*Inducted at Brevard NC   on Oct 3, 1917

Place of birth: Brevard NC   Age or date of birth: 21 4/12 yrs.

Organizations served in, with dates of assignments and transfers: 323 F Hosp to Nov 26/17; Base Hosp Camp Jackson SC to disch

Grades, with date of appointment: Pvt

Engagements:

Wounds or other injuries received in action: None.
Served overseas from † NO to † , from † to †
Honorably discharged on demobilization Mch 30, 19 19
In view of occupation he was, on date of discharge, reported 0 per cent disabled.
Remarks:

7/15/1954
NEWTON L. HEATH

Newton Lee Heath, 58, died in Transylvania Community Hospital Wednesday, July 7th after a brief illness. He was born and reared in Transylvania County and been employed by the Carr Lumber Company for the last 11 years.

Survivors include the widow, Mrs. Nora Heath; two sisters: Mrs. Cora Byars and Mrs. Nettie Chasteen; three stepchildren: Montez, Annie Mae and Cpl. Aaron Masters.

Funeral services were conducted at Carr's Hill Baptist Church Thursday, July the 8th. Burial was in the church cemetery.

Robert Elzie HEATH

Born:	15 Jul 1896, Transylvania County, NC
Died:	12 Aug 1991, Oteen VA Hospital, Buncombe County; age 95
Buried:	Dunn's Creek Baptist Church Cemetery
Spouse(s):	**Ethel WALKER, Minnie RAMEY**
Father:	**Americus HEATH**
Mother:	**Athalinda McCALL**
Draft Registration:	21, working with his father

[Documentation: Buncombe County DC, Spouses' DC, Ancestry.com]

Heath	Robert E	4 480 512	* White * ~~Colored~~
(Surname)	(Christian name)	(Army serial number)	

Residence: RFD#1   Pisgah Forest   NORTH CAROLINA
(Street and house number)   (Town or city)   (County)   (State)

*Inducted: Brevard NC   on Aug 26 1918

Place of birth: Brevard NC   Age or date of birth: July 16 1896

Organizations served in, with dates of assignments and transfers:
3 Regt FARD to disch

Grades, with date of appointment:
Pvt

Engagements:

Wounds or other injuries received in action: None.
Served overseas from none to †_____, from †_____ to †_____
Honorably discharged on demobilization .. Dec 11/18 , 19_____
In view of occupation he was, on date of discharge, reported __0__ per cent disabled.

R. Elzie Heath
Eileen Summey Photo

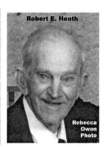

Robert E. Heath
Rebecca Owen Photo

SRC Notes: FARD (Field Artillery Reserve Department)

26 Aug 1918   Brevard News
TWELVE MORE MEN LEFT MONDAY
The following men were entrained for Camp Jackson Monday afternoon:. . . Robert E. Heath, ...

Hendersonville Times-News
8/14/1991
ROBERT E. HEATH

Robert Elzie Heath, 95, of Pisgah Forest died Monday, 12 Aug 1991, in the Asheville VA Medical Center. He was a native of Transylvania County and the son of the late Americus and Athalinda McCall Heath. He was an Army veteran of World War I and a member of Dunn's Creek Baptist Church.

Survivors include his wife, Minnie Ramey Heath; two sons: Robert H. and John Heath; four daughters: Betty Barton, Mary Ball, Becky Owen and Vera Calloway; three stepsons: Glen Davis, Jack Davis and Jim Davis; and four stepdaughters: Lona Mae LaGrant, Mary Rehburg, Diane Baxter and June Owen

The funeral will be held at 2 p.m. Thursday in Moore Funeral Home Chapel in Brevard. Burial will follow in Dunn's Creek Baptist Church Cemetery, with military graveside rites conducted by the American Legion Monroe Wilson Post 88 and Veteran of Foreign War Lewis Earl Jackson Post 4309

NATIONAL ARMY CANTONMENT (CAMP)

Camp Taylor   Location: Louisville, KY   Organization: 84th Division
Troops from Indiana and Kentucky

James Jeter HEDDEN

Born:	1 Jul 1893, Jackson County, NC
Died:	Apr 1965, probably South Carolina; age 71
Buried:	Undetermined
Spouse:	**Irene WHITAKER**
Father:	**Elisha HEDDEN**
Mother:	**Sarah C PARKER**
Draft Registration:	22, single, working in lumber at Pisgah Forest
Note:	James' wife is buried at Hillcrest Cemetery, Pickens, SC

[Documentation: SSDI, 1900-1940 Censuses, Ancestry.com]

Hedden, James J. 2,616,787 * White ~~Colored~~ 1
(Surname) (Christian name) (Army serial number)

Residence: _____ Pisgah Forest NORTH CAROLINA
(Street and house number) (Town or city) (County) (State)

* ▮▮▮▮▮▮▮▮ *Inducted at Transylvania Co N C on Sept 5, 1918
Place of birth Jackson Co N C   Age or date of birth: July 1/1893

Organizations served in, with dates of assignments and transfers: _____
_____ Engr Tng Regt Camp Humphreys Va to disch _____

Grades, with date of appointment: _____
Pvt

Engagements: _____

Wounds or other injuries received in action: None.
Served overseas from † None to † _____, from † _____ to † _____
Honorably discharged on demobilization Dec 18/18, 19_____
In view of occupation he was, on date of discharge, reported 0 per cent disabled.
Remarks: _____

Form No. 724-1, A. G. O.   * Strike out words not applicable.   † Dates of departure from and arrival in the U. S.

SRC Note: Engr Tng Regt (Engineers Training Regiment)

4/8/1965
JIM HEDDEN

Word has been received here of the death of James Jeter Hedden, 71, of Pickens, S.C. Mr. Hedden was a former resident of Transylvania County.

Funeral services will be held at the First Baptist Church in Pickens Wednesday afternoon.

Apr 1918   Brevard News

RED CROSS TO ENTER
NEW FIELD OF SERVICE IN
ARMY CAMPS OF AMERICA

At the suggestion of Secretary of War Raker, the American Red Cross is about to enter a new field of service in the Army camps of the United States, a field in which they are already working in France, the Bureau of Communication between the man in the hospital and their families at home. This will necessitate building a Red Cross house in every Army camp in the country and securing for each house a man who will keep in personal touch with every man who is admitted to the camp hospital, as well as a sufficient stenographic force to handle the letters dictated by the men and keep their families constantly informed as to their condition and progress.

(long article that goes into detail of the chain of command)

Simon R. HELMICK

Born:	6 Oct 1899, Williams, W.VA
Died:	28 Dec 1923
Buried:	Undetermined
Father:	**Sampson HELMICK**
Mother:	**Ida THOMPSON**
Draft Registration:	No
Note:	Simon was born in West Virginia and 1920 census records have him back in West Virginia.

[Documentation: Ancestry.com]

Helmick   Simon R   1,406,225   White
    (Surname)   (Christian name)   (Army serial number) (Race: White or colored)

Residence: Rosman   NORTH CAROLINA
        (Street and house number)   (Town or city)   (County)   (State)

*Enlisted in   RA at Columbus Bks Ohio   Feb 17/17
†Born in   Williams W Va   _   18 4/12 yrs
Organizations: Tr H 13 Cav to June 1/17; Tr H 21 Cav (Btry D 79 FA)
        to disch

Grades: Pvt Feb 17/17; Hs Feb 19/18; Pvt Apr 15/18; Pvt lcl
        July 19/18; Hs May 12/19

Engagements: _

Wounds or other injuries received in action: None.
‡Served overseas: Aug 8/18 to June 20/19
§Hon. disch.   June 4/20 Abolishment of RA Res
Was reported   per cent disabled on date of discharge, in view of occupation.
Remarks: 0

1917 Columbus Barracks, Ohio

STREET SCENE, SHOWING LOCATION OF COMPANY BARRACKS.

Columbus Harrison HOLDEN

Born:	24 Apr 1897, Transylvania County, NC
Died:	31 May 1980, Transylvania County, NC; age 83
Buried:	Pisgah Gardens Cemetery
Father:	**Leander Jackson HOLDEN**
Mother:	**Arrie Bertha EUBANKS**
Draft Registration:	21, single, works with his father
Military Marker:	PVT US Army WW I

[Documentation: North Carolina Death Index, Discharge, Transylvania County BC, <u>Transylvania County Cemetery Survey</u>, Asheville CT obituary, Ancestry.com]

Holden, Columbus H.   4,480,511   White
(Surname)   (Christian name)   (Army serial number)

Residence: R.F.D. 1   Brevard *Transylvania*   NORTH CAROLINA
(Street and house number)   (Town or city)   (County)   (State)

Inducted at Brevard NC   on Aug 26, 1918

Place of birth: Brevard NC   Age or date of birth: Apr 24/1897

Organizations served in, with dates of assignments and transfers:
156 ep Brig to disch

Grades, with date of appointment: Pvt

Engagements:

Wounds or other injuries received in action: None.
Served overseas from †No   to †   , from †   to †
Honorably discharged on demobilization   Dec 16/18, 19
In view of occupation he was, on date of discharge, reported   0   per cent disabled.
Remarks:

Columbus Holden — Gene Baker Photo

26 Aug 1918   Brevard News
TWELVE MORE MEN LEFT MONDAY
The following men were entrained for Camp Jackson Monday afternoon:
. . . Columbus H. Holden, Brevard R.F.D. . . .

Asheville Citizen Times
6/2/1980
COLUMBUS HOLDEN

Columbus Harrison Holden, 83, of Island Ford Road, died Saturday in the Brevard hospital after a brief illness. He was a lifelong resident of Transylvania County, the son of the late Lee and Arrie B. Eubanks Holden. He was a World War I veteran and a retired farmer.

Services were held in Dunn's Rock Church, of which he was a member and trustee. Burial was in Pisgah Gardens Cemetery.

Surviving are two brothers: Ralph and Jackson Holden; six sisters: Della Mull, Flora Baker, Florence Baker, Florida Kilpatrick, Minerva Baynard and Carrie Holden

---

NATIONAL ARMY CANTONMENT (CAMP)

Camp Grant   Location: Rockford, Ill   Organization: 86th Division
Troops from Illinois

Spurgeon Montgomery HOLLAND

Born:	12 Sep 1896, Macon County, NC
Died:	13 Apr 1980, Oteen VA Hospital, Buncombe County; age 83
Buried:	Pisgah Gardens Cemetery
Spouse:	**Pauline PARKER**
Father:	**Anthony HOLLAND**
Mother:	**Sarah CRAWFORD**
Draft Registration:	No
Military Marker:	QM2 US Navy WW I

[Documentation: North Carolina Death Collection, <u>Transylvania County Cemetery</u> <u>Survey</u>, Hendersonville, T-N obituary, Ancestry.com]

4/15/1980
Hendersonville Times-News
S.M. HOLLAND

Spurgeon Montgomery Holland, 83, of Holland Road, Pisgah Forest, died Sunday in Asheville VA Medical Center after a long illness. Mr. Holland was a native of Macon Count, a son of the late Anthony and Sarah Crawford Holland. He was a Navy veteran of World War I where he served aboard the USS Pennsylvania. He was a member of Monroe Wilson American Legion Post, Veterans of Foreign Wars, and Barracks 0742. He had lived in Transylvania County for 40 years.

Surviving are his wife, Pauline Parker Holland; son, Corbett Holland; two daughters: Villa Freeman and Virta O'Connor; a brother, Lester Holland; and a sister, Charlotte Peek.

Services will be held Wednesday afternoon in the chapel of Moody-Connolly Funeral Home. Military graveside rites will be conducted by Monroe Wilson American Legion Post in Pisgah Gardens Cemetery.

Spurgeon Holland

Villa H. Freeman

Brevard News   Oct. 10, 1917

Liberty Loan Slogans

Don't cheer up the Kaiser—Buy a Bond.

Buy a Baby Bond for Baby.

If you are too old for the trenches, buy a Liberty Bond.

Soldiers give their lives—Others give their money.

If you cannot go across, come across— Buy a Liberty Bond.

If you can't fight, your DOLLARS can —Buy Liberty Bonds.

Be a bondholder in the United States Government.

Charles Montgomery HOLLINGSWORTH

Born: 14 Apr 1891 in Transylvania County, NC
Died: 5 May 1968, Honea Path, Anderson County, SC; age 78
Buried: Woodlawn Memorial Park, Greenville, SC
Spouse: **Julia SCOTT**
Father: **Thomas J. HOLLINGSWORTH**
Mother: **Mary Ann COLE**
Draft Registration: 26, single, self-employed farmer in Blantyre

[Documentation: Transylvania County Birth Index, findagrave.com Ancestry.com SSDI]

Hollingsworth   Charles M   4,159,455   *White *Colored.
(Surname)   (Christian name)   (Army serial number)

Residence: _____ Brevard _____ NORTH CAROLINA
           (Street and house number)   (Town or city)   (County)   (State)

*Enlisted _____ *Inducted at __Brevard N C_____ on __July 24, 18__
Place of birth: __Brevard N C__   Age or date of birth: __Apr 14, 1891__
Organizations served in, with dates of assignments and transfers: _____
_____ 53 Dep Brig to Oct 30/18; Co A 358 M G Bn to disch _____

Grades, with date of appointment: __Pvt_____

Engagements: _____

Wounds or other injuries received in action: None.
Served overseas from †__No_____ to †_____; from †_____ to †_____
Honorably discharged on demobilization __Dec 12/18_____, 19_____
In view of occupation he was, on date of discharge, reported ____0____ per cent disabled.
Remarks: _____

18 Jul 1918   Brevard News
23 MORE MEN TO LEAVE JULY 24, 1918 for Camp Hancock, Ga., who will leave on the 3:13 train:
. . . Charles Montgomery Hollingsworth, Blantyre . . .

Artillery Drill Camp Hancoc, Augusta, Ga.

James Charles HOLLINGSWORTH

Born:	9 Jun 1892
Died:	29 Dec 1953, Buncombe County, NC; age 61
Buried:	Kings Grove Church Cemetery, Henderson County, NC
Spouse:	**Pansy DRAKE**
Father:	**Alec HOLLINGSWORTH**
Mother:	**Mandy CARVER**
Draft Registration:	21, single, worked as a yardman for the Brevard Tanning Company

[Documentation: Buncombe County DC; Ancestry.com findagrave.com; Hendersonville T-N obituary]

1

Hollingsworth   James C   303,539   • White • Colored.

CAROLINA

Residence: _____ Pisga Forest   Transylvania NO.TH
(Street and house number)   (Town or city)   (County)   (State)

_____ •Inducted at Brevard N C _____ on Oct. 3, 1917

Place of birth: Asheville N C _____ Age or date of birth: 22 4/12 yrs

Organizations served in, with dates of assignments and transfers: _____
_____ M D to disch _____

Grades, with date of appointment: Corp May 1/18 _____

Engagements: _____

Wounds or other injuries received in action: None.
Served overseas from † Nov 12/1 to † Apr 17/19, from † _____ to † _____
Honorably discharged on demobilization Apr 30/19 , 19___
In view of occupation he was, on date of discharge, reported O _____ per cent disabled.
Remarks: _____

12/29/1953

JAMES HOLLINGSWORTH

James C. Hollingsworth, 61, a resident of Hendersonville, RFD 2, died last night at Oteen Hospital after a long illness. He had been a patient at the hospital for almost three years.

The funeral service will be held Thursday at 3 p.m. at the Edneyville Methodist Church. Members of Hedricks-Rhodes VFW post will conduct the graveside service.

Mr. Hollingsworth was a veteran of WWI, having served overseas in the Medical Corps for 18 months.

Surviving are a daughter, Mrs. James Young of RFD 2; the brother, Randolph Hollingsworth; and three sisters: Mrs. D.D. Anderson, Mrs. Coralee Brackett and Mrs. Maggie Grice.

Postmarked 1918 Postal Card

Ambulance Field Hospital Camp Hancock, Ga.

Lawrence Anderson HOLT

Born: 16 Apr 1901, Burlington, NC
Died: 4 May, 1978, Transylvania County, NC; age 77
Buried: Gillespie-Evergreen Cemetery
Spouse: **Lucy WHITMIRE**
Father: **Young Anderson HOLT**
Mother: **Minnie ALBERTIE**
Draft Registration: No
Military Marker: PVT US Army WW I

[Documentation: NC Death Collection, <u>Transylvania County Cemetery Survey</u>, 1940 Census, Ancestry.com]

Lawrence Holt

Lucille C. Cooper Photo

Prior to the Armistice only 15,000 men had returned to the United States. With the signing of the Armistice the War Department announced a policy to send home certain auxiliaries to set up the procedures to start shipping our troops home without delay. On December 21 the War Department announced by cable that it had decided to begin immediately the return of our forces and continue as rapidly as transportation would permit. The lack of military housing at the ports and the shortage of ships created a big challenge for the top administration.

James Fred HONEYCUTT

Born;	2 Jun 1897
Died:	11 Mar 1968, Veteran's Hospital, Johnson City, TN; age 70
Buried:	Jason McCall Cemetery
Occupation:	Textile worker
Spouse:	**Ethel Phoebe McCALL**, m. 21 Mar 1918, Transylvania County, NC
Mother:	**Mary Jane HONEYCUTT**
Draft Registration:	22, single, laborer for F.E. Allen at Gloucester
Military Marker:	NC PCT BTRY C 5 DEV BN WW I

[Documentation: SSDI; <u>Transylvania County Cemetery Survey</u>; TT obituary]

Honeycutt, James F. 3,277,110   • White • Colored.
(Surname)   (Christian name)   (Army serial number)
Residence: _____ Brevard   Transylvania NORTH CAROLINA
        (Street and house number)   (Town or city)   (County)   (State)
                    Brevard N C June 25/18
            •Inducted at _____ on _____, 19___
Place of birth: ___ Ashville N C ___ Age or date of birth: ___ June 2/1896 ___
Organizations served in, with dates of assignments and transfers: _____
        156 Dep Brig to Aug 30/18; Aux Rmt Dep 315 te disch

Grades, with date of appointment: _____
            Pvt

Engagements: _____

Wounds or other injuries received in action: None.
Served overseas from †No to † _____, from † _____ to † _____
Honorably discharged on demobilization _____ Dec 18/18 ____, 19____
In view of occupation he was, on date of discharge, reported ____0____ per cent disabled.

Note: Aux RMT Depot (Auxiliary Remount Depot) The procurement and training of horses and mules for military use.

21 Jun 1918   **Brevard News**
WHITE REGISTRANTS WHO ARE TO LEAVE FOR CAMP JACKSON, S.C.
TUESDAY, JUNE 25th, 1918 AT 3:13 P.M.
. . . James Fred Honeycutt, Balsam Grove . . .

3/14/1968
James F. Honeycutt

James Fred Honeycutt, 72, of Brevard, died in a Johnson City, TN hospital after a long illness. He was a retired textile worker and veteran of World War I.

Surviving are his wife, Mrs. Ethel McCall Honeycutt; three sons: Jack, James and John; four daughters: Mrs. Pauline Ellis, Mrs. Delphia Brown, Mrs. Marce Hughes and Mrs. Myrtice Whiteside; and two half-brothers: Vennie and Alvin Hollifield.

Funeral services were held Wednesday afternoon in the Chapel of Frank Moody Funeral home. Burial was in the McCall Cemetery at Balsam Grove.

Walter Grady HOOPER, Sr.

Born:	24 Oct 1891, Jackson County, NC
Died:	9 May 1975, Transylvania County, NC; age 83
Buried:	Pisgah Gardens Cemetery
Occupation:	Farmer
Spouse:	**Eva PACE**
Father:	**John HOOPER**
Mother:	**Ruth HOOPER**
Draft Registration:	Henderson County, 25, single and farming
Military Marker:	PVT US Army WW I

[Documentation: NC Delayed Birth Index, Transylvania County Cemetery Survey, Ancestry.com]

Walter G. Hooper, Sr.

Walter G. Hooper, III Photo

5/12/1975
W.G. HOOPER

Walter Grady Hooper, Sr., 83, died at the home of a son, Thomas L. Hooper of Brevard, after a period of declining health. A native of Jackson County, he had lived in Brevard since 1946 and was a veteran of World War I. He was a member of American Legion Post No. 88 and was an inactive deacon of Mt. Moriah Baptist Church. He was a retired farmer.

Surviving in addition to the son are the widow, Eva Pace Hooper; another son, Walter Grady Hooper, Jr.; and a daughter, Ruth Bresnahan.

Services were held Sunday in the chapel of Moore Funeral Home. Burial was in the Pisgah Gardens Cemetery.

---

17 Aug 1917   Brevard News
200 MEN CALLED FOR EXAMINATION
Fearing that Transylvania County would not be able to furnish its quota of 78 men on the first call from the 200 examined last week, the exemption board has called for 200 more men to appear on next Monday, Tuesday, Wednesday and Thursday, 50 each day, to appear at the city hall for physical examination.

(Readers were referred to the list printed earlier to determine the 200 next men).

George E. HOWARD

Born:	25 Aug 1896, North Carolina
Died:	17 Jun 1948, Greenville, South Carolina; age 51
Buried:	Blue Ridge Baptist Church Cemetery
Spouse:	**Bell Zonnie SUMMEY**, m. 11 Feb 1939, Greenville, SC
Father:	**Andrew HOWARD**
Mother:	**Molly PATTERSON**
Draft Registration:	No
Military Marker:	SC PVT 156 Depot WW I

[Documentation: <u>Transylvania County Cemetery Survey</u>, Application for Veteran's Headstone, Greenville County SC marriage record, Ancestry.com]

Greenville News (SC)
6/18/1948
GEORGE E. HOWARD

George E. Howard, 53, died last night at his home after having been in declining health nine months and seriously ill five months. He lived at Mills Mill the past four years and prior to that time made his home at Franklin Mill for eight years. He was engaged in textile work. During World War I he was a military policeman in a depot brigade.

He was a son of the late Andrew and Mollie Patterson Howard and a native of Greenville County. His first wife was the late Sarah Woodward Howard. From that union tow children survive: Ruby Lane and G.A. Howard. His second wife, Bell Summey Howard survives with seven stepchildren.

The average American soldier who went to France received six months training in this country before he sailed. After he landed overseas he had two months training before entering the battle line in a quiet sector where he remained one month before going into an active sector and taking part in hard fighting. Orcutt, Louis E., **The Great War Supplement**, published 1920, p. 69

Jason HUGGINS

Born:	25 Apr 1893, Henderson County, NC
Died:	3 Oct 1978, Transylvania County, NC; age 85
Buried:	Pisgah Gardens Cemetery
Spouse:	**Myrtle TOWNSEND**, m. 1 Jul 1917, Transylvania County, NC
Father:	**William HUGGINS**
Mother:	**Naomi MIDDLETON**
Draft Registration:	Henderson County, 24, single, working at Transylvania Tannery

[Documentation: North Carolina Birth Index, North Carolina Death Collection, Discharge, Transylvania County Cemetery Survey, Ashevile CT obituary, Ancestry.com]

Huggins, Jason   718,378   Henderson   1¼   White

Residence: Hendersonville NORTH CAROLINA
(Street and house number) (Town or city) (County) (State)

Enlisted in: NG at Hendersonville N C   July 1/15

Born in: Henderson Co N C   23 yrs

Organizations: 6 Co CAC NC NG 6 Co Cape Fear CAC Ft Caswell to Jan 25/18; Btry C 2 QM Bn to May 14/18; 12 Co Cape Fear CAC Ft Caswell to Nov 14/18; 3 Co Cape Fear CAC Ft Caswell to disch

Grades: Pvt 1cl July 17/17; Corp Sept 25/18

Engagements: —

Wounds or other injuries received in action: None.
Served overseas: None
Hon. disch. Apr 17/19 on demobilization
Was reported 0 per cent disabled on date of discharge, in view of occupation.
Remarks: —

SRC Notes: CAC NC NG (Coast Artillery Corps North Carolina National Guard)

21 Sep 1917   Brevard News
Mrs. Jason Huggins left this week to join her husband who is with the Coast Artillery Corps at Fort Caswell.

18 Jan 1918   Brevard News
Mrs. Jason Huggins left Wednesday morning to join her husband who is stationed at Fort Caswell.

12 Oct 1918   Brevard News
FORT CASWELL NEWS
Editor Brevard News:
    Probably it will be interesting to your readers do have a few items from Fort Caswell, as several of the Transylvania boys are or have been here.
    I arrived at Caswell on 31 August, 1917 and have seen boys from different parts of the state coming and going, but so far it is been my misfortune to be left behind. Most of my company has gone across with the exception of about fifteen. The 6th Company from Hendersonville was composed of boys from Transylvania and Henderson mostly, and to my sorrow after some months there will be quite a number transferring to different seagoing organizations which will be leaving soon afterwards. After two months there will be another transfer made which will take most all of the remaining ones. The boys that have left are as follows: A.K. Lewis, Thomas Bagwell, Roy Crary, Roy Marr, Henry Scruggs, Claude and Benjamin Staggs, Carl Hardin, Overton Erwin and James Garren, all of Brevard, and those that are left here are Henry Garren, Everett Osteen and myself. And since arriving here it has been one continuous squad "right and left" flavored with K. P. (kitchen police) and other work that is connected with an Army post.

Some boys try to shun the work and there are numerous ways of doing it. Some get sick, others hide while still others seek office work and to be orderlies for officers, but I believe that Company Clerk is the best-known remedy for getting out of work. No one but Privates hold these positions and are usually kept busy sweeping the floor for the First Sergeant, but that is some better than using the muscle.

I have been everything from a Private in the rear rank to the Mess Sergeant and the latter excels for all liberty and good eating as they have access to all the "grub." And I have the pleasure of acting Mess Sergeant at this time.

While walking up the street some time ago I came up with Ervin Galloway which was a surprise and I was glad to see someone from home.

The Spanish influenza has been raging here for some time but is about under control at present There have been several deaths since its appearance.

Thanking you for this valuable space, I beg to remain,

Yours truly,
Cpl. Jason Huggins

Asheville Citizen Times
10/5/1978
JASON HUGGINS

Jason Huggins, 85 died Tuesday in the Asheville VA Hospital after an extended illness. A native of Henderson County, he was a son of the late William and Naomi Middleton Huggins and was an Army veteran of World War I. A retired postal employee, he was a member of Brevard First Baptist Church, Dunn's Rock Masonic Lodge and the American Legion.

Mr. Huggin's wife, Myrtle Townsend Huggins, died in 1976.

Masonic graveside rites were conducted in Pisgah Gardens Cemetery. The Dunn's Rock Masonic Lodge officiated.

Surviving are three sons: William F., Jack L. and Robert J. Huggins; a daughter, Kathryn Orr; and a sister, Mrs. John Drake.

NOON DAY MESS.

1919 Postal Card

Jessie B. HUGGINS

Born: 24 Apr 1889, Henderson County, NC
Died: 29 Jun 1955, Transylvania County, NC; age 66
Buried: Greenwood Cemetery
Spouse: **Catherine AIKEN**, m. 22 Oct 1920 Transylvania County, NC
Father: **Andrew L. HUGGINS**
Mother: **Salena SENTELLE**
Draft Registration: 27, single, self-employed farmer at Calvert
Headstone inscription: NC Pvt Co D Engr Tng Regt WW I

[Documentation: Transylvania County Cemetery Survey, TT obituary, Cowart's Index to Marriages. Ancestry.com]

7/7/1955
JESSIE HUGGINS

Funeral services for Jesse B. Huggins, 63, were held last Friday morning in the Cherryfield Calvert Baptist Church. Burial was in the Greenwood Cemetery.

Mr. Huggins died at his home at Cherryfield last Wednesday night. A native of Henderson County, he had lived in Transylvania most of his life.

Survivors include the widow; one sister, Mrs. Louse Sprouse and one brother, Marshall Huggins.

26 Aug 1918   Brevard News
TWELVE MORE MEN LEFT MONDAY
The following men were entrained for Camp Jackson Monday afternoon:
. . . Jesse B. Huggins, Cherryfield . . .

---

27 Jun 1918   Brevard News

NAMES TO BE PUBLISHED
At the meeting of the Township chairmen of the War Savings drive, it was decided to print the names of every person in the county with the amount of War Stamps they have subscribed for. You will be able to see whether your neighbor is a slacker or not. In subscribing for these War Stamps no one gives anything; they had just agreed to save that much before January 1, 1919. The stamps are as good as money and draw 4% interest compounded every 3 months, which means a little better than 4 1/2% tax-free, which again means about 6 1/2% on your money. These certificates will be registered at the Post Office so no one but you, yourself, can get the money on Stamps. You can get your money at any time after 10 days notice to the postmaster.

John Marshall HUGGINS

Born:	2 Nov 1895, Henderson County, NC
Died:	31 Jan 1973, Transylvania County, NC; age 77
Buried:	Greenwood Cemetery
Occupation:	Farmer and textile worker
Spouse:	**Ethel AIKEN**, m. 22 Jul 1920, Transylvania County, NC
Father:	**Andrew L. HUGGINS**
Mother:	**Salena SENTELLE**
Draft Registration:	21, single, self-employed farmer living at Calvert
Military Marker:	VA Wagoner US Army WW I

[Documentation: Transylvania County DC; Transylvania County Cemetery Survey; TT obituary, Cowart's Index to Marriages]

```
_____Huggins, Marshall_____731,231_____ * White * Colored
      (Surname)      (Christian name)    (Army serial number)

Residence: _____Calvert Transylva N C    NORTH CAROLINA
              (Street and house number)  (Town or city)  (County)      (State)

_____, *Inducted at _Brevard NC_  on_Nov 5_, 19_17_
Place of birth: ___Henderson Co SC_  Age or date of birth: ___21 yrs_
Organizations served in, with dates of assignments and transfers: _____
_____Co B 324 Inf to Feb 5/18; Sup Co 6 Inf to disch_____

Grades, with date of appointment: _____
_____Wag Feb 19/18_____

Engagements: _____
_____

Wounds or other injuries received in action: None.
Served overseas from †_Apr 11/18_ to †_July 22/19_, from †_____ to †_____
Honorably discharged on demobilization _____July 29/19_____, 19____
In view of occupation he was, on date of discharge, reported ___0___ per cent disabled.
Remarks: _____
```

2 Nov 1917   Brevard News
LOCAL BOARD ORDERS THIRTEEN MORE MEN to report to the Local Board at 5 P.M. on Monday, November 5, 1917 for transportation for Camp Jackson. They will leave for Camp November 6 at 8 A.M.
. . . Marshall Huggins . . .

2/8/1973
J.M. HUGGINS

John Marshall Huggins, 77, Brevard, died last Wednesday evening in Transylvania Community Hospital after a lingering illness.

Funeral services were held Friday afternoon in the Mt. Moriah Calvert Baptist Church. Burial was in the Greenwood Cemetery on the Rosman Highway.

He was a native of Henderson County and a veteran of World War I. He was a retired farmer and had been employed by several textile mills.

Surviving is the wife, Mrs. Ethel Aiken Huggins; two sons: Charles M. and John F.; and one sister, Mrs. Eloise Sprouse.

---

25 Jul 1918   Brevard
RED CROSS CALLS FOR HELP
The local Red Cross has received an order from headquarters for a case of five-yard gauze rolls to

Van Elliott HUGGINS

Born:	1 Dec 1893, Henderson County, NC
Died:	17 Nov 1981, Buncombe County, NC; age 87
Buried:	Cathey's Creek Baptist Church Cemetery
Occupation:	Tannery
Spouse(s):	**Rosa McCALL**, m. 4 Jul 1922, Transylvania County, NC
	Lula Blanche OWEN
	Martha E. Olivia STEPP, m. 14 Sep 1941, Transylvania County, NC
Father:	**John Elliott HUGGINS**
Mother:	**Mary REVIS**
Draft Registration:	23, single, cutting acid wood
Military Marker:	PVT US Army WW I

[Documentation: NC Birth Index, NC Death Collection, <u>Transylvania County Cemetery Survey</u>, Discharge, Hendersonville T-N obituary, Family Search.org]

Van Elliot Huggins, Sr.

Rhonda Huggins Photo

Huggins, Van		1,322,762		White
(Surname)	(Christian name)	(Army serial number)	(Race: White or colored)	
Residence:		Henderson	NORTH CAROLINA	
(Street and house number)	(Town or city)	(County)	(State)	

* Enlisted in	N G at Brevard N C	July 9/17
† Born in	Henderson Co N C	22 7/12 Yrs
Organizations:	MG Co 1 Sep Sq Cav N C N G to --; Co A 115 M G Bn to disch	
Grades:	Pvt 1cl Sept 15, 17; Pvt Dec 1/17	
Engagements:	—	—

Wounds or other injuries received in action: None. —
‡ Served overseas: May 11/18 to Mch 22/19 —
§ Hon. disch. Apr 2/19 on demobilization —
Was reported 0 per cent disabled on date of discharge, in view of occupation. —
Remarks:

Form No. 724-1½, A. G. O.
March 12, 1920.
3—7688

* Insert " R. A.," " N. G.," " E. R. C.," " N A.," as case may be, followed by place and date of enlistment. † Give place of birth and date of birth, or age at enlistment.
‡ Give dates of departure from and arrival in the United States. § Give date.

SRC Notes: MG Co (Machine Gun Company)

Hendersonville Times-News
11/19/1981
Van E. Huggins, Sr.

VAN ELLIOTT HUGGINS SR., 87, of Brevard, a native of Henderson County, died Tuesday in Asheville Veterans Administration Medical Center after a period of declining health. Mr. Huggins was a son of the late John Elliott and Mary Revis Huggins. He had lived in Transylvania County most of his life. He was an Army veteran of World War I and was a retired employee of Transylvania Tannery. He was a former member of Selica Baptist Church.

Surviving are four sons: Van Elliott Huggins Jr., Russell E. and Gary E. and Ronald E.; and two daughters: Patricia Owen and Rosalie Passmore.

Services will be held at 11 a.m. Friday in Rosman Baptist Tabernacle. Burial will be in Cathey's Creek Cemetery. American Legion Post 88 will conduct military graveside **rites.**

David Lutterich HUNT

Born:	8 Oct 1896, Transylvania County, NC
Died:	1 Sep 1964, Pinellas, FL; age 67
Buried:	Undetermined
Spouse:	**Anne**
Father:	**Dr. Charles HUNT**
Mother:	**Henrietta ANDERSON**
Draft Registration:	No

[Documentation: Ancestry.com, Transylvania County Birth Index, SSDI]

```
         Hunt    David L            1,165,040    white              1¼
      (Surname)      (Christian name)   (Army serial number) (Race: White or colored)
Residence:_____ Brevard        NORTH CAROLINA
         (Street and house number)    (Town or city)    (County)      (State)
*Enlisted in    NG Charlotte NC         Apr 25/17
†Born in        Brevard NC        —     20 6/12 yrs              —
 Organizations:  Co B 105 Engrs to Nov 22/17; Co A 115 MG Bn 2 Corps Repl
                 Bn AEF France to disch

Grades:  Corp May 10/17; Corp Oct 13/17; Sgt July 6/17; Sgt Nov
         22/18; Pvt Sept 16/17
Engagements:                      —                              —

Wounds or other injuries received in action: None.
‡Served overseas: May 10/18 to Apr 5/18                         —
§Hon. disch.  Apr 16/19    on demobilization                    —
Was reported   0           per cent disabled on date of discharge, in view of occupation.
Remarks:                                                        —
```

SRC Notes: Engrs (Engineers) MG (Machine Gun) Repl Bn AEF (Replacement Battalion American Expeditionary Forces)

27 Apr 1917   Brevard News
MORE TRANSYLVANIANS READY FOR WAR
   Last week the News published the names of those who, to its knowledge, had offered their services to the government in various branches . . . David Hunt.

12 Oct 1917   Brevard News
David Hunt of the 125th Engineers, stationed at Camp Sevier, near Greenville, was at home for the weekend.

26 Sep 1918   Brevard News
FROM A BREVARD BOY OVER THERE
(Quotations from a letter written by David Hunt to Dr. and Mrs. C. W. Hunt)
   "I received your newspaper clippings and enjoyed them very much. We have no news from the US except through an occasional English paper.
   We can't tell, of course, which one of us will be next. All of the Germans that I have seen are nothing but little boys or very old men.
   I am in charge of the machine gun and squad. I am in the trenches at Ypres (in Belgium), shallow trenches and embraced works. If the trenches are deep the water rises. The Huns are scared to death of the French-Americans.
   Gerry (Germans) is still bombing hospitals. That is due to the fact that Gerry and the allies began painting large red crosses on some of their ammunition dumps and it was discouraged eventually.

While coming over we all wore life preservers all the time. We got plenty of cigarettes. They are British made and no good. I received some magazines from Rev. C.D. Chapman and enjoyed them very much. Please thank him for them.

Yes, I can carry on an incorrectly simple conversation in French. I do not find it hard to learn, having studied Latin.

The last time that I was on the line I had orders to move my machine gun and squad to a certain place and fire on a certain crossing of railroad and a trail where Gerry usually crosses in bringing up his reserves. We got our elevation and direction from a map. According to orders we used three hours to fire 2,000 shots, firing bursts of irregular sizes at irregular intervals. Monroe Wilson, the gunner of my squad did most of the firing and I did some of it to keep in practice. It is fun to fire. Monroe is one of the best gunners and soldiers in the company and absolutely fearless. That night we might have killed a pile of Germans or we might not have killed any. Gerry was circulating around that section that night. We concealed the flash of our gun with a wet fire screen. We had to keep our heads low on account of snappers. We would fire a while, five or six seconds, then a German sniper with a machine gun would answer us, firing about a foot over our heads. We were in a hole and behind a bank. We would simply laugh at him, because he could not hit us. He would skin over the edge of the bank. It is very easy to tell where a machine gun is and in what direction it is firing. On the front that we are on we are almost surrounded by Gerry, just as Rhelms used to be.

You are right, there is nothing that looks natural over here except the stars. The other night some of the boys commented upon that very fact. The poem you sent me is right; give me "America." These people over here are so far behind time that they don't know they are living. They have two-wheeled dump carts for buggies. There are only one or two decent looking vehicles in Paris.

All of our work is done at night. When we get through we sleep and eat and smoke and tell big lies and do all we can to make each other wish that he were at home, all for mental occupation.

We sit around and watch air battles, watch "Gerry" shoot "whizz bangs" at our planes and watch ours shoot at his. We see them brought down in flames sometimes. It is very hard to hit them. Gerry is deathly afraid of our aircraft and anti-aircraft guns.

If you hang around the trenches for a while you become very indifferent and fearless of shells and bullets and don't pay any attention to them, but of course it will not do to allow yourself to be careless.

14 Feb 1919   Brevard News
LETTER FROM OVER THERE

In A Letter To His Father Sgt. David L. Hunt Gives An Outline Of His Trip To France

On May 5th, 1917, the 115th Machine Gun Battalion under the command of Maj. William R. Robertson started on its trip to help "Get the Kaiser." On May 11th, 1917 we sailed from Philadelphia and after a trip of four days we reached the harbor of Halifax, Nova Scotia, stayed there one day and joined the fleet of eleven other transports before we started across the sea, which was a trip of ten days.

Our English ship was partly loaded with chickens, apples, and candies. But our food for the sixteen days was tea, half cooked goat meat (not mutton), Army hard bread (hard tacks), pickles and a few teacakes occasionally. We paid 25 cents apiece for the apples and about the same for the chocolates, etc. Why did we pay that price? Because we had to live. The government allots 41 cents per day for food to each soldier.

When the convoy reached the war zone, a distance of about 500 miles from Europe, we were joined by six American submarine destroyers, which escorted us until we landed. It was about 1 o'clock in the morning May 25th, 1917 as we were drawing near the middle of the Irish Sea, when two submarines attacked our fleet. Our chasers sank the two submarines.

We landed in Liverpool and our next move was by rail to Dover. This was a mainline of English railroad and made exceptionally good speed. It made at least thirty miles an hour, which is "running some" for a train in Europe. If you go from one section to another, you must get out on the ground 1st. The trainmen get on the roof and put their hands through a trapdoor to light the gas lamps.

When the English soldiers are aboard these trains, they stop at every good-sized village in order that hot tea can be issued to the "Fighting Tommies." From Dover we crossed the English Channel and landed in Calais, France. Marched from the dock to a so-called "Rest Camp" with the name rest entirely misleading, because there is nothing restful about any rest camp.

Judging by the way that the French people stared at us, they probably had never seen any American soldiers. After "promenading" around the "Burg" we return to the camp to rest, which was named "Camp Sands" by a member of the company, appropriately named too, as the sand was ankle deep. When our supper was over, which was the same as breakfast and dinner, corned beef and hard bread, "Bully Beef and hard tack" we played cards and had our evening smokes. And had talks concerning the large guns, which we could hear booming in the distance, the first that we had heard.

It was about 12 o'clock when the "Gerry" (the popular name that applies to any Germans in general) woke us up with bombs which were raining down everywhere, and the roar of the anti-aircraft guns all around Calais, one would naturally think that there would be no town or camp left by morning.

A few days later we were detrained near St. Omer. The Corporals and Sergeants were sent to special machine gun schools before the 30th division, "Old Hickory" was scheduled to go to the front. I was sent to Camlers, France where the "General Headquarters Base Machine Gun School" was located. I had a course of thirty days at the school before we went to the front.

In a machine gun company, a Corporal is in charge of the squad of seven men and one gun. A Sergeant is in charge of a section, which is composed of two squads. The gunner of each squad must be entirely reliable and efficient. The best gunner in our company was Monroe Wilson from Transylvania County.

After the armistice was signed, I was sent to the 40th division (The Sunshine Division), which was from California. We are now at Bordeaux with orders to take the 1st available transport to the US.

On account of their initiative, alertness, and swiftness, the Americans are the best soldiers in France. The Australians, Canadians, and Scotch soldiers lack those three qualities to the degree of the Americans and for that reason cannot be placed on the same footing as the soldiers from the U.S.A. Next are the French soldiers. They were splendid soldiers but are too slow and not aggressive enough. Very good on defense and can hold the line but don't have much success when they go over after "Gerry." Judging by what I have heard, the Italians rank next to the French. Next the Belgians and at the bottom of the list we find the "Fighting English." The English do well on aircrafts and did much of the transporting American troops.

I have been trying to find out why they called this "Sunny France." If they would call it muddy France or rainy France there would be no puzzle to the phrase. During the eight months I have been over here we have had some good weather. I will venture to say we have had at least 23 to 27 clear sunshiny days during the eight months, and no two or three days consecutively.

The people from Western Belgium are almost uncivilized. They would run and hide, etc. And they would take the handles off the pumps in order that we couldn't get water to drink. They live in huts of two rooms, they live in one room and the horses, and pigs, etc. live in the other room with the chickens patrolling the dining table. The people of northern France are civilized but very slouchy looking. The towns and houses of northern France are very unsanitary. And the height of these peoples ambition is to cheat a soldier out of as much money as possible. In southern France there is rather a good class of people, comparatively speaking. Their homes are clean, and they have barns for their horses, cows, etc. They are very kind, generous and courteous with American soldiers. With the exception of sanitation, the towns of France are all alike. Cobblestones for pavement and the only place where they have sidewalks that are wide enough to walk on is Paris. Some of the towns have a streetcar system but none of them are any good. Nearly all of the buildings are of stone and brick and no buildings over there over three or four stories tall. even in the wonderful famous city of Paris. Paris covers a large area of ground. A few of the streets are wide and paved with asphalt and in comparison with the streets of other towns they seem quite pretty. They have a fairly large streetcar system but very old timing and slow. You can catch a car "ever now and then". They don't have a schedule in France. There is a pretty good subway station in Paris although the cars are much smaller, lighter, and slower than those in the United States.

The people of Southern France (not northern France) are very courteous and polite always say good morning, good day, Sir - never leave off the "Sir." All they want is to get back to real country once more. They will know how to appreciate a good home and country.

2 May 1919   Brevard News
David Hunt has returned to his home here from overseas. He spent eleven months in France and says that Paris doesn't look a bit like it sounds. He likes Main Street, Brevard much better.

Garfield HUNTSINGER

Born:	13 Apr 1896, Madison County, NC
Died:	20 Feb 1970, Oteen VA Hospital, Buncombe County; age 73
Buried:	West Memorial Park Cemetery, Weaverville, NC
Occupation:	Sawmill worker
Spouse:	**Macie DILLINGHAM**
Father:	**Tom HUNTSINGER**
Mother:	**Rebecca PEGG**
Draft registration:	22, single, worked as a logger for L.R. Dillingham, Gloucester

[Documentation: Buncombe County DC, Ancestry.com, SSDI, findagrave.com]

huntsinger Garfield 1,872,945 * White ~~Colored~~
(Surname) (Christian name) (Army serial number)

Residence: _____ Balsam Grove _____ N.RTH CAROLINA
(Street and house number) (Town or city) (County) (State)

_____ *Inducted at __ Brevard NC _____ on Apr 26, 19__ 18

Place of birth: __ Madison NC __ Age or date of birth: ____ 23 1/12 yr

Organizations served in, with dates of assignments and transfers: _____
_____ M D Camp Greenleaf Ga to disch. _____

Grades, with date of appointment: _____
_____ Pvt 1cl Oct 1/18 _____

Engagements: _____

Wounds or other injuries received in action: None.
Served overseas from † no ___ to † _____, from † _____ to † _____
Honorably discharged on demobilization ___ Nov 4/19 ___, 19___
In view of occupation he was, on date of discharge, reported ___ 0 ___ per cent disabled.
Remarks: _____

Asheville Citizen-Times
2/21/1970
JAMES HUNTSINGER

James Garfield Huntsinger, 75, Barnardsville, died Friday in a Buncombe County hospital after a long illness. He was a retired farmer, lumberman and a veteran of World War I.

Surviving are two sons, Harry and James Huntsinger; two sisters, Mrs. Albert Crowder and Mrs. Laura Dixon; and a half-brother, Mitchell Dillingham.

Services will be held Sunday in Dillingham Presbyterian Church and burial will be in West Memorial Park, Weaverville.

---

5 Sep 1918   Brevard News

MISS GASH RECEIVES APPOINTMENT

Miss Annie Jean Gash has been notified by the National Red Cross office in Washington of her appointment by the government as official dietician for Transylvania County.

By this appointment Miss Gash becomes supervisor of all branches of dietetic instruction given by the government or the Red Cross in this county.

She will maintain headquarters at Brevard and Rosman and will begin her work sometime about the first of October.

William Walker HURST

Born: 20 Nov 1893, North Carolina
Died: 31 Oct 1958, VAH Kecaughtan, VA; age 64
Buried: Hampton National Cemetery, Hampton, VA
Married: **Dora CONLEY,** m. 23 Dec 1919, Transylvania County
Father: **William Walter HURST**
Mother: **Martha OSBORNE**
Draft registration: 23, single, worked as a spinner for Maurice Hook, Pisgah Silk Mill
Military Marker: NC PVT 2 WG CONC BRIG AIR SERVICE WW I

[Ancestry.com, findagrave.com, FamilySearch.org, U.S. National Cemetery Interment Control Form]

Hurst	William	1 080 109	White
(Surname)	(Christian name)	(Army serial number)	(Race: White or colored)

Residence: Brevard   Transylvania   NORTH CAROLINA
           (Street and house number)   (Town or city)   (County)   (State)

Enlisted in RA at Ft Thomas Ky   Nov 14/17
Born in   Brevard NC   2311/12 yrs
Organizations: Av 12 Det Sig C Kelly Field Tex to July 9/18; Dt Med
            Dept AS Kelly Field Tex to Feb 1/19; AS Unassigned
            Camp Wadsworth SC to disch

Grades: Pvt

Engagements:

Wounds or other injuries received in action: None.
Served overseas: none
Hon. disch. Feb 5/19   on demobilization
Was reported 0   per cent disabled on date of discharge, in view of occupation.

23 Nov 1917   Brevard News
W.W. HURST ENTERS AVIATION SERVICE

The following taken from a recent issue of the Asheville Citizens will be of interest to the friends of Walter Hearst:

William W. Hearst left last night for Ft. Thomas, Kentucky, being one of the men accepted by Capt. Dennis yesterday. He enlisted in the aviation service and will go from Ft. Thomas to Ft. Sam Houston, Texas.

30 Nov 1917   Brevard News
WALTER HURST WRITES ON MILITARY TRAINING

Walter Hurst, who recently enlisted in the aviation service, makes the following observations on the training of a soldier, and the letter written from Fort Thomas, Ky.

If a young man has not learned self-reliance prior to his coming here he will have ample opportunity to acquire the art before leaving. At this and all other Army camps a chap has to win his spurs. However, in spite of the rigid discipline that exists at Ft. Thomas, there is no lack of levity and enthusiasm. I have observed that when a recruit wears Uncle Sam's uniform he, at once becomes a man of poise and appreciates fully that he is going on a new endeavor. It is the goal of the men to teach Kaiser Bill a lesson that he will never forget.

1 Aug 1918   <u>Brevard News</u>
A SOLDIER'S LETTER

Am now working in the office of the Flight Surgeon, and am not busy just at this time. There is no flying done on Wednesday afternoons, so guess we will have it pretty soft this afternoon.

Yesterday I was very assiduously engaged in writing up the proceedings of the Board, which investigated several airplane accidents within the past few weeks. One fellow's ship was burned up, but he and his passenger escaped with just a few bruises. Another fellow broke his propeller. Another was a complete wreck, and another drove his nose into a bank (this does not mean his own nose, but the nose of his ship).

The weather is very fine now. If anyone had told me that San Antonio had such an even climate during the summer as I was enduring the sweltering heat last spring, I would've not believed it.

It seems that the Americans have given the Germans a sound beating. May the good work progress until the Huns are eliminated.

There is nothing happening here just now. Of course the routine would be exciting to a casual observer of life, the planes doing various stunts at all times during the day from sun up to dark, but it has become rather commonplace to us.

Sincerely,
Walter Hurst
San Antonio, Texas

14 Feb 1919   <u>Brevard News</u>
W.W. Hurst, who has seen several months of service in the Aviation Corps, San Antonio, Tex. is at his home here.

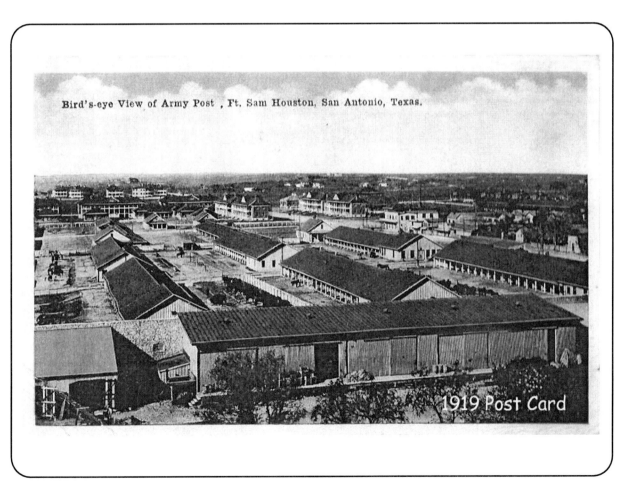

Bird's-eye View of Army Post , Ft. Sam Houston, San Antonio, Texas.

1919 Post Card

George Meyer ISRAEL

Born:	23 Oct 1891, Henderson County, NC
Died:	26 Apr 1951, Oteen VA Hospital, Buncombe County; age 59
Buried:	Whitmire Cemetery, Flat Creek Road
Occupation:	Owned Israel Grocery and had worked at Toxaway Tanning Co
Spouse:	**Hasse WHITMIRE**, m. 11 Sep 1921, Transylvania County, NC
Father:	**Edwin W. ISRAEL**
Mother:	**Alice Mary GUICE**
Draft Registration:	25, single, salesman
Military Marker:	NC Wagoner 321 INF 81 DIV WW I

[Documentation: Buncombe County DC, Upper Transylvania County, NC Remembered, FamilySearch.org, Application for Veteran Headstone, Ancestry.com, TT obituary, Cowart's Index to Marriages]

Israel, George M   1,857, 908   *White *Colored*
(Surname)   (Christian name)   (Army serial number)

Residence: 102 1/2 Patton Ave Asheville-   NORTH CAROLINA
(Street and house number)   (Town or city)   (County)   (State)

▓▓▓▓▓▓. *Inducted at Asheville N C   on Sept 18 19 17

Place of birth: Hendersonville N C   Age or date of birth: 25 11/12 Yrs

Organizations served in, with dates of assignments and transfers: Co I 321 Inf to May 13/18; Su Co 32 1 Inf to disch.

Grades, with date of appointment: Wag May 1/19

Engagements:

Wounds or other injuries received in action: None.
Served overseas from †July 31/18 to †June 20/19 from †_____ to †_____
Honorably discharged on demobilization Aug 14/19 , 19_____
In view of occupation he was, on date of discharge, reported 0 per cent disabled.
Remarks:

George M. Israel

Ila Israel Photo

5/3/1951
G.M. ISRAEL

Final rites for George Meyer Israel, 60, who died in the Veterans hospital at Swannanoa last Friday night, were held Saturday at the Zion Baptist Church at Rosman. Members of the Monroe Wilson Post of the American Legion conducted military services and interment was in the Whitmire Cemetery.

Mr. Israel, a native of Henderson County, had resided at Rosman for 31 years. A very active church worker, he was a deacon and also taught Sunday school. A former employee of the Toxaway Tanning company, he was the owner of the Israel Grocery Store on the Pickens Highway.

Survivors include the widow, Mrs. Hassie Whitmire Israel; one daughter, Mrs. Eva Duckett; one son, Albert; one brother, E.W. Israel; one half-brother, O.C. Israel; and one sister, Mrs. T.A. Christenberry.

NATIONAL ARMY CANTONMENT (CAMP)

Camp Grant   Location: Rockford, Ill.   Organization: 86th Division
Troops from Illinois

Glover JACKSON

Born:	17 Apr 1898, Henderson County, NC
Died:	9 Sep 1974, Oteen VA Hospital, Buncombe County; age 76
Buried:	Gillespie-Evergreen Cemetery
Spouse:	**Sallie HESTER**
Father:	**Zeb JACKSON**
Mother:	**Elizabeth CASE**
Draft Registration:	No
Military Marker:	PFC US Army WW I

[Documentation: Buncombe County DC, NC Birth Index, Transylvania County Cemetery Survey, Discharge, Ancestry.com]

Jackson Glover   717,786   White
(Surname)   (Christian name)   (Army serial number)   (Race: White or colored)

Residence: Hendersonville   NORTH CAROLINA
           (Street and house number)   (Town or city)   (County)   (State)

Enlisted in: N G at Hendersonville N C on June 2/16

Born in: Dana N C 21 2/12 yrs

Organizations: 6 Co C A C N C N G to Jan 25/18; 10 Co San Francisco C A C to July 26/18; Btry F 59 Arty C A C to Nov 26/18; 232 Co 116 Bn M P C to Dec 16/18; 231 Co 116 Bn*

Grades: Pvt 1 cl Dec 7/16; Corp June 6/18; Sgt July 10/18; Pvt 1 cl Apr 9/19

Engagements: —

Wounds or other injuries received in action: None.

Served overseas: Oct 6/18 to July 23/19

Hon. disch. July 28/19 on demobilization

Was reported 10 per cent disabled on date of discharge, in view of occupation.

SRC Note: C A C N C N G (Coast Artillery Corps North Carolina National Guard}

9/12/1974
GLOVER JACKSON

Glover Jackson, 76, died Monday in an Oteen hospital after an extended illness. He was a native of Henderson County but had resided in Transylvania County most of his life. He was a retired employee of Olin Corporation with 24 years service and a veteran of World War I, having served in the US Army in Europe. He was a member of the Lewis Earle Jackson V.F.W. Post.

Surviving are the wife, Sallie Hester Jackson; and two sons, Richard Kimsey and Vance Jackson.

Services were held Wednesday in the Moore Funeral Home Chapel and burial followed in the Gillespie-Evergreen Cemetery.

William JACKSON

Born:	28 Mar 1898, Transylvania County, NC
Died:	26 May 1967, Oteen VA Hospital, Buncombe County; age 69
Buried:	Mt. Moriah Calvert Baptist Church Cemetery
Spouse:	**Ila WILBANKS**
Father:	**William H. JACKSON**
Mother:	**Mary MEECE**
Draft Registration:	No
Military Marker:	NC PFC CO A 115 MG BN WW I

[Documentation: Buncombe County DC, Ancestry.com (family file), Transylvania County Cemetery Survey, TT obituary]

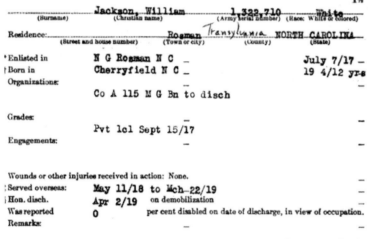

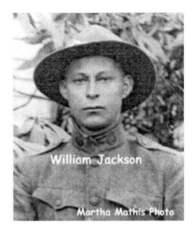

William Jackson

Martha Mathis Photo

SRC Note: MG (Machine Gun Battalion)

12 Apr 1918   Brevard News
William Jackson was at home recently on a furlough from Camp Sevier.

25 Apr 1919   Brevard News
We are all very glad to again have in our midst the following who spent ten months in France working faithfully for Uncle Sam: Pick Whitmire, William Jackson, Elbert Whitmire and Lee Nicholson.

Excerpt of Discharge
Battles, engagements, skirmishes, expeditions Occupation Ypres, sailent Jult 15th. to Aug. 31,1918. Doormeyeeleand Mt. Kemmel Engagement Aug. 31 to Sept. 5, 1918. Hindenburg Line, Bellicourt, Nauroy, Engagement Sept 29, to Oct. 2nd. 1918. Premount, Vaux-Andigny Engagement Oct. 8th. to 12th. 1918. Selle River Engagement Oct. 17th. to 21st. 1918

1/1/1967
WILLIAM JACKSON

Funeral services for William Jackson, 69, Rosman, were held Monday afternoon in the Rosman Methodist Church. Burial was in the Mt. Moriah Cemetery. Mr. Jackson was a veteran of World War I, assigned with the 30th Division. He was a former employee of the Toxaway Tanning Company.

Survivors are the widow, Mrs. Ila W. Jackson; a son, Tom; a daughter, Mrs. Amos Chandler; three sisters: Mrs. Lloyd Bryson, Mrs. Dorsey Paxton, Mrs. Ernest Howell; and one brother, John Jackson.

Paul Emmit JOHNSON

Born:	3 Apr 1888, Blanchester, Ohio
Died:	2 Aug 1962, Transylvania County, NC; age 74
Buried:	Pisgah Gardens Cemetery
Spouse:	**Ruth McCRUM**
Father:	Undetermined
Mother:	**Sarah JOHNSON**
Draft Registration:	Hamilton County, OH, 29, married, chauffeur
Military Marker:	Ohio MM1 US Navy

[Documentation: Transylvania County DC, Application for Veteran's Headstone, Transylvania County Cemetery Survey, 1900 Census, TT obituary, Ohio Military Soldiers, Ancestry.com]

Ohio Soldiers in WWI, 1917-1918 about PAUL EMMIT JOHNSON
Name: Paul Emmit Johnson
Age: 30
Race: White
Birth Date: 3 Apr 1888
Birth Location: Blanchester, Ohio, USA
Enlistment Date: 10 Apr 1918
Enlistment County: Recruiting Station Cincinnati
Enlistment State: Ohio
Enlistment Division: United States Navy

Comments:
Naval Training Camp Charleston
Summary Court to 24 June 1918;
Receiving Ship Pensacola Fla to 11 Nov 1918.
Landsman for Quartermaster (Aviation) 174 days;
Machinist's Mate, Second Class Hydroplane 41 days.
Ordinary Discharge 8 July 1919. Demobilization Pittsburgh Pa.

8/9/1962
PAUL JOHNSON

Funeral services for Paul Emmit Johnson, 74, of Inglewood, Florida, were held Saturday in the chapel of Moore-Kilpatrick Funeral home. Burial followed in the Pisgah Garden Cemetery.

Mr. Johnson died Thursday night at his home following a long illness. He was a native of Blanchester, Ohio and a retired employee of the city of Cincinnati, Ohio. He was a veteran of World War I. Since his retirement he had spent much of the time here in Brevard.

He is survived by the widow, Mrs. Ruth McCrum Johnson.

NATIONAL ARMY CANTONMENT (CAMP)

Camp Pike   Location: Little Rock, Ark.   Organization: 87th Division
Troops from Arkansas, Louisiana, and Mississippi

Elbert Emerson JONES

Born:	28 Mar 1892, Transylvania County, NC
Died:	8 Aug 1966, Oteen VA Hospital, Buncombe County; age 70
Buried:	Blue Ridge Baptist Church Cemetery
Father:	**James JONES**
Mother:	**Elmina Jane BISHOP**
Draft registration:	21, single, a farmer living at Cedar Mountain
Military Marker:	NC PFC Medical Dep WW I

[Documentation: Buncombe County DC, Ancestry.com, Transylvania County Cemetery Survey, TT obituary]

Jones   Elbert ?   1,878,521   • White • Colored.   **1**
(Surname)   (Christian name)   (Army serial number)

Residence: Cedar Mountain   Transylvania-   N.C.LT.
     (Street and house number)   (Town or city)   (County)   (State)

Enlisted .... In ducted at: revard NC   on Sep. 18 19 17

Place of birth: ...... Cedar Mountain NC   Age or date of birth: ...... 25 6/12   yrs.

Organizations served in, with dates of assignments and transfers: ML field H sp 324 to
     Jan1/18;   Sn Det 156 Dep Brig to Disch.

Grades, with date of appointment: Pvt 1cl Mar 14/18.

Engagements: ....

Wounds or other injuries received in action: None.

Served overseas from † No e   to † .... , from † .... to † ....

Honorably discharged on demobilization ...... June 10/19 ......, 19......

In view of occupation he was, on date of discharge, reported ...... 0 ...... per cent disabled.

SRC Note: Sn Det (Sanitation Detachment) Dep Brig (Depot Brigade)

---

21 Sep 1917   Brevard News
THIRTY-ONE MEN TO CAMP JACKSON
   . . .Elbert Emerson Jones . . .

8/11/1966
E.E. JONES

Mr. Jones died August 7th at the veteran's hospital in Oteen after a long illness. He was a native of Transylvania County.

Surviving is one sister, Mrs. Roy Robinson and one brother, Seldon Jones.

Funeral services for Elbert Emerson Jones, 54, were held at Blue Ridge Baptist Church Wednesday afternoon. Burial followed in the church cemetery.

SANITARY TRAIN

Each division had a Sanitary Train (today's Medical Battalion), which consisted of an ambulance section, a field hospital section and a medical supply unit. In all, a division's Sanitary Train totaled 1,331 men and 991 of that number were enlisted personnel

Ginn, Richard V.N. The History of the U.S. Army Medical Service Corps, p. 43

Fred JONES

Born:	7 Jun 1894, Pickens County, SC
Died:	Undetermined
Buried:	Undetermined
Race:	Colored
Father:	Undetermined
Draft Registration:	23, single working for the railroad
Note:	No further information has been located for Fred

[Documentation: 1900 Census, Ancestry.com]

Jones,   Fred   1,858,257   • ~~White~~ • Colored.
(Surname)   (Christian name)   (Army serial number)

Residence: _____ Brevard Transylvania   NORTH CAROLINA
            (Street and house number)   (Town or city)   (County)   (State)
                                        Breva N C   Apr 30/18
• ▬▬▬▬▬▬▬▬▬▬ •Inducted at _____ on _____, 19___
Place of birth: Pickens S C _____   Age or date of birth: 21 11/12 yra.
Organizations served in, with dates of assignments and transfers: _____
        156 Dep Brig to May 23/18; Co D 321 Serv Bn to disch

Grades, with date of appointment: _____
        Prt lcl Oct 15/18 _____

Engagements: _____
_____
_____

Wounds or other injuries received in action: None.
Served overseas from † __Aug 2/18__ to † __July 7/19__ from † _____ to † _____
Honorably discharged on demobilization __July 1 /19__, 19_____
In view of occupation he was, on date of discharge, reported __0_____ per cent disabled.

SRC Note: Dep Brig (Depot Brigade)   Serv Bn (Service Battalion)

Harlen Eugene JONES

Born:	26 May 1890, Transylvania County, NC
Died:	5 Apr 1965, Greenville, South Carolina; age 74
Buried:	Reedy River Baptist Church Cemetery, Greenville County, SC
Spouse:	**Lucille HUDSON**, m. 17 Sep 1933, Greenville County, SC
Father:	**James L. JONES**
Mother:	**Elmina Jane BISHOP**
Draft Registration:	27, single, farmer at Cedar Mountain

[Documentation: South Carolina findagrave.com, discharge, SSDI, Ancestry.com]

```
                                                                    1
    Jones, Harlen E.                xx              • White • Colored
    (Surname)        (Christian name)   (Army serial number)
Residence: _____xx_____      Cedar Mountain,        NORTH CAROLINA
              (Street and house number)  (Town or city)  (County)    (State)
• Enlisted R.E.C. • E.R.C. • Inducted at __Brevard, N. C.__ on Sept. 18, 19 17
Place of birth: _____Cedar Mountain, N.C.__ Age or date of birth: _27 - 4/12 yrs._
Organizations served in, with dates of assignments and transfers: _Fld. Hosp. 324 Camp_
Jackson, S. C. to-; 10 Co. 3 Tng. Bn. 156 Dep. Brig. to disch.

Grades, with date of appointment: _Pvt._


Engagements: _____xx_____


Wounds or other injuries received in action: None.
Served overseas from † __none__ to † _____, from † _____ to † _____
Honorably discharged on demobilization _____ Mch. 29, 19 19
In view of occupation he was, on date of discharge, reported ____0____ per cent disabled.
Remarks: _____xx_____
```

SRC Note: Tng (Training Center) Fld. Hosp. (Field Hospital)

21 Sep 1917   Brevard News
THIRTY-ONE MEN TO CAMP JACKSON
Alternates: . . Harlan Eugene Jones . . .

Two of the men, Roy Lamance and Barney Jackson Chapman had failed to report and the alternates Lauder B. Lyday and Harlen Eugene Jones took their place.

The Greenville News (SC)
4/ 6/1965
HARLEN E. JONES

Funeral services for Harlen Eugene Jones of Route 7, Greenville, will be conducted at 4:30 p.m. today at Reedy River Baptist Church. Burial will be in the church cemetery. Mr. Jones had been in failing health for four years. He was stricken at his home on Parker Road and died suddenly at 7 a.m. Monday.

He was born May 26, 1890, a son of the late James and Jane Bishop Jones of Cedar Mountain, North Carolina. The greater part of his life was spent in Greenville County; he was a plumber for many years. Mr. Jones was a veteran of World War I. He was a member of Blue Ridge Baptist Church at Cedar Mountain.

Surviving are his wife, Mrs. Lucille Hudson Jones; one daughter, Mrs. Marion Jones Swanger; one son, Eugene Jones; one sister, Mrs. Rosa Robinson; two brothers, Emerson and Seldon Jones.

> At the declaration of war all German ships in American ports were seized and approximately 3,000 men and a few wives were interned for the duration of the war.

Seldon Elzie JONES

Born:	28 Mar 1892, Transylvania County, NC
Died:	3 Mar 1970, Oteen VA Hospital, Buncombe County; age 77
Buried:	Unknown but in Transylvania County
Spouse:	**Nellie LEE**, m. 16 Sep, 1923, Transylvania County, NC
Father:	**James L. JONES**
Mother:	**Elmina Jane BISHOP**
Draft registration:	25, single, worked as a carpenter for Furman University, lived at Cedar Mountain

[Documentation: Buncombe County DC, Ancestry.com, TT obituary, Cowart's Index to Marriages

3/15/1970
SELDON JONES

Seldon Elzie Jones, 77, of Cedar Mountain, died Tuesday afternoon in an Asheville hospital after an extended illness. He was a lifelong resident of Transylvania County, a retired carpenter and a member of Blue Ridge Baptist Church. He was a veteran of World War I.

Mr. Jones is survived by his wife, Nellie Lee Jones; one sister, Mrs. Rosa Robinson; one daughter, Helen Fowler; and one son, Alvin Jones.

3 Oct 1918   Brevard News
If You Were To See The Ghastly Battle Fields

To hear the roaring of guns, the shrieking of shells, the gasping for breath, the pitiful cry of infants, the terrified scream of the mother. If you were to hear and see all these things right here in Old North Carolina, what would you not do to stop it? You wouldn't stand back and let the other fellow do your share, while you lived amid these beautiful hills in PEACE, LOVE, LUXURY AND HAPPINESS. Listen! Don't say it isn't possible. Remember those submarines operated right off our very coast, sank helpless non-combatants without warning. If you thought that by loaning your money to the grandest government (your government) on earth, in order to save the civilization of the world, wouldn't you give all you have even life itself? Your Government asks you to come forward like your forefathers, like a real genuine American who can feel the flap of "Old Glory" in the breeze, and LOAN, not give, for your own protection a few paltry dollars. WILL YOU DO IT? Or are so petrified with selfishness that you will let the greatest hour of your life pass without an effort to do YOUR DUTY. STAND BY YOUR COUNTRY, GOD'S OWN PARADISE. Go to our banker and subscribe to the fourth Liberty Loan. Sacrifice some luxury, if you have to, and loan your money at over four per cent interest. DO IT NOW! Protect your Independence, Country, Home and Loved Ones. You'll feel like a real American and will have done something to blot out the dastardly child and woman slayers.

BREVARD PRINTERY   **BREVARD NEWS**

Wm. A. Band   C.B. Osborne

Vardry C. JONES

Born:	20 Feb 1892, Transylvania County, NC
Died:	1 Oct 1937, Oteen VA Hospital, Buncombe County; age 45
Buried:	Blue Ridge Baptist Church Cemetery
Father:	**Solomon JONES**
Mother:	**Martha McCRARY**
Draft Registration:	24, single, farmer
Note:	Discharge papers: Enlisted 5 Nov 1917; Discharged 11 Nov 1917, by reason of physical disability incurred prior to entry into service.

[Documentation: Buncombe County DC, Application for Veteran's Headstone, <u>Transylvania County Cemetery Survey</u>, Discharge, TT obituary, Ancestry.com]

10/7/1937
VARDRY C. JONES

Funeral services were held last Saturday at Cedar Mountain for Vardry C. Jones who died at Oteen Hospital. Mr. Jones was given military honors at the service. He was an ex-service man, having served a short time in Co. E 32nd Infantry but was discharged on account of his health.

2 Nov 1917   Brevard News

LOCAL BOARD ORDERS THIRTEEN MORE MEN to report to the Local Board at 5 P.M. on Monday, November 5, 1917 for transportation for Camp Jackson. They will leave for Camp November 6 at 8 A.M.   . . . Verdry C. Jones . . .

---

7 Nov 1918   Brevard News

CHRISTMAS PARCELS FOR THE SOLDIERS

Cartons have been received at the Red Cross rooms for inclosing Christmas presents for the soldiers overseas. These cartons are for free distribution and everyone who has received a label is asked to come at once and get the box, as the time is growing very short in which these packages may be mailed.

Remember the amount of shipping space is so limited that only one parcel may go to each man and that from the person to whom he sends the label provided him overseas. All parcels must be packed in these cardboard boxes, 3 x 4 x 9 inches in size.

Do not mail the box yourself. When packed, take it to the Red Cross rooms where it will be examined and weighed. The box must contain neither explosives nor liquids; nothing packed in glass and must not weigh over two pounds, 15 oz. nor must contain any written matter.

The sender furnishes the postage to carry the parcel to Hoboken, N.J. The cost from here will be about fifteen cents for the full weight package.

Samuel Josh KEATON

Born:	5 Oct 1886, Burke County, NC
Died:	21 Sep 1972, Transylvania County, NC; age 85
Buried:	Pisgah Gardens Cemetery
Spouse:	**Mary Edna STAMEY**, m. 28 Jun 1923, Transylvania County, NC
Father:	**John KEATON**
Mother:	**Mary McCALL**
Draft Registration:	Burke County, 30, single in the lumber business
Military Marker:	S.C. PVT US Army WW I

Documentation: Transylvania County DC, Transylvania County Cemetery Survey, 1900-1940 Censuses, TT obituary, Ancestry.com, Cowart's Index to Marriages]

Keaton S(amuel) J   1,893,198   * White * Colored.
(Surname)   (Christian name)   (Army serial number)

Residence: _____ Morgantown   NORTH CAROLINA _____
(Street and house number)   (Town or city)   (County)   (State)

* ▓▓▓▓▓▓▓▓▓▓▓ *Inducted at Morgantown N C _____ on May 25, 1918

Place of birth: Morgantown N C   Age or date of birth: Oct 5,1886

Organizations served in, with dates of assignments and transfers: 156 Dep Brig to June 24 /18; Co C 324 Inf to Aug 3/18; Aux Rmt Dep 310 to disch

Grades, with date of appointment: Pvt

Engagements: _____

Wounds or other injuries received in action: None.
Served overseas from † None to † _____ , from † _____ to † _____
Honorably discharged on demobilization May 12 /19 , 19_____
In view of occupation he was, on date of discharge, reported 0 per cent disabled.

SRC Note: Aux Rmt Dep (Auxiliary Remount Depot)

9/28/1972
SAMUEL KEATON

Samuel Keaton, 84, of Kings Creek Road died unexpectedly in his home last Thursday evening. Mr. Keaton was a veteran of World War I and was retired from Brevard Tannery.

Surviving is the widow, Mrs. Mary Keaton; four daughters: Mrs. Virginia Rogers, Mrs. Ruth Goldsmith, Mrs. Nell Reid and Mrs. Jane Evett; two sons: Jim and Burt Keaton; and two sisters, Mrs. Callie Weeks and Mrs. Betty Padgett.

Funeral services were held Saturday in the Chapel of Frank Moody Funeral Home. Burial followed in the Pisgah Gardens Cemetery.

---

22 Aug 1918   Brevard News

MEN 21 SINCE JUNE 5TH REGISTER AUGUST 24TH

All male persons who have reached their twenty-first birthday since June 5, 1918, and on or before August 24, 1918 must register August 24, 1918. These men should consult with local draft boards as to how and when they should register.

The place of registration will be Office of Local Board at Brevard, N.C. Office will be open from 7:00 a.m. to 9 p.m., August 24, 1918.

J.I. Watson, Chief Clerk

John Harrison KEENER

Born:	1 Nov 1888, Macon County, NC
Died:	11 Nov 1984, Buncombe County, NC; age 96
Buried:	Woodlawn Memorial Park, Macon County
Occupation:	Retired farmer
Spouse:	**Dana NICHOLSON**
Father:	**Melvin KEENER**
Mother:	**Martha Caroline HOLLAND**
Draft Registration:	28, single, Field Assistant with Forest Service, Macon County
Discharge:	Enlisted 17 Sep 1917, Asheville, NC; served overseas in France from 22 Jan 1918 until 23 May 1919, discharged 29 May 1919, Camp Lee, Va

[Documentation; NC Death Collection; 1900, 1910 and 1930 Censuses; obit]

11/12/1984
JOHN H. KEENER

John Harrison Keener, 96, of Brevard, died Sunday, Nov. 11, 1984, in the Asheville VA Medical Center. A Macon County native, Keener was the son of the late Melvin Brownlow and Martha Holland Keener. He was a retired farmer and a member of Franklin First Baptist Church, a World War I veteran and a member of the American Legion.

Surviving are his wife, Dana Nicholson Keener; four daughters: Carolyn Fisher, Hazel Haynes, Pauline Kirkland and Viola Poteet; two sons, Harold and Eugene Keener; and a sister Charlotte Talley.

Services were held Wednesday in the chapel of Bryant Funeral Home in Franklin and the burial was in Woodlawn Memorial Park.

John Harrison Keener

Darel C. Keener Photo

MOTORCYCLES

During World War I the military role of the motorcycle was rapidly developed. As well as being widely used for the delivery of dispatches and the rapid movement of key personnel, it had a direct operational role as a machine-gun carrier. The Machine-Gun Corps used a Vickers-Cline motorcycle powered by a 5/6hp V-twin engine. It had a Vickers machine-gun, which was protected by an armored shield, mounted on a sidecar chassis, which also accommodated the gunner on a low seat. The motorcycle machine-gun combination could reach a required position quickly, make a strike and retreat quickly.

William Enoch KENNEDY

Born: 14 Oct 1890, Seagrove, NC
Died: 16 Jun 1977, Randolph County, NC; age 86
Buried: Midway Wesleyan Church Cemetery, Randolph County, NC
Spouse: **Ethel STALKE**
Father: **Dennis KENNEDY**
Mother: **Sarah LATHAM**
Draft registration: 26, single, employed as a farmer by Brevard Institute, lived in Brevard

[Documentation: Ancestry.com, findagrave.com, SSDI]

Kennedy, William E   1,876,250   • White • Colored
(Surname)   (Christian name)   (Army serial number)   NORTH CAROLINA

Residence: _____ Brevard _Transylvania_ _____
(Street and house number)   (Town or city)   (County)   (State)

• ▓▓▓▓▓▓▓▓▓▓ . •Inducted at __Brevard NC_____ Sept 18/17.
Place of birth: _____Seagrove NC_____ Age or date of birth: __26 11/12 yrs__
Organizations served in, with dates of assignments and transfers: _____
Amb Co 324 - 306 Sn Tn to disch.

Grades, with date of appointment: _____
Pvt 1cl Feb 12/18; Corp Sept 15/18

Engagements: _____

Wounds or other injuries received in action: None.
Served overseas from † __Aug 8/18__ to __June 20/19__ from † _____ to † _____
Honorably discharged on demobilization __June 29/19__ , 19____
In view of occupation he was, on date of discharge, reported __0__ per cent disabled.
Remarks: _____

SRC Note: Amb Co (Ambulance Corps)

21 Sep 1917   Brevard News
THIRTY-ONE MEN TO CAMP JACKSON
   . . . William Enoch Kennedy . . .

MOTOR TRANSPORTATION CORPS

   The requirement for a great number of vehicles caused the Medical Department to establish the Motor Ambulance Supply Depot in 1917 at Louisville, Kentucky. Its goal was to provide ambulance supply, repair and salvage, as well as a school of mechanics.

   The department shipped to Europe 3,070 GMC and 3,805 Ford ambulances. The vehicles were sent unassembled in two sections, the chassis and the body, because assembled vehicles were often damaged in shipping.

   A motor ambulance assembly detachment located at St. Nazaire, France would prepare the ambulance for combat service starting with completing four per day in January 1918 and increasing it until they were completing 15 per day. In September 1918 their title changed to Motor Transportation Corps (MTC).

Ginn, Richard V.N., **The History of the U.S. Army Medical Service Corps**, p. 51

Thomas Fred KILPATRICK

Born:	31 Jan 1895, Transylvania County, NC
Died:	2 Jun 1954, Transylvania County, NC; age 59
Buried:	Gillespie-Evergreen Cemetery
Occupation:	Brick mason
Spouse:	**Miriam POOR**
Father:	**Charles KILPATRICK**
Mother:	**Mary Alice TERRY**
Draft registration:	22, single, lived in Brevard, self-employed as a brick mason

[Documentation: Transylvania DC, Ancestry.com, Transylvania County Cemetery Survey, TT obituary]

```
                                                                        1
        Kilpatrick, Thomas F        1,891,627    * White  Colored
        (Surname)      (Christian name)    (Army serial number)

Residence: _____ Brevard Transylvania  NORTH CAROLINA
           (Street and house number)  (Town or city)  (County)    (State)

* Enlisted  R. A. N. G. or N. A. Inducted at Brevard N C May 24/18 on _____, 19___
Place of birth: Grange N C          Age or date of birth: 23 4/12 yrs

Organizations served in, with dates of assignments and transfers: _____
        156 Dep Brig to Dec 16/18; Utilities Div QMC Camp
        Jackson S C to disch _____

Grades, with date of appointment: _____
        Sgt Feb 20/19

Engagements: _____
        _____
        _____

Wounds or other injuries received in action: None.
Served overseas from † NO _____ to † _____, from † _____ to † _____
Honorably discharged on demobilization ___ May 10 /19 ____, 19___
In view of occupation he was, on date of discharge, reported ___ 0 ___ per cent disabled.
```

SCR Note: Dep Brig (Depot Brigade) QMC (Quartermaster Corps)

6/3/1954
FRED KILPATRICK

Thomas Fred Kilpatrick, 56, well known brick mason and native of Transylvania County, died suddenly of a heart attack Wednesday morning at his home on England Street. A veteran of World War I, he was the son of Charles and Alice Kilpatrick of the Little River section.

Survivors include the widow, Mrs. Miriam Poor Kilpatrick; one son, Charles; one sister, Mrs. Tom Allen; and one brother, L.F. Kilpatrick.

Last rites will be conducted Thursday afternoon at the Brevard-Davidson River Presbyterian Church. Burial will follow in the Gillespie-Evergreen Cemetery.

---

22 Aug 1918   Brevard News
RED CROSS LOOKS AFTER PRISONERS

"If unlucky enough to get captured, send your first prison camp post card to the American Red Cross at Berne." This is the substance of the advice, which the War Department is having all officers give the men of the American Expeditionary Forces before they go to the front in France. By sending this post card to the Bureau of Prisoners Relief of the Red Cross at Berne, the captured man sets in motion the machinery which will cause his family to be notified promptly and also enables the Red Cross to begin shipments to him of twenty pounds of food every week, and clothing, tobacco, toilet articles and other comfort and luxuries as they are needed

Elmer Adolph KILSTROM

Born:	23 Jun 1895, Chicago, Illinois
Died:	17 Aug 1966, Henderson County, NC; age 71
Buried:	Little River Baptist Church Cemetery
Occupation:	Protestant minister
Spouse:	**Reba ORR**
Father:	**Sven KILSTROM**
Mother:	**Matilda NELSON**
Draft Registration:	Chicago, 21, single, draftsman for Western Electric Co., Inc.
Military Marker:	ILL. SGT BTRY A 333 FLD ARTY WW I

[Documentation: Henderson County DC, <u>Transylvania County Cemetery Survey</u>, FamilySearch.org, Hendersonville T-N obituary, Ancestry.com]

Hendersonville Times-News
18 Aug 1966
REV. ELMER A. KILSTROM

Rev. Elmer A. Kilstrom, 71, a resident of Transylvania County for the past 22 years recently living in Penrose, died unexpectedly Wednesday in Pardee Memorial Hospital. He was a native of Chicago IL and was a retired Protestant minister. A veteran of World War I, he was the son of the late Sven and Matilda Nelson Kilstrom.

Funeral services will be held at 2 p.m. Friday in the Little River Baptist Church. Interment will take place in the church cemetery

Surviving are his wife, Reba Orr Kilstrom; two sons, Fred E. and Harry H. Kilstrom; and a daughter, Grace Grub.

Elmer Kilstrom
Fred Kilstrom Photo

NOTICE TO APPEAR FOR PHYSICAL EXAMINATION

Local Board for ....Local Board for Division #27......

(Date.)

You are hereby directed to appear before this Local Board

for physical examination at ...8. P.M. m. on ....
(Date)

Failure to do so is a misdemeanor, punishable by not to exceed

one year's imprisonment, and may also result in your losing

valuable rights and your immediate induction into military

service.

FORM 1009—PMGC
(See Soc. 122, S. S.)

Member of Local Board.

Courtney Lee KING

Born: 6 Sep 1889, Transylvania County, NC
Died: 18 Aug 1941, Union City, NJ; age 51
Buried: King-Old Town Cemetery
Father: **Pinkney S. KING**
Mother: **Mary Belle MILLER**
Draft registration: 27, single, a resident of Brevard, working for Remington Arms Co. of Eddys-
                 town, PA
Military Marker: SGT 32 Y INF 81 DIV

[Documentation: Ancestry.com, Transylvania County Cemetery Survey, TT obituary]

| King, Coat L. | 1,858,831 | | **1** |
| (Surname) (Christian name) | (Army serial number) | | • White • Colored |

Residence: _____ Brevard   Transylvania NORTH CAROLINA
            (Street and house number)   (Town or city) (County)   (State)
                              Brevard N C Nov 5/17
_____. *Inducted at _____ on _____, 19__
Place of birth: ____Brevard N C____   Age or date of birth: ___27-1/12 Yrs.
Organizations served in, with dates of assignments and transfers: _____
            Co E 324 Inf to disch

Grades, with date of appointment:
            Pvt 1c1 Apr 5/18; Corp May 24/18;
                 Sgt July 1/18

Engagements: _____

Wounds or other injuries received in action: None.
Served overseas from † __Aug 6/18__ to † __June 18/19__ from † _____ to † _____
Honorably discharged on demobilization ___June 23/19___, 19__
In view of occupation he was, on date of discharge, reported ____0____ per cent disabled.

---

2 Nov 1917   Brevard News
LOCAL BOARD ORDERS THIRTEEN MORE MEN

All men whose names appear here are ordered to report to the Local Board at 5 P.M. on Monday, November 5, 1917 for transportation for Camp Jackson. They will leave for Camp on November 6 at 8 A.M. . . . Coat L. King . . .

8/21/1941
C.L. KING

Funeral services will be held Thursday afternoon at the First Baptist Church in Brevard for Courtney Lee King, 52, who died at his home in Union City, N.J. on Monday. Death was due to heart trouble. Interment will be in the family burial ground near the Brevard Episcopal Church.

Mr. King, unmarried, was the son of the late Pinkney S. King and Mary Belle King of Bre-

vard. He had made his home in New Jersey since World War I. He was a member of the firm King Auto Supply.

Survivors are the following brothers: Henry Mitchell King, Samuel B. King, James Alonzo King, John Monroe King; and three sisters: Mrs. Fred J. Langley, Mrs. J.F. McKinney and Mrs. J.M. Tutson.

Frank Charles KING

Born:	6 Dec 1899, Transylvania County, NC
Died:	22 Jun 1965, Transylvania County, NC; age 65
Buried:	Gillespie-Evergreen Cemetery
Spouse:	**Lillian GIBBS**
Father:	**Alexander KING**
Mother:	**Hessie CLAYTON**
Draft registration:	18, a student at the University of NC at Chapel Hill

[Documentation: Transylvania County DC, Ancestry.com, Transylvania County Cemetery Survey, TT obituary]

King, Frank C   4,467,423   • White • Colored
       (Surname)   (Christian name)   (Army serial number)

Residence: _____ Brevard   Transylvania NORTH CAROLINA
       (Street and house number)   (Town or city)   (County)   (State)

_____. •Inducted at Chapel Hill NC ____ on Oct 14/18

Place of birth: ___ Bre vard NC ___   Age or date of birth: Dec 6/1899

Organizations served in, with dates of assignments and transfers: _____
       Students Army ¹ng C University of NC to disch

Grades, with date of appointment: _____
       Pvt

Engagements: _____

Wounds or other injuries received in action: None.

Served overseas from † __No__ to † _____, from † _____ to † _____

Honorably discharged on demobilization ___ Dec 9/18 ___, 19_____

In view of occupation he was, on date of discharge, reported ___ 0 ___ per cent disabled.

6/24/1965
FRANK KING

Frank Charles King, 64, former tax collector of Transylvania County, died in a local hospital early Tuesday morning after a short illness. He was a native of Transylvania County and a realtor by profession.

Mr. King was a veteran of World War I and he was a member of the First Baptist Church. He was on the North Carolina Commission for the Blind of Raleigh and a member of the Brevard Lions Club.

Funeral services were conducted at the First Baptist Church in Brevard Wednesday afternoon. Burial was in the Gillespie-Evergreen Cemetery.

<u>18 Jul 1918</u>   <u>Brevard News</u>

WAR COURSES

**In response to the Government's call for superior trained men the
University is offering an addition to its popular courses in
ACADEMIC, CIVIL, CHEMICAL, ELECTRICAL, HIGHWAY AND
MINING ENGINEERING, LAW, MEDICINE AND PHARMACY**

WAR ENGINEERING

**Courses and Military Training under
U.S. Army IX Division
Officers Reserve Training Courses**

University of North Carolina

John Monroe KING

Born:	10 Feb 1894, Transylvania County, NC
Died:	15 Jul 1968, Transylvania County, NC; age 74
Buried:	Gillespie-Evergreen Cemetery
Occupation:	Business owner
Spouse:	**Mary BANTA**
Father:	**Pinkney S. KING**
Mother:	**Mary Belle MILLER**
Draft Registration:	No

[Documentation: Roster of WWI Veterans from American Legion 50th Anniversary celebration; NC Death Certificate; 1900-1940 Censuses; Transylvania County Cemetery Survey; obit]

7/18/1968
JOHN M. KING

John Monroe King, age 74, died Tuesday morning in the local hospital after a short illness. Mr. King was a native of Transylvania County and a veteran of World War I. He was a summer resident of Brevard and a winter resident of Orlando, Florida. He was a member of the First Presbyterian Church and of the Yowell's Young Presbyterian Class of Orlando, Florida. He had been in business for himself in Atlanta GA before retirement.

Surviving are the widow, Mary Banta King of the home; one son, John Monroe King, Jr.; one daughter, Catherine King Wiseman; three sisters: Della Langley, Azilee McKinney and Lillian Tatum.

Funeral services will be held Thursday in the Brevard-Davidson River Presbyterian Church. Burial will be in Gillespie-Evergreen Cemetery.

Mustering out 1919

The United States in the Great War
pub. 1920, page 287

Jerry Verdell KINSEY

Born:	27 Jun 1891, Cleveland, GA
Died:	19 Sep 1965, Oteen VA Hospital, Buncombe County; age 74
Buried:	Reid Cemetery at Oakland
Spouse:	**Delphia AIKEN**
Father:	**Thomas H. KINSEY**
Mother:	**Sarah CANTRELL**
Draft registration:	26, single, a resident of Pisgah Forest, employed as a logger for Carr Lumber Company

[Documentation: Ancestry.com, findagrave.com, Buncombe County DC, Upper Transylvania County, NC Remembered]

Kinsey, Jerry		1,024,504	White	1½
(Surname)	(Christian name)	(Army serial number)	(Race: White or colored)	

Residence: _____ Brevard *Transylvania* NORTH CAROLINA
(Street and house number)   (Town or city)   (County)   (State)

Enlisted in   NG Brevard NC   July 19/17   —
Born in   Rabun Ga   — 26 7/12 ys   —
Organizations: Btry F 1 FA NC NG (Btry F 113 FA) to ~ay 18/18; Co I 321 Inf to Aug 25/18; Co M 165 Inf to disch.

Grades: Pvt   —   —

Engagements: —   —

Wounds or other injuries received in action: None.   —
Served overseas Jul" 3/18 to Fe ' 2 2 /19   —
Hon. disch.   Mch 8/19   on demobilization   —
Was reported   0   per cent disabled on date of discharge, in view of occupation.   —
Remarks: —   —

SCR Notes: NG (National Guard) Btry (Battery) FA (Field Artillery) NC (North Carolina)

Company Scene, 118th Infantry

Alexander Hoke KIZER

Born:	19 Apr 1892, Lincoln, North Carolina
Died:	23 Mar 1962, Transylvania County, NC; age 69
Buried:	St. Paul-in-the-Valley
Spouse:	**Dorothy McKEE**, m. Sep 1926, Sylva, NC
Father:	**George KIZER**
Mother:	**Sarah PIERCY**
Draft Registration:	25, single, secretary for Carr Lumber Co
Note:	Discharge states he was inducted July 30, 1918 and was discharged from the draft by reason of physical unfitness.

[Documentation: Transylvania County DC, Ancestry.com, 1900-1940 Censuses; Discharge, TT obituary, Heritage of Transylvania County NC, Vol 3:241-42, TC Library Kizer family files]

A young man by the name of Alex Hoke Kizer was sent away by the local Board to do limited service but returned from a northern camp after being away just a few days and he claims the officers found him unfit for military service of any kind. One of the names sent may be meant for the last mentioned young man as there is no other name on the list in any way similar to Hekekizer. There has been some mistake as to spelling of the names I believe or the man mentioned may come from a different locality.

Sincerely,

Mrs. J.L. Silversteen, Chairman Civilian Relief

(note found in Mrs. Silversteen folder, TCPL, NC Room, no date)

3/29/1962
ALEX KIZER

Funeral services for Alex Kizer, age 69, of Brevard, were conducted Sunday afternoon at St. Philip's Episcopal Church. Burial was in the St. Paul's in the Valley Cemetery.

Mr. Kizer died in the local hospital early Friday morning following an illness of several days. A native of Lincolnton, he had made his home in Transylvania County since 1913. An auditor by profession, he had served as county accountant and as clerk of the Town of Brevard. From 1934 through 1937, he was State Auditor for the Emergency Relief Administration.

He was also engaged in summer camp activities, having built and founded Camp Cherryfield in the late 20's and was at one time director of Rockbrook Camp. From 1945 until he retired in 1957, he was recreational supervisor of Camp Straus. For many years, Mr. Kizer served as secretary of the Transylvania chapter of the American Red Cross and for two years after his retirement at Ecusta, he was business manager of Camp Carolina. He was a director of the Brevard Chamber of Commerce for many terms and he also served as treasurer for several years. At the time of his death, he was U.S. District Commissioner.

He was a veteran of World War I, a former member of the Brevard Kiwanis Club and a member of St. Philip's Episcopal Church.

Surviving are his widow, Dorothy McKee Kizer; two daughters: Mrs. J.P. Mather and Mrs. S.C. Marcinko; one son, Alex Kizer, Jr.; and two brothers: Fred R. Kizer and Vernon Kizer

Luther William KUYKENDALL

Born: 3 Jan 1897, Haywood County, NC
Died: 18 Aug 1970, Hamilton, OH; age 73
Father: **Pleasant KUYKENDALL**
Mother: **Anna BLACKWELL**
Draft Registration: No

[Documentation: NC Birth Index, Ancestry.com, Ohio Death Index, 1900-1940 censuses]

Kuykendall   Luther William   4,070,832 • White • C█████d.
(Surname)   (Christian name)   (Army serial number)

Residence: ___ General Delivery   Pisgah Randolph NORTH CAROLINA
                (Street and house number)   (Town or city)   (County)   (State)

██████████████████. •Inducted at Transylvania Co, NC on Aug 5 , 19 18
Place of birth: Cruso, NC _____   Age or date of birth: Jan 3/1897
Organizations served in, with dates of assignments and transfers: Co M 5 Pion Inf to
___ Aug 25/18; 55 Pion Inf to Nov 8/18; Gd Co 101 ASC ¿
___ to disch

Grades, with date of appointment: _____
_____ Pvt _____

Engagements: _____

Wounds or other injuries received in action: None.
Served overseas from Sept 15/18 to †July 7/19, from †_____ to †_____
Honorably discharged on demobilization ___ July 21/19 , 19____
In view of occupation he was, on date of discharge, reported ___ 0 ___ per cent disabled.
Remarks: _____
_____

Form No. 724-1, A. G. O.   •Strike out words not applicable.   †Dates of departure from and arrival in the U S

SRC NOTES: Pion Inf (Pioneer Infantry)   Pisgah is in Transylvania County, not Randolph

**Augustus Bagwell's Group
Co 316 Field Artillery somewhere in France**

**Ann Stamey &
Judy Bagwell Photo**

Roy LAMANCE

Born:	15 Mar 1891, Transylvania County, NC
Died:	25 Jan 1974, South Carolina; age 82
Buried:	Hillcrest Memorial Park, Pickens, SC
Spouse:	**Olivene GALLOWAY**, m. 3 Sep 1921, Transylvania County, NC
Father:	**John W. LAMANCE**
Mother:	**Nancy C. BRACKEN**
Draft registration:	26, single, lists his occupation as a laborer for Goodyear Rubber Co. of Akron, OH, asks for a draft deferment because he was not physically fit.

[Documentation: Ancestry.com, findagrave.com, Cowart's Index to Marriages]

Lamance, Roy 1,863,420 *White ~~Colored~~ 1
(Surname) (Christian name) (Army serial number)

Residence: Cherryfield NORTH CAROLINA
(Street and house number) (Town or city) (County) (State)

*Inducted at Brevard, NC on Sept 23, 19 17
Place of birth: Balsam Grove, NC Age or date of birth: 26 6/12 yrs
Organizations served in, with dates of assignments and transfers: MD Amb Co. 324
to Nov 26/17., Bas Hosp Camp Jackson SC to disch.

Grades, with date of appointment: Ck Mch 1/18.

Engagements:

Wounds or other injuries received in action: None.
Served overseas from None to † from † to †
Honorably discharged on demobilization July 18/19, 19
In view of occupation he was, on date of discharge, reported 0 per cent disabled.

SRC Note: MD Amb Co (Medical Department Ambulance Corps Ck (Cook)

21 Sep 1917 <u>Brevard News</u>
THIRTY-ONE MEN TO CAMP JACKSON
. . .Roy Lamance . . .

28 Sep 1917 <u>Brevard News</u>
   The number of men that left last week was 31 of which three were alternates. Walter Whitmire was omitted by mistake. He went as a substitute for a man to go in a later contingent.
   Two men who failed to report on Tuesday of last week, Barney Chapman and Roy Lamance, both appeared later and have gone on to Camp Jackson. Both had excuses for their delay that was acceptable to the local exemption board.

Greenville News (SC)
1/26/1974
ROY LaMANCE

Roy LaMance, of Rt. 1, Pickens Highway, died Friday. Born in Transylvania County, NC, son of the late John W. and Carolyn Brackens LaMance, he was a retired farmer, a World War I veteran, member of the American Legion and Six Mile Baptist Church.

Surviving are his wife, Olive Galloway LaMance; a daughter, Mrs. J. S. Garrett; three sons: Clinton L., J. Lester and Elmo LaMance; and one brother, John LaMance.

Funeral services will be Saturday at Dillard Funeral Home and burial in Hillcrest Memorial Park.

Elbert Garnard LANCE

Born:	21 Apr 1896, Transylvania County, NC
Died:	4 Oct 1966, Johnson City, Tennessee; age 70
Buried:	Tolletts Chapel Cemetery, Crossville, TN
Spouse:	**Tersey STANCIL**
Father:	**Julius L. LANCE**
Mother:	**Arminta ANDERS**
Draft Registration:	No
Military Stone:	NC PVT CO A 115 MACH GUN BN WW I

[Documentation: Ancestry.com, findagrave.com, Tennessee DC]

Lance	Elbert G	1,322,767	White
(Surname)	(Christian name)	(Army serial number)	(Race: White or colored)

Residence: Selica NORTH CAROLINA
(Street and house number) (Town or city) (County) (State)

Enlisted in NG At Canton N C June 5/17

Born in Quebec N C 21 1/12 yrs

Organizations: Co H 1 Inf N C NG to Oct 24/17; Co A 115 M G Bn to disch

Grade: Pvt

Engagements:

Wounds or other injuries received in action: None.

Served overseas: May 11/18 to Mch 23/19

Hon. disch. Apr 2/19 on demobilization

Was reported 0 per cent disabled on date of discharge, in view of occupation.

18 Sep 1918   Brevard News
Mrs. Lance of this place has received a letter from her son Elbert from France, who has been on the firing lines three times, and says he sure does enjoy it.

9 May 1919   Brevard News
Corp. Elbert Lance has arrived at home with an honorable discharge. Corp. Lance was in service two years for Uncle Sam.

---

22 Aug 1918   Brevard News
SURGEON GENERAL CALLS FOR NURSES

Surgeon General Gorgus of the U.S. Army has called upon the American Red Cross to enroll for military service at home and abroad a thousand nurses a week for eight weeks. The Red Cross has just announced from National Headquarters that it has set its organization machinery in motion to comply with this request.

The eight thousand nurses thus called for by the government in groups of one thousand are in addition to more than twelve thousand nurses already supplied by the American Red Cross to the government for active war service.

Only graduate nurses are eligible for military service. However, any woman who wishes to serve the government may enter the Town and County Nursing Reserves or may enter a civilian hospital for training and thereby, release a graduate nurse for military service.

Full information in regard to these branches of service may be obtained at County Red Cross Headquarters.

Fred LANCE

Born:	1 May 1894, Transylvania County, NC
Died:	30 Mar 1964, Oteen VA Hospital, Buncombe County; age 69
Buried:	Lance Cemetery, East Fork area
Spouse:	**Della SEARCY**, m. 9 Dec 1920, Transylvania County, NC
Father:	**Charles E. LANCE**
Mother:	**Emma J. ELLENBURG**
Draft registration:	24, single, resident of Brevard, worked as a teamster at the sawmill of Sam Gillespie

Documentation: Buncombe County DC, Ancestry.com, <u>Transylvania County Cemetery Survey</u>, TT obituary]

Lance, Fred   3,277,154   • White • Colored

Residence: RFD #1   Brevard   Transylvania   NORTH CAROLINA

• E_____. •Inducted at Brevard NC   June 25, 1918

Place of birth: Brevard NC   Age or date of birth: May 1/1894

Organizations served in, with dates of assignments and transfers:
156 Dep Brig to Oct 22/18; 5 Engrs Camp Humphreys Va to disch

Grades, with date of appointment:
Pvt

Engagements:

Wounds or other injuries received in action: None.
Served overseas from † None to †_____, from †_____ to †_____
Honorably discharged on demobilization   Dec 27, 19 18
In view of occupation he was, on date of discharge, reported   0   per cent disabled.

SRC Note: Dep Brig (Depot Brigade) Engrs (Engineer)

21 Jun 1918   Brevard News
WHITE REGISTRANTS WHO ARE TO LEAVE FOR CAMP JACKSON, S.C. TUESDAY, JUNE 25th, 1918 AT 3:13 P.M.
ALTERNATIVES:
. . . Fred Lance, Brevard . . .

4/2/1964
FRED LANCE

Funeral services for Fred Alfred Lance, 69, Rosman, were held Wednesday afternoon at the Rosman Church of God. The burial was in the East Fork Cemetery. Mr. Lance died in an Asheville hospital Monday afternoon after a long illness. He was a native of Transylvania County and a retired employee of Gloucester Lumber Company.

Survivors include the widow, Mrs. Delia Searcy Lance; two daughters: Bonnie Jones and Dorothy Jane Lineberry; seven sons: Roy, Frank, Robert, Carl, Charles, Earl and T.L.; six sisters: Mrs. Hershel Meece, Mrs. Bud Nicholson, Mrs. L.J. Whitmire, Mrs. Etta Rice, Mrs. Loney Searcy, and Mrs. Louise Barton; and three brothers: Jim, Bob and Ben Lance.

Wales Perineau LANKFORD

Born:	13 Apr 1899, Transylvania County, NC
Died:	24 Apr 1976, Oteen VA Hospital, Buncombe County; age 77
Buried:	Woodlawn Memorial Park, Greenville County, SC
Spouse:	**Frances**
Father:	**Wales S. LANKFORD**
Mother:	**Hattie JUSTUS**
Draft Registration:	No

[Documentation: Ancestry.com, Buncombe County DC, findagrave.com]

Lankford, Wales P   1,324,525   white
(surname)   (Christian name)   (Army serial number) (Race: White or colored)

Residence:
(street and house number)   Brevard Transylvania NORTH CAROLINA
Morganville   (Town or city)   (County)   (State)

Enlisted in   NG at Brevard N Car   July 19/17
Born in   Transylvania N Car   18 4/12 yrs
Organizations: Btry F 1 FA NG (Btry F 113 FA) to May 18/18· Sch for
Mtrs & Cks Camp Sevier S C to Aug 5/18· 1 Dev Bn
Camp Sevier S C to Sept 27/18· Co A ' Prov Dec Bn
to disch
Grades: Pvt

Engagements:

Wounds or other injuries received in action: None.
Served overseas: No
Hon. disch.   Dec 11/18   on demobilization

SRC Note: Btry FA NG (Battery Field Artillery National Guard)

16 Nov 1917   Brevard News
Horace Davis, Ralph Duckworth, Perineau Lankford and Mack Sitton came from Camp Sevier for a visit home at the weekend.

15 Feb 1918   Brevard News
Perineau Lankford has returned to Ft. Caswell after spending his furlough at home.

7 Mar 1919   Brevard News
Perineau Lankford has gone to Fayetteville, NC where he is engaged in government work for Camp Bragg.

3 Aug 1917   Brevard News

LOCAL RED CROSS FORMS ORGANIZATION
At Well Attended Meeting Monday Night Organization Was Made Permanent And Various Committees Will Enter Upon Work

Although considerable work has been done for the Red Cross in Brevard the permanent organization was not official until Monday night, when a well-attended meeting was held at the courthouse.

J.S. Silversteen presided over the meeting and told of encouraging things he had learned about the handling of the Red Cross funds while in New York recently.

(article illegible)

Joe LATTIMORE

Born: 5 Dec 1900, Rabun County, GA
Died: 12 Sep 1965, Transylvania County, NC; age 64
Buried: Pisgah Gardens Cemetery
Occupation: Saw mill worker
Spouse: **Patsy Pallie SHULER** m. 17 Jan 1935 Dillsboro, NC
Father: **Thomas LATTIMORE**
Mother: **Sallie LATTIMORE**
Draft Registration: No
Military Marker: NC PVT CO D 114 Machine Gun BN WW I

[Documentation: Transylvania County DC, Transylvania County Cemetery Survey, Family History (Ancestry.com), Ancestry.com]

9/16/1956
JOSEPH LATTIMORE

Funeral services for Joseph Lattimore, age 64, of Lake Toxaway, were held Wednesday morning at the Crab Creek Baptist Church. Rev. Jack Plemmons officiated and burial was in Pisgah Gardens. Mr. Lattimore died Sunday night at his home after a period of declining health. A native of Rabun County GA, he was a World War I veteran.

He is survived by his widow, Pallie Shuler Lattimore; three sons: Joe, Frank and Paul Lattimore; five daughters: Florence Heath, Bonnie Morris, Inez Owens, Brenda Lattimore and Jeraldine Lance; and two sisters: Sadie Koreach and Vadia McMahan.

Haywood County Digital Collection

Battery C 113th Field Artillery at Drill

Walter Webb LEDBETTER

Born:	20 Apr 1897, Henderson County, NC
Died:	24 Apr 1957, Oteen VA Hospital, Buncombe County; age 60
Buried:	Gillespie-Evergreen Cemetery
Occupation:	Truck driver
Spouse:	**Marie BROWN**, m. 2 Jun 1928, Transylvania County, NC
Father:	**James D. LEDBETTER**
Mother:	**Carrie BRANK**
Draft registration:	21, worked for Miller Supply Co. of Brevard

[Documentation: Buncombe County DC, US Headstone Application Form, Ancestry.com, Transylvania County Cemetery Survey, Cowart's Index to Marriages]

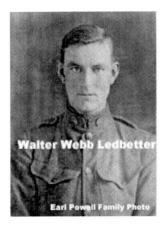

Ledbetter   Walter W   4,070,965   • White • Colored
(Surname)   (Christian name)   (Army serial number)

Residence: _____ Brevard *Transylvania* ___ NORTH CAROLINA
(Street and house number)   (Town or city)   (County)   (State)

Inlisted N. A. • N. G. • E. R. C. *Inducted at* Transylvania Co NC on Aug 5, 19 18

Place of birth: ___ Mills River NC ___ Age or date of birth: Apr 20/1897

Organizations served in, with dates of assignments and transfers: _____
___ Co C 56 Pion Inf to disc. _____

Grades, with date of appointment: _____
___ Pvt _____

Engagements: _____

Wounds or other injuries received in action: None.
Served overseas from † Sept 4/18 to † June 25/19 from † _____ to † _____
Honorably discharged on demobilization July 5/19 , 19 _____
In view of occupation he was, on date of discharge, reported ___ 0 ___ per cent disabled.

Walter Webb Ledbetter
Earl Powell Family Photo

SRC Notes: Pion Inf (Pioneer Regiment Infantry)

4 Apr 1919   Brevard News
P.L. Gallamore's brother, Walter Ledbetter, now with the Army of Occupation in Germany writes that the Army life agrees with him, in fact he has gained fifty pounds since he joined. He says: "That the country over there will do, but old N.C. is good enough for him."

4/25/1957
Walter W. Ledbetter

Funeral services for Walter Webb Ledbetter, 60, who died yesterday in an Asheville hospital after a long illness, will be held today at 2 p.m. in Brevard Methodist Church. Burial will be in Evergreen Cemetery. Graveside rites will be conducted by members of Dunn's Rock Masonic Lodge of which Ledbetter was a member.

A resident of Brevard for the past 35 years, he was a native of Henderson County. He had been in the coal and ice business here for 19 years and was a World War I veteran with service in Europe.

He is survived by his widow, Marie Brown Ledbetter; two daughters: Mrs. Earl Powell and Catherine; and one sister, Mrs. Beulah Cogdill.

NATIONAL ARMY CANTONMENT (CAMP)

Camp Sherman   Location: Chillicothe, Ohio   Organization: 83rd Division
Troops from Ohio and West Virginia

Raleigh C. LEDFORD

Born:	3 Jan 1893, Haywood County, NC
Died:	1 May 1980, Oteen VA Hospital, Buncombe County; age 87
Buried:	Caldwell Cemetery, Haywood County
Spouse(s):	**Jessie Effie CALDWELL**
	Wilma Lee MESSER
Father:	**Daniel LEDFORD**
Mother:	**Florence SUTTLES**
Draft registration:	24, single, a resident of Pisgah Forest, occupation listed as day laborer for John Pressley of Davidson River

[Documentation: Buncombe County DC, Haywood County Delayed BC, Ancestry.com, findagrave.com, Asheville CT obituary]

```
      Ledford Raleigh C          1,315,358        * White xxxxxx.
       (Surname)    (Christian name)    (Army serial number)
Residence: ___ xx _____ Transylvania _____ NORTH CAROLINA
              (Street and house number)   (Town or city)   (County)        (State)
* Enlisted * xxxxxxxxxx .Inducted at ___ Brevard N C ___ Oct 4     17
Place of birth: Haywood Co N C ___ Age or date of birth: 24 10/12 yrs 19
Organizations served in, with dates of assignment and transfer:
      Hq Co 316 F A to Oct 16/17; Co D 119 Inf to desertion

Grades, with date of appointment: _____
      Pvt

Engagements xx _____

Wounds or other injuries received in action:  None.
Served overseas from † no        to † _____ from † _____    to † _____
Deserted: ___ Mch 15 _____, 18 _, at __ Cp Sevier, S.C. _____
         (Date)                      (Place)
Remarks: _____
```

SRC Note: FA (Field Artillery)

Asheville Citizens Times
5/2/1989
R.C. LEDFORD

Raleigh Cleveland Ledford, 87, died Thursday in an Asheville nursing home. Mr. Ledford was a native of Haywood County, a son of the late Daniel and Florence Suttles Ledford and was a retired farmer.

Surviving are his wife, Wilma Lee Messer Ledford; two sons, Robert and Martin Ledford; a daughter, Mary Ann Teague; a brother, Lee Ledford; and a sister, Annie Mae Southers.

Services were held in the chapel of Crawford Funeral Home, Waynesville with burial in Caldwell cemetery.

---

12 Apr 1918   Brevard News
REWARD OFFERED FOR TRANSYLVANIA DESERTERS

The following man from Transylvania County has deserted from Camp Sevier, South Carolina:

Ledford, Raleigh C., Company D, 119th Infantry, deserted March 18, 1918, age 21, height 6 ft. 8 in., black hair, brown eyes, weight 150 lbs. home address, Transylvania, NC; relative to be notified in case of emergency, Mrs. Florence Ledford, Union, S.C.

A reward of $50.00 will be paid to any person for the delivery of the above deserter to the nearest army post or camp.   William G. Green   Capt. 119th Infantry

Daniel Weldon LEE

Born:	3 Apr 1894, Transylvania County, NC
Died:	11 Sep 1960, Transylvania County, NC; age 66
Buried:	Rocky Hill Cemetery
Occupation:	Carpenter
Spouse:	**Ellen CRANE**
Father:	**R.W. LEE**
Mother:	**Alice Louise BURNS**
Draft Registration:	23, single and farming
Note:	Grave marker gives NO military information
	Transylvania DC states he served in WW I

[Documentation: Transylvania County DC, <u>Transylvania County Cemetery Survey</u>, TT obituary, Ancestry.com]

18 Jul 1918   Brevard News
23 More Men To Leave July 24, 1918

Following is a list of white registrants for induction on July 24th, 1918 for Camp Hancock, Ga., who will leave on the 3:13 train:

. . . Daniel Waldon Lee, Cedar Mountain . . .

9/15/1960
DANIEL W. LEE

Last rites for Daniel Weldon Lee, 65, of Cedar Mountain were held Tuesday morning at the Rocky Hill Baptist Church. Burial followed in the church cemetery. Mr. Lee died Sunday afternoon following a short illness. A native of Transylvania County, he was a retired contractor and a member of the Rocky Hill Baptist Church.

Survivors include the widow, Mrs. Ellen Crane Lee; one son, Ralph; and one sister, Mrs. Seldon Jones.

Alexander Kennedy LEWIS

Born:	3 Mar 1896, Pickens County, SC
Died:	31 Jul 1973, Greenville, South Carolina; age 77
Buried:	Woodlawn Memorial Park, Greenville County, SC
Spouse:	**Cordelia Irene ERWIN**, m. 10 Sep 1925, Transylvania County
Father:	**Andrew F. LEWIS**
Mother:	**Martha Louella ENGLISH**
Draft registration:	21, single, a resident of Brevard, worked as a clerk for O.L. Erwin in Brevard

[Documentation: Findagrave.com, Ancestry.com, SSDI, 1900- 1930 Censuses, Cowart's Index to Marriages]

```
                                                                      1½
          Lewis,    Alexander K          707,527          White
      (Surname)       (Christian name)   (Army serial number)  (Race: White or colored)
Residence:                      Brevard Transylvania    NORTH CAROLINA
      (Street and house number)     (Town or city)    (County)      (State)
Enlisted in    NG  Hendersonville NC June 11/17
Born in        Central S C  21 2/12 yrs                          —
Organizations: 6 Co CA NC NG to May 11/18; 9 A A Btry to disch.  —

Grades:       Pvt 1 cl Feb 5/18   —                              —

Engagements:                      —                              —


Wounds or other injuries received in action: None.
Served overseas:  July 14/18  to Mch 7/19                        —
Hon. disch.       Mch 24/19    on demobilization                 —
Was reported      0            per cent disabled on date of discharge, in view of occupation.
Remarks:                       —                                 —
```

SRC Notes: CA NC MG (Coast Artillery North Carolina Machine Gun)

8/9/1973
A.K. LEWIS

Alexander Kennedy Lewis, 75, died last Tuesday in Greenville, S.C. Born in Central, son of the late Fielding Andrew and Ella English Lewis, he was a retired sales representative, a veteran of World War I and a member of Buncombe Street United Methodist Church. He was a third degree Mason and Shriner and a member of Sons of Confederate Veterans.

Surviving are his wife, Mrs. Irene Erwin Lewis; a daughter, Mrs. Charles W. Long; a son, Overton Alexander Lewis; and two sisters: Mrs. Helen Lewis Terry and Miss Mattie E. Lewis.

Graveside services were held in Woodlawn Memorial Park last Thursday

---

National Army Cantonment (Camp)

Camp Dodge   Des Moines, Iowa   Organization: 89th Division
Troops from Minnesota, Iowa, Nebraska, North Dakota and South Dakota

Lamar English LEWIS

Born:	10 Jun 1892, Central, SC
Died:	7 Feb 1950, Greenville, South Carolina; age 57
Buried:	Gillespie-Evergreen Cemetery
Spouse:	**Margaret L ERWIN**, m. 3 Jan 1923, Transylvania County, NC
Father:	**Andrew F. LEWIS**
Mother:	**Martha Louella ENGLISH**
Draft registration:	24, a resident of Brevard, worked as a clerk for O.L. Erwin of Brevard, single with his mother and sister listed as dependents.

[Documentation: Greenville SC DC, US Headstone application, Ancestry.com, Transylvania County Cemetery Survey, Cowart's Index to Marriages]

Lewis, Lamar E   1,891,638   • White • Colored

Residence: _____ Brevard Transylvania NORTH CAROL
          (Street and house number)   (Town or city)   (County)   (State)

• _____ C. *Inducted at ___ Brevard N Car ___ on May 24, 1918
Place of birth: ___ Central S Car ___ Age or date of birth: ___ 26 y'rs
Organizations served in, with dates of assignments and transfers: _____
          Co B 324 Inf to disch

Grades, with date of appointment: ___ Pvt 1cl Aug 24 /r

Engagements: _____

Wounds or other injuries received in action: None.
Served overseas from †___ Aug 5/18 ___ to †___ June 18/19 ___ from †___ to †___
Honorably discharged on demobilization ___ June 27 ___, 19 19
In view of occupation he was, on date of discharge, reported ___ 0 ___ per cent disabled.

2/9/1950
LAMAR LEWIS

Funeral services for Lamar English Lewis, 57, who died at his home in Greenville, S.C. on Tuesday morning were held at the Brevard Methodist Church Wednesday afternoon. Burial followed in the Evergreen Cemetery.

Mr. Lewis, who retired some years ago because of ill health, made his home in Brevard, Raleigh and Greenville, S.C. and for 24 years traveled for the International Shoe Company.

He is survived by widow, Mrs. Louise Erwin Lewis; one daughter, Verena Lamar Lewis; two sisters, Helen Terry and Mattie Lewis.

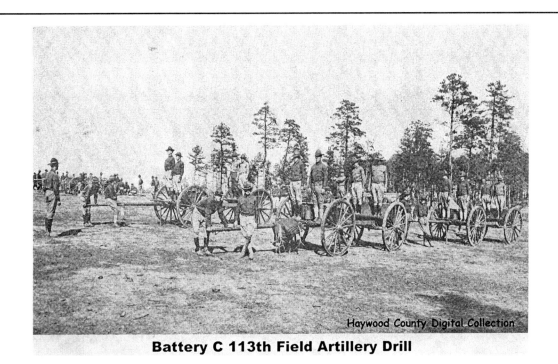

Haywood County Digital Collection

Battery C 113th Field Artillery Drill

243

Zeftius LITMAN

Born: 20 Oct 1897, Oconee County, SC
Died: 9 Dec 1968; age 71
Buried: Wildwood Memorial Park, Oconee County, SC
Race: Colored
Occupation: Cook at the Aethelwold Hotel, Brevard
Father: **Frank LITMAN**
Mother: **Lula**
Draft Registration: 21, single, cook at the Aethelwold Hotel

[Documentation: Ancestry.com, 1910 census, usgwarchives.net/sc/Oconee/cemeteries]

Litman, Zeftius   1,888,256   • White • Colored.
(Surname)   (Christian name)   (Army serial number)

Residence: _____ Brevard Transylvania NORTH CAROLINA
(Street and house number)   (Town or city)   (County)   (State)

_____. *Inducted at Brevard N C   on Apr 30, 19 18
Place of birth: ___ Oconee Co S C ___ Age or date of birth: 21 6/12 yrs

Organizations served in, with dates of assignments and transfers:
156 Dep Brig to May 23/18; Co D 321 Serv Bn to disch

Grades, with date of appointment: _____ Pvt

Engagements: _____

Wounds or other injuries received in action: None.
Served overseas from † Aug 7/18 to † July 7/19, from † _____ to † _____
Honorably discharged on demobilization July 18, 19 19
In view of occupation he was, on date of discharge, reported ___ 0 ___ per cent disabled.
Remarks: _____

SRC Notes: Serv Bn (Service Battalion)

Nearly 400,000 Negro Soldiers served in the United States Army in the Great World War. About 367,710 of these came into the service through the operation of the Selective Draft Law.

The instant of the declaration of war, there were nearly 20,000 soldiers of the Negro race in the United States, uniformed, armed, equipped, drilled, trained and ready to take the field against the foe. Proportionately to the total Negro population of America, this was a splendid showing.

Negro Troops in the Post of Honor

Of particular interest, is the fact that on March 25, 1917, the Secretary of War, by order of the President, called for the First Separate Battalion, District of Columbia Infantry, National Guard to be mustered into federal service to guard the White House, Capitol and other Federal buildings. It became their responsibility to defend the National Capitol. This was even before a formal declaration of war. While it is estimated that 1/3 of all labor troops in Europe were African Americans, it is not true that all were assigned to labor units.

Scott, Emmett, **American Negro The World War**, 1919.

Louie Carlisle LOFTIS

Born:	9 Apr 1896, Transylvania County, NC
Died:	17 Jul 1974, undetermined; age 78
Buried:	Highland Cemetery, Alabama
Education:	Four years college
Spouse:	**Nola ROBERTS**
Father:	**Tyrell LOFTIS**
Mother:	**Emma SUMMEY**
Draft registration:	21, single, lived in Brevard, self-employed electrician in Brevard
	WW II Draft Registration: age 46, employed at Bendix Radio Co., Montgomery County, MD
	SSDI records last residence as Baltimore, Maryland.

[Documentation: Ancestry.com, Alabama findagrave.com, 1940 census]

Name LOFTIS- LOUIE CARLISLE   Service Number   181-74-28

Enlisted at RECRUITING STATION RALEIGH N C   Date 6-11-17   U. S. N.

Age at Entrance 20 YRS 2 MOS   Rate LANDSMAN ELECTRICIAN GENERAL

Home Address XX   Town BREVARD

M   County TRANSYLVANIA   State N C

Served at	From	To	Served as	No. Days
RECEIVING SHIP AT NEW YORK N Y	6-11-17	2-20-18	LANDSMAN FOR ELECTRICIAN G	204
USS CUYAMA	2-20-18	11-11-18	ELECTRICIAN 3 CLASS G	1ω1
			ELECTRICIAN 2 CLASS G	92
			ELECTRICIAN 1 CLASS G	41

Remarks:

Date Discharge 3-29-19 USS CUYANA AT   ELECTRICIAN 1 CLASS G
Place XXXXXXX PORT ARTHUR TEX   Rating at Discharge

7 Nov 1918   Brevard News

Louie Loftis has been spending a ten-day furlough with his family. Louie has crossed the ocean seven times as electrician on an oil tanker.

9 May 1919   Brevard News

Louie Loftis has purchased the stock of electrical supplies formerly handled by Brevard Hardware Co. He will move the goods to the Five and Ten Cent Store on Broad Street where he expects to install adequate equipment to look after the electrical supply needs of the town. He was head electrician on one of Uncle Sam's troopships that made seven trips overseas with fighting men and munitions.

7/25/1974
LOUIS LOFTIS

Louis Carlisle Loftis, 78, of Baltimore, MD, died in Baltimore Wednesday, July 17th, after a long illness. He was a native of Brevard and had resided in Baltimore for a number of years. He was an electrical engineer and contractor. He was a member of Dunn's Rock Masonic Lodge for 54 years and a member of the Scottish Rites and Eoomi Shrine Temple of Baltimore.

He is survived by the wife, Nola Roberts Lofits; one son, James Loftis; one daughter, Mrs. Nathan Churn; one brother, Hume Loftis.

Graveside rites were conducted in Piedmont, Ala., last Monday.

George B. LONDON

Born:	4 Apr 1894, Macon County, NC
Died:	27 Jul 1960, Oteen VA Hospital, Buncombe County; age 66
Buried:	Whitmire Cemetery, Eastatoe
Spouse:	**Kannie G GALLOWAY**, m. 13 Nov 1920, Transylvania County, NC
	Myrtle McGEE, m. 23 Oct 1936, Transylvania County, NC
Father:	**John LONDON**
Mother:	**Dixie HUGGINS**
Draft Registration:	No

[Documentation: Buncombe County DC, Application for Military Headstone, Ancestry.com, Cowart's Index to Marriages]

London, George B. 58,206 * White * Colored.
(Surname)   (Christian name)   (Army serial number)

Residence: _____ Rosman   NORTH CAROLINA
(Street and house number)   (Town or city)   (County)   (State)

* Enlisted * R. A. * N. G. * E. R. C. * Inducted at Ft Thomas Ky on Mch 30, 19 17
Place of birth: Franklin NC   Age or date of birth: 22 11/12 yrs
Organizations served in, with dates of assignments and transfers: Co I 28 Inf to furlough
to reserve

Grades, with date of appointment: _____
Corp

Engagements: _____

Wounded in action (degree and date) slightly Oct. 9 a bout Oct 26, 1918
Served overseas from † June 14/17 to † Sept 4/19 from † _____ to † _____
* Honorably discharged on demobilization Furloughed to reserve Mch 31/20, 19 __
(If separated for other cause give reason)
In view of occupation he was, on date of discharge, reported _____ per cent disabled.
Remarks: _____ Also wounded slightly Nov 8, 18

8/4/1960
George London

George B. London, 66, of Rosman, died last Wednesday night in an Asheville hospital after a long illness. Mr. London was a native of Macon County, but had lived in Transylvania County for several years. He was a retired timber worker.

Surviving is a sister, Mrs. Alma Eubanks.

Services were held Friday in Rosman Church of God and the burial was in the Whitmire Cemetery near Rosman.

APPLICATION FOR HEADSTONE OR MARKER

LONDON, George B.

Whitmire Cenetary, Rosman, N.C.

Corporal, Co. 1, 28th.Infantry

James Edmond LONDON

Born:	29 Sep 1887, Macon County, NC
Died:	3 May 1948, Transylvania County, NC; age 60
Buried:	Mt. Moriah Baptist Church Cemetery
Spouse(s):	**Ida McCALL**, m. 24 Apr 1918, Transylvania County, NC
	Myrtle PETTIT
FATHER:	**John LONDON**
Mother:	**Dixie HUGGINS**
Draft Registration:	29, logging, had a child as a dependent
Note:	Gravestone has NO military information

[Documentation: Transylvania County DC, Cowart's Index to Marriages, Transylvania County Cemetery Survey, 1940 Census, Ancestry.com]

<u>18 Jul 1918</u>   <u>Brevard News</u>
23 More Men To Leave July 24, 1918
. . . James Edmond London, Rosman . . .

German Tank and Gun on display   **Hal Hart Photo**

Andrew Virgil LYDAY

Born:	9 Jun 1892, Transylvania County, NC
Died:	25 Jun 1973, Oteen VA Hospital, Buncombe County; age 81
Buried:	Enon Baptist Church Cemetery
Occupation:	Accountant for US Postal Service in Washington, DC
Father:	**George LYDAY**
Mother:	**Elizabeth SURRETTE**
Draft Registration:	24, single, self-employed farmer who claims both father and mother as dependents.

[Documentation: Buncombe County DC, 1900-1930-1940 Censuses, <u>Transylvania County Cemetery Survey</u>]

```
              Lyday, Andrew V              1,876, 493      * White  *Colored.*
            (Surname)        (Christian name)    (Army serial number)
Residence: ____RFD  2_____Brevard_____NORTH CAROLINA___
            (Street and house number)    (Town or city)    (County)        (State)

_____. *Inducted at Brevard N C_____ on Oct 4___, 1917
Place of birth: ___Transylvania___NC_____ . Age or date of birth: _25_3,12_Yrs___
Organizations served in, with dates of assignments and transfers: _____
          F H 324  -  306 ₅n Tn to qisch_____

Grades, with date of appointment: _____

          Corp July 9,18;_____
Engagements: _____

Wounds or other injuries received in action: None.
Served overseas from †Aug 8,18 to †une 20,19, from †_____ to †_____
Honorably discharged on demobilization _____June 29, 19__, 19_____
In view of occupation he was, on date of discharge, reported ____0_____ per cent disabled.
Remarks: _____

Form No. 724-1, A. G. O.   *Strike out words not applicable.   † Dates of departure from and arrival in the U. S.
```

SRC Notes: Sn Tn (Sanitation Train)

21 Jun 1918   Brevard News
A.V. Lyday, of Camp Jackson, son of County Commissioner Lyday, is at home on a furlough for a few days.

26 Sep 1918   Brevard News
Mr. and Mrs. Geo. T.. Lyday have received news that their sons, A. Virgil and Lander B. Lyday, have landed safely overseas.

6/27/1973
ANDREW V. LYDAY

Andrew Virgil Lyday, 80, died in Oteen Veterans Hospital Monday morning after an extended illness. He was a native of Transylvania County and had made his home in Washington, D.C. for the past 38 years where he was employed in the U.S. Postal Service until retirement. He was an Army veteran of WW I and the son of the late George T. and Elizabeth Surrette Lyday.

One sister, Mrs. J.R. Allison; and one brother, L.B. Lyday, survive him.

Services were conducted Wednesday afternoon at Enon Baptist Church of which he was a member and burial was in the church cemetery.

Joseph William LYDAY

Born:	5 Oct 1899, Transylvania County, NC
Died:	1 Oct 1981, Henderson County, NC; age 81
Buried:	Oakdale Cemetery, Henderson County, NC
Spouse:	**Ruth Elizabeth ALLISON**, m. 18 Dec 1926, Transylvania County, NC
Father:	**John F. LYDAY**
Mother:	**Ella ORR**
Draft Registration:	18, single, student

[Documentation: Transylvania County BC, Henderson County DC, Ancestry.com, Cowart's Index to Marriages]

Lyday Joseph W.   4,467,426   * White * ~~Colored~~
(Surname)   (Christian name)   (Army serial number)

Residence: Brevard   Transylvania   NORTH CAROLINA
(Street and house number)   (Town or city)   (County)   (State)

*Inducted at Chapel Hill NC   Oct. 14, 1918

Place of birth: Brevard NC   Age or date of birth: Oct. 5, 1899

Organizations served in, with dates of assignments and transfers:
Students Army Tng C University of NC Chapel Hill NC to disch

Grades, with date of appointment:

Pvt

Engagements:

Wounds or other injuries received in action: None.

Served overseas from † None to † , from † to †

Honorably discharged on demobilization Dec 9/18, 19

In view of occupation he was, on date of discharge, reported 0 per cent disabled.

Remarks:

Hendersonville Times-News
10/1/1981
JOSEPH LYDAY, SR.

Joseph William Lyday, 81, former owner of Houston Furniture Company, died Thursday in a Hendersonville hospital after a long illness. Mr. Lyday was a native of Brevard, a son of the late John F. and Ella Orr Lyday. He was a graduate of Brevard High School and attended UNC at Chapel Hill. Retiring in 1965, he had been involved in the furniture business since 1925.

He was a member of Hendersonville First United Methodist Church and a former member of Kiwanis Club, a member of Kedron Lodge 387, AF & AM, a life member of the Oasis Shrine Temple of Charlotte and a member of Hendersonville Shrine Club.

Surviving are his wife, Ruth Allison Lyday; a son, Joseph Lyday, Jr.; four sisters: Pearl Brittain, Mamie Moore, Doris Edwards and Inez Mueller; and two brothers, Frank and John H

Funeral services will be held at 2 p.m. Saturday in Shepherd's Church Street Chapel. Burial will be in Oakdale Cemetery.

National Army Cantonment (Camp)

Camp Fuston   Location: Fort Riley, Kansas   Organization: 89th Division
Troops from Kansas, Missouri and Colorada

Lauder Bernard LYDAY

Born:	23 Dec 1894, Transylvania County, NC
Died:	9 Feb 1982, Buncombe County, NC; age 87
Buried:	Little River Baptist Church Cemetery
Occupation:	Clerk for Southern Railroad
Spouse:	**Lora McCALL**
Father:	**George LYDAY**
Mother:	**Elizabeth SURRETTE**
Draft Registration:	22, single, employed by Southern RR in Asheville, NC

[Documentation: Buncombe County DC, Ancestry.com, Asheville C-T obituary, <u>Transylvania County Cemetery Survey</u>]

```
          Lyday  Lauder B            1,876,507              * White * Colored
          (Surname)    (Christian name)    (Army serial number)

Residence: _____ Brevard  Transylvania   NORTH CAROLI
          (Street and house number)      (Town or city)    (County)       (State)

_____ *Inducted at Brevard NC _____ on Sept 18 1917
Place of birth: Boyd NC _____ Age or date of birth: ____ 22 10/12yrs
Organizations served in, with dates of assignments and transfers: _____
          Med Dept to disch _____

Grades, with date of appointment: _____
          Pvt 1cl Sept 14/18

Engagements: _____

Wounds or other injuries received in action: None.
Served overseas from †Aug 8/18 to †June 20/19 from †_____ to †_____
Honorably discharged on demobilization ____ June 29/19 ____, 19____
In view of occupation he was, on date of discharge, reported ____0____ per cent disabled.
Remarks: _____
```

21 Sep 1917 Brevard News
THIRTY-ONE MEN TO CAMP JACKSON was ordered to report on Tuesday at 5 P.M. at the office of the local enlistment board and to leave for Camp Jackson, S.C. Wednesday morning.
Alternates: . . . Lauder R. Lyday . . .

26 Sep 1918 Brevard News
Mr. and Mrs. Geo. F. Lyday have received news that their sons, A. Virgil and Lander B. Lyday, have landed safely overseas.

Asheville Citizen Times
2/10/1982
Lauder Lyday

Lauder Bernard Lyday, 87, of 35 Oakley Road, Asheville, died Tuesday in an Asheville health care center after a period of declining health. He was a native of Transylvania County, who had resided in Buncombe County for the past 60 years. He was a son of the late George and Elizabeth Surrette Lyday. He was a U.S. Army veteran of World War I and a retired clerk of Southern Railroad.

Surviving are his wife, Lora McCall Lyday; a daughter, Mary Frances Havener; and a sister, Pearl Allison.

Services will be held Thursday afternoon in the Little River Baptist Church and burial will follow in the church cemetery.

Dr. George Boyce LYNCH

Born:	11 Jan 1887, Buncombe County, NC
Died:	11 Dec 1978, Oteen VA Hospital, Buncombe County; age 91
Buried:	Gillespie-Evergreen Cemetery
Occupation:	Physician and was Transylvania County's Health Officer
Spouse:	**Ada WILLISON**
Father:	**George W. LYNCH**
Mother:	**Elmyra TOMS**
Draft Registration:	30, married and was a physician
Military Marker:	1st Lt. US Army WW I

[Documentation: Buncombe DC, Transylvania County Cemetery Survey, Discharge, Ancestry.com]

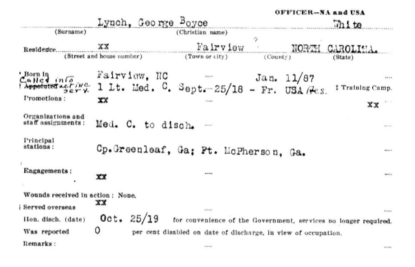

12/12/1978
DR. GEORGE B. LYNCH

Dr. George Boyce Lynch, 91, retired Brevard physician, died Monday in Asheville VA Medical Center after a period of declining health. He was a veteran of World War I, having served in the U.S. Army Medical Corps.

Dr. Lynch was a native of Fairview and a 1914 graduate of the University of Maryland School of Medicine. He was a resident surgeon at St. Joseph's Hospital in Baltimore, MD. He served as superintendent of Kernan Hospital for Crippled Children in Baltimore for two years. He passed the N.C. State Medical Board in 1920 and practiced medicine in Rosman for four years. In 1924 he moved to Brevard where he practiced until his retirement in 1974.

During his practice in Brevard, he was county coroner for two years, county physician for 12 years and county health officer for four years. He was part owner of the former Brevard Hospital, now known as Transylvania Community Hospital.

He served seven years on the Transylvania County Selective Service Board and received special commendations signed by both President Franklin D. Roosevelt and President Harry S. Truman.

He was vice president of the 10th District Medical Society and a charter member of the Brevard Kiwanis Club. He was a master Mason and held 14 degrees in Scottish Rite Masonry.

Memorial services will be held Wednesday in St. Phillip's Episcopal Church, where he was a member.

Fate L. MAHAFFEY

Born:	8 May 1891, Haywood County, NC
Died:	12 Dec 1968, Transylvania County, NC; age 77
Buried:	Turkey Creek Cemetery
Spouse:	**Annie ALEXANDER**, m. 30 Mar 1919, Transylvania County, NC
Father:	**George MAHAFFEY**
Mother:	**Mary GROGAN**
Draft Registration:	26, single, farming
Note:	Grave marker gives NO military information

[Documentation: Transylvania County DC, <u>Cowart's Index to Marriages</u>, <u>Transylvania County Cemetery Survey</u>, Ancestry.com]

Hendersonville Times – News
2/21/1968
FATE L. MAHAFFEY

Fate L. Mahaffey 76, a Haywood County native and local resident died Wednesday at the home of his daughter, Mrs. Ralph Brown of Pisgah Forest. He was a retired farmer and had lived in Transylvania County for several years. Mr. Mahaffey was a member of Turkey Creek Baptist Church. Funeral services will be held at 2 o'clock Saturday at the Church and the burial will follow in Turkey Creek Cemetery.

Surviving in addition to his daughter, Mrs. Brown are two sons: Lenor and L.G.(Lyday G.) Mahaffey; two sisters, Mrs. Fred Anders and Mrs. Sam Stamey;and a brother Arthur Mahaffey of Alexander.

Fate Mahaffey Family

Aileen

Aileen M. Brown Photo

Fate mailed this bullet shaped postal card from Camp Wadsworth to his sweetheart who became his wife 30 Mar 1919.

The message he inscribe in the *Soldiers Dispatch* is "**Layfaett Mahaffey
Round is the ring
That has no end
I hope some day
To see you again.
Put on the pan
And fry my will
It will be the scalp
Of Kaiser Bill.**

*Inscriptions preprinted on the card:
Be an American First, Last and All the Time*

WAR DECLARED April 6, 1917

First US Troops Landed in France June 27

WE'LL WIN LIBERTY FOR ALL

Roy French MARR

Born:	1 Jan 1895, Asheville, NC
Died:	19 Mar 1985, Pinellas, FL; age 90
Buried:	Undetermined
Spouse:	Gladys
Father:	**Thomas F. MARR**
Mother:	**Kannie ZACHARY**
Draft Registration:	22, single, working as a self-employed farmer in Brevard

[Documentation: 1900, 1940 Censuses, Florida Death Index, FamilySearch.org, Ancestry.com]

Marr Roy F	718,069 White	1½
(Surname) (Christian name)	(Army serial number) (Race: White or colored)	
Residence:	Brevard Transylvania NORTH CAROLINA	
	(Street and house number) (Town or city) (County) (State)	

Enlisted in: NG Hendersonville NC Aug 14/17

Born in: Asheville NC 22 8/12 yrs

Organizations: Co 6 CAC NC NG (6 Co. Cape Fear) to Jan 5/18; 8 AA Btry CAC to disch

Grades: Pvt 1cl Sept 30/17; Corp Dec 15/17; Sgt Apr 6/18

Engagements:

Wounds or other injuries received in action: None.

Served overseas: June 10/18 to Mch 7/19

Hon. disch. Mch 24/19 on demobilization

Was reported 0 per cent disabled on date of discharge, in view of occupation.

Remarks:

SRC Notes: CAC NC NG (Coast Artillery Corps North Carolina National Guard)

28 Mar 1919   Brevard News

Sgt. Roy Marr, who was one of the first Transylvanian volunteers after the U.S. declared war against Germany, has arrived at Camp Lee, Va. from overseas. He expects to be mustered out of the service this week. After a visit to relatives in Charlotte he will come to Brevard for the summer.

MOTOR SUPPLY TRAIN CAMP LEE, VA.

Camp Lee Camp Booklet

William Perry MASTERS

Born:	22 Jan 1888, Transylvania County, NC
Died:	11 May 1980, Transylvania County, NC; age 92
Buried:	Masters Cemetery, Transylvania County
Father:	**Perry T. MASTERS**
Mother:	**Rachael L. CHASTAIN**
Draft Registration:	28, single and farming

[Documentation: Transylvania County DC, FamilySearch.com, Ancestry.com]

Masters, William Perry 3,277,171 • White • Colored.
(Surname)   (Christian name)   (Army serial number)

Residence: _____ XX _____ Bevard _____ NORTH CAROLINA
(Street and house number)   (Town or city)   (County)   (State)

• Enlisted • R. A. • N. G. • E. R. C. • Inducted at Bevard N.C. _____ on June 25, 1918
Place of birth: _____ Bevard N.C. _____ Age or date of birth: Jan 22/88
Organizations served in, with dates of assignments and transfers: 51 Co 8 Tr Bn, 156 Dep
_____ Brig to disch _____

Grades, with date of appointment: Pvt _____

Engagements: _____ XX _____

Wounds or other injuries received in action: None.
Served overseas from † _____ no _____ to † _____, from † _____ to † _____
Deserted: _____ July 19 19 18 at _____ Cp Jackson SC
(Date)   (Place)
Remarks: _____

SRC Notes: Tn Bn (Train Battalion)

Asheville Citizen Times
5/12/1980
WILLIAM MASTERS

William Perry Masters, 92, of the Ford community died Sunday in the Brevard hospital. Mr. Masters was a lifelong resident of Transylvania County and the son of the late Perry and Rachel Chastain Masters. He was a retired farmer.

Services were held in the chapel of Moore Funeral Home. Burial was in the Masters Cemetery.

He is survived by a sister, Ester M. Masters.

---

21 Jun 1918   **Brevard News**
WHITE REGISTRANTS WHO ARE TO LEAVE FOR CAMP JACKSON, S.C.
TUESDAY, JUNE 25th, 1918 AT 3:13 P.M.
. . . William Perry Masters, Brevard . . .

---

18 Jul 1918   **Brevard News**

LOCAL RED CROSS COMMENDED

The Transylvania Red Cross has this week been visited by an inspector from the Red Cross headquarters who gave the entire system of Red Cross work in the County a thorough inspection.

Mrs. Clauise, who was sent from Atlanta to Brevard for that purpose, stated that she had been visiting several small county chapters for the past 6 months and "not one that I have seen equals the Transylvania Chapter in the efficiency of its organization and the quality of its output of hospital supplies."

She spoke to the members of the executive committee at a special meeting on Monday evening. She also held a conference with the directors of the Women's Work Department on Tuesday morning. To the workers who came from all parts of the county she gave special instructions for the important work, which they will be expected to carry on during the next few months.

Charles Edgar McCALL

Born:	1 Apr 1897, Transylvania County
Died:	31 Mar 1927, Henderson County; age 29
Buried:	Little River Baptist Church Cemetery
Spouse:	**Creolee COLLINS**
Father:	**Nick McCALL**
Mother:	**Mattie KILPATRICK**
Draft Registration:	Henderson County, 21, employed by Green River Mfg. Co.

[Documentation: FamilySearch.org , Ancestry.com, Henderson County DC, <u>Transylvania</u> <u>County Cemetery Survey</u>]

McCall   (Charles) Edgar   4,070,922   *White *Colored.
(Surname)   (Christian name)   (Army serial number)

Residence: __RFD1__   __Brevard__   __Transylvania__ NORTH CAROLINA
(Street and house number)   (Town or city)   (County)   (State)

*Inducted at __LB Henderson Co NC__ on __Aug 5__ 19 __18__

Place of birth: __Transylvania Co NC__   Age or date of birth: __Apr 1/1897__

Organizations served in, with dates of assignments and transfers:
Co M 5 Pion Inf to Aug 25/18; Co M 4 Pion Inf to Sept
1/18; 55 Pion Inf to Dec 7/18; Co K 106 Inf to disch

Grades, with date of appointment: Pvt

Engagements:

Wounds or other injuries received in action: None.
Served overseas from †__Sept 15/18__o †__March 6/19__, from † _____ to † _____
Honorably discharged on demobilization __Apr 4/19__ , 19 ____
In view of occupation he was, on date of discharge, reported __0__ per cent disabled.

Note: Pion Inf (Pioneer Regiment Infantry)

Pioneer Infantry Regiments

The United States Army formed many Pioneer Infantry Regiments for World War I. They were cross-trained in combat engineering and infantry tactics. They were trained to perform engineering and construction tasks. One officer described them as "they did everything the Infantry was too proud to do and the Engineers were too lazy to do."

The Pioneer Regiments included such specialist as mechanics, carpenters, farriers and masons. The primary role of pioneer units was to assist other arms in task such as the construction of field fortifications, military camps, bridge construction and road building. The pioneers were often engaged in the construction and repair of military railroads. They received standard infantry training so they could defend themselves. They were rarely involved in battle.

Doughboy Center, **Story of the American Expeditionary Forces**
Wikipedia.com

Crate McCALL

Born:	20 Jun 1895, Jackson County, NC
Died:	1 Mar 1965, Seneca, SC; age 69
Buried:	Jackson County, NC
Spouse:	**Sallie McKINNEY**, m. 3 Oct 1925, Transylvania County, NC
Mother:	**Ida McCALL**
Draft Registration:	21, single, logging and claimed mother and brother as dependents

[Documentation: Delayed Jackson County BC, Cowart's Index to Marriages, Discharge, TT obituary, Ancestry.com]

McCall   Crate   2,594,073   • White • Colored:
(Surname)   (Christian name)   (Army serial number)

Residence: _____ Grimshawes   Jackson   NORTH CAROLINA
(Street and house number)   (Town or city)   (County)   (State)

• ▓▓▓▓▓▓▓▓▓▓▓. •Inducted at Brevard NC _____ on May 10, 19 18
Place of birth: Grimshawes NC _____ Age or date of birth: 22 11/12 yrs

Organizations served in, with dates of assignments and transfers: _____
_____ Co F 54 Inf to disch _____

Grades, with date of appointment: _____
_____ Pvt 1cl June 1/19 _____

Engagements: _____

Wounds or other injuries received in action: None.
Served overseas from †July 6/18 to †June 10/19 from † _____ to † _____
Honorably discharged on demobilization _____ June 24/19 _____, 19 _____
In view of occupation he was, on date of discharge, reported _____ O _____ per cent disabled.

3/4/1965
CRATE McCALL

Funeral services for Crate McCall, Sr., 71, of Cashiers, were held Tuesday March 2nd at the Pleasant Grove Baptist Church in Cashiers. Burial followed in the church cemetery. A native of Cashiers, Mr. McCall was a retired carpenter and a veteran of World War I.

Surviving are the widow, Mrs. Sally McKinney McCall; one son, Crate, Jr.; and a half-brother Clinton McCall of Cashiers.

Mr. McCall died of injuries received during an affray while he was visiting in the home of Ray Cox in Seneca, SC. According to Oconee County Sheriff Floyd Owens, Mr. Cox has been charged with murder.

---

3 Aug 1917   Brevard News

LADIES IN TROUSERS
BOOST THE RED CROSS

The Red Cross fund was appreciably boosted to the tune of about $150 on Tuesday when a number of ladies appearing in man's attire and men in woman's garb displayed their baseball playing skills on the Franklin lawn to the amusement of the on-lookers. It was an enjoyable event and sufficiently ludicrous to cause the coins to flow more freely than common, as was desired by those promoting the event.

Flave Garland McCALL

Born:	24 Mar 1897, Henderson County, NC
Died:	1 Jan 1972, Henderson County, NC; age 74
Buried:	Holly Springs Baptist Church Cemetery, Henderson County, NC
Occupation:	Employee of G.F.Jones, Chester, SC
Father:	**John A. McCALL**
Mother:	**Matilda HAMILTON**
Draft registration:	21, home address of Etowah, NC, worked for G.F. Jones of Chester, SC, occupation not listed. WW II Draft Registration: Employed by G.F. Jones at Mars Hill, NC

[Documentation: NC Delayed BC, Henderson County DC, Ancestry.com]

McCall Flave G 4,480,514 · White · ~~Colored~~ 1

(Surname) (Christian name) (Army serial number)

Residence: RFD 1 Etowah Transylvania NORTH CAROLINA

(Street and house number) (Town or city) (County) (State)

~~Hinsbee T. A.~~ *Inducted at Brevard N C on Aug 26/18 , 19

Place of birth: Etowah N C Age or date of birth: Mch 24/1897

Organizations served in, with dates of assignments and transfers: 156 Dep Brig to disch

Grades, with date of appointment: Pvt

Engagements:

Wounds or other injuries received in action: None.

Served overseas from † No to † , from † to †

Honorably discharged on demobilization Dec 11 , 1918

In view of occupation he was, on date of discharge, reported 0 per cent disabled.

Remarks:

SRC Notes: Dep Brig (Depot Brigade)

26 Aug 1918   Brevard News
TWELVE MORE MEN LEFT Monday for Camp Jackson Monday afternoon:
. . . Flave G. McCall, Etowah . . .

"Sawing wood for the cook" Camp Grant, Rockford, Ill.

257

Frank McCALL

Born:	18 Feb 1893, Jackson County, NC
Died:	18 Sep 1976, Jackson County, NC; age 83
Buried:	Pinhook Baptist Church Cemetery, Jackson County, NC
Father:	**Walker McCALL**
Mother:	**Mary OWEN**
Draft Registration:	No

[Documentation: North Carolina Death Collection, 1930 Census, Parent's NC Marriage record, Ancestry.com]

McCall, Frank ✗ ✗ * White * Colored.
(Surname) (Christian name) (Army serial number)

Residence: Balsam Grove, NORTH CAROLINA
(Street and house number) (Town or city) (County) (State)

* Enlisted XXXXX XXXXXXXXXX *Inducted at Brevard, N. Car. on Nov. 5, 1917

Place of birth: Gloucester, N. Car. Age or date of birth: 22 yrs.

Organizations served in, with dates of assignments and transfers: Co E 324 Inf to Dec 15/17; Hq 81 Div to Dec. 31/17; Co E 324 Inf to Disch.

Grades, with date of appointment: Pvt.

Engagements: XX

Wounds or other injuries received in action: None.

Served overseas from † None to † , from † to †

Honorably discharged: Jan. 3, 19 18 On SCD
(Date) (Cause)

In view of occupation he was, on date of discharge, reported 10 per cent disabled.

Note: SCD (Surgeons Certificate of Disability)

2 Nov 1917   Brevard News
LOCAL BOARD ORDERS THIRTEEN MORE MEN

All men whose names appear here are ordered to report to the Local Board at 5 P.M. on Monday, November 5, 1917 for transportation for Camp Jackson. They will leave for Camp November 6 at 8 A.M.

. . . Frank McCall . . .

9 Nov 1917   Brevard News

"An unusual incident took place in exemption with the present draft. Fred McCall, twin brother to Frank McCall, one of the drafted men, accompanied the latter when he came to report and requested the local board that he be allowed to go with his brother to the camp. The brothers resemble each other very much and were dressed to minute details. Hard as it was the duty of the board the request had to be refused."

To follow up on the newspaper article Pat Owen told me the family story that Fred went home very hurt and angry that he did not get to go with Frank to camp. Frank did go to Camp Jackson but he was also very angry that Fred had been turned away. Frank was determined to get discharged so he informed his superiors that he could not stay in the Army because he had poor eyesight. The officers did not buy the story and put him on the shooting range for target practice. He could only hit the target one time out of every six shots. Family tradition is that all six bullets hit the exact same spot but the Army did not realize this was the case so he was discharged with a 10% disability. Looking at his Service Record Card above he did enter the Army 5 Nov 1917 and was discharged 3 Jan 1918. The two brothers remained bachelors and lived together their entire lives in the Pinhook area.

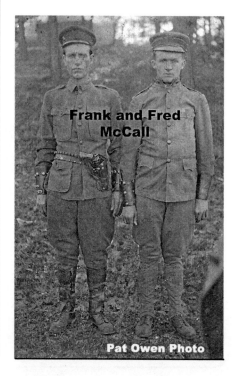

Frank and Fred McCall

Pat Owen Photo

Gilbert Clyde McCALL

Born:	18 Jun 1894, Balsam Grove, NC
Died:	24 Mar 1974, Transylvania County, NC; age 79
Buried:	Mt. Moriah Calvert Baptist Church Cemetery
Spouse:	**Mary E. GALLOWAY**, m. 11 Apr 1921, Transylvania County, NC
Father:	**Harvey McCALL**
Mother:	**Clarissa C. McCALL**
Draft registration:	23, single, a resident of Cherryfield, NC, self-employed farmer

[Documentation: Ancestry.com, Transylvania County DC, Cowart's Index to Marriages]

McCall Gilbert C 3,277,169 • White • ~~Colored~~.
(Surname) (Christian name) (Army serial number)

Residence: _____ Cherryfield Transylvania NORTH CAROLINA
(Street and house number) (Town or city) (County) (State)

▬▬▬▬▬ *Inducted at Brevard NC on June 25, 1918
Place of birth: Balsam Grove NC Age or date of birth: June 18/1893

Organizations served in, with dates of assignments and transfers:
156 Dep Brig to July 19/18; Co H 53 Pion Inf to Sept
10/18; Prov Salvage Co QMC Le Mans Sarthe France to
disch

Grades, with date of appointment:
Pvt

Engagements: _____

Wounds or other injuries received in action: None.
Served overseas from † Aug 4/18 to † July 13/19 from † _____ to † _____
Honorably discharged on demobilization July 24/19 _____, 19 ____
In view of occupation he was, on date of discharge, reported __O__ per cent disabled.

SRC Notes: Dep Brig (Depot Brigade) Pion Inf (Pioneer Infantry) Prov Salvage Co QMC (Provisional Salvage Company Quartermasters Corps)

21 Jun 1918   Brevard News
WHITE REGISTRANTS WHO ARE TO LEAVE FOR CAMP JACKSON, S.C.
TUESDAY, JUNE 25th, 1918 AT 3:13 P.M.
. . . Gilbert Clyde McCall, Cherryfield . . .

3/28/1974
GILBERT C. McCALL

Gilbert Clyde McCall, 79, of Route #2, died Sunday evening in Transylvania Community Hospital after a lingering illness. Mr. McCall was a life-long resident of Transylvania County and a retired farmer. He was a veteran of World War I.

Surviving are one daughter, Edith Buchanan; and one sister, Mrs. Wilburn Galloway.

Funeral services were held Tuesday in the Cherryfield Baptist Church of which he was a member. Burial followed in the Mt. Moriah Calvert Cemetery.

NATIONAL ARMY CANTONMENT (CAMP)
Camp McClellan   Location: Anniston, Ala.   Organization: 29th (old 8th) Division
Troops from New Jersey, Virginia, Maryland, Delaware and District of Columbia

---

Homer Nelson McCALL

Born:	17 Jun 1896, Transylvania County, NC
Died:	3 Oct 1973, Henderson County, NC; age 77
Buried:	Oak Grove Baptist Church Cemetery, Quebec, NC
Occupation:	Railroad conductor
Spouse:	**Bessie ROBINSON**
Father:	**Thomas McCALL**
Mother:	**Lydia GALLOWAY**
Draft Registration:	21, single and working for W.J. Owen
Discharge:	Homer was inducted 10 Nov 1918, the Armistice was signed 11 Nov 1918; discharged 14 Nov 1918 as the draft had been cancelled.

[Documentation: Henderson County DC, Upper Transylvania County, NC Remembered, Ancestry.com]

14 Nov 1918   Brevard News
   On Monday morning a crowd of relatives, friends and well-wishers were at the depot to bid God Speed to the following young men who were leaving for Camp Green, Charlotte:
. . . Homer Nelson McCall . . .
(He was discharged in Charlotte the same day this notice was published)

10/11/1973
HOMER N. McCALL

Homer Nelson McCall, 77, died in a Hendersonville hospital last Wednesday after an extended illness. A prominent civic and religious leader, he was a life-long resident of Transylvania County. He retired after 44 years as a Southern Railway Freight Conductor. He was a graduate of Western Carolina University and taught school for a few years in Transylvania County. He was a former member of the Transylvania County School Board, a Mason and Shriner, and a director in the Community Action program.

Surviving are the wife, Bessie Robinson McCall; two sons, Homer, Jr. and James Broadus McCall; and one brother Loon R. McCall.

Funeral services were conducted last Friday at Oak Grove Quebec Baptist Church and burial followed in the church cemetery.

4/25/1919 Brevard News

BE SURE AND HEAR RETURNED SOLDIER AT BREVARD INSTITUTE SATURDAY AT EIGHT O'CLOCK P. M.

James Luther McCALL

Born:	1 Jan 1896, McDowell County, NC
Died:	1 Jan 1977, Oteen VA Hospital, Buncombe County; age 81
Buried:	New French Broad Cemetery
Occupation:	Contractor
Race:	Colored
Spouse:	**Geneva SMITH**, m. 28 Dec 1922, Transylvania County, NC
Mother:	**Harriet McCALL**
Military Marker:	PVT US Army WW I

[Documentation: Hendersonville T-N obituary, Ancestry.com, 1920 Census,Cowart's Index to Marriages]

Hendersonville Times-News
1/29/1977
JAMES LUTHER MCCALL

James Luther McCall, 82, of Jackson Road in Marion, died Thursday in a Buncombe County VA hospital after a long illness. He was a retired contractor and an Army veteran of World War I.

Surviving are the widow, Ivory Conley McCall; three sons: James Luther McCall Jr., Joseph McCall and Eugene Waters McCall; two daughters: Beatrice Walker and Dorothy Camp; and a stepson, Roy Conley.

Services will be held at 2:30 p.m. Sunday at New French Broad Baptist Church in Transylvania County. Burial will be in the church cemetery.

Jasper Warrior McCALL

Born: 11 May 1892, Transylvania County, NC
Died: 25 Apr 1967, Oteen VA Hospital, Buncombe County; age 74
Buried: Pisgah Gardens Cemetery
Spouse: **Hettie Oda ENGLISH**, 20 Jan 1918, Transylvania County, NC
Father: **Jasper McCALL**
Mother: **Alice DUNN**
Draft Registration: 25, single, farming with his father Jasper McCall

[Documentation: Transylvania County BC, Buncombe County DC, TT obituary, Transylvania County Cemetery Survey, Ancestry.com, Cowart's Index to Marriages]

McCall	Warrior		1,324,532	White	
(Surname)	(Christian name)		(Army serial number)	(Race: White or colored)	

Residence: Pisgah Forest   NORTH CAROLINA
              (Street and house number)   (Town or city)   (County)   (State)

*Enlisted in   NG Pisgah Forest N.C   July 19/17   —
†Born in   Gloucester N C   —   25 2/12 yrs   —
Organizations: —   —
                Btry F 1 FA N C NG (Btry F 113 FA) to Apr 29/18;
                Hq Tr 20 Div to disch
Grades: Ck Jan 11/19 .   —   —

Engagements: —   —

Wounds or other injuries received in action: None.   —
‡Served overseas: No   —
§Hon. disch.   Feb 27/19   on demobilization   —
Was reported   0   per cent disabled on date of discharge, in view of occupation.

Note: NG (National Guard) Hq Tr (Headquarters Troop) Ck (cook)

4/27/1967
J. WARRIOR MCCALL

     Funeral services for Jasper Warrior McCall, 73, of Brevard, will be conducted Thursday at 11 AM at Calvary Baptist Church. Burial will be in Pisgah Garden Cemetery.

     Mr. McCall died Tuesday in the Veterans Hospital at Oteen. He was retired from Olin Chemical Corp. and was a member and deacon of Calvary Baptist Church.

     Surviving are his wife, Mrs. Oda English McCall; three daughters: Mrs. Raymond Burgess, Mrs. Melvin Mull, and Mrs. Ted Dalton; and three sons: Roy, Dewitt and William.

Special Rations of World War I

1. Reserve ration –enough food for one day carried by each soldier.

2. Emergency ration- concentrated food, packaged in a tin that would fit into a pocket and was carried by each soldier

3. Trench rations – As its name implies, it was designed to provide subsistence under conditions of trench warfare. The unit consisted of sufficient canned meats and canned hard bread to provide 25 men with food for one day. The canned meats were roast beef, corned beef, salmon and sardines. Other items included salt, sugar soluble coffee, solidified alcohol and cigarettes. The unit was packed in large galvanized containers designed to protect the contents from poison gas.

John Allen McCALL

Born:	17 Aug 1893, Transylvania County, NC
Died:	10 Feb 1976, Transylvania County, NC; age 78
Buried:	Mack McCall Cemetery
Spouse:	**Harriett FISHER**, m. 30 Dec 1916, Transylvania County, NC
Father:	**William M. McCALL**
Mother:	**Juda OWEN**
Draft Registration:	23, married, employed as a carpenter by Owens & Clayton on the waters of the French Broad River

[Documentation: FamilySearch.org, Ancestry.com, Transylvania County DC, Cowart's Index to Marriages]

McCall   John A   733,233   • White • Colored
(Surname)   (Christian name)   (Army serial number)

Residence: Lake Toxaway   Transylvania   NORTH CAROLINA
(Street and house number)   (Town or city)   (County)   (State)

•Inducted at Brevard N C   on Nov 5, 1917

Place of birth: Gloucester N C   Age or date of birth: 23 10/12 yrs

Organizations served in, with dates of assignments and transfers:
Co E 324 Inf to Feb 5/18; Co H 6 Inf to disch

Grades, with date of appointment: Pvt

Engagements:

Wounds or other injuries received in action: None.
Served overseas from † May 22/18 to July 22/19, from † _____ to † _____
Honorably discharged on demobilization July 29/19, 19_____
In view of occupation he was, on date of discharge, reported 0 per cent disabled.

John Allen McCall
Pat Owen Photo

2 Nov 1917   Brevard News

LOCAL BOARD ORDERS THIRTEEN MORE MEN are ordered to report on Monday, November 5, 1917 for transportation for Camp Jackson. They will leave for Camp November 6 at 8 A.M.
. . . John A. McCall . . .

2/12/1976
J.A. McCall

John Allen McCall, 82, of Rt. 2, Brevard, died Tuesday in a Brevard hospital after a long illness. A native of Transylvania County, he was a retired carpenter and a WWI veteran. He was a son of the late Monroe and Judy Owen McCall.

Surviving are the widow, Harriett Fisher McCall; two sons: Donald Lawrence McCall; and two daughters: Mrs. Almond Hall and Mrs. Clinton McCall

Services were held Thursday at Macedonia Baptist Church of which he was a member and deacon. Burial was in Mack McCall Cemetery

---

After the men finished their course of training in the US camps they were shipped to Europe. In both England and France there were other instruction camps in which the men were taught more precisely the rudiments of war under the instruction of foreign officers fresh from the front and with many years of experience in battle. The instruction in the European camps was from the first briefer than had been planned. The need for their presence on the battle line was already pressing. Their real education came in the trenches beside other soldiers.

Ralph McCALL

Born:	8 Dec 1895, Cashiers, NC
Died:	7 May 1951, Buncombe County, NC; age 55
Buried:	Lower Zachary Cemetery, Jackson County
Spouse:	**Roxanna BRYSON**
Father:	**Willie Hix McCALL**
Mother:	**Daisy Texanna FOWLER**
Draft registration:	21, single, lived at Pisgah Forest, logging for the Carr Lumber Co.

[Documentation: 1900, 1940 Censuses, findagrave.com, Buncombe County, Death Index, Ancestry.com]

McCall Ralph 4,159,452 • White
(Surname) (Christian name) (Army serial number)

Residence: Brevard Transylvania NORTH CAROLINA
(Street and house number) (Town or city) (County) (State)

• *Inducted at Brevard, N. C. on July 24, 1918

Place of birth: Jackson Co., NC Age or date of birth: Dec. 8, 1895

Organizations served in, with dates of assignments and transfers: MG Tng Camp, Camp Hancock, Ga to Oct 30/18; Co B 358 MG Bn to disch.

Grades, with date of appointment: Pvt

Engagements:

Wounds or other injuries received in action: None.
Served overseas from † none to †___, from †___ to †___.
Honorably discharged on demobilization Dec 10/18, 19___.
In view of occupation he was, on date of discharge, reported -0- per cent disabled.
Remarks:

Note: MG Tng (machine gun training)

18 Jul 1918   Brevard News
23 MORE MEN TO LEAVE JULY 24, 1918 for Camp Hancock, Ga., who will leave on the 3:13 train:
Alternates:
. . . Ralph McCall, Cashiers . . .

---

12 July 1918   Brevard News
JUNIOR RED CROSS BEGINS WORK

The Brevard Junior Red Cross held its 1st meeting at Transylvania Red Cross headquarters last Tuesday morning. The first thing in order was the election of officers. Ms. Agatha Deaver was elected Chairman, Ms. Ethel Hays, Vice-Chairman, Ms. Dorothy Silversteen, Secretary and Ms. Virginia Stradley, Treasure.

After disposing of several important business matters, which came before the meeting, those present set eagerly to work under the direction of Ms. Louise Brunot and Ms. Violet Henry. These young ladies sewed and the young gentleman made pillows

All the officers and the following members were present: Amelia Galloway, Marguerite Watson, Elizabeth Shipman, Blanche Dole, Joe Poole, E.C.Neal, Jr., O'Dell Nicholson, Inez Nicholson, Helen Duckworth, Geneva Neil, L. King, and Evelyn Townsend.

The next meeting will be held in the local Red Cross room Tuesday morning July 16 at 10 o'clock. Every girl and boy in the town who wishes to do something to help with the war efforts is urged to be present.

Thomas Wilson McCALL

Born:	26 Oct 1894, Transylvania County, NC
Died:	3 Feb 1973, Oteen VA Hospital, Buncombe County; age 78
Buried:	Boylston Cemetery, Henderson County, NC
Spouse:	**Frances Pauline ALLISON**
Father:	**Thomas P. McCALL**
Mother:	**Mary Elizabeth BALL**
Draft registration:	22, worked for his father, a farmer in Transylvania County. He asked for a draft exemption stating that his father and mother were totally dependent upon him working the farm.

[Documentation: Ancestry.com, FamilySearch.org, Buncombe County DC, findagrave.com, Hendersonville T-N obituary]

McCall   Thomas Wilson   4,070,953 • White • Colored.
(Surname)   (Christian name)   (Army serial number)

Residence: _____ Etowah ___ Transylvania NORTH CAROLINA
          (Street and house number)   (Town or city)   (County)   (State)
_____ •Inducted at ___ Transylvania Co N C __ on ___ Aug 5/18 __ 19.

Place of birth: Brevard N C   Age or date of birth: Oct 26/1894

Organizations served in, with dates of assignments and transfers: ___
_____ 5 Corps Arty Pk Pk Btry to Sept 15/18; Btry F 61 FA
_____ to disch

Grades, with date of appointment: _____
_____ Pvt

Engagements: _____

Wounds or other injuries received in action: None.
Served overseas from Nov 2/18 to Jan 18/19, from † _____ to † _____
Honorably discharged on demobilization _____ Feb 18, 19 19
In view of occupation he was, on date of discharge, reported _____ 0 _____ per cent disabled.

Note: Pk (Park) Btry (Battery) FA (Field Artillery)

Hendersonville Times-News
2/1/ 1973
THOMAS W. McCALL

Thomas Wilson McCall, 78, of Penrose, died Saturday afternoon in an Asheville hospital. He was a native of Transylvania County but had spent most of his life in Henderson County. A veteran of World War I, he was a member of Hedrick-Rhodes VFW Post No. 5206 and the Hubert M. Smith American Legion Post 77 and was associated with Gossett Furniture Company prior to his retirement.

He is survived by one daughter, Dorothy Shipman.

Funeral services will be held Tuesday in the Chapel of Jackson Funeral Home. Burial will be in Boylston Baptist Church Cemetery.

---

10 Aug 1917   **Brevard News**

DIED SUBJECT TO DRAFT

James Hinkle of the Sapphire section, died on Friday after an illness of three days. He was buried on Saturday, the Rev. Nolde conducting the funeral ceremony.

He was the son on Perry Hinkle and was 25 years old. Being of the draft age, he would have been examined on Tuesday by the examining board.

William Frank McCALL

Born:	16 Jun 1888, Henderson County, NC
Died:	1 Nov 1961, Oteen VA Hospital, Buncombe County; age 73
Buried:	Reid Cemetery at Oakland
Spouse:	**Jennie Sue NORTON**, m. 30 Aug 1925, Transylvania County, NC
Father:	**William P. McCALL**
Mother:	**Nancy Adaline BIRD**
Draft Registration:	Charlotte, 23, single, employed as a brakeman for Southern Railroad Company
Military Marker:	NC 106 Ordnance Depot Co WW I

[Documentation: Henderson County Delayed BC, Buncombe County DC, US Headstone Application, Upper Transylvania County, NC Remembered, TT Obituary, Cowart's Index to Marriages]

McCall William Frank 3,277,446 *White *Colored.
(Surname) (Christian name) (Army serial number)

Residence: _____ Fletcher Henderson NORTH CAROLINA
(Street and house number) (Town or city) (County) (State)

_____ *Inducted at Charlotte NC on June 24 19 18
Place of birth: Fletcher NC Age or date of birth: June 16/1888
Organizations served in, with dates of assignments and transfers: _____
156 Den Brig to disch _____

Grades, with date of appointment: _____
Corp Nov 25/18

Engagements: _____

Wounds or other injuries received in action: None.
Served overseas from †__No__ to †_____, from †_____ to †_____
Honorably discharged on demobilization __July 3/19__, 19____
In view of occupation he was, on date of discharge, reported __0__ per cent disabled.

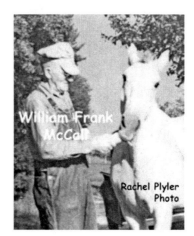
Rachel Plyler Photo

11/9/1961
McCALL RITES HELD

Funeral services for William Frank McCall, 73, of Route 1, Lake Toxaway, were held Friday afternoon at the Lake Toxaway Baptist Church. Burial followed in the Reid Cemetery of Lake Toxaway.

Mr. McCall died Wednesday night at the Oteen Veteran's Hospital. A retired railroad worker, he was a veteran of World War I and a member of the Mills River Methodist Church.

Survivors include the widow, Mrs. Jennie Sue Norton McCall; three sisters: Mrs. N.E. Posey, Mrs. Gertrude McCall and Mrs. Eloise Flanagan; and one brother, M. L. McCall.

---

27 Jun 1918   **Brevard News**

PICTURES FOR RED CROSS BENEFIT

Frank D. Clement has very kindly agreed to turn over the use of the auditorium to the Red Cross every Tuesday and Thursday during the months of July and August. Some of the best pictures on the road have been booked for the shows and the artists will include Mary Pickford, Dustin Farnam and others.

The 1st picture will feature Dustin Farnam in "Reaching for the Moon" and will be shown either July 3 or 4th, as the Odd Fellows have the auditorium on the 4th.

William Henry McCALL

Born:	6 May 1895, Henderson County, NC
Died:	16 Jul 1954, Henderson County, NC; age 59
Buried:	Little River Baptist Church Cemetery
Occupation:	Rural mail carrier
Spouse:	**Hazel PATTERSON**
Father:	**Gaston McCALL**
Mother:	**Dorcus HAMILTON**
Draft Registration:	No
Military Marker:	NC CPL BTRY A ARTY CAC WW I

[Documentation: Henderson County DC, <u>Transylvania County Cemetery Survey</u>, Application for Veteran's Headstone, TT obituary, Ancestry.com]

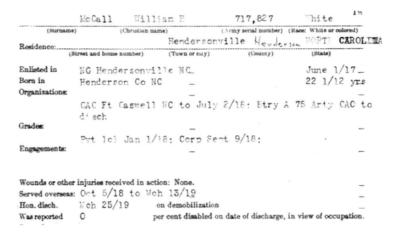

Note: CAC (Coast Artillery Corps)

7/22/1954
HENRY McCALL

Funeral services for William Henry McCall, 59, were held Tuesday afternoon in the Thomas Shepherd Funeral Home chapel in Hendersonville. Following the service, Mr. McCall was buried in the Little River Cemetery. He was a native of Transylvania County. He died last Friday in the Hendersonville hospital. Mr. McCall was a rural mail carrier at Penrose.

Survivors include the widow, Hazel Patterson McCall; one daughter, Mrs. Sam King; and one son, Fred McCall.

William Jason McCALL

Born:	21 Jun 1892, Transylvania County, NC
Died:	1 Dec 1979, Transylvania County, NC; age 87
Buried:	Jason McCall Cemetery
Spouse:	**Rosetta OWEN**, m. 4 Jul 1921, Transylvania County, NC
Father:	**Rufus E. McCALL**
Mother:	**Elvira P. OWEN**
Draft Registration:	24, single, worked as a farmer
Military Marker:	WAGR US Army WW I

[Documentation: Transylvania County BC, Transylvania County DC, Transylvania County Cemetery Survey, Ancestry.com, Cowart's Index to Marriages]

McCall William J   1,876,294   • White • Colored.
(Surname)   (Christian name)   (Army serial number)

Residence: _____ Balsam Grove Transylvania NORTH CAROLINA
(Street and house number)   (Town or city)   (County)   (State)

• _____ •Inducted at Brevard NC   on Sept 18, 19 17
Place of birth: Gloucester NC _____ Age or date of birth: 25 3/12 yrs

Organizations served in, with dates of assignments and transfers: _____
MD to disch

Grades, with date of appointment: _____
Wag Feb 22/19

Engagements: _____

Wounds or other injuries received in action: None.
Served overseas from † Aug 8/18 to † June 20/19, from † _____ to † _____
Honorably discharged on demobilization June 29/19 _____, 19 ____
In view of occupation he was, on date of discharge, reported ____ 0 ____ per cent disabled.

SRC Notes: MD (Medical Department)

21 Sep 1917   Brevard News
THIRTY-ONE MEN TO CAMP JACKSON was ordered to report on Tuesday at 5 P.M. at the office of the local enlistment board and to leave for Camp Jackson, S.C. Wednesday morning.
. . . William Jason McCall . . .

12/3/1979
WILLIAM McCALL

William Jason McCall, 87, died last Saturday in Brevard Residential Care Center after an extended illness. A native of Transylvania County, he was the son of the late Rufus E. and Elvira P. Owen McCall. He was married to Rosetta Owen McCall, who died in July. He was a veteran of World War I and served as wagoner for the U.S. Army. He was a member of Shoal Creek Baptist Church.

Surviving are two sons, Joseph C. and L.C. McCall; a daughter, Violet Smith; tow brothers, Richard and Ira C. McCall; and a sister Irona Crisp.

The American Legion Post No. 88 of which he was a member for 41 years held full military services Monday in the Moody-Connolly Funeral Home Chapel. Burial was in the Jason McCall Cemetery.

NATIONAL ARMY CANTONMENT (CAMP)
Camp Jackson   Location: Columbia, SC   Organization: 81st Division
Troops from Tennessee, North Carolina, South Carolina and Florida

---

Hugh T. McCARRELL

Born:	16 Aug 1891, Transylvania County, NC
Died:	1 Mar 1930, Richmond County, GA; age 38
Buried:	Gillespie-Evergreen Cemetery
Spouse:	**Rose ANDERSON**
Father:	**Samuel P. McCARRELL**
Mother:	**Sarah DUCKWORTH**
Draft Registration:	No
Military Marker:	NC SGT 1CL 638 AERQ SODN

[Documentation: Discharge, Georgia Death Index, <u>Transylvania County Cemetery Survey</u>, FamilySearch.org, Brevard News obituary]

```
                McCarroll, Hugh T        1,330,194        White        1½
              (Surname)      (Christian name)     (Army serial number)  (Race: White or colored)
Residence:    R #3           Asheville                         NORTH CAROLINA
              (Street and house number)   (Town or city)        (County)        (State)
* Enlisted in  NG at Asheville NC         Dec 4/14
† Born in      Brevard NC                 24 yrs
Organizations: Co K 1 Inf NC NG to Sept 12/17; 55 Dep Brig to Oct 24/17
               Co G 120 Inf to Nov 17/17; Co C 105 F Sig Bn to Aug 8/18
               1102 Aero Sq to Aug 31/18; 638 Aero Sq to disch
Grades:        Sgt July 26/17; Pvt Nov 17/17; Pvt 1cl Nov 8/17; Corp Dec
Engagements:   1/17; Sgt Feb 3/18; Sgt 1cl Apr 1/19

Wounds or other injuries received in action:  None.
‡ Served overseas: Aug 8/18 to June 25/19
§ Hon. disch.    July 16/19    on demobilization
  Was reported   0            per cent disabled on date of discharge, in view of occupation.
```

SRC Notes: Sig Bn (Signal Battalion) Aero Sq (Air Squadron)

3/5/1930
HUGH McCARRELL

Hugh T. McCarrell, former resident of Brevard, died last Saturday evening in the Veterans Hospital, Augusta, Ga., and the remains were brought here for interment. Funeral services were conducted Tuesday morning at the home of the deceased's sister Mrs. S.W. Radford, and burial was made in the Gillespie Cemetery. The deceased was a World War I veteran, having seen much active service overseas. Death was result of shocks and nervous breakdown as a result of these experiences

The widow and one child, two years of age, survive. In addition to Mrs. Radford, two other sisters and one brother survive: Mrs. T.E. Hume, Mrs. M.M. Howard and Harold McCarrell.

.

---

17 Oct 1918   Brevard News

Private Jim Mitchell of Company A died Oct 8th of pneumonia. The remains were shipped Saturday to his mother, Mrs. Nellie Mitchell, at Nelson, SC, accompanied by an attendant. Funeral services were held previous to shipment at the undertaking establishment of Kilpatrick & Sons by Rev. John R. Hay of the Camp Y.M.C.A.

William McKinley McCONNELL

Born: 7 Jul 1896, Hiwassee, Georgia
Died: 29 Mar 1964, Transylvania County, NC; age 67
Buried: Mt. Moriah Calvert Baptist Church Cemetery
Occupation: Lumbering
Spouse: **Mary Nan PRATHER**
Father: **Elisha McCONNELL**
Mother: **Lillia Adeline ELLIOTT**
Draft Registration: Berrien County, GA, 21, farming
Note: Death Certificate states WW I

[Documentation: Transylvania County DC, Discharge, FamilySearch.org, Ancestry.com, TT obituary]

4/2/1964
WILLIAM M. MCCONNELL

Funeral services for William McKinley McConnell, 67, of Brevard were held Tuesday at the Mt. Moriah Calvert Baptist church. Burial followed in the church cemetery. Mr. McConnell died Sunday morning in the Transylvania Community hospital after a long illness. A native of Hiwassee, Georgia, he had resided in Transylvania County for the past 30 years. He was in the lumbering business.

Survivors include a daughter, Mrs. Charles Lance; six sons: Claude, Frank, Carl, Eugene, Odean and Dennis McConnell; a brother, Homer McConnell; and a sister, Mrs. Stella Kirby.

Montfaucon   Remains of a church
38
Robert Merrill Collection

Columbus "Lum" McCRARY

Born:	18 Nov 1893, Transylvania County, NC
Died:	22 Feb 1934, Greenville, South Carolina; age 40
Buried:	Rocky Hill Cemetery
Father:	**Alexander McCRARY**
Mother:	**Nancy THOMAS**
Draft Registration:	24, single and farming

[Documentation: South Carolina DC, 1900 Census, Transylvania County Cemetery Survey, TT obituary]

McCrarey, Lum   4,159,462   *Transylvania* 1
(Surname)   (Christian name)   (Army serial number)   * White *Colored.

Residence: _____ **Cedar Mount** **NORTH CAROLINA**
(Street and house number)   (Town or city)   (County)   (State)

*█████████████ *Inducted at **Brevard NC** _____ on **July 24, 1918**
Place of birth: **Henderson Co NC** _____ Age or date of birth: **Nov 19, 1893**

Organizations served in, with dates of assignments and transfers: _____
53 Dep Brig to disch

Grades, with date of appointment: _____
Pvt

Engagements: _____

Wounds or other injuries received in action: None.
Served overseas from † **no** to † _____, from † _____ to † _____
Honorably discharged on demobilization **Dec 21/18** , 19 _____
In view of occupation he was, on date of discharge, reported **0** per cent disabled.

SRC Note: Dep Brig (Depot Brigade)

18 Jul 1918   BrevardNews
23 More Men To Leave July 24, 1918 for Camp Hancock, Ga.:
. . . Lum McCrary, Cedar Mountain . . .

3/1/1934
COLUMBUS McCRARY

Funeral services for Columbus McCrary, 41, who was burned to death at his home near Marietta, S.C., late last Thursday, were held Saturday morning from the Rocky Hill Baptist Church at Cedar Mountain. Interment was made in the church cemetery.

His parents Mr. and Mrs. A.L. McCrary, Cedar Mountain; three sisters: Mrs. William Fisher, Misses Mary and Nannie Sue McCrary; and three brothers: Sanford, Francis and Manning, survive Mr. McCrary.

The deceased was burned to death when his three room house two miles northwest of Marietta went up in flames. Coroner George W. McCoy who investigated said he did not think an inquest would be necessary.

Edward Turner who lives near the McCrary house said he visited McCrary during the afternoon and when he left, the man was building a fire in the fireplace of the house. Soon he saw heavy smoke coming from the house ran over and found McCrary lying on a bed and the flames spreading rapidly over one side of the room.

Turner told the coroner he got McCrary to the door and there the man, who weighted about 180 pounds jerked loose from his rescuer and ran back into the blazing room. Turner said the flames had spread so far he could not make his way back into the room. After the building burned Mr. McCrary's charred body, burned beyond recognition, was found in the heap of ashes.

Ellison K McCRARY

Born:	30 Aug 1896, Transylvania County, NC
Died:	3 Jul 1976, Oteen VA Hospital, Buncombe County; age 79
Buried:	Dunn's Creek Baptist Church Cemetery
Spouse:	**Lula Mae HEATH**, m. 18 Jun 1922, Transylvania County, NC
Father:	**Volney C. McCRARY**
Mother:	**Ellen Rachel RAXTER**
Draft Registration:	No

[Documentation: Transylvania County BC, Buncombe County DC, <u>Transylvania County Cemetery Survey</u>, Ancestry.com, <u>Cowart's Index to Marriages</u>]

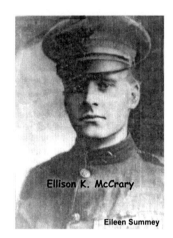

McCrary	Ellison K		1,039,637		White 1½
(Surname)	(Christian name)		(Army serial number)		(Race: White or colored)
Residence:		Cedar Mountain		NORTH CAROLINA	
	(Street and house number)	(Town or city)	(County)	(State)	

Enlisted in RA at Ft Screven Ga Nov 3/17

Born in Cedar Mountain NC 21-2/12 yrs

Organizations:
Btry A 11 FA to Disch

Grades:
Wag Jan 4/19

Engagements:

Wounds or other injuries received in action: None.
Served overseas: July 14/18 to June 10/19
Hon. disch. June 24/19 on demobilization
Was reported 0 per cent disabled on date of discharge, in view of occupation.
Remarks:

Ellison K. McCrary
Eileen Summey

SRC Note: FA (Field Artillery)

7/8/1976
E.K. McCRARY

Ellison K. McCrary, 79, died Saturday, June 3, 1976, in the Oteen Hospital at Asheville after an extended illness. He was a lifelong resident of Transylvania County and a son of the late Volney C. and Ellen Raxter McCrary. He was a retired farmer, a member of Carrs Creek Baptist Church, a veteran of World War I, a member of the Brevard V.F.W., a 32nd degree mason and a member of the Dunn's Rock Masonic Lodge.

Survivors include his widow, Lula Heath McCrary; four sons: John Allen, Frederick Eugene, Jack L. and Ellison K., Jr.; five daughters: Eileen Summey, Louella Merrill, Thalia Queen, Helen Channell and Joanne Black; three brothers: Foster, Bill and Gus McCrary; and one sister, Leota McCarthy.

Services were held Monday in the Moody-Connolly Funeral Home Chapel and burial followed in the Dunn's Creek Cemetery with full military rites.

PARACHUTES

Among American pilots in World War I parachutes were not used. An American invented the "packed" parachute before the war began but the War Department of the United States did not like the idea of pilots wearing parachutes. They believed that a pilot might bail out too quickly in an emergency leaving his plane to crash while he survived. They felt the plane might be saved and brought down safely if the pilots were forced to stay onboard.

There were pilots that agreed with the War Department and thought that wearing a parachute showed signs of fear and lack of confidence in their own skills.

Judson McCRARY

Born:	19 Oct 1896, Henderson County, NC
Died:	8 Apr 1939, Transylvania County, NC; age 42
Buried:	Gillespie-Evergreen Cemetery
Occupation:	Saw miller
Spouse:	**Dora Mildred REECE**
Father:	**William J. McCRARY**
Mother:	**Mary E. HAMILTON**
Draft Registration:	21, single, unemployed well driller

[Documentation: Transylvania County DC, <u>Transylvania County Cemetery Survey</u>, Ancestry.com, TT obituary]

McCrary, Judson   1,891,641   • White • Colored
(Surname)   (Christian name)   (Army serial number)

Residence: _____ Penrose Transylvania NORTH CAROLINA
(Street and house number)   (Town or city)   (County)   (State)

_____. *Inducted at Beard N C _____ on May 24, 19__ 18
Place of birth: Hendersonville N C__ Age or date of birth: 21 7/12 yrs
Organizations served in, with dates of assignments and transfers: _____
156 Dep Brig to June 28/18; Co B 324 Inf to July 15/18; 55 Dep Brig to Oct 15/18; Provost Gds Co Camp

Grades, with date of appointment: _____
Pvt

Engagements: _____
Remarks (continued): _____
Sevier S C to disch

Wounds or other injuries received in action: None.
Served overseas from †None____ to †_____ from †_____ to †_____
Honorably discharged on demobilization __ Mch 21/19 ___, 19_____
In view of occupation he was, on date of discharge, reported __0__ per cent disabled.

Judson McCrary TT Photo

SRC Note: Provost Gds Co Camp (Military Police Guard Company)

4/13/1939
JUDSON McCRARY

Funeral services were held Sunday afternoon from the residence on Maple Street and interment followed in the Gillespie Cemetery. Mr. McCrary was a veteran of the World War and belonged to the Provost Guard Company stationed at Camp Sevier, Greenville. After his military service he spent several years in the well drilling business in South Carolina. He came to Brevard in 1921 and established the McCrary Motor Company and in 1926 he established the Brevard Realty Company, later adding insurance and rentals to his business. Through his efforts the Wheeler Silk Hosier Mill was located in Brevard and he was also one of the men assisting in locating the new paper industry in the county. He was known as an active "pusher" for civic progress both in the town and the county.

Surviving are the widow and one son, Judson, Jr.; the mother, Mrs. W.J. McCrary; and three sisters: Mrs. Sam. M. Turner, Mrs. Belva McCray, and Mrs. Herman Rhodes; and three brothers: Virgil, Joe, and Avery McCrary. The father died ten years ago and his eldest son, Billy, died nine years ago.

NATIONAL ARMY CANTONMENT (CAMP)

Camp Travis   Location: Fort Sam Houston, Tex.   Organization: 90th Division
Troops from Texas, Arizona, New Mexico and Oklahoma

Virgil McCRARY

Born:	24 Jan 1889, Transylvania County, NC
Died:	20 Jun 1957, Transylvania County, NC; age 68
Buried:	Little River Baptist Church Cemetery
Spouse:	**Ida McCALL**
Father:	**William J. McCRARY**
Mother:	**Mary E. HAMILTON**
Draft Registration:	28, single, employed as a well driller for Green River Mfg. Company

[Documentation: Transylvania County DC, Ancestry.com, Transylvania County Cemetery Survey, TT obituary]

McCrary, Virgil   2,587,023   • White •Colored.
(Surname)   (Christian name)   (Army serial number)

Residence: _____ Penrose Transylvania NORTH CAROLINA
(Street and house number)   (Town or city)   (County)   (State)

N.C.R.C. *Inducted at Transylvania CoNC on July 5 19 18
Place of birth: Henderson Co N C   Age or date of birth: 29 6/12 yrs
Organizations served in, with dates of assignments and transfers: _____
15 Bn Camp Greenleaf Ga to July 23/18; 2 Motor Co Camp
Greenleaf Ga to Aug 2/18; Motor Co 4 Sec B Camp Green-
Grades, with date of appointment: _____
Pvt

Remarks (continued): _____
leaf Ga to Aug 22/18; Bn Det 109 Inf to disch

Wounds or other injuries received in action: None.
Served overseas from †Sept 1/18 to †May 3/19, from † _____ to † _____
Honorably discharged on demobilization May 16/19 , 19 ___
In view of occupation he was, on date of discharge, reported 0 per cent disabled.

11 Jul 1918   Brevard News

Twelve Transylvania boys left on last Saturday for Fort Oglethorpe, Ga., to begin their careers as defenders of democracy. The boys left on the afternoon train . . .
. . .Virgil McCrary, Penrose . .

6/27/1957
VIRGIL McCRARY

Final rites for Virgil McCrary, 68, one of Western North Carolina's pioneer well drillers, were held Saturday afternoon in the Little River Baptist Church. Mr. McCrary died Thursday night at his home at Penrose following a lingering illness.

Mr. McCrary had been engaged in well drilling in the area for over 40 years. He had lived most of his life in Transylvania County.

Active in civic affairs he was a member of the American Legion, the Veterans of Foreign Wars and the local Elks Lodge. He was a veteran of World War I. McCrary was a 32nd degree Mason and a member of the Dunn's Rock Lodge for 37 years. He was a member of the Scottish Rites bodies of Asheville. He was also a member of the Oasis Temple in Charlotte and a charter member of the Transylvania Shrine Club.

Surviving are the widow, Mrs. Ida McCrary; six daughters: Mrs. G.T. Shipman, Mrs. J.F. Duckworth, Mrs. W.M. Case, Mrs. R.W. Misenheimer, Mrs. Clifton Moore and Mary McCrary; two sons, Thomas and Charles; two brothers, Joe and Avery McCrary; and three sisters: Mrs. Herbert Rhodes, Mrs. A.R. Wellwood and Mrs. Sam M. Turner.

Warren Lafayette McCRAW

Born:	30 Jan 1895, Cherokee, SC
Died:	Jul 1945, Pinellas County, FL; age 50
Buried:	Oakland Cemetery, Gaffney, SC
Spouse:	**Bessie**
Draft Registration:	No
Father:	**J. Carb McCRAW**
Mother:	**Sallie Amanda COOPER**
Note:	**Very few clues for this fellow and no idea what he was doing in Transylvania County at the time of his enlistment.**

[Documentation: FamilySearch.org, Ancestry.com, South Carolina Delayed BC, Florida Death Index, findagrave.com]

McCraw	Warren L	715,478	White 1½
(Surname)	(Christian name)	(Army serial number)	(Race: White or colored)

Residence: _____ Brevard *Transylvania* NORTH CAROLINA
(Street and house number) (Town or City) (County) (State)

Enlisted in NG at Gaffney SC June 4/17

Born in Cherokee Co SC 21-4/12 yrs

Organizations:
8 Co CA Ft Moultrie SC to Feb 1/18; Btry B 61 CAC to Disch

Grades: Ck Sept 7/17; Pvt Feb 1/18; Ck Feb 1/18; Sgt Aug. 3/18; Mess Sgt Aug 4/18

Engagements:

Wounds or other injuries received in action: None.

Served overseas: July 17/18 to Feb 17/19

Hon. disch. Mch 3/19 on demobilization

Was reported 0 per cent disabled on date of discharge, in view of occupation.

Remarks:

SRC Note: CAC (Coast Artillery Corps) Ck (Cook)

Field Kitchen

1917 Post Card

Ernest P. McDONALD

Born:	1 Mar 1891, Mississippi City, Mississippi
Died:	7 Apr 1957, Houston, Texas; age 66
Buried:	Woodlawn Garden of Memory, Houston, TX
Occupation:	Electrical Engineer
Father:	**William McDONALD**
Mother:	**Margaret**
Draft Registration:	Cado, Mississippi, 26, single, Gulf Oil refinery worker

[Documentation: Ancestry.com, FamilySearch.org, US Headstone Application, Texas DC]

McDonald Ernest P   4,431,889 . White . Colored.   1
(Surname)   (Christian name)   (Army serial number)

Residence: _____ Brevard Transylvania NORTH CAROLINA
(Street and house number) (Town or city) (County) (State)

_____ . Inducted at ____ Gulfport Miss ___ 13th Aug 13, 19__18
Place of birth: McHenry Miss. ____ Age or date of birth: 1st 1/91

Organizations served in, with dates of assignments and transfers: _____
Student Army Trng C Ala Polytechnic Institute Auburn Ala
to Disch

Grades, with date of appointment: _____
Pvt

Engagements: _____

Wounds or other injuries received in action: None.
Served overseas from † no to † ____, from † ____ to † ____
Honorably discharged on demobilization ____ Dec 9 ____, 19__18
In view of occupation he was, on date of discharge, reported ____0____ per cent disabled.

Mar 1918   Brevard News
TRANSYLVANIA'S PATRIOTIC WOMEN

Within a fortnight after the Congress almost unanimously declared war, twenty-one representative women of Transylvania County bonded themselves together to form a branch of the National League of Women's Service in this county.

From the beginning this organization has justified its existence by utilizing for the national defense energies of a numbers of women who longed to do something helpful but failed to recognize services which they might give in their daily lives from home.

Especially did the league emphasized the importance of food conservation—the canning and drying of fruits and vegetables. It is estimated that over 15,000 pounds of food was conserved in this community last summer through the direct efforts of the league.

However, the members of this organization did not let this work, vital as it was, interfere with their thoughtful provision for the comfort of the Transylvanian soldiers. Of the boys who went from Transylvania to fight for our country, each individual received from the League of Women, a well-stocked comfort kit.

In this benevolent work the race distinctions weren't made and the women of the County raised statistical sums of money to help in supplying items for the comfort kits presented to each soldier, both colored and white.

Not only did the League provide for the immediate comfort of the departing soldiers, but it also forwarded several boxes of hospital supplies to New York for shipment to France.

Their work did not stop with this. Benevolent services went still further and compiled complete records, so far as possible, of the Transylvania boys who went into the national services. These records are to be preserved in the archives of the organization.

Wade McGAHA

Born:	15 Feb 1897, Transylvania County, NC.
Died:	25 Sep 1966, Oteen VA Hospital, Buncombe County; age 69
Buried:	Mud Creek Baptist Church Cemetery, Henderson County
Occupation:	Farmer
Spouse:	**Winnie PATTERSON**
Father:	**James E. McGAHA**
Mother:	**Sarah E. MOORE**
Draft registration:	21, single, resident of Pisgah Forest, worked for C. Clough of Pisgah Forest

*[Documentation: Buncombe County DC, <u>Henderson County Cemetery Book</u>, ancestry.com,
Hendersonville T-N obituary]*

McGaha, Wade   4,480,515-   * White
 (Surname)   (Christian name)   (Army serial number)

Residence: RFD 2   Pisgah Forest   NORTH CAROLINA
           (Street and house number)   (Town or city)   (County)   (State)

*   . *Inducted at   Brevard NC   on Aug 28, 19 18
Place of birth: Little Rock NC   Age or date of birth: Feb 15, 1897

Organizations served in, with dates of assignments and transfers:
Co L 4 Prov Regt 156 Dep Brig to Sept 20/18; Btry D
118 FA to Oct 2/18; Co A 2 Bn 1 Prov Dev Bn FA Repl
Grades, with date of appointment Draft Camp Jackson SC to Disch
Pvt

Engagements: None

Wounds or other injuries received in action: None.
Served overseas from † None   to †   , from †   to †
Honorably discharged: Dec 27, 19 18   on SCD
                     (Date)   (Cause)
In view of occupation he was, on date of discharge, reported 12½ per cent disabled.

*SRC Note: Dep Brig (Depot Brigade) FA (Field Artillery) FA Repl (Field Artillery Replacement)
SCD (Surgeons Certificate of Disability)*

26 Aug 1918   Brevard News
TWELVE MORE MEN LEFT MONDAY
The following men were entrained for Camp Jackson Monday afternoon:
...Wade McGaha, Pisgah Forest R.F.D. ....

Hendersonville Times News
Sep. 26, 1966
WADE L. MCGAHA

Funeral services for Wade Leo McGaha, 69, will be held at Jackson Funeral Home Chapel, Tuesday at 2 pm. Interment will follow at Mud Creek Baptist Church Cemetery.

Mr. McGaha died at Oteen Veteran's Hospital Sunday night following a lengthy illness. He was a retired farmer and a resident of Henderson County since 1950. Prior to that he was a resident of Transylvania County. McGaha was a member of Little River Baptist Church. He was a veteran of WWI.

He is survived by his wife, Winnie Patterson McGaha; daughter, Kathleen Thompson; step-son, Kenneth King; one brother, Sylvester McGaha; and five sisters: Mildred Gray, Mae Blackwell, Flora Jones, Annis McGaha and Sallie Hill.

William Ernest McGUIRE

Born:	15 May 1890, Macon County, NC
Died:	12 Mar 1960, Winston-Salem, NC; age 69
Buried:	Shepherd's Memorial Park, Henderson County
Occupation:	Structural engineer for Builder's Lumber Co.
Spouse:	**Kathleen NORRYCE**, m. 14 Jul 1915, Anderson, SC
Father:	**Joseph Alexander McGUIRE**
Mother:	**Nancy Catherine HILL**
Draft Registration:	27, married, structural engineer

[Documentation: North Carolina DC, 1900-1940 Censuses, Ancestry.com, Application for Veteran's headstone, Henderson County Cemetery Book.]

The following letters were shared by Mac Morrow, the grandson of R.H. Morrow.

7 Nov 1917 Letter from William E. McGuire, Co. C 318 MG BN, Camp Jackson, SC
To: Mr. R.H. Morrow, Brevard, NC

Dear Mr. Morrow,

Well here I am a full fledged soldier and getting along very well, in fact, much better than I expected to before I came down here. The barracks are good buildings and will be well heated when they get the stoves installed. The mess is fairly good, we get plenty but it is the sameness that hurts.

I have been assigned to a machine gun battalion and they are trying to make a machine gunner out of me, which is slow work. I have been promoted to a petty officer, which I was glad to get for it lets me out of lots of disagreeable detail work. I can get a transfer to the engineers any time I want it but I think that I will stay where I am for my chances are better to get something later on, for in the engineers there are men drilling in the rear ranks that are graduates from some of the best colleges and lots of experience. There is one fellow that put in four years on the Culebra Cut at Panama as an engineer and he had been back home only three months when he was drafted and now he is a private working at digging up stumps in these pine woods.

Men can be found here from all walks of life in some cases it is amusing and some that are very pitiful. Most of the men in my company are a pretty good sort for nearly all of them are farmer boys from middle Tenn. and they haven't got rough yet.

I surely hope you are getting some hunting in this fall for you haven't had any in two or three years. I would certainly like to spend a while in the mountains now.

Kathleen is staying in Columbia and I get two afternoons off during the week and Sundays to spend with her.

I wish you would please send me a bushel of apples the first chance you get for I get mighty hungry for a mountain apple. Send them to Kathleen at 1624 Senate Street, Columbus, S.C. and send me the bill for them and I will appreciate it very much if you will do this for me.

I had the gun sent to you from Anderson some time ago which please keep until I get back from France, if I ever do, if not the gun is yours along with the little 22 rifle.

Please give Mrs. Morrow and my very best wishes for your self I am

Your friend   Will McGuire

19 Nov 1917 Letter from William E. McGuire, Sanitary Detachment, 318 M.G. Bn. Camp Jackson, S.C.
American Expeditionary Forces. .S.A. P.O. #791
To: Mr. R.H. Morrow, Brevard, NC

Dear Mr. Morrow,

I received your letter Saturday saying that you was thinking of coming down here on a little trip and I want to insist on your coming for there are lots of things of interest to see and I want you to see how the construction work is handled. This is said to be the largest camp in the US. and I guess it is for I haven't seen it all yet.

I have been transferred into the Sanitary Detachment since I wrote you. I have been in it about a week now but I haven't been able to find out what we are supposed to do when
we go across. I like the change and I think I have improved conditions some.

When you get to Columbia, go to the army office on the 9th floor of the Union National Bank Building and ask for a pass to visit the camp and you will find me in J-42 Infirmary of the 318th M.G. Bn. on the infantry side of the camp. Come out on a cantonment car and the guards at the car line will direct you how to find me. I will be able to get off to show you all over the camp while you are here. Kathleen is staying with the Banks at 1624 Senate Street, if you want to look her up before you come out to camp.

Be sure to come for I am looking forward to your visit and I know you will enjoy seeing the camp and every thing connected with it.

Mama writes me that Walker was on a bear hunt a couple of weeks ago and the crowd got three, Walker getting one big one this time. I reckon he feels pretty good over it. I certainly wish we could have been along with him

Don't let any thing keep you from coming down.

Sincerely,
Will McGuire

P.S. I heard from R.E. Wood the other day and G.L. is a Major in the Foresters in active service in France.

Sep 1918 Letter from Somewhere in France
From: Sgt. William E. McGuire, Sanitary Detachment, 318 Machine Gun Bn.
To: Mr. R.H. Morrow, Brevard, North Carolina, U.S.A.

Dear Mr. Morrow,

I bet you are finding something to take you up about the Rainy Knobs these days for the squirrels are bound to be cutting on the hickory nuts down in the cove below the bungalow. I would certainly like to be there with you but I have something more urgent just now but I hope to be able to put in a month there with you sometime batching and having a good time once more.

I had a great trip across and enjoyed every minute of the whole trip for a fellow feels all the time like he does in a deer stand expecting a buck to bob up at any time. I got across in fine shape without any un-due excitement.

I got to see a good bit of England and quite a bit of France while we were on the move but I can't tell you anything just yet about what I saw. For the present we are billeted in a small village where we are very comfortable but this is only for the time being.

This is a great country and it is wonderful to see the amount of work the women are able to do. Of course all the men are at the front but the women certainly keep things moving. The people are all very cheerful but you can see the effects of the war wherever you look.

Wine is the most plentiful thing that I have found since I hit France. I don't believe the people here ever drink any water, for which I don't blame them for it absolutely is no good. The wine that is used is very mild and doesn't have much of a kick. I am sorry to say that I don't like the stuff but I do enjoy a little champagne once in a while which is very cheap.

We are all working hard taking intensive training and everybody is in splendid health and full of pep. The morale is fine and I never saw a better behaved bunch of men.

Please give my best to Mrs. Morrow and the youngsters and let me hear from you as often as you can for I get hungry for the news.

Will

John Crawford McKELVEY

Born:	11 Oct 1892, Transylvania County, NC
Died:	9 Jun 1956, Veteran Hospital, Murfreesboro, TN; age 63
Buried:	Enon Baptist Church Cemetery
Spouse:	**Lila May SURRETTE**
Father:	**William T. McKELVEY**
Mother:	**Martha E. NEELEY**
Draft registration:	26, single, worked as a farmer in the Dunn's Rock Township, listed his mother as a dependent. He did not request draft deferment.

[Documentation: Tennessee DC, 1900 Census, <u>Transylvania County Cemetery Survey</u>, TT obituary, Ancestry.com]

SRC Note: MG Tng (Machine Gun Training)

18 Jul 1918   Brevard News
23 MORE MEN TO LEAVE JULY 24, 1918
Following is a list of white registrants for induction on July 24th, 1918 for Camp Hancock, Ga., who will leave on the 3:13 train:

. . . John Crawford McKelvey, Brevard . . .

6/14/1956
JOHN C. McKELVEY

John C. McKelvey, 63, of Route 1 Brevard, died Saturday in a veteran's hospital in Murfreesboro, Tenn. He had been in ill health for sometime.

Surviving are the widow Mrs. Lil Mae Surrette McKelvey; four daughters: Mrs. Dave Whitson, Mrs. D.C. Stanley, Misses June and Hazel McKelvey; three sons: John R., Jack and Bill McKelvey; two sisters: Misses Minnie and Margaret McKelvey; and two brothers: W.H. and S.N. McKelvey.

Graveside rites were held Monday afternoon at the Enon Baptist Church Cemetery. Members of the Monroe Wilson Post of the American Legion conducted graveside services. Mr. McKelvey was a native of Transylvania County and a veteran of World War I.

Thomas G. McKILLOP

Born:	15 Feb 1893, Henderson County, NC
Died:	7 Dec 1976, Gastonia, NC; age 83
Burial:	Gaston Memorial Park, Gastonia, NC
Spouse:	**Callie Mae COLLINS,** married 3 Jan 1927, Transylvania County
Father:	**James McKILLOP**
Mother:	**Sarah M. JACKSON**
Draft Registration:	24, single, employed at Brevard Tannery

[Documentation: Transylvania County BC, North Carolina Death Index, Cowart's Index to Marriages, Ancestry.com, FamilySearch.org]

McKillop, Thomas G   1,319,694   * White * Colored.
        (Surname)   (Christian name)   (Army serial number)

Residence: _____ Transylvania CoNORTH CAROLINA
          (Street and house number)   (Town or city)   (County)   (State)

_____. *Inducted at Brevard, N C _____ on Oct 4/, 1917

Place of birth: Henderson Co N C ____ Age or date of birth: 24 8/12 yrs.

Organizations served in, with dates of assignments and transfers: _____
        Btry A 316 FA to Oct 16/17 ; Co B 120 Inf to disch

Grades, with date of appointment: _____
        Pvt

Engagements: _____

Wounds or other injuries received in action: None.
Served overseas from †May 12/18 to † Apr 11/19, from †_____ to †_____
Honorably discharged on demobilization __Apr 17/19___, 19___
In view of occupation he was, on date of discharge, reported ___0___ per cent disabled.

SRC Notes: Btry FA (Battery Field Artillery)

John Young McKINNEY

Born:	6 May 1886, Henderson County, NC
Death:	12 Aug 1960, Florence, SC; age 74
Burial:	Mt. Hope Cemetery, Florence, SC
Spouse:	**Louise C. HOWELL** m. 22 Sept 1934, Transylvania County
Father:	**George McKINNEY**
Mother:	**Mary HEFNER**
Note:	1940 Census has a John Young McKinney as a practicing dentist in Florence, SC.

[Documentation: Ancestry.com, Cowart's Marriage Index, FamilySearch.org, 1940 Census, findagrave.com]

```
                                                  OFFICER—ORC
          McKinney,    John Young                     White
          (Surname)                                          .
Residence                            Brevard          NORTH CAROLINA
          (Street and house number)      (Town or city)   (County)     (State)
• Born in          Horseshoe N C    May 6/1886                        —
‡ Called into active service as   1 Lt DC June 27/18 fr ORC    xxxxxxxxxxx
Promotions:        none                            ....              —

Organizations and
staff assignments:  DC to c1sch       ....                           —

Principal
stations:          Camp Jackson SC    ....                           —

Engagements:       none              ....                            —

Wounds received in action : None.
‡ Served overseas    no             ....                            —
‡ Hon. disch.       Dec 6/18         for convenience of the Government, services no longer required.
Was reported        xx              per cent disabled on date of discharge, in view of occupation,
Remarks:                             ....                            —
```

SRC Note: DC (Dental Corps)

7 Dec 1917   Brevard News
Dr. J.Y. McKinney this week received a commission of First Lieutenant for the dental section. He is now subject to call at any time.

21 Jun 1918   Brevard News
Dr. J.Y. McKinney has been called to the service of the Government. The following telegram explains the whole matter, as received from Washington, D.C.:
"Dr. J.Y. McKinney, First Lieutenant, You will receive orders assigning you to active duty in about 10 days. Arrange to comply."

10 Oct 1918   Brevard News
Lieut. and Mrs. J.Y. McKinney , who spent a ten-day leave here, left Monday for Camp Jackson.

30 May 1919   Brevard News
After the first of next July Dr. T. J. Summey and Dr. J.Y. McKinney will occupy offices together for the practice of their profession. Dr. McKinney will devote his time to dental work and Dr. Summey expects to give his entire attention to diseases of the nose and throat.

Dr. J.Y. McKinney came to Brevard several years ago from Henderson County. He gave up a large dental practice here to volunteer for military service. He was made first lieutenant and spent most of his time while in the Army at Camp Jackson. After his discharge last spring he returned to Brevard and resumed his practice, which is winning for him an enviable reputation throughout the county.

Dr. Pascal Carothers McLAIN

Born:	12 Sep 1895, Newport, SC
Died:	1 Oct 1977, Transylvania County, NC; age 82
Buried:	Hollywood Cemetery, Gastonia, NC
Occupation:	Business owner
Spouse:	**Berthel M. MITCHELL**
Father:	**Rev. James M. McLAIN**
Mother:	**Mary Ellen CAMPBELL**
Draft Registration:	21, single, attending veterinary college
Note:	ROSTER VETERINARY COMPANY NO 1
	CAMP GREENLEAF 1918
	Pascal C. McLain - Enlisted December 22 1917 and reported to duty August 14
	1918

[Documentation: Roster of WWI Veterans from American Legion 50th Anniversary celebration; NC Death Collection; 1900-1940 Censuses; obit]

10/6/1977
Dr. P.C. McLAIN

Dr. Pascal C. McLain, 82, died Saturday in a Brevard hospital after a short illness. Dr. McLain was a native of Newport, S.C. and was the son of the late Rev. J.M. and Mary Ellen Campbell McLain. He was a graduate of Kansas City Veterinary College in 1918 and practiced veterinary medicine in Gastonia, Charlotte and High Point before retiring and moving to Brevard in 1965.

He was past president of the NC Veterinarian Association and was also secretary-treasurer of the Veterinarian Examining Board for NC for 20 years. A charter member of the Gastonia Rotary Club, he was also a veteran of World War I.

Surviving are the widow, Mrs. Berthel M. McLain and several nieces and nephews.

Graveside services were held at 2 p.m. Monday in Hollywood Cemetery in Gastonia. A memorial service will be held at 3 p.m. Tuesday in Brevard-Davidson River Presbyterian Church, of which he was a member.

Fred Iva McNEELY

Born:	10 Oct 1895, Burke County, NC
Died:	4 Jan 1957, Longview, Washington; age 61
Buried:	Willamette National Cemetery, Portland, OR
Spouse:	**Hazel McCALL**, m. 11 Oct 1919, Transylvania, NC
	Edna OWEN
Father:	**Charles McNEELY**
Mother:	**Fannie J GANT**
Draft Registration:	No

[Documentation: NC Death Index, WA Death Index, US Veteran's Gravesites, <u>Cowart's Index to Marriages</u>, Ancestry.com]

McNeely, Fred			1,333,133	White	1½
(Surname)	(Christian name)		(Army serial number)	(Race: White or colored)	
Residence:		Lake Toxaway		NORTH CAROLINA	
	(Street and house number)	(Town or city)	(County)	(State)	
*Enlisted in	N G Canton NC	—	May15/17		—
†Born in	Burk Co NC		22 7/12 Yrs		—
Organizations:	Amb Co 1 M C N G	—			—
	Sn Tn to disch		to	: Amb Co 118 – 1p5	
Grades:	Wag Dec 3/17	—			—
Engagements:		—			—

Wounds or other injuries received in action: None. — —
‡Served overseas: June 4/18 to Apr 3/19 —
‡Hon. disch. Apr 7/19   on demobilization —
Was reported 0   per cent disabled on date of discharge, in view of occupation.

SRC Notes: Amb Co (Ambulance Corps) Sn Tn (Sanitary Train) Wag (Wagoner)

7 Jul 1917   <u>Brevard News</u>
Fred McNeely of Camp Sevier, Greenville, SC, visited his parents recently.

17 Jan 1957   <u>Transylvania Times</u>
This community was saddened by the death of Mr. Fred M. McNeely of Kelso, Washington. Mr. McNeely was a former resident of Oakland.

Restored World War I Ambulance

Robert Lee McNEELY

Born: 24 Mar 1892, Morganton, NC
Died: 3 Sep 1949, Richland County, SC; age 57
Buried: Woodlawn Memorial Park, Greenville County, SC
Spouse: **Nell DUFFIE**
Father: **Samuel McNEELY**
Mother: **Mary Elizabeth DALE**
Draft Registration: 25, single, employed as express messenger for Southern Express Company, Spartanburg & Columbia Southern RR

[Documentation: South Carolina DC, FamilySearch.org, findagrave.com, US Headstone Application, Ancestry.com]

Mc Neely Robert L	1,323,836	White	
(Surname) (Christian name)	(Army serial number)	(Race: White or colored)	
Residence:	Lake Toxaway	NORTH CAROLINA	
(Street and house number) . (Town or city)	(County)	(State)	

* Enlisted in   NG Ashville NC   _   July 30/17   —
† Born in   Morgan NC   25 5/12yrs
Organizations: Co K 1 Inf NCNG to Sept 12/17; 55 Dep Brig to Oct 24,
                 17; Btry C 113 FA to Aug 12/18; Sup Co 113 FA to
                 disch
Grades: Pvt lcl Aug 2/17; Corp Dec 1/17; Pvt July 9/18;
                 Pvt lcl Aug 1/18
Engagements: —   —

Wounds or other injuries received in action: None.   —
‡ Served overseas: May 27/18 to Mch 19/19   —
§ Hon. disch.   Mch 26/19   on demobilization   —
Was reported   0   per cent disabled on date of discharge, in view of occupation.
Remarks:

SRC Notes: NC NG (North Carolina National Guard) FA (Field Artillery) Sup Co (Supply Company)

18 Apr 1919   Brevard News
Robert McNeely is with his father after serving for some time on the battlefront with the 30th Division in France. Mrs. McNeely is with him.

9/8/1949
Robert L. McNeely

Funeral services for Robert Lee McNeely, 55, were held Monday afternoon at the Markey Mortuary in Greenville, SC. Interment was in Woodlawn Memorial Park.

Mr. McNeely died Saturday night in the Veterans Hospital in Columbia, SC, a few minutes after he was admitted. His death was attributed to pneumonia. He had been in declining health for a number of years.

Surviving are the widow, one sister, Miss Carrie McNeely and one brother, Fred McNeely.

A native of Morganton, NC he served for four years as postmaster of Westminster and before moving to Greenville a number of years ago he operated a grocery store at Tryon. He lived in Transylvania County for about 30 years. He served in World War I.

The duties of the engineers included providing water supplies, operating both light and standard gauge railroads, keeping the roads in good repair, building bridges--sometimes just in time to have them blown up again--- and providing electricity. Engineers built pillboxes for machine guns, laid barbed wire entanglements, laid out the white tape to guide the infantry going over the top of the trenches and cleared mud out of the trenches.

Elza E. MEECE

Born:	22 Nov 1891, Transylvania County, NC
Died:	30 Jul 1948, Bronx, New York; age 56
Buried:	Woodlawn Cemetery, Bronx, NY
Spouse:	**Eugenia KUNZELMAN**
Father:	**James MEECE**
Mother:	**Martha SIMMS**
Draft Registration:	25, single, self-employed photographer

[Documentation: NC Birth Index, US Headstone Application, 1900 Census, NY Findagrave, FamilySearch.org, Ancestry.com]

Elza Ervin Meece

Jim Meece Photo

SRC Note: Aeo Sq (Aviation Squadron) AS (Air Service)

<u>2 Nov 1917</u>   **Brevard News**
LOCAL BOARD ORDERS THIRTEEN MORE MEN on Monday, November 5, 1917 for transportation for Camp Jackson. They will leave for Camp November 6 at 8 A.M.
. . . Elza E. Meece . . .

Ossie Elum MERRELL

Born:	2 Oct 1895, Transylvania County, NC
Died:	19 Apr 1975, Buncombe County, NC; age 79
Buried:	Little River Baptist Church Cemetery
Occupation:	Farmer
Father:	**William E. MERRELL**
Mother:	**Sula LINDSEY**
Draft Registration:	21, single and farming with his dad
Military Marker:	PVT US Army

[Documentation: Discharge, Buncombe County DC, Transylvania County Cemetery Survey, Discharge, Ancestry.com]

Ossie E. Merrell

Walt Hart Photo

Merrell Ossie E   1 856 171   • White • Colored

(Surname)   (Christian name)   (Army serial number)

Residence: __Route 1__   __Etowah__ *Henderson* __NORTH CAROLINA__

(Street and house number)   (Town or city)   (County)   (State)

•Enlisted • R. A. • N. G. • E. R. C. •Inducted at __Brevard NC__ on __Dec 14__, 19__17__

Place of birth: __Brevard NC__   Age or date of birth: __22 yrs__

Organizations served __156 Dep Brig to Jan 28/18; Co M 323 Inf to disch__

Grades, with date of appointment: __Pvt__

Engagements: ____

Wounds or other injuries received in action: None.

Served overseas from † __no__ to † ____, from † ____ to † ____

Honorably discharged __Feb 2__, 19 __18__ per __SCD__

(Date)   (Cause)

In view of occupation he was, on date of discharge, reported __0__ per cent disabled.

SCR Note: SCD (Surgeons Certificate of Disability)

2 Nov 1917   Brevard News
LOCAL BOARD ORDERS THIRTEEN MORE MEN
All men whose names appear here are ordered to report to the Local Board at 5 P.M. on Monday, November 5, 1917 for transportation for Camp Jackson. They will leave for Camp November 6 at 8 A.M. . . . Ossie E. Merrill . . .

4/21/1975
O.E. MERRELL

Ossie Elum Merrell, 79, died in an Asheville hospital Saturday after a brief illness. He was a farmer and a member of Little River Baptist Church.

Surviving are two sisters, Flora Merrell and Anna Merrell. Services will be held Tuesday at the Little River Baptist Church and burial will follow in the church cemetery.

22 Dec 1917   Brevard News
ROSMAN GIVES 32 NEW MEMBERS TO RED CROSS SERVICE
TOWN GIVES GOOD ATTENDANCE TO SPEAKERS

Benjamin Franklin MERRILL

Born:	30 May 1893, Transylvania County, NC
Died:	1 Jun 1974, Henderson County, NC; age 81
Buried:	Little River Baptist Church Cemetery
Occupation:	Construction with Southern Bell
Father:	**Ben Perry MERRILL**
Mother:	**Rachel MERRILL**
Draft Registration:	24, single, farrier and claimed mother and brother as dependents
Military Marker:	SGT. US ARMY WW I

[Documentation: North Carolina BC, Henderson County DC, findagrave.com, Discharge, Hendersonville T-N obituary, Ancestry.com]

Benjamin Franklin Merrill

Sandra Lyday Reid Photo

11 Jul 1918   Brevard News

   Twelve Transylvania boys left on last Saturday for Fort Oglethorpe, Ga., to begin their careers as defenders of democracy. The boys left on the afternoon train
. . . Benjamin Franklin Merrill, Etowah . . .

Hendersonville Times-News
6/3/1974
B. FRANK MERRILL

   Benjamin Frank Merrill, 81, of the Little River Community died Saturday morning in a Hendersonville hospital of a short illness. He was a lifelong resident of Transylvania County and was a construction foreman for Southern Bell Telephone Co. for over 40 years and a farmer. He was a veteran of World War I and was a Mason and Shriner for over 50 years.

   Mr. Merrill is survived by one sister, Emma Beddingfield and three brothers: George, David and Ernest Merrill.

   Funeral services were at 11 a.m. today at Little River Baptist Church Burial was in Little River Cemetery.

NATIONAL ARMY CANTONMENT (CAMP)
Camp Lewis   Location: American Lake, Wash.   Organization: 91st Division
Troops from Washington, Oregon, California, Nevada, Utah, Idaho, Montana and Wyoming

---

Harley Merrimon MERRILL

Born:	15 Dec 1889, Transylvania County, NC
Died:	14 Nov 1967, Transylvania County, NC; age 77
Buried:	Little River Baptist Church Cemetery
Occupation:	Farmer
Spouse(s):	**Stella I. MERRILL**
	Armeture MERRILL
Father:	**Perry MERRILL**
Mother:	**Miriam KITCHENS**
Draft Registration:	27, single and farming
Note:	Grave marker gives NO military information

[Documentation: North Carolina Birth Index, Transylvania County DC, Discharge, <u>Transylvania County Cemetery Survey</u>, Ancestry.com]

Merrell, Harley M   4,159,467   *White *~~Colored~~
(Surname)   (Christian name)   (Army serial number)

Residence: R #1   Etowah   Henderson   NORTH CAROLINA
(Street and house number)   (Town or city)   (County)   (State)

~~▆▆▆▆▆▆▆▆▆▆▆▆▆~~. *Inducted at Brevard NC   on Jul 24, 19 18

Place of birth: Transylvania Co NC   Age or date of birth: Dec 15/1890

Organizations served in, with dates of assignments and transfers: _____
66 Co MTD 6 Group to Sept 19/18; Co D 365 MG Bn to Disch.

Grades, with date of appointment: _____
Pvt

Engagement: _____

Wounds or other injuries received in action: None.
Served overseas from † No to † _____, from † _____ to † _____
Honorably discharged on demobilization   Dec 18/18, 19 _____
In view of occupation he was, on date of discharge, reported   O   per cent disabled.
Remarks: _____

SRC Notes: MTD (Motor Transportation Department) MG Bn (Machine Gun Battalion)

18 Jul 1918   Brevard News
23 MORE MEN TO LEAVE JULY 24, 1918
Following is a list of white registrants for induction on July 24th, 1918 for Camp Hancock, Ga.
. . . Harley Meremon Merrell, Etowah . . .

Hendersonville Times-News
11/16/ 1967
HARLEY M. MERRILL

Harley M. Merrill, 77, of the Little River Community, died Tuesday night after a brief illness in a Transylvania County hospital. He was a Transylvania County native, a retired farmer and a veteran of World War I.

Funeral services will be held at 3 p.m. Friday in the Little River Baptist Church. Burial will take place in the church cemetery.

Surviving are the widow, Mrs. Armetures Merrill; and two daughters, Syble McCrary and Miriam Rice.

The draft drawing started in Washington, D.C. on July 20, 1917, and lasted for almost seventeen hours. When it ended more than 1.3 million men had been called into military service, making it the largest army in U.S. history.

Robert Leroy MERRILL

Born:	2 Jul 1893, Penrose, NC
Died:	8 Oct 1970, Oteen VA Hospital, Buncombe County; age 77
Buried:	Little River Baptist Church Cemetery
Occupation:	Well driller
Spouse:	**Myra PICKELSIMER**, m. 27 Dec 1925, Transylvania County, NC
Father:	**William F. MERRILL**
Mother:	**Sula LINDSEY**
Draft Registration:	23, single, teamster for J. A. Getford
Military Marker:	NC PVT HQ CO 360 INF WW I

[Documentation: Discharge, Buncombe County DC, Transylvania County Cemetery Survey, Cowart's Index to Marriages, Ancestry.com]

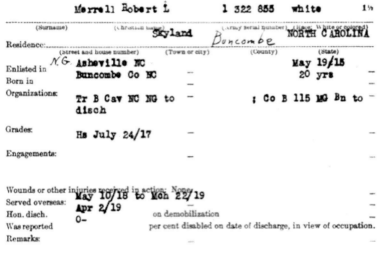

SCR Note: Tr B Cav NC NG (Troop B Cavalry North Carolina National Guard) MG (Machine Gun)

Hendersonville Times-News
10/10 /1970
ROBERT L. MERRILL SR

Robert L. Merrill Sr., 77, of Penrose died Thursday night in an Oteen hospital after a long illness. He was a lifelong resident of Transylvania County and before his retirement was self-employed as a water pump installer and repairman. He was a veteran of World War I and a member of Hedrick-Rhodes VFW Post No. 3206.

Surviving are his widow, Myra Pickelsimer Merrill; two sons: Robert L. Jr. and Thomas W.; a brother, Ossie E. Merrill; and three sisters: Flora and Ann and Julia Allison.

Services will be held at 2 p.m. Sunday in Little River Baptist Church, of which he was a member. Burial will be in the church cemetery.

---

18 Jun 1917   **Brevard News**

HOW SHALL WE PAY FOR THE WAR?
A Constructive Criticism on the House Revenue Bill
LOANS BETTER THAN TAXES

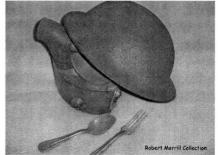

No. ?? Motor Transport Corps
Chauffeur's Authority

Merrill Robert L. Pvt.

The person to whom this card is issued is authorized to operate government motor vehicles as indicated hereon.

Signature of Bearer: By Command of Maj. Gen. Bundy:

Pvt Robert L Merrill
M.T.C. Co 671
Rank and Organization   Motor Transport Officer
                                   Col. McGuire

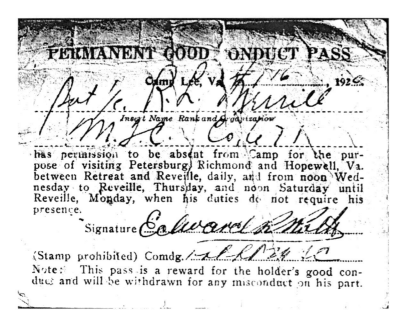

PERMANENT GOOD CONDUCT PASS

Camp Lee, Va. ?? 16 192?

Pvt/c R. L. Merrill
M.T.C. Co 671
Insert Name Rank and Organization

has permission to be absent from Camp for the purpose of visiting Petersburg, Richmond and Hopewell, Va. between Retreat and Reveille, daily, and from noon Wednesday to Reveille, Thursday, and noon Saturday until Reveille, Monday, when his duties do not require his presence.

Signature Edward R. Smith

(Stamp prohibited) Comdg. ?????

Note: This pass is a reward for the holder's good conduct and will be withdrawn for any misconduct on his part.

Virgil MERRILL

Born:	20 May 1894, Transylvania County, NC
Died:	30 Aug 1966, Oteen VA Hospital, Buncombe County; age 72
Buried:	Little River Baptist Church Cemetery
Spouse:	**Rhuemma J. SHIPMAN,** 13 Oct 1936, Transylvania County
Father:	**John Baxter MERRILL**
Mother:	**Florida GALLOWAY**
Draft Registration:	23, single, mechanic for Perfection Spring Co., Cleveland, Ohio

[Documentation: Buncombe County DC, Transylvania County Cemetery Survey, Cowart's Index to Marriages, FamilySearch.org, Ancestry.com]

Merrill Virgil   1,876,253   • White • Colored   1

Residence: R#1   Etowah   Transylvania   NORTH CAROLINA

N.G. • E.R.C • Inducted at Brevard NC on Sept 18 19 17

Place of birth: Orange • C   Age or date of birth: 23 4/12 yr

Organizations served in, with dates of assignments and transfers: M D to disch.

Grades, with date of appointment: Pvt 1cl Feb 12/18; Wag Mch 15/18

Engagements:

Wounds or other injuries received in action: None.
Served overseas from † Aug 8/18 to † June 20/19 from † ___ to † ___
Honorably discharged on demobilization June 29, 1919
In view of occupation he was, on date of discharge, reported 0 per cent disabled.

Virgil Merrill
Nina Miller Photo

SCR Note: MD (Medical Department)

21 Sep 1917   Brevard News
THIRTY-ONE MEN TO CAMP JACKSON
Forty percent of the certified draft, making 31 men, was ordered to report on Tuesday at 5 P.M. at the office of the local enlistment board and to leave for Camp Jackson, S.C. Wednesday morning.
. . . Virgil Merrell . . .

7 Nov 1918   Brevard News
"SOMEWHERE IN FRANCE" (See John Luke Osteen for complete letter)
. . . Wags. Virgil Merrill, Coy A. Surrett and King S. Whitaker by their faithful work are considered among the best wagoners in the company. . . .

9/8/1966
VIRGIL MERRILL

Funeral services for Virgil Merrill, 72, of Little River were held September 1st in the Little River Baptist Church. Burial followed in the church cemetery. Mr. Merrill died August 30th in the Oteen Veteran's Hospital. He was a lifelong resident of Transylvania County, a retired farmer and a veteran of World War I.

Surviving are the widow, Mrs. Rhuemma Shipman Merrill and one brother, John Merrill.

Ernest Otto MILLER

Born:	13 Oct 1895, Buncombe County, NC
Died:	18 Jul 1934, Transylvania County, NC; age 38
Buried:	Oak Grove Cemetery, Brevard
Occupation:	Cement worker
Father:	**Herbert M. MILLER**
Mother:	**Laura Lee SUMMEY**
Draft Registration:	21, single, self-employed as a plasterer and cement worker

[Documentation: Transylvania County DC, <u>Transylvania County Cemetery Survey</u>, Ancestry.com, obituary]

```
      i ler, _rnest O          1,876, 232                              1
      (Surname)      (Christian name)      (Army serial number)     • White • Colored

Residence: _____ Brevard _____ NORTH CAROLINA _____
               (Street and house number)     (Town or city)    (County)      (State)

            *Inducted at  Brevard NC            on Sept 7, 19 17
Place of birth: Asheville NC            Age or date of birth: 21 11,12 Yrs
Organizations served in, with dates of assignments and transfers;
            Camp Jackson SC to Nov 11,17;  Amb Co  324 to disch

Grades, with date of appointment: Pvt 1 Cl Dec 1,17; Cor Feb 12,18; Sgt Apr 1,18;

Engagements: _____

Wounds or other injuries received in action: None.
Served overseas from † Aug 8,18  to † June 2_,19 from † _____ to † _____
Honorably discharged on demobilization    June 29, 19 , 19____
In view of occupation he was, on date of discharge, reported ____0____ per cent disabled.
```

14 Sep 1917   Brevard News
THE GOING OF SOLDIERS FOUR
. . . Ernest Miller . . . ., the first of the regular draft to be called to the colors left Saturday morning for Camp Jackson, Columbia, S.C.

7 Nov 1918   Brevard News
"SOMEWHERE IN FRANCE" (See John Luke Osteen for complete letter)
. . . Sgt. Ernest O. Miller for business purposes is away from the company, but is expected to return soon.
. . .

7/19/1934
ERNEST OTTO MILLER

Ernest Miller, 39 year old local man died Wednesday afternoon from apoplectic stroke while he was engaged in superintending construction work at the Brevard Municipal park. Mr. Miller had been sitting beside Coach Ernest Tilson and Dr. Jimmy Cob on the edge of the pool for several minutes, and had just gotten up to speak to one of the laborers when he sank to the ground.

One of the workers applied artificial respiration to the heart, keeping the stricken man alive for several minutes, but by the time Dr. E.S.

English arrived moments after being summoned, Mr. Miller had passed away.

Mr. Miller has been in charge of construction work in the park, being an experienced construction man. He was a member of the Brevard Methodist Church and took an active part in veteran's affairs. He served nine months overseas in the World War.

Surviving are the parents, Mr. and Mrs. H.M. Miller and three sisters: Mrs. Mae Johnson, Mrs. W.O. Cowan and Miss Nellie Miller.

Noah Carson MILLER

Born:	31 Oct 1892, Transylvania County, NC
Died:	8 Sep 1996, Transylvania County, NC; age 103
Buried:	Oak Grove Baptist Church Cemetery, Quebec, NC
Spouse(s):	**Anna YOUNG**, m. 20 Aug 1920, Transylvania County, NC
	Anna PAXTON, m. 20 Aug 1936, Transylvania County, NC
Father:	**David H. MILLER**
Mother:	**Rachel L. HENDERSON**
Draft Registration:	No

[Documentation: Upper Transylvania County, NC Remembered, Transylvania DC, Cowart's Index to Marriages, Ancestry.com]

Noah Carson Miller

Carolyn T. Owen Photo

21 Sep 1917   Brevard News
Noah Miller, who enlisted in the Navy last March and has been stationed at Paris Island, near Port Royal, SC, as a member of the Marine Hospital Corps, is visiting his home at Sapphire on leave of absence.

9/8/1996
NOAH C. MILLER

Noah Carson Miller, 103, died Sunday, Sept. 8, 1996, at Ivy Hill Health and Retirement Center in Brevard. He was the son of the late David H. and Louisa Henderson Miller. He was also preceded in death by his wives: Dorothy Young Miller and Annie Mae Paxton Miller and also two daughters: Annie Van Buren and Lois Romanczky. He was a U.S. Navy veteran of World War I, a member of Dunn's Rock Masonic Lodge 267, a 32nd Degree Scottish Rites Mason and a member of Little Cove Baptist Church.

Surviving are three sons: Noah C, Jr., David F., and Ralph F. Miller; one daughter, Hazel Pocher; and one brother, Floyd K Miller.

Services will be held Thursday, Sept. 12 at Moore Funeral Home Chapel. Burial will be at Oak Grove Cemetery in Quebec with a Masonic graveside service.

The USS Kittery was a captured German Transport, refitted for Naval service and commissioned 6 July 1917 at Philadelphia, Pa. She operated out of Charleston, SC making monthly trips to transport troops, cargo and supplies to the American forces for the remainder of the war.

Scadin Alvin MILLER

Born:	19 Jul 1898, Transylvania County, NC
Died:	19 Nov 1963, WNC Sanatorium, Buncombe County; age 65
Buried:	Pisgah Gardens Cemetery
Occupation:	Caretaker for Old Sapphire Estate
Spouse:	**Annie McCALL**, m. 28 Nov 1923, Transylvania County, NC
	Alice HAUPERT
Father:	**David H. MILLER**
Mother:	**Rachel L. HENDERSON**
Note:	18 Sep 1924 Scadin arrived in the port of Seattle, WA from Kobe, Japan, aboard the troop transport ship the USS President Grant.

[Documentation: Buncombe County DC, Transylvania County Cemetery Survey, Cowart's Index to Marriages, Ancestry.com]

Name MILLER –SCADIN ALVIN   Service Number 143-00-95
Enlisted at N/VY RECRUITING STATION –RALEIGH N.C. Date 3-23-17
Age at Entrance 16 YRS. 8 MO . Rate PPRENTICE SEAMAN   U.S.N. R.F.
Home Address --- Town SAPPHIRE
County 0   State N.C.

Served at	From	To	Served as	No. Days
RECEIVING SHIP NORFOLK VA.	4-6-17	4-14-17	APPRENTICE SEAMAN	7
NAVAL HOSPITAL NORFOLK VA.	4-14-17	5-4-17	SEAMAN 2 CLASS	577
RECEIVING SHIP NORFOLK VA.	5-4-17	5-8-17		
U.S.S. TALLAHASSEE	5-8-17	6-14-17		
U.S.S. PREBLE	6-14-17	7-4-17		
U.S.S. PAUL JONES	7-4-17	7-25-17		
U.S.S. PERRY	7-25-17	9-25-17		
U.S.S. HANNIBAL	9-25-17	11-11-18		

Date Discharge 7-26-19 RECEIVING SHIP
Place in NEW YORK N.Y.   Rating at Discharge SEAMAN

11/28/1963
S.A. MILLER

Funeral services for Scadin A. Miller, 65, Sapphire, were held Thursday afternoon in the chapel of the Frank Moody Funeral Home. The Rev. T.F. Rose officiated and burial was in Pisgah Gardens.

Mr. Miller died early last Tuesday morning in a Western North Carolina Sanatorium after a long illness. A native of Transylvania county, he was the caretaker for the Old Sapphire Estate.

He is survived by the widow, Mrs. Alice Miller; two sisters: Mrs. Ethel Senora Johnson and Mrs. Louise Harrison; and two brothers: Noah Carson and Floyd Miller.

The *USS Hannibal*, a converted steamer, was commissioned by the Navy 16 April 1898. After an overhaul in early 1918, she became a tender to submarine chaser at Plymouth, England. The *Hannibal* served in English waters until December, when she sailed for Azores via Gibraltar as a sub-chaser escort. In early 1919, she resumed sub-tender duties and visited England, France and Portugal and returned to the United States in August.

The *USS Hannibal* was decommissioned 20 August 1944 and was sunk as a bombing target on 1 March 1945, in the Chesapeake Bay.

Crowell MILLS

Born:	1899, probably Transylvania or Haywood County, North Carolina
Died:	29 Jul 1933, Los Angeles, California; age 34
Buried:	VA Administration Facility, Los Angeles, CA
Race:	Colored
Father:	Unknown
Mother:	Unknown
Draft Registration:	No
Note:	1900 Census has Crowell living in Waynesville with an uncle Henry Thompson. 1920 Crowell is living in Arizona. 1930 he has moved to Los Angeles, California. All census records indicate he was single.
	The request for his military headstone was made by the cemetery administrator to identify an unmarked grave.

[Documentation: 1900, 1920, 1930 Censuses, US Veteran Gravesites, Application for Military Headstones, Ancestry.com]

Mills	Crowell	335,384	Colored
(Surname)	(Christian name)	(Army serial number)	(Race: White or colored)

Residence: _____ Brevard _Transylvania_ NORTH CAROLINA

     (Street and house number)   (Town or city)   (County)   (State)

*Enlisted in RA Schofield Bks H T Apr 25/17

†Born in Transylvania N C 28 yrs

Organizations: Co C 25 Inf to disch

Grades: Pvt 1cl Apr 1/17; Corp Apr 20/17

Engagements:

Wounds or other injuries received in action: None.

‡Served overseas NO

§Hon. disch. Apr 15/19 to re-enlist

Was reported O per cent disabled on date of discharge, in view of occupation.

Remarks:

SCR Note: Provisional Early Discharge to Re-enlist

Name	Rank	Company	U.S. Regiment, State Organization, or Vessel	Date of Death
MILLS, Crowell	Corp	C	25th U.S. Inf.,	July 29,1933

Name of Cemetery	Located in or near		If World War Veteran		
	City	State	Division	State	Emblem
Veterans Administration Facility	Los Angeles,	Cal.,	NONE	N.C.	Christian Hebrew None

To be shipped to: Manager, Veterans Administration Facility, West Los Angeles, Cal.,

Whose post-office address is: National Military Home, Cal.,

To A.G.O. JAN 31 1934

Ordered

From TATE, GEORGIA MAR 7 1934

B.L. 4/3-34 684700

This application is for the UNMARKED grave of a veteran. It is understood the stone will be furnished and delivered at the railroad station or steamboat landing above indicated, at Government expense, freight prepaid. I hereby agree to promptly accept the headstone at destination, remove it and properly place same at decedent's grave at my expense.

JAMES F. McKINLEY
Major General
The Adjutant General

Dewey Lonzo MILLS

Born:	27 Mar 1898, Transylvania County, NC
Died:	22 Sep 1959, undetermined; age 61
Buried:	Cooper Cemetery
Race:	Colored
Father:	**W. Brice MILLS**
Mother:	**Winnie PAYNE**
Draft Registration:	Aurora, IL, 21, single, working with Ed Robinson
Military Marker:	CPL Co. C. 803 Pioneer Inf. WW I

[Documentation: 1900-1920 Censuses, Application for Veteran's Headstone, Transylvania County Cemetery Survey, Ancestry.com]

Pioneer Infantry regiments were organized in the summer of 1918 and given standard infantry training so that if necessary they could be used in combat.

Pioneer infantry regiments worked behind the front lines in the Argonne Forest and at St. Mihiel where they built narrow and wide gauge railroads and macadam roads for the movement of light and heavy artillery and supplies.

The Pioneers worked through the night with shells falling around them. Some also worked in burial details, often under shellfire. 7 of the 17 African American Pioneer Infantry Regiments were entitled to wear battle clasps on the Victory medals whereas of the other 20 Pioneer Infantry regiments, only 8 were so entitled.

In France, African American troops were welcomed, and treated with respect by the French. The 803rd Infantry Band worked hard to raise the spirits of fighting soldiers by playing music, and the 365th, one of the few all-black regiments that saw combat, fought heroically and tenaciously.

Scott, Emmett J., **The American Negro in the World War**, 1919.

John T. MILLS

Born:	15 Oct 1898, Transylvania County
Died:	Undetermined
Buried:	Undetermined
Spouse:	**Hazel**
Father:	**John W. MILLS**
Mother:	**Mary J. HAMPTON**
Note:	Unable to find anything for John after the 1940 Census

[Documentation: NC Birth Index, 1900-1940 Censuses, Ancestry.com]

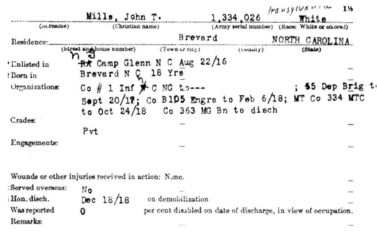

SCR Notes: MT Co (Motor Transport Company) MTC (Motor Transport Corps) MG (Machine Gun)

12 Oct 1917   Brevard News
A party of boys from Camp Sevier, Greenville, came home for a short visit Saturday, returning Sunday afternoon. There were . . . J.T. Mills. . . .The boys seemed to be in good spirits and enjoying camp life.

12 Apr 1918   Brevard News
J.T. Mills came up from Camp Sevier to spend Sunday with his mother.

22 Aug 1918   Brevard News
J.T. Mills of Camp Sevier, Greenville, is in the city spending some time with his mother, Mrs. J.W. Mills.

14 Feb 1919   Brevard News
J.T. Mills, who has been in military service for several months, is at home now.

21 Feb 1919   Brevard News
J.T. and Charles Mills left Tuesday for Fayetteville where they have accepted positions at Camp Bragg.

> The Motor Transport Corps was responsible for the supervision of all motor vehicles. The were responsible for the salvage and evacuation of damaged motor vehicles. It was their responsibility to store, maintain and replace all motor vehicles. The preparation of plans for hauling cargo and personnel over military roads, or roads under military control were under the control of the Motor Transport Corps. Motor Vehicle was defined as bicycles, motorcycles, automobiles, trucks and trailers. Tanks were excluded.

Walter B. MILLS

Born:	28 Oct 1889, Transylvania County, NC
Died:	7 Jul 1972, Dade County, Florida; age 82
Buried:	Undetermined
Race:	Colored
Father:	**W. Brice MILLS**
Mother:	**Winnie PAYNE**
Draft Registration:	No

[Documentation: 1900-1940 Censuses, Florida Death Index, Ancestry.com]

Mills Walter B   3,450,874   * White- * Colored.
(Surname)   (Christian name)   (Army serial number)

Residence: _____ Brevard Transylvania NORTH CAROLINA
(Street and house number)   (Town or city)   (County)   (State)

_____. *Inducted at Aurora Ill _____ on June 25 19 18
Place of birth: _____ Brevard NC _____ Age or date of birth: _____ Oct 26/1 88 9
Organizations served in, with dates of assignments and transfers: _____
_____ Med Dept to disch _____

Grades, with date of appointment: _____
_____ Pvt _____

Engagements: _____

Wounds or other injuries received in action: None.
Served overseas from † No _____ to † _____, from † _____ to † _____
Honorably discharged on demobilization _____ Jan 8/19 _____, 19 _____
In view of occupation he was, on date of discharge, reported _____ 0 _____ per cent disabled.
Remarks: _____

Nurses at the Camp Hospital

Edward Clarence MITCHEM

Born: 5 Nov 1890, Gaston County, NC
Died: 21 Feb 1973, Transylvania County, NC; age 82
Buried: Pisgah Gardens Cemetery
Occupation: Merchant
Spouse: **Mae RHINEHART**
Father: **David MITCHEM**
Mother: **Martha WILLETT**
Draft Registration: Gaston County, 26, single and farming
Military Marker: NC PVT US Army WW I

[Documentation: Discharge, Transylvania County DC, <u>Transylvania County Cemetery Survey, Ancestry.com</u>]

Mitchem, Edward C.   4,155,605   • White • Colored.
(Surname)   (Christian name)   (Army serial number)

Residence: _____ Lowell Gaston   NORTH CAROLINA
            (Street and house number) (Town or city) (County) (State)

_____ Lowell N C •Inducted at Gastonia N C on Aug 26, 19 18
Place of birth: _____ Lowell N C _____ Age or date of birth: Nov 5/90 ____

Organizations served in, with dates of assignments and transfers: _____
_____ 156 Dep Brig to disch _____

Grades, with date of appointment: _____
_____ Pvt _____

Engagements: _____
_____

Wounds or other injuries received in action: None.
Served overseas from † __No__ to † ____ from † ____ to † ____
Honorably discharged on demobilization __Dec 13/18__, 19 ___
In view of occupation he was, on date of discharge, reported __0__ per cent disabled.

3/1/1973
E.C. MITCHEM

Edward C. Mitchem, 82, died in a local hospital Wednesday morning after a short illness. He was a native of Lowell and a retired merchant. He had resided in Transylvania County since 1933.

He was a member of the Balsam Camp of the Woodman of the World, a veteran of World War I and a member of the Monroe Wilson American Legion Post. In addition to his mercantile business he was in the real estate business and developed Mitchem's Lake near Brevard.

He is survived by the wife, Mae Rhinehart Mitchem; two sons: Robert E. and E.C. (Mike) Mitchem; and one sister, Mrs. C.F. Abbott.

Funeral services were conducted last Friday morning in the First Baptist Church of which he was a member. Burial was in Pisgah Garden Cemetery.

<u>23 Nov 1917</u>   <u>Brevard News</u>
TRAINING CLASS TAKES EXAMINATION
Red Cross Class Of 19 Members Equipped For Efficient Service;
Box Of Dressings Recently Shipped:
Work Of Chapter Highly Praised

The Red Cross class in surgical dressing, taught by Ms. Birdie Blankenship, came to a close after a 10-day session last Saturday with examinations which were taken by 19 ladies. The examinations are oral, written, and practical.

Carl Jerome MOLTZ

Born: 23 Jan 1893, Williamsport, Pennsylvania
Died: 16 May 1961, Transylvania County, NC; age 78
Buried: E. Wildwood Cemetery, Lycoming Co. PA
Spouse: **Lucy Mae CAMP**
Father: **Jerome MOLTZ**
Mother: **May GOULD**
Draft Registration: 24, single, Supt. of Moltz Lumber Company

[Documentation: Transylvania County DC, PA Veteran Burial Card, FamilySearch.org, Ancestry.com]

Moltz Carl J 175,099 *Transylvania* White
(Surname) (Christian name) (Army serial number) (Race: White or colored)
Residence: Lake Toxaway NORTH CAROLINA
(Street and house number) (Town or city) (County) (State)
Enlisted in NA Washington D C Dec 12/17
Born in Williamsport Pa 24 11/12 yrs
Organizations: Co B 5 Bn 20 Engrs to Aug 15/18; 14 Co 20 Engrs to disch

Grades: Sgt Feb 19/18; Sgt 1cl May 1/18

Engagements: —

Wounds or other injuries received in action: None.
Served overseas Jan 31/18 to June 14/19
Hon. disch., June 23/19 on demobilization
Was reported per cent disabled on date of discharge, in view of occupation.
Remarks: 0

SCR Note: Engrs (Engineers)

Carl J. Moltz

Marlene Brand Photo

Commonwealth of Pennsylvania Department of Military Affairs	RECORD OF BURIAL PLACE OF VETERAN	LYCOMING COUNTY GM	
NAME Moltz, Carl J. 175 099		DATE OF BIRTH 1/23/93	DATE OF DEATH 5/15/61
VETERAN OF WW 1	WAR	SERVED IN ☒ ARMY ☐ NAVY	☐ MARINE CORPS
DATES OF SERVICE 12/12/17 6/23/19	ORGANIZATION (S) 14th Co. 20th Engrs.	RANK Sgt. 1/C	
CEMETERY OR PLACE OF INTERMENT NAME E. Wildwood LOCATION Loyalsock Twp.			5/19/61
LOCATION OF GRAVE IN CEMETERY SECTION F LOT No. 252 RANGE GRAVE No. 61	HEADSTONE GOVERNMENT ☐ COUNTY ☐ FAMILY ☐		
INFORMATION GIVEN BY Recorder's Office Lyc. Co., Vol. 1, Page 483 DATE 7/31/61	REMARKS Residence at death Lake Toxaway, N. C.		

5/19/1961
CARL J. MOLTZ

Carl Jerome Moltz, 68, passed away in the local hospital Tuesday morning after a lengthy illness. A native of Williamsport, Pa., he had resided in Transylvania County since 1917. He was a retired lumberman.

Funeral services will be conducted later this week and burial will be in the family cemetery in Williamsport, Pa. Mr. Moltz is survived by his wife, Lucy Camp Armstrong Moltz, of Lake Toxaway.

---

25 Jul 1918   Brevard

HOSPITALS CALLING FOR HELP

Old white rags, consisting of sheets, pillowcases and also old blankets are urgently needed by the Red Cross hospitals in the Southern division. They will gladly be received at Transylvania Red Cross headquarters and forwarded for distribution.

Edgar MOONEY

Born:	25 Feb 1894, Transylvania County, NC
Died:	22 Dec 1959, Henderson County, NC; age 65
Buried:	Oakdale Cemetery, Henderson County, NC
Race:	Colored
Spouse:	**Exie HAMILTON**
Father:	**Parrish MOONEY**
Mother:	**Susan SMITH**
Draft Registration:	No

[Documentation: Henderson DC, Application for Military Headstone, <u>Henderson County Cemeteries</u>, Ancestry.com]

SCR Notes: Dep Brig (Depot Brigade) Sup Co (Supply Company) Pion Inf (Pioneer Infantry)

Enormous supply lines slowly came into being as the American Expeditionary Forces, finding that the French could not provide adequate ports or railroads or camps or warehouses, began building its own. All this involved much manpower. Pershing estimated that of the first million men that arrived in France no more than five hundred thousand would be available for the front lines. Thus it was that hundreds of thousands of men found themselves assigned to the Services of Supply, filling vital needs but seldom seeing active combat.

Lester MOONEY

Born:	7 Mar 1896, Transylvania County, NC
Died:	29 May 1972, Cleveland, Ohio; age 76
Buried:	Highland Park Cemetery, Cuyahoga, OH
Race:	Colored
Father:	**Anderson MOONEY**
Mother:	**Laura HENDERSON**
Draft Registration:	21, single, laborer for Carr Lumber Company

[Documentation: Transylvania County BC, Ohio Death Index, Dept. of Veterans Affairs BIRLS Death File, findagrave, FamilySearch.org, Ancestry.com]

Mooney Lester   1 888 259   * Colored.
(Surname)   (Christian name)   (Army serial number)
Residence: _____ brevard Transylvania NORTH CAROLINA
(Street and house number) (Town or city)   (County)   (State)
* Enlisted R. A. * N. G. * E. R. C. Inducted at Durham N Car on Apr 30, 1918
Place of birth: brevard N C   Age or date of birth: 22 yrs
Organizations served in, with dates of assignments and transfers:
11 Co 3 Tng Bn 156 Dep Brig to May 21/18. 323 Lab
Bn QMC to disch
Grades, with date of appointment: Pvt
Engagements: _____
Wounds or other injuries received in action: None.
Served overseas from No to †_____, from †_____ to †_____
Honorably discharged on demobilization Dec 30, 1918
In view of occupation he was, on date of discharge, reported 0 per cent disabled.

SCR Notes: Tng Bn (Training Battalion) Dep Brig (Depot Brigade) Lab Bn QMC (Laboratory Battalion Quartermasters Corps)

Haywood County Digital Collection
Delivery Meat to Company Kitchens

George Ernest MOORE

Born:	17 Feb 1897, Transylvania County, NC
Died:	14 Apr 1973, Oteen VA Hospital, Buncombe County; age 76
Buried:	Gillespie-Evergreen
Spouse:	**Delitha MORRISON**
Father:	**Philetus MOORE**
Mother:	**Elvira GALLOWAY**
Draft Registration:	21, employed by Tellico River Lumber Company, Tellico Plains, Tennessee

[Documentation: Buncombe County DC, <u>Transylvania County Cemetery Survey</u>, 1900 Census, Ancestry.com]

George Moore

Linda Anders Photo

Author's Note: SRC says NO overseas service and the <u>Brevard News</u> reports "just returned from France"

<u>2 May 1919</u>   <u>Brevard News</u>

George Moore, who has just returned from France, was seen in Calvert last Sunday.

4/19/1973
GEORGE E. MOORE

George Ernest Moore, 76 died in an Oteen hospital last Saturday after a long illness. He was a native of Transylvania County and for years was employed by Carr Lumber Company in Pisgah Forest as a sawyer. He was a veteran of World War I, having served in the U.S. Army.

Surviving are the wife, Mrs. Delitha Morrison Moore; one son, Jack Moore; two sisters: Mrs. Christine Smith and Mrs. Kathleen Bailey; and four brothers: Furman, Charlie, Gen and Emmett Moore.

Funeral services were conducted Sunday at Zion Baptist Church where he was a member. Burial followed in Gillespie-Evergreen Cemetery.

<u>19 Sep 1918</u>   <u>Brevard News</u>

NAVY RECRUITING OFFICE

A Navy recruiting office has been opened in the Macfie-Brodie Drug Store. The Navy offers one of the best opportunities of the day for patriotic service. The young men of Transylvania County are expected to make a prompt response to this call for recruits in this branch of Uncle Sam's line of defense.

Lewis MOORE

Born:	29 Dec 1892, Transylvania County, NC
Died:	10 Oct 1970, Morganton, NC; age 77
Buried:	Pisgah Gardens Cemetery
Spouse:	**Bessie A. ALLISON**, m. 25 Dec 1920, Transylvania County, NC
Father:	**Volney C. MOORE**
Mother:	**Eunice WHITMIRE**
Draft Registration:	24, single, employed as a carpenter for Toxaway Lumber Co.

[Documentation: Burke County DC, <u>Transylvania County Cemetery Survey, Cowart's Index to Marriages,</u> Ancestry.com]

Lewis Moore

Martha Cantrell Cremer Photo

10/15/1970
LEWIS MOORE

Lewis Moore, 77, died last Saturday after a long illness. He was a native of Transylvania County, a retired carpenter and a veteran of World War I. He was a member of Carr's Hill Baptist Church. Graveside services were held Tuesday at Pisgah Gardens Cemetery.

Surviving are three daughters: Euna Leigh Cantrell, Frankie Wagoner and Lois Roberson; a son, Farrell Moore; a sister, Mrs. Wesley Holtzclaw; and two brothers, Dewey and Richard Moore.

Gas claimed a notable number of casualties during its early use, but once the crucial element of surprise had been lost, the overall number of casualties quickly diminished. Deaths from gas after about May 1915 were relatively rare. Gas victims often led highly debilitating lives thereafter with many unable to seek employment once they were discharged from the army.

Between 1917 and 1920, chemical warfare research in the United States involved more than 1900 scientists and technicians, making it at that time the largest government research program in American history. By the time the war ended, historians estimate more than 5500 university-trained scientists and technicians and tens of thousands of industrial workers on both sides of the battle lines worked on chemical weapons. Both the military use and industrial production of chemical weapons presented a number of health risks.

Dan Pinkney MORGAN

Born:	16 Apr 1894, Transylvania County, NC
Died:	26 Dec 1928, DeKalb County, GA; age 34
Buried:	Old Toxaway Baptist Church Cemetery
Spouse:	**Beulah HENDRICKS**, m. 13 Mar 1920, Transylvania County, NC
Father:	**John D. MORGAN**
Mother:	**Narcissa AIKEN**
Draft registration:	23, single, laborer for Heilmon Lumber Co.

Morgan, Dan P   4,159,448   * White * Colored
(Surname) (Christian name) (Army serial number)

Residence: Rosman / NORTH CAROLINA
(Street and house number) (Town or city) (County) (State)

M. O. E. R. C. *Inducted at Brevard NC on July 24, 19 18

Place of birth: Rosman NC   Age or date of birth: Apr 16/1894

Organizations served in, with dates of assignments and transfers:
Main Ing Depot MG Ing Center Camp Hancock Ga to Oct 30/
18: 358 MG Bn to Disch.

Grades, with date of appointment: Pvt

Engagements:

Wounds or other injuries received in action: None.
Served overseas from † No to † , from † to †
Honorably discharged on demobilization Dec 12/18 , 19
In view of occupation he was, on date of discharge, reported 0 per cent disabled.

1/3/1929
DAL MORGAN

Mr. Dal Morgan, son of D. Morgan of Middle Fork section, died of diabetes in a government hospital in Atlanta on December 20. Mr. Morgan was a World War veteran and had been in the hospital for the past five years.

Funeral services were held at the Old Toxaway Baptist Church Saturday, December 22.

The deceased is survived by his wife, Mrs. Beulah Hendricks, daughter of Ed Hendricks of Old Toxaway section; and two children; also his father, D. Morgan; brother, Lee Morgan; and sister, Mrs. Norman Murphy.

18 Jul 1918   Brevard News
23 MORE MEN TO LEAVE JULY 24, 1918 for Camp Hancock, Ga.,:
. . Dan Pinkney Morgan, Rosman . . .

Special Notes: Dan's obituary is typed just as it appeared in the **Brevard News.** The name appears to be mispelled as well as his date of death. The application for a military grave marker stated December 26th as the date of death.

View in Camp Hancock Augusta, Ga.   Postal Card

Gus MORGAN

Born:	27 Oct 1897, Transylvania County, NC.
Died:	11 Oct 1965, Wrens, GA; age 67
Buried:	Holden Cemetery
Occupation:	Retired farmer
Spouse:	**Dovie A. KUYKENDALL**, m. 26 Jan 1918, Transylvania County, NC
Father:	**Humphrey MORGAN**
Mother:	**Debbie CARVER**
Draft Registration:	21, self-employed

[Documentation: Georgia Death Index, <u>Transylvania County Cemetery Survey</u>, <u>Cowart's Index to Marriages</u>, findagrave.com, Ancestry.com]

Morgan, Gus   4,070,966   * White * Colored.
(Surname)   (Christian name)   (Army serial number)

Residence: _____ R.F.D. #1   Brevard _____ NORTH CAROLINA
(Street and house number)   (Town or city)   (County)   (State)

_____ C. *Inducted at Brevard N.C. _____ on AUG 2 , 1918

Place of birth: _____ XX _____ Age or date of birth: 22 yrs.

Organizations served in, with dates of assignments and transfers: 2 Dev 3n Med Det to disch

Grades, with date of appointment: PVT

Engagements: _____ XX

Wounds or other injuries received in action: None.

Served overseas from † _____ no _____ to † _____ , from † _____ to † _____

Honorably discharged: _____ Dec 2 , 19 18 S.C.D.
(Date)

In view of occupation he was, on date of discharge, reported 20 _____ (Cause) _____ per cent disabled.

Gus Morgan

Marie M. Golden Photo

SRC Notes: Med Det (Medical Detachment) SCD (Surgeons Certificate of Disability)

10/14/1965
GUS MORGAN

Last rites for Augustus Gus Morgan, 67, were held Wednesday afternoon at the Dunn's Creek Baptist Church. Burial was in the Holden Cemetery. He died early Monday morning at Wrens, Georgia after a lingering illness.

Mr. Morgan was a retired farmer. He was active in the Dunn's Creek Baptist Church and served as deacon and trustee. He was a veteran of World War I.

Survivors are as follows: the widow, Mrs. Dovie Kuykendall Morgan; three daughters: Ellaree Wilson, Marie Golden and Anna Lee Barton; four sons: Eli, Richard, Gentry, and William Morgan; and one sister, Mrs. Lillie Eubanks.

Food shortages in Europe, as well as Americans fighting the war, brought about a successful campaign at home to get loyal Americans to cut down on the amount of meat, sugar and bread that they normally ate. President Wilson had a Victory Garden planted in one corner of the White House lawn and even brought in sheep to graze, allowing gardeners who kept the lawn mowed, to enlist in the Army.

The American farmers were asked to feed the Europeans as well as the U.S. civilians and soldiers fighting in Europe. Herbert Hoover was appointed to watch over the nation's food supply. Hoover and the newly formed U.S. Food Administraton asked Americans to cut down on the amount of meat, sugar and bread they normally ate. One day a week was to be "meatless", another "sugarless", etc.

John Posey MORGAN

Born:	21 Mar 1893, Transylvania County, NC
Died:	20 Aug 1952, Transylvania County, NC; age 59
Buried:	Old Toxaway Baptist Church Cemetery
Father:	**Lewis Harmon MORGAN**
Mother:	**Delia F. POWELL**
Draft Registration:	23, single, farming
Military marker:	NC PVT Medical Dept. WW I

Documentation: Transylvania County DC, <u>Transylvania County Cemetery Survey</u>, Discharge, Ancestry.com, TT obituary]

Morgan, John P   2,395,171   White

(Surname)   (Christian name)   (Army serial number)

Residence: x x Transylvania Co   Rosman   NORTH CAROLINA

(Street and house number)   (Town or city)   (County)   (State)

*Inducted at Brevard N C   on Sept. 18, 19 17

Place of birth: Rosman, N C   Age or date of birth: 23 6/12

Organizations served in, with dates of assignments and transfers: Med Dept F H to 11/11/17; Cp Jackson F H 825 Cp Jackson S C Nov 26/17; Base Hosp to disch

Grades, with date of appointment: **Pvt**

Engagements: x x

Wounds or other injuries received in action: None.

Served overseas from † x x to † _____, from † _____ to † _____

Honorably discharged Aug. 18, 1918 S C D

(Date)

In view of occupation he was, on date of discharge, reported 0 (Cause) per cent disabled.

SRC Notes: F H (Field Hospital) SCD (Surgeon's Certificate of Disability)

8/21/1952
J.P. Morgan

John P. Morgan, 59, of Rosman, died in his sleep Tuesday night of a heart attack and funeral services will be held Thursday afternoon at Old Toxaway Baptist Church. Burial will be in the church cemetery.

A native of this county, Mr. Morgan was engaged in farming in the upper end of Transylvania.

He is survived by four brothers: Marcus, Goldie, Justin and Lewis; and three sisters: Mrs. Hall Chappell, Mrs. George Chappell and Mrs. Jim Aiken.

21 Sep 1917   **Brevard News**
THIRTY-ONE MEN TO CAMP JACKSON leave on Wednesday morning.
. . .John Posey Morgan . . .

12 Jul 1918   **Brevard News**
RETURN VOLUNTARILY
   John Posey Morgan, who left camp Jackson about Christmas, sent word to our local board that he would like to return to camp. He reported June 30 in his uniform and was accompanied to the camp at Spartanburg, by J. L. Watson, chief clerk of the local board. Morgan's sorrow for his conduct and his willingness to return to camp will probably save him from severe punishment

---

GRAVE REGISTRATION SERVICE

   The graves registration service, under the Quartermaster Corps, was charged with the acquisition cemeteries, the identification and reburial of our dead, and the correspondence with relatives of the deceased. Central cemeteries were organized on the American battlefields. All territory over which our troops fought was examined by this service, and cemeteries and the graves marked with a cross or six-pointed star and photographed. A few bodies were buried where they fell or in neighboring French or British cemeteries. Wherever the soldier was buried his identification tag, giving his name and Army serial number was fastened to the marker. A careful location of each grave was kept.

   Orcutt, Louis E., **The Great War Supplement**, published 1920, p. 279

William Sword MORGAN

Born:	29 Jul 1895, Transylvania County, NC
Died:	31 May 1945, Greenville County, SC; age 49
Buried:	Old Toxaway Baptist Church Cemetery
Spouse:	**Hattie KEITH**
Father:	**Martin MORGAN**
Mother:	**Lucy BOWEN**
Draft Registration:	22, single, farming
Discharge Record:	Drafted 19 Sep 1917; discharged by reason of physical defects existing prior to the draft; poor general development.

[Documentation: South Carolina DC, Discharge, Ancestry.com]

21 Sep 1917   Brevard News
THIRTY-ONE MEN TO CAMP JACKSON

Forty percent of the certified draft, making 31 men, was ordered to report on Tuesday at 5 P.M. at the office of the local enlistment board and to leave for Camp Jackson, S.C. Wednesday morning. . . .William Sword Morgan . . .

Greenville News (SC)
6/1/1945
WILLIAM S. MORGAN

William S. Morgan, 51, died suddenly yesterday morning at his home at Augusta Road. He had lived in Greenville for the past year and a half, moving here from Rosman, NC, where he lived for some years. Born and reared at Old Toxaway, NC, his parents were the late Mart and Lucy Bowen Morgan.

His wife, Hattie Keith Morgan survives him with a stepson, Charles Morgan; two sisters, Isabell Morgan and Morrie Galloway; two brothers, J.H. and Avery Morgan.

The body was sent to Brevard, NC for services and burial there Saturday at the Old Toxaway Baptist Church and cemetery.

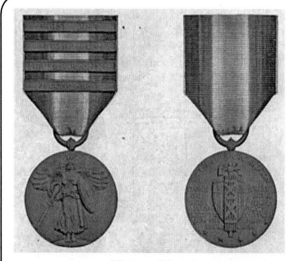

Victory Medal

The World War I **Victory Medal** was awarded to any member of the U.S. Military who had served int the armed forces between the following dates, in the following locations:

1. 6 Apr 1917 to 11 Nov 1918 for any military service
2. 12 Nov 1918 to 5 Aug 1919 for service in European Russia
3. 23 Nov 1918 to 1 Apr 1920 for service with the American Expeditionary Force Siberia

Zarkegrate G. MORGAN

Born:	21 Apr 1895, Transylvania County, NC
Died:	17 Aug 1951, Transylvania County, NC; age 56
Buried:	Old Toxaway Baptist Church Cemetery
Occupation:	Farmer
Spouse:	**Aurie CHAPMAN**, m. 26 May 1918, Transylvania County, NC
Father:	**Lewis Harmon MORGAN**
Mother:	**Delia F. POWELL**
Draft Registration:	No
Note:	Grave marker gives NO military data

[Documentation: Transylvania County DC, Transylvania County Cemetery Survey, Cowart's Index to Marriages, 1930 Census, TT obituary, Ancestry.com]

21 Jun 1918   Brevard News
WHITE REGISTRANTS WHO ARE TO LEAVE FOR CAMP JACKSON, S.C.
TUESDAY, JUNE 25th, 1918 AT 3:13 P.M.
ALTERNATIVES:
. . . Zark Morgan, Rosman . . .

8/23/1951
ZARKEGRATE H. MORGAN

Zarks H. Morgan, 56, of Old Toxaway died Friday morning at his home in Eastatoe Township following a brief illness. Mr. Morgan was a farmer and a member of the Old Toxaway Baptist church.

Survivors include the widow, Mrs. Aurie Chapman Morgan; one son, Dennis Morgan; one daughter, Tessie Morgan; and six brothers and three sisters.

Funeral services were conducted at the Old Toxaway Baptist Church with interment in the church cemetery.

Company 120th Infantry Supply House

Leo Lenoir MORRIS

Born:	3 Oct 1895, Transylvania County, NC
Died:	27 Feb 1958, Oteen VA Hospital, Buncombe County; age 62
Buried:	Oakdale Cemetery, Henderson County, NC
Spouse:	**Janie LESLIE**
Father:	**Waverly MORRIS**
Mother:	**Mary L. Annie CAGLE**
Draft Registration:	21, single, timber cutter in Pisgah Forest

[Documentation: Buncombe County DC, Application for Military Headstone, <u>Henderson County Cemeteries</u>, Ancestry.com]

Morris, Leo L   1,324,454   *Transylvania* white 1½

(surname)	(Christian name)	(army serial number)	(race: White or colored)

Residence: Pisgah Forest   NORTH CAROLINA

(Street and house number)	(Town or city)	(County)	(State)

*Enlisted in NG Davidson River NC   July 18/17

†Born in Davidson River NC   21 8/12 yrs

Organization: Btry F 1 FA NC NG (113 FA) to disch

Grades: Pvt 1cl Jan 21/18

Engagements:

Wounds or other injuries received in action: None.

‡Served overseas May 26/18 to "ch 19/19

§Hon. disch ~~Sarg 28/19~~ *Feb 2 8/19* on demobilization

Was reported *0* per cent disabled on date of discharge, in view of occupation.

Remarks:

SRC Notes: FA (Field Artillery) NG (National Guard)

Hendersonville Times News
2/26/1958
LEO L. MORRIS

Leo Lenoir Morris, 62, a resident of Spring Street, died yesterday morning at the Veterans Administration Hospital at Swannanoa after a period of declining health.

Mr. Morris was a retired safety officer for the TVA at Fontana. He was a veteran of World War I and a member of the Hedrick-Rhodes Post of the VFW. He was a member of Fontana American Legion and a Mason and Shriner. He was a member of Valley Hill Baptist Church.

Funeral services will be held Saturday at 2 p.m. in the chapel of Thomas Shepherd Funeral Home. Interment will follow in Oakdale Cemetery.

Surviving are the wife, Mrs. Janie Leslie Morris; two sons: Leo L. and James H. Morris; four brothers: Jamie, Carlos, William and Waverly; two sisters: and Beatrice Lauler and Mrs. Lem Daniels.

---

21 Jun 1918   Brevard News

NEGRO CAMP ON GOVERNMENT RESERVATION

A Negro camp has been located on the Government reservation for the purpose of cutting timber. The former Vanderbilt Estate, so long undisturbed by human invasion, now becomes for a season at least, alive with the melodious voices of the southern Negro. The wild animals of this region will doubtless be charmed, if not alarmed, at their presence.

Tom MORRISON

Born:	24 Jul 1892, Hartwell, GA
Died:	24 Nov 1961, Transylvania County, NC; age 69
Buried:	Cooper Cemetery
Race:	Colored
Parents:	Unknown
Draft Registration:	No
Military marker:	Georgia PVT Co A 327 Labor BMC QMC WW I

[Documentation: Transylvania County DC, <u>Transylvania County Cemetery Survey</u>, Application for Veteran's Headstone, Discharge, Ancestry.com]

Morrison Thomas M   720,465 White
(Surname)   (Christian name)   (Army serial number) (Race: White or colored)

Residence: RFD 1   Edneyville Henderson NORTH CAROLINA
(Street and house number)   (Town or city)   (County)   (State)

Enlisted in   RA Ft Screven Ga Mch 9/18   —
Born in   Hendersonville NC 21 5/12 yrs   —
Organizations: 17 Bln Co to disch   —

Grades: Pvt 1cl July 5/18   —

Engagements: —   —

Wounds or other injuries received in action: None.   —
Served overseas: Oct 21/18 to My 3/19   —
Hon. disch.   May 10/19   on demobilization   —
Was reported   0   per cent disabled on date of discharge, in view of occupation.   —
Remarks: —   —

SRC Notes: Bln Co (Balloon Company)
Special Note: Charles Kilpatrick of Moore-Kilpatrick Funeral home applied for a military headstone for Tom.

Type R Observation Balloon   Wikepedia.org

Buford Dall MULENEX

Born:	2 May 1895, Transylvania County, NC
Died:	7 Jan 1967, Oteen VA Hospital, Buncombe County; age 71
Buried:	Davidson River Cemetery
Occupation:	Retired grocer
Spouse:	**Florence KINSEY**
Mother:	**Annie Lousia MULENEX**
Draft Registration:	22, single, worked for Carr Lumber Company
Military Marker:	NC PVT 159 Ambulance Co WW I

[Documentation: Buncombe County DC, findagrave.com, Transylvania County Cemetery Survey, Ancestry.com]

Buford Mulenex

Helen Reynolds Photo

11 Jul 1918   Brevard News

Twelve Transylvania boys left on last Saturday for Fort Oglethorpe, Ga., to begin their careers as defenders of democracy. The boys left on the afternoon train
. . . Daniel Buford Mulenex, Pisgah Forest . . .

1/15/1967
"POP" MULENEX

Buford D. Mulenex, 78, of Old Camp Road, Greenville, SC, died in the Veteran's hospital at Oteen early last Saturday morning after an extended illness. He was a native of Transylvania County but had lived in Greenville for 18 years where he was in the grocery and meat business. He was a veteran of World War I.

Surviving are his wife, Florence Mulenex; three daughters: Mrs. Ellen Marsh, Mrs. John Reynolds and Mrs. Fred Wright; two sons: Harvey Emanuel and Edward J. Mullenex; and one sister, Miss Effie Mulenex.

Funeral services were conducted January 10th, 1967 in the chapel of Moore Funeral Home of Brevard and the burial followed in the Davidson River Cemetery.

NATIONAL ARMY CANTONMENT (CAMP)

Camp Lewis   Location: American Lake, Wash.   Organization: 91st Division
Troops from Washington, Oregon, California, Nevada, Utah Idaho, Montana and Wyoming

Elzie Alvin MULL

Born:	27 Jun 1895, Transylvania County, NC
Died:	26 Oct 1982, Mecklenburg County, NC; age 87
Buried:	Gillespie-Evergreen
Spouse:	**Ruby Lee RUSHING**
Father:	**James A. MULL**
Mother:	**Mattie JUSTUS**
Draft Registration:	21, single and self-employed farmer

[Transylvania County BC, Mecklenburg County DC, Transylvania County Cemetery Survey, Ancestry.com]

Mull Elzie A.   4,159,461   • White • *colored/*
(Surname)   (Christian name)   (Army serial number)

Residence: __XX__   Selica, __   Transylvania Co   NORTH CAROLIN
(Street and house number)   (Town or city)   (County)   (State)

• Enlisted • R. A. • N. G. • E. R. C. •Inducted at __Brevard, N.C.__ on July 24, 19 18
Place of birth: __Selica, N.C.__   Age or date of birth: __23 1/12 yrs.__
Organizations served in, with dates of assignments and transfers: _____
____19th Co Rct Rec Dep M.G.T.C. Camp Hancock Ga. to Aug____
____30, 1918; 71st 6th Group M; T.D. to Nov 3, 1918 12th Pro____
Grades, with date of appointment: (12th Prov Co. Camp Hancock Ga. to disch.

____Pvt.____
Engagements: _____
____XX____

Wounds or other injuries received in action: None.
Served overseas from † __XX__ to † _____, from † _____ to † _____
Honorably discharged on demobilization __Dec 29, 1918.__ 19 _____
In view of occupation he was, on date of discharge, reported _____ per cent disabled.

SRC Notes: RA (Regular Army) ERC (Enlisted Reserve Corps) MCTC (Machine Gun Training Corps)

18 Jul 1918   Brevard News
23 MORE MEN TO LEAVE JULY 24, 1918
Following is a list of white registrants for induction on July 24th, 1918 for Camp Hancock, Ga., who will leave on the 3:13 train: . . .
. . . Elzie Alvin Mull, Selica . . .

17 Jan 1919   Brevard News
Chester Fenwicke, Elzie Mull and Monroe Eubanks have returned home from the training camps. Their many friends are glad to see them home again.

14 Feb 1919   Brevard News
Pvt. Elzie Mull has recovered from the mumps and visited his sister Mrs. C.R. Sharp Sunday.

10/28/1982
ELZIE MULL

Elzie Alvin Mull, 87, died Tuesday in a Charlotte hospital. Born in Selica in Transylvania County, he was the son of the late J.A. and Mattie Mull. He was a retired motel manager and an Army veteran of World War I.

Surviving is a son, James Richard Mull. Graveside services were held Thursday in Gillespie Evergreen Cemetery in Brevard.

Carl Leonida MYNATT

Born: 22 Apr 1893, Talladega, Alabama
Died: 14 Dec 1919, Pulaski, Arkansas; age 26
Buried: Little Rock National Cemetery, Little Rock, AK
Parents: Undetermined
Draft Registration: 24, single, student at Brevard Institute

[Documentation: Arkansas Death Index, US Veteran Gravesite, Ancestry.com]

Mynatt,   Carl Leonidas 2,339,765   • White • Colored.
(Surname)   (Christian name)   (Army serial number)

Residence: _____ Brevard _____ NORTH CAROLINA
(Street and house number) (Town or city) (County) (State)

• Enlisted • R. A. • N. G. • E. R. C. • Inducted at Ft Thomas Ky on June 16, 17, 19__

Place of birth: Talladega Ala   Age or date of birth: 24 1/12 yr

Organizations served in, with dates of assignments and transfers: _____
Co L 4 Inf to

Grades, with date of appointment: _____
Corp June 12/18; Bn Sgt Maj Aug 23/19

Engagements: _____

Wounded in action (degree and date) Degree Undetermined about July 24, 19 18
Served overseas from †Apr 6/18 to †Aug 22/19 from † ____ to † ____
• Honorably discharged on demobilization ror Immediate Reenlistment Aug 28/919
(If separated for other cause give reason)
In view of occupation he was, on date of discharge, reported _____ per cent disabled.

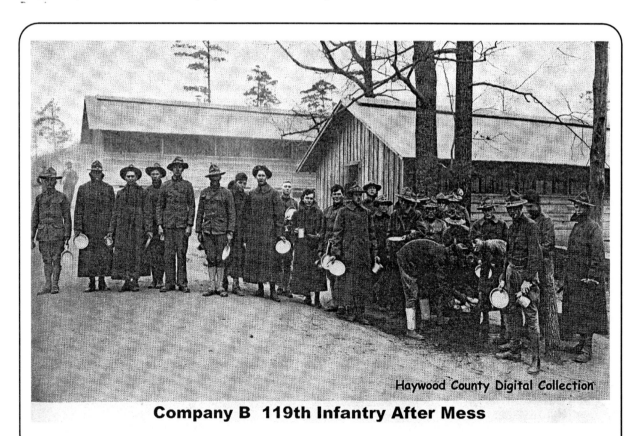

Company B 119th Infantry After Mess

Haywood County Digital Collection

Robert Mitchell NEELEY

Born:	29 May 1896, Transylvania County, NC
Died:	19 May 1966, Oteen VA Hospital, Buncombe County; age 69
Buried:	Gillespie-Evergreen Cemetery
Occupation:	Butcher
Spouse:	**Roxie REECE**
Father:	**Robert D. NEELEY**
Mother:	**Susan SOUTHERN**
Draft Registration:	21, single, was a chauffeur

[Documentation: Transylvania County BC, Buncombe County DC, <u>Transylvania County Cemetery Survey</u>, Ancestry.com]

Neeley, Robert M   1,320,323   · White · Colored
(Surname)   (Christian name)   (Army serial number)

Residence: _____ **Brevard** _____ **NORTH CAROLINA**
(Street and house number) (Town or city) (County) (State)

_____C. *Inducted at **Brevard N C** _____ on **Oct 4**, 19**17**
Place of birth: _____ **Brevard N C** _____ Age or date of birth: **21 4/12 yrs**
Organizations served in, with dates of assignments and transfers:
Btry C 318 FA to Oct 16/17; Btry E 120 Inf to disch

Grades, with date of appointment: _____
Corp Feb 21/18

Engagements: _____

Wounds or other injuries received in action: None.
Served overseas from † **May 12/18** to † **Apr 13/19**, from † _____ to † _____
Honorably discharged on demobilization _____ **Apr 18** _____, 19**19**
In view of occupation he was, on date of discharge, reported _____ **0** _____ per cent disabled.

SRC Note: FA (Field Artillery)

5/26/1966
Mitch Neely

Funeral services for Robert Mitchell Neely, 69, were held Saturday in the First Baptist Church. Burial followed in Gillespie-Evergreen Cemetery. Mr. Neely died in the Veterans Hospital at Oteen last Thursday night after a lingering illness.

Survivors include the wife, Roxanne Reece Neely; two sisters: Mrs. Pat Poor and Mrs. Fred Grogan.

Mr. Neely was a veteran of World War I, having served in Europe with the 120th Infantry Division. He attended Brevard College and was a member of the Dunn's Rock Masonic Lodge, Pisgah Order of the Eastern Star and Woodman of the World. He also served as an alderman for the Town of Brevard for six years. For 30 years he was connected with Carr Lumber Company

A new and dreaded weapon was used for the first time in this world war---poison gas. There were several types of gas that was fired in shells at the enemy. Tear gas caused blindness; chlorine gas suffocated the soldiers and mustard gas, an oily, smoky substance that was most commonly used was particularly horrible. It caused burns and great mustard-colored blisters, often caused blindness and difficulty breathing. Many men suffered ill health for years following the war as a result of having been gassed.

Avery NEILL

Born:	2 Nov 1890, Transylvania County, NC
Died:	23 Jul 1981, Henderson County, NC; age 91
Buried:	Pisgah Gardens Cemetery
Spouse:	**Minnie**
Father:	**John G. NEILL**
Mother:	**Lydia S ENGLISH**
Draft Registration:	26, single, listed both parents as dependents, worked at Carr Lumber Co

[Documentation: Henderson County DC, <u>Transylvania County Cemetery Survey</u>, 1900-1930 Censuses, Ancestry.com, Hendersonville Times News obituary]

Neill Avery C   1 334 021   white
(Surname)   (Christian name)   (Army serial number) (Race: White or colored)

Residence: Pisgah   Randolph   NORTH CAROLINA
                (Street and house number) (Town or city) (County) (State)

Enlisted in   NC Ashville NC —   July 23/17 —
Born in   Transylvania NC —   '   27 9/12 yrs —

Organizations: Co F 1 Inf NC NG to¯ ; Co B 105 Engrs to Jan 15/18
                Motor Trk Co 334 to July 16/18 ; 328 Labor Bn to
Grades: disch
                Pvt 1 cl   ¯ Corp Dec 1/17; Pvt Jan 4/18; —
Engagements: Corp June 22/18; Sgt July 24/18 —

Wounds or other injuries received in action: None. —
Served overseas: No —
Hon. disch.   Jan 15/19   on demobilization —
Was reported 0   per cent disabled on date of discharge, in view of occupation.
Remarks: —   —

Hendersonville Times News
7/25/1981
AVERY C. NEILL

Avery C. Neill, 90, died Thursday in Carolina Village. He was a native of Transylvania County and a veteran of WW I. He was a son of the late John and Savannah Neill.

He is survived by two daughters: Sally Candiano and Mrs. W.H. McCulloch and a son, Avery C. Jr.

Services will be held Sunday in the English Chapel at Pisgah Forest. Burial will be in Pisgah Gardens Cemetery.

SRC Notes: NG (National Guard) Engross (Engineers) Motor Trk Co (Motor Truck Company)

<u>**5 May 1917**</u>   <u>**Brevard News**</u>

While coupling cars on the Carr Lumber Company's railroad recently, Avery Neill had a finger of his left hand badly mashed. He is recovering rapidly from the accident.

U.S. Army Truck Company

Postal Card

Arthur S. NELSON

Born:	11 Aug 1892, Morris, PA
Died:	19 Dec 1953, Unknown; age 61
Buried:	Soldier's Home National Cemetery, Washington, DC
Father:	**Albert NELSON**
Draft Registration:	No
Note:	Can find no connection to Transylvania County other than his Service Record Card gives Pisgah Forest as his address. Suppose he was here working with timber industry.

[Documentation: Ancestry.com, US Veterans Gravesites, US National Cemetery, Interment Control form]

SRC Notes: CAC (Cost Artillery Corps) MT (Motor Transport) Rep Unit (Repair Unit) FA (Field Artillery)
RA (Regular Army)

One of the many responsibilities of the Motor Transportation Corps was receiving new vehicles into service. This was done at the Reception Parks. Vehicles were unloaded, uncrated and assembled at these parks, then assigned a registration card and markings. Detailed records were kept on each vehicle's whereabouts and conditions. Vehicles and spare parts collected in these parks awaited assignments to specific army units as requested.

Maintenance and repair was a major responsibility that was done in the Overhaul parks. These parks were to occupy permanent or semi-permanent structures and were to be located 30 miles behind the fighting zone (40 miles if behind a "thinly held sector"). When the cost of a repair exceeded 30% of the first cost of the vehicle, they were to be sent to a reconstruction park for salvage.

The reconstruction parks were permanent facilities equipped for large-scale rebuilding and salvage operations. A temporary park in Nevers was relocated in July 1918 to a permanent facility in Verneuil, Nièvre, 30 miles east of Nevers. The M.T.C. Reconstruction Park covered approximately 1,000 acres and consisted of five steel shops averaging 25,000 sq. ft. each and a large warehouse for storage of spare parts. The park was staffed by three units of approximately 1,150 men each (Units 301, 302, and 303). German prisoners also supplied some labor.

Wikepedia.com

Zero Walond NICHOLS

Born:	19 May 1897, Transylvania County
Died:	Undetermined
Buried:	Undetermined
Spouse:	**Ottille**
Father:	**Zero NICHOLS**
Mother:	**Leslie ATKINS**
Draft Registration:	No
Note:	1930 Census had Zero living in Washington, DC and 1940 had him in Asheville, NC

[Documentation: Transylvania County BC, 1900-1940 Censuses, Ancestry.com]

Nichols, Zero W Jr   612,547   * White * Colored.—
(Surname)   (Christian name)   (Army serial number)

Residence: _____ Brevard *Transylvania* NORTH CAROLINA
(Street and house number)   (Town or city)   (County)   (State)

* Enlisted * R. A. * N. G. * E. R. C. *Inducted at Ft Monroe Va on Oct 3/, 19 15
Place of birth: Brevard NC   Age or date of birth: 18-?/12 yrs
Organizations served in, with dates of assignments and transfers:

(69 Co CAC to — ; 4 Co C Chesapeake Bay CAC to disch)

Grades, with date of appointment: _____

(Pvt 1 c Aug 1/16; Mec Nov 5/17; Pvt Fob 1/18)

Engagements: _____

Wounds or other injuries received in action: None.
Served overseas from † No to † _____, from † _____ to † _____
Honorably discharged: June 4/, 19 20 abolition of Br-ies
(Date)   (Cause)
In view of occupation he was, on date of discharge, reported 0 per cent disabled.

SRC Notes: CAC (Coast Artillery Corps)

14 Nov 1918   Brevard News
Z.W. Nichols, Jr., who has been stationed in Washington, DC is now in General Hospital No. 22, Richmond College, VA, recuperating from Flu.

4 Apr 1919   Brevard News
Z.W. Nichols, Jr., of Washington City is here for a visit to his parents.

General View, Approach to Fort Monroe, Va.

Postal Card

Lee NICHOLSON

Born:	1 Jul 1893, Transylvania County, NC
Died:	11 Nov 1968, Oteen VA Hospital, Buncombe County; age 75
Buried:	Pisgah Gardens Cemetery
Spouse:	**Ethel R. COLLINS**, m. 10 Aug 1919, Transylvania County, NC
Father:	**Wade H. NICHOLSON**
Mother:	**Maggie REID**
Draft Registration:	No
Military Marker:	NC CPL CO A 115 MG BN WW I

[Documentation: Transylvania County Birth Index, Buncombe County DC, Transylvania County Cemetery Survey, Cowart's Index to Marriages, Ancestry.com]

Nicholson, Lee		1,322,677	White	1½
(Surname)	(Christian name)	(Army serial number)	(Race: White or colored)	
Residence: xx	Rosman		NORTH CAROLINA	
	(Street and house number) (Town or city)	(County)	(State)	

Enlisted in	N G Roseman N C	July 10/17
Born in	Transylvania Co N C	24 yrs
Organizations:	Co A 115 M G Bn to Disch	

Grades: Corpl Sept 15/17; Pvt 1c July 1/18; Corp Aug 9/18; Sgt Nov 14/18; Corp Dec 31/18

Engagements: Flanders; Ypres Lys; Somme Offensive

Wounds or other injuries received in action: None.

Served overseas: May 11/18 to Mch 22/19

Hon. disch. Apr 2/19 on demobilization

Was reported 0 per cent disabled on date of discharge, in view of occupation.

Remarks: xx

SRC Notes: MG Bn (Machine Gun Battalion)

11 Apr 1919   Brevard News
Lee Nicholson has returned to his home after several months work in France for Uncle Sam.

25 Apr 1919   Brevard News
We are all very glad to again have in our midst the following who spent ten months in France working faithfully for Uncle Sam: Pick Whitmire, William Jackson, Elbert Whitmire and Lee Nicholson.

---

7 Dec 1917   Brevard News
WAR CANNOT LAST FOREVER
PEACE MUST COME SOME TIME

And when peace comes, a long line of American soldiers can make their way homeward from the depths of this German manufactured hell. Some of these fighters will be minus an eye, maybe two; an arm, or maybe two. These men, who have placed the uttermost offering upon the alter of patriotism, will sometimes give reminiscent talks of the battles which saved America. If we, who stay in the protected shelter of our homes, give OUR BEST SERVICE to the AMERICAN NATIONAL RED CROSS we can listen unashamed to details of the struggle, for we will know that we have helped defeat the foe. If we have done nothing for the RED CROSS, or almost nothing in a half-hearted way, when the boys come back from the trenches, we'll have to hang our head and feel like ----!

Carl Fanning NORRIS

Born:	12 Sep 1895, Haywood County, NC
Died:	13 Jan 1979, Oteen VA Hospital, Buncombe County; age 83
Buried:	Pisgah Gardens Cemetery
Spouse:	**Ola GALLOWAY**, 26 Aug 1922, Transylvania County, NC
Father:	**James H. NORRIS**
Mother:	**Laura SEARCY**
Draft Registration:	Haywood County, 21, single, employed by Champion Fiber Co

Documentation: North Carolina Delayed Birth Index, Buncombe County DC, Transylvania County Cemetery Survey, Cowart's Index to Marriages, Ancestry.com]

Norris Carl F   4,480,940   * White ~~Colored~~
    (Surname)   (Christian name)   (Army serial number)

Residence: _____ Chennyfield   Transylvania NORTH CAROLINA
            (Street and house number)   (Town or city)   (County)   (State)

~~_____~~ *Inducted at___Waynesville N C_____ on _Aug 30_ 19_18_

Place of birth: __Canton N C__   Age or date of birth: _____Sept. 12 1895___

Organizations served in, with dates of assignments and transfers: _15° Dep Brig to Oct 3/18_
          Oct Aut Repl Draft to disch

Grades, with date of appointment: _Pvt_____

Engagements: _____

Wounds or other injuries received in action: None.
Served overseas from †_Oct 28/18_ to †_June 5/19_, from †_____ to †_____
Honorably discharged on demobilization ___June 18___, 19_19_
In view of occupation he was, on date of discharge, reported _____0_____ per cent disabled.

SRC Notes: Aut Repl (Auto Replacement)

Asheville Citizen-Times
1/15/1979
CARL F. NORRIS

Carl Fanning Norris, 83, of Lake Sega Rd. died Saturday in Asheville VA Medical Center after a brief illness. A native of Haywood County, he was the son of the late Jim and Laura Norris. He was a veteran of World War I and a retired employee of Olin Corp.

Mr. Fanning is survived by two sons: James A. Jackson and Robert E. Norris; a brother, Jamie Norris; and three sisters: Agnes Taylor, Ruby Taylor and Myrtle Gaddy.

Services were held in Glady Branch Baptist Church, of which he was a member, with burial in Pisgah Gardens.

---

26 Sep 1918   **Brevard News**
MAKERS OF SURGICAL DRESSINGS BUSY

Mrs. H.N. Carrier, director of Woman's Work of the Transylvania Red Cross has received an order for 840 cotton pads to be shipped to Atlanta by the twentieth of October. The workrooms are open every morning and afternoon in the week and every woman in the town is urged to lend a hand toward getting this order off by the scheduled time.

Charlie Isaac NORRIS

Born:	6 Apr 1893, Haywood County, NC
Died:	24 Oct 1973, Oteen VA Hospital, Buncombe County; age 80
Buried:	Macedonia Church Cemetery
Spouse:	**Mary GALLOWAY**, m. 24 Apr 1922, Transylvania County, NC
Father:	**James H. NORRIS**
Mother:	**Laura SEARCY**
Draft Registration:	24, single, employed as a laborer at Davidson River

[Documentation: Buncombe County DC, Transylvania County Cemetery Survey, Cowart's Index to Marriages, Ancestry.com]

Norris, Charlie   717516   White
(Surname)   (Christian name)   (Army serial number)   (Race: White or colored)

Residence: _____ Cherry field   NORTH CAROLINA
            (Street and house number)   (Town or city)   (County)   (State)

*Enlisted in N G at Hendersonville N.C   June 11/17   —
†Born in   Cherryfield NC   —   24 2/12 yrs   —
Organizations: —   —

Grades: 6 Co C A C N C NG (6 Co Cape Fear) CAC to July 26/18
           Btry F 50 Arty C A C to disch
           Pvt 1 cl Feb 1/18; Corp Feb 9/18   —

Engagements: —   —

Wounds or other injuries received in action: None.   —
‡Served overseas: Oct 7/18 to Feb 14/19   —
‡Hon. disch. Mch 4/19   on demobilization   —
Was reported   0   per cent disabled on date of discharge, in view of occupation.
Remarks: —   —

SRC Notes: CAC NC NG (Coast Artillery Corps North Carolina National Guard)

21 Mar 1919   Brevard News
Charles Norris just returned from France is visiting friends here.

Hendersonville Times News
10/19/1973
CHARLIE I. NORRIS

Charlie Isaac Norris, 80, of Etowah, died Wednesday at Oteen VA Hospital after a long illness. A native of Canton, he had lived in Rosman for 60 years. He was a member of Cherryfield Baptist Church and a veteran of World War I.

Mr. Norris is survived by one son, Tinsley Norris; four brothers: Carl, Everette, James and Neal Norris; three sisters: Ruby Taylor, Agnes Taylor and Myrtle Gaddy; ; three grandchildren and two great-grandchildren.

Funeral services were conducted at 2 p.m. today at Macedonia Baptist Church near Rosman. Burial was in the church cemetery.

NATIONAL ARMY CANTONMENT (CAMP)

Camp Greene Location: Charlotte, NC Organization: 26th Division (Old 5th)
Troops from Maine, New Hampshire, Vermont, Massachusetts, Rhode Island and Connecticut.

Clarence Fisher NORTON

Born:	27 Feb 1896, Transylvania County, NC
Died:	18 Apr 1982, Oteen VA Hospital, Buncombe County; age 86
Buried:	Reid Cemetery at Oakland
Spouse:	**Launia Grace GRAY**
Father:	**Lee Fisher NORTON**
Mother:	**Nancy Jane REID**
Draft Registration:	Cedar Grove, W VA, 21, single, working in the coal mines
Military Marker:	PVT US Army WW I

[Documentation: Discharge, Transylvania County BC, Buncombe County DC, <u>Upper Transylvania County, NC Remembered</u>, Ancestry.com, Asheville C-T obituary]

Asheville Citizen-Times
4/20/1982
CLARENCE NORTON

Clarence Fisher Norton, 86, of Lake Toxaway, died Sunday in the Asheville VA Medical Center. A lifelong resident of Transylvania County, he was a son of the late Lee F. and Nancy Reid Norton. He was a World War I Army veteran and a farmer. He was the husband of the late Launia Gray Norton.

Services were held in Lake Toxaway Baptist church with burial in the Reid cemetery.

Surviving are six sons: Marty, Dr. Jerry, Larry, David, Leroy and Bill Norton; two daughters: Nan Turner and Mary Queen; three sisters: Emily Fisher, Edrei Matheson and Ola Sanders.

Clarence Norton

Mary Norton Pangle Photo

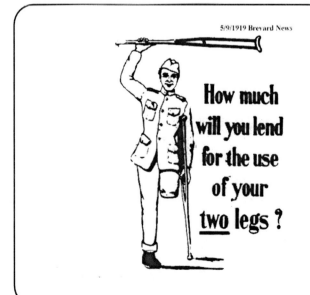

5/9/1919 Brevard News

How much will you lend for the use of your two legs?

4/18/1918 Brevard News

With THEM— to the VERY LAST

Brevard Banking Co.

Hillard OLIVER

Born:	11 Feb 1894, Henderson County, NC
Died:	18 Jan 1979, undetermined; age 84
Buried:	Pisgah Gardens Cemetery
Spouse:	**Flora HUGGINS**, m. 1 Nov 1912, Henderson County, NC
Father:	**William OLIVER**
Mother:	**Julia Ann SCOTT**
Draft Registration:	Henderson County, 23, single and farming
Military Marker:	PVT US Army WW I

[Documentation: SSDI, <u>Transylvania County Cemetery Survey</u>, <u>Cowart's Index to Marriages</u>, Huggin Family Genealogy, Ancestry.com]

```
                                                                          1
              Oliver, Hillard          4,159,428        • White •XXXXXX
         (Surname)      (Christian name)    (Army serial number)
Residence: _____ Route 1 _____ Etough ·_____ NORTH CAROLINA ___
         (Street and house number)  (Town or city)  (County)    (State)
• H____ R. A. • N. G. • E. R. ___•Inducted at ___ Hendersonville NC on July 24, 19_18
Place of birth: ___ Henderson Co NC ____  Age or date of birth: _ 25 5/12 yrs __
Organizations served in, with dates of assignments and transfers:
         71 Co 6 Gr MTD MG TC Camp Hancock Ga to Sept 23/18;
         Dev Bn MG TC to Oct 9/18
Grades, with date of appointment: _____
                           Pvt

Engagements: _____ None _____

Wounds or other injuries received in action: None.
Served overseas from † _ None ___ to † _____, from † _____ to † _____
Honorably discharged on demobilization _____ Mch 20 ____, 19__19
In view of occupation he was, on date of discharge, reported ___ 0 ___ per cent disabled.
```

SRC Notes: MTD MG TC (Motor Transport Depot Machine Gun Transportation Corps)

Hendersonville Times-News
1/19/1979
HILLARD OLIVER

Hillard Oliver, 84, of Pelzer SC, a native of Henderson County, died Thursday morning in a Fountain Inn SC hospital after a period of declining health. He had lived in the Etowah area before moving to Pelzer about eight years ago. He was an Army veteran of World War I and a retired farmer. His wife was the late Flora Ship- man Oliver who died in 1970. He is survived by a granddaughter, Shelia Oliver of Etowah and a number of nieces and nephews.

Services will be held at 11 a.m. Saturday in Pleasant Grove Baptist Church Burial will be in Pisgah Gardens

---

First Draft Number Drawn
20 Jul 1917
#258

In Washington, D.C. on July 20, 1917 President Wilson, Secretary of War, Baker, and other officials gathered to draw the numbers for the draft. Secretary Baker, blindfolded, drew the first number from a fishbowl---#258. In all 4,557 precincts around the country, men with #258 had officially become soldiers.

Avery McEver ORR

Born: 13 Dec 1895, Transylvania County, NC
Died: 31 May 1933, Oteen VA Hospital, Buncombe County; age 37
Buried: North Pacolet Baptist Church Cemetery, Spartanburg, SC
Spouse: **Lucy BLACKWELL**
Father: **Lambert ORR**
Mother: **Harriet N. KITCHEN**
Draft Registration: 21, single, mechanic for Carr Lumber Company

[Documentation: Buncombe County DC, findagrave.com, 1900 census, Ancestry.com]

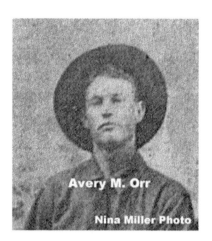

Orr, Avery M   1,876,254   • White • Colored
(Surname)   (Christian name)   (Army serial number)

Residence: Davidson River   NORTH CAROLINA
(Street and house number)   (Town or city)   (County)   (State)

*Inducted at Brevard NC   on Sept. 14 17
Place of birth: Brevard NC   Age or date of birth: 21 11/12 yrs
Organizations served in, with dates of assignments and transfers:
MD t disch

Grades, with date of appointment:
Pvt 1st Cl Feb 12/1 ; Corp Apr 1/18; Sgt May 1/18;

Engagements:

Wounds or other injuries received in action: None
Served overseas from † Aug 6/18 to † June 20/19 , from † _____ to † _____
Honorably discharged on demobilization   June 29/19 , 19
In view of occupation he was, on date of discharge, reported 0 per cent disabled.
Remarks:

Avery M. Orr
Nina Miller Photo

SRC Notes: MD (Medical Department)

21 Sep 1917   Brevard News
THIRTY-ONE MEN TO CAMP JACKSON

Forty percent of the certified draft, making 31 men, was ordered to report on Tuesday at 5 P.M. at the office of the local enlistment board and to leave for Camp Jackson, S.C. Wednesday morning.
. . . Avery McEver Orr . . .

The men reported to the local exemption board Tuesday J.L. Osteen was put in command until the arrival at Camp Jackson and he selected Avery Orr as his assistant.

Tuesday night at the Aethelwold Mrs. J. S. Silversteen, Chairman of the National League of Woman's Service, presented the men with comfort kits prepared by the women of the league.

On Wednesday morning 31 men formed a line at the rooms of the War Department and marched to the depot. There was no roll of drums nor blare of horns but it was, nevertheless, an impressive spectacle. A large crowd was on hand for the good-byes and the young men were cheerful.

7 Nov 1918   Brevard News
"SOMEWHERE IN FRANCE" (See John Luke Osteen for complete letter)
. . . Sgt. Avery M. Orr had the pleasure of visiting the front recently with a detail for purpose of rescuing a wrecked ambulance. . .

> There were a significant number of famous authors that were ambulance drivers during World War I. They included Ernest Hemingway, W. Somerset Maugham, and E.E. Cummings. Most of these drivers volunteered prior to the United States entering the war and drove for the Red Cross and Great Britain.

Charlie C. ORR

Born:	10 Jun 1899, Transylvania County, NC
Died:	8 Jul 1969, Greenville, South Carolina; age 70
Buried:	Oak Grove Cemetery at Brevard
Spouse:	**Jennie May DUCKER**, m. 5 Jan 1920, Transylvania County, NC
Father:	**William ORR**
Mother:	**Elizabeth OSTEEN**
Draft Registration:	No

[Documentation: <u>Transylvania County Cemetery Survey</u>, <u>Cowart's Index to Marriages</u>, SSDI, Ancestry.com, obituary]

Orr, Charlie		1,322,775	white	1½
(Surname)	(Christian name)	(Army serial number)	(Race: White or colored)	

Residence: _____ Brevard _____ NORTH CAROLINA

	(Street and house number)	(Town or city)	(County)	(State)
Enlisted in	NC Brevard NC		July 7/7	
Born in	Transylvania Co NC —		18 1/12 yrs —	
Organizations:	NC Tr 1 Dep Sq C NG (Co A 115 MG Bn) to disch			—

Grades: Pvt 1cl Sept 15/17; Pvt Dec 1/17 —

Engagements: — —

Wounds or other injuries received in action: None. —
Served overseas: May 11/18 to —ch 22/19 —
Hon. disch. Apr 2/19   on demobilization   —
Was reported 0   per cent disabled on date of discharge, in view of occupation. —
Remarks: — —

SRC Notes: MG TR (Machine Gun Troops

7/17/1969
CHARLES C. ORR

Charlie C. Orr, 70, Travelers Rest, S.C., formerly of Transylvania County died last Tuesday in a Greenville, S.C. hospital after a long illness. He was a retired tannery worker, veteran of World War I and a member of Travelers Rest Church of God.

Survivors are the widow, Jennie Ducker Orr; seven sons: Charlie Jr., Paul, Ernest, Bernard, Robert, Sgt. William and Reece Orr; three daughters: Mrs. Mace Britt, Mrs. Margaret Grayson and Mrs. Vera Holden; and a sister, Mrs. Ellen McCall.

Services were held last Thursday in Brevard Church of God. Burial was in the Oak Grove Cemetery.

---

2 May 1919   Brevard News
SOMETHING SHOULD BE DONE

Dr. C.W. Hunt, in his article on the question of a memorial to our soldier boys, touches upon a subject, which should be of personal interest to every loyal citizen of Transylvania County. A matter of vital concern to all those in whose memories the victory of America and her allies will be marked as the close of a period of immeasurable suffering. It is unthinkable that Transylvania will fail to build some lasting memorial to her soldiers in the cause of freedom and some definite action should be taken at once.

Clarence Ehler ORR

Born:	28 Jun 1896, Transylvania County, NC
Died:	19 Dec 1972, Oteen VA Hospital, Buncombe County; age 76
Buried:	Turkey Creek Baptist Church
Occupation:	Carpenter and operated Orr's Store
Spouse:	**Emma BROWN**, m. 11 Apr 1920, Transylvania County, NC
Father:	**Samuel ORR**
Mother:	**Mary Emma LYDAY**
Draft Registration:	22, single, farming with his father

[Documentation: Transylvania County BC, Buncombe County DC, Transylvania County Cemetery Survey, TT obituary, Cowart's Index to Marriages, Ancestry.com]

Orr, Clarence E   1,322,760   white
(Surname)   (Christian name)   (Army serial number)   (Race: White or colored)

Residence: _____ Brevard _____ NORTH CAROLINA
         (Street and house number)   (Town or city)   (County)   (State)

Enlisted in NC Gastonia NC   —   July 25/17
Born in   Transylvania Co NC   22 1/12 yrs
Organizations: MG Troop 1 Sep Sq NC NG (Co A 115 MG Bn) to disch

Grades: Pvt 1cl Sept 1/17; Pvt Dec 1/17;

Engagements: —

Wounds or other injuries received in action: None.
Served overseas: May 11/18 to Mch 22/19
Hon. disch. Apr 2/19   on demobilization
Was reported 0   per cent disabled on date of discharge, in view of occupation
Remarks:

SRC Notes: NC NG (North Carolina National Guard) MG Bn (Machine Gun Battalion)

12/21/1972
CLARENCE ORR

Clarence E. Orr, 76, of Pisgah Forest died Tuesday afternoon in Oteen Veterans Hospital after a lengthy illness. He was a lifelong resident of Transylvania County and operated Orr's Store for many years. He was an Army veteran of World War I, having served in Europe with the 30th (Old Hickory) Division. He was active in church affairs and a member of Turkey Creek Baptist Church. Graveside services were conducted Wednesday in Turkey Creek Cemetery.

Surviving are a son, Ralph A. Orr; a brother, Earl Orr; and a sister, Mrs. Marybell Drake.

---

27 Jul 1917   **Brevard News**

HOLDS CHARM FOR RED-BLOODED MEN
Navy With Its High Ideals and Splendid Record, Justifies Nation's Pride
MEN NEEDED FOR SERVICE
Uncle Sam Pays All Expenses and Monthly Wages

"There Is Always Room At The Top" True of the Navy

Harrison Raymond ORR

Born:	25 Mar 1896, Transylvania County, NC
Died:	17 Jun 1981, Oteen VA Hospital, Buncombe County; age 85
Buried:	Oak Forest Cemetery, Etowah
Spouse:	**Ida Lee SHOOK**
Father:	**Robert B. ORR**
Mother:	**Rosanna COLE**
Draft Registration:	Henderson County, 21, single, self-employed farmer

Documentation: Transylvania County BC, Buncombe County DC, findagrave.com, Henderson County Cemetery Book, Ancestry.com]

Orr, Harrison R   3,278,394   1
(surname)   (Christian name)   (Army serial number)   • White • Colored.
Residence: _____ Blantyre   Transylvania   NORTH CAROLINA
(Street and house number)   (Town or city)   (County)   (State)
_____. •Inducted at LB 1 Hendersonvil e NC Jun 25 19 18
Place of birth: Transylvania Co NC   Age or date of birth: Mch 25 1896
Organizations served in, with dates of assignments and transfers: 156 Dep Brig to Nov 26/18;
55 Guard Co Army Serv to June 19/19; 52 Guard Co Army Serv

Grades, with date of appointment: _____
Pvt 1cl Mch 3/19

Engagements: _____

Wounds or other injuries received in action: None
Served overseas from Aug 22/18 to Sept 15/19
Honorably discharged on demobilization   Sept 23/19   from __ to __ , 19___
In view of occupation he was, on date of discharge, reported   0   per cent disabled.

SRC Notes: Dep Brig (Depot Brigade)

Asheville Citizen- Times
6/18/1981
RAYMOND ORR

Raymond Orr, 85, of Horse Shoe, died Wednesday in the Asheville VA Medical Center after an extended illness. A native of Transylvania County, the son of the late Robert and Rosie Ann Cole Orr, he had lived most of his life in Henderson County. He served in the U.S. Army during World War I and worked at Moland-Drysdale Brick Corp. for 36 years before retiring in 1961.

Surviving are his wife, Ida Shook Orr; three sons: Marvin, Raymond Jr. and Samuel Orr; four daughters: Virginia Stepp, Patty Orr, Clair Whitmire and Margie Crane; and a sister, Zenia Justus.

Services were held at the Etowah Baptist Church of which he was a member with burial following in Oak Forest cemetery.

---

18 Jul 1918   Brevard News

Robert Maxwell, a Negro soldier in camp near Pisgah Forest, was drowned in Davidson River Saturday evening while bathing. His body was recovered shortly afterward and was sent to his home at Ranlowles, SC on Monday.

Henry Samuel ORR

Born:	20 Dec 1889, Transylvania County, NC
Died:	18 Jan 1970, Greenville, South Carolina; age 80
Buried:	Greenville Memorial Gardens, Greenville, SC
Spouse(s)	**Julia M. LEDBETTER**, m. 12 Nov 1922, Transylvania County, NC
	Janie McKINNEY
Father:	**Robert B. ORR**
Mother:	**Rosanna COLE**
Draft Registration:	Henderson County, 25, single, self-employed farmer

[Documentation: Ancestry.com, findagrave.com, 1900-1930 Censuses, Cowart's Index to Marriages]

Orr, Henry S		3,278,396	• White • ~~Colored~~	1
(Surname)	(Christian name)	(Army serial number)		

Residence: _____ Blantyre ~~Henderson~~ NORTH CAROLINA
(Street and house number)   (Town or city)   (County)   (State)

~~_____~~ *Inducted at_ Hendersonville NC _____ June 25 18
Place of birth: Transylvania Co NC _____ Age or date of birth: ~~08 20 1892~~ 19___

Organizations served in, with dates of assignments and transfers: FA Repl Dep Camp Jack ___
_____ deen 30 to Aug 8/18; 5 Btry F Repl Regt to disch _____

Grades, with date of appointment: _____
Pvt

Engagements: _____

Wounds or other injuries received in action: None.
Served overseas from †_Aug 21/ 8_ to †_May 1/19_ from †_____ to †_____
Honorably discharged on demobilization ____ May 13/19 _____, 19____
In view of occupation he was, on date of discharge, reported _0_____ per cent disabled.

SRC Notes: FA Repl Dep (Field Artillery Replacement Depot)

Greenville News (SC)
1/19/1970
HENRY S. ORR

Henry Samuel Orr, 78, Standing Springs Community, Greenville, died Sunday. Born in Transylvania County, NC, he was a son of the late Robert and Rosie Cole Orr. He moved to Greenville County in 1938 and lived in the Marietta section before moving to the Standing Springs Community 20 years ago. During World War I, he served with the US Army. He was a member of Pleasant Grove Baptist Church near Hendersonville, NC. His first wife was the late Julia Maybelle Ledbetter Orr.

Surviving are his wife, Janie McKinney Orr; and a son, O. Franklin Orr.

Burial will be in the Greenville Memorial Gardens, Greenville, SC.

> **Dec 1917**   **Brevard News**
> ### LOCAL RED CROSS TO FURNISH 5000 WIPES
> **Telegram From Headquarters In Atlanta Asked For 5000 Gauze Wipes Within Three Weeks**
> Mrs. H.N. Carrier has just received a telegram from the Red Cross headquarters asking this chapter to furnish 5000 wipes for surgical dressings. These are wanted within three weeks. This will necessitate keeping the workroom open every morning and afternoon and very likely 2 or 3 hours every evening. Additional workers will be needed for this emergency work. Anyone willing to help should communicate with Mrs. Carrier.

Robert Lewis ORR

Born:	12 Apr 1893, Transylvania County, NC
Died:	14 Oct 1974, Transylvania County, NC; age 81
Buried:	Davidson River Cemetery
Occupation:	Retired from Carr Lumber Company
Spouse:	**Ida S. R. LYDAY**, m. 25 Aug 1923, Transylvania County, NC
Father:	**Robert B. ORR**
Mother:	**Rosanna COLE**
Draft Registration:	Henderson County, 24, single, logger in Transylvania County

[Documentation: Transylvania County DC, <u>Cowart's Index to Marriages</u>, <u>Transylvania County Cemetery Survey</u>, Ancestry.com]

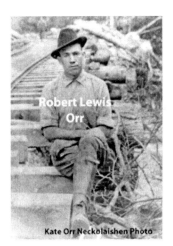

Orr. Robert L. 4,159,430 * White * ~~Colored~~.
(Surname) (Christian name) (Army serial number)

Residence: _____ Blantyre NORTH CAROLINA
(Street and house number) (Town or city) (County) (State)

~~Enlisted in N. C.~~ *Inducted at Hendersonville, NC on July 24 19 18
Place of birth: Transylvania, Co. NC Age or date of birth: Apr 12, 1893
Organizations served in, with dates of assignments and transfers: MG Tng Centre Camp
Hancock Ga to disch.

Grades, with date of appointment: Pvt.

Engagements: _____

Wounds or other injuries received in action: None.
Served overseas from † None to † Jan 13/19. from † _____ to † _____
Honorably discharged on demobilization _____ O , 19_____
In view of occupation he was, on date of discharge, reported _____ per cent disabled.

Kate Orr Neckolaishen Photo

SRC Note: MG Tng (Machine Gun Training)

Hendersonville Times-News
12 Oct 1974
ROBERT L. ORR

Pisgah Forest- Robert L. Orr, 81, of Pisgah Forest, died Monday in a Brevard hospital after a short illness. He was a retired employee of Carr Lumber Co., a WW 1 veteran and a member of Pleasant Grove Baptist Church.

Mr. Orr is survived by four daughters: Mrs. B.C. Brown, Mrs. C.W. Spates, Mrs. J.W. Hud-son and Mrs. Frank E. Tinsley; three sons: Clyde, James L. and Robert E.; two sisters: Mrs. Turley Justice and Mrs. Merrit Duncan; and one brother, Raymond Orr

Funeral services will be at 2 p.m. Wednesday at Pisgah Forest Baptist Church. . Burial will be in Davidson River Cemetery.

Robert Merrill Collection

Sylvester ORR

Born:	20 Apr 1887, Transylvania County, NC.
Died:	26 Sep 1956, Transylvania County, NC; age 69
Buried:	Little River Baptist Church Cemetery
Spouse:	**Eva HOLDEN**
Father:	**Azra ORR**
Mother:	**Lovenia MOORE**
Draft Registration:	30, single, farming and listed his mother as his dependent

[Documentation: Transylvania County DC, <u>Transylvania County Cemetery Survey</u>, Ancestry.com, TT obituary]

Orr, Sylvester 1,863,459 *White
(Surname) (Christian name) (Army serial number)
Residence: RFD 1 Etowah Henderson Transylvania NORTH CAROLINA
(Street and house number) (Town or city) (County) (State)
* Enlisted * R. A. * N. G. * E.R.C. *Inducted at Brevard N C on Sept. 18, 1917
Place of birth: Crab Creek N C Age or date of birth: 30 5/12 yrs
Organizations served in, with dates of assignments and transfers:
Cas Det MD Fld Hosp Cp Jackson SC to Nov 11/17; Fld
Hosp 323 to disch
Grades, with date of appointment:
Ck Aug 1/18

Engagements: xx

Wounds or other injuries received in action: None.
Served overseas from † xx to † , from † to †
Honorably discharged on demobilization Aug 23/19 , 19
In view of occupation he was, on date of discharge, reported 0 per cent disabled.

SRC Notes: Cas Det MD Fld (Casualty Detachment Medical Field)

9/29/1956
SYLVESTER ORR

Funeral services for Sylvester Orr were held Tuesday afternoon at the Little River Baptist Church and burial was in the Little River Cemetery. Mr. Orr died on Sunday while working at his barn. He had been in declining health for some time.

The widow and one brother, C.C. of Penrose survive.

21 Sep 1917   Brevard News
THIRTY-ONE MEN TO CAMP JACKSON Wednesday morning.
. . . Sylvester Orr . . .

Staff Officers at Field Hospital

Haywood County Digital Collection

John Luke OSTEEN

Born:	12 Jun 1892, Transylvania County, NC
Died:	22 Oct 1980, Greensboro, NC; age 88
Buried:	Forest Lawn Cemetery, Greensboro, NC
Spouse:	**Ruth TATUM**
Father:	**Lafayette OSTEEN**
Mother:	**Esther BANTHER**
Draft Registration:	24, single, farming

[Documentation: North Carolina Death Index, findagrave.com, Ancestry.com]

Osteen, John L   1,876,289   • White • Colored.
(Surname)   (Christian name)   (Army serial number)

Residence: Selica   *Transylvania*   NORTH CAROLINA
                (Street and house number)   (Town or city)   (County)   (State)

*Enlisted • R. A. •N. G. • E. R. C. •Inducted at   Brevard N C   on Sept 19, 19 17
Place of birth: New Brevard N C   Age or date of birth: 24 3/12 yrs

Organizations served in, with dates of assignments and transfers:
     M D Amb Co 324; 306 Sn Tn to disch

Grades, with date of appointment:
          Pvt

Engagements:

Wounds or other injuries received in action: None.
Served overseas from   Aug 8/18   to   May 29/19   , from †   to †
Honorably discharged on demobilization   June 3/19   , 19
In view of occupation he was, on date of discharge, reported   0   per cent disabled.

John Luke Osteen

SRC Notes: Amb Co (Ambulance Company) Sn Tn (Sanitation Train)

21 Sep 1917   Brevard News
THIRTY-ONE MEN TO CAMP JACKSON

Forty percent of the certified draft, making 31 men, was ordered to report on Tuesday at 5 P.M. at the office of the local enlistment board and to leave for Camp Jackson, S.C. Wednesday morning.

. . . John Luke Osteen . . .

The men reported the local exemption board Tuesday J.L. Osteen was put in command till the arrival at Camp Jackson and he selected Avery Orr as his assistant.

On Wednesday morning 31 men formed a line at the rooms of the War Department and marched to the depot. There was no roll of drums nor blare of horns but it was, nevertheless, an impressive spectacle. A large crowd was on hand for the good-byes and the young men were cheerful.

14 Dec 1917   Brevard News
VISIT TO CAMP JACKSON

LaFayette Osteen of Selica last week made a pleasant visit to his son J.L. Osteen and other soldier boys at Camp Jackson, spending Sunday at the camp. He says that he was shown the greatest respect by both officers and men and was hospitably entertained, sleeping in a comfortable bed in the barracks and taking meals, which were all one could expect, with the boys. Mr. Osteen found his son was not having good health.

10 May 1918   Brevard News
J. L. OSTEEN WRITES FROM CAMP JACKSON

The following letter, written September 29th to G. E. Lathrop and published with his permission, will be of interest to NEWS readers.

Your cheerful letter received and should have been answered before this, but our mail was hung up because the postman did not have the number of our barrack. We boys have been very fortunate indeed thus far. We are assigned to the Hospital Corps and that is considered one of the best branches of the service. Most of the boys are happy and enjoying camp life to the fullest extent. We have splendid officers. They treat us like men in every respect. Our Lieutenant tells us that, in comparison with the practical experience, which we have had, we are doing the best drilling of any company in the camp. I consider this very complimentary since it was spoken by such a high official.

I was absolutely mistaken in my estimation of camp life. I surely thought it would be rough and tough from beginning to end, but I am forced to confess that I was mistaken. The utmost of kindness exists between the boys, and the officers are very kind and gentlemanly towards the boys.

Tell the other boys that the anticipation of the trip is the greatest burden; that after they reach here they will meet officers who are interested in their personal welfare. Tell the parents not to worry, for their boys will receive the best of care.

We are permitted to attend church on Sundays and that is something a lot of the folks didn't expect. Last night we had preaching here in our barrack, also again tonight.

In regard to Morgan, I have just talked to the Lieutenant about his condition, and he seems to think we can make a soldier out of him. He only got lost instead of running away from camp.

Don't you know I feel somewhat dignified this evening, Sergeant Noble has gone to Columbia and left me in his position.

Mr. Lathrop, let me extend to you my sincere thanks for your past favors and for the assurance of your aid at any time in the future.

In behalf of myself and the other boys I thank you for the magazines. We have read them thoroughly, and at any time we shall be glad to have these things.

Yours sincerely,
John Luke Osteen
Casual Detachment Field Hospital
Barrack No. A 2
Columbia, S.C.

15 Feb 1918   Brevard News
LETTER FROM TRANSYLVANIA   BOY AT CAMP JACKSON
Dear Editor:

Permit a Transylvania boy a short space in your splendid paper and I will give you some idea of what the boys at Camp Jackson are doing. Things at this place are moving along rapidly. Everything is working like machinery. To be out on the drill ground and watch the boys use their rifles, and then stroll to the trenches and watch others, as they successfully do the present trench work, and then as you are almost suddenly deafened by the loud cry out of the big guns not far away it begins to appear like a real business. Skirmishes at night are continually going on, and let not the Calvary men be forgotten, for he is getting thorough training each day.

The writer, with 18 others from Ambulance Co. 321, were sent to the base hospital three months ago from special service and we are still retained. Most of the boys are working in wards. For two months I worked in a ward and found the work rather fascinating, however, at times we had some very sick boys. I am now bookkeeper in the supply office and must confess that I like the official work better than the ward work.

The consoling part to the folks at home will be to know that the sickness in the camp is rapidly decreasing and death rate is much lower than it was three weeks ago. Surely with the coming of the beautiful spring weather everyone will rise up from his bed of affliction. The Transylvania boys are enjoying reasonably good health and no one has been seriously ill since entering camp

Nearly all the Transylvania boys have been taking advantage of the splendid insurance offer made by the government.

Just a word in behalf of the Red Cross. It is doing a great work for the boys in camp. Most of the boys in camp are awarded sweaters and other necessary articles to ward off the cold weather by this grand organization.

And let not the Y.M.C.A. be forgotten. It is wonderful to be telling what this helpful organization is doing for the soldiers. The "Y" furnishes free stationery, ink, pens, pencils and in fact, all things necessary for writing. Also, almost every night entertainments are given for the pleasure of the soldiers. Religious services are held frequently and are largely attended. The "Y" also has a free library, which is used by the soldiers.

We received a copy of the news most every week and it's just like having a letter from home.

Best wishes to all my friends.

John Luke Osteen
Base Hospital, Camp Jackson
Columbia South Carolina

8 Oct 1918   Brevard News
"SOMEWHERE IN FRANCE"
Dear Editor:

I am sure the friends of the Transylvania boys who on active service in France with Ambulance Co 324 will be very happy to hear that they are enjoying the very best of health, as well as the many interesting things of France. France is a wonderful country and we are getting much pleasure from our stay as well as hard work. We don't mind hard work when it's for a just and righteous cause and when we realize that the patriotic people at home are sacrificing so much for the righteous cause.

The spirit that exists among the Transylvanian boys is clearly demonstrated by the fact that when the call comes for volunteers to go near the front for the purpose of rendering first aid work every boy responds, but to our sad disappointment, all are not accepted.

The boys with the immediate company have been very fortunate in that we have been together since their enlistment on September 18, 1917. We consider it grand and often wonder why we have been so fortunate. Our case is about the only one in which so many homeboys were kept together. It certainly has been a pleasure sharing many happy hours describing the exciting things that happened during our boyhood days among those hills of old Transylvania. And, too, it has been a pleasure from the standpoint of news, for when one hears from home he relates the news to the others. Since our arrival bugler Harold Hardin has received one copy of the Brevard News and even though the date was a little old it was handed from boy to boy and each column scanned very closely. It was just like a long letter from home. Never before did we realize the pleasure obtained from our splendid home paper.

Wags. Virgil Merrill, Coy A. Surrett and King S. Whitaker, by their faithful work, are considered among the best wagoners in the company. Cook Walter C Whitmire can make biscuits almost equal to any Transylvania girl. Going some isn't he? Sgt. Avery M. Orr had the pleasure of visiting the front recently with a detail for purpose of rescuing a wrecked ambulance. Sgt. Ernest O. Miller is away from the company for business purposes, but is expected to return soon.

We are all well clad, well fed, and in fact we are well cared for in every respect. Our officers are very much interested in our welfare and favor us in every way possible.

We wish to extend a sincere thanks to our home people for the contributions they have given the Red Cross. The marvelous work done by the Red Cross cannot be described; therefore I shall only say that in our estimation the Red Cross has done more than any other organization towards the comfort of the soldiers.

Let not the faithful Y.M.C.A. workers be forgotten for where ever we are located there is a "Y" man ready to furnish information, all writing material and in fact, aided every way possible. "Y" workers are continually giving amusing entertainment and adding to the pleasures of soldier life. Last Sunday we had two religious services and the hall was packed with eager hearers.

You should see us and the Sammys conversing, or rather trying to, for with most of us our vocabulary is very limited with our French comrades and especially with the Mademoiselles. I fear you would consider it rather comical and consider us more like actors than conversationalists for it seems as if we make more motions than we say in words.

Cheer up, dear friends, for the time of victory is coming and we shall come proudly marching home to parents and friends and live in peace and unity for the days to come. May time speed that day.

John Luke Osteen

John L. Osteen of Selica is now in the Medical Corps of the victorious American Army en route to Berlin.

7 Feb 1919   Brevard News
FROM ACROSS THE WATER

Dear Editor:

Since the strenuous hand of censorship has been lifted to a certain extent, and since we have been permitted to give some of the details of our voyage and experience, I presume the home people will be interested in hearing of some of our actual happenings "over here."

As this is now New Year's Day and we have the afternoon "off" I shall spend my time in writing and shall say in the beginning that I wish for all the folks at home 365 perfectly pleasant days.

How well we remember that memorable day of August 8th 1918 when we set sail for a foreign country not pleasure seeking as many had previous to the out break of the war nor were we permitted the comfort and luxuries of a first class passenger transport. We sailed on an English transport (Nester) accompanied by 14 other troop ships, being guarded by a number of chasers and destroyers. After leaving sight of our own beloved land the first land we saw was Ireland, and let me say, from what we saw of Ireland it is a most wonderful country. The most picturesque hills you ever saw. The next land was the long beard of Scotland; we were very favorably impressed by its magnificent scenery. Having been upon water several days we were homesick for land. We saw many beautiful homes and much farming land; several times we saw laborers tilling the soil near Scotland. We were met by more guards, and about forty chasers and destroyers and also an observation balloon. On our voyage we saw one big iceberg, and many flying fish, small ones of course, also a number of real large swimming ones.

We got off the ship in Liverpool and paraded the city. The people were very enthusiastic and cheered much. We paraded hurriedly and soon left on our voyage by rail. We passed through some of the large cities of England, viz. Birmingham, Derby and others. England is a beautiful country. Everything seems to be uniform.

We landed in a so-called "Rest Camp" but we didn't consider it so for most of the time was spent in taking long hikes, and doing detail work. But really those hikes gave more pleasure than you might think for we always went a new route and visited several places of interest, such as the home of Oliver Cromwell, etc.

We stayed in England about a week and left for France. We went by way of South-Hampton, passed the home of Priscilla, which is spoken of in the "Courtship of Miles Standish." We were less than one night crossing the English Channel, landed in Cherbourg, France then to another "Rest Camp." Spent very little time there. From there we caught a train and rode two days and nights on "Side door Pullmans," crossing the northern part of France, not knowing where we were going. From then on it was a continued move until we landed on the front, in the Lorraine sector on Sept. 21 and here we saw our first actual service. The night of our landing our company relieved another such company. The greatest excitements were air raids most every day or two, enemy planes would come over and soon the aircraft guns would open up. Occasionally Jerry would be brought down. The most exciting air-dual I saw and the one that struck me most forcibly was between a German bombing plane and an English scouting plane. For almost an hour the battle continued but finally the large plane was brought down by the smaller one.

From that sector we went to the western front near Verdun and there we found what we had read of for the past four years. The afternoon of our landing 54 allied planes passed over in battle formation going after Jerry, I suppose. It was impressive to see how systematically they flew. We had entered the zone of war; yes war in every meaning of the word. It was an easy matter to go out on any knoll and watch the shelling of roads. The doleful cry of the cannon ball soon became a common thing as well as a continuous one. It was so wonderful to see how calm both the American and French went about their tasks even if the pensive cry of the shell was about the only thing audible. It was war in the first degree; what we had learned in the past was only a dream. Oh! All the battles I have heard the veterans of the 60th tell of and those I have read of on the pages of history flashed vividly thru my mind. But what I got in reality will stay with me longest. Indeed, "Experience is the greatest school of life."

Our Division 81st (better known as the Wild Cat Division) went over the top at 5:30 A.M. on Friday before the war ceased on the following Monday and the battle never ceased for one hour until 11:00 o'clock sharp on Monday November 11. We made great advancement and took a number of prisoners.

After the signing of the Armistice the rumor soon began that we would leave the front immediately, and sure enough we did, we left hiking, carrying full equipment too. We were on the hike 14 days making over 125 miles. But not a word of resentment did you hear even if at night our closest neighbors were the sweet scented goat and the clucking hen, for we were told we are on our way home.

We are now located in a small town by the name of MussySur-Seine and well cared for but our happiest day will be when orders come to pack up and leave on our homeward voyage.

JOHN LUKE OSTEEN

10/30/1980
JOHN L. OSTEEN

Word has been received here of the death on October 22 of **John Luke Osteen**, 88, a native of Transylvania County, a former state senator and for 30 years chief probation officer of the U.S. Middle District of N.C. Court, at his home in Greensboro.

Mr. Osteen, former principal of Lake Toxaway School left Transylvania County in 1924 to become Deputy Probation Administrator for Western N.C. in Salisbury. In 1928 he moved to Greensboro where he served for 30 years as Chief Probation Officer of the U.S. Middle District Court until his retirement in 1962.

After his retirement, Osteen served a three-year stint as probation officer for Guilford Coun-

run successfully for the state senate. From 1966 to 1968 he was Guilford County's only Republican senator and was minority leader of the Senate during his term. He served as District Chairman of the Republican Party form 1969 to 1970.

Mr. Osteen, who married the former Ruth Tatum of Salisbury, was the father of Attorney William Osteen and Major General John L. Osteen, Jr. Also surviving are four sisters: Belle Rogers, Rita Bryson, Mae Smith and Emma Lance.

Burial in Forest Lawn Cemetery, Greensboro NC

Subchaser #273

SC.273

Naval History Archives

Thomas Everett OSTEEN

Born:	3 Feb 1895, Transylvania County, NC
Died:	1 Jul 1940, Oteen VA Hospital, Buncombe County; age 45
Buried:	Mt. Moriah Baptist Church Cemetery
Spouse(s):	**Goldie McCALL**, m. 28 May 1921, Transylvania County, NC
	Alma LONDON SOUTHERN
Father:	**Joseph H. OSTEEN**
Mother:	**Lydia HARRISON**
Draft Registration:	22, single, farmer

[Documentation: Buncombe County DC, Transylvania County Cemetery Survey, Transylvania County Marriages, US Headstone Application Ancestry.com]

SRC Notes: CAC NC NG (Coast Artillery Corps North Carolina National Guard)

24 Jan 1919   Brevard News
Pvt. Everett Osteen returned home Monday night from France. We were very proud to see him at home again and are hoping to see others returning soon.

14 Feb 1919   Brevard News
Pvt. Everett Osteen, who returned home from France a few weeks ago, is suffering with mumps.

Thomas Zachery OSTEEN

Born:	8 Sep 1889, Transylvania County, NC
Died:	15 May 1928, Oteen VA Hospital, Buncombe County; age 38
Buried:	Oak Grove Cemetery, Brevard
Occupation:	Electrician
Spouse:	**Sallie Rose OWENS**
Mother:	**Nancy OSTEEN**
Draft Registration:	No
Military Marker:	SC PVT 168 Inf. 42 DIV

[Documentation: Buncombe County DC, Application for Veteran's Headstone, Discharge, <u>Transylvania County Cemetery Survey</u>, Ancestry.com]

Osteen, Thomas J 4,159,426 • White ~~Colored~~ 1
(Surname) (Christian name) (Army serial number)

Residence: Etouah Henderson NORTH CAROLINA
(Street and house number) (Town or city) (County) (State)

Place of birth: Henderson Co N C *Inducted at Hendersonville NC on July 24, 1918

Age or date of birth: Oct 21/90

Organizations served in, with dates of assignments and transfers: 53 Dep Brig to disch

Grades, with date of appointment: Pvt

Engagements:

Wounds or other injuries received in action: None.
Served overseas from † no to † from † to †
Honorably discharged on demobilization Dec 29/18, 19
In view of occupation he was, on date of discharge, reported 0 per cent disabled.

2 May 1919   Brevard News
Mrs. T.Z. Osteen has received a telegram announcing the safe arrival of Mr. Osteen from overseas. Mr. Osteen is at Camp Upton, N.Y., and is expected home soon.

5/17/1928
ZACH OSTEEN

Thomas Zachary Osteen, 32, died Tuesday at Oteen Veteran's Hospital. Funeral services will be held in the Oak Grove Chapel and burial will follow in the church cemetery.

Mr. Osteen had been in declining health since suffering injuries while working for the Brevard Light & Power Company at the Sapphire Cotton Mill, on July 2, 1926. A post mortem examination was held by the government doctors at Oteen and disclosed cancerous growth of the intestines. He was a soldier in the World War and was a devout member of the American Legion.

Surviving are his mother, Mrs. Nancy Osteen; his wife and six children, the oldest being 10 years of age.

NATIONAL ARMY CANTONMENT (CAMP)

Camp Wadsworth   Location: Spartanburg, SC   Organization: 27th Division (old 6th)
Troops from New York

Arthur Edward OVENDEN

Born:	23 May 1895, Pittsburgh, PA
Died:	19 Feb 1976, Transylvania County, NC; age 80
Buried:	Gillespie-Evergreen Cemetery
Spouse:	**Clyde GLINN**
Father:	**Thomas OVENDEN**
Mother:	**Edith**
Draft Registration:	Cleveland, OH, 22, an accountant
Military Marker:	PFC US Army WW I

[Documentation: North Carolina Death Collection, <u>Transylvania County Cemetery Survey</u>, 1900-1940 Censuses, Ohio Soldiers in WW I, Ancestry.com]

Name:	**Arthur E. Ovenden**
Age:	23 2/12 Years
Race:	White
Birth Date:	abt 1895
Birth Location:	Pittsburgh, Pennsylvania, USA
Enlistment Date:	2 Aug 1918
Enlistment County:	Cleveland
Enlistment State:	Ohio
Enlistment Division:	National Army
Decorations and Awards:	
Rank:	
Advancement:	
Comments:	13 Service Company Signal Corps to 24 Aug 1918; Co A 220 Field Signal Battalion to Discharge Private, first class 1 Oct 1918. Honorable discharge 1 Feb 1919.

Ohio Soldiers in WW I entry for Arthur E. Ovenden.

2/19/1976
A.R. OVENDEN

Arthur Edward Ovenden, 80, died in a Brevard hospital Thursday morning. He was a native of Pittsburg, Pennsylvania and had resided in Brevard for 26 years. He was a veteran of World War I and was formerly connected with Continental Music Company. He was a member of the Brevard Elk's Lodge.

His wife, Clyde Glinn Ovenden, survives him. Graveside services will be held in Gillespie-Evergreen Cemetery Friday.

Army officers knew that to become good soldiers men had to do more than learn to salute, march in formation and use weapons. A sense of unity and camaraderie builds trust in one another. One method that was extremely effective in trust building was singing. A number of songs became popular among the men at base camps, although some were merely nonsense songs with a good marching beat.

Berlin OWEN

Born:	19 May 1897, Transylvania County, NC
Died:	26 Nov 1977, Oteen VA Hospital, Buncombe County; age 80
Buried:	Pisgah Gardens Cemetery
Spouse:	**Bettie OWEN**, m. 8 Aug 1919, Transylvania County, NC
Father:	**Elijah D. OWEN**
Mother:	**Samantha MOORE**
Draft Registration:	21, single, employed at Toxaway Lumber Company

[Documentation: Transylvania County BC, Buncombe County DC, Transylvania County Cemetery Survey, Ancestry.com, Cowart's Index to Marriages, Asheville C-T obituary]

				1
Owen	Berlin	4,430,516	• White •Colored:	
(Surname)	(Christian name)	(Army serial number)		

Residence: ___R F D #1___ ___Lake Toxaway___ *Transylva..* ___NORTH CAROLINA___
(Street and house number) (Town or city) (County) (State)

•_____ *Inducted at __Brevard N C__ ____ on __Aug 26__, 19__18__
Place of birth: __Lake Toxaway N C__ Age or date of birth: ____ __May 19/97__
Organizations served in, with dates of assignments and transfers: _____
___F A Repl Draft Camp Jackson S C to Dec 12/18;___
___Btry C 60 F A to disch___

Grades, with date of appointment: _____
___Pvt___

Engagements: _____

Wounds or other injuries received in action: None.
Served overseas from †___no___ to †_____, from †_____ to †_____
Honorably discharged on demobilization ___Jan 3/19___, 19_____
In view of occupation he was, on date of discharge, reported ___0___ per cent disabled.

Berlin Owen
1923
Inez Owen Photo

SRC Notes: FA Repl (Field Artillery Replacement)

26 Aug 1918   Brevard News
TWELVE MORE MEN LEFT Monday for Camp Jackson Monday afternoon:
. . . Berlin Owen, Lake Toxaway . . .

Asheville Citizen-Times
11/28/1977
BERLIN OWEN

Berlin Owen, 80, of Lake Toxaway died Saturday in Asheville VA Hospital after a period of declining health. He was a lifelong resident of Transylvania County and the son of the late Elijah D. and Samantha Moore Owen. He was a veteran of World War I, a retired farmer and a merchant. He was also a member of the United Methodist Church.

Mr. Owen is survived by two sons, A. L. Owen and Ray Owen.

Graveside services were held in Pisgah Gardens Cemetery.

---

22 Jun 1917   **Brevard News**
FAVOR DRAFTING PHYSICIANS ALSO
Need For More Medical Men in the Army Very Imperative

DOCTORS NOT VOLUNTEERING

Samuel Kie OWEN

Born:	8 Mar 1896, Haywood County
Died:	12 May 1968, unknown location; age 72
Buried:	Williamette National Cemetery, Portland, OR
Spouse:	**Pearl STATON**, m. 4 Jul 1920, Transylvania County, NC
Father:	**Leander OWEN**
Mother:	**Addie Adeline BYRD**
Draft Registration:	21, single, fireman at the Rosman Extract plant

[Documentation: Haywood County Delayed BC, US Veteran's Gravesite, findagrave.com, Ancestry.com, Cowart's Index to Marriages]

Owen, Samuel Kie 3,277,190 Indian 1
(Surname) (Christian name) (Army serial number) White Colored.

Residence: Rosman Transylvania NORTH CAROLINA
(Street and house number) (Town or city) (County) (State)

*Inducted at Brevard NC on June 25 19 18

Place of birth: Waysinville NC Age or date of birth: Mch 8 1896

Organizations served in, with dates of assignments and transfers:
FA Repl Dep Camp Jackson SC to disch

Grades, with date of appointment:
Pvt

Engagements:

Wounds or other injuries received in action: None,
Served overseas from † Aug 22/18 to † Apr 26/19 from † _____ to † _____
Honorably discharged on demobilization May 13/19 , 19 _____
In view of occupation he was, on date of discharge, reported 0 per cent disabled.

SRC Notes: FA Repl Dep (Field Artillery Replacement Depot)

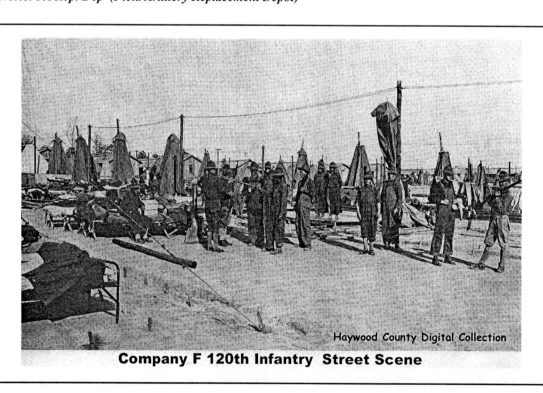

Haywood County Digital Collection

Company F 120th Infantry Street Scene

Samuel Roland OWEN

Born:	13 Jun 1892, Transylvania County, NC
Died:	29 Jun 1970, Oteen VA Hospital, Buncombe County; age 78
Buried:	Gillespie-Evergreen
Occupation:	Retired lumber worker
Spouse:	**Pearl BRACKEN**
Father:	**Elijah D. OWEN**
Mother:	**Samantha MOORE**
Draft Registration:	24, single, farmer

[Documentation: 1900-1920 Censuses, Buncombe County DC, <u>Transylvania County Cemetery Survey</u>, Ancestry.com]

Roland Owen

E.D. Owen Family Photo

SRC Notes: Postal Det (Postal Detachment) FA (Field Artillery)

21 Jun 1918   **Brevard News**
WHITE REGISTRANTS WHO ARE TO LEAVE FOR CAMP JACKSON, S.C.
TUESDAY, JUNE 25th, 1918 AT 3:13 P.M.
. . . Samuel Owen, Rosman . . .

7/2/1970
ROLAND OWEN

Roland Owen, 78, died Monday afternoon in a Buncombe County hospital after a long illness. Services were conducted in the chapel of Frank Moody Funeral Home. Burial was in Gillespie-Evergreen cemetery with members of Brevard VFW Post conducting military graveside rites.

A lifelong resident of Transylvania county, he was a retired farmer and lumberman. He had been elected Register of Deeds for Transylvania County at one time. Mr. Owen was a veteran of World War I.

Surviving are the widow, Mrs. Pearl B. Owen; two sisters: Mrs. Penira Owen and Mrs. Dovie Fisher; and a brother, Berlin Owen.

NATIONAL ARMY CANTONMENT (CAMP)

Camp Hancock   Location: Augusta Ga.   Organization: 28th Division (old 7th)
Troops from Pennsylvania

William McKinley OWEN

Born:	19 Feb 1894, Transylvania County, NC
Died:	4 Apr 1971, Transylvania County, NC; age 77
Buried:	Shoals Creek Cemetery
Occupation:	Farmer
Spouse(s)	**Dora Bertha MORRIS, Julia Mae WOODS**
Father:	**Jack OWEN**
Mother:	**Maggie PARKER**
Draft Registration:	No

[Documentation: Transylvania County DC, 1900-1930 Censuses, TT obituary, Ancestry.com]

11/11/1971
WILLIAM M. OWEN

William McKinley Owen, 77, of Pisgah Forest died last Thursday in Transylvania Community Hospital. He was a retired farmer and a veteran of World War I. He was born in Jackson County but had resided in Transylvania County most of his life. Funeral services were held in the Shoal Creek Baptist Church and burial followed in the church cemetery.

Survivors include his wife, Julia Mae Woods Owen; two stepdaughters: Mrs. Ethel Kilpatrick and Mrs. Corlee Binford; two stepsons: Arthur Riddle and Oscar Riddle; two brothers: Sam Owen and Henson Owen; and one sister, Mrs. Viny Shelton.

William Wiley OWEN

Born:	9 Mar 1894, Transylvania County, NC
Died:	23 Feb 1977, Transylvania County, NC; age 82
Buried:	Macedonia Church Cemetery
Spouse:	**Florence OWEN**
Father:	**Merritt OWEN**
Mother:	**Sarah Dora L. PARKER**
Draft Registration:	23, single, farming

[Documentation: North Carolina Death Collection, <u>Transylvania County Cemetery</u> <u>Survey</u>, findagrave.com, Ancestry.com]

7 Dec 1917   Brevard News
COUNTY CITIZEN VISITS CAMP BOYS

R.M. Powell of Rosman was here last week in his return from Columbia, SC, where he had been to visit some of the Transylvania boys at Camp Jackson. The boys to whom he made a special visit were his son, <u>Wiley Owen</u>, . . . Mr. Powell spent three days in camp and was much pleased with what he saw, especially with the good treatment the boys were receiving from Uncle Sam.

Jess Madison OWENBY

Born:	11 Apr 1896, Transylvania County, NC
Died:	31 Dec 1972, Henderson County, NC; age 76
Buried:	Boylston Baptist Church Cemetery, Henderson County, NC
Occupation:	"Dolphing" in textile industry
Spouse:	**Ruth TURNER**
Father:	**Joseph N. OWENBY**
Mother:	**Martha R. McKINNA**
Draft Registration:	21, single, worked at Brevard Cotton Mill

[Documentation: Henderson County DC, Henderson County Cemeteries, Ancestry.com. Discharge]

Jess Madison Owenby

Harold Turner Photo

Hendersonville Times News
1/2/1973
Jess M. Owenby

Jess Madison Owenby, 76, of 213 Vance Street, died Sunday morning in a Hendersonville hospital after a long illness. He was a native of Transylvania County and had lived in Hendersonville for the past 30 years. He was a member of Calvary Baptist Church and the American Legion.

He is survived by his wife, Ruth Turner Owenby; three sons: Mitchell, Clyde and Roger Owenby; and one sister, Sarah Vaughn

Funeral services were conducted today at Shepherd Memorial Chapel. Burial was in Boylston Baptist Church Cemetery.

No Date   Brevard News

65 DOZEN EGGS FROM RURAL ROUTES

The Woman's National Service League has sprung a new and very clever idea in raising funds for comfort kits for the boys who are about to leave for camps. They have asked every family on the two rural routes to give as many eggs as there are members in the family.

Those who have not had any part in this noble work may send in their eggs at once and they will be gratefully received.

Route No. 1 has furnished 35 ½ dozen eggs and $1.00 in cash.

Route No. 2 has contributed 30 dozen and 2 eggs, one pound of butter and $1.51 in cash.

The eggs are on sale at Brevard Hardware Store.

Herman PARKER

Born:	25 Nov 1896, Transylvania County, NC
Died:	4 Nov 1965, Oteen VA Hospital, Buncombe County; age 68
Buried:	Pisgah Garden Cemetery
Occupation:	Worked in lumber and timber
Spouse:	**Nettie B. CORN**, m. 19 Feb 1921, Transylvania County, NC
Father:	**John H. PARKER**
Mother:	**Rebecca ALLISON**
Draft Registration:	21, single, worked at Carr Lumber Co., claimed his parents and sister as dependents

[Documentation: Buncombe County DC, Transylvania County Cemetery Survey, Cowart's Index to Marriages, FamilySearch.org, Ancestry.com, TT obituary

Herman Parker

Fred Parker Photo

Parker, Herman — 1,863,461 — •White •Colored
(Surname) (Christian name) (Army serial number)

Residence: Penrose TRANSYLVANIA NORTH CAROLINA
(Street and house number) (Town or city) (County) (State)

•Enlisted •R. A. •N. G. •E. R. C. •Inducted at Brevard NC on Sept 18 19 17
Place of birth: Penrose NC Age or date of birth: 22 10/12 yrs
Organizations served in, with dates of assignments and transfers:
324 Amb Co to Nov 26/17; MD Base Hosp Camp Jackson
SC to Disch

Grades, with date of appointment:
Pvt 1cl July 2/18

Engagements:

Wounds or other injuries received in action: None.
Served overseas from † NO to † , from † to †
Honorably discharged on demobilization Mch 27, 19 19
In view of occupation he was, on date of discharge, reported 0 per cent disabled.

SRC Notes: Amb Co (Ambulance Corps) MD (Medical Department)

21 Sep 1917   Brevard News
THIRTY-ONE MEN TO CAMP JACKSON Wednesday morning.
. . . Herman Parker . . .

11/11/1965
HERMAN O. PARKER

Funeral services for Herman O. Parker, 69, were held Saturday at the Pisgah Forest Baptist church with interment in Pisgah Gardens Cemetery. Mr. Parker died Thursday in an Asheville hospital after a long illness. He was a native of Transylvania County and was a retired employee of Carr Lumber Company. He was a veteran of World War I and a member of Pisgah Forest Baptist church.

Survivors include the widow, Mrs. Nettie Corn Parker; 3 sons: A.J., Vella and Fred Parker; 2 brothers: Sam and Vella Parker; and two sisters: Mrs. Belle Corn and Mrs. Dovie Sentelle.

Apr 1918   Brevard News   TRANSYLVANIA'S PATRIOTIC DAY
Commencement Turned Into Patriotic Celebration: County School Children From All Over County Parade Streets; Many Prizes Awarded: Good Speakers at Auditorium

Vella Andrew PARKER

Born: 20 Feb 1893, Transylvania County, NC
Died: 13 May 1982, Transylvania County, NC; age 89
Buried: Enon Baptist Church Cemetery
Spouse: **Katherine Lenora OWENBY**
Father: **John H. PARKER**
Mother: **Rebecca ALLISON**
Draft Registration: Wayne County, MI, 24, single, fireman for Michigan Central RR
Note: Grave marker gives NO military information
Discharge: Inducted 20 Sep 1917 at Detroit, Mich., discharged 3 Jun 1919 at Camp Custer, Mich. CPL. In rank with M.T. Co. #306 (Motor Transport Corps)

[Documentation: North Carolina Birth Index, North Carolina Death Collection, 1900-1930 Censuses, Transylvania County Cemetery Survey, Discharge, Ancestry.com]

5/17/1982
VELLA PARKER

Vella Andrew Parker, 90, died Thursday in Transylvania Community Hospital. He was a native of Transylvania County, a retired woodworker for Carr Lumber Company and a son of the late John Andrew and Rebecca Allison Parker. He was also a veteran of World War I.

Surviving are his wife, Katherine Owenby Parker; and two daughters, Arvella Chambers and Naia Parker.

Services were held last Saturday at Enon Baptist Church of which he was a member. Burial followed in the church cemetery.

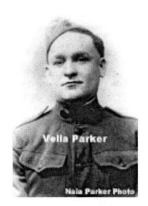

<u>11 May 1917</u>   <u>Brevard News</u>
MORE TRANSYLVANIANS READY FOR WAR

Last week the News published the names of those who, to its knowledge, had offered their services to the government in various branches.

This list has been increased by Dr. E.W. Blythe, Ralph H. Fisher, Rev. John R. Hay, Elda Hallenburg, Robert L. Gash, David Hunt.

Dr. T.J. Summey last week successfully passed the mental and physical examinations in Asheville for the medical corps. While he could render an acceptable service at this time he will be giving up his medical practice unless the call but physicians should become urgent.

The following names were given last week: T.H. Shipman, J.S. Silversteen, Ora L. Jones, W.E. Breese and Thomas Teague. Meynardie Walter Cloud enlisted in the Navy at Brooklyn, NY.

Charlie Y. PATTON

Born:	1 Dec 1895, Transylvania County
Died:	18 Jul 1968, Transylvania County, NC; age 72
Buried:	Davidson River Cemetery
Occupation:	Farmer and merchant
Spouse:	Mrs. **Dora McLEOD**, m. 7 Jan 1924, Transylvania County, NC
Father:	**Joseph J. PATTON**
Mother:	**Anna YONGUE**
Draft Registration:	21, single, merchant
Note:	Death Certificate states 16 Dec 1895 as birth date, draft registration states 16 Oct 1895

[Documentation: Transylvania County DC, Discharge, <u>Cowart's Index to Marriages</u>, <u>Transylvania County Cemetery Survey</u>, TT obituary, Ancestry.com]

Patton, Charlie Y.   4,155,473   • White •Colored

(Surname)   (Christian name)   (Army serial number)

Residence: _____ Davidson River _____ NORTH CAROLINA

(Street and house number)   (Town or city)   (County)   (State)

•_____ •Inducted at Brevard NC _____ on July 24 19 18

Place of birth: Davidson River NC   Age or date of birth: 22 7/12 yrs

Organizations served in, with dates of assignments and transfers: _____

_____ MG Tng C Camp Hancock Ga to Disch _____

Grades, with date of appointment: _____

Sgt Oct 10/18

Engagements: _____

Wounds or other injuries received in action: None.

Served overseas from † No _____ to † _____, from † _____ to † _____

Honorably discharged on demobilization _____ Dec 21, 1918

In view of occupation he was, on date of discharge, reported _____ per cent disabled.

SRC Notes: MG Tng (Machine Gun Training)

7/25/1968
C.Y. PATTON

Charlie Youngue Patton, 72, died last Thursday night in the local hospital after a short illness. He was a lifelong resident of Transylvania County and the son of the late Joseph J. and Annie Yongue Patton. He was engaged in farming and the automotive and service station business before retiring several years ago. He was a veteran of World War I.

Surviving are a daughter, Betty Combs; a son, Charlie Yongue Patton, Jr.; the stepmother, Mrs. Amanda Walker Patton; two sisters: Miss Annie Mae Patton and Mrs. Arch Graham; and two brothers, Joe Patton McLeod and Walker Patton.

Memorial services were held at the Brevard-Davidson River Presbyterian Church of which he was a member, last Saturday.

> In 1912 Congress sactioned the allowance of the War Department of four machine guns per regiment. In 1919, as a result of the experience of the war, the new Army plans provided for an equipment of 336 machine guns per regiment.
>
> The total number of machine guns of American manufacture produced to the end of 1918 was 226,557. In addition there were secured from France and Great Britain 5,300 heavy machine guns.
>
> Orcutt, Louis, **GREAT WAR SUPPLEMENT**, published 1920.

William M. PATTON

Born: 14 Mar 1896, Transylvania County, NC
Died: 20 May 1917, military base; age 21
Buried: Boylston Baptist Church Cemetery, Henderson County, NC
Father: **James PATTON**
Mother: **Caroline SIMPSON**
Draft Registration: No
Note: Service Record Card states he died of an accident at military base

[Documentation: Henderson County Cemeteries, findagrave.com, Ancestry.com]

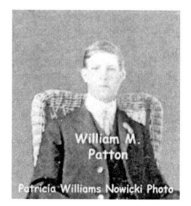

Patton, William M.
(Surname)   (Christian name)   (Army serial number)   * White *Colored*

Residence: _____ Brevard *Transylvania* NORTH CAROLINA
(Street and house number)   (Town or city)   (County)   (State)

* Enlisted * R. A. *N. G. * R. C. *Inducted* Columbus Bks Ohio   on June 26, 19 15
Place of birth: Brevard N.C.   Age or date of birth: 18 3/12 yrs
Organizations served in, with dates of assignments and transfers:
    134 Co CAC Ft H G Wright N.Y. to(   ); 1 Co CAC Ft
    H G Wright N.Y. to death

Grades, with date of appointment:
    Pvt; Pvt lcl ---

Engagements:
    xxx

Wounds or other injuries received in action: * None.
Served overseas from † xxx   to †   , from †   to †
Died of _____ shock from fracture (Accident.) _____ May 20 19 17
                        (Cause and date of death)
Person notified of death: James M Patton   Father
                (Name)   (Degree of relationship)
    RR 2   Brevard   N C.
(No. and street or rural route)   (City, town, or post office)   (State or country)

SRC Notes: CAC (Coast Artillery Corps) William died from shock from a fracture due to an accident.

Of every 100 American soldiers who took part in the war with Germany, two were killed or died of disease during the period of hostilities.

Killed in action:	34,180	
Died of wounds:	14,729	
Total dead:		48,909
Wounded severly	80.130	
Wounded slightly	110,544	
Wounded, degree undetermined	39,400	
Total wounded		230,074
Missing in Action:		2,913
Taken Prisoner:		4,434
Grand Total		286,330

Orcutt, Louis E., **GREAT WAR SUPPLEMENT**, published 1920, p. 119.

Robert PEAHUFF

Born:	9 Jun 1890, Transylvania County, NC
Died:	19 Nov 1955, Transylvania County, NC; age 65
Buried:	Orr Cemetery
Spouse:	**Mary LANDRETH McGAHA**
Father:	**Benjamin PEAHUFF**
Mother:	**Mary Ann CORN**
Draft Registration:	No
Military marker:	NC PVT 318 Field Arty BN WW I

[Documentation: North Carolina Death Collection, <u>Transylvania County Cemetery Survey</u>, Application for Veteran Headstone, Ancestry.com, TT obituary]

1

Peahuff   Robert   1,865,836   • White • ~~Colored~~.
(Surname)   (Christian name)   (Army serial number)

Residence: ____RFD 2_____Brevard___Transylvania_NORTH CAROLINA___
(Street and house number)   (Town or city)   (County)   (State)

• ~~R. A. N. G. E. R. C.~~ •Inducted at _Brevard, NC_____ on_Apr 1_, 19 18
Place of birth: _Brevard, NC_____ Age or date of birth: _____June 17/92__

Organizations served in, with dates of assignments and transfers: _____
_____Btry E 318 FA to disch_____

Grades, with date of appointment: _____
_____Pvt_____

Engagements: _____
_____

Wounds or other injuries received in action: None.
Served overseas from †_Aug 8/18_ to †_June 11/19_ from †_____ to †_____
Honorably discharged on demobilization _June 22/19_____, 19____
In view of occupation he was, on date of discharge, reported ____0_____ per cent disabled.

SRC Notes: FA (Field Artillery)

11/25/1955
ROBERT PEAHUFF

Robert Peahuff, age 65, died suddenly at his Little River home Saturday. Funeral services were held at the Little River Baptist Church, of which he was a member, with burial in the Orr Cemetery. A native of Transylvania County, Mr. Peahuff was a farmer and a veteran of World War I, serving with the 318th Field Artillery Battalion.

He was the son of Mr. and Mrs. Ben Peahuff of Transylvania County.

Survivors include the widow, Mrs. Mary McGaha Peahuff; four sisters: Mrs. Beck Andrews, Mrs. Mamie Powell, Mrs. Sally Patterson and Mrs. Martha Laughton.

Army officers knew that to become good soldiers men had to do more than learn to salute, march in formation and use weapons. A sense of unity and camaraderie builds trust in one another. One method that was extremely effective in trust building was singing. A number of songs became popular among the men at base camps, although some were merely nonsense songs with a good marching beat.

William Henry PERKINS

Born:	11 Jan 1891, Morganton, NC
Died:	15 May 1942, Oteen VA Hospital, Buncombe County; age 51
Buried:	Undetermined Brevard cemetery
Race:	Colored
Occupation:	Logger
Spouse:	**Nina SMITH**, m. 23 Oct 1922, Transylvania County, NC
Father:	**Sandy PERKINS**
Mother:	**Ellen MOORE**
Draft Registration:	25, married, working for Carr Lumber Co

[Documentation: Buncombe County DC, Ancestry.com, Cowart's Index to Marriages, 1900-1930 Censuses]

Perkins William Henry   1 888 236   * ~~White~~ * Colored.
(Surname)   (Christian name)   (Army serial number)

Residence: _____ Brevard   Transylvania NORTH CAROLINA
            (Street and house number)   (Town or city)   (County)   (State)

* ~~xxxxxxxxxxxxx~~ *Inducted at Morganton N C ___ on Apr 30, 1918

Place of birth: __Morganton N C__   Age or date of birth: __27 4/12 yrs__

Organizations served in, with dates of assignments and transfers: _____
_____ Co C 321 Serv Bn to disch _____

Grades, with date of appointment: _____
        Pvt

Engagements: _____

Wounds or other injuries received in action: None.
Served overseas from † __Aug 7/18__ to † __July 7/19__, from † _____ to † _____
Honorably discharged on demobilization __July 18/19__, 19___
In view of occupation he was, on date of discharge, reported ___0___ per cent disabled.

SRC Notes: Serv Bn (Service Battalion)

Monkey Meat and Other Delights

" One of the biggest complaints the Doughboys on the western front had was about the food. The mess sergeant, whose job it was to feed the troops, was regarded as the constant enemy of each soldier. Doughboys loved to complain about the food they were served.

The most hated part of their diet was canned, fatty, corned beef. It was know by a variety of names "corned Willy," "slum," and most commonly, "monkey meat." One soldier wrote home, "The stuff is barely edible when it is hot, but cold it'll kill you."

Unfortunately, most food was eaten cold, at least in the trenches. Fires were strictly forbidden because they gave the enemy an easy target. Sometimes, food was heated in small stoves far behind the lines and brought to the trenches. Usually, however, it was cold by the time it got to the men.

Every once in a while, the men in the front trenches were treated to a cup of coffee. This was prepared by the machine gunner. After he fired off several hundred shots, he would then use the hot gun barrel to instantly boil water."

Stewart, Gail B., **World War I**, Lucent Books, 1991, p. 44

John Lusk PERRY

Born:	13 Jan 1888, Transylvania County, NC
Died:	9 Jan 1955, Oteen VA Hospital, Buncombe County; age 66
Buried:	Dunn's Rock-Connestee Cemetery
Occupation:	Farmer
Spouse:	**Ila HOLDEN**, m. 14 Jan 1920, Transylvania County, NC
Father:	**James B. PERRY**
Mother:	**Synthy Evelyn McCALL**
Draft Registration:	30, married with no children, farming

[Documentation: Buncombe County DC, Transylvania County Birth Index, <u>Transylvania County Cemetery Survey</u>, <u>Cowart's Index to Marriages</u>, Discharge, Application for Veteran Headstone, TT obituary, Ancestry.com]

Perry, John B.   3,215,516. White Colored.   1

Residence: Brevard   Transylvania NORTH CAROLINA
(Street and house number)   (Town or city)   (County)   (State)

...N.C.E.R.C. *Inducted at Brevard N C   Sept 18 19 17
Place of birth: Brevard N C   Age or date of birth: 29 9/12 Yrs

Organizations served in, with dates of assignments and transfers:
Fld Hosp 324 306 Sn Tn to disch

Grades, with date of appointment: Pvt

Engagements:

Wounds or other injuries received in action: None.
Served overseas from † Aug 8/18 to † June 20/19 from † ___ to † ___
Honorably discharged on demobilization   June 29, 19 19
In view of occupation he was, on date of discharge, reported ___ 0 ___ per cent disabled.

John Lusk Perry

Ruth Barton Photo

SRC Notes: Fld Hops (Field Hospital) Sn Tn (Sanitation Train)

<u>21 Sep 1917</u>   <u>Brevard News</u>
THIRTY-ONE MEN TO CAMP JACKSON Wednesday morning.
. . . John Lusk Perry . . .

1/13/1955
JOHN PERRY

John Lusk Perry, 67, died Sunday night in the Veterans' Hospital in Swannanoa following an illness for the past three years. He was a farmer, a native Transylvanian and a veteran of World War I.

Survivors include the widow, Mrs. Ila Holden Perry; one son, Lester; two brothers, Will and James Perry; and three sisters: Mrs. Frank Ball, Mrs. Charlie Hogsed and Mrs. Alice Dixon.

Funeral services for Mr. Perry were held at the Church of God in Brevard and burial followed in the Dunn's Rock cemetery. Legionnaires of the Monroe Wilson post of the American Legion conducted graveside services.

The Rolls Royce was the most successful armored car of the First World War. They became the most extensively used armored car of the war, serving in widely scattered locations - France, Egypt, Gallipoli, South West Africa and East Africa. Operated successfully even under very unfavorable conditions, the Rolls Royce became the standard British type.

McKinley PERRY

Born:	19 Mar 1895, Jackson County, NC
Died:	17 Aug 1937, Transylvania County, NC; age 42
Buried:	Dunn's Creek Baptist Church.
Occupation:	Farmer
Spouse:	**Viola MATHIS**
Father:	**James B. PERRY**
Mother:	**Synthy Evelyn McCALL**
Draft Registration:	No
Military marker:	NC PVT PROVOST Guard CO WW I

[Documentation: Transylvania County DC, Application for Veteran's Headstone, Discharge, <u>Transylvania County Cemetery Survey</u>, Ancestry.com, TT obituary]

McKinley Perry

Ruth Barton Photo

8/19/1937
MACK PERRY

McKinley (Mack) Perry, 41, died Tuesday at the home of his brother, Will Perry, in the See-Off section, from either a weak heart or over-drinking of whiskey. The sheriff and coroner were summoned, and after investigating the matter, decided than an inquest was unnecessary.

Miles Perry, who was at the home of his father the evening before, said that Mack went down to the creek below the house shortly after dark; that Mack had been in a rather nervous and weakened condition due in part to over-drinking; that he and his sister went down to the creek and brought the ill man back to the Will Perry porch where he asked to be laid.

He was left on the porch, apparently the worse for drinking and was discovered there the next morning by Will Perry. He was dead when discovered.

He had been living in South Carolina and had been brought to the Will Perry home by a man who said he would return the next day. This man left the home, presumably to send a doctor from Brevard but a doctor never came.

Mack McKinley was an ex-soldier who enlisted in the Army on Aug. 7 1918 and was honorably discharged on Feb. 18, 1919.

Funeral services were held from the Dunn's Creek church and interment was in the cemetery nearby.

He had a wife and three small children in South Carolina. His mother, three brothers and two sisters also survive him.

Ralph E. PETRIKIN

Born:	22 Nov 1893, Johnstown, PA
Died:	11 Sep 1958, Oteen VA Hospital, Buncombe County; age 64
Buried:	Lakeside Cemetery
Occupation:	Postmaster
Spouse:	**Alberta BURGESS**
Father:	**Albert PETRIKIN**
Mother:	**Caroline BLACKWELL**
Draft Registration:	No
Military marker:	Honorably volunteered Served his country in 2 World Wars US Army 1917-1919 US Marine Corps 1942-1944

[Documentation: Buncombe County DC, Upper Transylvania County, NC Remembered, Ancestry.com, TT obituary]

9/19/1958
RALPH E. PETRIKIN

Last rites for Ralph E. Petrikin, 64, were held at the Lake Toxaway Baptist Church with burial in the church cemetery. Mr. Petrikin died Friday at the Oteen hospital after a brief illness. A native of Johnstown, PA Mr. Petrikin had resided in the Oakland section of Transylvania County for the past 12 years.

Survivors include the widow, Mrs. Alberta Burgess; one son, Thomas Petrikin; and two sisters: Mrs. Dorothy Wilson and Mrs. Ruth Rhodes.

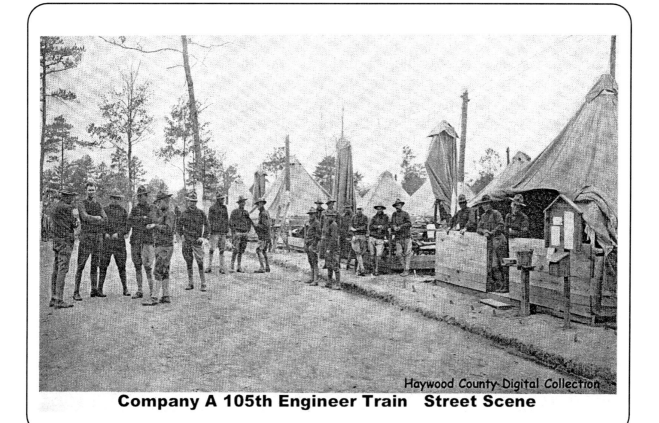

Company A 105th Engineer Train   Street Scene

Jennings Bryan PETTIT, Sr.

Born: 25 Jan 1897, Transylvania County, NC
Died: 16 May 1973, Buncombe County, NC; age 76
Buried: Gillespie-Evergreen Cemetery
Occupation: Shoe repairman
Spouse: **Lottie Mae NORTON**
Father: **Frances Marion PETTIT**
Mother: **Lydia GALLOWAY**
Draft Registration: Pickens, SC, 21, single
Military Marker: NC PVT US Army WW I

[Documentation: Discharge, Buncombe County Death Certificate, Transylvania County Cemetery Survey, Ancestry.com, TT obituary]

5/24/1973
JENNINGS B. PETTIT, Sr.

Jennings Bryan Pettit, Sr., 76, died in an Asheville hospital Wednesday after a short illness. He was a native of Transylvania County and an Army veteran of World War I with service overseas in Europe. He was founder and owner of Pettit's Shoe Shop Service for many years. He was a member of the Monroe Wilson Post, American Legion No. 68, and V.F.W. Post No. 4309.

Services were conducted in the First Baptist Church of which he was a member, and burial was in Gillespie-Evergreen cemetery.

Surviving are the wife, Mrs. Lottie Mae Norton Pettit; two daughters: Mrs. Alice McCall and Mrs. Eleanor Tinsley; two sons: Bruce and Bryan Pettit; two bothers: John F. and James M. Pettit; and one sister, Mrs. Mary Lee Tinsley.

---

21 Mar 1919   Brevard News

SHALL WE WELCOME THE BOYS HOME?

When the 1st group of Transylvania boys who responded to the Selective Draft call were ready to leave Brevard, a farewell mass meeting was held to hearten them, and they appreciated it. Most of the other groups who left later were accompanied to the train by a procession, and presented with Comfort Kits, etc. The leaving show had to be done, but we ought not to leave the return undone.

When the boys who volunteered without waiting to be drafted went away to become a part of the now famous 30th and other divisions, little interest was shown in their departure because at that stage of the War our country had not caught the spirit of those volunteers.

The 30th division is now on its way home. Is it not time that we plan to give these boys a royal welcome back to Brevard in Transylvania County? Those who are already here can be included in this first special reception, and later a general Homecoming Welcome can be given when the last of our boys come back.

In both of these programs of welcome, the Women's League should have a part, for they were the first to begin ministering to the boys; the Red Cross should have a part for it ministered to bodily welfare and comfort of the boys in khaki; the church should be a part for it administered to the spiritual welfare, strengthened the morale of the fighting man while it kept the home-fires burning; and the County itself should have a part in it because it gave of its sturdy sons to turn the tide backward, break the Hindenburg line and with it the spirit of the Hun. Let there be no delay in beginning preparation for welcoming our heroes home.

W.E. Poovey

Sherman PHILLIPS

Born:	17 Mar 1895, Jackson County, NC
Died:	2 Mar 1969, Henderson County, NC; he was 73
Buried:	Rock Bridge Cemetery, Jackson County
Occupation:	Farmer and timber worker
Spouse:	**Birdie ASHE**, m. 19 Jun 1925, Transylvania County
Father:	**John Wesley PHILLIPS**
Mother:	**Artie Jane CRAWFORD**
Draft Registration:	22, single and farming

[Documentation; Henderson County DC, 1900-1940 censuses, Ancestry.com, findagrave.com]

Hendersonville Times News
3/4/1969
SHERMAN PHILLIPS

Sherman Phillips, 73, of Brevard, died Sunday. Services will be held at 2 p.m. Wednesday in Wolf Creek Baptist church, of which he was a member and former deacon. Burial will be in Canada Cemetery.

Surviving in addition to Mrs. Galloway are four sons: Talmadge, Tillman, Carrell and Theodore Phillips; three sisters: Mrs. Howard Owen, Mrs. Margaret Brown and Miss Stella Phillips; and two brothers: George and John Phillips.

Mr. Phillips had lived in the Canada section of Jackson County until he moved to Brevard four years ago where he made his home with a daughter, Mrs. Mildred Galloway.

---

25 July 1918   Brevard News
25,000 WOMEN WANTED AS NURSES

The government is calling for 25,000 young women to join the United States Student Nurse Reserve and hold themselves in readiness training for service as nurses. The war is creating unprecedented demand for nurses. Only those who have taken full training course are eligible for service with our forces overseas. These nurses are being drawn largely from hospitals at home. Student nurses enrolled for the full training course of from two to three years must fill their places. Every young woman who enrolls in the United States Student Nurse Reserve is releasing a nurse for service at the front and swelling the home Army which we must rely on to act as air our 2nd line of hospital defense.

The call is for women between the ages of nineteen and thirty -five. Intelligent, responsible women of good education and sound mind are wanted--the pick of the country. A college education is a valuable asset and many hospitals will give credit for it. Credit will also be given for special scientific equipment or for preliminary training in nursing, such as that given in special courses now being conducted at various colleges and schools. Some schools, on the other hand, do not even require a full high school education.

Women will be given an opportunity to enroll in the United States Student Nurse Reserve in any one of the 3 ways:

(1) As engaging to hold themselves in readiness until April 1, 1919, to accept assignments to nurses training schools.

(2) As desiring to become candidates for the Army nursing school recently established by authority of the war Department, with branch schools in selected military hospitals.

(3) As engaging to hold themselves in readiness until April 1, 1919, to accept assignments to either a civilian training school or the Army Nursing School.

Arthur H. PLEMONS

Born:	26 Sep 1890, Buncombe County, NC
Died:	12 Dec 1944, South Carolina; age 54
Buried:	Friendship Baptist Church Cemetery, Lyman, SC
Father:	**John PLEMONS**
Mother:	**Martha Susana REED**
Draft Registration:	No
Military Marker:	South Carolina PVT 21 ENGRS

[Documentation: Ancestry.com, findagrave.com, Application for Veteran Headstone]

Plemons,	Arthur H.	176,435	White	1¼
(Surname)	(Christian name)	(Army serial number)	(Race: White or colored)	

Residence: _____ Blantyre _Transylvania_ NORTH CAROLINA
(Street and house number)   (Town or city)   (County)   (State)

* Enlisted in   NA Ft Bliss Tex   Dec 4/17   —
† Born in   Asheville N.C.   27 2/12 yrs   —
Organizations: Co F 21 Engrs to disch   —

Grades: Pvt   —   —

Engagements: —   —

Wounds or other injuries received in action: None.   —
‡ Served overseas: Dec 26/17 to June 9/19   —
§ Hon. disch.   June 21/19   on demobilization   —
Was reported   0   per cent disabled on date of discharge, in view of occupation.   —
Remarks: —   —

SRC NOTES: Engrs (Engineers)

Greenville News (SC)
ARTHUR H. PLEMMONS
12/13/1944

Arthur H. Plemmons, 54, died at a Veterans Hospital at Lake City, Florida this morning after two years of declining health. The body will arrive in Greer Thursday and funeral plans will be announced.

He is survived by two brothers, L.B. and E.J. Plemmons; and four sisters: Mrs. B.C. Comer, Mrs. A.B. Davis, Mrs. W.L. Ivey and Mrs. Leonard Wood.

Note: found Plemmons spelled with single and double M's.

---

2 Nov 1917   **Brevard News**   ANNOUNCEMENT

The recent War Tax on Theaters and Moving Pictures necessitates an increase in the price of admission. The law requires that all children not in arms as well as adults shall pay this tax. The greater part of exhibitors have advanced their 10 cents admission to 15 cents and are keeping the 5 cents admission the same.

Whether we can give you a high-class feature at 15 cents remains to be seen, but we shall endeavor to do it. The admission for a time will be adults 15 cents. Children not in arms and under 12 years of age 5 cents.

Brevard Amusement Co.
F.D. Clement, Manager

Judson L. PLOTT

Born:	11 Aug 1894, Jackson County, NC
Died:	3 Dec 1966, Oteen VA Hospital, Buncombe County; age 72
Buried:	Pisgah Gardens Cemetery
Occupation:	Machine tender
Spouse:	**Sallie OSTEEN**, m. 11 Jul 1923, Transylvania County, NC
	Billie Cecilia NICHOLSON
Father:	**Robert PLOTT**
Mother:	**Margaret CRAWFORD**
Draft Registration:	22, single, brakeman on Gloucester Lumber Co. train
Military Marker:	NC PFC 83 CO Trans Corps WW I

Documentation: Buncombe County DC, <u>Cowart's Index to Marriages</u>, <u>Transylvania County Cemetery Survey</u>, Discharge, Ancestry.com, TT obituary]

```
                                                                            1
Plott, Judson L.              1,872,942        • White • Colored:
      (Surname)       (Christian name)    (Army serial number)

Residence: _____ Rosman  Transylvania  NORTH CAROLINA
            (Street and house number)  (Town or city)  (County)  (State)
████████████████████, •Inducted at  Brevard, N.C. Apr 26/18
                                              on _____, 19__
Place of birth: __Balsam, N.C.__   Age or date of birth: __23 8/12 yrs__
Organizations served in, with dates of assignments and transfers: _____
      Co A 51 Engrs to Dec 1/18; 83 Co TC to disch

Grades, with date of appointment: _____
      Pvt lcl May 13/19

Engagements: _____

Wounds or other injuries received in action: None.
Served overseas from † June 26/18 † July 16/19 from † _____ to † _____
Honorably discharged on demobilization __July 27/19__ , 19__
In view of occupation he was, on date of discharge, reported ___0___ per cent disabled.
```

SRC Notes: TC (Transportation Corps)

12/8/1966
JUDSON L. PLOTT

Judson Lee Plott, 72, Pisgah Forest, died in an Asheville hospital December 3rd following a long illness. He was a native of Jackson County but he had lived in Transylvania County for a number of years. He was a veteran of World War I and a retired employee of Olin Mathieson Chemical Corporation.

Surviving are the wife, Billie Cecilia Plott; four sisters: Adelia Hawkins, Annie Bryson, Harriett Lowery and Marcella Brooks; one half brother, Guy Jones; three stepsons: Tom and Sam Jordan and Emmett Weeks; and one stepdaughter, Julia Winchester.

Funeral services were held in the chapel of Frank Moody Funeral Home December 5th and burial followed in the Pisgah Gardens Cemetery

---

NATIONAL ARMY CANTONMENT (CAMP)

Camp Sevier   Location: Greenville, SC   Establishment: 30th (Old 9th) Division
Troops from Tennessee, North Carolina and South Carolina

Clarence Franklin POOLE

Born:	11 Sep 1895, Jellico, TN
Died:	28 May 1957, Transylvania County, NC; age 61
Buried:	Gillespie-Evergreen Cemetery
Occupation:	Rail road clerk
Spouse:	**Maude BRYSON**, m. 27 Feb 1921, Transylvania County, NC
Father:	**Newton POOLE**
Mother:	**Linda Mae SMITH (Transylvania County DC)**
Draft Registration:	21, single clerking for Southern Railroad
Note:	Grave marker gives NO military information

[Documentation: Transylvania County DC, Transylvania County Cemetery Survey, Cowart's Index to Marriages, Ancestry.com, TT obituary]

5/30/1957
C.F. POOLE

Funeral services for Clarence Franklin Poole, 62, who died last Saturday after a long illness, were held Sunday afternoon here at the First Baptist Church. Burial followed in the Gillespie-Evergreen Cemetery with Masonic Rites.

Surviving are his wife, Maude Bryson Poole; a son, C.F. Russ Poole; two daughters: Dorothy Plemmons and Joan Holman; his mother, Brenda Mae Fuller; a brother, Herbert; and a half brother, Joe Poole.

Mr. Poole worked for the past 35 years for the Southern Railway. He was a member of the First Baptist Church and the Dunn's Rock Masonic Lodge.

Semaphore Signaling Camp Jackson, Columbia, SC

Edwin Ally POOR

Born:	24 Jan 1894, Transylvania County, NC
Died:	30 Jan 1932, Transylvania County, NC; age 38
Buried:	Davidson River Cemetery
Occupation:	Carpenter
Father:	**Edwin POOR**
Mother:	**Margaret J. PATTON**
Draft Registration:	23, single and farming

[Documentation: Transylvania County DC, <u>Transylvania County Cemetery Survey</u>, Ancestry.com, Brevard News obituary]

SRC Notes: NG (National Guard) M G Trp (Machine Gun Troops)

2/4/1932
E.A. POOR

E.A. Poor, 38, son of Maggie Poor, who died at his home Saturday from a heart attack was buried at Davidson River cemetery Sunday afternoon.

Mr. Poor is of a very prominent family and he was well known in Transylvania County. He was taken suddenly ill Saturday morning, his condition growing worse as the day passed. He was a carpenter by trade and a veteran of World War I.

Survivors include his mother, Mrs. Maggie Poor; one sister, Mrs. Alfred Allison; and three brothers: A.P., Eugene and Jack Poor

---

FACTS FOR US SOLDIERS FOR WORLD WAR I

Prisoners:	Unaccounted for	15	
	Died	147	
	Repatriated	<u>4,270</u>	
	Total Prisoners		4,432

Orcutt, Louis, **THE GREAT SUPPLEMENT**, pub. 1920, p. 286

Carl Burrell POWELL

Born:	8 Feb 1897, Transylvania County, NC
Died:	28 Aug 1956, Buncombe County, NC; age 59
Buried:	Shepherd Memorial Park Cemetery, Henderson County, NC
Occupation:	Building contractor
Spouse:	**Augusta HOOTS**
Father:	**John E. POWELL**
Mother:	**Alice McCALL**
Draft Registration:	24, single working at Brevard Tanning Company

[Documentation: Buncombe County DC, <u>Henderson County Cemeteries</u>, Application for Veteran Headstone, Ancestry.com]

Powell, Carl B. 4,483,286 *White *~~Colored~~

(Surname) (Christian name) (Army serial number)

Residence: _____ Blantyre _____ NORTH CAROLINA

(Street and house number) (Town or city) (County) (State)

~~Enlisted~~ N.C. *Inducted at Hendersonville NC on Aug 26, 18

Place of birth: Blantyre, N.C. Age or date of birth: 21 6/12 yrs

Organizations served in, with dates of assignments and transfers:

Co I 4 Prov Regt 156 D.B. to Sept 5/18; Btry E 2 Regt ARD to Oct 17/18; Btry C 2nd Regt FARD to Nov 7/18;

Grades, with date of appointment: 6 Btry NARD to Nov 21/18; Btry C 2nd Regt

Remarks (continued): FARD to disch.

Engagements: xx

Wounds or other injuries received in action: None.

Served overseas from † None to † _____, from † _____ to † _____

Honorably discharged on demobilization Dec 23/18, 19___

In view of occupation he was, on date of discharge, reported 0 per cent disabled.

SRC Notes: Prov Regt (Provost Regiment) FARD (Field Artillery Replacement Depot) NARD (National Army Replacement Depot)

APPLICATION FOR HEADSTONE OR MARKER

POWELL, CARL BURRELL

ENLISTMENT DATE: 8-26-18 DISCHARGE: 12-23-18

SERVICE NO.: 4 483 286 xc PENSION OR VA CLAIM NO.: 1 538 301

STATE: N.C. GRADE: Pvt.

BRANCH OF SERVICE: Btry C 2nd Regt F.A. Rpl. Dept ARMY

DATE OF BIRTH: 2-18-97 DATE OF DEATH: 8-28-56

SHIP TO: Shepherd Memorial Park, Inc. Hendersonville, N.C.

FREIGHT STATION: Hendersonville, N.C.

NAME AND LOCATION OF CEMETERY: Shepherd Memorial Park, Henderson C

SIGNATURE: M. Shepherd DATE: 20Aug57

RECEIVED: AUG 23 1957

RL. 3980 JAS H. MATTHEWS Co. PITTSBURGH, PA.

ORDERED: 17 SEP 1957

NAME AND ADDRESS OF APPLICANT: Betty S. Powell 155½ Pennsylvania Ave. Asheville, NC

SIGNATURE OF APPLICANT: Betty S. Powell DATE: 7-31-57

NATIONAL ARMY CANTONMENT (CAMP)

Camp Wheeler Location: Macon, Ga. Establishment: 31st (old 10th) Division
Troops from Georgia, Alabama and Florida

Roman Cornelius POWELL

Born:	14 May 1894, Transylvania County, NC
Died:	29 Sep 1985, Transylvania County, NC; age 91
Buried:	Galloway Cemetery in East Fork
Spouse:	**Annie MEECE**, m. 8 Nov 1923, Transylvania County, NC
Father:	**Robert M POWELL**
Mother:	**Texana MORGAN**
Draft Registration:	23, single and farming

[Documentation: North Carolina Death Collection, Cowart's Index to Marriages, 1910-1930 Censuses, Discharge, findagrave.com, Ancestry.com]

Roman Cornelius Powell

Dorene Mahoney Photo

7 Dec 1917   Brevard News
COUNTY CITIZEN VISITS CAMP BOYS
R.M. Powell of Rosman was here last week in his return from Columbia, SC, where he had been to visit some of the Transylvania boys at Camp Jackson. The boys to whom he made a special visit were his son R.C. Powell, Pierce Aiken, Wiley Owen, Walter Whitmire and Bill Bowman. Mr. Powell spent three days in camp and was much pleased with what he saw, especially with the good treatment the boys were receiving from Uncle Sam.

Author's Note: From all information gathered from the Brevard News articles, visitors to the a military base were allow to live in the barracks and eat meals in the dining room with the soldiers.

10//3/1985
R.C. POWELL
Roman Cornelius Powell, 91, died Sunday at his residence. He was a native of Transylvania County and a son of the late R.M. and Texanna Morgan Powell. He was a World War I Army veteran and a farmer.

Surviving are his wife, Annie Meece Powell; two daughters, Josephine P. Chappell and Norma P. Raines; three sons: Ernest, Melvin L. and Charles W. Powell; a sister, Rhoda P. Chapman; and two brothers, Fields and Leason Powell.

Services were Wednesday in Middle Fork Baptist Church. Burial will be in the church cemetery with American Legion conducting military rites.

Homer PRICE

Born:	16 Jan 1896, Henderson County, NC
Died:	3 Feb 1975, Transylvania County, NC; age 79
Buried:	Cooper's Cemetery
Race:	Colored
Spouse:	**Tena BAILEY**
Father:	**Richard PRICE**
Draft Registration:	21, single, worked for Joseph Silversteen

[Documentation: Transylvania County DC, Discharge, 1930 Census, Ancestry.com]

Price, Homer   1,888,255   ~~White~~ * Colored.
(Surname)   (Christian name)   (Army serial number)

Residence: _____ Breward _____ NORTH CAROLINA
    (Street and house number)   (Town or city)   (County)   (State)

_____. *Inducted at Breward N.C. on Apr 30, 19 18
Place of birth: Breward N.C.   Age or date of birth: 22 4/12 yrs

Organizations served in, with dates of assignments and transfers: _____
    156 Dep Brig to July 25/18; 152 Dep Brig to disch

Grades, with date of appointment: _____
    Pvt

Engagements: _____

Wounds or other injuries received in action: None.
Served overseas from †None to †_____, from †_____ to †_____
Honorably discharged on demobilization   Feb 20/19, 19___
In view of occupation he was, on date of discharge, reported _____ per cent disabled.

Hendersonville Times News
2/6/1976
HOMER PRICE

Homer Price of Cedar Crest Apt. 2, died Monday at his home. A veteran of World War I, he had lived in Brevard for many years. He is survived by his daughter, Martha L. Jeter of Menlo Park CA; a niece, Marjorie Logan of New York; and a nephew, John Gash of Pittsburgh PA;

Funeral services will be at 2 p.m. Friday at Bethel Baptist Church, of which he was a member. Burial will be in Cooper Cemetery.

---

12 Jul 1918   Brevard News
HOME SERVICE WORK OF LOCAL RED CROSS

The Transylvania chapter of the American Red Cross has provided a place where information concerning allotments, allowances, power of attorney, insurance, etc., for families of men in service can be obtained. Anyone interested may call at the U. D.C. library at Brevard on any Tuesday morning between the hours of 10:30 and 12:30, and any Friday afternoon from 4 to 6 o'clock, beginning Tuesday morning, July 16th.

Members of soldiers families or young men who are to enter the Army or Navy may come and find out, free of charge all about your rights under this new law.

The home service committee is glad to be of service to you in this way, just as we stand solid to help or advise you in any matter which may be troubling you because of the absence of a man from your family.

Mrs. Joseph S. Silverstein,   Chairman of the Home Service Committee

Jesse L. QUINN

Born:	19 Jan 1897, McDowell County, NC
Died:	11 Jun 1953, Oteen VA Hospital, Buncombe County; age 56
Buried:	Piney Grove Baptist Cemetery, Old Fort, NC
Occupation:	Brick mason
Spouse:	**Pearl MORROW**
Father:	**James S. QUINN**
Mother:	**Susie PITTMAN**
Draft Registration:	McDowell County, 21, single and farming in Transylvania County

[Documentation: Buncombe County DC, Application for Veteran Headstone, findagrave.com, Ancestry.com]

Quinn, Jesse L   4,136,076   • White •Colored•
(Surname)   (Christian name)   (Army serial number)

Residence: _____ Rosman _Transylvania_ NORTH CAROLINA
          (Street and house number) (Town or city) (County) (State)
                    Marion N C Aug 25/18
•_____ •Inducted at _____, 19__
Place of birth: _Graphiteville N C_   Age or date of birth: __June 2/97__
Organizations served in, with dates of assignments and transfers: _____
          156 Dep Brig to disch

Grades, with date of appointment: _____
          Pvt

Engagements: _____

Wounds or other injuries received in action: None.
Served overseas from † __None__ to † _____ from† _____ to † _____
Honorably discharged on demobilization _____ Dec 7/18 _____, 19____
In view of occupation he was, on date of discharge, reported ____0____ per cent disabled.

FACTS FOR FATALITIES FOR US SOLDIERS

Killed in Action:	34,248
Died of Disease:	23,430
Died of Wounds:	13,700
Died of Accidents:	2,019
Drown:	300
Suicide:	272
Murder:	154
Executed by Court Martial:	10
Other Known Causes:	489
Causes Undetermined:	1,839
Presumed Dead:	650
Total Dead:	77,118

Author's Notes:
1. Found no explanation for "Other Known Causes".
2. Three categories: "Presumed Dead" and "Missing in Action" "Unaccounted For" were listed in the facts section and all had different numbers. There was no explanation to verify the numbers that were posted.
3. "Causes Undetermined" gives one reason to question how that category was defined.

365

Abner Ewart RAINES

Born: 23 Sep 1888, Henderson County, NC
Died: 11 Dec 1974, Oteen VA Hospital, Buncombe County; age 86
Buried: Crab Creek Baptist Church Cemetery, Henderson County, NC
Occupation: US Forestry Service
Father: **Robert L. RAINES**
Mother: **Sarah SENTELL**
Draft Registration: 28, single, listed both parents as dependents

[Documentation: Buncombe County DC, Discharge, Ancestry.com]

Raines, Abner E.   4,159,480   * White * Colored
(Surname)   (Christian name)   (Army serial number)

Residence: _____ Route 2 _____ Brevard _Transylvania_ NORTH CAROLINA
            (Street and house number)   (Town or city)   (County)   (State)

*Inducted at Brevard Transylvania NC July 24 18
Place of birth: Henderson Co NC   Age or date of birth: Sept 23/88
Organizations served in, with dates of assignments and transfers: MG Tng Center Camp
Hancock Ga to Dec 11/18; 53 Dep Brig to disch

Grades, with date of appointment: Pvt

Engagements:

Wounds or other injuries received in action: None.
Served overseas from † NO ____ to † ____, from † ____ to † ____
Honorably discharged on demobilization ____ Mch 20, 19 19
In view of occupation he was, on date of discharge, reported ____ 0 ____ per cent disabled.

SRC Notes: MG Tng (Machine Gun Training)

18 Jul 1918   Brevard News
23 MORE MEN TO LEAVE JULY 24, 1918
Following is a list of white registrants for induction on July 24th, 1918 for Camp Hancock, Ga., who will leave on the 3:13 train:
. . . Abner Ewart Raines, Brevard R. 2 . . .

12/16/1974
E.A. RAINES

Ewart Abner Raines, 86, died in the Veterans Hospital at Oteen Wednesday. He was a native of Henderson County since childhood. He was the son of the late Robert and Sarah Sentell Raines. He was a retired employee of the US Forestry Service. He was an Army veteran of World War I. For some time he had resided with a niece, Mrs. Catherine R. Corn.

Services were held at Turkey Creek Baptist Church and the burial was in Crab Creek Cemetery in Henderson County.

> Georgia played a giant role during World War I. The state was home to more training camps than any other state and by the war's end had contributed more than 100,000 soldiers to the war. The state had five major Federal military installations when the US declared war in 1917. Fort McPherson, the oldest, located near Atlanta, Fort Oglethorpe constructed near the Tennessee border, Fort Screen at Type Island, Augusta housed the oldest federal arsenal, the Arsenal of Augusta and the army's second military airfield, Camp Hancock was also at Augusta, Georgia.

Louis Buford RAINES

Born:	25 Nov 1892, Transylvania County, NC
Died:	2 Nov 1918, Camp Hancock, Augusta, GA; age 25
Buried:	Galloway Cemetery in East Fork
Father;	**Robert T. RAINES**
Mother:	**Clarinda A. GALLOWAY**
Draft Registration:	No
Note:	Grave marker does NOT give military information

[Documentation: Transylvania County Cemetery Survey, 1900 Census, Ancestry.com]

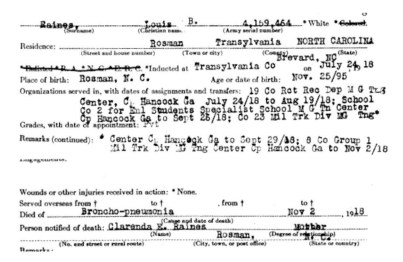

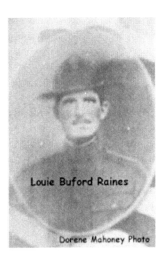

Louie Buford Raines

Dorene Mahoney Photo

SRC Notes: Rct Rec Dep MG Trg (Railroad Transportation Corps Receiving Depot Machine Gun Training) Mil Trk Div MG Tng (Military Truck Division Machine Gun Training)

18 Jul 1918   Brevard News
23 MORE MEN TO LEAVE JULY 24, 1918
Following is a list of white registrants for induction on July 24th, 1918 for Camp Hancock, Ga., who will leave on the 3:13 train:
. . . Louie Raines, Rosman . . .

Clarinda A. Galloway Raines

Louis Buford Raines

Dorene Mahoney Photo

> A family story that was shared to me is that Mrs. Clarinda Raines had lost her husband some years prior to the war and had raised the family with modest means. Louis was drafted and served from 24 July 1918 until his death 2 Nov 1918 of bronchial pneumonia at Camp Hancock, Georgia. At the time of his death she had never had photo made of the two of them together. She paid a photographer to make her photo with the military photo of Louis on a table beside her. This was the only photo she had "of the two of them together."
>
> No obituary has been found for his death.

Samuel Clemay RAINES

Born: 29 Oct 1892, Henderson County, NC
Died: 7 Jul 1964, Transylvania County, NC; age 71
Buried: Crab Creek Baptist Church Cemetery, Henderson Co. NC
Occupation: Farming
Spouse: **Eva BROWN**
Father: **Robert Lewis RAINES**
Mother: **Sarah E. SENTELLE**
Draft Registration: 25, single and farming
Discharge: Inducted 26 Aug 1918 at Brevard, NC and discharged 10 Dec 1918 at Camp Jackson, SC. He was a Private in Battery D 7th Regiment Field Artillery United States Army.

[Documentation: Transylvania County DC, findagrave.com, Discharge, Ancestry.com, TT obituary]

<u>26 Aug 1918</u>   <u>Brevard News</u>
TWELVE MORE MEN LEFT MONDAY
The following men were entrained for Camp Jackson Monday afternoon:
….Samuel Clemsey Raines, Brevard R.F.D. . . . .

7/9/1964
SAMUEL C. RAINES

Samuel Clemmey Raines, 71, died Tuesday at his home in Pisgah Forest after a brief illness. A native of Henderson County, he had lived in Transylvania County most of his life. He served in the U.S. Army during World War I and had worked for the Vanderbilt Estate and the U.S. Forestry Service.

Survivors include the widow, Mrs. Eva Brown Raines; a daughter, Mrs. CaLenne Corn; a son, William C. Raines; and a brother, Abner Ewan Raines.

Funeral services for Samuel Raines were held Thursday at the Turkey Creek Baptist Church with burial in the Crab Creek cemetery.

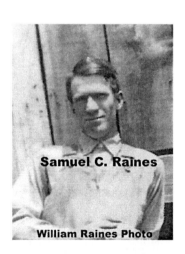

Samuel C. Raines

William Raines Photo

Photo # NH 78919 Crewmen on USS E 2 WW I

Naval History Archives

Ralph Heyward RAMSEY, Jr.

Born:	7 Apr 1900, Greenville County, SC
Died:	17 Jan 1984, Transylvania County, NC; age 83
Buried:	Gillespie-Evergreen Cemetery
Occupation:	Attorney
Spouse:	**Mary Dick ALFORD**
Father:	**Ralph Heyward RAMSEY, Sr.**
Mother:	**Una WELLS**
Draft Registration:	19, single, student in Wedgefield, Sumter, SC

[Documentation: Roster of WWI Veterans from American Legion 50ᵗʰ Anniversary celebration; NC Death Collection; findagrave.com; 1900, 1930 and 1940 Censuses; obit]

1/19/1984
RALPH RAMSEY

Ralph Heyward Ramsey, Jr., 83, died Tuesday afternoon. He was a native of Wedgefield, S.C. and attended the University of South Carolina. He set up a law practice here in 1926 and was the senior member of the Ramsey, Smart, Ramsey and Pratt law firm. In 1976, he received the N.C. bar award for 50 years continuous service as an attorney in North Carolina. In 1979, he received the Brevard Chamber of Commerce Outstanding Citizens Award.

Surviving are his wife, Mary Dick Alford Ramsey; two daughters, Mary Ann Norris and Sarah Martha Nifong; and two sons, Ralph Heyward, III and Gayle Edward Ramsey.

Services were held Thursday at Brevard First Baptist Church. Burial was in the Gillespie-Evergreen Cemetery.

Mayor Ralph H. Ramsey

Brevard News 1932

WHAT IS A W. S. S. ?

IT IS A WAR SAVINGS STAMP
THERE ARE TWO KINDS—UNITED STATES THRIFT
STAMPS TWENTY-FIVE CENTS EACH, AND UNITED
STATES WAR SAVINGS STAMPS, FOUR DOL-
LARS AND TWELVE CENTS EACH.
BOTH ARE DEBTS OF THE UNITED STATES GOVERN-
MENT TO REPAY YOUR MONEY JANUARY 1ST, 1923,
WITH INTEREST ON THE WAR SAVINGS STAMPS AT
THE RATE OF 4 PER CENT. A GOOD WAY TO SAVE.
AN EXCELLENT INVESTMENT—AND HELPS WIN THE
WAR. FOR SALE AT THE POSTOFFICE AND BANK.

WAR SAVINGS COMMITTEE
TRANSYLVANIA COUNTY

Major RAMEY

Born:	4 Oct 1896, Rabun County, GA
Died:	25 Apr 1957, Walhalla, SC; age 60
Buried:	Double Springs Methodist Church Cemetery, Walhalla, SC
Spouse:	**Bonnie TEAGUE**
Mother:	**Elizabeth RAMEY**
Draft Registration:	21, single, farming

[Documentation: South Carolina findagrave, Application for Military Headstone, 1910 census, Ancestry.com]

application cancelled 6/13/57 at request of applicant

DUPLICATE

APPLICATION FOR HEADSTONE OR MARKER

1. Name of deceased—last—first—middle: Ramey, Major Redmond
2. Enlistment date: 23 July 1918
3. Discharge date: Nov. 11, 1918
4. Service no.: 4121945
5. Pension or VA claim no.: C-316482
6. State: S.C.
7. Grade: Pvt.
8. Medals:
9. Branch of service, company, regiment, and division or ship: 156th Depot Brigade
10. Date of birth: October 4, 1894
11. Date of death: April 25, 1957
12. Emblem: Christian (Latin Cross)
13. Check type required: Flat marble marker
14. Ship to: W.D. Thomason Jr. & Anel Funeral Home
15. Freight station: Walhalla, S.C.
16. Name and location of cemetery: Double Springs Cemetery, Mountain Rest S.C.
17. I certify the applicant for this stone or marker has made arrangements with me to transport same to the cemetery. Signature: W.D. Thomason Jr. April 29, 1957
18. Name and address of applicant: Mrs. Bonnie T. Ramey, Mountain Rest S.C., Star Route
19. I certify this application is submitted for a stone or marker for the unmarked grave of a deceased member or former member of the Armed Forces of the United States, soldiers of Union and Confederate Armies of the Civil War. I hereby agree to accept responsibility for properly placing the stone or marker at the grave at no expense to the Government.
Signature of applicant: Mrs. Bonnie T. Ramey April 29, 1957

DO NOT WRITE HERE
Received: MAY 3 1957
Verified:
B/L:
Ordered:

MAY 13 1957

DD FORM 646 — IMPORTANT—Reverse Side Must Be Completed

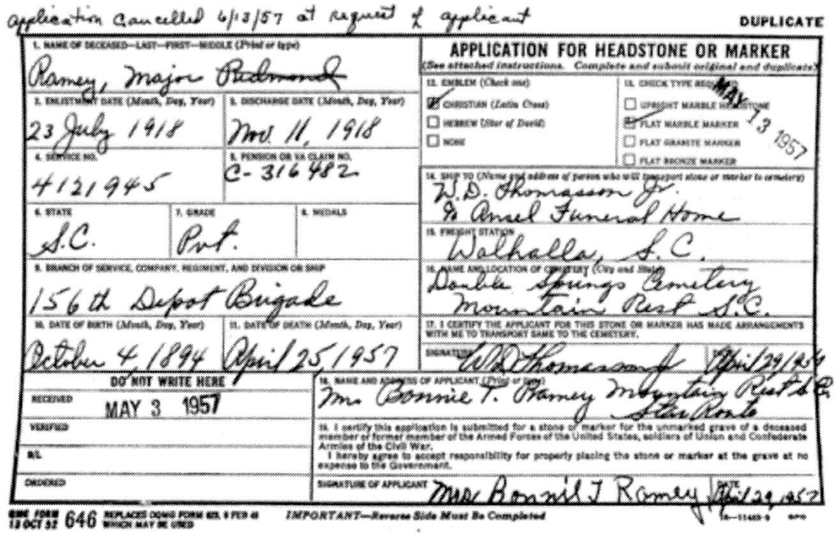

Greenville News (SC)
M.R. RAMEY
4/26/1957

Major Redmon Ramey, 62, died suddenly Thursday at the Veterans Hospital in Columbia, where he had gone for treatment Monday. Mr. Ramey was born in Rabun County, Georgia but had lived practically his entire life in Oconee County. He was a veteran of World War I and a member of the America Legion.

Surviving are his wife, Bonnie Teague Ramey; Three sons: Redmon, John and Tommy Ramey; three daughters: Thelma Ledwell, Grace Edwards and Fannie Durham; and one sister, Mae Kirby.

Funeral services will be conducted Saturday at Double Springs Baptist Church near Mt. Rest and the burial will be in the church cemetery.

15 Feb 1918 **Brevard News**

FIRST-CLASS PLUMBING SHOP

In the Walker McGaha Building on Main Street

And we will be pleased to have our friends call and see us. We are both expert plumbers, having been wiht W.E. Bishop & Co. For several years, therefore we are able to take care of your wants.

In connection with our plumbing, steam and hot water fitting, we will do tin and sheet-metal work.

Nicholson & Duclos

Expert Plumbers

Clifford RAXTER

Born:	20 Oct 1890, Transylvania County, NC
Died:	26 Jun 1988, Transylvania County, NC; age 97
Buried:	Boylston Baptist Church Cemetery, Henderson County, NC
Spouse(s):	**Ava Vashti ALLISON**, m. 4 May 1919, Transylvania County, NC
	Susan E. SMITH, m. 10 Nov 1923, Transylvania County, NC
Father:	**James Henry RAXTER**
Mother:	**Sarah HAMET**
Draft Registration:	26, single, carpenter for T.B. Summey Co

[Documentation: North Carolina Death Collection, Henderson County Cemeteries, Cowart's Index to Marriages, Ancestry.com]

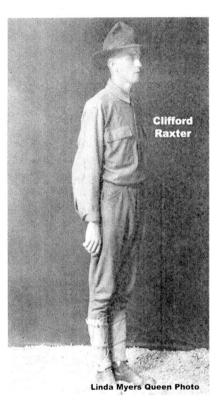

Clifford Raxter

Linda Myers Queen Photo

Raxter, Clifford		white	
(Surname) (Christian name)		(Army serial number) (Race: White or colored)	
Residence:	Brevard	NORTH CAROLINA	
	(Street and house number) (Town or city)	(County) (State)	
Enlisted in	NG Hendersonville N C June 18/17		—
Born in	Brevard N C 26 7/12 yrs		—
Organizations:	6 Co CAC N C NG to disch		—
Grades:	Pvt	—	—
Engagements:		—	—

Wounds or other injuries received in action: None.   —
Served overseas no   —   —
Hon. disch. Aug 29/17 SCD   —   —
Was reported not shown   per cent disabled on date of discharge, in view of occupation.
Remarks: —   —

SRC Notes: CAC (Coast Artillery Corps) SCD (Surgeon's Certificate of Disability)

6/30/1988
CLIFFORD A. RAXTER

Clifford A. Raxter, 97, of Brevard died Sunday at his residence. A lifelong resident of Transylvania County, he was the son of the late James H. and Sarah Hamet Raxter and was the husband of the late Susan Elizabeth Smith Raxter. He retired from Ecusta Corporation.

Surviving are two daughters: Willow Faye Myers and Opal McCormick; and a son R.E. Raxter.

Services were held Wednesday in Carr's Hill Baptist Church of which he was a member. Burial was in Boylston Baptist Church Cemetery.

Fayette RAXTER

Born:	19 May 1892, Transylvania County, NC
Died:	1 Nov 1972, Anniston, Alabama; age 80
Buried:	Forest Lawn Gardens, Anniston, Alabama
Spouse:	**Flossie Marie TAYLOR**
Father:	**James Henry RAXTER**
Mother:	**Sarah HAMET**
Draft Registration:	No
Discharge:	Enlisted 2 Feb 1917 at Fort Royal, SC in the US Marine Corps. Served on USS Wyoming 12 May 1917 to 28 Aug 1920. Discharged 1 Feb 1921.

Battles, engagements, skirmishes, expeditions; Served with the British Grand Fleet in foreign waters on board the U.S.S. Wyoming from 7 Dec 1917 to 1 Dec 1918; took part in surrender of German High Seal Fleet, 21 Nov 1918. Took part in Presidential escort into Brest, France, 13 Dec 1918. Served on board U.S.S. Wyoming in connection with first Trans-Atlantic Aero plane Flight, Lat 40⁰ N Long 2⁰ West.

[Documentation: Discharge, North Carolina Birth Index, Alabama Death & Burial Index, TT obituary, Ancestry.com]

11/9/1972
FAYETTE RAXTER

Fayette Raxter, 80, of Anniston, AL died November 1st after a short illness. Funeral services were held the 3rd at Bray Brown Funeral Service with burial in Forest Lawn Gardens.

Mr. Raxter was a native of Brevard and lived in Calhoun County for the past 15 years. He was a member of Carr's Hill Baptist church and a veteran of World War I.

Survivors include his wife, Mrs. Flossie Marie Taylor Raxter; two daughters: Mrs. James Rhodes and Mrs. Richard Bryson; a son, Robert Henry Raxter; and one brother, Cliff Raxter.

U.S.S. Wyoming

Naval Military Archives

William Leslie RAY

Born:	6 Mar 1894, Transylvania County, NC
Died:	3 Dec 1949, Transylvania County, NC; age 55
Buried:	Holly Springs Baptist Church Cemetery, Henderson County, NC
Father:	**W.J. RAY**
Mother:	**Sara RICE**
Draft Registration:	23, single and farming with his father

[Documentation: Transylvania County DC, Application for Veterans Headstone, TT obituary, Ancestry.com]

Ray, William L(esley)   2,616,786   * White * Colored   **2**
(Surname)   (Christian name)   (Army serial number)

Residence: R.F.D.1.   Pisgah Forest   NORTH CAROLINA
(Street and house number)   (Town or city)   (County)   (State)

. *Inducted at Brevard N C Sept 5/18 on____, 19__
Place of birth: Transylvania N C   Age or date of birth: Mch 6, 1894
Organizations served in, with dates of assignments and transfers:
7 Engr Tng Regt to Sept 25/18; 8 Engr Tng Regt to Nov 16/18; 5 Engr Tng Regt to disch

Grades, with date of appointment: Pvt

Engagements: ____

Wounds or other injuries received in action: None.
Served overseas from †____no____ to †____, from †____ to †____
Honorably discharged: Dec 2, 19 18 SCD
(Date)   (Cause)
In view of occupation he was, on date of discharge, reported 25 per cent disabled.

SRC Notes: Engr Tng Regt (Engineer Training Regiment)

12/8/1949
WILLIAM LESLIE RAY

William Leslie Ray, 55, farmer and native of the Little River community, died Saturday afternoon after a short illness. Funeral services were held Monday morning in Holly Springs Baptist Church with burial in Holly Springs Cemetery.

Surviving are four brothers: Carl, Claud, Miles and Hal; and three sisters: Mrs. Lenoir Odem, Mrs. Elsie Reed and Mrs. Grace Smith.

George Wallace REECE

Born:	8 May 1896, Transylvania County, NC
Died:	4 Aug 1977, Henderson County, NC; age 81
Buried:	Shepherd Memorial Park, Henderson County, NC
Occupation:	Building contractor
Spouse(s):	**Donnie Mae MOORE**, **Pauline LIVERETTE**
Father:	**Larkin REECE**
Mother:	**Juda E. HENDERSON**
Draft Registration:	21, single, brakeman on Southern RR

[Documentation: North Carolina Death Collection, 1930 Census, Ancestry.com, Hendersonville T-N obituary]

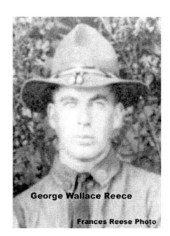
George Wallace Reece

Frances Reese Photo

SRC Note: MD (Medical Department)

18 Jul 1918   Brevard News
George W. Reece of the Quebec Community left last Saturday for Greenleaf Camp, near Chattanooga, Tenn., where he is to take training for service in the world war.

21 Jan 1919   Brevard News
George Reece of Quebec, who has just returned from training camp visited relatives and friends here last week.

Hendersonville Times News
8/5/1977
GEORGE W. REECE

Services for **George Wallace Reece**, 81, who died Thursday after a long illness, will be held at 11 a.m. Saturday in Shepherd's Church Street Chapel. Burial will be in Shepherd Memorial Park.

Mr. Reese was a native of Transylvania County and a former resident of Haywood County and had lived in Henderson County since 1941. He was a retired building contractor. He was an Army veteran of WW 1 and a member of First Baptist Church in Hendersonville and Hubert M. Smith Post 77, American Legion.

Surviving are the widow, Mrs. Pauline Liverette Reese; three sons: Vernon, Russel and Ted Reese; three sisters: Mrs. John Smith, Mrs. Mitchell Neely and Mrs. Belvin Simmons.

Daniel Marrion REID

Born:	13 Sep 1896, Transylvania County, NC
Died:	21 Apr 1975, Pinellas County, FL; age 78
Buried:	Gulf Pines Memorial Park, Englewood, FL
Occupation:	Operated restaurant, service station and motel – Mt. Toxaway Lodge
Spouse:	**Myrtle MILLER**
Father:	**Elijah Dillard REID**
Mother:	**Annie Sarah ALEXANDER**
Draft Registration:	No

[Documentation: Transylvania County BC, Florida Death Collection, Florida Divorce Index, findagrave.com, 1940 Census, Ancestry.com]

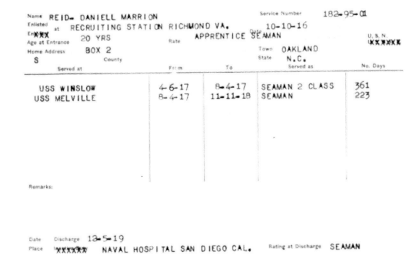

23 Nov 1917   Brevard News
Mr. E. D. Reid said that his son Daniel M. Reid had the distinction of being the 1st Transylvania boy to be on actual service in France.

Samuel Welch REID

Born:	18 Jan 1893, Transylvania County, NC
Died:	10 Feb 1979, Cowiltz County, WA; age 86
Buried:	Bunker Hill Cemetery, Cowiltz County, WA
Spouse:	**Azalea MILLER**, m. 15 Oct 1922, Transylvania County, NC
	Eva L. MILLER, m. 12 Oct 1925, Transylvania County, NC
Father:	**Jefferson D. REID**
Mother:	**Mary Louise LOWE**
Draft Registration:	Chehalis, WA, 24, single and a merchant

[Documentation: Discharge, Washington findagrave.com, 1900-1940 Censuses, <u>Cowart's Index to Marriages</u>, Ancestry.com

<u>Jun 1918</u>   <u>Brevard News</u>
FROM OVER THERE

Somewhere in France, May 20, 1918

I get the Brevard News weekly and noticed the names of many of my Transylvania friends in it and I'm glad to know they are still keeping the wheels of industry rolling in my home county. It may be interesting to them to know I'm with the boys in France and we're getting along fine, enjoying the best of health and ready for anything that may come.

Although I've been away from Transylvania for years, my home is still there, near Oakland, in the free hills of as fine a country as the sun ever shined upon. I've enlisted with the U.S. Engineers at Portland, Oregon last fall and came to France two months later. I've been over quite a bit of France and seen many interesting things, such as the old battlefields where the world's greatest battles were fought and I was stationed in one of the forts where Napoleon trained one of his armies. The Americans are looked upon as a restless, fast-living people. If you could see us here you would think we owned France by the liberties we have, and when you see the US motor truck pop around the corner and start down one of the narrow streets you just ought to see the Frenchman clear out.

We boys in France have much more enjoyment than you people can realize. We have the Y.M.C.A. entertainments, the Red Cross, with all its care and kindness, daily and weekly papers, plenty of good literature to read, and seems just like home follows us everywhere we go. We are treated with great kindness and hospitality by the French people. When we disembark from the transport and march out through the streets the girls throw flowers to us from the windows, while the men stand with their hats off as we pass and the children call us good Americans. A young French soldier spoke to us at one of the Y's one night. He said when America entered the war it seemed like the sun was shining again after darkness and with the help of America, France would be saved and democracy made safe.   We heartily appreciate the kindness and friendship of the French people, but what we like best of all is the letters we get from home. If you want to drive the blues away and make the boys in France happy just send them a letter from home.

S. W. Reid   20th Eng. Co., A–3rd Bn., A C F

Longview, Oregon
2/22/1978
SAMUEL REID

Samuel Welch Reid, 86, died February 20, 1979 in a local hospital. He had come to the Longview-Kelso area from Transylvania County, NC in 1925. A veteran of World War I, he was a self-employed logger and a member of the Longview Assembly of God Church.

Reid is survived by his wife, Eva; six sons: Howard R., Ronald T., S. Carrol, Gerald H., Allen K. and Burt W. Reid; a daughter, Nelda M. Moyer; and two brothers, Lamon and Frank Reid.

Interment was at the Bunker Hill Cemetery.

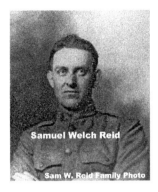
Samuel Welch Reid

Sam W. Reid Family Photo

6/1/1917   Brevard News
INTERNED GERMANS TO BE NEAR BREVARD
Camps For Both Hot Springs And Brevard

The camp for Brevard never happened but there was a camp at Hot Springs in Madison County. Jackie Painter has published **The German Invasion of Western North Carolina**, an excellent history of that camp.

18 May 1917   Brevard News
3000 GERMANS COMING TO DAVIDSON RIVER
GOVERNMENT PROPOSES TO ESTABLISH MODEL INTERIOR CAMP
FOR GERMANS IN PISGAH NATIONAL FOREST
4 MILES FROM BREVARD PENDING WAR WITH GERMANY

About 2 weeks ago the government decided upon Kanuga Lake, near Hendersonville, but when it became known that the title to the property was clouded, the lease was canceled and the government officials visited the Davidson River section for the 2nd time and practically decided upon the location of the camp for the Germans near the Young place about 4 miles from Brevard and 2 miles from Pisgah Forest. This will be a model prison camp for about 3,000 interned Germans.

The government proposes to build houses for sheltering the Germans and to enclose them in the stockade so that their presence or movements will not be a menace. The site decided upon is an isolated community sparsely settled and within the borders of the government's forest land.

"To this camp will be consigned the 1800 officers and men from the German entered ships which have been temporarily held at Ellis Island, Boston, Philadelphia and New Orleans. In addition there are approximately 1200 individuals who have been held at the immigration stations who must be cared for. There are alien enemies, alien neutrals and alien allies who have come to this country through the regular channels of immigration, but are inadmissible under our laws.

"Under the Hague treaty this government is empowered to work the interned men or to farm them out to individuals or corporations. When worked by the government they will receive the pay of soldiers and when farmed out they will be remunerated at prevailing wage rates. After making deduction for their maintenance, the men will be given, at the time of their discharge, by the government whatever sums they have earned.

"The men in the camp of North Carolina will be used to clear the grounds, and will be farmed out for lumbering and road building. In view of the necessity for guards the two latter occupations appear to be the only ones in which they can be conveniently worked by private capital.

"Arrangements have been made already with the Department of Agriculture for the employment of a number of men and road building on the Vanderbilt track that adjoins the camp which is been taken over by the department as a forest reserve."

Original statement from the United States Government concerning interned Germans:
When it was decided to locate the Germans at Kanuga, Secretary of Labor Wilson of Washington gave out the following statement as to the status of the Germans and the government's purposes: "With the coming of warm weather, it was realized that opportunities should be provided that would afford the individuals interned a chance to work and obtain recreation; apparently they would enjoy greater liberties than are possible at the various immigration stations where they are now interned. This government desires to treat interned persons with the greatest courtesy and make the conditions under which they must live as pleasant as possible."

Walter Jordon REID

Born:	28 Aug 1893, Transylvania County, NC
Died:	11 Jun 1946, Miami, Florida; age 52
Buried:	Cremation
Spouse(s):	**Virginia**
	Helen GRAVES
Father:	**Elijah Dillard REID**
Mother:	**Annie Sarah ALEXANDER**
Draft Registration:	Madison County, 24, single working at Mt. Park Hotel

[Documentation: Transylvania County BC, 1900-1940 Censuses, SSDI, Ancestry.com, FamilySearch.org, TT obituary]

```
              Reid  Walter J          1 317 457   white
          (Surname)        (Christian name)     (Army serial number)  (Race: White or colored)

Residence:                 Lake Toxaway          NORTH CAROLINA
              (Street and house number)   (Town or city)   (County)    (State)

*Enlisted in      NG Knoxville Tenn  -            Aug 1/17      -
†Born in          Transylvania Co NC -            25 yrs        -
Organizations:

                  Brig Hq Tenn NG to      ; Hq 119 Inf to Mch 22/18
                  Hq Troop 30 Div to Nov 20/18; Postal Det 30 Div to
Grades:           disch              -                           -

Engagements:      Pvt lcl Aug 4/17; Mess Sgt       ; Pvt Oct 31/18

Wounds or other injuries received in action: None.              -
‡Served overseas: May 10/18 to Apr 2/19                          -
§Hon. disch.      Apr 8/19        on demobilization              -
Was reported      0              per cent disabled on date of discharge, in view of occupation.
Remarks:                         -                               -

Form No. 724-1¼, A. G. O.    *Insert "R. A.", "N. G.", "E. R. C.", "N. A.", as case may be, followed by place and
    March 12, 1920.            date of enlistment.    †Give place of birth and date of birth, or age at enlistment.
    3—7088                    ‡Give dates of departure from and arrival in the United States.   §Give date.
```

23 Nov 1917   Brevard News
SOUTHERN HOSPITALITY SHOWN CAMP BOYS

E. D. Reid of Oakland was in town Saturday. He was accompanied by his son, Walter J. Reid, who is stationed at Camp Sevier, Greenville. Walter is highly pleased with camp life there. He says the people of Greenville are the most hospitable he has ever met and that out of the 30,000 soldiers stationed at Camp Sevier not one has failed to receive an invitation from some family in the city to dinner.

6/20/1946
WALTER JORDAN REID

Walter J Reid, 52, a native of the Oakland section of Transylvania County, died of a heart attack at his home in Miami, FL, June 11. He operated the Fairfield Inn last summer, and at the time of his death was managing the Tropical Hotel, at Ft. Lauderdale, FL. Mr. Reid was actively engaged in the hotel and brokerage business for many years, starting as a clerk at the Old Toxaway Inn when he was 14.

He received his education in the public schools of Transylvania County, Fruitland Institute, the University of Nevada, and Leland Stanford University. He was a veteran of World War I.

Surviving are his wife, Mrs. Helen Graves Reid; his mother, Mrs. Annie Reid; two sisters: Mrs. Grace Stewart and Mrs. Lula Ducker; and two brothers: J.C. Reid and Dan Reid.

In accordance with previously expressed wishes, his body was cremated.

Suel RHINEHART

Born:	18 Oct 1896, Haywood County, NC
Died:	16 Jun 1985, Oteen VA Hospital, Buncombe County; age 88
Buried:	Ridgeway Baptist Church Cemetery, Candler, NC
Spouse:	**Nellie WILSON**
Father:	**Ellis RHINEHART**
Mother:	**Mary P. MULL**
Draft Registration:	21, single, working at Transylvania Tanning Company

[Documentation: Haywood County Delayed BC, NC Death Collection, findagrave.com, Ancestry.com]

1

Rhinehart, Suel   4,480,518   * White *Colored
(Surname)   (Christian name)   (Army serial number)

Residence: ___RFD 1____ ___Brevard___ Transylvania ___NORTH CAROLINA___
(Street and house number)   (Town or city)   (County)   (State)

*Enlisted ____ *Inducted at __Brevard NC____ on __Aug 26__, 19_18_

Place of birth: __Waynesville NC____ Age or date of birth: _Oct 28/1896_

Organizations served in, with dates of assignments and transfers: _____
____156 Dep Brig to Oct 3/18; Camp Jackson SC Oct Aut____
____Repl Draft to   ;²Btry FA Repl Regt APO 778 to Disch____

Grades, with date of appointment: _____
____Pvt_____

Engagements: _____

Wounds or other injuries received in action: None.
Served overseas from †_Oct 28/18_ to _May 21/19_, from †_____ to †_____
Honorably discharged on demobilization __May 26/19__, 19____
In view of occupation he was, on date of discharge, reported ___0___ per cent disabled.

SRC Notes; Dep Brig (Depot Brigade)   FA Repl Regt (Field Artillery Replacement Regiment)

30 Aug 1918   Brevard News
Twelve more men left for Camp Jackson Monday afternoon.
. . . Suel Rhinhart, Brevard . . .

Asheville Citizen Times
6/18/1985
SUEL RHINEHART

Suel Rhinehart, 88, died Sunday in the Asheville VA Medical Center. A lifelong resident of Haywood County, his parents were the late Elias "Sonny" and Polly Mull Rhinehart. He retired from Champion Papers and was a World War I Army veteran. Rhinehart was an ordained deacon and member of Dutch Cove Baptist Church.

Surviving are his wife, Nellie Wilson Rhinehart; two daughters: Irene Livingstone and Doro

thy Dockery; four sons: J. Earl Rhinehart, Ray C. Rhinehart, Russell Rhinehart, and Max "Tony" Rhinehart; two sisters: Margaret Harkins and Tisha Belle Elliott; and a brother, B. H. Rhinehart.

Services were in the chapel of Wells Funeral Home with burial in Ridgeway Baptist Church cemetery.

The American aviators brought down in the course of their few months of active service 755 enemy planes. Our losses in combat were 357 planes.

Orcutt, Louis E., **The Great War Supplement**, published 1920, p. 98.

Ed RHODES

Born: 30 Mar 1897, Transylvania County, NC
Died: 14 Jul 1980, Henderson County, NC; age 83
Buried: Pisgah Gardens Cemetery
Spouse: **Evelyn BOLDING**
Father: **Zeb RHODES**
Mother: **Mattie DALTON**
Draft Registration: Anderson, SC, 21, single and working for Pelzer County
Military Marker: PVT US Army WW I

[Documentation: North Carolina Death Index, <u>Transylvania County Cemetery Survey</u>, Hendersonville T-N obituary, Ancestry.com]

Hendersonville Times News
7/15/ 1980
ED RHODES

Ed Rhodes, 83, of Mills River, died Monday at his home after a long illness. Mr. Rhodes was a native of Transylvania County, a son of the late Zeb and Mattie Dalton Rhodes. He was an Army veteran of World War I and a retired textile worker.

Surviving are his wife, Evelyn Bolding Rhodes; two sons, Billy Rhodes and Ed Rhodes, Jr. a daughter, Bertia Lee Rhodes; and three sisters: Estella Cobbison, Elvida Smith and Carrie Liberato.

Services will be held at 2 p.m. Thursday in the Church of God of Prophecy of which he was a member. Military graveside rites will be conducted by Monroe Wilson Post 88, American Legion, Pisgah Gardens.

Company B 114th Machine Gun Battery Building Chimney

Roe O. RICE

Born:	24 Feb 1893, Transylvania County, NC
Died:	19 Nov 1993, Transylvania County, NC; age 100
Buried:	Old Toxaway Baptist Church Cemetery
Spouse:	**Inez PENLAND**
Father:	**Nathaniel RICE**
Mother:	**Addie GALLOWAY**
Draft Registration:	No
Note:	Was unable to verify military service

[Documentation: NC Death Collection, 1900-1940 Censuses, Ancestry.com]

11/19/1993
R.O. RICE

R.O. Rice, 100, died Friday in the Transylvania Community Hospital. He was a native of Pickens, S.C. and had resided in Brevard for the past 22 years. His wife, Inez Penland Rice died in 1971. He was the son of Nathaniel and Addie Galloway Rice. He retired from Cannon Mills as a machine operator in the card room.

Surviving is one sister, Beulah Rice Meece.

A funeral service was held Sunday, Nov. 21 at the Old Toxaway Baptist Church and interment was in the church cemetery.

Haywood County Digital Collection

General Camp View

John RICHIE/RICHEY

Born: 19 Apr 1893, South Carolina
Died: 5 Mar 1921, Buncombe County, NC; age 24
Buried: Walhalla, SC
Father: **Frank RICHEY**
Mother: **Margaret SWAYNGIM**
Draft Registration: Oconee, SC, 24, single, farming
Note: His death was the result of respiratory injuries from mustard gas

[Documentation: Buncombe County DC, Census, Ancestry.com]

Richie, John	2,337,812	White
(Surname) (Christian name)	(Army serial number)	(Race: White or colored)

Residence: Pisgah Forest *Transylvania* NORTH CAROLINA
(Street and house number)   (Town or city)   (County)   (State)

Enlisted in   RA Ft Thomas Ky June 16/17
Born in   Transylvania Co NC 20 3/12 yrs
Organizations: Sup Co 4 Inf to disch

Grades: Wag Nov 8/17;

Engagements:

Wounds or other injuries received in action: None.
Served overseas: Apr 15/18 to disch
Hon. disch.   June 21/19 for immediate reenlistment
Was reported   0   per cent disabled on date of discharge, in view of occupation.
Remarks:

SRC Notes: Sup Co (Supply Company)   Wag (Wagoneer)

Y.M.C.A. at Fort Thomas, Kentucky   Postal Card

Lewis H. RIGDON

Born: 9 Mar 1894, Sylva, North Carolina
Died: 7 Jun 1947, Oteen VA Hospital, Buncombe County; age 53
Buried: Lakeside Cemetery
Occupation: Truck driver
Spouse: **Mamie GALLOWAY**
Father: **James M. RIGDON**
Mother: **Charlotte OWEN**
Draft Registration: Jackson County, 25, single, teamster for a construction company
Military marker: 101 First AM TRAIN AEF SERIAL No. 206451

[Documentation: Buncombe County DC, <u>Upper Transylvania County, NC Remembered</u>, Ancestry.com, TT obituary]

6/12/1947
RIGDON RITES HELD

Funeral services were held Monday at Lake Toxaway Baptist Church for Lewis Rigdon, who died at Moore General Hospital Saturday, after an illness of several weeks. Burial followed in the church cemetery.

Mr. Rigdon was a native of Jackson County but had lived here for several years where he had made many friends. He was a veteran of World War I.

Surviving are the widow, Mrs. Mamie Galloway Rigdon; one son, Ray; and two daughters; Louise and Mae Rigdon.

The cost of the personal articles for our military personnel serving overseas was valued at more than I trillion dollars.

A short summary of just a few the items that were shipped and distributed to the men were as follows:

Wool stockings	pairs	131,800,000
Undershirts		85,000,000
Under drawers		83,600,000
Shoes pairs		30,700,000
Flannel shirts		26,500,000
Wool breeches		21,700000
Wool coats		13,900,000
Overcoats		8,300,000
Blankets		21,700,000

Wool coats last about three months in active service. Two million men overseas required something like 8 million coats.

Orcutt, Louis E., **The Great War Supplement**, published 1920, p. 79.

Mall Henry RIGSBY

Born: 22 Jul 1892, Madison County, NC
Died: 4 Aug 1982, Transylvania County, NC; age 90
Buried: Lakeside Cemetery
Occupation: Lumberman
Spouse: **Cora ALVIS**, m. 24 Jul 1920, Hawkins County, TN
Father: **Jesse J. RIGSBY**
Mother: **Sidney McDOWELL**
Draft Registration: No

[Documentation: NC Death Index, Tenn. Marriage Index, <u>Upper Transylvania</u> <u>County, NC Remembered</u>, Ancestry.com]

Mall Rigsby

Lovada Rigsby Photo

Rigsby, Mall H 2,994,006   1
(Surname) (Christian name) (Army serial number) • White • ~~Colored~~

Residence: ___ Marshall _Madison_ NORTH CAROLINA
   (Street and house number) (Town or city) (County) (State)

• ~~~~ •Inducted at ___ Asheville NC June 3/18 ___ on ___, 19___

Place of birth: __ Marshall NC Age or date of birth: __ July 22/93

Organizations served in, with dates of assignments and transfers: ___
156 Dep ~rig to June 24/18; MG Co 322 Inf to disch

Grades, with date of appointment: ___
___ Saddler May 6/19 ___

Engagements: ___

Wounds or other injuries received in action: None.
Served overseas from † _July 31/18_ † _June 18/19_ from † ___ to † ___
Honorably discharged on demobilization ___ June 25/19 ___, 19___
In view of occupation he was, on date of discharge, reported ___ 0 ___ per cent disabled.

SRC Notes: Saddler (he worked directly with the horses).

8/8/1982
HENRY RIGSBY

Mall Henry Rigsby, 90, died last Wednesday at his home after an extended illness. He was a native of Madison County and the son of the late Jesse J. and Sidney McDowell Rigsby. He was the husband of the late Cora Lee Alvis Rigsby and a member of the North Toxaway Baptist Church.

Surviving are two sons: Frank J. and Charles E. Rigsby; and two daughters, Clara Wilson and Dorothy Rigsby.

Services were held Friday in the Moody-Connolly Funeral Home Chapel and burial followed in the Lakeside Cemetery.

President Wilson appointed a department to handle the switching of peacetime economy to a war-time one. He named Bernard Baruch, a Wall Street millionaire to head this War Industries Board (WIB) and they began assembling information about the amount of steel, chemicals, fuel and other materials available for manufacturers. They also helped many manufacturers convert factories into plants capable of producing needed products for waging war.

Baruch and the WIB learned that more than eight thousand tons of steel was used each year to make corsets. Before the war "ribs" made of steel were added to corsets to give them extra strength. Baruch refused to let so much steel be used this way and he announced that a couple of battleships would be built each year by using the corset steel.

Frederick Joseph ROACH

Born:	30 Aug 1896, New York
Died:	11 Feb 1967, Buncombe County, NC; age 70
Buried:	Little River Baptist Church Cemetery
Occupation:	Sales manager for Holland Furnace Co of New York
Spouse:	**Mamie TURNER**
Father:	**Frederick ROACH**
Military Marker:	NY CRM USNR WW I & II

[Documentation: Buncombe County DC, <u>Transylvania County Cemetery Survey</u>, British Army WW I Pension Records, Ancestry.com, TT obituary]

2/16/1967
F.J. ROACH

A Requiem Mass was said Tuesday at Sacred Heart Catholic Church for Frederick J. Roach, 67, of Pisgah Forest, who died in an Asheville hospital after an illness of several weeks. Burial was in the Little River Cemetery.

He was a native of New York City and had resided in Transylvania County for four years. He was manager of the Little River Camping Resort. He was a veteran of World War I and World War II, having served with the U.S. Navy as a radio technician. Before coming to this county he was with the Holland Furnace Company as sales manager.

Surviving are his wife, Mrs. Mary Turner Roach; one step-daughter, Edith Mediager; and two sisters: Mrs. Ray R Pengene and Mrs. Madeline Roach.

Photo #NH 95082 Yeomen enlistees receive telegraphy training

Naval History Archives

Adger ROBINSON

Born:	17 Jan 1896, South Carolina
Died:	22 Aug 1974, Douglas, OR; age 78
Buried:	Roseburg National Cemetery, Roseburg, OR
Spouse:	**Elsie WOODS**
Father:	**Charles ROBINSON, Sr.**
Mother:	**Pomelia PACK**
Draft Registration:	21, single, lumberman with West Va. Pulp and Paper Company

[Documentation: North Carolina Birth Index, Oregon Death Index, US Veteran's Gravesites, Ancestry.com]

Robinson, Adger   3,277,210   2
(Surname)   (Christian name)   (Army serial number)   * White * Colored
                                                            North
Residence: RFD 2 Pisgah Forrest Transylvnia SOUTH CAROLINA
        (Street and house number) (Town or city) (County) (State)
                        Brevard N C   June 25 19 18
                *Inducted at   Jan 17/ 1896
Place of birth: Marietta SC   Age or date of birth:
Organizations served in, with dates of assignments and transfers:
        156 Dep Brig to Aug 10/18; Btry D 76 FA to disch

Grades, with date of appointment:

Engagements:

Wounds or other injuries received in action: None.
Served overseas from † Aug 22/18 to † Disch , from † ___ to † ___
Honorably discharged: July 29, 19 19 Immediate reenlistment
            (Date)   (Cause)
In view of occupation he was, on date of discharge, reported ___ 0 per cent disabled.

SRC Notes: Dep Brig (Depot Brigade)   FA (Field Artillery)

21 Jun 1918   Brevard News
WHITE REGISTRANTS WHO ARE TO LEAVE FOR CAMP JACKSON, S.C. TUESDAY, JUNE 25th, 1918 AT 3:13 P.M.
. . . Adger Robinson, RFD 2, Pisgah Forest . . .

AUGUST 1974
GEORGE A. ROBINSON

George Adger Robinson, 78, of Canyonville, died at a Roseburg hospital 22 Aug 1974. Born 17 Jan 1896 at Marietta SC, he was a veteran of World War 1. He had resided in Canyonville for 27 years, moving there from Akron OH. Before retiring, he had been employed as a logger with Chappel Logging Co.

Survivors: wife, Elsie Robinson; son, Homer Woods and two granddaughters, Lynnia and Laveida Woods of Canyonville; one sister, Kate Taylor of Greenville SC.

Graveside services will be held at Roseburg National Cemetery on Tuesday, 27 Aug 1974.

NATIONAL ARMY CANTONMENT (CAMP)

Camp Wheeler   Location: Macon, Ga.   Organization: 31st (old 10th) Division
Troops from Georgia, Alabama and Florida

Charles Alexander ROBINSON, Jr.

Born:	3 Oct 1895, Transylvania County, NC
Died:	7 Jul 1971, Oteen VA Hospital, Buncombe County; age 75
Buried:	Blue Ridge Baptist Church Cemetery
Occupation:	Farmer
Spouse:	**Sadie HARRIS**
Father:	**Charles ROBINSON, Sr.**
Mother:	**Pomelia PACK**
Draft Registration:	No
Military Marker:	NC PVT 89 Inf WW I

[Documentation: Buncombe County DC, Transylvania County Cemetery Survey, Hendersonville T-N obituary, Ancestry.com]

Robison Charles A Jr   2,993,187   • White •Colored

(Surname)   (Christian name)   (Army serial number)

Residence: RFD 2   Pisgah Forest   Transylvania   NORTH CAROLINA
(Street and house number)   (Town or city)   (County)   (State)

• .... *Inducted at Brevard NC .... on May 24 19.18
Place of birth: Cedar Mt NC .... Age or date of birth: 23 9/12 yrs
Organizations served in, with dates of assignments and transfers: ....
156 Dep Brig to disch

Grades, with date of appointment: ....
Pvt

Engagements: ....

Wounds or other injuries received in action: None.
Served overseas from none none to † ...., from † .... to † ....
Honorably discharged on demobilization Mch 18/19 , 19......
In view of occupation he was, on date of discharge, reported 0 per cent disabled.
Remarks: ....

SRC Notes: Dep Brig (Depot Brigade)

Hendersonville Times News
7/1971
CHARLES A. ROBINSON

Charles Alexander Robinson, 76, of Horse Shoe died early Wednesday in a Buncombe County hospital after a long illness. He was a native of Transylvania County and had lived in Henderson County for the past 22 years. He was a retired truck farmer and a veteran of World War I.

Surviving are the widow, Sadie Harris Robinson; a stepson, Marshall Burrell; a brother, Adger Robinson; and a sister, Mrs. Kate Taylor Services will be held at 2 p.m. Friday in Blue Ridge Baptist Church, of which he was a member. Burial will be in the church cemetery.

One of the jobs of the Army's new shoe repair shops is to furnish the railroad troops and hospital attendants with hobnail-less shoes. If there are not enough of the russet garrison shoes the hobnails simply have to be removed by hand. The railroaders claim that the hobnails slip as they climb about on the engines and causing disastrous falls. The hospital attendant's objection to studs and heel plates is primary one of noise.
STARS AND STRIPES 1918

Alvin ROCKWOOD

Born:	25 Apr 1899, Weymouth, Mass
Died:	Jun 1943, Tampa, FL; age 44
Buried:	Gillespie-Evergreen Cemetery
Spouse:	**Jessie Mae KING**
Father:	**George A. ROCKWOOD**
Mother:	**Harriett BAKER**
Draft Registration:	South Raintree, Mass., 18, single, ship worker
Note:	Grave marker gives NO military information

[Documentation: Mass. Vital Records, Discharge, TT obituary]

7/1/1943
ALVIN ROCKWOOD

The body of Alvin Rockwood, 45, well-known Brevard man who drowned near Tampa, FL last week, is expected to arrive today and funeral services arrangements are pending because definite information could not be obtained as to when the body would reach here. When arrangements are made the services will be held at the First Baptist Church.

Tuesday afternoon Mrs. Rockwood received a telegram from a funeral home in Tampa, stating that her husband drowned last Thursday and the body was recovered on Saturday. "We postponed notifying you, pending positive proof." the message said. He went to Tampa to help in Coast Guard work and may have been on a patrol when he drowned.

The deceased was a native of Massachusetts, but had lived in Brevard most of the time for the past several years. He sustained permanent injuries in the First World War and was unable to work full time. However, he was active in civic affairs and served as Commander of the Legion post here. Members of the Monroe Wilson Post will assist in conducting the funeral.

He is survived by his wife, Jessie Mae King Rockwood and one daughter, Dorothy Gay.

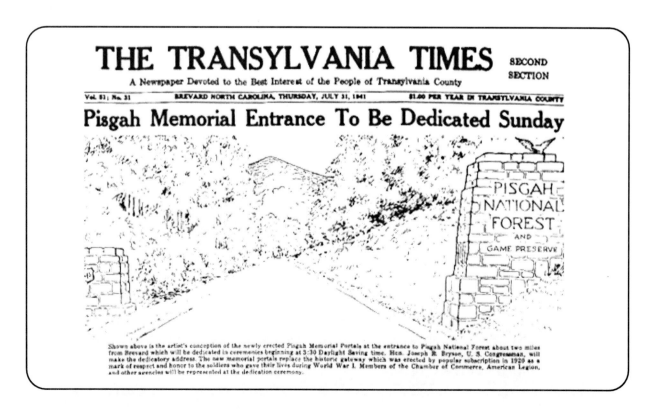

THE TRANSYLVANIA TIMES SECOND SECTION

A Newspaper Devoted to the Best Interest of the People of Transylvania County

Vol. 51; No. 31   BREVARD NORTH CAROLINA, THURSDAY, JULY 31, 1941 $1.00 PER YEAR IN TRANSYLVANIA COUNTY

Pisgah Memorial Entrance To Be Dedicated Sunday

PISGAH NATIONAL FOREST AND GAME PRESERVE

Shown above is the artist's conception of the newly erected Pisgah Memorial Portals at the entrance to Pisgah National Forest about two miles from Brevard which will be dedicated in ceremonies beginning at 3:30 Daylight Saving time. Hon. Joseph R. Bryson, U. S. Congressman, will make the dedicatory address. The new memorial portals replace the historic gateway which was erected by popular subscription in 1920 as a mark of respect and honor to the soldiers who gave their lives during World War I. Members of the Chamber of Commerce, American Legion, and other agencies will be represented at the dedication ceremony.

Boyd Wiley ROSS

Born:	4 Apr 1887, Transylvania County, NC
Died:	18 Oct 1918, Augusta, GA; age 31
Buried:	Mt. Moriah Cemetery
Father:	**Thomas J. ROSS**
Mother:	**Martha PEACE**
Draft registration:	30, single, self-employed farmer

[Documentation: Transylvania County Cemetery Survey, Brevard News obituary, Ancestry.com]

Ross, Boyd   4,159,468 * White * Colored.
(Surname)   (Christian name)   (Army serial number)

Residence: Selica   Transylvania   NORTH CAROLINA
(Street and house number)   (Town or city)   (County)   (State)

*Enlisted * R. A. * N. G. * E. R. C. *Inducted at Brevard N.C.   on July 24 1918
Place of birth: Transylvania Co N.C.   Age or date of birth: Apr 4, 1887
Organizations served in, with dates of assignments and transfers: 19th Co Rct Receiving
Depot M G T C Camp Hancock Ga July 24/30 to Aug 30/18.
71 Co 6th Group M. Truck Div Camp Hancock to Oct 18/18.
Grades, with date of appointment: Pvt

Engagements:

Wounds or other injuries received in action: * None.
Served overseas from †   to †   , from †   to †
Died of   Influenza , Broncho pneumonia   Oct. 18 , 19 18
(Cause and date of death)
Person notified of death: Edwin J Ross   Brother
(Name)   (Degree of relationship)
Selica Transylvania Co   NC
(No. and street or rural route)   (City, town, or post office)   (State or country)
Remarks:

SRC Note: M G T C (Machine Gun Training)

18 Jul 1918   Brevard News
23 More Men To Leave July 24, 1918
Following is a list of white registrants for induction on July 24th, 1918 for Camp Hancock, Ga., who will leave on the 3:13 train: . . .
. . .Boyd Ross, Selica . . .

10/24/1918
BOYD ROSS DIES IN CAMP

Boyd Ross, son of the late Mr. and Mrs. Tom J. Ross of Cherryfield, died at the hospital at Camp Hancock, Ga. last Saturday. His body was shipped to Cherryfield Wednesday, accompanied by PVT. John C. McKelvey, where it was laid to rest in Mt. Moriah Cemetery.

Owing to the epidemic of influenza only the family and a few friends were present at the interment. Mr. Ross was 31 and had been in service for about one year. His superior officer said he was a soldier of high order, always obedient and true. Four sisters survive him: Madame's Bryson and Waldrop, Misses Ora and Nora Ross; and one brother, Edwin Ross.

> Factories in the United States produced 5,400,000 gas masks and 2,728,000 steel helmets by the end of Nov. 1918
> Orcutt, Louis E., **The Great War Supplement**, published 1920, p. 79.

Wallace B. RUSTIN

Born: 10 Nov 1891, Savannah, GA
Died: 8 Oct 1923, Gaston County, NC; age 31
Burial: Savannah, GA
Occupation: Secretary for Haverty-Rustin Furniture Co., Columbia, SC
Spouse: **Ina TALLEY**, m. 9 Oct 1917, Transylvania County, NC
Father: **Sidney B. RUSTIN**
Mother: **Mary**
Draft registration: 25, single, secretary and manager of Haverty-Rustin Furniture Co., Columbia, SC

[Documentation: Georgia Birth Record, Gaston County DC, Cowart's Index to Marriages, Ancestry.com]

Rustin W B		3,351,934	*Transylvania*	1
(Surname)	(Christian name)	(Army serial number)	*White *Colored*	

Residence: _____ Penrose   NORTH CAROLINA
           (Street and house number) (Town or city) (County) (State)

_____. *Inducted at Columbia SC July 16/18_____, 19__
Place of birth: ___Savannah Ga___ Age or date of birth: ___Nov 10 1891___
Organizations served in, with dates of assignments and transfers: _____
_____ Co C 57 Pion Inf to July 29/18; Co I 53 Pion Inf to
_____ disch
Grades, with date of appointment: _____
_____ Corp Sept 2/18

Engagements: _____

Wounds or other injuries received in action: None.
Served overseas from †Aug 6/18 to † May 6/19, from †_____ to †_____
Honorably discharged on demobilization _____ May 17/19, 19__
In view of occupation he was, on date of discharge, reported ___0___ per cent disabled.

SRC Notes: Pion Inf (Pioneer Infantry)

3 Oct. 1918   Brevard News

Friends and relatives of Mrs. W.B. Rustin, nee Miss Ina Talley, will be interested to know she has received the first letter from her husband since he landed in France, about August 20th. Mr. Rustin is now serving as company clerk. He has been in the service two months, having served two weeks at Camp Wadsworth before going across. Mrs. Rustin, who is visiting her husband's parents in Savannah, GA, for some time expects to return to her former home at Penrose very soon.

25 Jan 1919   Brevard News

Mrs. Wallace Rustin of Savannah, Ga., is spending the winter with her father Mr. N.L. Tally, while her husband is in France.

---

6 Apr 1917   Brevard News

PRESIDENT WILSON ASKS FOR WAR

Congress convened in extra session Monday and was urged by President Wilson to declare war on Germany. Congress is debating the matter and will most likely declare a state of war while big war-like preparations are being made.

Champ Clark was elected Speaker of the House.

Farmer Herbert SANDERS

Born:	31 Mar 1894, Westminister, SC
Died:	15 Nov 1964, Transylvania County, NC; age 70
Buried:	Orr Cemetery
Occupation:	Steam fitter
Spouse:	**Minnie MERRILL**
Father:	**James M. SANDERS**
Mother:	**Johanna KENNEDY**
Note:	Military Marker: SC E2 USNRF WW I.

[Documentation: <u>Transylvania County Cemetery Survey</u>, TT obit, Ancestry.com]

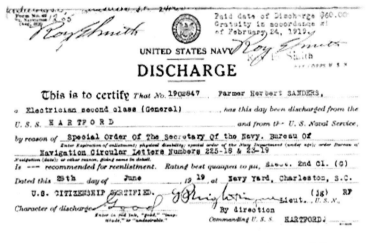
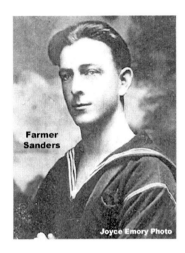

Anderson, SC
11/16/1964
F.H. Sanders

Brevard, N.C. ~ Farmer Herbert Sanders, 70, of Pisgah Forest, died early Sunday at his home. Mr. Sanders was born in Westminster, SC, the son of the late James Marion Sanders and Johanna Kennedy Sanders. He was a retired steamfitter, a member of Pleasant Grove Baptist Church, VFW, American Legion and Local No. 10 Plumbers and Steamfitters Union.

Survivors include one son, Rev. Joseph M. Sanders and his wife Doris; one daughter, Joyce Sanders Emory and her husband, John; one granddaughter, Debra Jo Sanders; one grandson, Herbert Lee Emory; three sisters: Iola S. Carlton, Roxie S. Evans and Lillie Sanders; and one brother, Tilmon Jethro Sanders.

Funeral services will be held Tuesday at Pleasant Grove Baptist Church. Burial will be Orr Cemetery.

This is a very colorful button with the photograph centered in the design shared by his daughter, Joyce Farmer Emory.

John Luna SANDERS

Born:	24 Jun 1890, Oakland, NC
Died:	27 Dec 1964, Transylvania County, NC; age 74
Buried:	Toxaway Lakeside Cemetery
Spouse:	**Virdee WILSON**
Father:	**Samuel SANDERS**
Mother:	**Mahulda MILLER**
Draft registration;	27 years, single, farmer in Oakland, SC
Military marker:	NC PVT HQ DET 156 Depot Brig WW I

[Documentation: Transylvania County DC, <u>Upper Transylvania County, NC Remembered</u>, Discharge, Ancestry.com, TT obituary]

Sanders, John Luna   1,864,320   *White *Colored.
(Surname)   (Christian name)   (Army serial number)

Residence: Oakland Transylvania NORTH CAROLINA
(Street and house number) (Town or city) (County) (State)

*Inducted at Brevard N C on Apr 1 19 18

Place of birth: Oakland N C Age or date of birth: 28 10/12 yrs

Organizations served in, with dates of assignments and transfers:
156 Dep Brig to disch

Grades, with date of appointment:
*ag June 1/18

Engagements:

Wounds or other injuries received in action: None.
Served overseas from None to † from † to †
Honorably discharged on demobilization Dec 7, 19 18
In view of occupation he was, on date of discharge, reported 2 per cent disabled.

John L. Sanders

Lois Beshears Photo

12/31/1964
JOHN L. SANDERS

Funeral services for John Luna Sanders, 74, of Route 1, Lake Toxaway, were held Tuesday in the Lakeside Baptist Church, where he was a member. Burial followed in the church cemetery. Mr. Sanders died Sunday night in the Transylvania County Hospital after a long illness.

A native of Transylvania County, he was a retired sawmill worker and a veteran of World War I.

Survivors include his widow, Virdree Wilson Sanders; two sisters: Mamie Reed and Mrs. L.M. Lyday; and a brother, Savannah Sanders.

The Army shipped 68,984 horses and mules to France. The military mainly used horses for logistical support during the war; they were better than mechanized vehicles at traveling through deep mud and over rough terrain. Horses were used for pulling artillery, ambulances and supply wagons. The presence of horses often increased morale among the soldiers at the front but the animals contributed to disease and poor sanitation in camps, caused by their manure and carcasses. The value of horses and the increasing difficulty of replacing them were such that by 1917 some troops were told that the loss of a horse was a greater tactical concern than the loss of a human soldier. Horses were not transported back to the United States at the end of the war.

Orcutt, Louis E., **The Great War Supplement**, published 1920.

392

Frank Winthrop SCRUGGS

Born:	29 Apr 1891, Transylvania County, NC
Died:	28 Dec 1961, Transylvania County, NC; age 70
Buried:	Gillespie-Evergreen Cemetery
Spouse:	**Helen JUSTUS**, m. 12 Mar 1924, Transylvania County, NC
Father:	**Lemuel R. SCRUGGS**
Mother:	**Lou Ella KUYKENDALL**
Draft Registration:	26, single and farming
Military Marker:	NC PVT US Army WW I

[Documentation: Cowart's Index to Marriages, Transylvania County Cemetery Survey, Discharge, Transylvania County DC, Application for Veteran's Headstone, Ancestry.com]

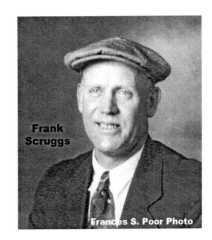

Frank Scruggs

Frances S. Poor Photo

SRC Notes: MD (Medical Department)

12/28/1961
FRANK W. SCRUGGS

Frank Winthrope Scruggs, 70, died in a local hospital Thursday morning after a brief illness. Mr. Scruggs was a native of Transylvania County and a veteran of World War I. He had been retired from Duke Power Company for the past five years due to ill health.

He is survived by the widow, Helen Justice Scruggs; one daughter, Mrs. L.C. Poor; one sister, Mrs. Flave Holden; and four brothers: Hampton, Charlie, Tom and Harry Scruggs.

Funeral services will be held Friday at the First Baptist Church and burial will follow in the Gillespie-Evergreen Cemetery.

---

11 Jul 1918   Brevard News

Twelve Transylvania boys left on last Saturday for Fort Oglethorpe, Ga., to begin their careers as defenders of democracy. The boys left on the afternoon train . . .

. . .Frank Winthrop **Scruggs**, Brevard . . .

---

7 July 1917   Brevard News

MANY LOCAL RECRUITS FOR MACHINE GUN CORPS

Henry J. SCRUGGS

Born:	20 Aug 1894, Transylvania County, NC
Died:	24 Dec 1983, Odessa, Tx; age 89
Buried:	Undetermined
Father:	**Lemuel R. SCRUGGS**
Mother:	**Lou Ella KUYKENDALL**
Draft Registration:	22, single, machinist at Dan Merrill Garage in Brevard
Last residence:	Ft. Stockton, Pecos, TX

[Documentation: BIRLS Death Files, 1900-1930 Censuses, Discharge, Ancestry.com]

<table>
<tr><td colspan="4">Scruggs Henry J   717,520   White   1½</td></tr>
<tr><td>(Surname)</td><td>(Christian name)</td><td>(Army serial number)</td><td>(Race: White or colored)</td></tr>
<tr><td colspan="4">Residence: Brevard   Transylvania   NORTH CAROLINA</td></tr>
<tr><td>(Street and house number)</td><td>(Town or city)</td><td>(County)</td><td>(State)</td></tr>
</table>

* Enlisted in   NG   Hendersonville NC   June 14/17

† Born in   Transylvania Co NC   22 10/12 yrs

Organizations: 6 Co CAC NC NG (6 Co Cape Fear) to July 18/18; Btry B 50 Arty CAC to disch

Grades: Pvt 1cl Dec 24/17; Mec Jan 1/18

Engagements: —

Wounds or other injuries received in action: None.

‡ Served overseas: Oct 6/18 to Feb 14/19

§ Hon. disch.   Mch 2/19   on demobilization

Was reported   0   per cent disabled on date of discharge, in view of occupation.

Remarks: —

SRC Notes: CAC NC NG (Coast Auxiliary Corps North Carolina National Guard)

Name:	**Henry Scruggs**
Gender:	Male
Birth Date:	20 Aug 1894
Death Date:	24 Dec 1983
SSN:	449500130
Branch 1:	ARMY
Enlistment Date 1:	4 Jun 1917
Release Date 1:	2 Mar 1919

U.S. Department of Veteran's Affairs BIRL Death File

12/29/1983
J. HENRY SCRUGGS

J. Henry Scruggs, 89, of Ft. Stockton, Texas, died in an Odessa Texas hospital Dec. 24 after an illness of several months. Funeral services and burial were in Ft. Stockton.

Surviving are two brothers: Hamp and Tom Scruggs.

A native of Brevard, son of the late L.R. and Ella Kuykendall Scruggs, had lived in Texas most of his life. He was retired from the Wist-Pyle Cattle Co.

Jesse Carl SCRUGGS

Born:	12 Apr 1896, Transylvania County, NC
Died:	14 May 1933, Oteen VA Hospital, Buncombe County; age 37
Buried:	Glazener Cemetery
Occupation:	Carpenter
Spouse:	**Annie Iantha BROWN**, m. 9 Jun 1918, Transylvania, NC
Father:	**Lemuel R SCRUGGS**
Mother:	**Lou Ella KUYKENDALL**
Draft registration:	21, single, bridge carpenter for the Southern Rail Road

[Documentation: Buncombe County DC, <u>Cowart's Index to Marriages</u>, <u>Transylvania County Cemetery Survey</u>, Discharge, Ancestry.com, TT obituary, Application for Veteran's Headstone]

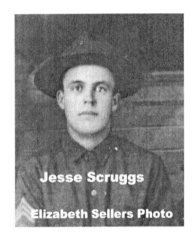

Jesse Scruggs
Elizabeth Sellers Photo

Scruggs Jesse C   1,876,443   • White • Colored
(Surname)   (Christian name)   (Army serial number)   1

Residence: _____ Brevard *Transylvania* NORTH CAROLINA
(Street and house number) (Town or city) (County) (State)

*Enlisted • • • • • *Inducted at_ Brevard NC _ on Sept 18 19 17
Place of birth: ___ Brevard NC ___ Age or date of birth: __ 21 5/12 yrs

Organizations served in, with dates of assignments and transfers:
F Hosp 323 306 Sn Tn to dis ch

Grades, with date of appointment: Ck Oct 16/17; Sgt Feb 19/18

Engagements: _____

Wounds or other injuries received in action: None.
Served overseas from †Aug 8/18 to † June 2/19 from † _____ to † ____
Honorably discharged on demobilization June 21/19 _____, 19 ____
In view of occupation he was, on date of discharge, reported ___0___ per cent disabled.

SRC Notes: Hosp (Hospital Company) Sn Tn (Sanitation Train)

21 Sep 1917   Brevard News   THIRTY-ONE MEN was ordered to report on Tuesday at 5 P.M. at the office of the local enlistment board and to leave for Camp Jackson, S.C. Wednesday morning. . . . Jesse Carl Scruggs . . .

14 Jun 1918   Brevard News
J.L. Scruggs, of Camp Sevier, is at home for a short stay with parents and friends.

5/18/1933
JESSE CARL SCRUGGS

Funeral services for Jesse Carl Scruggs were held at the home Tuesday morning with interment in the Glazener cemetery. Members of the American Legion acted as pallbearers at the burial.

Mr. Scruggs, aged 37, died at Oteen VA hospital early Sunday night where he had been a patient for less than one week, although he had been in ill health for several months.

Ranking as sergeant in the American Expeditionary Forces, the Brevard man saw action at St. Die, Meuse and Argonne, having spent a year in France. Discharged after peace had been declared, Sergeant Scruggs returned to Brevard where he had been employed at Transylvania Tanning Company until several months ago when his health failed him.

Surviving are the wife Mrs. Inatha Brown Scruggs and three small children: Nelle, Carl and Carolyn; the parents, Mr. and Mrs. L.R. Scruggs; six brothers: Charlie, Frank, Hampton, Robert, Henry and Thomas; and one sister, Mrs. Flave Holden.

Carl Eugene SEARCY

Born:	31 Mar 1895, Transylvania County, NC
Died:	15 Oct 1978, Transylvania County, NC; age 83
Buried:	Mt. Moriah Cemetery
Spouse:	**Maude GALLOWAY**, m. 2 Dec 1922, Transylvania County, NC
Father:	**Harve M. SEARCY**
Mother:	**Eliza Jane LANCE**
Draft registration:	21, single, farmer working for T. C. Galloway in Cherryfield, NC
Grave stone:	PVT US Army WW I

[Documentation: North Carolina Death Collection, <u>Cowart's Index to Marriages</u>, <u>Transylvania County Cemetery Survey</u>, Discharge, Ancestry.com]

1

Searcy, Carl E   2,993,189 • White • Colored.
(Surname)   (Christian name)   (Army serial number)

Residence: Rosman   Transylvania NORTH CAROLINA
(Street and house number)   (Town or city)   (County)   (State)

• ~~Enlisted R. A. N. G. E. R. C.~~ •Inducted at Brevard NC   on May 24, 18

Place of birth: Rosman NC   Age or date of birth: 23 3/12 yrs.

Organizations served in, with dates of assignments and transfers:
156 Dep Brig to July 30/18; 2 Ord Guard Co to Aug 17/18
9 Ord Guard Co to disch

Grades, with date of appointment: Pvt

Engagements:

Wounds or other injuries received in action: None.
Served overseas from † **No** to † , from † to †
Honorably discharged on demobilization   Apr 11/19   , 19
In view of occupation he was, on date of discharge, reported   **0**   per cent disabled.

SRC Notes: Dep Brig (Depot Brigade) Ord Guard Co. (Ordnance Guard Company)

Asheville Citizen Times
10/16/1978
CARL EUGENE SEARCY

Carl Eugene Searcy, 83, died Sunday in the Brevard hospital after an extended illness. A lifelong resident of Transylvania County, he was the son of the late Harve and Eliza Lance Searcy. He was a retired farmer and an Army veteran of World War I.

He is survived by the wife, Maudie Galloway Searcy; a son, Harold E. Searcy; five daughters: Nina Bumgarner, Dot Duncan, Margaret Smith, Trudy Crenshaw and Martha Savage; two brothers: Louie and Vernon Searcy; and five sisters: Dela Lance, Nora Pettit, Edith Tinsley, Cora Wolfe and Dora Reece.

Services were held in Mount Moriah Cherryfield Baptist Church with graveside services conducted by the American Legion in Mount Moriah Calvert Cemetery.

> ### NATIONAL ARMY CANTONMENT (CAMP)
>
> **Camp Fremont**   Location: Palo Alto, Cal.   Organization: 41st (old 20th) Division
> Troops from Washington, Oregon, Montana, Idaho and Wyoming

Clyde Franklin SEARCY

Born:	12 Nov 1893, Transylvania County, NC
Died:	1 Jan 1979, Pickens County, SC; age 85
Buried:	Undetermined
Spouse:	**Lucy McCALL**
Father:	**John H. SEARCY**
Mother:	**Elizabeth V WALDROP**
Draft registration:	21, single, farmer working for Van Waldrop in Cherryfield, NC

[Documentation: SSDI, 1900-1940 Censuses, Discharge, BIRLS Death File, Ancestry.com]

Searcy, Clyde F   2,594,087   • White • Colored
(Surname)   (Christian name)   (Army serial number)

Residence: _____ Cherryfield / Transylvania NORTH CAROLINA
           (Street and house number)   (Town or city) (County)   (State)

• R_____. *Inducted at __Brevard NC_____ on __May 19, 18

Place of birth: __Cherryfield NC_____ Age or date of birth: __22 6/12 yrs_

Organizations served in, with dates of assignments and transfers: _____
        Co F 6 Am Tn to disch

Grades, with date of appointment: _____
        Pvt 1cl May 19/19

Engagements: _____

Wounds or other injuries received in action: None.
Served overseas from † July 14/18 † June 11/19 from † _____ to † _____
Honorably discharged on demobilization ____June 19/19____, 19___
In view of occupation he was, on date of discharge, reported ____0____ per cent disabled.

SRC Notes: Am Tn (Ammunition Train)

3 Oct. 1918   Brevard News

Clyde F. Searcy of Cherryfield who is now in France, writes that he is charmed with life in that country and that he is enjoying good health, but that life is incomplete without the Brevard News.

Greenville News (SC)
CLYDE SEARCY
1/2/1979

Clyde Franklin Searcy, 85, Camp Creek Community, widower of Leecie McCall Searcy, died Monday. Born in Transylvania County, NC, he was a retired farmer and a member of the Camp Creek Baptist Church.

Surviving are sisters, Ella Mae Smith and Beulah Revis; and a brother, Spann Searcy.

Services will be held Wednesday at Camp Creek Baptist Church and burial will follow in Greenlawn Memorial Park in Easley.

---

17 Sep 1917   Brevard News

Patriotic Rally of Citizens and Soldiers

Friday at the Court House 2:30 PM: Parade of Transylvania soldiers
With Citizens; Music and Speeches

Louie Ernest SEARCY

Born:	20 Jul 1888, Transylvania County, NC
Died:	27 Oct 1983, Oteen VA Hospital, Buncombe County; age 95
Buried:	Lance Cemetery
Spouse:	**Anna Bertha LANCE**, m 4 May 1918, Transylvania County, NC
Father:	**Harve M. SEARCY**
Mother:	**Eliza Jane LANCE**
Draft Registration:	29, single, worked on public works
Military Marker:	PVT US Army WW I

[Documentation: NC Death Collection, Transylvania County Cemetery Survey, Cowart's Index to Marriages, 1900-1930 Census, Discharge, FamilySearch.org, Ancestry.com]

Searcy   Louie E   3,277,233   • White • Colored.

Residence: RFD 1   Brevard   Transylvania   NORTH CAROLINA
                (Street and house number)   (Town or city)   (County)   (State)
                                    Brevard   N C   June 25/18
        *Inducted at   on   , 19
Place of birth: Brevard   N C   Age or date of birth: July 20/1887
Organizations served in, with dates of assignments and transfers:
        156 Dep Brig to July 26/18; Co B 53 Pion Inf to
        July 30/18; 52 Dep Brig to disch
Grades, with date of appointment:
        Pvt

Engagements:

Wounds or other injuries received in action: None.
Served overseas from †   NO   to †   , from †   to †
Honorably discharged on demobilization   Mch 1   , 19   19
In view of occupation he was, on date of discharge, reported   5   per cent disabled.
Remarks:

SRC Notes: Dep Brig (Depot Brigade) Pion Inf (Pioneer Infantry)

21 Jun 1918   Brevard News
WHITE REGISTRANTS WHO ARE TO LEAVE FOR CAMP JACKSON, S.C.
TUESDAY, JUNE 25th, 1918 AT 3:13 P.M.
. . . Louie Ernest Searcy, Calvert . . .

10/31/1983
LOUIE E. SEARCY

Louie Ernest Searcy, 95, died Thursday in the VA Medical Center. A native of Transylvania County, he was the son of the late Mr. and Mrs. Harve Searcy and was the husband of the late Bertha Lance Searcy. He was a veteran of World War I and a farmer for many years.

Surviving are two sons: Monroe and Bud Searcy; four daughters: Carrie Whitmire, Ruby Reid, Edna Mae Cox and Bonnie Outlaw; a sister, Mrs. Walt Reese; and four half-sisters: Edith Pensley, Cora Wolf, Mrs. Pettitt and Stella Lance. Services were held Saturday at the Rosman Church of God and burial followed in the Lance Cemetery.

Marion Filmore SEARCY

Born:	24 May 1881, Transylvania County, NC
Died:	2 May 1969, Burke County, NC; age 87
Buried:	Pisgah Gardens Cemetery
Spouse:	**Mary Ann MORRIS**
Father:	**William G. SEARCY**
Mother:	**Elmira Jane MEDLOCK ALEXANDER**
Draft Registration:	No
Discharge Notes:	Inducted 5 Nov 1918; Discharged from draft by reason of fistula of tear sac; placed in Class C-2

[Documentation: SSDI, Discharge, TT obituary, Ancestry.com]

5/8/1969
MARION F. SEARCY

Marion Filmore Searcy, 87, of Brevard, died in a Morganton hospital last Friday following a lingering illness. Mr. Searcy was a retired textile worker and a veteran of World War I.

Survivors include the wife, Mary Morris Searcy; two daughters: Mrs. B.F. Cox and Mrs. Grover Duvall; one son, Summett Searcy; one sister, Ida Ward; and one brother, George Searcy.

Funeral services were conducted Sunday in the Frank Moody Funeral Home Chapel and burial followed in the Pisgah Gardens Cemetery.

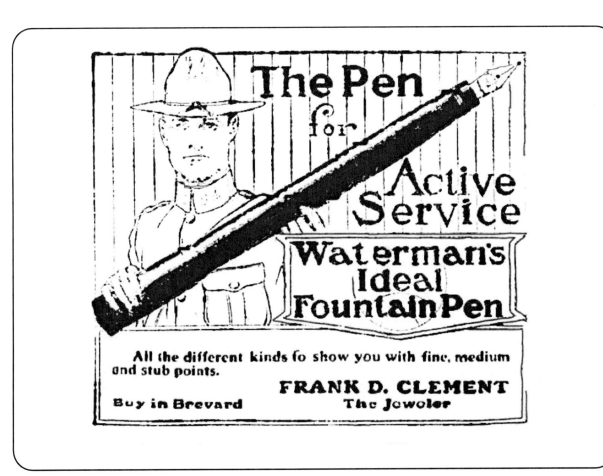

Andrew M. SHARP

Born:	10 Dec 1896, South Carolina
Died:	15 Jan 1937, Oteen VA Hospital, Buncombe County; age 40
Buried:	Cooper Cemetery
Race:	Colored
Occupation:	Mechanic
Father:	**Condrey SHARP**
Mother:	**Susan MILLS**
Military Stone:	NC WAGR 505 SVC BN Engr. Corps WW I

[Documentation: [Buncombe County DC, Application for Veteran's Headstone, Transylvania County Cemetery Survey, Ancestry.com]

---

2 May 1918   **Brevard News**

A MONUMENT TO OUR TRANSYLVANIA SOLDIERS

I take it for granted that each county in North Carolina should and will erect a monument to their "Soldier Boys."

I would suggest that we use rough granite rock blasted out of the cliffs on the Connestee Road, our native stone from the Blue Ridge, and build on the Court House Square, a pyramid about fifty or sixty feet high at the base. It would have an inside chamber with an arched opening or doorways at both the front and back.

In this chamber, on either side of the pass way, place two long marble slabs; on one engrave all the names of the Transylvania boys who entered the military services of the Army and Navy. On the other put the names of all who died in service. A monument of this kind would be unusual, unique and handsome. As an inscription over the arched entrance the following words:

In Proud and Affectionate Remembrance, to her Valorous and Beloved Sons, Who Fought and Gave Their Lives for Truth and Liberty on the Seas and the Battle Fields of Europe, Transylvania Erects This Monument.

C.W. Hunt

Samuel SHARP

Born:	11 Oct 1893, Transylvania County, NC
Died:	21 Jan 1929, undetermined; age 35
Buried:	Cooper Cemetery
Race:	Colored
Father:	**Condrey SHARP**
Mother:	**Susan MILLS**
Draft Registration:	Allegheny, PA, 24, single, laborer for Armstrong Cork Co
Military Stone:	PVT Co B 505th SB, Enlisted Oct. 26, 1917, Discharged May 27, 1919

[Documentation: 1900-1940 Censuses, Transylvania County Cemetery Survey, Ancestry.com]

---

1 Jun 1917   **Brevard News**

YEAR'S IMPRISONMENT FOR THOSE FAILING TO REGISTER FOR ARMY DRAFT ON JUNE 5

All Men, White Or Black, Feeble Or Strong, Between Ages Of 21 And 31 Years Required To Register On June 5

Will Be Subject To One Year's Imprisonment By Federal Government: The President's Proclamation.

NO ONE EXCUSED FROM REGISTERING

President Wilson's proclamation for selective draft registration of eligibles for military service has become a state and local matter by Gov. Bickell's appointing a registration board in every county. This board consists of the Sheriff, Clerk of the Court and the County physician, and is empowered to appoint precinct registrars, whose duty it will be beginning on June 5 to register eligibles for service in the Army - that is, men who have reached their 21st and who have not yet reached her 31st birthday.

The hours for registration will be from 7 o'clock in the morning to 9 o'clock in the evening.

In obedience to the proclamation the Sheriff, the Clerk of the Court and the County physician organized and made appointments of the registrars on Tuesday for each precincts as follows:

Brevard – F.F. Shuford, T.H. Hampton, Bill Jones
Boyd – L.F. Lyday
Cathy's Creek – L.W. Brooks, J.L. Waldrop
Cedar Mountain - Ralph L. Lee
Dunn's Rock – William Maxwell
Eastatoe - Jordon Whitmire
East Fork – Charlie Gravely
Gloucester – J.H. House
Hogback – W.H. Nicholson
Rosman – J.M. Zachary
Little River – H.P. Nicholson

The local registration board, the Sheriff, Clerk of Court and health officer have decided to give their services to the government on June 5. The matter of registration is not a plaything. It is a serious matter and all persons failing to register will face heavy penalty. Registration will take place at or near the voting places.

(This very long article explains the selective draft program that is necessary to build an army to protect our country.)

Luther Webster SHIPMAN

Born:	18 Oct 1890, Henderson County, NC
Died:	14 Oct 1959, Oteen VA Hospital, Buncombe County; age 68
Buried:	Little River Baptist Church Cemetery
Occupation:	Farmer
Father:	**Martin L. SHIPMAN**
Mother:	**Margaret PICKELSIMER**
Draft Registration:	Greenville, SC, 28 single and farming
Military Marker:	NC PVT 4 CO Casual DET WW I

[Documentation: Application for Veteran's Headstone, Buncombe County DC, Discharge, <u>Transylvania County Cemetery Survey</u>, Discharge, Ancestry.com]

Company H 117th Infantry Attention

Martin C. SHIPMAN

Born:	1 Sep 1889, Transylvania County, NC
Died:	3 Feb 1979, Transylvania County, NC; age 90
Buried:	Little River Baptist Church Cemetery
Spouse:	**Sue HEATH**, m. 5 May 1920, Transylvania County, NC
Father:	**Caleb SHIPMAN**
Mother:	**Henrietta ORR**
Draft Registration:	28, single and a farrier
Military Marker:	Farrier US Army WW I

[Documentation: NC Death Collection, <u>Transylvania County Cemetery Survey</u>, Discharge, <u>Cowart's Index to Marriages</u>, Ancestry.com]

2/7/1979
MARTIN SHIPMAN

Martin C. Shipman, age 89, died unexpectedly last Saturday in Transylvania Community Hospital. Mr. Shipman was a lifelong resident of Transylvania County and was the son of the late Caleb and Henrietta Jane Orr Shipman. He was a veteran of WWI, a retired farmer and cattleman and a member of the board of trustees of Little River Cemetery.

Survivors include the wife, Sue Heath Shipman; a daughter, Gladys Hitzroth; and a grandson, Thomas Hitzroth.

Services were held Monday in the Little River Baptist Church of which he was a member and deacon for 55 years. Burial was in Little River Cemetery.

Martin Shipman

Little River Church Archives

Thad SILER

Born:	18 Sep 1892, Transylvania County, NC
Died:	13 Aug 1974, Butte County, California; age 81
Buried:	Memorial Park Cemetery, Butte County, California
Spouse:	**Lula BRUNER**
Draft Registration:	Charlotte, Virginia, 24, single, farming and listed his grandmother as a dependent
Note:	All census records have him in his Siler grandparent's home with no father or mother listed

[Documentation: California Death Index, findagrave.com, 1910-1930 Censuses, Ancestry.com]

1

Siler, Thad	4,159,545	*White *~~Colored~~
(Surname) (Christian name)	(Army serial number)	

Residence: _____ Quebec *Transylvania* NORTH CAROLINA
(Street and house number) (Town or city) (County) (State)

*E~~████~~ ~~████~~ *Inducted at _____ Brevard NC ___ on July 24, 19 18

Place of birth: _____ Transylvania Co NC ___ Age or date of birth: _____ Sept 18/92

Organizations served in, with dates of assignments and transfers: _____
_____ 12 Prov Co Camp Hancock Ga to disch _____

Grades, with date of appointment: _____
_____ Pvt _____

Engagements: _____

Wounds or other injuries received in action: None.

Served overseas from †____~~No~~____ to †_____, from †_____ to †_____

Honorably discharged on demobilization _____ Dec 29 ____, 19 18

In view of occupation he was, on date of discharge, reported _____ 0 _____ per cent disabled.

SRC Notes: Prov Co (Provost Company)

Provost Guards Searching Visitors Camp Devens, Ayer, Mass.

1918 Postal Card

James Arvol SIMPSON

Born:	3 Aug 1889, Mitchell County
Died:	5 Jan 1973, Transylvania County, NC; age 83
Buried:	Gillespie-Evergreen Cemetery
Spouse:	**Effie McCRARY**
Father:	**Jarrett David SIMPSON**
Mother:	**Martha BRYANT**
Draft Registration:	Henderson County, 27, single, farming, lists parents as dependents
Military Marker:	NC SGT US Army WW

[Documentation: Transylvania County DC, <u>Transylvania County Cemetery Survey</u>, Discharge, 1900-1940 Censuses, Ancestry.com, Hendersonville TN obituary]

Simpson, James A.   1,860,832   •White •Colored.
(Surname)   (Christian name)   (Army serial number)

Residence: RFD 2   Horseshoe Henderson NORTH CAROLINA
(Street and home number) (Town or city) (County) (State)

•Inducted at Hendersonville NC on Sept 18, 1917
Place of birth: Mitchell Co NC   Age or date of birth: 28 1/12 yrs.
Organizations served in, with dates of assignments and transfers:
Btry A 316 FA to disch.

Grades, with date of appointment:
Pvt 1cl Mch 1/18 Sgt Aug 13/18 1 Sgt Aug 14/18
Sgt Nov 15/18

Engagements:

Wounds or other injuries received in action: None.
Served overseas from † No to † , from † to †
Honorably discharged on demobilization Jan 11, 1919
In view of occupation he was, on date of discharge, reported 0 per cent disabled.
Remarks:

SRC Notes: FA (Field Artillery)

Hendersonville Times News
1/7/1973
JAMES A. SIMPSON

James Arvol Simpson, 83, Brevard, died Friday morning at his home following a lingering illness. A native of Mitchell County, he had lived in Brevard a number of years. He was one of the founders of the Osborne-Simpson Funeral Home and retired in 1957. He was a veteran of World War I and a member of the First Baptist Church.

Funeral services will be held Sunday afternoon in the Frank Moody Funeral Home chapel. Burial will be in the Gillespie-Evergreen Cemetery.

He is survived by his wife, Effie M. Simpson; one daughter, Katherine Bagwell; two sons: Ray and Paul Simpson; one sister Elzora Simpson; and one brother, Leonard Simpson.

A new tactic evolved in this conflict---trench warfare. With the development of machine guns and quick-loading rifles it was suicide to try mass charges, as had been done in previous battles. Instead, deep trenches were dug to accommodate men and their supplies as a way to defend the ground that they had won. By late November, 1914 two lines of trenches, one German and one Allied, stretched from the border of Switzerland to the North Sea, almost five hundred miles.

James Elis SIMPSON

Born:	24 May 1889, Transylvania County, NC
Died:	4 Feb 1961, South Carolina; age 71
Buried:	Woodlawn Memorial Park, Greenville County, SC
Spouse:	**Ada WHITMIRE**, m. 2 Dec 1922, Transylvania County, NC
Father:	**Jacob SIMPSON**
Draft Registration:	27, single and farming
Military Marker:	PVT PROVOST GUARD CO WW I

[Documentation: 1910-1930 Censuses, findagrave.com, Ancestry.com, Cowart's Index to Marriages]

Simpson, James E.   1,891,678   • White • Colored.
(Surname)   (Christian name)   (Army serial number)

Residence: RFD#2   Brevard   *Transylvania*   NORTH CAROLINA
(Street and house number)   (Town or city)   (County)   (State)

• ~~ENLISTED RG, N.C.~~ *Inducted at* Brevard NC   on May24 19_18

Place of birth: Brevard NC   Age or date of birth: 28 yrs.

Organizations served in, with dates of assignments and transfers:
156 Dep Brig to disch.

Grades, with date of appointment:
Pvt.

Engagements:

Wounds or other injuries received in action: None.
Served overseas from †NO   to †   , from †   to †
Honorably discharged on demobilization   Mch 21   19.19
In view of occupation he was, on date of discharge, reported   0   per cent disabled.
Remarks:

SRC Notes: Dep Brig (Depot Brigade)

---

19 Oct 1917   Brevard News

REGISTRATION OF WOMEN COMPLETED ON FAIR DAY

Next Wednesday, Oct. 2nd, will be Registration Day for women in Transylvania County. On that day the school buildings of the state will be open from 9 a.m. to 1 p.m. for the Food Campaign and also for the registration of all women who are loyal to America, without age limit.

It has been decided by the Woman's Committee of the Council for National Defense to make October 21-31 inclusive Registration Week. The pastors of churches or Sunday school superintendents where church services are held on the 21st, are requested on that day to appoint one woman from each church to assist the teachers in registration. The teachers are also asked to bring registration blanks to Brevard on October 31st, as the Fair Day will offer a good opportunity for registering.

Miss Georgia Bell is chairman of the registration committee and will furnish the blanks to the teachers.

The purpose of this registration is to secure a record of the womanpower of the country, but it is purely voluntary and no woman will be asked for service outside her home unless she so desires. However, it will place trained women who can volunteer for service in line for good positions and will provide training classes for others where there is a demand for it. It is earnestly hoped that every woman will go to her nearest school building and state what work she can do best, no matter how humble it may be so that our county will go on record with a big registration of its loyal and patriotic women.

Leonard McKinley SIMPSON

Born:	10 Dec 1897, Mitchell County
Died:	1 Nov 1973, Transylvania County, NC; age 75
Buried:	Gillespie-Evergreen Cemetery
Occupation:	Barber
Spouse:	**Lillian BYRD**
Father:	**Jarrett David SIMPSON**
Mother:	**Martha BRYANT**
Draft Registration:	22, single, ratchet setter for Carr Lumber Co
Military Marker:	NC SGT US Army WW I

[Documentation: Transylvania County DC, Transylvania County Cemetery Survey, Discharge, Ancestry.com]

Simpson, Leonard   2,616,788   • White • ~~Colored~~.
(Surname)   (Christian name)   (Army serial number)

Residence: RFD #2 Box 33   Horse Shoe   Henderson   NORTH CAROLINA
(Street and house number)   (Town or city)   (County)   (State)

Place of birth: Mitchell Co NC   •Inducted at   Transylvania Co NC   on Sept 5 19 18
Age or date of birth: Dec 10/1895

Organizations served in, with dates of assignments and transfers:
Engr Tng Regt Camp Humphreys to Nov17/18 Co B 447
Res Lab Bn to disch.

Grades, with date of appointment:
Corp Oct 14/18 Sgt oct 29/18 1 st Sgt Feb18/19

Engagements:

Wounds or other injuries received in action: None.
Served overseas from no   to †   , from †   to †
Honorably discharged on demobilization   Apr 12   , 19 19
In view of occupation he was, on date of discharge, reported   0   per cent disabled.

SRC Notes: Engr Tng Regt (Engineer Training Regiment) Res Lab Bn (Reserve Laboratory Battalion)

11/8/1973
LEONARD SIMPSON

Leonard McKinley Simpson, 75, died in the local hospital last Thursday after an extended illness. He was a retired barber, a native of Mitchell County and had resided in Transylvania County for a number of years. He was a veteran of World War I with service in the US Army and a member of the First Baptist Church of Brevard.

Surviving are the wife, Lillian Byrd Simpson; one daughter, Ilaleet Johnson; two sons, James and Leonard P. Simpson; and one sister, Elzora Godshaw.

Graveside services were held at Gillespie-Evergreen Cemetery in Brevard last Friday.

<u>3 Aug 1917</u>   <u>Brevard News</u>
LOCAL RED CROSS FORMS ORGANIZATION
At Well Attended Meeting Monday Night Organization Was Made Permanent And Various Committees Will Enter Upon Work

Although considerable work has been done for the Red Cross in Brevard the permanent organization was not official until Monday night when a well-attended meeting was held at the courthouse.

J.S. Silversteen presiding over the meeting, told of encouraging things he had learned about the handling of the Red Cross funds while in New York recently.

(article illegible)

Charlie Thomas SIMS

Born:	22 Dec 1893, Transylvania County, NC
Died:	30 Sep 1971, Tiffin, OHIO; age 77
Buried:	Fairmount Cemetery, Tiffin, OH
Spouse:	**Juanita NORMAN,** m. 26 Mar 1921, Spartanburg, SC
Father:	**Thomas B SIMS**
Mother:	**Sarah A. ALLISON**
Draft Registration:	24, single, farming

[Documentation: Ohio Death Index, Discharge, <u>Heritage of Transylvania County, NC Vol 2:272:763</u>, Ancestry.com]

Sims Charlie T 4,159,466 / Transylvania 1
(Surname) (Christian name) (Army serial number) • White •Colored-

Residence: R #2 Blantyre NORTH CAROLINA
(Street and house number) (Town or city) (County) (State)

• N. G. R. R. G. •Inducted at Brevard N C on July 24 19 18
Place of birth: Transylvania Co N C Age or date of birth: Dec 22/93
Organizations served in, with dates of assignments and transfers:
Main Tng Dep M G Tng Camp Camp Hancock Ga to disch

Grades, with date of appointment: Pvt

Engagements:

Wounds or other injuries received in action: None.
Served overseas from † none to † , from † to †
Honorably discharged on demobilization Jan 9/19 , 19
In view of occupation he was, on date of discharge, reported O per cent disabled.

SRC Notes: MG Tng (Machine Gun Training)

<u>18 Jul 1918</u>   <u>Brevard News</u>
23 MORE MEN TO LEAVE JULY 24, 1918 for Camp Hancock, Ga.
. . . Charlie Thomas Sims, Brevard Rt. 2 . . .

<u>31 Jan 1919</u>   <u>Brevard News</u>
Charlie Sims, one of our residents has returned home after several month in training at Camp Hancock.

Greetings from Camp Gordon, Atlanta, Ga.
Machine Gun attached to Motorcycle

Eskel Lewis SIMS, Sr.

Born:	18 Oct 1896, Transylvania County, NC
Died:	22 Jan 1970, Oteen VA Hospital, Buncombe County; age 82
Buried:	Gillespie-Evergreen Cemetery
Spouse:	**Blanche OSBORNE**
Father:	**David SIMS**
Mother:	**Maggie FOWLER**
Draft Registration:	24, single, working at the sawmill at Carr Lumber
Military Marker:	WW I, WW II, Korean War

[Documentation: Buncombe County DC, <u>Transylvania County Cemetery Survey</u>, Ancestry.com, TT obituary]

(Surname)	(Christian name)	(Army serial number)	(Race: White or colored)
Sims,	Eskel L	1,324,546	White

Residence: Brevard — NORTH CAROLINA
(Street and house number) (Town or city) (County) (State)

* Enlisted in: NC Brevard NC July 18/17
† Born in: Brevard NC 22 10/12 yrs
Organizations: Btry F 1st FA (Btry F 113 FA) to disch

Grade: Pvt

Engagements: —

Wounds or other injuries received in action: None.
‡ Served overseas: May 26/18 to Mch 19/19
§ Hon. disch.: Mch 28/19 on demobilization
Was reported 0 per cent disabled on date of discharge, in view of occupation.
Remarks:

SRC Notes: NG (National Guard) FA (Field Artillery)

1/29/1970
ECK SIMS

Eskel Lewis Sims, 73, died in the Veterans Hospital at Oteen last Thursday after a long illness. He was a native of Transylvania County and a veteran of World War I, World War II and the Korean War.

He was a former Register of Deeds of Transylvania County, a Deputy Sheriff and had been connected with the NC Highway Department.

The wife, Blanche Osburne Sims, survives him.

Funeral services were conducted Sunday at the First Baptist Church of which he was a member. Burial was in the Gillespie-Evergreen Cemetery.

<u>17 Aug 1917</u>   <u>Brevard News</u>
RED CROSS BOOSTED BY 816 ARTICLES

Mrs. J.S. Silversteen, chairman of the National League of Woman's Service, recently shipped to the Red Cross supply depot at New York a box of articles prepared by the women of the league.

The box contained 816 articles for the use of Army hospitals and was valued at $70. The list included arm slings, fracture pillows, head, abdominal and T Bandages, and many plain bandages—nearly enough to supply one Army hospital for a week.

Henry Coy SIMS

Born:	5 Sep 1890, Transylvania County, NC
Died:	16 Jul 1947, undetermined; age 56
Buried:	Arlington National Cemetery, Arlington, VA
Spouse:	**Olivia KERBY**
Father:	**Thomas B SIMS**
Mother:	**Sarah A. ALLISON**
Draft Registration:	26, single, farming

[Documentation: NC Delayed Birth Index, US Cemetery Interment Control Form, <u>Heritage of Transylvania County, NC Vol</u> 2:272:763, Ancestry.com]

Sims, Henry C 1,878,471 * White

Residence: RFD #2 Brevord Transylvania NORTH CAROLINA
(Street and house number) (Town or city) (County) (State)

*Inducted at Brevord NC on Oct 4 19.
Place of birth: Brevord NC Age or date of birth 26 1/12 yrs

Organizations served in, with dates of assignments and transfers:
Btry D 316 FA to ; Hq Co 317 FA to disch

Grades, with date of appointment: Pvt 1cl Jan 15/18; Wag Mch 7/18; Pvt Oct 1/18

Engagements:

Wounds or other injuries received in action: None.
Served overseas from Aug 5/18 t. t May 30/19. from t to t
Honorably discharged on demobilization June 21/19 , 19
In view of occupation he was, on date of discharge, reported 0 per cent disabled.

SRC Notes: FA (Field Artillery)

7/24/1947
HENRY COY SIMS

News has been received here of the recent death of H.C. Sims, former resident of Transylvania , although he has been residing in Rockville, MD, for the past 15 years.

Funeral services were held in Rockville with interment in the Arlington, VA cemetery.

Besides his wife, Mrs. Olivia Kerby Sims, he is survived by his 91-year-old mother, Mrs. Sara Allison; a sister, Mrs. Leta Brown; and a brother, Charles T. Sims.

INTERMENT IN THE ARLINGTON NATIONAL CEMETERY	

TO: THE QUARTERMASTER GENERAL, WASHINGTON 25, D. C.

ORIG...

Sims, Henry C. (white) N. Carolina
Wagoner
1878471
Hdqrs. Co., 156th Federal Artillery, U.S. Army

DATE OF BIRTH			DATE OF DEATH			DATE OF INTERMENT			GRAVE LOCATION			DATES OF SERVICE		
Sept.	5	1891	July	16	1947	July	18	1947	17	-23 2367		10/4/17	6/21/19	

Headstone requires - Protestant Chaplain
Form mailed
No subsequent service
No medals

3046703

RAILROAD STATION FOR FREIGHT
Cameron, Virginia

POST OFFICE ADDRESS

ROBERT A. SPENCE, SUPERINTENDENT

QMC FORM 14

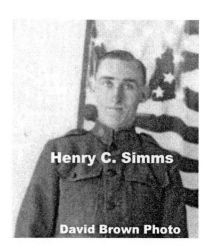

Henry C. Simms
David Brown Photo

---

6 Apr 1917 - 11 Nov 1918
About 4 million men served in the Army of the United States during the war. The total number of Army, the Navy, the Marine Corps and other services numbered to 4,800,000 men and women.

Orcutt, Louise E., **The Great War Supplement**, published 1920, p. 65.

James Columbus SINIARD

Born:	4 Feb 1894, Transylvania County, NC
Died:	1 May 1981, Tennessee; age 87
Buried:	Oak Hill Cemetery, Kingsport, TN
Spouse:	**Ruby Lee TINSLEY**, m. 20 Jan 1918, Transylvania County, NC
Father:	**Columbus M SINIARD**
Mother:	**Lillie E MACKEY**
Draft Registration:	23, single, farming

[Documentation: Transylvania County BC, Cowart's Index to Marriages, BIRLS Death File, findagrave.com, SSDI, Discharge, Ancestry.com]

James C. Siniard

Bill Siniard Photo

Siniard, James C.   1,891,679   * White *Colored*
(Surname)   (Christian name)   (Army serial number)

Residence: _____ Brevard *Transylvania* NORTH CAROLINA
(Street and house number) (Town or city) (County) (State)

*Inducted at Brevard N.C. on May 24, 1918

Place of birth: Brevard N.C.   Age or date of birth: 24 3/12 yrs

Organizations served in, with dates of assignments and transfers:
Co B 324 Inf to disch

Grades, with date of appointment:
Pvt

Engagements:

Wounds or other injuries received in action: None.
Served overseas from †Aug 5/18 to †June 18/19, from † _____ to † _____
Honorably discharged on demobilization June 23/19, 19
In view of occupation he was, on date of discharge, reported 0 per cent disabled.
Remarks:

SRC Notes: Inf (Infantry)

21 Aug 1918   Brevard News
C.M. Siniard has received word that his son J.C. Siniard has arrived safely in France.

5/14/1981
JAMES C. SINIARD

James C. Siniard, 87, of Kingsport, Tennessee, died last Friday, May 1 at his home. A native of Transylvania County, he was a son of the late Columbus Millard and Lillie Mackey Siniard. He was a member of Lynn Gardens Presbyterian Church and was retired from the Tennessee Press. He was a veteran of World War I.

Surviving are his wife, Ruby Tinsley Siniard; four daughters: Marjorie Poe, Nell Turpin, Josephine Rutledge and Dorene Dixon; a son, James I. Siniard; a sister, Henrietta Sprouse; and three brothers: Jerome, Joseph and Robert Siniard.

Services were May 3 in the Oak Hill Chapel and burial followed at the Oak Hill Cemetery.

NATIONAL ARMY CANTONMENT (CAMP)

Camp Logan   Location: Houston, Texas   Organization: 32nd (old 12th) Division
Troops from Illinois

411

Robert Gaston SINIARD

Born:	30 May 1890, Transylvania County, NC
Died:	27 Jun 1981, Marion County, FL; age 91
Buried:	Good Shepherd Memorial Gardens, Marion County, FL
Spouse:	**Emma WATTS**, m. 27 Oct 1923, Transylvania County, NC
Father:	**Columbus M SINIARD**
Mother:	**Lillie E MACKEY**
Draft Registration:	27, single, chauffeur
Note:	Family story is that Robert was a fur trader in western North Carolina, buying furs from trappers and then reselling them to merchants.

[Documentation: Transylvania County BC, <u>Cowart's Index to Marriages</u>, Florida Death Index, findagrave.com]

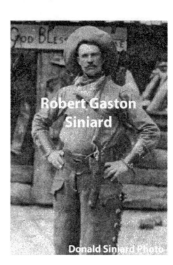

Robert Gaston Siniard

Donald Siniard Photo

	Sinard	Robert G	168,819	White	1½
(Surname)		(Christian name)	(Army serial number) (Race: White or colored)		

Residence: Brevard /Transylvania NORTH CAROLINA
(Street and house number) (Town or city) (County) (State)

Enlisted in: NA Knoxville Tenn — July 6/17 —
Born in: Brevard NC — 27 1/12 yrs —

Organizations: 7 Engrs to _____; Camp Greenleaf Det 17 Engrs to disch

Grades: Pvt 1cl Oct 1/18 —

Engagements: — —

Wounds or other injuries received in action: None.
Served overseas: July 28/17 to Mch 25/19
Hon. disch. Apr 11/19 on demobilization
Was reported 0 per cent disabled on date of discharge, in view of occupation.
Remarks: —

SRC Notes: Engrs (Engineers)

28 Sep 1917   Brevard News
HOME BOYS IN FRANCE
C. M. Siniard received a letter this week from his son Robert, who is with the American Expeditionary Forces somewhere in France. He and Will Fortune, both of whom left here almost two months ago, are in a regiment of engineers.

19 Oct 1917   Brevard News
C.M. Siniard has heard for a second time from his son Robert in France. The letter said that he was running an engine and that Will Fortune was with the electric line workers.

30 Nov 1917   Brevard News
It is always interesting to hear from the homeboys who have left to serve their country. Mr. and Mrs. C.M. Siniard have just received a third letter from Robert. He is engaged in the important business of pulling a train that supplies the fighting men with provisions and is delighted with his work.

21 Jun 1918   Brevard News
C.M. Siniard received a long letter from Robert somewhere in France. Robert says the Huns won't have much chance when our boys all get over there. He sent a paper printed right in the trenches, which is well edited and has some very humorous jokes, etc., in it. He also sent some very nice gifts to his parents.

17 Jan 1919   Brevard News

Robert Siniard, who was one of the first Transylvania boys to reach France, recently sent to friends here a pair of wooden shoes, which he states he wore during November in France. These shoes are on display in C. Doyle's window.

14 Mar 1919   Brevard News

We have just received from Robert Siniard a copy of the "Oa La La Times," the unofficial newspaper of the 17th U.S. Engineers. This issue of the paper, which is a weekly publication, contains reports of the camp life of the men of the Seventeenth and also an account of a visit paid the company by General Pershing.

7/2/1981

ROBERT G. SINIARD, Sr.

Robert Gaston Siniard, Sr., 91, Summerfield, Florida, died last Saturday at his home. A native of Brevard, he had lived in Summerfield since 1925. A retired farmer, he was a member of Pedro Baptist Church, Woodmen of the World of NC and the Veterans of W.W. I, Belleview Barracks, #3150.

Survivors include three sons: McDonald, Clarence and Robert G., Jr., one daughter, Mrs. Louise Warnock; two brothers, Jerome and Joe Siniard; and one sister, Henrietta Sprouse.

American Participation in World War I

Total number that registered in draft	24,234,021
Total soldiers in the armed forces, including Army Navy Marine Corps	4,800,000
Total men in the Army	4,000,000
Men who went over seas	2,086,000
Men who fought in France	1,390,000
Greatest number sent in one month	306,000
Greatest number returning in one month	333,000
Greatest number inducted in one month	400,000
Graduates of Line Officer's Training schools	80,468
Battles fought by American troops	13
Months of American participation in the war	19
Days of battle	200
American battle deaths in war	50,000
American wounded in war	236,000
American deaths by disease	56,991
Total deaths in the Army	112,422

Orcutt, Louis E., **The Great War Supplement**, published 1920, p. 64

Allen Monroe SISK

Born:	12 Apr 1893, Newport, TN
Died:	17 Jul 1967, Transylvania County, NC; age 74
Buried:	Mt. Moriah Baptist Church Cemetery
Occupation:	Lumber man
Spouse:	**Kitty BATSON**, m. 28 Mar 1926, Transylvania County, NC
Father:	**Loonie SISK**
Mother:	**Amanda MORGAN**
Draft Registration:	20, single, brake man on RR for Gloucester Lumber Co
Note:	Grave marker gives NO military information

[Documentation: Transylvania County DC, Cowart's Index to Marriages, Transylvania County Cemetery Survey, Discharge, Ancestry.com, TT obituary]

Sisk, Allen M.   1,872,947   • White •Colored.

(Surname)   (Christian name)   (Army serial number)

Residence: _____ Rosman *Transylvania* NORTH CAROLINA

(Street and house number)   (Town or city)   (County)   (State)

• ~~Enlisted~~ ~~R.~~ •Inducted at __Brevard N Car Apr 26/18__ on ____, 19__

Place of birth: __Parrottsville Tenn__   Age or date of birth: __24 yrs__

Organizations served in, with dates of assignments and transfers: _____
306 TM Btry to disch

Grades, with date of appointment: _____
Pvt

Engagements: _____

Wounds or other injuries received in action: None.
Served overseas from †__July 31/18__ to __Mch 20/19__, from †____ to †____
Honorably discharged on demobilization __Apr 3/19__, 19___
In view of occupation he was, on date of discharge, reported __0__ per cent disabled.

SRC Notes: TM Btry (Trench Mortar Battery)

7/20/1967
MAYOR ALLEN SISK

Mayor Allen Monroe Sisk, 74, of Rosman, died suddenly Monday morning in the Transylvania Community Hospital. He had served three years as Mayor of Rosman and had been reelected to serve two more years.

He was a retired employee of Gloucester and Carr Lumber Companies, a member of the Lions Club, a veteran of World War I and a member of the Zion Baptist Church.

Surviving are three daughters: Elizabeth Mull, Mamie Owens and Jane Pangle; three sons: Allen, Loonie and Paul; one sister, Ella Clark; and two brothers: Ira and Frank Sisk.

Funeral services were held Wednesday at Zion Baptist Church and the burial was in the Mt. Moriah Cemetery.

NATIONAL ARMY CANTONMENT (CAMP)

Camp MacArthur   Location: Waco, Texas   Organization: 32nd (old 11th) Division
Troops from Michigan and Wisconsin

Paul W. SITTON

Born:	1 Dec 1894, Transylvania County, NC
Died:	27 Aug 1942, Mountain Home, Tennessee; age 47
Buried:	Mountain Home National Cemetery, Mountain Home, Tennessee
Occupation:	Fruit dealer
Father:	**J.M. SITTON**
Mother:	**Nevada COCHRAN**
Note:	Death Certificate states he was divorced at time of death

[Documentation: TN Death Index, Application for Veteran's Headstone, Ancestry.com]

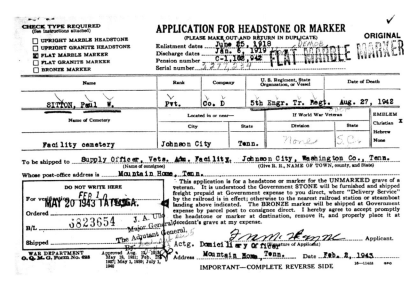

Tennessee State Marker
NATIONAL SOLDIERS HOME

"Approved by an Act of Congress on January 28, 1901, the Mountain Branch of the National Home for Disabled Volunteer Soldiers was created through the work of Tennessee Congressman Walter P. Brownlow. Known locally as Mountain Home, the original site comprised 447 acres and opened in October 1903. Peek enrollment reached over 2,500 Civil War and Spanish-American War veterans. In 1930 the National Soldiers' Home system became part of the Veterans Administration."

Willie K. SIGMORE

Born: 12 Sep 1895, Haywood County, NC
Died: 30 May 1950, San Francisco, California; age 54
Buried: Golden Gate National Cemetery, CA
Spouse: **Mary FOLMSBY**
Father: **Robert SIZEMORE**
Mother: **Harriet MURRAY**
Draft Registration: Henderson County, 21, married and a farmer

[Documentation: 1910 Census, California, San Francisco Funeral Home, Ancestry.com]

SRC Notes: Dep Brig (Depot Brigade) M D (Medical Department)

Authors Note: While researching Willie K. Sizemore it was discovered that his name had changed to SIGMORE for his military marker. The Godeau Funeral Home, San Francisco, gave his name as Willie Kirk SIZEMORE but his wife elected to use SIGMORE and applied for the marker in the new assumed name. If you should go to the Golden Gate National Cemetery you would not find Willie K. SIZEMORE but instead Willie K. SIGMORE.

Charles Hasting SLATTEN

Born:	14 Apr 1888, Jackson County, NC
Died:	14 Apr 1921, Transylvania County, NC; age 33
Buried:	Enon Baptist Church Cemetery
Spouse:	**Azalea BROWN**, m. 22 Dec. 1919, Transylvania County, NC
Father:	**Dick SLATTEN**
Mother:	**Sarah HOOPER**
Draft Registration:	30, single, cutting acid wood for Carr Lumber Co
Military Marker:	NC PVT 120 Inf 30 Div

[Documentation: Transylvania County DC, Transylvania County Cemetery Survey, Cowart's Index to Marriages, Discharge, Ancestry.com]

Slatten   Charles H   1,880,300   • White • Colored.
(Surname)   (Christian name)   (Army serial number)

Residence: _____ Brevard   Transylvania   NORTH CAROLINA
            (Street and house number) (Town or city) (County) (State)

•~~Enlisted in N.G.~~• E.R.C. •Inducted at Brevard, NC on Apr 1, 19 18
Place of birth: Tuckaslegee, NC   Age or date of birth: 31 yrs
Organizations served in, with dates of assignments and transfers:
            156 Dep Brig to Apr 25/18;
            Co B 120 Inf to disch

Grades, with date of appointment:
            Pvt

Engagements:

Wounds or other injuries received in action: None.
Served overseas from May 12/18 to † Apr 11/19, from †_____ to †_____
Honorably discharged on demobilization Apr 17/19 , 19___
In view of occupation he was, on date of discharge, reported 0 per cent disabled.

SRC Notes: Dep Brig (Depot Brigade)

2 Nov 1917   Brevard News
LOCAL BOARD ORDERS THIRTEEN MORE MEN

All men whose names appear here are ordered to report to the Local Board at 5 P.M. on Monday, November 5, 1917 for transportation for Camp Jackson. They will leave for Camp November 6 at 8 A.M. . . . Charlie Slatton . . .

The draft drawing started in Washington, D.C. on July 20, 1917, and lasted for almost seventeen hours. When it ended more than 1.3 million men had been called into military service, making it the largest army in U.S. history.

The draft had been tried once by the North in 1863 and it was violently unsuccessful. By making certain citizens in each community responsible for making sure that all eligible young men enlisted it was hoped that having friends and neighbors in charge would make the draft more acceptable. These citizens were known as the Selective Service Board. It was a group of five citizen volunteers whose mission was to decide who among the registrants in their community could receive deferments, postponements, or exemption from military service based on the individual registrant's circumstances and beliefs.

Julius Walter SLATTON

Born: 1 Apr 1890, Transylvania County, NC
Died: 12 Oct 1958, Transylvania County, NC; age 68
Buried: Macedonia Church Cemetery
Occupation: Caretaker for private residence
Spouse: **Lizzie HAMILTON**
Father: **Harlon SLATTON**
Mother: **Annie OWEN**
Draft Registration: 27, single, logging
Military Stone: M RH Base Hosp WW I

[Documentation: Transylvania County DC, <u>Transylvania County Cemetery Survey</u>, Discharge, Application for Veteran's Headstone, Ancestry.com, TT obituary]

Slatton Julius W	1,863,478		• White • ~~Colored.~~
(Surname) (Christian name)	(Army serial number)		

Residence: _____ Balsom Grove Transylvania NORTH CAROLINA
(Street and house number)   (Town or city)   (County)   (State)

• ~~N~~ .*Inducted at Brevard N C _____ on Sept 18/19 17
Place of birth: _____ Transylvania Co N C _____ Age or date of birth: ___ 27 5/12 yrs
Organizations served in, with dates of assignments and transfers: _____
_____ Med Dept to disch _____

Grades, with date of appointment: _____
_____ pvt 1cl May 17/18 _____

Engagements: _____

_____
_____

Wounds or other injuries received in action: None.
Served overseas from †_____ no _____ to †_____, from †_____ to †_____
Honorably discharged on demobilization _____ Mch 18/19 _____, 19_____
In view of occupation he was, on date of discharge, reported _____ 0 _____ per cent disabled.

SRC Notes: Med Dept (Medical Department)

10/16/1958
JULIUS WALTER SLATTON

Final rites for Julius Walter Slatton, 68, who died Sunday night in the Old Toxaway section, after a brief illness, were held in the Macedonia Baptist Church. Burial was in the church cemetery.

Mr. Slatton was a native of Transylvania and a veteran of World War I.

Survivors include one daughter, Mrs. Christine Kuykendall; one sister, Mrs. Emma Jane Carson; and one brother, Zollie Shelton.

---

21 Sep 1917   **Brevard News**
THIRTY-ONE MEN to leave for Camp Jackson, S.C. Wednesday morning.
. . .Julius Walter Slatton . . .

---

9 Jun 1932   **Brevard News**
BREVARD VETERANS IN BIG BONUS ARMY

Brevard's Bonus Army of 12 World War I veterans returned Sunday after a trip to Washington to confer with United States Congressmen in regard to the Soldier's bonus, plans for which are now being considered by that body.

The local army included: Streeter Fisher, Jude Albert, Alvin Rockwood, Wilson McCall, Elmer Gillespie, Fred Hunnicutt, Knute Heath, Julian Allison, Ruel Aiken, Fred Kilpatrick, Bill Fortune and Louie Raines left for Washington, D.C. Thursday morning at 4:30 and arrived in Washington Friday morning.

It has been said that more than 5000 veterans registered in camps in Washington while as many were reported to be located in boarding houses, hotels and private homes of the capitol city. The veterans went to Capitol city Friday where they conferred with the US Congressmen and succeeded in getting 145 of them to sign the petition which makes it necessary for the bonus question be carried to a vote before Congress June 16.

Alvin Taylor SMITH

Born: 21 Dec 1901, Fairfield, Ohio
Died: 3 Sep 1973, Transylvania County, NC; age 71
Buried: Pisgah Gardens Cemetery
Spouse: **J. Wythel SCOTT**
Father: **Van B. SMITH**
Mother: **Frances TAYLOR**
Military Marker: Ohio SEA US Navy WW I

[Documentation: Ohio Birth Index, Transylvania County DC, Ohio Soldiers in WW I, <u>Transylvania County</u> <u>Cemetery Survey</u>, Ancestry.com]

Ohio Soldiers in WWI, 1917-1918
Name: Alvin Taylor Smith
Age: 19
Race: White
Birth Date: 21 Dec 1899
Birth Location: Big Plane, Ohio, USA
Enlistment Date: 4 Mar 1918
Enlistment County: Recruiting Station Cincinnati
Enlistment State: Ohio
Enlistment Division: United States Navy
Comments: Naval Training Station Great Lakes Ill to 16 May 1918;
                      Naval Operating Base Norfolk Va to 24 May 1918;
                      United States Ship Connecticut to 11 Nov 1918. AS (active service) 89 days;
                      Seaman, Second Class 163 days.
                      Honorable discharge: 19 Aug 1919.
                      Expiration. Navy Demobilization

9/6/1973
ALVIN T. SMITH

Alvin Taylor Smith, 71, died in the local hospital Monday afternoon after a short illness. A native of London, Ohio, he had resided in Pompano Beach, Florida before coming to Transylvania County ten years ago. He was a World War I veteran of the U.S. Navy and a retired barber.

He is survived by the wife, J. Wythel Scott Smith; and four daughters: Shirley, Patricia, Deborah Lynn and Robin Melanie Smith.

Services were held in the Moore Funeral Home Chapel on Wednesday and burial was in the Pisgah Gardens Cemetery.

419

Carl Murray SMITH

Born: 12 Dec 1892, Transylvania County, NC
Died: 23 Jan 1973, Transylvania County, NC; age 80
Buried: Pisgah Gardens Cemetery
Occupation: Self-employed trucker
Spouse: **Lillie Mae GALLOWAY**
Father: **James Mack SMITH**
Mother: **Loura WILSON**
Draft Registration: No
Military Marker: NC CPL US Army WW I

[Documentation: Transylvania County BC, Transylvania County DC, <u>Transylvania</u> <u>County Cemetery Survey</u>,
<u>Ancestry.com</u>]

Carl Smith

Nancy Hughes Photo

Smith Carl *M.*	1,328,307		White	1"
(Surname) (Christian name)	(Army serial number)		(Race: White or colored)	

Residence: _____ Cullowhee _Jackson_ NORTH CAROLINA
(Street and house number) (Town or city) (County) (State)

*Enlisted in   NG Camp Glenn NC July 12/16   —
†Born in   Bravard NC 23 yrs   —   —
  Organizations:
              Hq Co 105 Engrs to disch

Grades: Wag July 12/16   —   —

Engagements: —   —

Wounds or other injuries received in action: None.
‡Served overseas: May 25/18 to Apr 13/19   —
§Hon. disch. Apr 18/19   &on demobilization   —
  Was reported   per cent disabled on date of discharge, in view of occupation.
  Remarks: 0   —   —

SRC Notes: Engrs (Engineers)

1/25/1973
CARL M. SMITH

Carl Murray Smith, 80, died at his home Tuesday after a long illness. He was a native of Transylvania County, an Army veteran of World War I and a member of VFW Post No. 4309. He was a retired trucking operator.

Surviving are the wife, Mae Galloway Smith; two daughters, Thelma Bryson and Phoebe Hooper; three sons: Jimmy, Marvin and Billy Smith; one sister, Gertrude Honaker; one half sister, Ruth Wallace; and one half-brother, H.K. Johnson.

Funeral services will be conducted Thursday at the Pisgah Forest Baptist Church and the burial will be in Pisgah Gardens Cemetery.

HEALTH AND CASUALTIES

Of every 100 American soldiers who took part in the war with Germany, 2 were killed or died of disease during the period of hostilities. The American losses were not as severe as other countries due to the fact that our armies were only in heavy fighting for 200 days. The chances of death were much heavier in the Infantry than in any other branch of the service. Of each 1,000 enlisted men in the Infantry 46 were killed or died of wounds.

Orcutt, Louis E., **The Great War Supplement**, published 1920, p. 112.

Ernest SMITH

Born:	10 Jul 1896, Transylvania County, NC
Died:	22 Sep 1963, Hartford, CT; age 67
Buried:	Cooper Cemetery
Race:	Colored
Spouse:	**Ada MOONEY**
Father:	**John SMITH**
Mother:	**Vernla McJUNKIN**
Draft Registration:	21, married and working at Brevard Tanning Co
Military marker:	NC PVT 347 Labor BN QMC WW I

[Documentation: Cowart's Index to Marriages, Transylvania County Cemetery Survey, NC Death Index, FamilySearch.org, Ancestry.com]

```
          Smith, Ernest               4,630,748    •White •Colored.
        (Surname)      (Christian name)    (Army serial number)
Residence: _____ Davidson River       NORTH CAROLINA
             (Street and house number) (Town or city) (County)   (State)
•H_____ •Inducted at   Bernard NC _____ on Sept 1 ,19 18
Place of birth: Transylvania Co NC _____ Age or date of birth: June 10 1896
Organizations served in, with dates of assignments and transfers: _____
        155 Dep Brig to Oct 14/18; Co D 355 Labor Bn to Oct 18/
        18; Co B 347 Serv Bn to disch
Grades, with date of appointment: _____
        Pvt
Engagements: _____

Wounds or other injuries received in action: None.
Served overseas from †Oct 21/18 to †June 29/19, from †_____ to †_____
Honorably discharged on demobilization    July 14/19 _____ , 19_____
In view of occupation he was, on date of discharge, reported ___0___ per cent disabled.
```

SRC Notes: Dep Brig (Depot Brigade) Labor Bn (Labor Battalion) Serv Bn (Service Battalion)

September 25, 1963
ERNEST E. SMITH

Ernest Edward Smith died 22 Sept. 1963 in the VA Hospital, Newington, Hartford, Connecticut. He was a native of Transylvania County, the son of John and Rena Henry Smith. He had worked at the Tannery in Brevard. Mr. Smith was a veteran of World War I.

Survivors include the widow, Ada Mooney Smith; two daughters, Johnsie Lee and Josephine; and one son, Ernest Smith, Jr.

Services were held September 27th at the Bethel Baptist Church and the burial followed in the Cooper Cemetery.

African American Statistics

The first African Americans in military service to be in combat zones were in the U.S. Navy and were among the service personnel landing the first troops of the American Expeditionary Forces in France.

While it is estimated that 1/3 of all labor troops in Europe were African Americans, it is not true that all were assigned to labor units.

Frederic Lansing SMITH

Born:	21 Nov 1886, Transylvania County, NC
Died:	Dec 1965, Mendota, VA; age 78
Buried:	Mendota, VA
Spouse:	**Bonnie EARLY**
Father:	**John Erwin SMITH**
Mother:	**Melinda S. SITTON**
Draft Registration:	28, single, college student at Berea College, KY

[Documentation:, Ancestry.com, FamilySearch.org, SSDI]

Frederic L. Smith

Lucy S. Parris Photo

Smith Frederic L 1,876,475 • White • Colored.
(Surname) (Christian name) (Army serial number)

Residence: _____ Brevard Transylvania NORTH CAROLINA
(Street and house number) (Town or city) (County) (State)

• _____ *Inducted at Brevard NC _____ on Sept 18, 19 17
Place of birth: ___ Brevard NC _____ Age or date of birth: ___ 30 10/12 yrs

Organizations served in, with dates of assignments and transfers: _____
MD F Hosp 324 506 Sn Tn to July 16/18; 55 Dep Brig to
Dec 18//18; 156 Dep Brig to June 27/19; MD Con Hosp 6

Grades, with date of appointment: _____ to disch
Ck Oct 16/17; Pvt July 2/18; C k Sept 7/18; Pvt Fob 1/
, 19

Engagements: _____

Wounds or other injuries received in action: None.
Served overseas from †no _____ to † _____, from † _____ to † _____
Honorably discharged: Aug 8/19, 19 _____ per SCD
(Date)
In view of occupation he was, on date of discharge, reported ___ 12(Cause)/2 ___ per cent disabled.

SRC Notes: MD (Medical) Sn Tn (Sanitation Train) Dep Brig (Depot Brigade)

21 Sep 1917   Brevard News

THIRTY-ONE MEN was ordered to report on Tuesday at 5 P.M. at the office of the local enlistment board and to leave for Camp Jackson, S.C. Wednesday morning.
. . .Fred Lansing Smith . . .

THE TANK

Among the new weapons introduced in World War I was the tank. It was a British invention and its development was top secret. The Allied commanders wanted something that could break the deadlock on the western front and they believed that a huge land battleship that could charge on special treads would be the ideal thing.

Keeping the tank a secret during its development was difficult. The machines were huge and they needed to be taken from place to place without attracting lots of attention. Rather than call them land battleships the inventors told everyone they were water carriers. These large water carriers were being built for the troops fighting in the Sinai Desert. Even the factory workers assembling the weapons were told that they were working on large water tank so the name stuck.

Up to the time of the Armistice 64 6-ton tanks had been produced in the United States and the total completed to March 31, 1919 was 778. A co-operative effort to producte 30-ton tanks were concentrated by the United States furnishing the Liberty motors and the rest of the driving mechanism while the British furnished the armor plate for 1,500 tanks for the 1919 campaign.

For immediate use in France the United States received 64 heavy tanks from the British.

Orcutt, Louis E., **The Great War Supplement**, published 1920, p. 89

Joe SMITH

Born:	18 Aug 1893, Transylvania County
Died:	16 Jun 1960, Oteen VA Hospital, Buncombe County; age 66
Buried:	New French Broad Cemetery
Occupation:	Custodian
Race:	Colored
Spouse:	**Willie Mae WILSON**, m. 3 Apr 1920, Transylvania County, NC
Father:	**Charles SMITH**
Mother:	**Mary CLANTON**
Draft Registration:	25, single and farming
Military Marker:	NC PVT CO C 426 Labor BN QMC WW I

[Documentation: Buncombe County DC, <u>Transylvania County Cemetery Survey</u>, <u>Cowart's Index to Marriages</u>, Application for Veteran's Headstone, Ancestry.com]

SRC Notes: Dep Brig (Depot Brigade) QMC (Quartermaster Corps) Res Lab (Reserve Labor)

Lewis William SMITH

Born:	29 Feb 1896, North Carolina
Died:	17 Oct 1969, Transylvania County, NC; age 73
Buried:	Pisgah Gardens Cemetery
Occupation:	Employed by the City of Brevard
Spouse:	**Alice WOOD**
Father:	**John SMITH**
Mother:	**Eliza YOUNG**
Draft Registration:	No
Military Marker:	NC PVT 120 Infantry WW I

[Documentation: Discharge, Transylvania County DC, Transylvania County Cemetery Survey, TT obituary, Ancestry.com]

10/23/1969
LEWIS W. SMITH

Lewis William Smith, 73, died last Friday at a local hospital after a long illness. He was a retired employee of the Town of Brevard and a veteran of World War I.

Surviving are his widow, Mrs. Alice Wood Smith; two daughters: Mrs. Robert Brown and Mrs. Mary Peek; a son, Clarence Smith; four sisters; Mrs. J.D. Vaughn, Mrs. Cliff Robinson, Mrs. Minnie Wood and Mrs. Lela Bohanon; and a brother, Jeff Smith.

Services were held in Morningside Baptist Church, of which he was a member and burial followed in the Pisgah Gardens Cemetery.

Loading and Firing Drill 118th Infantry

William Henry Harrison SMITH

Born:	26 May 1889, Henderson County, NC.
Died:	27 Feb 1958, Balbo Heights, Panama; age 64
Occupation:	Career military
Spouse:	**Marion WALKER**
Father:	**John Erwin SMITH**
Mother:	**Melinda S SITTON**

[Documentation: obituary]

			2½
S-ith William H	693,755	White	
(Surname) (Christian name)	(Army serial number)	(Race: White or colored)	

Residence: _____ Brevard _____ NORTH CAROLINA
(Street and house number) (Town or city) (County) (State)

Enlisted in RA at Ft Monroe, Va — July 14/14 —
Born in Henderson Co, N C — 25 1/12 yrs —
Organizations 69 Co CAC to disch —

Grades: Pvt —

Engagements: —

Wounds or other injuries received in action: None.
Served overseas: None —
Hon. disch. Apr 7/19 Immediate re-enlistment —
Was reported 0 per cent disabled on date of discharge, in view of occupation.
Remarks: —

William Henry H. Smith

Lucy S. Parris Photo

SRC Notes: CAC (Coast Auxiliary Corps)

3/6/1958
WILLIAM H. SMITH

Word has been received here of the sudden death of Maj. W.H. Smith, Western North Carolina native, in Balboa Heights, Panama. The body is being returned to the states for burial.

Mr. Smith, who traveled extensively, retired four years ago after 34 years of service in the armed forces. For some 28 years he was in the Air Force and the remainder of his years of service were in the Army artillery.

He saw action in many theatres of the world, and at the time of his death, he was spending the winter in Panama.

A native of Horse Shoe, Mr. Smith attended Brevard High School and Brevard Institute, which is now Brevard College.

He was a direct descendent of the Sittons, of the upper Mills River section, who were famous for making iron; also the Gillespies, who were noted for the early "Gillespie" rifles.

He is survived by the widow; three daughters: Malinda, Billie and Joyce Smith; two sisters, Mrs. L.N. Edmundson and Mrs. S. L. Cagle; four brothers: Jess A., John W., R. L. and Fredrick Smith.

The Control of Disease
Some of the outstanding causes of the remarkable low disease death rate in the war against Germany are: (1) a highly trained medical personnel, (2) compulsory vaccination of the entire Army against typhoid fever, (3) thorough camp sanitation and control of drinking water, and (4) adequate provision of hospital facilities. On December 1, 1918, there were available in Army hospitals 399,510 beds or 1 bed for every 9 men in the Army.
Orcutt, Louis E., **The Great War Supplement**, published 1920, p. 117

Harvey SNYDER

Born:	7 Apr 1897, Rabun County, GA
Died:	13 Oct 1987, Henderson County, NC; age 90
Buried:	Oak Forest Cemetery, Henderson County, NC
Spouse:	**Lottie HOLDEN**, m. 18 May 1918, Transylvania County, NC
Father:	**Arl SNYDER**
Mother:	**Mary BURRELL**
Draft Registration:	No

[Documentation: <u>Cowart's Index to Marriages</u>, Hendersonville T-N obituary, Ancestry.com]

Snyder, Harvey   4,070,826   • White •Colored.
(Surname)   (Christian name)   (Army serial number)

Residence: _____ Pisgah Forest   NORTH CAROLINA
(Street and house number)   (Town or city)   (County)   (State)

•T.R.C. •Inducted at Transylvania NC   on Aug 5 19 18
Place of birth: Rabun Co Ga   Age or date of birth: Apr 7/1897

Organizations served in, with dates of assignments and transfers: Co 5 Pion Inf to Aug 25/18. 55 Pion Inf to Nov 1/18; 331 Inf to Dec 19/18; Co I 14 Inf to disch

Grades, with date of appointment: Pvt

Engagements: _____

Wounds or other injuries received in action: None.
Served overseas from †Sept 15/18 to †Apr 2/19 from †_____ to †_____
Honorably discharged on demobilization Apr 12/19 , 19_____
In view of occupation he was, on date of discharge, reported 0 per cent disabled.

Harvey Snyder

Capps Family Collection

SRC Notes: Pion (Pioneer Infantry)

Hendersonville Times News
10/16/1987
HARVEY S. SNYDER

Harvey S. Snyder, 90, Etowah, died Tuesday, Oct. 13, 1987 at Pardee Hospital. A native of Rabun County GA, he had lived in Henderson County for the past 72 years. He was the son of the late Arl and Mary Burrell Snyder and a WW I veteran. He was a member of Etowah Baptist Church and Hendersonville VFW Post #5206.

Survivors include his wife, Lottie H. Snyder; two sons: Jesse and Jimmy Snyder; two daughters: Ruth Harrison and Mildred McCall; a brother, Sam Snyder; and two sisters: Ellen and Lela Snyder.

Funeral services will be held Friday afternoon in Moody-Connelly Funeral Home Chapel and burial will be in the Oak Forest Cemetery in Etowah.

One of the most gruesome aspects of trench warfare in World War I was that the dead were seldom attended to. The fighting between lines of trenches went on for many months. Many soldiers were killed in the trenches and because there was no clear cut times when shelling or firing stopped, the dead simply remained where they fell.

Dewitt Talmadge SOUTHER

Born:	6 Dec 1893, Henderson County, NC
Died:	7 Dec 1963, Henderson County, NC; age 70
Buried:	Campground Cemetery, Henderson County, NC
Spouse:	**Reba Pearl CASE**, m. 20 Apr 1919, Transylvania County, NC
Father:	**John SOUTHER**
Mother:	**Nancy MAHAFFEY**
Draft Registration:	22, single and farming for Carl Case

[Documentation: Henderson County, DC, findagrave.com, Ancestry.com]

1

Souther, Dewitt T.   4,159,465   • White • ~~Colored~~.
(Surname)   (Christian name)   (Army serial number)

Residence: _____ Pisgah Forest   Transylvania   NORTH CAROLINA
(Street and house number)   (Town or city)   (County)   (State)

• ~~[REDACTED]~~ •Inducted at Brevard NC _____ on July 24 19 18
Place of birth: Henderson Co NC ____ Age or date of birth: Dec 6/95

Organizations served in, with dates of assignments and transfers: _____
_____ MG Tng Center Camp Hancock Ga to disch _____

Grades, with date of appointment: _____
_____ Corp Oct 10/18 _____

Engagements: _____

Wounds or other injuries received in action: None.
Served overseas from No ____ to † _____ , from † _____ to † _____
Honorably discharged on demobilization _____ Dec 21/18 , 19 _____
In view of occupation he was, on date of discharge, reported ____ 0 ____ per cent disabled.

SRC Notes: MG Tng (Machine Gun Training Center)

18 Jul 1918   Brevard News
23 MORE MEN TO LEAVE JULY 24, 1918
Following is a list of white registrants for induction on July 24th, 1918 for Camp Hancock, Ga., who will leave on the 3:13 train:
. . . Dewitt Talmage Souther, Pisgah Forest . . .

Hendersonville Times News
12/7/1963
D.T. SOUTHER

Dewitt Talmadge Souther, 70, died early this morning at his home. Mr. Souther was a retired carpenter and farmer, a veteran of World War I and a member of the Horse Shoe Baptist Church. He was the son of the late John and Nancy Mahaffey Souther.

Funeral services will be held Sunday in the Thomas Shepherd Memorial Chapel. Interment will be in the Campground Cemetery.

Survivors of Mr. Souther are his wife, Reba Case Souther; five sons: John D., Robert R. Thomas W., Floyd H. and Franklin D. Souther; two daughters: Mrs. James L. Clay and Mrs. Cameron Houk; and four brothers: Harvey, Fred, Spurgeon and Luther Souther.

Air Strength at Armistice
At the signing of the Armistice, there were on the front 20 pursuit squadrons, 18 observation squadrons, and 7 squadrons of bombers with 1, 238 flying officers and 740 service planes. There were also 23 balloon companies. Orcutt, Louis E., **The Great War Supplement**, published 1920, p. 98

Willie Kay SPROUSE

Born: 25 Dec 1896, McDowell County, NC
Died: 3 Sep 1954, Transylvania County, NC; age 57
Buried: Gillespie-Evergreen Cemetery
Occupation: Foreman at Transylvania Tannery
Spouse(s):   **Mary VICKERS**
                            Eloise HUGGINS
Father: **Charles W. SPROUSE**
Mother: **Mary Jane CHRISTIE**
Draft registration: 22, McDowell County, single, teamster for Taylors Lumber Co.
Note: Death Certificate states he served in World War I
                            Grave marker has NO military information

[Documentation: Transylvania County DC, <u>Transylvania County Cemetery Survey</u>, Ancestry.com, TT obituary]

9/9/1954
WILLIE SPROUSE

Willie Kay Sprouse, 59, an employee of Transylvania Tanning Company for 25 years died early Friday morning at his home in North Brevard after a lingering illness. Funeral services were held Sunday afternoon at the Mt. Moriah Calvert Baptist Church of which he was a member. Burial was in the Gillespie Cemetery.

Survivors include his widow, Mrs. Eloise Gillespie Sprouse; three daughters: Mrs. Sims Blanton, Mrs. Kenneth Sentelle and Mrs. Floyd Goodson; three brothers: Ed, Ben and Monroe; two sisters: Mrs. Nora Williams and Mrs. Ernest Hardin; one stepson, Fred Gillespie; and one stepdaughter, Mrs. Clyde Summey.

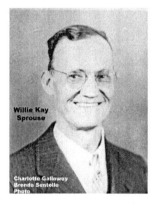

Willie Kay Sprouse

Charlotte Galloway
Brenda Sentelle
Photo

Claude W. STAGGS

Born:	22 Oct 1898, Henderson County, NC
Died:	17 Jun 1946; Richmond, VA, age 47
Buried:	Arlington National Cemetery, Arlington, VA
Spouse:	**Thelma**
Father:	**John W. STAGGS**
Mother:	**Maggie SHIPMAN**
Draft Registration:	No

[Documentation: findagrave.com, 1900 and 1930 Census, Ancestry.com]

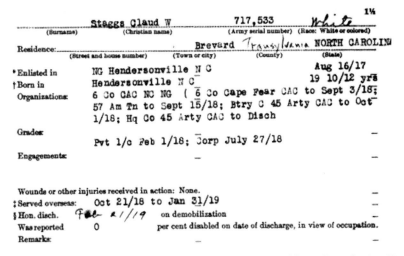

SRC Notes: NG (National Guard) CAC (Coast Auxiliary Guard) Am Tn (Ammunition Train)

6/27/1946
CLAUDE W. STAGGS

Funeral services for Claude Wilkerson Staggs, 48, resident engineer for the Virginia Highway department who died in the Medical College Hospital, Richmond, VA, last week, was held in the Manassas Baptist church and burial followed in the Arlington National Cemetery. He was a mason and a member of the American Legion.

Mr. Staggs was born in Hendersonville, N.C. and graduated from the Brevard high school. He lived in Transylvania County until he was called into service in the First World War.

Mr. Staggs had been engineer for several districts in Virginia before being named resident engineer in 1944. He was a veteran of 23 years with the department, having begun work as an inspector, July 23, 1923. Previously he had been employed since 1919 by the North Carolina State Highway Department, after service in World War I.

Surviving are his wife and young son, C. W. Jr.; and his mother, Mrs. Patrick Henry; and a brother, W.J. Staggs.

The Regular Army consisted of Divisions 1 through 10. These were in place prior to the Declaration of War.

The National Guard was made up of Divisions 26 through 42, while the National Army was 76th Division through the 93rd Division.

Joseph B. STAGGS

Born: 6 May 1899, Henderson County, NC
Died: 8 Oct 1927, Virginia; age 28
Buried: Oakdale Cemetery, Henderson County, NC
Father: **John W. STAGGS**
Mother: **Maggie SHIPMAN**
Draft Registration: No

[Documentation: Henderson County Cemetery Book, 1900 Census, Ancestry.com, Brevard News obituary]

Staggs, Joseph B		717,755		White
(Surname)	(Christian name)	(Army serial number)		(Race: White or colored)

Residence: Brevard Transylvania   NORTH CAROLINA
           (Street and house number)   (Town or city)   (County)   (State)

*Enlisted in   NG at Hendersonville NC   Aug 13/17
†Born in   Hendersonville NC   ‾   18 3/12 yrs
Organizations: 6 Co CAC NC NG Ft Caswell NC to Feb 10/18; CAC 9 Co‾
             Ft Caswell NC to Sept 28/18; CAC Btry D 6 TM Btry to
             disch

Grade: Corp Sept 25/18

Engagements:

Wounds or other injuries received in action: None.
‡Served overseas: Nov 2/18 to Jan 8/19
§Hon. disch.   Jan 19/19   on demobilization
Was reported   0   per cent disabled on date of discharge, in view of occupation.
Remarks:

SRC Notes; CAC NC NG (Coast Auxiliary Corps North Carolina National Guard) TM (Trench Mortar)

10/13/1927
JOSEPH B. STAGGS

Relatives and friends in the community were saddened Monday on hearing of the sudden death of Joseph Ben Staggs, 28, the second son of Mrs. Patrick Henry of Brevard. His death having been the result of the car which he was driving plunged off an embankment in the mountain section of Virginia, near his home, killing him instantly. The body was brought to Hendersonville, his former home, where funeral services were held Tuesday morning at the Methodist church. Interment was made in the Oakdale Cemetery.

Mr. Staggs was connected with a concrete bridge construction company in Virginia, and was on his way to take one of the young men of the working force to a doctor's appointment, when it is thought, the steering wheel became unmanageable, causing the machine to plunge over the embankment on the dangerous mountain pass. Mr. Staggs was a young man of splendid Christian character and of high standing in the community in which he lived. He also leaves many warm friends in Brevard to mourn the untimely death.

The immediate family surviving are his wife and six-month old baby, his mother and two brothers, Claude and Jeff.

Before the signing of the Armistice 42 American military Divisions were trained and sent overseas. The training of 12 more was well advanced and there were 4 others being organized. The plans on which the Army was acting called for 80 divisions overseas before July 1919 and 100 divisions by the end of the year.

Cager Green STAMEY

Born:	5 Nov 1893, Macon County, NC
Died:	13 Jan 1943, Oconee, SC; age 49
Buried:	Alexander Cemetery
Spouse:	**Lela McCOY**, m. 26 May 1918, Transylvania County, NC
Father:	**Charlie W. STAMEY**
Mother:	**Addie FULCHER**
Draft Registration:	22, single

[Documentation: NC Delayed Birth Certificate, South Carolina findagrave, 1900-40 censuses, Cowart's Index to Marriages, Application for Military Headstone, Ancestry.com]

Greenville News (SC)
CAGER G. STAMEY
6/15/1943

Cager Green Stamey, 50, a veteran of World War I, died at his home Sunday night. He is survived by his wife, Lela Stamey; five children: Otha, Ernest, Carlie, Ned and J.B. Stamey; one sister, Celia Patterson; and two brothers, Fred and Reid Stamey.

Funeral services were conducted Monday at Alexander burying ground.

BARRAGE BALLOONS

Balloon barrages were among the new defensive measures against aerial attack developed during World War I. Barrages were established around a number of European cities in 1917-18 and they were also used to protect industrial sites in Germany. The barrage protecting London, which was 51 miles long, was one of the most elaborate. Established in 1918, it consisted of groups of three balloons, set at an altitude, which made it difficult for enemy planes to fly above them. They were interconnected by means of steel cables; from these a number of lighter cables hung vertically, providing a formidable barrier for German bombers to negotiate.

Plato STANCIL

Born: 18 Dec 1891, Transylvania County, NC
Died: 8 Aug 1936, Transylvania County, NC; age 44
Buried: Oak Grove Cemetery Brevard
Occupation: Farmer
Father: **John STANCIL**
Mother: **Alice ELLENBURG**
Draft Registration: No

[Documentation: Transylvania County DC, Ancestry.com

| Stancil | Plate | 3,277,336 | 1 |
| (Surname) | (Christian name) | (Army serial number) | * White *Colored* |

Residence: _____ Brevard   Transylvania   NORTH CAROLINA
            (Street and house number) (Town or city) (County)   (State)

* Enlisted * R. A. * N. G. * E. R. C. *Inducted at Brevard N C _____ on June 25, 19 18

Place of birth: ___Old Taxaway N C___   Age or date of birth Sept 2/1889

Organizations served in, with dates of assignments and transfers: _____
          156 Dep Brig to disch

Grades, with date of appointment: _____
          Pvt

Engagements: _____

Wounds or other injuries received in action: None.
Served overseas from none _____ to †_____, from †_____ to †_____
Honorably discharged on demobilization ___Nov 30___, 19 18
In view of occupation he was, on date of discharge, reported ___0___ per cent disabled.

SRC Notes: Dep Brig (Depot Brigade)

21 Jun 1918   Brevard News
WHITE REGISTRANTS WHO ARE TO LEAVE FOR CAMP JACKSON, S.C.
TUESDAY, JUNE 25th, 1918 AT 3:13 P.M.
. . . Plato Stancil, Brevard . . .

8/13/1936
PLATO STANCIL

Plato Stancil, 56 year-old Brevard ex-service man, died as the result of an altercation with Clarence Stamey and Lester Bowen of this county. Stancil died late Saturday afternoon at the home of his father, John Stancil, near Brevard, from knife wounds, which were alleged to have been inflicted by Stamey on Thursday afternoon.

Funeral services were held Sunday afternoon at Oak Grove Methodist church, North Brevard. Interment was made in the church cemetery. Stancil was a member of the 81st Division in the World War and therefore given burial by the United States Army fund provided for in case of death of a veteran.

Women had little power in 1918 and remember, they were not allowed to vote in national elections. With the men being drafted women entered the work force and proved they were excellent workers. They worked in hospitals as nurses and technicians; they made uniforms and rolled bandages. Thousands of women worked as "munitionettes," filling shell casings with explosives. Many of these women were called "yellow girls" because the powdery explosives turned their skin a bright yellow.

John STEPP

Born:	9 Nov 1895, Henderson County, NC
Died:	13 Feb 1960, Greenville, South Carolina; age 64
Buried:	Judson Cemetery, Greenville County, SC
Spouse:	**Flora Lee STEPP**, m. 8 Oct 1916, Transylvania County, NC
	Sallie HARNETT
	Tenie ARROWOOD
Father:	**Mitchell STEPP**
Mother:	**Lena BEDDINGFIELD**
Draft Registration:	21, married and working at Carr Lumber Co

[Documentation: Henderson County BC, <u>Cowart's Index to Marriages</u>, Application for Veteran's Headstone, Ancestry.com]

```
                Stepp John                              • White • Colored.      2
            (Surname)      (Christian name)      (Army serial number)
Residence:  XX-         Pisgah Forest            NORTH CAROLINA
            (Street and house number)  (Town or city)  (County)  (State)
• ENTERED N.A.N.G.N.C. •Inducted at  Brevard N C      on Sept 18, 19 17
Place of birth: Davidson River N C   Age or date of birth: 21 11/12 yrs
Organizations served in, with dates of assignments and transfers: _____
            M D 20 Engrs  to disch

Grades, with date of appointment: _____
            Pvt

Engagements: XX

Wounds or other injuries received in action: None.
Served overseas from no    to †_____, from †_____ to †_____
Honorably discharged: Dec 18, 19 17 SCD
                      (Date)
In view of occupation he was, on date of discharge, reported  1 9/16    per cent disabled.
```

SRC Notes: MD Engrs Mortar Department Engineers) SCD (Surgeons Certificate of Disability)
Authors Note: John only served three months and was discharged with a Surgeon's Certificate of Disability. The percent of disability was 1 9/16 or one and one-half percent disability.

21 Sep 1917   Brevard News
THIRTY-ONE MEN was ordered to report on Tuesday at 5 P.M. at the office of the local enlistment board and to leave for Camp Jackson, S.C. Wednesday morning.
. . . John Stepp . . .

Greenville News (SC)
J.A. Stepp
2/15/1960

Funeral services for John Albert Stepp, 64, will be conducted at the Mackey Mortuary. Burial will be in the Judson Cemetery. Mr. Stepp died Saturday at his home following an illness of one year. He was a native of Henderson County, NC and a son of the late Mitchell F. and Selena Beddingfield Stepp.

He moved to Greenville 50 years ago from Hendersonville and was a retired carpenter. He was a veteran of World War I and a member of Turkey Creek Baptist Church.

Mr. Stepp was married first to Flora Stepp, who died some years ago. From this union the following children survive: Mrs. Harold Wood, Albert John and Edward Stepp. His second wife, Sallie Harnett Stepp also died some years ago. He is survived by his widow, Tenie Arrowood Stepp.

Emory S. STROUP

Born:	20 Dec 1886, Henderson County, NC
Died:	13 Jun 1949, Wayside, Md.; age 62
Buried:	Wayside Cemetery, Wayside, MD
Spouse:	**Emma**
Father:	**Zebulon STROUP**
Mother:	**Carrie RUSSELL**
Draft Registration:	Hendersonville, 30 single, banker at Newport News, VA

[Documentation: Henderson County BC, Application for Veteran's Headstone, Ancestry.com]

Stroup   Emory S   4,159,443   * White * Colored.
(Surname)   (Christian name)   (Army serial number)

Residence: Rosman   Rosman   *Transylvania*   NORTH CAROLINA
(Street and house number)   (Town or city)   (County)   (State)

*Inducted Hendersonville NC-   on Jul 24 19 18
Place of birth: Henderson Co NC   Age or date of birth: Dec 20 1886

Organizations served in, with dates of assignments and transfers:
Main Tng Dep Camp Hancock Ga to di ch

Grades, with date of appointment:
Pvt

Engagements:

Wounds or other injuries received in action: None.
Served overseas from †none   to †   , from †   to †
Honorably discharged on demobilization   Dec 29/18
In view of occupation he was, on date of discharge, reported 0   per cent disabled.

SRC Notes: Tng Dep (Training Depot)

"Candy Cigars or Cigarettes"   Camp Hancock, Ga.

Dr. Thomas Johnson SUMMEY

Born:	20 May 1887, Transylvania County, NC
Died:	22 Jan 1980, Richmond, Virginia; age 92
Buried:	Hollywood Cemetery, Richmond City, VA
Spouse:	**Jane MOSELEY**
Father:	**Thomas B. SUMMEY**
Mother:	**Harriett BRYSON**
Draft Registration:	No

[Documentation: 1900-1940 Censuses, findagrave.com, Heritage of Transylvania County, Ancestry.com]

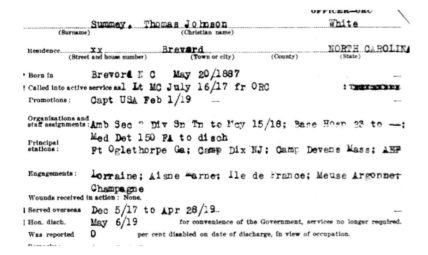

Thomas J. Summey
Dunn's Rock Masonic Lodge Archives

Summey, Thomas Johnson, first lieutenant, Medical Corps, 23d Ambulance Company, 2d Division.

French Croix de Guerre with silver star, under Order No. 13,573 "D", dated February 9, 1919, General Headquarters, French Armies of the East, with the following citation:

"On October 8 and 9, 1918, near Somme-Py he displayed coolness and courage in directing a group of litter bearers under a violent bombardment.
Residence at appointment: Brevard, N. C.

SRC Notes: Sn Tn (Sanitation Train)

27 Apr 1917   Brevard News
MORE TRANSYLVANIANS READY FOR WAR
Last week the News published the names of those who, to its knowledge, had offered their services to the government in various branches.

Dr. T.J. Summey last week successfully passed the mental and physical examinations in Asheville for the medical corps. While he could render an acceptable service at this time he will not be giving up his medical practice unless the call for physicians should become urgent.

25 May 1917   Brevard News
Dr. T.J. Summey, who recently tendered his services to the government, has received his commission of First Lieutenant from the Secretary of War. If war conditions demand, Dr. Summey will be called into service in the Medical Corps.

24 Aug 1917   Brevard News

Dr. T.J. Summey is now at Fort Oglethorpe in the Medical Officers Training Corps, Company 7, where he expects to remain for six weeks.

30 May 1919   Brevard News

After the first of next July Dr. T. J. Summey and Dr. J.Y. McKinney will occupy offices together for the practice of their profession. Dr. McKinney will devote his time to dental work and Dr. Summey expects to give his entire attention to diseases of the nose and throat.

Dr. Summey was the first Transylvanian to enlist for overseas service after the declaration of war in 1917. He received a First Lieutenant's commission and was sent to Camp Sevier where he served several months on the examining board. From Sevier he was transferred to Ft. Oglethorpe from which place he went to France in the fall of 1918. Here he had charge of a front line dressing station in close proximity to the Hindenburg Line. At the close of the Argonne Drive Lt. Summey was decorated for distinguished service, and before his return to the U.S. he was promoted the rank of Captain. Dr. Summey left here Tuesday after a visit of ten days to his parents, for Philadelphia where he will take a post-graduate course in the branches of medicine that have particular bearing on the work in which he expects to specialize.

1/31/1980
THOMAS SUMMEY

Word has been received here of the death of Brevard native Dr. Thomas Johnson Summey, 92, last week in a Richmond, Virginia hospital. Dr. Summey, a surgeon, was born in Brevard in 1887 and first practiced medicine here.

Survivors include the widow, Jane Moseley Summey; and a brother, T.B. Summey, Jr.,

Services were held last Friday at Westminster Canterbury Chapel in Richmond and burial was also in Richmond at Hollywood Cemetery.

Haywood County Digital Collection

Major F.E. Scott & Staff at Base Hospital

Andrew Coy SURRETTE

Born:	16 Jul 1894, Transylvania County, NC
Died:	12 May 1985, Transylvania County, NC; age 90
Buried:	Pisgah Garden Cemetery
Spouse:	**Beulah McGUIRE**, m. 20 Dec 1924, Transylvania County, NC
Father:	**Perry C. SURRETTE**
Mother:	**Jerusha LYDAY**
Draft Registration:	22, single, lived near Brevard, self-employed farmer

[Documentation: NC Death Collection, 1900-1940 Censuses, Ancestry.com]

Surrette, Andrew C   1,876,263   • White • Colored.
(Surname)   (Christian name)   (Army serial number)

Residence: RFD 2   Brevard   Transylvania   NORTH CAROLINA
(Street and house number)   (Town or city)   (County)   (State)

• Enlisted R. A. N. G. or N. A.   *Inducted at   Brevard NC   on Sept 18, 17
Place of birth: Brevard NC   Age or date of birth: 22 2/12 yrs

Organizations served in, with dates of assignments and transfers:
306 Sn Tn Camp Lee VA to disch

Grades, with date of appointment:
Wag Mch 15/18

Engagements:

Wounds or other injuries received in action: None.
Served overseas from † Aug 8/18 to † June 20/19 from † _____ to † _____
Honorably discharged on demobilization   June 29/19   , 19____
In view of occupation he was, on date of discharge, reported   0   per cent disabled.

Coy A. Surrette

Nina Miller Photo

SRC Notes: Sn Tn (Sanitation Train) Wag (Wagoner)

21 Sep 1917   Brevard News
THIRTY-ONE MEN TO CAMP JACKSON
Forty percent of the certified draft, making 31 men, was ordered to report on Tuesday at 5 P.M. at the office of the local enlistment board and to leave for Camp Jackson, S.C. Wednesday morning.
. . .Andrew Coy Surrette . . .

30 Aug 1918   Brevard News
Mr. and Mrs. P.C. Surrette have received word that their son Coy Surrette has safely landed over seas.

7 Nov 1918   Brevard News
"SOMEWHERE IN FRANCE"-(See John Luke Osteen for complete letter)
. . . Wags. Virgil Merrill, <u>Coy A. Surrett</u> and King S. Whitaker by their faithful work are considered among the best wagoners in the company. . . .

Asheville Citizen Times
5/14/1985
ANDREW C. SURRETT

Andrew Coy Surrett, 90, of Lyday Creek Rd., died in a Hendersonville hospital last Sunday. A native of Transylvania County, his parents were the late Perry and Jerusha Lyday Surrett. He farmed before his retirement and was a member of Enon Baptist church.

Surviving are his wife, Beulah McGuire Surrett; and a son, William A. Surrett.

Graveside services were held Wednesday in Pisgah Gardens.

Frank Bangs SUTHERLAND

Born:	9 Dec 1896, Jackson, Michigan
Died:	15 Jul 1986, Transylvania County, NC; age 89
Buried:	Cremation
Occupation:	Retired engineer with Atlantic Refining Oil Company
Spouse:	**Frances DREW**
Father:	**George SUTHERLAND**
Mother:	**Mary BANGS**
Draft Registration:	No

[Documentation: Roster of WWI Veterans from American Legion 50th Anniversary celebration; obit]

7/17/1986
FRANK SUTHERLAND

Frank Bangs Sutherland, 89, died Tuesday in Transylvania Community Hospital. A native of Jackson, Michigan, he was the son of the late George and Mary Bangs Sutherland. Sutherland was a retired engineer with Atlantic Refining Oil Company and a 1924 graduate of the University of Pennsylvania. He had resided in the area since 1966.

Survivors include his wife, Frances Drew Sutherland; one son, George D. Sutherland; one daughter, Frances S. Kirk; and one brother, Sanborn Sutherland.

Memorial services will be held Saturday at St. Philip's Episcopal Church, of which he was a member.

Red Cross Ambulances   1920 Postal Card

Dahl SWANGIM

Born:	22 May 1894, Henderson County, NC
Died:	19 Dec 1964, Transylvania County, NC; age 70
Buried:	Pisgah Gardens Cemetery
Spouse:	**Nellie ALLEN**
Father:	**Thomas SWANGIM**
Mother:	**Dovie CLAYTON**
Draft Registration:	No
Military Marker:	NC PVT CO D 115 MG BN 30 DIV WW I

[Documentation: Transylvania County DC, <u>Transylvania County Cemetery Survey</u>, 1900-1940 Censuses, Ancestry.com, TT obituary]

Dahl Swangim

Jean S. Galloway Photo

SRC Notes: NG (National Guard) MG Bn (Machine Battalion) Mec (Mechanic)

<u>19 Oct 1917</u>   <u>Brevard News</u>

Lieut. Eugene Allison, Ralph Duckworth, Horace Davis, Carl and George Fortune and Dahl Swangim of Camp Sevier, Greenville, spent Saturday night and Sunday in Brevard, returning Sunday night.

12/24/1964
DAHL SWANGIM DIES FOLLOWING ACCIDENT

Last rites for Dahl Swangim, 74, were held Monday at the Frank Moody Funeral Home chapel with burial in Pisgah Memorial Gardens. Mr. Swangim was a veteran of World War I.

Mr. Swangim died about 9:30 Saturday night of injuries he suffered when struck by an automobile on Caldwell Street about an hour earlier. A coroner's jury ruled Monday that Mr. Dahl Swangim's death was due to an unavoidable accident and the driver of the car, Peter Surrett, 16, was absolved of all blame.

Surviving are the widow, Mrs. Nellie Allen Swangim; four daughters: Jean, Nannie, Mrs. V.J Ashe and Mrs. Don Peebles; three sons: Tommy, Allen and Russell; and one brother, Frank.

> ### Did you know
> The Army shipped 68,984 horses and mules to France during World War I and did NOT bring any back to the United States at the end of the war?

Frank SWANGIM

Born:	16 Apr 1899, Henderson County, NC
Died:	24 Mar 1968, Oteen VA Hospital, Buncombe County; age 68
Buried:	Pisgah Gardens Cemetery
Father:	**Thomas SWANGIM**
Mother:	**Dovie CLAYTON**
Draft Registration:	No
Military Marker:	NC PFC US Army WW I

[Documentation: Buncombe County DC, <u>Transylvania County Cemetery Survey</u>, Ancestry.com]

Swangim, Frank   1,324,418   White
(Surname)   (Christian name)   (Army serial number)   (Race: White or colored)

Residence: _____ Pisgah   Forest   NORTH CAROLINA
(Street and house number)   (Town or city)   (County)   (State)

Enlisted in   Ho Charlotte N July20/17

Born in   Pisgah Forest NC 18 yrs

Organizations: Btry 1 FA NC NG (Btry F 113 FA) to disch

Grades: Pvt   —

Engagements: —

Wounds or other injuries received in action: None.
Served overseas: May 26/18 to Mch19/19
Hon. disch.   Apr 17/19   on demobilization
Was reported   0   per cent disabled on date of discharge, in view of occupation.
Remarks: —

SRC Notes: FA NC NG (Field Artillery North Carolina National Guard)

Hendersonville Times-News
3/26/1968
FRANK SWANGIM

Frank Swangim, 68, died Sunday in a Buncombe County hospital after a long illness. He was a retired farmer and World War I veteran. He was a member of the American Legion Post here. A number of nieces and nephews survive.

Funeral services were held today in the chapel of Frank Moody Funeral Home. Burial took place in Pisgah Gardens Cemetery.

Field Bakery

440

Fuller B. TAYLOR

Born:	4 Jul 1894, North Carolina
Died:	15 Apr 1941, Oteen VA Hospital, Buncombe County; age 46
Buried:	Oak Forest Cemetery, Henderson County, NC
Occupation:	Railroad work
Spouse:	**Lula Lucinda CRANE**, m. 17 Oct 1920, Transylvania County, NC
Father:	**James David TAYLOR**
Mother:	**Mary COFFEE**
Draft Registration:	23, single, lived in Pisgah Forest; worked for Carr Lumber Company on the railroad
Military Marker:	PVT US ARMY 14TH GRAND DIVISION TRANSPORATION CORPS WW I

[Documentation: Buncombe County DC, Application for Veteran's Headstone, Discharge, Ancestry.com, Cowart's Index to Marriages]

Taylor, Fuller B   1,872,944   1 • White • Colored.
(Surname)   (Christian name)   (Army serial number)

Residence: _____ Pisgah Forest _____ NORTH CAROLINA
(Street and house number)   (Town or city)   (County)   (State)

• Enlisted • R A • N G • ... C. •Inducted at ___ Brevard N C ___ on Apr 26, 19 18
Place of birth: ___ Weaverville N C ___ Age or date of birth: 24 9/12 yrs

Organizations served in, with dates of assignments and transfers: _____
156 Dep Brig to June 2/18;163 Dep Brig to Dec 17/18; 17
Co 14 Grand Div TC to June 19/19;12 Co TC to disch.

Grades, with date of appointment: Pvt

Engagements: _____

Wounds or other injuries received in action: None.
Served overseas from † Aug 30/18 to † July 17/19 from † _____ to † _____
Honorably discharged on demobilization _____ July 23, 19 19
In view of occupation he was, on date of discharge, reported ___ 0 ___ per cent disabled.

SRC Notes: Dep Brig (Depot Brigade) TC (Transportation Corps)

CAMP JACKSON, COLUMBIA, S. C.

Motorcycle Corps.   Postal Card

Albert TEASTER

Born:	3 Feb 1894, Madison County, NC
Died:	6 Jan 1966, Oteen VA Hospital, Buncombe County; age 71
Buried:	Catawba County, NC
Occupation:	Lumberman
Spouse:	**Dorothy TIPTON**
Father:	**Samuel TEASTER**
Mother:	**Nellie HICKS**
Draft Registration:	21, single, laborer at Gloucester Lumber Company

[Documentation: Ancestry.com, Buncombe County DC]

NOTICE TO TAX-PAYERS

I OR MY DEPUTY WILL BE AT THE FOLLOWING PLACES ON THE DATE GIVEN, FROM 10 A. M., TO 3 P. M., FOR THE PURPOSE OF RECEIVING TAXES, AND TRUST THAT ALL TAX-PAYERS WILL PREPARE TO MEET ME AND SETTLE THEIR TAXES:——

GLOUCESTER TOWNSHIP, MACEDONIA CHURCH, MONDAY, OCT. 21st.

HOGBACK TOWNSHIP, C. R. McNEELY'S STORE, TUESDAY, OCT. 22nd.

EASTATOE TOWNSHIP, L. M. GLAZENER'S SHOP, WEDNESDAY, OCT. 23.

EAST FORK PRECINCT, BAPTIST CHURCH, THURSDAY, OCT. 24th.

CATHEY'S CREEK TOWNSHIP, J. C. WHITMIRE'S STORE, FRIDAY, OCT. 25th.

CEDAR MOUNTAIN PRECINCT, H. GARREN'S STORE, SATUR., OCT. 26.

LITTLE RIVER TOWNSHIP, MERRELL'S STORE, MONDAY, OCT. 28th.

BOYD TOWNSHIP, TALLEY'S STORE, TUESDAY, OCT. 29th.

DUNN'S ROCK TOWNSHIP, T. D. ENGLAND'S STORE, WED., OCT. 30th.

BREVARD TOWNSHIP OFFICE WILL BE OPEN ALL DURING TAX PAYING TIME.

CALL ON ME AND SETTLE YOUR TAXES ON THE ABOVE DATES AND SAVE YOURSELF COST, AS I AM GOING TO LEVY AND COLLECT ALL UNPAID TAXES.

COS PAXTON,
Sheriff and Tax Collector.

Avery Clarence TERRY

Born:	10 Oct 1892, Cumberland County
Died:	26 Aug 1918, killed in action; age 25
Buried:	Oak Grove Cemetery-Brevard
Spouse:	**Florence G. BLACKWELL**, 3 Jun 1917, Transylvania County, NC
Father:	**Newton J. TERRY**
Mother:	**Mary TERRY**
Draft Registration:	None
Military Marker:	NC PVT CO K 119 Inf WW I

[Documentation: Transylvania County Cemetery Survey, Application for Veteran's Headstone, NC Marriage Index, Familysearch.org, Brevard News obituary]

Terry, Avery C. 1,317,588 * White *Colored*
(Surname) (Christian name) (Army serial number)

Residence: Bessemer City Gaston NORTH CAROLINA
(Street and house number) (Town or city) (County) (State)

* Enlisted *R.A.* N. G. *E.R.C. Inducted* at Shelby N.C on June 21, 1916
Place of birth: Burk Co N C Age or date of birth: 24 Yrs
Organizations served in, with dates of assignments and transfers: Co G 1 Inf NC NG June 21/16 to † ; Co C 4 Tng Bn 55 Dep Brig to Sept 19/17; 1 Co 105 MP to Dec 5/17; Co K 119 Inf to Aug 26/18.
Grades, with date of appointment: Pvt June 21/16; Corp Sept 19/17; Pvt Dec 2/17.

Engagements:

Served overseas from † May 12/18 to † Aug 26/18 from † to †
Killed in action Aug 26 , 19 18
Other wounds or injuries received in action none
Person notified of death: Mrs. Florence G. Terry (If none, so state) wife
(Name) (Degree of relationship)
Brevard N. C.
(No. and street or rural route) (City, town, or post office) (State or country)
Remarks :

SRC Notes: NC NG (North Carolina National Guard) Tng Bn (Training Battalion) MP (Military Police)

4/22/1921
AVERY C. TERRY

The remains of Avery C. Terry will arrive from France in Brevard at noon on Thursday, April 21st. This lad hailed from Cumberland County originally; but was a citizen of Transylvania County when he became a soldier in his country's army. He married a Brevard girl and came here to live.

He was a member of that grand organization, the 119th Regiment Infantry and appeared in action at Soissons Fismes and Chateau-Thierry. No American regiment fought more bravely or lost so heavily as did this valiant outfit. He was killed on August 26th, 1918 and was the only soldier from Transylvania County killed in actual battle.

The people of Brevard will meet the remains of this gallant Carolinian and will do honor to his memory. The funeral will be at Oak Grove Cemetery on Friday at 2:30. He leaves a widow and a three-year-old daughter; five brothers: Joe, Willie, Charlie, Edgar and Frank and one sister, Mrs. Susie Shuford; and both parents to mourn their loss.

Note: Avery's remains were returned three years after his death.

Sampson Abraham THOMAS

Born:	27 Jul 1890, Salem, SC
Died:	20 Sep 1936, Pickens County, SC; age 46
Buried:	Mt. View Cemetery, Pickens County, SC
Spouse:	**Winnie WHITMIRE**, m. 12 Jan 1919, Transylvania County, NC
Father:	**West POWELL**
Mother:	**Rachel THOMAS**
Draft Registration:	Pickens County, SC., 26, single; self-employed farmer living in Nimmons, SC

[Documentation: South Carolina Death Index, Cowart's Index to Marriages, Application for Veteran's Headstone, Ancestry.com]

Thomas, Sampson A. 2,999,088 * White * Colored

Residence: Nossman NORTH CAROLINA
(Street and house number) (Town or city) (County) (State)

Enlisted R.A. N.G. *E.R.C. *Inducted at Pickens SC on June 23, 19 18
Place of birth: Nossman SC Age or date of birth: July 27/1890

Organizations served in, with dates of assignments and transfers:
156 Dep Brig to disc.

Grades, with date of appointment:
Pvt

Engagements:

Wounds or other injuries received in action: None.
Served overseas from None to †, from † to †
Honorably discharged Nov 4, 19 18 on SCD
(Date) (Cause)
In view of occupation he was, on date of discharge, reported 25 per cent disabled.

SRC Notes: Dep Brig (Depot Brigade) SCD (Surgeons Certificate of Disability)

Greenville News (SC)
9/2/1936
SAMPSON A. THOMAS

Sampson A. Thomas, 46, died at a local hospital this morning. He was a native of Oconee County and had lived in Pickens for 10 years. He was a member of Boone's Creek Baptist Church and was a World War I veteran.

He is survived by his widow, Winnie Whitmire Thomas; six daughters: Miriam Nix, Helen, Ella Mae, Barbara, Evelyn and Nellie Thomas; two sons, Walter and Lloyd Thomas; two sisters, Mrs. Pliner O'Bryant and Irene Rotan; and one brother, Luther Thomas.

Funeral services will be held at Mountain View Baptist Church Monday afternoon and interment will follow in the Mountain View Cemetery.

NATIONAL ARMY CANTONMENT (CAMPS)

Camp Logan   Location: Houston, Texas   Organization: 32nd (old 12th) Division
Troops from Illinois

Rev. Benjamin Walter THOMASON

Born:	15 Aug 1893, Greenville, SC
Died:	Mar 1987, Transylvania County, NC; age 93.
Buried:	Pisgah Gardens
Occupation:	Retired Baptist minister
Spouse(s):	**Janette MARTIN**
	Mary HARRIS
Father:	**Benjamin Arnold THOMASON**
Mother:	**Emma LEAKE**
Draft Registration:	23, single, ministerial student in Greenville, SC

[Documentation: PoliticalGraveyard.com; obit; 1990, 1910, 1930 and 1940 Censuses; NC Death Collection]

3/30/1987
Rev. B.W. THOMASON

The Rev. Benjamin Walter Thomason, 93, mayor of Brevard from 1961 to 1965, died Saturday in Transylvania Community Hospital. A native of Greenville, S.C., he moved to Brevard in 1940. He earned his bachelor's degree from Furman University and a Th.M. degree from Southern Baptist Theological Seminary. He was a retired Baptist Minister and a veteran of World Wars I and II. He served churches in Summerville, S.C., Bishopville, S.C. and First Baptist Church in Brevard until his retirement in 1958.

A 32nd degree Mason, he was a member of Dunn's Rock Masonic Lodge. He served in the 1965 session of the North Carolina House of Representatives and also served in the North Carolina Senate.

Surviving are his wife, Mary H. Thomason; two sons, Ben W., Jr. and William M. Thomason; and a daughter, Jeanne Newton.

Services will be held at 2 p.m. Tuesday in First Baptist Church of Brevard. Burial will be in Pisgah Gardens.

B. W. THOMASON

In August 1917 the first 200 men called for the draft under went a physical examination in Brevard to determine their physical fitness to serve as soldiers. The physical exams were administered by local physicians but adhered to the standards mandated by the United States Military.

No record has been located to indicate that the physical examinations ever took place locally after the initial draft call. From that date the men were officially inducted into the Army and rode the train to the assigned military base where they underwent their first official physical examination.

The Service Record Cards and Discharge Records indicate in some cases, that some individuals were found physically unfit for military service and discharged with as few as five days military duty.

Because these individuals had been officially sworn into the military service they automatically became eligible for all military benefits granted to soldiers that served in the military. This included medical benefits, pension benefits and a military headstone

Ulysses V. THRIFT

Born:	8 May 1898, Transylvania County, NC
Died:	15 Mar 1966, Washington County, TN; age 67
Buried:	Monte Vista Cemetery, Johnson City, TN
Spouse:	**Susie Mae ORR**
	Thelma
Father:	**James A. THRIFT**
Mother:	**Amanda E. LYDAY**
Draft Registration:	No

[Documentation: SSDI, Family History from Ancestry.com, Hendersonville T-N obituary]

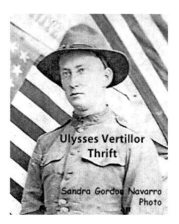

Ulysses Vertillor Thrift

Sandra Gordon Navarro Photo

Thrift, Ulysses V		1,324,552	white	1½
(Surname)	(Christian name)	(Army serial number)	(Race: White or colored)	

Residence: ___ Brevard Transylvania NORTH CAROLINA
(Street and house number) (Town or city) (County) (State)

* Enlisted in   NG Brevard N C _   July 24/17

† Born in   Transylvania Co N C _   19 2/12 yrs

Organizations: Btry 1 FA NC NG (Btry 113 FA) to disch

Grades: Pvt

Engagements:

Wounds or other injuries received in action: None.
‡ Served overseas: May 26/18 to Mch 19/19
§ Hon. disch.   Mch 28/19   on demobilization
Was reported   ___ per cent disabled on date of discharge, in view of occupation.
Remarks: 0

SRC Notes: FA NC NG (Field Artillery North Carolina National Guard)

11 Apr 1919   Brevard News
Pvt. Ulysses Thrift who belonged to the famous "30th" has received his honorable discharge. We are all glad that he is with us again.

18 Apr 1919   Brevard News
Ulysses Thrift of Pisgah Forest was a visitor to Toxaway last week having just returned home from France.

Hendersonville Times News
3/17/1966
ULYSSES V. THRIFT

Ulysses V. Thrift, 67, of Johnson City, Tenn., died Tuesday in a VA hospital.

He is survived by the wife, Mrs. Thelma Thrift; two sons: Finley and Norman Thrift; two daughters: Mrs. Ruby Neal and Mrs. Anna Mae Camp; one stepson, Don J. Adams; and one stepdaughter, Mrs. Robert Stout.

Funeral services were from the Kiser-Woodall Chapel with burial in Monte Vista Cemetery.

NATIONAL ARMY CANTONMENT (CAMP)

Camp Cody   Location: Deming, New Mexico   Organization: 34th (old 13th) Division
Troops from Minnesota, Iowa, Nebraska, North Dakota and South Dakota

---

John Wesley TINSLEY

Born:	19 Apr 1894, Transylvania County, NC
Died:	10 Apr 1965, Oteen VA Hospital, Buncombe County; age 70
Buried:	Flat Rock Baptist Church Cemetery, Liberty, SC
Occupation:	Construction worker
Spouse:	**Mary PETTIT**
Father:	**George H. TINSLEY**
Mother:	**Mary LAMANCE**
Draft Registration:	Easley, SC 23, single and farming

[Documentation: Buncombe County DC, SC findagrave.com, Ancestry.com]

Greenville News (SC)
4/11/1965
JOHN W. TINSLEY

John Wesley Tinsley, 70, died yesterday at the Veterans Hospital at Oteen, NC, after a sudden attack. For some time he had been in declining health. He was born and reared in Brevard, NC, a son of the late George Harrison and Mary LaMance Tinsley. In early life he moved to Liberty and lived before coming to Greenville 15 years ago. He was a construction foreman and superintendent with Daniel Construction before retirement. During World War I he served in the Army.

Surviving are his wife, May Pettit Tinsley; a daughter, Elaine Jaynes; two sons, Blanton C. and Arlie L. Tinsley. Also surviving are six sisters: Emma Conley, Florence Fox, Elsie Holliday, Jessie Smith, Georgia Holliday and Alice Hamlin; and four brothers: Monroe, Jeff, G.N. and R.A. Tinsley.

6/10/1918

WAR!
HEROIC FRANCE
8-BIG REELS-8

Hot from the battlefield where OUR BOYS are fighting. Real battle scenes. Actual fighting. This great picture was made on the WAR FRONT in the midst of furious fighting on land and in the air and shows our brave boys and our allies meeting the enemy.

See Big Guns Booming in World's Biggest Battle

This superb War Picture will be shown at

THE SAPPHIRE THEATRE

Opposite Post Office   Brevard, N. C.

MONDAY, JUNE 10, 1918

Matinee 1:30 P. M.   Special Show 10 A. M.   Night 7:30
Admission: Children 10 cents   Adults 20 cents

Columbus C. TOWNSEND

Born:	8 Jul 1894, Transylvania County, NC
Died:	8 Aug 1948, Oteen VA Hospital, Buncombe County; age 54
Buried:	Oakdale Cemetery, Henderson County, NC
Occupation:	Engineer
Spouse:	**Ada COOPER**
Father:	**George TOWNSEND**
Mother:	**Adeline TURNER**
Draft Registration:	23, married with a stepchild, train fireman

[Documentation: Buncombe County DC, FamilySearch.org]

Townsend, Lum   1 876 354   • White • ~~Colored~~
(Surname)   (Christian name)   (Army serial number)

Residence: _____ Brevard _____ NORTH CAROLINA
(Street and house number) (Town or city) (County) (State)

• ~~N. G.~~ ~~E. R. C.~~ •Inducted at Brevard NC _____ on Sept. 19 17

Place of birth: _____ Brevard NC _____ Age or date of birth: 23 11/12 yrs

Organizations served in, with dates of assignments and transfers: _____
_____ MD to Nov 11/17;F Hosp 324 to disch _____

Grades, with date of appointment: _____
_____ Cfr Mch 20/18;Pvt May 1/18;Pvt 1 cl Sept 14/18;
_____ Corp Apr 14/19 _____

Engagements: _____
_____
_____

Wounds or other injuries received in action: None.
Served overseas from †Aug 8/18 to †June 20/19 from †_____ to †_____
Honorably discharged on demobilization June 26/19 _____, 19_____
In view of occupation he was, on date of discharge, reported _____ 0 _____ per cent disabled.
Remarks: _____

SRC Notes: MD (Medical Department) Cfr (Chauffeur)

21 Sep 1917   Brevard News
THIRTY-ONE MEN was ordered to report on Tuesday at 5 P.M. at the office of the local enlistment board and to leave for Camp Jackson, S.C. Wednesday morning.
. . . Lum Townsend . . .

MUD IS A "NATURAL" THREAT

In addition to the bombs and poison gas there were other "natural" threats that made trench life dangerous and equally unbearable. One of the worst natural threats was MUD. The trenches were constructed of packed dirt and the dirt was almost always wet. Heavy rainfall in the fall and winter months turned the trenches into water-filled mud baths.

In addition to being dirty the mud was extremely dangerous. Thousands of soldiers drowned in the mud, often the result of falling when being shot. The mud literally swallowed up the men, as they were unable to get any traction to pull themselves to higher ground.

Mud was also an obstacle that had to be dealt with in the transportation department. Roads were impossible to keep in good repair. Motor vehicles would become stuck to the axles and horses would sink deeply into the mud. Once a vehicle was stuck all the vehicles that followed were in trouble because the roads were so narrow it was almost impossible to pass the stranded vehicle. Often horses and mules would drown in the mud because they could not free themselves from their harness and wagons.

Clifford Otto TURNER

Born: 27 Apr 1895, Waycross, Georgia
Died: 23 Oct 1955, South Carolina; age 60
Buried: Greenlawn Cemetery, Columbia, SC
Spouse: **Lucy SAVAGE**
Father: **George TURNER**
Mother: **Minnie WILSON**
Draft Registration: 24, single, a resident of Brevard; worked as an auto mechanic in Hendersonville, NC

[Documentation: South Carolina Death Index, Ancestry.com, FamilySearch.org]

Turner, Clifford O   1,876,269   * White * Colored.
     (Surname)   (Christian name)   (Army serial number)
Residence: __Main St_____Brevard_____NORTH CAROLINA__
     (Street and house number)   (Town or city)   (County)   (State)
                          Brevard N C Nov 5/17
* E_____ *Inducted at _____ on _____, 19__
Place of birth: _Waycross Ga_____ Age or date of birth: __24 7/12 yrs__
Organizations served in, with dates of assignments and transfers: _____
_____Co E 324 Inf to Jan 31/18; 324 Amb Co #306 Sn Tn to___
_____disch_____
Grades, with date of appointment:: _____
_____Pvt 1cl Feb 12/18; Mec Moh 1/19_____

Engagements: _____
_____

Wounds or other injuries received in action: None.
Served overseas from †Aug 8/18__ to †_June 20/19from †_____ to †_____
Honorably discharged on demobilization _____June 29/19_____, 19_____
In view of occupation he was, on date of discharge, reported ____0_____ per cent disabled.

SRC Notes: Inf (Infantry)   Amb Co (Ambulance Corps)   Sn Tn (Sanitation Train)

2 Nov 1917   Brevard News
LOCAL BOARD ORDERS THIRTEEN MORE MEN will leave November 6 at for Camp Jackson.
. . . Clifford Turner . . .

Company H 118th Infantry   Cleaning Grounds

Thomas Joseph TURNER

Born:	21 Jun 1895, Transylvania County, NC
Died:	21 Dec 1917, Augusta, GA; age 22
Buried:	Cathey's Creek Baptist Church Cemetery
Father:	**Thomas Fair TURNER**
Mother:	**Laura Jane HAMLIN**
Draft Registration:	21, single, lived in Selica, NC; laborer on public works employed by Lester B. Wilson
Military Marker:	NC PVT US Army WW I

[Documentation: <u>Transylvania County Cemetery Survey</u>, 1900 Census, Ancestry.com, Brevard News obituary]

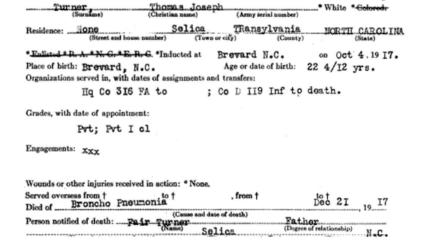

Thomas Joseph Turner

Harold Turner Photo

28 Dec 1917   Brevard News
DIED AT CAMP JACKSON
The body of Tom Turner, one of the county's drafted men who died recently at Camp Jackson, Columbia, SC, was brought home on Christmas Day. He was the son of Fair Turner of Selica and was a young man of good record and much promise. This is the first death of a Transylvanian soldier at camp.

---

18 July 1918   Brevard News
RED CROSS DRIVE AT ROSMAN

Dear editor:

Please published the following report of the W.S.S. Drive in Cathy's Creek Township: the committee made a thorough canvass and nearly everyone subscribed.

Selica subscribed... ...	$2365
Calvert subscribed....	$1195
Cherrryfield subscribed...	$2250
Rosman subscribe...	<u>$4695</u>
total........	$10,505

Rosman district committee solicited the town thoroughly and not a single residence that the committee could think of failed to subscribe. The schoolhouse meeting proved to be a great success.

Robert Kent VANDEUSEN

Born:	29 Aug 1889, Brooklyn, New York
Died:	16 Oct 1983, Transylvania County, NC; age 94
Buried:	Pisgah Gardens
Occupation:	Retired architectural draftsman
Spouse:	**Sophia HEYAN**
Father:	**Henry VANDEUSEN**
Mother:	**Annie MOREAU**
Draft Registration:	No

[Documentation: Roster of WWI Veterans from American Legion 50th Anniversary celebration; obit; NC Death Collection; 1900-1940 Censuses]

10/20/1983
ROBERT K. VANDEUSEN

Robert Kent Van Deusen, 94, died Sunday in Transylvania Community Hospital. A native of Brooklyn, New York and a resident of Transylvania County since 1961, he was a son of the late Henry and Annie Moreau Van Deusen. He was an Army veteran of World War I.

Van Deusen formerly worked as an architectural draftsman in New York, N.Y. and was employed by the New York Custom Service. He was adjutant and historian of the American Legion Post in Plainfield, N.J. and was one of the organizers of Dunn's Rock Community Center.

He was a member of Holland Society of New York, Dunn's Rock Masonic Lodge No. 167, Brevard Post American Legion and the Brevard Chapter of AARP.

Surviving is his wife, Sophia Heyen Van Deusen.

Graveside services were held Wednesday in Pisgah Gardens with Masonic graveside rites conducted by Dunn's Rock Masonic Lodge No. 267.

Camouflaged tank for battle

The United States in the Great War
published 1920, page 210

William Joseph WALLIS

Born:	30 Oct 1898, Transylvania County, NC
Died:	11 Apr 1967, Transylvania County, NC; age 68
Buried:	St. Paul's in the Valley
Occupation:	Farmer
Spouse:	**Nancy EASLEY**
Father:	**Dr. Joseph WALLIS**
Mother:	**Lucy BOSWELL**
Draft Registration:	19, single, recent graduated of the Citadel

[Documentation: Transylvania County BC, Transylvania County DC, Discharge, <u>Transylvania County Cemetery Survey</u>, TT obituary, Ancestry.com]

OFFICER 2A ARM USA

Wallis, William Joseph
(Surname)   (Christian name)

Residence ___XX___   Brevard _____   NORTH CAROLINA
(Street and house number)   (Town or city)   (County)   (State)

* Born in   Brevard, NC   Oct 30/1898
† Appointed   2 Lt Inf Sept 16/18 fr CL; Plattsburg Bks Training Camp.
Promotions: none

Organizations and
staff assignments: SATC to disch

Principal
stations: Oxford Ga; Cp Lee Va

Engagements: xx

Wounds received in action : None.
‡ Served overseas   xx
Hon. disch. (date) Mch 20/18   for convenience of the Government, services no longer required.
Was reported   0   per cent disabled on date of discharge, in view of occupation.
Remarks :

SRC Notes: SATC (Student Army Training Corps)

17 Oct 1918   Brevard News

Lieut. William Wallis has been appointed by the government as Military Instructor at Emory University, Oxford, GA.

4 Apr 1919   Brevard News

Lt. William Wallis is the guest of his parents Dr. and Mrs. W.J. Wallis.

4/13/1967
WILLIAM WALLIS

Last rites for William J. Wallis, 68, prominent Transylvania County resident will be held Thursday afternoon at the St. Philip's Episcopal Church with the burial in the St. Paul's in the Valley Cemetery. Mr. Wallis died Tuesday afternoon in the local hospital after a lengthy illness.

He was a native of Transylvania County and a former alderman of the Town of Brevard. He received his education at the Citadel, Charleston, SC.

Surviving are the widow, Mrs. Nancy Easley Wallis; three stepsons: Dr. Carol Johnson, Rev. Robert Johnson and Allen Johnson; and a sister, Mrs. Eliza Wallis Persher.

Emmett Lee WARD

Born:	27 Nov 1895, Saluda, NC
Died:	29 May 1950, Transylvania County, NC; age 54
Buried:	Oak Grove Cemetery-Brevard
Occupation:	Day laborer for coal company
Spouse:	**Ola Euphemia BAYNE**
Father:	**William Erwin WARD**
Mother:	**Mary Alice WARD**
Draft Registration:	Polk County, 21, single and working as a brakeman on the railroad
Military Marker:	NC PVT 166 INF 42 Div WW I

[Documentation: Transylvania County DC, Application for Veteran's Headstone, <u>Transylvania County Cemetery Survey</u>, Ancestry.com, TT obituary]

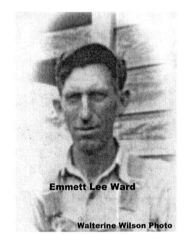

Emmett Lee Ward

Walterine Wilson Photo

SRC Notes: Dep Brig (Depot Brigade) Inf (Infantry) PL (Post Laundry)

6/1/1950
E.L. WARD

Last rites for Emmett Lee Ward, 55, were held at the Church of God on Wednesday with burial in Oak Grove cemetery. Mr. Ward died very suddenly at his home Monday morning. He had been an employee of Purity Products for many years.

Survivors include the widow, Ola Bayne Ward and the following children: Melvin L., James. M., Grady, Bobby, Larry, Walterine Wilson, Nina Raxter, Mildred Ward, Janie Lee Ward, Charlotte Ward, Patricia, Helen and Virginia Ward.

The Lewis Earl Jackson post of the VFW was in charge of military rites at the cemetery.

The excessive rainfall caused the soldiers to get a disease called trench foot. It was the result of standing for hours or days in the wet trenches without being able to put on dry socks or boots. It was not uncommon for soldiers to stand for many days in water as high as their chests. A soldier with trench foot would first notice that his toes were turning blue or red and becoming numb. Eventually, the foot would begin to rot and the only way to save the soldier's life was to amputate the foot.

Ernest Hardy WEBB

Born:	8 Mar 1893, Buncombe County, NC
Died:	24 Sep 1970, Henderson County, NC; age 77
Buried:	Oak Grove Cemetery, Brevard
Occupation:	Engineer for state highway department
Spouse(s):	**Virginia ALLISON**
	Jacksie McGAHA
Father:	**David Hardy WEBB**
Mother:	**Wilhemena WUSTROW**
Draft Registration:	24, working for Citizen Lumber Company in Mill Springs, NC

[Documentation: Roster of WWI Veterans from American Legion 50th Anniversary celebration; NC Death Certificate; 1920 and 1930 Censuses; obit; Transylvania County NC Cemetery Survey]

10/1/1970
ERNEST H. WEBB

Ernest Hardy Webb, age 78, died in a Henderson County hospital last Thursday after an extended illness. He was a native of Buncombe County and had resided in Brevard for a number of years. He had served as District Engineer of the N.C. Highway Department for 30 years before retirement several years ago. He was a veteran of World War I, having served in the U.S. Army.

He is survived by his wife, Mrs. Jacksie Webb of the home; one stepdaughter, Mrs. Rose Ruer; two stepsons, Howard Wolfe and Charles Wolfe; and two sisters, Mrs. Florence W. Burrows and Sadie Webb.

Funeral services were conducted Sunday at the First United Methodist Church of which he was a member. Burial was in Oak Grove Cemetery, Brevard.

Field Hospital US Army   Post Card

Walter Alexander WEILT

Born:	10 Dec 1887, Altoona, Pennsylvania
Died:	4 Jun 1984, Transylvania County, NC; age 96
Buried:	Oak Grove Cemetery Brevard
Father:	**William Penn WEILT**
Mother:	**Sarah Jane FISHER**
Draft Registration:	Altoona, PA, 27, single, carpenter

[Documentation: NC Death Index, FamilySearch.org]

6/7/1984
WALTER A. WEILT

Walter Alexander Weilt, 96, of the Cathey's Creek community, died Monday in Transylvania County Hospital. A native of Altoona, Pa., and a resident of Transylvania County since 1901, he was the son of the late William P. and Sarah Ann Fisher Weilt. He was a carpenter, a member of Oak Grove Independent Baptist Church and an Army World War I veteran.

Graveside services were held Wednesday in Oak Grove Cemetery, Brevard.

"Above is shown the prize bear killed two weeks ago by Walter Weilt on his hunting preserve near Brevard. This is the second bear Mr. Weilt has killed in Transylvania County this year. The first animal tipped the scales at 519 pounds, while the one shown above was estimated to go better than six hundred pounds."

"Above picture shows the fine moose head which was prize kill of Walter A. Weilt of Brevard in Jackson Hole, Wyoming recently. The huge moose weighed over 1,200 pounds and was said by rangers to be the largest killed in three years." October 20, 1938

Deloyd Samuel WELCH

Born:	20 Mar 1893, North Carolina
Died:	17 Mar 1966, Oteen VA Hospital, Buncombe County; age 72
Buried:	Pleasant Hill United Methodist Church Cemetery, Candler, NC
Occupation:	Construction worker
Spouse:	**Rebecca CASE**
Father:	**John N. WELCH**
Mother:	**Bell RUSSELL**
Draft Registration:	21, married with dependents, grade man for Carr Lumber Company
Military Marker:	North Carolina WAGR Co D 5 Ammo Train WW I

[Documentation: Buncombe County DC, findagrave.com, Ancestry.com]

Welch Deloyd S.   750,999   * White * Colored.
(Surname)   (Christian name)   (Army serial number)

Residence: Pisgot Forrest   NORTH CAROLINA
      (Street and house number)   (Town or city)   (County)   (State)

* ▉▉▉▉▉▉▉. *Inducted at   Brevard NC   on Nov 5 , 19 17
Place of birth: Candler NC   Age or date of birth: 24 4/12yrs

Organizations served in, with dates of assignments and transfers:
    Co E 324 Inf to Feb 5/18   Hq Co 6 Inf to Aug 21/18
    Co D 5th Am Tn to disch

Grades, with dates of appointment: Pvt 1/cl Mch 1/18 Wag Sept 2/18

Engagements: _____

Wounds or other injuries received in action: None.
Served overseas from Apr 9/18 to July 21/19, from † _____ to † _____
Honorably discharged on demobilization July 30 , 19 19
In view of occupation he was, on date of discharge, reported 0 per cent disabled.

SRC Notes: Inf (Infantry) Am Tn (Ambulance Train)

2 Nov 1917   Brevard News
LOCAL BOARD ORDERS THIRTEEN MORE MEN to report to the Local Board at 5 P.M. on Monday, November 5, 1917. They will leave for Camp November 6 at 8 A.M.
. . . Deloyd S. Welch . . .

NO DATE   Brevard News

NATIONAL LEAGUE W.S. HOLD MEETING
    An important business meeting of the National League of Woman's Service of Transylvania County was held on Thursday afternoon, June 20th, at the home of the chairman, Mrs. J.S. Silversteen. Various committees were appointed to carry on the general work taken up by the League and a motion passed to hold meetings on the fourth Thursday of each month at the home of the chairman. All members of the League are requested to attend these meetings, as they will, at such times, take up the business side of the work. All persons interested in making comfort kits for our boys and in food conservation will be most welcome.

                         Elizabeth M. Silversteen
                         Chairman

King Sullivan WHITAKER

Born:	23 Jun 1893, Henderson County, NC
Died:	6 Jan 1963, Buncombe County, NC; age 69
Buried:	Forest Lawn Cemetery, Enka, NC
Occupation:	Lumber inspector
Spouse:	**Blanche JONES**
Father:	**Solomon WHITAKER**
Mother:	**Elmina GRAY**
Draft Registration:	23, single, worked as a lumber inspector for Williams & Fulpin Lumber Company

[Documentation: Buncombe County DC, Application for Veteran's Headstone, 1900-1940 Censuses, Ancestry.com]

Whitaker   King S 1,876,261   1
  (Surname)   (Christian name)   (Army serial number)   • White • Colored.

                                      Brevard *Transylvania*   NORTH CAROLINA
Residence: _____
              (Street and house number)   (Town or city)   (County)   (State)

• E._____ •Inducted at Brevard, N.C.,   on Sept 18, 1917
Place of birth: _____ Mills River, N.C. or date of birth: __23 3/12 yrs__
Organizations served in, with dates of assignments and transfers: _____
_____ M.D. Amb Co 324 - 306 Sn Tn to disch _____

Grades, with date of appointment: _____
_____ Wag Mch 15/18 _____

Engagements: _____

Wounds or other injuries received in action: None.
Served overseas from †Aug 8/18 to †June 20/19, from †_____ to †_____
Honorably discharged on demobilization _____ June 29/19 , 19_____
In view of occupation he was, on date of discharge, reported _____0_____ per cent disabled.

SRC Notes: MD Amb Co (Medical Ambulance Company) Sn Tn (Sanitation Train)

21 Sep 1917   Brevard News
THIRTY-ONE MEN TO CAMP JACKSON
. . . King S. Whitaker. . .

7 Nov 1918   Brevard News
"SOMEWHERE IN FRANCE"-(See John Luke Osteen for complete letter)
. . .Wags. . . <u>King S. Whitaker. . . .</u> by their faithful work are considered among the best wagoner's in the company

> The airplane had been invented only eleven years before World War I. At first planes were used only for observation and reporting activity on the ground. In the beginning pilots would exchange friendly gestures in the sky and then they began to do combat with each other. The pilots would throw bricks and stones at each other and some even carried long lengths of chain that could be dropped on the enemy plane in hopes of it getting entangled with the propeller causing the plane to crash. Finally, guns were mounted on the sides of the plane and this proved to be ineffective and put the pilots at great risk, trying to fly the plane and man the gun. The first guns mounted inside the planes were directly behind the propeller and that proved to be fatal for many pilots. Fokker, a Dutch engineer designed a system for firing the gun and missing the propeller, giving the Germans a clear advantage until one of their planes was shot down and the Allies copied the mechanics of the gun.

Elihu Hamilton WHITE

Born:	10 Jun 1889, Jackson County, NC
Died:	29 May 1953, Transylvania County, NC; age 63
Buried:	Cathey's Creek Baptist Church Cemetery
Spouse:	**Cora Belle BARTON**, m. 18 Jun 1923, Transylvania County, NC
Father:	**Warren WHITE**
Mother:	**Martha DAVES**
Draft Registration:	27, married; employed as a cutter of acid wood for Carr Lumber Co.
Notes:	The first name on his NC Death Certificate is spelled ELIHUS, first name on WWI Draft Registration is spelled Eluhu; spelled Elibue on marriage record; birth date given on draft registration card is Oct. 6, 1889 and on death certificate it is June 10, 1889.

[Documentation: Transylvania County DC, Cowart's Index to Marriages, Transylvania County Cemetery Survey, Discharge, Ancestry.com]

Elihue White
Harold Turner Photo

SRC Notes: Med Det (Medical Detail) Sn Tn (Sanitary Train)

21 Sep 1917   Brevard News
THIRTY-ONE MEN TO CAMP JACKSON
. . . Elihu White . . .

MOTOR TRANSPORT CORPS

The quantity and importance of gasoline engine transportation in the war necessitated the creation of a new service known as the Motor Transport Corps. It was responsible for setting up motor vehicles received from the United States, their distribution, repair, and maintenance. Within the assigned area of the services of supply, the Motor Transport Corps controlled the use of motor vehicles and it gave technical supervision to their operation in the assigned area of the Army. It was responsible for the training and instruction of chauffeurs and other technical personnel. Due to the shortage of shipments from the United States, a large number of trucks, automobiles, and spare parts had to be purchased from France.

Orcutt, Louis E., **The Great War Supplement**, published 1920, p. 279.

William Rodrick WHITE

Born:	22 Aug 1896, Transylvania County, NC
Died:	27 Jun 1975, Transylvania County, NC; age 78
Buried:	Cathey's Creek Baptist Church Cemetery
Occupation:	Logger
Spouse:	**Alma LANCE**, m. 24 Dec 1917, Transylvania County, NC
Father:	**Warren WHITE**
Mother:	**Martha DAVES**
Draft Registration:	single, worked as a laborer for Mr. J. R. Sharpe in Cathy's Creek Township, listed his father and mother as dependents

[Documentation: Transylvania County DC, <u>Cowart's Index to Marriages</u>, <u>Transylvania County Cemetery Survey</u>, Discharge, Ancestry.com]

White, William R.   4,159,48.6   * White * ~~Colored~~   **1**

Residence: _____ Jolica *Transylvania* NORTH CAROLINA
(Street and house number) (Town or city) (County) (State)

* ~~_____~~ N.C. *Inducted at Brevard NC _____ on July 24, 19 18
Place of birth: Jackson Co NC _____ Age or date of birth: Aug 22/1896

Organizations served in, with dates of assignments and transfers: _____
Main Tng Dep MG Tng Camp Camp Hancock Ga to Nov 29/18; Ord Corps to Disch

Grades, with date of appointment: Pvt

Engagements: _____

Wounds or other injuries received in action: None.
Served overseas from †NO _____ to † _____, from † _____ to † _____
Honorably discharged on demobilization _____ Mch 21 _____, 19 19
In view of occupation he was, on date of discharge, reported _____ 0 _____ per cent disabled.

Roderick White
Cora Roess Photo

SRC Notes: Tng Dep (Training Depot) MG Tng (Machine Gun Training) Ord Corps (Ordnance Corps)

18 Jul 1918   Brevard News
23 MORE MEN TO LEAVE JULY 24, 1918
Following is a list of white registrants for induction on July 24th, 1918 for Camp Hancock, Ga., who will leave on the 3:13 train:

. . . William Rodie White, Selica . . .

6/30/1975
W.R. WHITE

William Rod White, 81, died in a local hospital Friday afternoon following a long illness. Mr. White was a retired logger and a veteran of World War I.

Survivors include four sons: Richard, Warren, Lee and Lynn White; two daughters: Gladys

Gerard and Martha Galloway; and one sister, Susie Carpenter.

Funeral services were held Sunday in the Frank Moody Funeral Home Chapel and burial was in the Catheys Creek Cemetery. The American Legion conducted military graveside rites.

NATIONAL ARMY CONTONMENT (CAMP)

Camp Bowie   Location: Fort Worth, Texas   Organization: 36th (old 15th) Division
Troops from Texas and Oklahoma

Mark David Whiteside

Born:	21 Apr 1895, Swain County, NC
Died:	11 Mar 1987, Buncombe County, NC; age 91
Buried:	Holly Springs Baptist Church Cemetery, Swain County, NC
Occupation:	Retired farmer and trucker
Spouse:	**Olar Clampitt**
Father:	**Elijah WHITESIDE**
Mother:	**Martha**
Draft Registration:	21, single, farmer in Bryson City, dependent parents

[Documentation; NC Death Collection;   1900, 1910, 1930 and 1940 Censuses; obit]

Asheville Citizen Times
3/13/1987
MARK D. WHITESIDE

Mark D. "Mack" Whiteside, 91, of Pisgah Forest, died Wednesday in Asheville VA Medical Center. A native and former resident of Swain County, he was a retired farmer and trucker and a veteran of World War I.

Surviving are his wife, Olar Clampitt Whiteside and a sister, Aileen Buchanan of Greenwood, SC.

Services will be at 11 a.m. Saturday in Holly Springs Baptist Church, where he was a member and deacon. Burial will be in the church cemetery.

Mark Whiteside

Transylvania Times Photo

460

Henry Leroy WHITESIDES

Born:	10 Jun 1890, Henderson County, NC
Died:	22 Sep 1967, Buncombe County; age 77
Buried:	Cooper Cemetery
Race:	Colored
Spouse:	**Marie SHARP**, m. 6 Sep 1912, Transylvania County, NC
Father:	**Andy WHITESIDES**
Mother:	**Rhoda MILLS**
Draft Registration:	No
Military stone:	New Jersey P.F.C. Infantry WW I

[Documentation: Transylvania County Cemetery Survey, Buncombe County DC, Ancestry.com, Cowart's Index to Marriages]

Whitesides Henry Leroy 3 098 835 ~~White~~ Colored.
(Surname) (Christian name) (Army serial number)

Residence: Brevard Transylvania NORTH CARLINA
(Street and house number) (Town or city) (County) (State)

P.F.C. Inducted at Transylvania N C on June 21, 1918.
Place of birth: Hendersonville N C Age or date of birth: 28 yrs

Organizations served in, with dates of assignments and transfers:
Co D 801 Pion Inf to disch

Grades, with date of appointment:
Pvt 1cl Nov 6/18

Engagements:

Wounds or other injuries received in action: None.
Served overseas from Sept 8/18 to June 5/19, from † ___ to † ___
Honorably discharged on demobilization June 13, 1919
In view of occupation he was, on date of discharge, reported 0 per cent disabled.

SRC Notes: Pion Inf (Pioneer Infantry)

21 Jun 1918   **Brevard News**
COLORED REGISTRANTS TO LEAVE FOR CAMP TAYLOR, KY
ON FRIDAY, JUNE 21, 1918.
. . . Henry Leroy Whitesides, Brevard . . .

Hendersonville Times-News
9/25/1967
HENRY L. WHITESIDE

Henry Leroy Whiteside, 77, a Henderson County native and long-time Transylvania County resident, died Friday in Oteen Veterans Hospital after a long illness. He was a brick mason and served in World War I in the U.S. Army. He operated a grocery store in Hendersonville in addition to several businesses in Brevard.

Funeral services were held at 2 p.m. today in Bethel A Baptist Church. Burial took place in Cooper Cemetery. Members of Monroe Wilson Post No. 88, American Legion, served as pallbearers and conducted graveside rites.

Surviving are his widow, Mary Sharp Whiteside; two daughters: Ophelia Hutchison and Mabel Marie Patterson; three sons: Luther L., Samuel M. and William Henry Whiteside; and one sister, Ura Mae Collins

Note: Found his name spelled both Whiteside and Whitesides.

Gilbert Cadamus WHITMIRE

Born:	26 Jul 1894, Transylvania County, NC
Died:	7 Jul 1985, Buncombe County, NC; age 90
Buried:	Whitmire Cemetery
Spouse:	**Bessie FISHER**, m. 29 Mar 1921, Transylvania County, NC
Father:	**William WHITMIRE**
Mother:	**Emma GALLOWAY**
Draft Registration:	No

[Documentation: North Carolina Birth Index, North Carolina Death Collection, Discharge, Ancestry.com, Cowart's Index to Marriages]

Whitmire, Gilbert C. 1,310,400 • White • Colored
(Surname) (Christian name) (Army serial number)

Residence: Lake Toxaway NORTH CAROLINA
(Street and house number) (Town or city) (County) (State)
Greenwood S C May 1/17

* Enlisted * R.A. * N.G. * E.R.C. Inducted at ____ on ____ , 19
Place of birth Lake Toxaway N C Age or date of birth: 21 10/12 yrs

Organizations served in, with dates of assignments and transfers:
Co b 1 Inf SC NG(Co B 111 Inf) to disch

Grades, with date of appointment:
Pvt 1 Cl July 1/18

Engagements:

Wounded in action (degree and date) Severely (Act 8) about Oct 10, 1918.
Served overseas from May 11/18 to Dec 23/18, from ____ to ____
* Honorably discharged on demobilization: Feb 5 /19 , 19
In view of occupation he was, on date of discharge, reported 0 per cent disabled.

SRC Notes: Inf SC NG (Infantry South Carolina National Guard)

14 Mar 1919   **Brevard News**
Gilbert L Whitmire who returned from France some time ago, is now visiting friends and relatives in Greenville, S.C.

Asheville Citizen Times
7/8/1986
GILBERT C. WHITMIRE

Gilbert "Cad" Whitmire, 93, of Brevard, died Sunday in Asheville VA Medical Center. A lifelong resident of Transylvania County, Whitmire was a son of the late William and Emma Galloway Whitmire. A World War I veteran, he gradated from Georgia Tech in 1926 and retired from Olin Corp. in 1958.

Surviving are his wife, Bessie F. Whitmire; three sons: Charles, Jimmy and Steve; two daughters, Gladys Whitmire and Cindy Compton; and a sister, Lela Whitted.

Services were held in Kingdom Hall of Jehovah's Witnesses, of which he was a member. Burial was in Whitmire Cemetery in Quebec.

NATIONAL ARMY CANTONMENT (CAMP)

Camp Sheridan   Location: Montgomery, Alabama   Organization: 37th (old 16th) Division
Troops from Ohio and West Virginia

Holbert Pickens WHITMIRE

Born:	20 Oct 1891, Transylvania County, NC
Died:	22 Aug 1954, Pickens County, SC; age 62
Buried:	Mt. Moriah Cemetery
Spouse:	**Mary Lou CURRENT**, m. 22 Dec 1919, Transylvania County, NC
Father:	**H.P. WHITMIRE**
Mother:	**Sarah E. PRICE**
Draft Registration:	26, single; lists occupation as self-employed fisherman at Rosman

{Documentation: Transylvania County BC, Cowart's Index to Marriages, Transylvania County Cemetery Survey, South Carolina Death Index, Ancestry.com]

Whitmire, Holbert P		1,322,684	white	1¼
(Surname)	(Christian name)	(Army serial number)	(Race: White or colored)	
Residence:		Rosman Transylvania	NORTH CAROLINA	
	(Street and house number)	(Town or city)	(County)	(State)
*Enlisted in	NG at Rosman NC		July 10/17	
†Born in	Rosman NC		26 9/12 yrs	
Organizations:	MG Tr 1 Cav NC NG (Co A 115 MG Bn) to disch			
Grades:	Mec July 25/17			
Engagements:				

Wounds or other injuries received in action: None.
‡Served overseas: May 11 /18 to Mch 22/19
§ Hon. disch. Apr 2/19 on demobilization
Was reported 0 per cent disabled on date of discharge, in view of occupation.
Remarks:

SRC Notes: MG Tr (Machine Gun Train) Cav NC NG (Calvary North Carolina National Guard)

25 Apr 1919   Brevard News
We are all very glad to again have in our midst the following who spent ten months in France working faithfully for Uncle Sam: Pick Whitmire, William Jackson, Elbert Whitmire and Lee Nicholson

8/24/1954
PICK WHITMIRE

Funeral services for Holbert Pickens Whitmire, 64, who died Sunday after a long illness, were held Monday afternoon at Mr. Moriah Calvert Baptist Church. Burial was in the church cemetery. Mr. Whitmire was a machinist by trade. He was the son of the late Mr. and Mrs. Holbert Whitmire and had resided in Transylvania County most of his life

Survivors are the widow, Mrs. Mary Lou Current Whitmire; two sons, Archie and Frank Whitmire; one daughter, Mrs. Frank McCall, Jr.; and one sister, Mrs. Ida Burrell

---

1 Aug 1918   Brevard News   WAR COMES CLOSE TO BREVARD
Friends have received a message Saturday morning as they left for camp that James H. Holmes has been killed by machine-gun fire while leading an attack on the Alsone-Marne front. Capt. Holmes, who was one of the founders of Camp French, had spent several summers here. He was a graduate of the Citadel and of West Point. He saw active service on the Mexican border and went to France in the 1st contingent of American forces.

John Leander WHITMIRE

Born:	9 Nov 1896, Transylvania County, NC
Died:	6 Nov 1964, Oteen VA Hospital, Buncombe County; age 67
Buried:	Gillespie-Evergreen Cemetery
Spouse:	**Betty OWEN**
Father:	**James L WHITMIRE**
Mother:	**Maggie LYON**
Draft Registration:	21, he was self-employed in Cherryfield, NC

[Documentation: Buncombe County DC, <u>Transylvania County Cemetery Survey</u>, US National Home for Disable Volunteers, TT obituary, Ancestory.com]

SRC Notes: Pion Inf (Pioneer Infantry)

25 Lbs. Net Weight
BOLTED
WATER GROUND
Corn Meal
FRESH
J. L. WHITMIRE
Route 1
Brevard, N. C.
Jimmy Whitmire Collection

464

Joseph Elbert WHITMIRE

Born:	4 Aug 1894, Transylvania County, NC
Died:	5 Jan 1994, Transylvania County, NC; age 99
Buried:	Pisgah Gardens Cemetery
Spouse:	**Ida L. MILLER**
Father:	**George Washington WHITMIRE**
Mother:	**Elizabeth GALLOWAY**
Draft Registration:	22, single, fireman for Gloucester Lumber RR

Documentation: North Carolina Delayed BC, Ancestry.com]

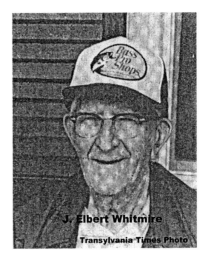

Whitmire, Elbert   1,322,607   white   1½
(Surname)   (Christian name)   (Army serial number)   (Race: White or colored)
                        Rosman   NORTH CAROLINA
Residence:
            (Street and house number)   (Town or city)   (County)   (State)
Enlisted in   NG · at Rosman NC   July 7/17
Born in   Quebec NC   22 11/12 yrs
Organizations: MG Co 1 Inf NC NG (Co A 115 MG Bn) to Nov 14/17
            Hq Co 115 MG Bn to disch
Grades: Corp Sept 15/17; Wag Nov 18/17
Engagements: —   —

Wounds or other injuries received in action: None.
Served overseas: May 11/18 to Mch 23/19
Hon. disch.   Apr 2/19   on demobilization
Was reported   0   per cent disabled on date of discharge, in view of occupation.
Remarks: —   —

J. Elbert Whitmire
Transylvania Times Photo

SRC Notes: MG NC NG (Machine Gun North Carolina National Guard)

25 Apr 1919   **Brevard News**
We are all very glad to again have in our midst the following who spent ten months in France working faithfully for Uncle Sam: Pick Whitmire, William Jackson, Elbert Whitmire and Lee Nicholson.

Asheville Citizen Times
1/6/1994
JOSEPH ELBERT WHITMIRE

J. Elbert Whitmire, 99, of Brevard died January 5th in the local hospital. A native of Transylvania County, he was married to Ida Miller Whitmire who died in 1991. He was an Army veteran of World War I and was a member of American Legion Monroe Wilson Post 88. He retired from the U. S. Postal Service in 1960.

He is survived by three daughters: Beulah Robinson, Carole Merrill and Margaret Guilkey; and two sons: Joseph E., Jr. and Ted Whitmire.

Services were held on Friday afternoon at Grace Baptist Church where he was a charter member and deacon. Burial was in Pisgah Gardens.

NATIONAL ARMY CANTONMENT (CAMP)

Camp Shelby   Location: Hattiesburg, Miss   Organization: 38th (old 17th) Division
Troops from Indiana and Kentucky

Oscar WHITMIRE

Born:	7 Jul 1898, Transylvania County, NC
Died:	9 Mar 1985, Oteen VA Hospital, Buncombe County; age 86
Buried:	Whitmire Cemetery, Flat Creek Rd.
Spouse:	**Hattie THOMAS**
Father:	**John C. WHITMIRE**
Mother:	**Dovie MURRAY**
Draft Registration:	No

[Documentation: NC Birth Index, NC Death Collection, Upper Transylvania County, NC Remembered, Ancestory.com, TT obituary]

Name WHITMIRE - OSCAR		Service Number 164-00-75		
Enroll'd at NAVY RECRUITING STATION RALEIGH N.C.				
Age at Entrance 20 YRS.	Rate SEAMAN 2 CLASS	Date 7-10-18		XXX U.S.N.R.F.
Home Address --		Town QUEBEC		
W County TRANSYLVANIA		State N.C.		

Served at	From	To	Served as	No. Days
NAVAL OPERATING BASE HAMPTON ROADS VA.	9-5-18	11-11-18	SEAMAN 2 CLASS	124

Remarks:

Date XXXXX 12-15-19
Place Inactive Duty USS WISCONSIN   Rating at Discharge SEAMAN 2 CLASS

3/9/1985
OSCAR WHITMIRE

Oscar Whitmire, 86, of Lake Toxaway, died Sunday in the Asheville VA Medical Center. He was a Transylvania County native, the son of the late John and Dovie Murray Whitmire. Survivors include his wife, Hattie Thomas Whitmire; two daughters: Jeanette Mason and Joan Holden; and a brother, Guy Whitmire.

Services will be held Tuesday in the Kingdom Hall of Jehovah's Witnesses and burial will follow in the Whitmire Cemetery at Quebec.

Photo #61955 USS Wisconsin

USS Wisconsin served as a midshipman's training ship in 1917 and 1918. She operated in the Chesapeake Bay-York River area, training recruits as oilers, watertenders and firemen.

One of her sources of men for training was the US Naval Academy at Annapolis.

Walter Clyde WHITMIRE

Born:	24 May 1894, Transylvania County, NC
Died:	16 Mar 1968, Transylvania County, NC; age 73
Buried:	Whitmire Cemetery, Eastatoe
Occupation:	Construction worker
Spouse:	**Ruth McCALL**
Father:	**Edward M. WHITMIRE**
Mother:	**Mary Emily GILLESPIE**
Draft Registration:	23, single; worked as a laborer for Rosman Tanning Company
Note:	Death Certificate stated he was divorced at time of death

[Documentation: Transylvania County DC, <u>Transylvania County Cemetery Survey</u>, discharge, Ancestry.com]

Whitmire, Walter C   1,876,291   • White • ~~Colored~~   1
(Surname)   (Christian name)   (Army serial number)

Residence: _____ Rosman *Transylvania* NORTH CAROLINA
(Street and house number)   (Town or city)   (County)   (State)

•~~_____~~C. *Inducted at _____ Brevard NC _____ on Sept 18, 19 17
Place of birth: __ Rosman NC _____ Age or date of birth: __ 23 4/12 yrs __

Organizations served in, with dates of assignments and transfers: _____
MD Camp Jackson SC to Nov 11/17; Amb Co 324 San Tr
306 to dfwch

Grades, with date of appointment: _____
Pvt lcl Oct 15/18; Cook Feb 1/19

Engagements: _____

Wounds or other injuries received in action: None.
Served overseas from **Aug 8/18** to † **June 20/19** from †_____ to †_____
Honorably discharged on demobilization _____ **June 29/19** , 19____
In view of occupation he was, on date of discharge, reported _____ **0** _____ per cent disabled.

SRC Notes: Amb Co (Ambulance Train) San Tr (Sanitation Train) Cook (Cook)

28 Sep 1917   Brevard News

The number of men of men that left last week was 31 of which three were alternates. Walter Whitmire was omitted by mistake, he went as a substitute for a man to go in a later contingent.

7 Nov 1918   Brevard News
"SOMEWHERE IN FRANCE" (See John Luke Osteen for complete letter)

. . . Cook <u>Walter C Whitmire</u> can make biscuits almost equal to any Transylvania girl. Going some isn't he? . . .

ARMISTICE

Terms for the suspension of fighting between the Allies and Germany were signed at Marshal Foch's headquarters, a <u>railway carriage</u> in the Forest of Compiegne, on 11 November 1918 (the eleventh hour of the eleventh day of the eleventh month).

Germany and Austro-Hungary had proposed an armistice to President Woodrow Wilson on 4 October 1918 but he would not accept their terms. The deteriorating military situation in Germany that threatened mutiny and revolution forced Germany's leaders to accept the Allied terms.

Frank Witcher WIKE

Born:	28 Apr 1889, Jackson County, NC
Died:	1961, Columbia, SC; age 71
Buried:	Lower Zachary Cemetery, Jackson County
Spouse:	**Lenora HOOPER**, m. 15 Sep 1922, Henderson County, NC
Father:	**David Monroe WIKE**
Mother:	**Elizabeth Alice NORTON**
Draft Registration:	Jackson County, single and farming

[Documentation: 1900-1940 Censuses, findagrave.com, Ancestry.com]

Wike Frank W. 4,159,544 * White * Colored:
(Surname) (Christian name) (Army serial number)

Residence: Sapphire *Transylvania* NORTH CAROLINA
(Street and house number) (Town or city) (County) (State)

*Inducted at Sylva NC on July 24, 1918
Place of birth: Sapphire NC Age or date of birth: Apr 28 1889
Organizations served in, with dates of assignments and transfers:
53 Dep Brig to disch

Grades, with date of appointment: Pvt .

Engagements:

Wounds or other injuries received in action: None.
Served overseas from none to †____, from †____ to †____
Honorably discharged on demobilization Dec 29, 19 18
In view of occupation he was, on date of discharge, reported 0 per cent disabled.

SRC Notes: Dep Brig (Depot Brigade)

American Soldiers with Gas Masks

Grover C. WILEY, Sr.

Born: 15 Dec 1893, Salisbury, NC
Died: 22 Dec 1976, Transylvania County, NC; age 83
Buried: Pisgah Gardens Cemetery
Spouse: **Tessa Prue CROWDER**
Father: **Thomas WILEY**
Draft Registration: Mecklenburg County, 24, single working as a repairman for Southern Power Co
Military Marker: CPL US Army WW I

[Documentation: NC Death Index, 1900-1940 Censuses, <u>Transylvania County Cemetery Survey</u>, Ancestry.com]

12/23/1976
GROVER WILEY

Grover C. Wiley Sr., age 83, died Wednesday morning in Transylvania Community Hospital after a brief illness. Mr. Wiley was a native of Salisbury, an electrician by profession and a veteran of WWI, having served in the US Army in France. Mr. Wiley was also a member of the American Legion and VFW posts of Brevard.

Surviving are his wife, Prue Crowder Wiley of the home; three daughters: Suzanne Hunt, Doris Bishop and Jeanne Hunter; and two sons, G.C. (Buddy), Jr. and Jack Wiley.

Graveside services will be held Friday in Pisgah Gardens.

---

14 Nov 1917   Brevard News

OUR HOME DEFENDERS ANSWER THE SUMMONS
Local Company Of Home Guards Organized Last Week
J. W. Burnett Elected Lieutenant
25 Men Selected From National Council Of Defense

A branch of the 38th division of home guards was organized at the rooms of the Brevard Club last Friday night by the enrollment of 25 representative men from this community as member of the body and by the election of J. W. Burnett as the 1st Lieut.

The men who were selected by the Council for National Defense as follows: J. W. Burnett, J. E. Waters, W. E. Breese, Robert Orr, Fred Johnson, P. H. Galloway, M. M. Chapman, J. S. Silversteen, W. W. Croushorn, E. F. Wellman, T. E. Patton, Jr., John O. Cantrell, B. J. Sitton, C. C. Yongue, J.A. Miller, Jr., J.M. Allison, E.F. Moffett, C.E. Orr, C.B. Deaver, R.L. Gash, C.M. Doyle and F.E. Slatton.

The members of the guard, as now constituted, are above the national draft age--their ages ranging from 34 to 45 years. They will be included in the Hendersonville Company and subject call from the captain of the company; but locally they will constitute an independent company, commanded by Mr. Burnett.

One other local officer has been appointed by Mr. Burnett, who will also appoint others. This officer is J. A. Miller, Jr., 1st Sgt.

J. S. Silversteen has offered the upper floor of the tannery as a meeting and drilling place for the company, and the men will assemble every Thursday night for military drill. This place has approximately an acre of floor space and has national advantages for training work.

Mr. Burnett elected 1st Lieut. and local commanding officer has had the advantage of military training that was taken in his college course.

Tessa Prue Crowder WILEY

Born:	14 May 1898, Gaston County, NC
Died:	24 Sep 1980, Oteen VA Hospital, Buncombe County; age 82
Buried:	Pisgah Gardens Cemetery
Husband:	**Grover C. Wiley**
Father:	**Caleb M. CROWDER**
Mother:	**Margaret A. SELLERS**
Draft Registration:	No
Military Marker:	YEO US Navy WW I

[Documentation: NC Death Index, BIRLS, 1900-1940 Censuses, <u>Transylvania County</u> <u>Cemetery Survey</u>, Ancestry.com]

Name:	**Prue Wiley**
Birth Date:	14 May 1898
Death Date:	24 Sep 1980
SSN:	414347470
Branch 1:	NAVY
Enlistment Date 1:	11 Oct 1918
Release Date 1:	11 Jul 1919

U.S. Department of Veterans Affairs
BIRLS Death File information

Asheville Citizen Times
1/25/1980
PRUE CROWDER WILEY

Prue Crowder Wiley, 82, died in Asheville VA Medical Center after a short illness. A native of Cherryville and a resident of Transylvania County since 1939, she was a daughter of the late Caleb and Margaret Sellers Crowder and the wife of the late Grover C. Wiley. She was a veteran of World War I, serving in the U.S. Navy. She was a member of the Brevard American Legion.

Surviving are three daughters: Suzanne Hunt, Doris Bishop and Jeanne Hunter; and two sons: G.C. Wiley, Jr. and Jack Wiley.

Graveside services were held in Pisgah Gardens.

Photo # NH105398 Yeomanettes at Main Navy Building 1918

When women entered the Navy as yeomen, no one knew what to call them. Nicknames: Yemenites, yeowomen, lady sailors, petticoat pets.

"If a women does a job, she ought have the name of the job. These women are as much a part of the general Navy as the men who have enlisted. They do the same work and are doing yeoman service." Rear Admiral McGowan.

The ladies were to be identified as **yeoman (F).**

Hasbrouck J. WILLIAMS

Born:	23 Jul 1899, Danbury, Connecticut
Died:	7 Jul 1954, Transylvania County, NC; age 54
Buried:	Gillespie-Evergreen Cemetery
Spouse:	**Ruth BRACKEN**, m. 17 Mar 1923, Transylvania County, NC
Father:	**William Roger WILLIAMS**
Mother:	**Irene (Rena)**
Draft Registration:	No
Military Marker:	NC PFC 116 BN MPC WW I

Documentation: NC Death Collection, 1900 and 1910 Censuses, Application for Veteran's Headstone, <u>Transylvania County Cemetery Survey</u>, TT obituary, FamilySearch.org, Ancestry.com, <u>Cowart's Indes to Marriages</u>]

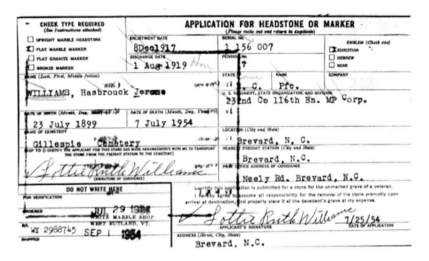

7/15/1954
HASBROUCK WILLIAMS

Last rites for Hasbrouck Williams, 54, were conducted last Friday at the First Baptist Church. The burial was in the Gillespie cemetery. Members of the Dunn's Rock Masonic Lodge were in charge of graveside rites. Mr. Williams died at Transylvania Community Hospital last Wednesday after a brief illness.

The widow, the former Ruth Bracken, and one daughter, Bertha of the home, survive him.

Mr. and Mrs. Williams had resided in Louisville, KY for many years where he was in the automobile business. They returned to Brevard several months ago and purchased a home on Neely Road.

In order to operate the transportation of supplies in France, a new system of communication had to be set up. At the time of the signing of the Armistice the Signal Corps was operating 282 telephone exchanges, 133 complete telegraph stations with 14,956 telephone lines, reaching 8,959 stations. More than 100,000 miles of wire had been strung.

Orcutt, Louis E., **The Great War Supplement**, published 1920.

Thomas Lewis WILLIX

Born: 10 Mar 1893, Cherokee County, NC
Died: 31 Mar 1976, Transylvania County, NC; age 83
Buried: Pisgah Gardens Cemetery
Occupation: Church of God minister, logger for Gennett Lumber Co.
Spouse: **Coy PHILLIPS**
Father: **William T. WILLIX**
Mother: **Martha CARPENTER**
Draft Registration: Single, section hand for RR, Andrews Mfg. Co
Military Marker: PVT US Army WW I

[Documentation: NC Death Index, Transylvania County Cemetery Survey, FamilySearch.org]

Willix Thomas L   2,594,226   • White • Colored.
(Surname)   (Christian name)   (Army serial number)

Residence: ___R F D 1_____ Andrews _Cherokee_ NORTH CAROLINA
(Street and house number)   (Town or city)   (County)   (State)

• _____ •Inducted at __Murphy N C___ on Apr 29, 19 18
Place of birth: _Robertsville N C___ Age or date of birth: _23 2/12 yrs_

Organizations served in, with dates of assignments and transfers: _____
Co G 54 Inf to disch

Grades, with date of appointment: __Pvt____

Engagements: _____

Wounds or other injuries received in action: None.
Served overseas from †July 7/18 to † July 10/19 from †_____ to †_____
Honorably discharged on demobilization __June 24/19__, 19____
In view of occupation he was, on date of discharge, reported ____0____ per cent disabled.

SRC Notes: Inf (Infantry)

Transylvania Times
4/1/1976
T.L. Willix

The Rev. Thomas Lewis Willix, 83, of the Dunn's Rock Community, died Wednesday in the Transylvania Community Hospital after an extended illness. A native of Graham County, he was a resident of Brevard for 17 years. He was a 1931 graduate of Bible Training School (now Lee College) in Cleveland TN and a retired Church of God minister. He had served churches in Tennessee, Georgia and North Carolina.

He was a World War I veteran, serving in Company G of the 54th Infantry, Sixth Division, Second Battalion. He was in overseas duty for 13 months, part of which was in the first line trench.

Surviving are his widow, Mrs. Coy Phillips Willix; two sons, Tommy Lee Willix and Robert Michael Willix; and a sister, Mrs. Hettie Pastell.

Services will be held at 2 p.m. Friday at the Church of God on French Broad, of which he was a member. Burial will be in Pisgah Gardens Cemetery.

Alvin Edgar WILSON

Born:	2 Mar 1894, Transylvania County, NC
Died:	3 Jul 1971, Pickens County, SC; age 77
Buried:	Cathey's Creek Baptist Church Cemetery
Spouse:	**Frances PARKER**, m. 14 Apr 1918, Transylvania County, NC
	Daisey Gertrude GALLOWAY
Father:	**Marcus WILSON**
Mother:	**Mary TINSLEY**
Draft Registration:	23, single, a mill hand at Champion Fiber Company in Canton, NC
Military Marker:	NC PVT US Army WW I

[Documentation: Transylvania County BC, Transylvania County Cemetery Survey, Cowart's Index to Marriages, Discharge, Ancestry.com]

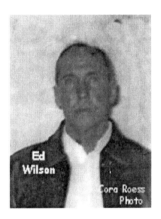

SRC Notes: MD (Medical Department)

11 Jul 1918   Brevard News

Twelve Transylvania boys left on last Saturday for Fort Oglethorpe, Ga.,
. . . Edgar Wilson, Selica . . .

14 Feb 1919   Brevard Times

Pvt. A.E. Wilson, who has been in service for his country since July 6 at Camp McClellan Base Hospital, received an honorable discharge January 29th and is at home. We are glad to see him back for he was missed very much by his many friends during his absence.

Greenville News (SC)
7/4/1971
ED WILSON

Ed Wilson, 77, died Saturday. A native of Brevard, NC, he moved to Easley 14 months ago. He was a veteran of World War I and a retired employee of the NC Highway Department.

Surviving are his wife Daisey G. Wilson; four daughters: Mrs. Mack Bell, Mrs. A.J. Theriault, Jr., Mrs. Rick Owen and Mrs. Earl Penninger; a son, Emmitt Wilson; two stepsons, Paul Barnes and Bob Barnes; and a sister, Geneva Jones.

Funeral services will be Monday in Cathey's Creek Baptist Church and burial will be in the church cemetery.

Dellie Monroe WILSON

Born: 5 Feb 1893, Transylvania County, NC
Died: 23 Jun 1919, Columbia, SC; age 26
Buried: Round Top Cemetery
Spouse: **Maude MURRAY**, m. 20 Apr 1918, Greenville, SC
Father: **Aaron WILSON**
Mother?   **Elmina RAINES**
Draft Registration: No
Military Marker: CO A 115 MCO

[Documentation: <u>Transylvania County Cemetery Survey</u>, Greenville County SC Marriage Records, 1900 Census, Ancestry.com, Brevard News obituary]

```
        ilson, Monroe              1,322,731       * White * Colored.
     (Surname)      (Christian name)     (Army serial number)

Residence: _____ Brevard  _____  NORTH CAROLINA
        (Street and house number)  (Town or city)  (County)     (State)

* Enlisted *R.A. * N. G. * E. R. C. *Inducted at Brevard N C      on July 7, 19 17
Place of birth: Transylvania Co N C      Age or date of birth: 25 11/12 yrs
Organizations served in, with dates of assignments and transfers: Co A 115 M C Bn to death


Grades, with date of appointment:
        Pvt; Pvt 1cl Sept 15/17


Engagements:
        Ypres;Voormezerle;Mt Kemmell;Hindenburg Line;Bellicourt
          Mauroy
Wounds or other inj... received in action: *None. Shrapnel wounds,head,Sept 29/18
Served overseas from May 11/18 to † Mch 23/19, from †        to †
Died of _____ cerebral embolism _____ June 23 , 19 19
                          (Cause and date of death)
Person notified of death: _____ Aaron Wilson _____ father
                (Name)    Brevard            (Degree of relationship) N.C.
     (No. and street or rural route)  (City, town, or post office)  (State or country)
Remarks :
```

SRC Notes: MG (Machine Gun Corps)

Sep 26, 1918   Brevard News
FROM A BREVARD BOY OVER THERE
(Quotations from a letter written by David Hunt to Dr. and Mrs. C. W. Hunt)

. . . .The last time that I was up the line I had orders to move my machine gun and squad to a certain place and fire on a certain crossing of railroad and a trail where Gerry usually crosses in bringing up his reserves. We got our elevation and direction from a map. According to orders we used three hours to fire 2,000 shots, firing bursts of irregular sizes and at irregular intervals. <u>Monroe Wilson</u>, the gunner of my squad, did most of the firing and I did some of it to keep in practice. It is also fun to fire. Monroe is one of the best gunners and soldiers in the company and absolutely fearless. That night we might have killed a pile of Germans or we might not have killed any. Gerry was circulating around that section that night. We concealed the flash of our gun with a wet fire screen. We had to keep our heads low on account of snipers. We would fire a while, five or six seconds, then a German sniper with a machine gun would answer us, firing about a foot over our heads. We were in a hole and behind a bank. We would simply laugh at him-because he could not hit us. He would skim over the edge of the bank. It is very easy to tell where a machine gun is and in what direction it is firing. . . . .

LETTER FROM OVER THERE

In A Letter To His Father Sgt. David L. Hunt Gives An Outline Of His Trip To France

. . . In a machine gun company, a corporal is in charge of the squad of seven men and one gun. A sergeant is in charge of a section, which is composed of two squads. The gunner of each squad must be entirely reliable and efficient. The best gunner in our company is <u>Monroe Wilson</u> from Transylvania County.

From the later part of September until about the middle of October the 30th (N.C., S.C., and Tenn.) 27th (New York) Divisions were driving the Germans out of St. Quentin and Cambria and were the 1st American troops to penetrate the Hindenburg line which was through those two towns. Both of the divisions were shot up. I was in charge of two machine guns and fourteen privates. Monroe Wilson of Brevard was slightly wounded in the hand by shrapnel. He was one of my gunners and a very good gunner. The 30th and 27th divisions won the war on the Western front when they broke the Hindenburg line in finishing Kaiser Bill. These two divisions were the 1st American troops in Belgium too. We wear a gold star for that. I have several decorations and stripes. . . . .(see David Hunt for complete Letter)

11 Apr 1919   Brevard News

Aaron Wilson has returned from Columbia, S.C., where he went to visit his son, Monroe Wilson, who is in the base hospital at Camp Jackson. He is suffering from the effects of shrapnel wound. The young man's father states that the hospital at Camp Jackson is a model in every area and he seems confident that Monroe is receiving the best of care. We hope for the young man's speedy recovery.

25 Apr 1919   Brevard News

Mr. Aaron Wilson left for Camp Jackson Wednesday morning in answer to a telegram, which stated that his son, Monroe Wilson, was not expected to live. Young Mr. Wilson went overseas with one of the first contingents of American soldiers. He received several severe shrapnel wounds and was sent to the base hospital at Camp Jackson. His father visited him a few weeks ago and came away with the assurance that his son was well on the road to recovery. The telegram received on Wednesday morning was the first undesirable news to reach him in regards to the young man's condition.

6/27/1919
PVT. MONROE WILSON

Pvt. Monroe Wilson, the son of Aaron Wilson, of Brevard, died Monday afternoon in the military hospital at Columbia, S.C. He was in one of the first groups of Transylvania boys to go to camp in the first draft. After three months at Camp Sevier the young man was sent to France with the famous 30th Division. He served overseas for ten months as a member of the 115th Machine Gun Battalion, Company A, and was pronounced by his officers the most efficient gunner in his company. He had a vital part in molding the history of the Old Hickory Division. In the Battle of Bellicourt he was gassed and sent to one of the base hospitals in France where he remained until March 1918 when he returned to this country to Camp Jackson. His father visited him shortly after his return and for several weeks prospects were bright for his recovery. But at length the chlorine gas did its work and death claimed another victim of Hun brutality.

Pvt. Wilson's body reached Brevard Wednesday on the 5:45 train. From the station the body was escorted to the dead soldier's former home near Wilson's Bridge. Thirty Transylvania boys who had served in France formed a guard of honor and marched with the remains of their dead comrade from the depot to the Wilson home.

The funeral was held in the Brevard Baptist church. Transylvania War Veterans, Members of the Red Cross, the National League for Women's Service, the Council of Defense and other patriotic organizations went as a body to the service, which was attended by people from all sections of Transylvania. Representatives from almost every community were present to pay tribute to the first Transylvania boy to lay down his life on the altar of freedom. The burial took place in the Round Top cemetery.

Donald Yearsley WILSON

Born:	21 Oct 1896, Vicksburg, Mississippi
Died:	28 Feb 1964, Transylvania County, NC; age 67
Buried:	Pisgah Gardens Cemetery
Occupation:	Mechanical engineer
Spouse:	**Beulah MORRIS**
Father:	**Harry WILSON**
Mother:	**Alice PAUL**
Draft Registration:	No
Military Marker:	Miss. PHN 3 USNRF WW I

[Documentation: Transylvania County DC, Transylvania County Cemetery Survey, TT obituary, Ancestry.com]

3/5/1964
D.Y. WILSON

Last rites for Donald Y. Wilson, 67, of Brevard and Balsam Grove were held Sunday at the St. Phillips's Episcopal Church. Burial followed in Pisgah Garden Cemetery. Mr. Wilson died in the Transylvania Community Hospital Friday after a long illness.

A native of Vicksburg, Mississippi he had lived in Texas before retiring. He was a Scottish Rite Mason. He was a veteran of World War I.

He is survived by the widow, Mrs. Beulah Morris Wilson; a daughter, Lecretia W. Weld; and a son, Don Y. Wilson, Jr.

---

20 Apr 1917   Brevard News

TRANSYLVANIA'S PLEDGE

Following the program of the Democratic Convention in Brevard Tuesday night those present remained and passed the following resolution prepared by the committee.

At this time of a crisis in the affairs of the Nation, when we find ourselves forced into a war that we have steadfastly sought to avoid, it is fitting that Americans should have the opportunity, as unquestionably they will have, to give assurance of their loyal support to the Government in its measures to uphold American rights and protect the lives of American citizens.

Therefore, Be it resolved by the citizens of Transylvania County, North Carolina, in mass meeting assembled, that as Americans, faithful to American ideals of justice, liberty and humanity, are confident the Government has exerted its most earnest efforts to keep us at peace with the world, we hereby declare our absolute and unconditional loyalty to the Government of the United States and pledge our undivided support to the President of the United States and offer our assistance in prosecuting for war with Germany and her allies to a final and satisfactory conclusion.

Unanimously adopted at Brevard, N.C. by a mass meeting of the citizens this 17th day of April 1917.

> G. H. TROWBRIDGE
> WELCH GALLOWAY
> ORA L. JONES
> Committee

Judson Lewis WILSON

Born:	7 May 1892, Buncombe County, NC
Died:	11 Aug 1953, Mecklenburg County, NC; age 61
Buried:	Evergreen Cemetery, Charlotte, NC
Spouse:	**Aileen BROYLES**
Father:	**Rufus WILSON**
Mother:	**Ella HAMPTON**
Draft Registration:	No

[Documentation: Mecklenburg County DC, Application for Veteran's Headstone, Ancestry.com]

Wilson, Judson L 48,801   *Transylvania*   White 2½
(Surname)   (Christian name)   (Army serial number)   (Race: White or colored)

Residence: _____ Pisgah Forest   NORTH CAROLINA
(Street and house number)   (Town or city)   (County)   (State)

* Enlisted in   RA Texas City Tex Lch 2 0/14

† Born in   Farview N C; 24 1/12 yrs

Organizations: Sup Co 23 Inf to disch

Grades: Pvt 1cl Nov 21/16; Sgt July 3/17; Ord Sgt July 11/19

Engagements:

Wounds or other injuries received in action: None.

‡ Served overseas: July 7/17 to Aug 4/19

§ Hon. disch.   Oct 9/19; re-enlistment

Was reported   0   per cent disabled on date of discharge, in view of occupation.

Remarks: *Cited for bravery*

Form No. 724-2½ A. G. O.   *Insert "R. A.", "N. G.", "E. R. C.", "N. A." as case may be, followed by place and
March 12, 1920.   date of enlistment.   † Give place of birth and date of birth, or age at enlistment.
‡ Give dates of departure from and arrival in the United States.   § Give date and cause.

SRC Notes: RA (Regular Army) Sup Co (Supply Company)

Company K 118th Infantry   Building Company Streets

Haywood County Digital Collection

477

Lester B. WILSON

Born: 12 Jun 1889, Transylvania County, NC
Died: 8 Apr 1936, Oteen VA Hospital, Buncombe County; age 46
Buried: Cathey's Creek Baptist Church Cemetery
Spouse: **Nora ROSS**, m. 25 Dec 1919, Transylvania County, NC
Father: **Marcus WILSON**
Mother: **Mary TINSLEY**
Draft Registration: 27, single, worked in construction for Mr. E.L. Gaston, Selica, NC,
                              father & mother were dependents.
Military Marker: NC PVT 323 INF 88 DIV

[Documentation: Buncombe County DC, <u>Transylvania County Cemetery Survey</u>, <u>Cowart's Index to Marriages</u>, Discharge, Ancestry.com]

Wilson Lester B   1,891,704   * White * Colored.
    (Surname)   (Christian name)   (Army serial number)

Residence: _____ Selica *Transylvania* NORTH CAROLINA
            (Street and house number)   (Town or city)   (County)   (State)

~~Enlisted R. A.~~ *Inducted at Brevard N C on May 24, 19 18
Place of birth: Selica N C _____ Age or date of birth 29 yrs
Organizations served in, with dates of assignments and transfers: _____
    Co D 323 Inf to Jan 15/19; Co B 144 Inf to disch

Grades, with date of appointment: Pvt

Engagements: _____

Wounds or other injuries received in action: None.
Served overseas from † Aug 1/18 to † Apr 27/19, from † _____ to † _____
Honorably discharged on demobilization May 10/19 _____, 19 __
In view of occupation he was, on date of discharge, reported 0 _____ per cent disabled.
Remarks: _____

SRC Notes: Inf (Infantry)

<u>28 Feb 1919</u>   <u>Brevard News</u>
Mrs. M.E. Wilson of Selica has received a letter from her son, L.B. Wilson, who is now in a military hospital in France. Young Wilson states that he expects to return to North Carolina in August.

<u>9 May 1919</u>   <u>Brevard News</u>
Mrs. M.E. Wilson has received notice that her son Lester has arrived from overseas. We all are hoping to see him home real soon.

4/9/1936
LESTER B. WILSON

Lester B. Wilson, 46, died at Oteen hospital Wednesday where he had been taking treatment for several weeks. Mr. Wilson worked for the state highway department prior to his last illness. He was a member of the 81st Division, and saw service in France during the World War.

Funeral arrangements were not complete as of this printing date, but will very probably be at the end of this week.

He is survived by his widow and three children: L.C., Ross and Mae; one sister, Mrs. Joseph Jones; and one brother, Ed Wilson.

Louislyn Pembroke WILSON

Born: 29 May 1896, Marietta, SC
Died: 6 Mar 1953, Yanceyville, NC; age 55
Buried: Carr's Hill Baptist Church Cemetery
Spouse: **Ossie GALLOWAY**, m. 29 May 1920, Transylvania County, NC
Father: **Luther WILSON**
Mother: **Dovie MOORE**
Draft Registration: 21, single; worked as a store clerk for Glazener Brothers Company, Rosman, NC; asked for draft exemption because he was 'not able'.

[Documentation: Transylvania County Cemetery Survey, Cowart's Index to Marriages, Discharge, TT obituary, Ancestry.com]

Wilson	Luoislyn P	1,315,421	White Colored.
(Surname)	(Christian name)	(Army serial number)	

Residence: _____ Rosman _____ NORTH CAROLINA
            (Street and house number) (Town or city) (County) (State)

Enlisted R. A. N. G. E. R. C. Inducted at ___ Brevard N C ___ on Oct 4 , 1917
Place of birth: ___ Marietta S C ___ Age or date of birth: 21 5/12 yrs
Organizations served in, with dates of assignments and transfers Hq Co 316 FA to ;
Co D 119 Inf to ; Co a 113 MG Bn to disch _____

Grades, with date of appointment: Pvt _____

Engagements: _____ xx _____

Wounds or other injuries received in action: None.
Served overseas from †none ___ to †_____ , from †_____ to †_____
Honorably discharged: May 5 , 1918. _____ S CD ____
                     (Date)   (Cause)
In view of occupation he was, on date of discharge, reported _____ per cent disabled.
Remarks:

SRC Notes: FA (Field Artillery) MG Bn (Machine Gun Battalion)

3/12/1953
LUOISLYN POMBROKE
WILSON

Funeral services for L. P. "Buck" Wilson, age 55, of Yanceyville and formerly of this county, were held at the Carr's Hill Baptist church with burial in the church cemetery.

Survivors include his widow, Ossie Galloway Wilson; one son, Gerald; one daughter, Mrs. Melvin Feldenhelmer; and three sisters: Mrs. Aston Heath, Mrs. Ben Allen and Mrs. Roy Bennett.

L.P. "Buck" Wilson
Louise Cotton Photo

12/7/1917

THIS WAR CANNOT LAST FOREVER; PEACE MUST COME SOME TIME

And when peace comes a long line of American soldiers will make their way homeward from the depths of this German manufactured hell. Some of these fighters will be minus an eye—maybe two; an arm, or maybe two; a leg, or maybe two. These men, who have placed the uttermost offering upon the altar of patriotism, will sometimes grow reminiscent and talk of the battles which saved America. If we who stay in the protected shelter of our homes give OUR BEST SERVICE to the AMERICAN NATIONAL RED CROSS we can listen unashamed to details of the struggle, for we will know that we have helped defeat the foe. If we have done nothing for the RED CROSS — or almost nothing in a half-hearted way — when the boys come back from the trenches, we'll have to hang our heads and feel like ____!

479

Sylvester WINCHESTER

Born: 21 Aug 1895, Pickens County, SC
Died: 22 Dec 1981, Pickens County, SC; age 86
Buried: Hillcrest Memorial Park, Pickens, SC
Occupation: Operated a garage in Rosman
Education: Studied mechanics in Kansas City, MO
Spouse(s):   **Florence RAXTER,** m. 23 Feb 1921, Transylvania County, NC
                    Vera Gertrude MCCALL m. 1938
Father: **James WINCHESTER**
Mother: **Hassie LOOPER**
Draft Registration: 21, single, working at Toxaway Tanning Co

[Documentation: SSDI, 1900-1930 Census, Family History on Ancestry.com), Ancestry.com, Pickens Sentinel obituary, Cowart's Index to Marriages]

Winchester, Sylvester   2,587,027   1
(Surname)   (Christian name)   (Army serial number)   * White * ~~Colored~~.

Residence: _____ Rossman *Transylvania* NORTH CAROLINA
            (Street and house number)   (Town or city)   (County)   (State)
_____C. *Inducted at _____Brevard ^ C_____ on _____July 6/₁₉ 18
Place of birth: _____Oconee Co S C_____ Age or date of birth: _____22 11/12 yrs
Organizations served in, with dates of assignments and transfers: _____
_____MD to disch_____

Grades, with date of appointment: _____
         Pvt

Engagements: _____

Wounds or other injuries received in action: None.
Served overseas from † _____**no**____ to † _____, from † _____ to † _____
Honorably discharged on demobilization _____Jan 10/19_, 1?_____
In view of occupation he was, on date of discharge, reported _____0_____ per cent disabled.
Remarks: _____

Sylvester Winchester

Frances Reese Photo

SRC Notes: MD (Medical Department)

11 Jul 1918   Brevard News

Twelve Transylvania boys left on last Saturday for Fort Oglethorpe, Ga., to begin their careers as defenders of democracy. The boys left on the afternoon train . . .
. . . Sylvester Winchester, Rosman . . .

20 Dec 1918   Brevard News

Sylvester Winchester, who spent several months at Camp Greenleaf, GA, spent Sunday and Monday here.

Pickens Sentinel
12/30/1981
SYLVESTER WINCHESTER

Roland "Vess" Sylvester Winchester, 86, of Route 2, husband of Vera McCall Winchester, died December 22. He was a retired lumberman and World War I veteran. He was a member of Antioch Baptist Church.

Surviving are his wife, Vera McCall Winchester; and a daughter, Jean Sinclair.

Services were December 24th in the chapel of the Dillard Funeral Home and burial followed in Hillcrest Memorial Park.

Demos WOOD

Born:	8 Mar 1896, Transylvania County, NC
Died:	26 Apr 1972, York County, SC; age 76
Buried:	Liberty United Methodist Church Cemetery, Whitney, SC
Father:	**John Massey WOOD**
Mother:	**Salena**
Draft Registration:	Jackson County, 21, single and farming
Military Marker:	SOUTH CAROLINA PVT US ARMY WW I

[Documentation: SSDI, findagrave.com, Discharge, Ancestry.com]

Wood Demos   1,319,489   • White • Colored.
(Surname)   (Christian name)   (Army serial number)

Residence: _____ "olfe Mt Jackson NORTH CAROLINA
(Street and house number)   (Town or city)   (County)   (State)

• _____ C. •Inducted at Sylvia NC _____ on Sept. 19, 19 17
Place of birth: Transylvania Co NC _____ Age or date of birth: 21 6/12 yrs

Organizations served in, with dates of assignments and transfers: _____
_____ Co L 321 Inf to Oct 15/17; Co A 120 Inf to disch

Grades, with date of appointment: _____
Pvt

Engagements: _____

Wounds or other injuries received in action: None.
Served overseas from † No _____ to † _____, from † _____ to † _____
Honorably discharged on demobilization _____ Apr 25/19 ., 19 _____
In view of occupation he was, on date of discharge, reported _____ 0 _____ per cent disabled.

SRC Notes; Inf (Infantry)

Company B 120th Infantry At Ease

George Frank WOODFIN

Born: 27 Sep 1898, Transylvania County, NC
Died: 4 Jan 1951, Richland County, SC; age 52
Buried: Mills River United Methodist Church Cemetery, Henderson County
Spouse: **Josephine NICHOLS**
Father: **Carson WOODFIN**
Mother: **Beulah WILSON**
Draft Registration: No

[Documentation: Henderson County NC Cemetery Book, SC Death Record, Discharge, Application for Veteran's Headstone, Ancestry.com]

```
Woodfin, Geroge F          613,823      Transy......  White    2½
    (Surname)       (Christian name)    (Army serial number) (Race: White or colored)
                            Pisgah Forest       NORTH CAROLINA
Residence:
        (Street and house number)  (Town or city)   (County)     (State)

*Enlisted in   RA Ft Oglethorpe Ga    -            Dec 14/17    -
†Born in       Henderson Co N C       -            21 3/12 yrs  -
Organizations: Btry E 60Arty CAC to --;  12 Co Chesapeake Bay CAC  -
               to Feb 23/18;  MD to disch

Grades:        Corp Feb 26/19         -                         -

Engagements:                          -                         -


Wounds or other injuries received in action: None.                -
‡Served overseas: Aug 30/18 to July 5/19                           -
§Hon. disch.  July 19/19  to reenlist                             -
Was reported  0           per cent disabled on date of discharge, in view of occupation.
Remarks:                              -                         -
```

SRC Notes: Arty CAC (Artillery Coast Auxiliary Corps)   MD (Medical Department)

12 Oct 1917   **Brevard News**
Frank Woodfin, whose letter in the News contains the surprising information of his enlisting in the aviation service, surprised his friends with a visit to his home at Little River this week.

12 Oct 1917   **Brevard News**
LETTER FROM TRANSYLVANIA BOY
Editor News:

Perhaps you know that I have been braking for the Baltimore & Ohio R. R. all summer. Now on the 14th of August while at Dover, Ohio, I became interested in an aeroplane a fellow had there, so I asked him to let me go with him and he took me. I was a little afraid at first, but the higher I got the better I felt. Since then I have made several trial trips on a hydroplane on Lake Erie with Captain Randall, Coast Guard. I like the profession and have joined the U.S. Aviation Corps, and am preparing to leave for Norfolk, Va. for training.

I believe I am the first Transylvania boy to join the "mosquito" fleet. Sure is great work and how thrilling when you get to a height so that the earth you live on looks like a tiny rubber ball. But it will be more thrilling to drop bombs on those German towns.

I will write you when I get located so I can get the NEWS, which I enjoy very much.

Wishing the NEWS and all my friends the greatest of success during war times. I remain a student aviator. Respectfully,

FRANK WOODFIN

8 Feb 1918   **Brevard News**

LETTER FROM FORT MONROE

Editor, Brevard News:

Although I am many miles from old Transylvania and the good people that dwell among the old historic hills of my childhood, my thoughts are of the good friends of my home country.

I am stationed at Fort Monroe, Va. in Battery E of the 60th Regiment of the 1st Artillery Corps. I like the Army life fine. I expect to be transferred either to Fort Moultrie, S.C. or to France inside of the next month, and as there is snow and sleet on the ground to the depth of 12 inches I would not object to the transfer at any time, although we have plenty of good clothes, shoes, comfortable quarters and religious officers, something that is usually scarce in the Army, and on top of all, we have the best rations going, which are never refused.

It has been said that the boys in khaki would not run from anything but they sure would run for the mess hall, and that is true so far as I have observed.

I want to say to the people of Transylvania and all other counties that the American Red Cross helped to make more soldiers happy at Christmas than any other organization on earth, and any man that wants to show patriotism to his country could not do a better thing than to contribute to the Red Cross fund. Another thing that contributes largely to the happiness and comfort of the soldiers is the Army Y.M.C.A. They furnish free stationery, shower baths, gymnasium, moving pictures, lecture or concert every night. The patriotic American people furnish all these things.

Fort Monroe is a great place to be located, for you are alongside the noted Hampton Roads, where, at least, half the Atlantic fleet lays at intervals. You see the Jackies in blue and at the same time you are only 14 miles from the Curtis aviation school at Norfolk also the largely filled aviation station, so you can see an aero plane, war ship and hear the huge 11 inch guns of old Battery Parrott roaring away at the same time.

Fort Monroe is the noted place where Jefferson Davis was held prisoner at the close of the Civil War. The casement is marked where he was held, also on the drill yard, is the big tree that he was tried under. There are also a number of brass cannon that were used in the War Between the States.

May your thoughts and daily prayers are with the American soldiers.

Respectfully

GEO. F. WOODFIN   Batt. E. 60th C. A. C.   Ft. Monroe, Va.

21 Jun 1918   **Brevard News**

Geo. W. Woodfin, who is with the medical detachment at Woodbridge, Va., was at home last week on a short leave of absence.

28 Aug 1918   **Brevard News**

SOLDIER BOYS LIKE HOME NEWS

Woodbridge, Va. 8-23-18

Editor Brevard NEWS:

As I have been in the good U.S.A. till it is thought that I have had enough training to go along with the rest of the fellows to the other side to do my bit there. I want the NEWS sent to me over there, so as we are all dressed up and ready to go, I want you to change my address to France via New York for the good old NEWS will be the same or better than a letter from home to me when I get there. I think that there is enough school teachers in the country to write up the weekly happenings of their respective districts, so that the boys in camp and the ones over there will hear things that are of interest to them. I have noticed a great shortage of such news for some time in our home paper so come on people, write often and see if the boys who are away from their homes and friends don't appreciate it and I know the editor will be glad to print all the county news that you will write to cheer us. [You bet he will. Anything for the soldier boys.]

This section of the country has been visited by a very hot spell, the worst that has ever been seen, so say the old residents of the place, but it has gotten real cool like good old fall of the year now.

As this is the last company of the regiment to cross, a new military school of mining has come to take up the camp that we are leaving which is located on the old camp ground, the Gen. Grant, the spot where he had his headquarters tent as marked by a marble tablet with the date of his encampment here before the battle of Bull Run, which took place only a few miles from here.

Wishing the NEWS and all its readers success in all their future undertakings, I am Respectfully,

Geo. F. Woodfin

25 Sep 1918   **Brevard News**

News has been received that Pvt. Geo. F. Woodfin has landed safely overseas.

21 Mar 1919   **Brevard News**

LETTER FROM FRANCE

Dear Sir:

Just to show you how much I appreciate the NEWS in France I will write you a few lines to publish while we are marking time waiting on a boat and an order to take us home. The weather is very cold here now, snow fell about two weeks ago and about every day a new two inches falls on what is already here, and the ground has been white since. Hope you good people of old Transylvania are having better weather than we are.

I was very glad to have my old friend, Guy M. Allison of the Boylston section stop and stay over night with me. We sat up and talked of the good times we had back home waiting for us, both were very home-sick and ready to come home at a minute's warning, so we call ourselves the "Minute men of the A. E. F."

After meeting some of the boys from home that were over here it was only a few weeks before I knew that the Company that I am with made the best time of any in getting from the states to the Great Front, for one month from the date we left the camp at Woodbridge, Va., we had two men killed in action and twelve wounded, so that they went to the hospital and some went to the U.S.A. and some got back with the organization, and I think that was the best time made by any Co. or Regt. that left the Camp in the states.

It has been a great mystery to the boys over here, why that the Y.M.C.A. is getting so much more of the money that is being given in the states, than the Salvation Army or the K. of C. for they are the two organizations that helped the boys that won the war, for they were always there at the front with Hot Chocolate and cigarettes and candy, for the boys, of course the Y.M.C.A. may have been doing good work back in the S.O.S., but the boys who came over here to win the war never got any benefits of anything back there, for they charged enormous prices for what they did sell, while other organizations gave away things or sold them at a little more than they would cost at home, and with all the money they are getting donated it is a plain problem for the men in the A.E.F. to study over and TRY to solve, for when they all get back there should be a real investigation by proper authorities to determine what all and how it was spent and from all the talk I have heard in this area; there will be a real report of it or the Y.M.C.A. is dead forever in the hearts of the American people.

Not that I favor one organization any more than another, do I write this, only I think it is proper for the people to know about these things, and as for taking my word you can easily get hundreds of men, in fact all of the largest per cent of men that have served in the Advance Zone. Just write any of them that have seen real active service and see if their opinion and mine are not just the same.

Hoping to see the people of my native land real soon, and that this reaches all in good health, and that the people may prosper in all of their undertakings, have good health in all ways.

I am as ever,

GEORGE F. WOODFIN

19 Apr 1919   **Brevard News**

LETTER FROM FRANCE

Editor Brevard NEWS:

Just a few lines to let you and the good people of Transylvania County how I am getting on in France and this is as the French say Tra-Bonne (or very good).

The weather the last few days has been just like our springtime. The farmers are all plowing and getting ready for a "Bumper Crop" under the conditions, and I often wonder if the farmers of our country ever stop to think of the difference in the conditions here and there, here they hitch the horses one in front of the other instead of double and I have seen 8 horses pulling one heavy plow, all were walking in the furrow, and yesterday a man was plowing near here on the old battle field of the St. Mihiel Salient, and his plow truck a German mine that the Salvage Corps had failed to explode, and the result was that his plow was blown about 100 yards and was in several different pieces when it was found and he was a little farther away and in many more pieces than his plow was. He was working three horses and the one in front was not killed outright but died soon after from the effect of the explosion and the other two were killed instantly. Now that is what the French farmers will have to contend with for years to come, in the battle area.

We were moved to this place from Laheycourt, and there is quite a difference between Laheycourt and Ruptdent St. Mihiel, as there is only about ten houses in this joint and there were over two hundred in Laheycourt.

Well, must close and will write a nice long letter and tell you about my experiences since leaving N.Y. if this one gets to the press and not to the wastebasket.

Wishing the NEWS and all its readers a prosperous year, good health and all like that that can be wished on a people. Hoping to receive the paper in the future as in the past, I am

Respectfully,
GEO. F. WOODFIN

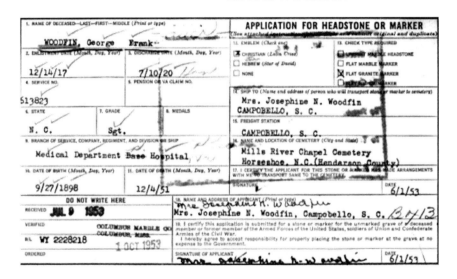

1/11/1951
George F. Woodfin

George Frank Woodfin, 52, veteran of World War I, died in the U.S. Veteran/s Hospital at Columbia, S.C., on Jan 4. A native of Transylvania County, Mr. Woodfin was born and reared at Enon. He was employed by the U.S. Department of Agriculture as a vegetable and fruit inspector, and made his home at Campobello, S.C.

Funeral services were held last Friday afternoon in the Mills River Methodist Church and burial followed in the church cemetery.

Survivors include the parents, Mr. and Mrs. C.F. Woodfin; his widow, and three brothers: Ralph, Davis and Nobel Woodfin.

NATIONAL ARMY CANTONMENTS

Camp Kearny   Location: Linda Vista, Cal.   Organization: 40th (old 19th) Division
Troops from California, Nevada, Utah, Colorada, Arizona and New Mexico

William Walter WOODRING

Born:	8 Mar 1894, Tuckasegee, NC
Died:	8 Sep 1976, Oteen VA Hospital, Buncombe County; age 82
Buried:	Mt. Moriah Baptist Church Cemetery
Spouse:	**Martha Berdine PATTERSON**, m. 2 Nov 1924, Transylvania County, NC
Father:	**Rufus WOODRING**
Mother:	**Mollie MIDDLETON**
Draft Registration:	No
Grave Stone:	PVT US Army WW I

[Documentation: North Carolina Death Collection, North Carolina Birth Index, Transylvania County Cemetery Survey, Discharge, FamilySearch.org, Ancestry.com, Cowart's Index to Marriages]

Woodring, William W(alter) 4,136,050 *White *Colored
(Surname) (Christian name) (Army serial number)

Residence: Tuckaseigee Jackson NORTH CAROLINA
(Street and house number) (Town or city) (County) (State)

*Enlisted *R. A. *N. G. *E. R. C. *Inducted at Sylva N C on Aug. 26, 19.18
Place of birth: Tuckasigee N C Age or date of birth: Mch 8 1897
Organizations served in, with dates of assignments and transfers:
Ordnance Guard Co Camp Raritan To Oct 4/18; Ord
Maintenance Repair School Raritan Arsenal NJ to
Grades, with date of appointment: Oct Jet Co to disch
Pvt
Engagements:

Wounds or other injuries received in action: None.
Served overseas from † None to † , from † to †
Honorably discharged on demobilization Apr 16/19 , 19
In view of occupation he was, on date of discharge, reported 0 per cent disabled.

W. Walter Woodring
Rufus Woodring Photo

9/13/1976
W.W. WOODRING

William Walter Woodring, 83, died Wednesday in a Buncombe County VA hospital after a period of declining health. A native of Jackson County and a Transylvania County resident most of his life, he was a retired railroad employee and an Army veteran of World War I.

Surviving are the widow, Birdeen Patterson Woodring; five sons: Eugene, Rufus, Carol, Junior and Elroy Woodring; a sister, Nellie Banther; and two brothers, Joe and Zeke Woodring.

Services were held Saturday at Mount Moriah Baptist Church and burial was in Calvert Cemetery. Members of the American Legion conducted graveside rites.

In January 1914, John J. Pershing arrived in El Paso, Texas and led the 8th Brigade in the search for Pancho Villo in the Mexican Revolution.

As American Expeditionary Forces (AEF) commander at Fort Bliss, Texas for two years (1917-1918) General Pershing was responsible to organize, train and supply an inexperienced force of men that grew from 27,000 to over 2 million to be known as the National Army of World War I.

Forest Alexander WOOTEN

Born:	27 May 1891, Buncombe County, NC
Died:	2 Oct 1974, Cleveland County, NC; age 83
Buried:	Sunnyside Baptist Church Cemetery, Bessemer City, NC
Spouse:	**Pansy GRANGER**
Father:	**Eber WOOTEN**
Mother:	**Elizabeth HARVEY**
Registration Card:	26 with a wife and one child; worked as a laborer in the Brevard Cotton Mill

[Documentation: North Carolina Death Index, findagrave.com, 1900-1930 Censuses, Ancestry.com]

Wooten, Forest A.   1,865,532   *White *Colored.
(Surname)   (Christian name)   (Army serial number)

Residence: _____ Brevard   Transylvania   NORTH CAROLINA
(Street and house number)   (Town or city)   (County)   (State)

Enlisted *R. A.* *N. G.* *E. R. C.* Inducted at   Brevard N C   Oct 6/17   on _____, 19__.

Place of birth: Buncombe Co N C   Age or date of birth: 26 4/12 yrs

Organizations served in, with dates of assignments and transfers: _____
_____ Co B 322 Inf to discharge _____

Grades, with date of appointment: _____
_____ Corp June 18/18 _____

Engagements: _____

Wounded in action (degree and date) Severely _____ about Sept 22, 19 18
Served overseas from July 31/18 to †Nov 15/18 , from † _____ to † _____
*Honorably discharged on demobilization: SCD   Feb 5/20 , 19__.
(If separated for other cause give reason)
In view of occupation he was, on date of discharge, reported ____ 50 ____ per cent disabled.

SRC Notes: SCD (Surgeon's Certificate of Disability)

Mess kitchens 120th Field Hospital

Haywood County Digital Collection

James R. WRIGHT

Born:	30 Sep 1895, Henderson County, NC
Died:	26 Aug 1959, Transylvania County; age 63
Buried:	Gillespie-Evergreen Cemetery
Occupation:	Brick mason
Spouse:	**Donnie Mae GILLESPIE**, m. 22 Jun 1921, Transylvania County, NC
Father:	**James WRIGHT, Sr.**
Mother:	**Sarah COUCH**
Draft Registration:	Henderson County, 21 single, brick mason
Note:	Grave marker gives NO military information

[Documentation: Transylvania County DC, Discharge, <u>Transylvania County Cemetery</u> <u>Survey</u>, <u>Cowart's Index to</u>
<u>Marriages</u>, Ancestry.com]

Wright, James Robert   3,034,295   • White • ~~Colored~~   1
   (Surname)   (Christian name)   (Army serial number)

Residence: Crab Creek St   Hendersonville   NORTH CAROLINA
            (Street and house number)   (Town or city)   (County)   (State)

                    *Inducted at   Hendersonville NC   on   July 13, 18
Place of birth: ____ Hendersonville NC   Age or date of birth: ____ Sept 30/95

Organizations served in, with dates of assignments and transfers: ____
       Btry B 6 T M Bn to disch

Grades, with date of appointment: ____
       Pvt

Engagements: ____

Wounds or other injuries received in action: None.
Served overseas from Nov 2/18 to Jan 8/19, from † ____ to † ____
Honorably discharged on demobilization ____ Jan 19, 19~~19~~
In view of occupation he was, on date of discharge, reported ____ 0 ____ per cent disabled.
Remarks: ____

SRC Notes: Btry (Battery) T M Bn (Trench Mortar Battalion)

9/3/1959
BOB WRIGHT

Funeral services for James Robert Wright, 64, were held Saturday in the chapel of Moody-Choate funeral home with burial in the Gillespie-Evergreen cemetery.

Mr. Wright, a brick and rock mason, died at his home on the Brevard Country Club Road. Some four years he suffered a heart attack and had been in declining health since that time. A native of Hendersonville, Mr. Wright had made his home in Brevard for the past 42 years. He was a veteran of World War I, a Woodman and an avid hunter.

Survivors include the following: Mrs. Donnie Mae Gillespie Wright; two sons: Carl and Pete; one daughter, Mrs. Charles Siniard; four brothers: John, Gene, Lee and Joe; and one sister, Mrs. Homer Pace.

NATIONAL ARMY CANTONMENT (CAMP)

Camp Beauregard   Location: Alexandria, La.   Organization: 39th (old 18th) Division
Troops from Louisiana, Mississippi and Arkansas

Howard Douglas WYATT

Born:	8 Sep 1896, Orange, NJ
Died:	10 Mar 1991, Transylvania, NC; age 94
Buried:	Gillespie-Evergreen Cemetery
Occupation:	Retired lumber inspector
Spouse(s):	**Beezie Bell BRACKEN, m.** 22 Mar 1924, Transylvania County
	Jettie FAHNESTOCK
Father:	**Irwing Washington WYATT**
Mother:	**Martha SEALANDER**
Notes:	PFC 113th Inf, 57th Inf Brg , 29th Inf Division

[Documentation: Roster of WWI Veterans from American Legion 50th Anniversary celebration; NC Death Collection; obit; 1900-1940 Censuses]

3/14/1991
HOWARD D. WYATT

Howard Douglas Wyatt, Sr., 94, died Sunday in the Brian Center. He was a native of Orange, N.J. and had lived most of his life in Transylvania County. He was the son of the late Irvin Washington and Martha Sealander Wyatt and the husband of the late Beezie Bracken Wyatt. He was a retired inspector with Carr Lumber Company, a veteran of World War I, a member of the American Legion Monroe Wilson Post #88 and was a member of the VFW Lewis Earl Jackson Post #4309.

Surviving are his wife, Jettie Allison Wyatt; one son, Kenneth Bell Wyatt; one stepson, Thomas E. Allison; and two stepdaughters, Betty Bush and Doti Cantrell.

Funeral services were held Tuesday in First Baptist Church. Burial was held at Gillespie-Evergreen Cemetery with military graveside rites conducted by American Legion Monroe Wilson Post #88 and VFW Lewis Earl Jackson Post #4309.

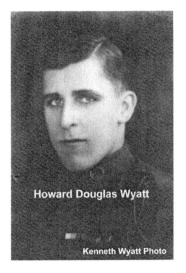

Howard Douglas Wyatt

Kenneth Wyatt Photo

Howard Wyatt, Sr. was wounded in the Argonne Forest October 27, 1918 while raising his arm to signal his men to attack the Germans. The doctors placed a silver plate in his shoulder and he required much medical attention for some years. The hospital in New York where he was receiving treatment closed and they sent him to Oteen Veterans Hospital in Asheville for further treatment. Having been trained in lumber grading he applied for a job with Carr Lumber Company in Brevard. It was in Brevard that he met and married Bees Bell Bracken. Howard lived his entire adult life in Brevard.

He was awarded a Purple Heart for his act of bravery in the Argonne Forest but through the years it disappeared. In 1991, the United States government replaced the medal but it took almost one year and much paper work. The original official records were destroyed in a fire at the National Archives but the Wyatt family had all the original documents as proof of the service and discharge. The American Legion had a ceremony September 8, 2011 to present the replacement Purple Heart to the Wyatt family.

Thomas Haywood YORK

Born:	1 Jul 1894, Buncombe County, NC
Died:	6 Feb 1959, Oteen VA Hospital, Buncombe County; age 64
Buried:	West Burnsville Baptist Church Cemetery, Yancey County, NC
Occupation:	Lumber inspector
Spouse:	**Willie Kate RAY**
Father:	**Sylvester S. YORK**
Mother:	**Robenia RUSSELL**
Draft Registration:	22, single; worked as a lumber stacker for Robert Orr in Brevard

[Documentation: Buncombe County DC, findagrave.com, 1900-1940 Censuses, Discharge, FamilySearch.org]

York, Thomas H   1,863,503   • White •
(Surname)   (Christian name)   (Army serial number)

Residence: _____ Brevard, Transylvania NORTH CAROLINA
(Street and house number) (Town or city) (County) (State)

*Inducted at Brevard, N C on Oct 3, 1917

Place of birth: Black Mountain N C   Age or date of birth: 23 3/12 yrs

Organizations served in, with dates of assignments and transfers: _____
M D to disch.

Grades, with date of appointment: _____
Ck Sept 1/18

Engagements: _____

Wounds or other injuries received in action: None.

Served overseas from † no _____ to † _____, from † _____ to † _____

Honorably discharged on demobilization Mch 6/19 , 19 ____

In view of occupation he was, on date of discharge, reported 5 per cent disabled.

SRC Notes: MD (Medical Department)

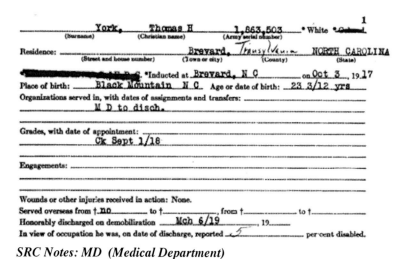

Abbott, W. US in the Great War   pub. 1919, p.38

Alfred Benjamin ZACHARY

Born:	31 Oct 1891, Jackson County, NC
Died:	25 May 1961, Transylvania County, NC; age 69
Buried:	Gillespie-Evergreen Cemetery
Spouse:	**Grace WATSON**
Father:	**William ZACHARY**
Mother:	**Nancy ALLISON**
Draft Registration:	25, single, worked as a locomotive fireman for Southern Rail Road in Brevard, listed his mother as a dependent
Military Marker:	NC Chauffeur 306 Sanitary TN WW I

[Documentation: Transylvania County DC, Application for Veteran's Headstone, <u>Transylvania County Cemetery Survey</u>, Ancestry.com, TT obituary]

```
                                                                              1
        Zachary Alfred B            1 873 361        • White • Colored.
        (Surname)      (Christian name)    (Army serial number)

Residence: _____ Brevard Transylvania      NORTH CAROLINA
          (Street and house number) (Town or city)  (County)      (State)

• _____ N. C. I.R.C. •Inducted at____Brevard N C____Sept 19__, 19 7
Place of birth: _____ Horsy Alley N C  Age or date of birth: ___25 11/22 yrs
Organizations served in, with dates of assignments and transfers: _____
        MD to disch

Grades, with date of appointment: _____
        Cpr Mar 24 /°

Engagements: _____

Wounds or other injuries received in action: None.
Served overseas from Aug 8/18  to June 20/19 , from †_____ to †_____
Honorably discharged on demobilization _____ June 29, 19 19
In view of occupation he was, on date of discharge, reported ____0___ per cent disabled.
```

SRC Notes: MD (Medical Department)

6/1/1961
ALFRED B. ZACHARY

Funeral services for Alfred Benjamin Zachary, 69, were held last Saturday at the Selica Methodist Church, of which he was a member, with burial in the Gillespie-Evergreen cemetery. Mr. Zachary died in the Transylvania Community Hospital, following a short illness.

Well-known in Transylvania County, he was a retired employee of the North Carolina Highway department, serving some 34 years as a foreman. He was also a veteran of World War I, a member of the American Legion, V.F.W., and the N.C. State Highway employees association.

Survivors are his widow, Mrs. Grace Watson Zachary; two daughters, Mrs. Howard Whitmire and Mrs. Ray McCall; three sons: Jack, Jon and William; and one sister, Mrs. Sam Allison.

NATIONAL ARMY CANTONMENT (CAMP)

Camp Mills   Location: Garden City, L.I., N.Y.   Organization: 42nd Division
Troops from Most of the Middle and far Western States

John McLean ZACHARY

Born:	13 Dec 1898, Transylvania County, NC
Died:	29 Nov 1963, Greenville, SC; age 64
Buried:	Gillespie-Evergreen Cemetery
Spouse:	**Ella HOUSTON**
Father:	**Ralph H. ZACHARY**
Mother:	**Carrie McLEAN**
Draft Registration:	19, clerking at the Macfie-Brodie Drug Company, Brevard
Military Marker:	NC PVT STU Army TNG Corps WW I

[Documentation: SSDI, 1900-1940 Censuses, Transylvania County Cemetery Survey, Ancestry.com]

Zachary John M(clean) 4 458 478   • White • Colored   1

Residence: _____ Brevard Transylvania   NORTH CAROLINA
                (Street and house number) (Town or city) (County) (State)

_____ C. *Inducted at Durham NC _____ Oct 21, 1918
Place of birth: _ Cherryfield N C _____ Age or date of birth: ___ Dec 13/1898

Organizations served in, with dates of assignments and transfers:
_____ Students Army Tng C Trinity Coll Durham N C to disch

Grades, with date of appointment: _____ Pvt _____

Engagements: _____

Wounds or other injuries received in action: None.
Served overseas from No _____ to † _____, from † _____ to † _____
Honorably discharged on demobilization _____ Dec 9, 1918
In view of occupation he was, on date of discharge, reported _____ 0 _____ per cent disabled.

SRC Notes: Student Army Training Corps at Trinity College in Durham, NC

12/3/1963
JACK ZACKARY

Funeral services for John McLean (Jack) Zachary, 64, of Greenville, SC were conducted Saturday at the gravesite in Gillespie-Evergreen Cemetery. Mr. Zachary died in a Greenville hospital. He had lived in Greenville for a number of years.

He was a member of Brevard Methodist Church, a member of the Revelers and Cotillion Clubs, the Chamber of Commerce, Downtown Association, the Masons and Shriners. He was a veteran of World War I.

Surviving are his wife, Mrs. Ella Houston Zachary; and one daughter, Mrs. James B. Gowan; and one brother, Ralph H. Zachary.

At mealtimes, to the call of the bugle, the men were marched to a mess hall, and there in single file carrying in their hands the metal plate and mug with which each must eat. They marched past the service table where the dishes of each were piled high with food and his cup filled with steaming coffee. The assortment and amount of food piled on each plate was overwhelming in quantity. The constant drilling, exercise and hard work did stimulate the appetite.

Abbott, Willis, **The United States in the Great War**, pub. 1919, p. 41.

John Robert ZACHARY

Born:	5 Oct 1893, Jackson County, NC
Died:	13 Apr 1959, Oteen VA Hospital, Buncombe County; age 65
Buried:	Gillespie-Evergreen Cemetery
Spouse:	**Bessie WATKINS**, m. 21 Jul 1926, Transylvania County, NC
Father:	**William ZACHARY**
Mother:	**Nancy ALLISON**
Draft Registration:	23, single; worked as a brakeman for Southern Rail Road, Brevard listed his mother as a dependent
Military Marker:	NC PVT ENG WW I

[Documentation: Discharge, Buncombe County DC, <u>Transylvania County Cemetery</u> <u>Survey</u>, Application for Veteran's Headstone, Ancestry.com, TT obituary, <u>Cowart's Index to Marriages</u>]

Zachary John R.   4 159 459   • White • Colored.
(Surname)   (Christian name)   (Army serial number)

Residence: _____ Brevard Transylvania _____ NORTH CAROL NA
(Street and house number)   (Town or city)   (County)   (State)

Inducted at _____ Brevard N C _____ July 24, 19 18
Place of birth: Jackson, N C   Age or date of birth: Oct 5/1893

Organizations served in, with dates of assignments and transfers:
716 M T Division Camp Hancock Ga to Nov 5 18
Co A 147 Engrs to disch

Grades, with date of appointment: Pvt

Engagements: _____

Wounds or other injuries received in action: None.
Served overseas from No _____ to † _____, from † _____ to † _____
Honorably discharged on demobilization _____ Dec 13, 19 18
In view of occupation he was, on date of discharge, reported _____ 0 _____ per cent disabled.

SRC Notes: MT (Motor Transport) Engrs (Engineers)

23 MORE MEN TO LEAVE JULY 24, 1918
Following is a list of white registrants for induction on July 24th, 1918 for Camp Hancock, Ga., who will leave on the 3:13 train:
Alternates:
. . . John Robert Zachary, Brevard . . .

4/16/1959

BOB ZACHARY

Funeral services for John Robert Zachary, 65, were at the Groce Funeral Home in Asheville Wednesday. Burial followed in the Gillespie-Evergreen Cemetery here in Brevard. Mr. Zachary died Monday in Moore General Hospital after a short illness.

He was a native of Jackson County and was the son of William and Nancy Allison Zachary. He retired in 1951 as conductor on Southern Railway. He had been affiliated with Southern for 37 years and had resided in Asheville for 30 years.

Mr. Zachary was a member of Haywood Street Methodist Church. He was a veteran of World War I and a member of the Brotherhood of Railway Trainmen.

Surviving are the widow, Mrs. Bessie Watkins Zachary, senior matron of Buncombe County jail; one brother, A.B. Zachary; and one sister, Mrs. S.B.Allison.

Charles Russel ZIEGLER

Born:	21 Sep 1890, Junction City, Kansas
Died:	1 Mar 1946, Guilford County, NC; age 55
Buried:	Gillespie-Evergreen Cemetery
Occupation:	Farmer
Spouse:	**Ruth ELLIOTT**
Father:	**J.C. ZIEGLER**
Mother:	**Mary J. OTTO**
Draft Registration:	Junction City, Kansas, 28, single, farming
Military Marker:	Kansas 1 SGT 164 Depot Brig

[Documentation: Transylvania County DC, Application for Veteran's Headstone, <u>Transylvania County Cemetery Survey</u>, Ancestry.com]

3/7/1946
CHARLES R. ZIEGLER

Charles Russel Ziegler, 55, of Brevard, died at the home of his father-in-law, J.O.Elliott, in Greensboro, last Friday morning. Mr. Ziegler went to Greensboro for medical treatment about three months ago. He was a patient for seven weeks at Wesley Long Hospital and was released to the Elliott home about six weeks ago.

Following funeral services held at Bethlehem Methodist Church near Climax on Sunday afternoon, the body was brought to Brevard where interment took place in Gillespie Cemetery here on Monday afternoon.

He was a native of Junction City, Kansas and came to North Carolina in 1923 with the Ziegler Road Construction Company. In recent years, he had been a farmer in the Brevard section. Mr. Ziegler was a veteran of World War I and a member of the Methodist church of Brevard.

Surviving are the widow, Mrs. Ruth Elliott Ziegler; one son, Charles Harrison Ziegler; three brothers: S.B Ziegler, Blake and Walter Ziegler; and two sisters, Mrs. Mae Glick and Mrs. Grace Saunders.

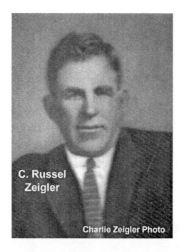

C. Russel Zeigler

Charlie Zeigler Photo

A wagoner was one who drove a wagon pulled by a horse or mule, usually in the Trains (Examples: Engineer, Sanitation, Food, Medical, Supply, Ammunition or Artillery.) Animal drawn vehicles were used throughout World War I but these modes of transportation were slowly being replaced by motorized vehicles due to the animal shortage. These men were responsible for moving supplies from the warehouses to the front line positions and to remove the injured from the battle. Being a wagoner was a duty description such as cook, bugler, cannon loader, etc. All Companies, Regiments and Divisions had wagoners.

Truck drivers were first known as wagoners.

Index

Index

Index

Index

Index

CPSIA information can be obtained at www.ICGtesting.com
Printed in the USA
BVOW052253140713

325910BV00003B/5/P